PRINCIPLES OF
LEARNING AND MEMORY

THE EXPERIMENTAL PSYCHOLOGY SERIES

Arthur W. Melton · Consulting Editor

MELTON AND MARTIN · Coding Processes in Human Memory, 1972

McGUIGAN AND LUMSDEN · Contemporary Approaches to Conditioning and Learning, 1973

ANDERSON AND BOWER · Human Associative Memory, 1973

GARNER · The Processing of Information and Structure, 1974

MURDOCK · Human Memory: Theory and Data, 1974

KINTSCH · The Representation of Meaning in Memory, 1974

KANTOWITZ · Human Information Processing: Tutorials in Performance and Cognition, 1974

LEVINE · A Cognitive Theory of Learning: Research on Hypothesis Testing, 1975

CROWDER · Principles of Learning and Memory, 1976

PRINCIPLES OF LEARNING AND MEMORY

Robert G. Crowder

YALE UNIVERSITY

LAWRENCE ERLBAUM ASSOCIATES, PUBLISHERS

1976   Hillsdale, New Jersey

DISTRIBUTED BY THE HALSTED PRESS DIVISION OF

JOHN WILEY & SONS

New York   Toronto   London   Sydney

Lawrence Erlbaum Associates, Inc., Publishers
62 Maria Drive
Hillsdale, New Jersey 07642

Distributed solely by Halsted Press Division
John Wiley & Sons, Inc., New York

Library of Congress Catalog Card Number: 76–7336

Printed in the United States of America

To
A. W. MELTON

Contents

Preface   xi

1. **Background Comments and Three Analytic Concepts** **1**
    Stage Analysis   4
    Coding Analysis   12
    Task Analysis   21
    Summary and Comment   26

2. **Iconic Memory** **29**
    Sperling's Research on Iconic Memory   30
    Evolution of a Process Model for Visual Memory Tasks   35
    Properties of Iconic Memory   41
    Summary   43

3. **Echoic Memory** **45**
    Demonstrations of Echoic Memory   45
       Recognition Methods   46
       Sampling Methods   47
       Masking Methods   53
       Further Properties of Echoic Storage   60
    Summmary and Comment   64

4. **Recoding by Speech in Short-Term Memory** **67**
    The Concept of Recoding   67
    Recoding of Visual Stimuli through Speech   70
    Summary   87

vii

5. **Nonverbal Memory** 89
   Eidetic Imagery   90
   Reproduction from Memory of Forms   95
   Functional Characteristics of Images in Short-Term Memory   97
      Visual Imagery in Speeded Matching   97
      Modality-Specific Interference   105
   Visual Imagery in Long-Term Memory   110
      Memory for Pictures   110
      The Pegword Technique   113
   Paivio's Dual-Trace Theory   120
   The Qualitative Nature of Images   127
   Summary   131

6. **Primary Memory** 132
   Process Dualism in Memory   133
      Historical Background on Process Dualism   133
      Modern Arguments for Process Dualism in Memory   137
      The Measurement of Primary Memory   146
      Individual Differences and Primary Memory   150
   The Nature of Primary Memory   151
      Is Primary Memory Phonological?   152
      Transfer between Primary and Secondary Memory   157
      Alternatives to Transfer   165
      More on the Recency Effect in Free Recall   170
   Summary   173

7. **Forgetting in Short-Term Memory** 175
   Theories of Forgetting   175
      Decay Theory   176
      Displacement and Interference   183
   The Brown–Peterson Task   195
      Retroactive Inhibition in Short-Term Memory   195
      Proactive Inhibition in Short-Term Memory   200
      Hypotheses for Proactive Inhibition   206
   Conclusions   215

8. **The Interference Theory of Forgetting in Long-Term Memory** 217
   Early Evolution of Interference Theory   218
      Consolidation Theory   219
      McGeoch's Response-Competition Theory   224
   The Unlearning Hypothesis and Spontaneous Recovery   229
   The Third Stage: Developments Since 1961   237
      Verification of the Spontaneous Recovery Hypothesis   238

Tests of the Response-Set Suppression Hypothesis   241
Verification of the Single-List Proactive-Inhibition Mechanism   246
Locus of Interference at the Level of the Individual Association   251
Independent Retrieval   252
Stimulus-Encoding Theory   256
Conclusions   260
Chapter Summary   260
Interference Theory Today   261

9. The Effects of Repetition on Memory   264
The Apparent Gradualness of Learning   264
All-or-None Memorization   265
Analytic Value of All-or-None Processes   271
Effects on Recall of Spacing Repetitions of Individual Items   273
Spacing of Repetitions in Free Recall   274
Theoretical Alternatives for Distribution and Lag Effects   277
Cued Recall in Continuous Paired-Associate Learning   291
Single-Item Short-Term Memory Techniques   309
Intraserial Repetition in Immediate-Memory Span   313
Summary of Repetition Effects on Recall   314
The Effects of Repetition on Judgments of Recency and Frequency   314
Summary   320

10. The Organization of Memory in Free Recall   322
Measurement of Organization in Free Recall   324
Slamecka's Independent Trace Storage Hypothesis   342
Summary   351

11. Retrieval   353
Sternberg's Memory-Scanning Paradigm   354
Some Explicit Models of Retrieval   355
Sternberg's Original Experiment   358
The Code of Comparisons   361
Boundary Conditions on Sternberg's Model   364
Recognition Memory   370
The Measurement of Memory   370
Process Models of Recognition   372
The Relation between Recognition and Recall   378
Variables with Opposite Effects on Recognition and Recall   379
The Anderson—Bower Retrieval Theory   381
Tulving's Encoding Specificity Principle   390
Summary   409

12. Serial Organization in Learning and Memory **411**

Historical Background   411
Philosophical Associationism   412
What Is Learned in Serial Learning?   417
Theories of Serial Learning Based on Paired-Associate
Learning   418
Language, Skill, and Lashley   424
Nonassociative Recoding into Higher-Order Responses   428
Multilevel-Associative Theories   434
Serial-Position Effects   445
Single-Process Analyses   446
Primacy and Recency in Two-Process Analyses   452
Other Sources of Serial-Position Data   456
Another Look at the Recency Effect   461
Linguistic Organization   464
Continuity between Word Lists and Sentences   464
Memory for Sentences   468
Summary   476

References **479**

Author Index   507
Subject Index   517

Preface

My intention in this book has been to present an organized review of the concepts that guide the current study of learning and memory. The basic organization is therefore theoretical, rather than historical or methodological. Fortunately, however, the ideas that experimental psychologists take seriously are usually anchored to some form of empirical accountability, and therefore there is a good deal of data here as well as theory.

Because psychology is subject to what sometimes seem to be capricious changes in fashion, it must be presumptuous of me to expect that many readers share just my organization of this field. Yet it is a firm conclusion of empirical research that some coherent organization is of great value in assimilating new material. Therefore, I have not hesitated to adopt a partisan attitude here and there, a tactic that allows (but does not guarantee) fitting as many findings as possible within a single conceptual scheme. Although a partisan attitude probably leads to selectivity in reporting experiments, I think that is preferable to the conceptual paralysis that results when all conflicting, anomalous, and possibly unreliable findings are included in the name of completeness. Therefore, although some may expect a judiciously partisan, theoretical approach to be abstract and so more difficult than a straight facts and figures approach, I am convinced it is the other way around in the long run.

This book grew out of lecture notes I developed over the years in both graduate and undergraduate versions of a course in human learning and memory at Yale. I expect it to be suitable for advanced undergraduate courses, as well as graduate courses, but perhaps not for courses following immediately on the undergraduate introduction to psychology. I have tried, however, to presume no prior knowledge of the subject matter on the part of the reader; technical terms are kept to a minimum, and I have made every effort to introduce them carefully when they first occur. I should state, also, my preference for giving thorough treatment to major experimental and theoretical statements (usually in the form initially offered by the author rather than as subject to minor later qualifications) at the expense of tracing out all subsequent ramifications of a problem area in order to provide a complete review of the literature.

It has not been possible for me to deal, even in passing, with the huge body of knowledge concerning learning among lower species of animal than man. It may turn out that the principles explained in this book can generalize to such organisms as rats and pigeons; certainly if one extends his reductionism to the level of neurochemical events there is an ultimate common process to all learning. However, such generality is not crucial for the principles in this book; it is rather to nonlaboratory instances of human learning and memory that we are anxious for these principles to apply. Generality in the other direction, the application of theory derived from lower species to humans, has, after a great expenditure of effort, talent, and money, been less successful than once hoped.

Another exclusion from the scope of this book is the new and active field of *semantic memory,* the system of memory that contains knowledge acquired in everyday life—knowledge that cars have wheels, that JEOPARDY is spelled with an E, that 4 + 8 = 12, and so on. It goes without saying that memory for information of this sort is a legitimate part of the domain announced by the title of this book and there are promising beginnings toward integrating semantic memory with more traditional experimental approaches. However, I have not undertaken to review semantic memory myself because others are better equipped to do so than I and because there is no shortage of material for a book within the domain chosen.

The overall organization of the book is as follows. There is an introductory chapter, providing a set of higher-order analytic strategies that are useful in studying learning and memory. The rest is organized into four broad sections. The first of these deals with the question of *coding* in memory, in particular, relations between memory and vision (Chapters 2 and 5), audition (Chapter 3) and speech (Chapter 4). Chapters 6 and 7 form a section that focuses on short-term memory. The third section is loosely organized around the topic of learning and includes chapters on interference and transfer (Chapter 8), the effects of repetition (Chapter 9), and organizational processes (Chapter 10). The final section includes two chapters that focus on the process of retrieval, with special attention to recognition (Chapter 11) and to serial organization (Chapter 12). Within these divisions it is quite important to preserve the order of chapters, because they cumulate to some extent. However, although there are some cumulative references between sections, the order of coverage from section to section is less crucial. Until I prepared this book, for example, I used to deal with the material in Chapters 8, 9, and 10 before the material in Chapters 6 and 7. The historical material, incidentally, is found in Chapters 8 and 12 almost exclusively because historical trends were organically related to the theoretical content of those chapters more than to the content of other chapters. There is certainly no reason to deal with the evolution of our science chronologically, especially when the whole enterprise is so recent.

It is a pleasure to acknowledge the large contribution of Arthur W. Melton to this book. His wise commentary on the manuscript penetrated points of syntax and points of interpretation with equal clarity. Working with him once again has been a rare experience.

The following people have been kind enough to read one or more chapters of the manuscript and to share their reactions with me, much to the benefit of the final product: James Antognini, Reid Hastie, Alice F. Healy, John L. Locke, James H. Neely, Frederick W. Sheffield, Henry L. Roediger, III, Endel Tulving, and Michael J. Watkins.

ROBERT G. CROWDER

**PRINCIPLES OF
LEARNING AND MEMORY**

1

Background Comments and Three Analytic Concepts

The experimental study of learning and memory is almost 100 years old as this book is being written. In this same period others of the life sciences, biology for example, have undergone mind-boggling changes—imagine the confusion of a nineteenth-century naturalist walking into a modern college class in cell biology. Gains within psychology have been more modest than that since the close of the 1870s, when Ebbinghaus first undertook to study the formation of associations in the mind, but still the psychologist has no reason to feel apologetic: Any science, biology included, has had to pass through a preliminary period of simple observation, quantification, and classification, with inevitable false starts, before reaching a rate of evolution with the potential for boggling many minds. As a specific example, research on the cause of cancer seems at present to be going through such a groping phase (although, of course, the treatment of cancer is another story).

In fact, impatience with the progress of psychology in such areas as learning and memory gives way to excitement at the possibilities for the future when it is appreciated how little total effort has been invested so far. As a measure of the youth of our enterprise, consider that there are now scientists still active whose graduate training included reading all of the experimental literature on learning and memory that had ever been published. It is no longer remotely feasible, even if it were desirable, to read all of the literature on even the subset of learning and memory research to be covered in this book. Nor is this book to be a guide to that literature in any comprehensive way. Instead, the intention here is to lead the reader through the most significant conceptual developments, with due consideration to the experimental foundations of these ideas and also to the historical context from which they have emerged.

The first chapter is focused on three somewhat abstract principles having to do with how learning and memory should be analyzed. These analytic principles are generally transcendental with regard to theoretical points but they provide an organized context from which to approach theory. The ideal topical outline for this book would be a three-dimensional solid defined by these analytic principles: stage analysis, coding analysis, and task analysis. A book must necessarily follow a linear ordering, however, so we shall try to weave them through the material wherever possible. First, however, a preview of what these principles entail is necessary.

Stage analysis denotes the separation of learning and memory processes into (1) acquisition—the placing of information into memory storage in the first place, (2) retention—the persistence of memory over passing time, and (3) retrieval—the extraction of information from memory storage when it is needed. Traditionally, the term "learning" has been assigned to experimental operations where primary focus is on the first of these stages and the term "memory" to the second and third stages.

Coding analysis addresses the problem of which aspects of experiences get recorded in memory. When we "remember" a dinner from the previous week, for example, are we remembering the actual flavors as such, the names of the dishes served, or both? The assumption is that all possible aspects do not invariably become the basis for memories of those experiences and therefore coding analysis is needed to cover the principal ones.

Task analysis is the process of decomposing complex skills into simpler constituent skills in the belief that these subskills may be more tractable to theory than the global task. For example, there are two logically separable tasks in associating names of strangers with their faces. First, it is necessary to learn the new name itself (which can pose problems with names from another language) and, second, there has to be a hooking up of the learned name with the proper face; it is at least possible (and testable through experimentation) that these two processes are independent.

We shall devote considerable time to going through concrete examples of each analytic principle from the published literature on human learning and memory. This survey has several goals. The experiments that have been selected are particularly vivid illustrations of the analytic principles, but they also serve to introduce the reader to many of the major research methods in the field as well as to some of the important basic results. First, however, a few more preliminary remarks are in order.

Learning, memory, and the scope of the book.   Any reasonable definition of "learning" includes many phenomena that lie outside the domain of the present book—habituation, the organization of receptive sensory fields, acquisition of strategies in problem solving, operant training, perceptual learning, the processes of abstraction in concept learning, and, of course, the data and theory that have come from the animal laboratory. These subjects are important and interesting and their exclusion from a book on learning is neither an act of derogation nor imperialism: Rather, the subject matter of this book is directed toward instances of learning that are (1) exclusively human and (2) largely symbolic, because these two restrictions define an area that is internally coherent and has historical continuity. The internal coherence of this field will hopefully become apparent through the organizing power of stage, coding, and task analysis and also through numerous theoretical and methodological concepts common to the various chapters and subheadings to be covered. The historical continuity of human symbolic learning and memory extends back to the preoccupation of ancient philosophers with the "higher mental processes" and their faith that the key to understanding the mind was in the analysis of these processes.

These Greek philosophers—and their descendants down through the nineteenth-century British empiricists (and ultimately including many of the scientists represented in this book) may have been wrong about the essentially experiential (learning and memory) and essentially symbolic (verbal and imaginal) basis for mind. Alternatively, they may have been correct in these two beliefs but their followers in current psychology may be wrong in expecting experimentally derived solutions for problems of mind (as opposed, for example, to solutions derived from such nonempirical fields as philosophy or artificial intelligence). In our present condition of basic ignorance about how the mind works, we can hardly decide between the ultimate usefulness of these different approaches. However, these considerations do provide a clear rationale for the content and approach of a book such as this one, to wit, the propositions (1) that psychology has a special responsibility to elucidate the mental processes of human beings among all of the other species, (2) that one distinguishing feature of human mental processes is their symbolic nature, and (3) that the main basis of symbolic mental processes is in learning and memory. These propositions have guided the content of this book.

There are some matters of terminology and definition that cannot be put off until later: One is what we mean by "learning" and "memory." Formulating a definition of *learning* is an instructive exercise, pondering the various inclusions and exclusions that must be added to any straightforward statement, but for the present purposes we may simply describe it as a change in the organism that occurs at a particular time as a function of experience. (Experience, of course, may also produce many other changes that are not learning.) The change in the brain that constitutes learning corresponds to what gets entered into memory. However, this change, learning, cannot itself be observed directly and therefore some indirect performance test must be used to infer that learning has occurred. The basic form of such a test is a comparison of performance that could reflect the learning experience with control performance, in which the critical experience is missing. Learning is inferred from a difference as a function of the experience. To recapitulate and anticipate the present sense of stage analysis, therefore, the acquisition process (learning) may be studied only through performance in a memory test (retention plus retrieval).

The term *memory* is often used in two different senses. When reference is to "a memory," the intention is to talk of the brain change that results from learning, the *memory trace,* that is, the hypothetical, unobservable product of experience to be inferred from performance. *Memory as a process,* in contrast, refers to the dynamic mechanisms associated with the holding of a memory trace over time and the retrieval of information about it in performance. In other words, the term "memory" is used for both the product of learning and the process of retention and retrieval. In this book the term "memory trace" is used for the product sense of the term. *Forgetting,* incidentally, has a technical reference to the loss of information in the retention stage; information is not forgotten if it has never been learned in the first place and it is not considered forgotten if it is just inaccessible to retrieval (although available in memory).

Stage Analysis

There must have been the inevitable Greek scholar who first conceived of separating acquisition, retention, and retrieval processes, but modern sources for this crucial distinction are Köhler (1947, p. 165) and especially Melton (1963a). If performance in a memory task is perfect, of course, one can be assured that information has been successfully learned by the subject, that it has been retained or held in storage from the time of acquisition until the time of attempted retrieval, and that the retrieval stage has contained no block itself. However, if performance in memory situations were always perfect, the world would be quite a different place.

The central problem occurs when there is a failure of retrieval. Such a failure brings up a very fundamental ambiguity: One has no idea whether the information has been (1) acquired adequately and retained adequately but is for some reason inaccessible at the time of attempted retrieval; (2) acquired adequately but then lost (forgotten) during the time elapsing between acquisition and retrieval; or finally (3) acquired inadequately in the first place so that there is nothing there to retain or retrieve. The big challenge is to tease possibilities apart through experimental means.

One of the most common applications of inferential problems related to stage analysis comes from the assessment of *forgetting,* the amount of information that does not persist between acquisition and a test of retrieval. It is a universal experience to try to recall a name or a word, without success, and to conclude that the missing item has been forgotten. However, the test of *recall*—which for the moment we can define as trying to reproduce information "out of the blue"—is only one of several, fallible measures of what has been retained. Often when the "forgotten" material is later discovered or somehow otherwise presented, people experience immediate, high confidence that they *recognize* it or find it familiar. Because recognition itself is a measure of retrieval, however, and therefore a performance test of retention, this must mean the information had indeed been retained. Sometimes, after years of disuse, people lament having forgotten a whole language, perhaps one they used as a child but not since; however, often the ostensibly forgotten material can be *relearned* at substantial savings, more quickly or easily than a totally new language. By this still more sensitive measure of retention, relearning, still more deeply inaccessible memory traces may therefore be recovered. From these commonplace demonstrations of the logic of stage analysis we turn now to examples from the laboratory.

Meaningfulness and forgetting.   Most laymen accept as self-evident the notion that meaningful material is forgotten more slowly, over time, than nonsense material. Pleas for "meaningful" as opposed to "rote" learning in the field of education are partly defended on this supposition. However, such truisms of folk psychology should not be accepted uncritically by psychologists. This particular problem yields, in an interesting way, to stage analysis, as explained originally by Underwood (1964).

For purposes of the present discussion, meaningfulness may be defined as the extent to which verbal materials resemble sensible English words or familiar letter sequences. Three-letter groups high in meaningfulness are ABC, POT, and THO, whereas comparable items low in meaningfulness are XVQ, HJI, and YWU. It should come as no surprise that subjects indeed perform better with items high on the meaningfulness dimension than with items low on it. The question is how to understand this advantage in terms of stages. Better performance on high-meaningful items may result from an advantage at any one of the three stages, from any pair of them or from all three. Our concern here is with separating *acquisition* and *retention* effects. It has been known since the earliest experiments on learning (Ebbinghaus, 1964, originally published in 1885) that meaningfulness bestows an advantage in learning (acquisition) but untangling the influence of meaningfulness on retention is more difficult.

Clearly it will not do to present high- and low-meaningful materials to two groups of subjects for a constant amount of study time, to excuse them for some retention interval, and then to call them back for a test of memory. In this hypothetical experiment the memory test would surely show a performance advantage for high meaningfulness, but because the fixed study time would have allowed better learning of the high-meaningful materials, than of the low-, it would be impossible to know whether there had also been a retention advantage.

A better solution is to measure the progress of acquisition in groups receiving high- or low-meaningful materials and to interrupt study at a *fixed criterion,* say 80% of all the information to be learned. Then, if all subjects are stopped and excused when they have just reached the 80% criterion, it may be supposed that acquisition has been equated and that any differences that show up after some subsequent time period are assignable to retention losses over that period.

However, Underwood (1964) has shown that even this method can lead to incorrect conclusions; the argument is rather too involved for coverage here, but it is explained carefully in his article.

The main problem is in knowing exactly how much each group—high and low meaningfulness—really knows at the beginning of a retention interval. Without this information it is not possible, then, to estimate what they have lost during the interval. The most elegant solution is to divide each experimental group into two subgroups, testing one subgroup at the beginning of the retention interval, right after the termination of study, and the other after the retention interval. Forgetting is estimated by comparing initial and delayed retrieval scores for each type of material.

Underwood's experiment. The experiment reported by Underwood (1964) illustrates this approach and answers our question about whether meaningfulness affects forgetting. Underwood's subjects were required to learn *paired-associate* lists of either high or low meaningfulness. We should pause to describe the task before continuing with the experiment. In paired-associate list learning a list of double items is presented in such a way that the subject has to learn, given one of the items in a pair, to provide the other member on his own. The given item is called the *stimulus term* and the item to be retrieved in response to it is called the *response term.* This is the same task as learning a foreign language vocabulary lesson such that, given an English word, the corresponding Spanish word can be reproduced. A *trial* in paired-associate learning consists of one learning experience for each pair on the list. Usually this experience includes both a test, where the stimulus term is given alone for a few seconds with the subject trying to supply the response himself, and an immediate feedback or study period in which the correct pairing is displayed. These trials are continued until all the pairs are correctly given by the subject, or until some fraction of them are given, at the discretion of the experimenter.

In Underwood's experiment, the items forming the pairs to be learned were single letters, not foreign-language equivalents. One paired-associate list consisted of easy, meaningful items, such as V–W and A–B; the subjects' job was to learn to say "W" given "V" or "B" given "A." On the other list, the low-meaningful one, the pairs did not reflect real-world associations (Z–J, N–Q, for example). There were four groups of subjects, two learning the low-meaningful list and two learning the high-meaningful list. All subjects were interrupted in acquisition just after the trial on which they first correctly anticipated (in response to the test with only a stimulus item showing) six of the nine pairs.

To reach the criterion of six out of nine pairs, the high-meaningfulness group required fewer than three trials through the list whereas the low-meaningfulness group required more than nine trials. There was indeed a difference in acquisition rate for these two lists, therefore. The subjects learning each list were then divided into two groups, one tested immediately and the other tested after 24 hr. The results are shown in Figure 1.1.

Consider the groups given an immediate test. It is clear from the figure that even though both the high-meaningfulness and the low-meaningfulness groups were allowed to study until a criterion of just six out of nine items was reached, still, on the following test, the high-meaningfulness group knew more. Subjects with the easier list, in fact, did much better than the six-item criterion, whereas subjects with the more difficult list were somewhat below it. The criterion "overshoot" for the high-meaningful subjects is understandable from the fact that the criterion trial, itself, included additional study on the entire list; because subjects have been learning at a very fast rate on the easier items, that single terminal trial can be expected to add an item or so. However, the subjects given the more difficult low-meaningful list, would not have been expected to over-shoot to this extent. In fact, these subjects dipped below six items slightly on the postcriterion trial, a decrement that could reflect experimental error, some slight forgetting, or, most probably, a statistical artifact called *postcriterial drop* (this is basically a special case of regression toward the mean; see Melton, 1936, for a full discussion).

The important point is that, between the two immediate-test groups and the two 24-hr test groups, the only procedural difference is the passage of time; they were tested in the same way and the same number of times. We can safely assume that each of the 24-hr groups, if they had been tested immediately after

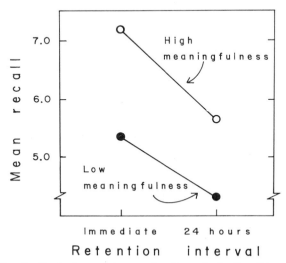

FIGURE 1.1 Recall of paired associates as a function of retention interval since learning. The upper and lower functions are for lists with high and low degrees of prior association between pair members, respectively. (After Underwood, 1964.)

acquisition, would have performed indistinguishably from the immediate groups. For either the easy or the hard materials, therefore, the difference between the immediate and the 24-hr performance is an uncontaminated measure of forgetting loss, free from any acquisition differences. As Figure 1.1 shows, the losses are quite comparable for the two types of lists. The loss was even slightly, although not significantly, larger with the high-meaningful materials than with the low-meaningful materials. In any case, there is absolutely no support for the intuitive expectation that the easier lists should be better retained.

The safest experimental design, therefore, for distinguishing whether a given variable affects retention when it is known to affect acquisition, is an arrangement with separate groups tested at the beginning and the end of the retention interval—a pair of such groups used for each level of the variable in question. Underwood and others have applied this research strategy to variables other than meaningfulness. For example, it has been shown to be *not* true that slow learners, as opposed to fast learners, receive Emersonian compensation for their toil by enjoying better retention over time: When the degree of original learning for fast and slow learners is taken into account, there is no difference in the rate of subsequent loss over time.

An experimental demonstration of the distinction between the retention and retrieval stages. We turn now to the problem of deciding whether forgotten information was lost through a failure in retention over time or through a failure in the retrieval process. It is a common experience, especially in old age, to have difficulty recalling a familiar name or place that we know for certain has been adequately registered at one time. Is this difficulty because the memory has since departed or is it still there but somehow hidden behind a retrieval block?

A study by Tulving and Pearlstone (1966) provides a particularly useful illustration of the distinction between failures of retention and failures of retrieval. These authors tested a group of 948 high-school students on memory for lists of categorized words.

Words within a category were presented together and preceded by the name of that category. During reception of a list, therefore, the subject heard an announcement of the name of each category—"part of clothing"—followed by a group of instances in that category—SHIRT, SOCKS, PANTS, BELT. The subjects in this experiment heard lists of either 12, 24, or 48 words, consisting of categories of size one, two, or four words. For example, students hearing the 12-word lists heard either 12 categories with one instance of each, six categories with two instances of each or four categories with three instances each. Combinations of total numbers of words in the list and their distribution into categories therefore created a total of nine conditions of presentation. In addition, for each presentation type, there were two conditions pertaining to the *testing* of memory. In one, the subjects were simply given a 2-min period in which to recall all the items, exclusive of category names, in any order they chose; this is the *free-recall* condition. In a second, *cued-recall* condition, other subjects were tested category by category; they heard the same category labels announced as they had during the original presentation of the list and they were given a period of time following each category name to supply the same words they had heard previously. This second group therefore received a test of recall in which the name of each category prompted the instances that had been received from it. The 948 subjects were therefore distributed over a total of 18 conditions.

An experiment as complicated as this naturally leads to a number of important outcomes. For present purposes, the important result is shown in Figure 1.2. Here we see a graph showing the number of words recalled as a function of the experimental conditions. The main result is the superior performance of the cued-recall subjects over the free-recall subjects. For every input condition subjects who received hints in the form of category labels recalled more of the critical target words than subjects who recalled on their own. (The authors' fine-grained analyses indicated that subjects did occasionally guess in the cued-recall conditions but that only a very tiny portion of the difference between cued and free recall could be accounted for by lucky guessing on the part of subjects who received category names.)

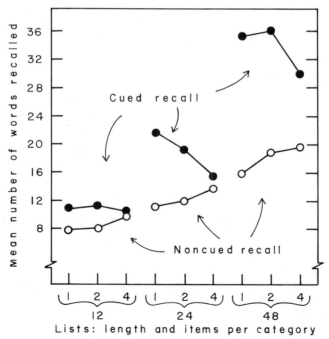

FIGURE 1.2 Mean number of words recalled in cued and noncued recall as a function of list length and number of items per category. (After Tulving & Pearlstone, 1966.)

How can we interpret this difference between cued and free recall? Tulving and Pearlstone introduced the distinction between *availability* of information in memory and *accessibility* to that information as a way of understanding the difference. The idea is that, because the cued- and free-recall subjects were treated identically until the moment of retrieval, they must have acquired and retained precisely equivalent amounts of information. Therefore, with respect to the availability of information, what has been called the "retention stage" here, there was no difference between free and cued groups. Instead, the dramatic differences between free- and cued-recall subjects in performance must logically be assigned entirely to mechanisms occurring during the retrieval stage, where recall was either free or cued. These procedures are considered by Tulving and Pearlstone to have produced differences in accessibility of the stored information. Access to stored information is presumed to be less difficult with such retrieval cues as category names than it is with no cues. The availability–accessibility distinction therefore exactly matches the retention–retrieval distinction.

The major lesson from the Tulving–Pearlstone study is that we cannot determine from observed performance in any memory test how much information the subject has stored in his brain; we can measure only that retained information that happens to be accessible under the particular retrieval conditions prevailing. Without the cued-recall test in this experiment one might have been tempted to conclude that the subjects had acquired and retained much less information than was actually the case. When a student misses an examination question it may not be because the information has been lost through forgetting over time; it may be only that available memories are somehow inaccessible to retrieval at that particular moment.

Also, there is a more subtle, yet more important, point to the Tulving–Pearlstone experiment. Without cued recall one would have been led to the wrong conclusion about the relationship between performance and the experimental variable of items per category. In free recall, performance was better the more items there were in each category, whereas in the cued-recall condition this was not the case. For theory construction it is even worse to be fooled about the direction in which a variable affects performance than it is to be fooled about the overall amount of stored information.

Stage analysis in amnesia. Leaving aside the unusually selective types of amnesia, which are seen mainly on television, the group of disorders that commonly falls under this term provides a rich application for stage analysis. We shall confine this discussion to general terms because related evidence is considered in detail in Chapters 6 and 7. Books by Talland (1968a), Talland and Waugh (1969), and Whitty and Zangwill (1966) are excellent sources on amnesia.

The point of departure for amnesia, as for all inquiries into memory, is an observed failure in retrieval. The main distinction to be made among disorders with this result is between *retrograde amnesia* and *anterograde amnesia:* both of these terms are defined with reference to some chronic or acute brain disorder. When memory for events prior to the disorder is lost, the term "retrograde amnesia" is used, and when memories for subsequent events are lost, the term "anterograde" is used. Amnesic effects associated with epileptic seizures include both types: Following the seizure, there is impaired memory for events occurring in the seconds, minutes, or sometimes hours before onset of the seizure and, for a brief period afterward new experiences seem to leave little or no trace.

The analysis of anterograde amnesia as a deficit in *acquisition* of new memory traces therefore seems quite natural. However, full consideration of the facts complicates this analysis. One type of anterograde amnesia occurs in patients with what is called the Korsakoff Syndrome, a pattern of disorders that occur along with brain damage caused by advanced alcoholism (actually the cause is basically suffocation of the brain through oxygen shortage). In tests of *immediate memory,* where the task is just to repeat back a moderately long sentence, Talland (1968a, p. 126) has found severe Korsakoff patients unimpaired, whereas in tests of the same material after 5-min distraction, the Korsakoff patients are markedly impaired compared to control subjects. In later chapters we shall be at pains to distinguish between two theoretically separate memory systems, *primary memory,* or *short-term storage,* versus *secondary memory,* or *long-term storage.* The suggestion of Talland's data is that Korsakoff deficits, and perhaps other anterograde amnesias, result from inadequate acquisition with respect to the long-term memory component. However, the unimpaired immediate memory suggests reasonably normal learning and memory within the short-term system.

Besides epilepsy and Korsakoff psychosis, amnesia results from various other brain-related types of damage, including especially head injuries. The most common types of retrograde amnesias are caused by such traumatic events as sports and motorcycle accidents. The typical phenomenon is complete inability, once the victim regains consciousness, to recall events leading up to the trauma. Sometimes the blank period is brief (in football, perhaps extending only to the play during which the accident happened) and sometimes the amnesia extends further back. The most simple view of these retrograde effects is that the traumatic event obliterates the previous memories. This would constitute an attribution of retrograde amnesia to the retention stage. However, a little reflection shows this view to be oversimplified, because there must be some reason amnesia is selective for memories from experiences just preceeding the traumatic event and leaves other memories intact. Perhaps memories from the recent past are in some sense more fragile than memories from the more distant past. This last proposition implies an old and important principle of memory— the *consolidation hypothesis.* According to the consolidation hypothesis (see Chapter 8) the process of acquisition extends longer in time than the experience itself; that is, there is a period of covert activity following a learning experience during which the memory trace is being somehow solidified in such a way as to be more persistent than it can have been without the additional activity. If a traumatic insult to the brain interrupts the process of consolidation, we should expect impaired recall for the events the consolidation of which has been interrupted. In concrete terms, at the time of a severe football head injury, the experiences leading up to it were in a fragile consolidatory state such that a permanent trace was never laid down, a deficit in acquisition.

There is also evidence, however, that at least some of the problem in retrograde amnesia can be related to retrieval. A common clinical observation (which has been verified with animals experimentally) is that the time lost shrinks with increasing delays after the original trauma. Immediately afterwards the amnesia extends farther back in time than it does days, weeks, or even years later. In other words, there is recovery of initially inaccessible memories. This must mean, on grounds of simple logic, that the recovered information has been present in memory storage all along but for some reason in a state where retrieval has not been possible. There are not enough systematic studies to allow estimation of what proportion of retrograde amnesia shows recovery with posttraumatic delay or whether the recovery observed is ever complete. However, the point here has not been to come up with a complete theory of amnesia but only to underline that here is an area where stage analysis is the indispensable starting point for development of theory.

Normal aging is frequently accompanied by impaired memory performance and the analysis of the impairment follows much the same logic as with amnesic disorders. Do the elderly actually forget new information more readily than younger people or is the problem one of retrieving available information or of acquiring new information in the first place? As with meaningfulness, there is evidence (Talland, 1968b) that the acquisition process is strongly affected but that retention is not at all affected. Other evidence suggests an age-related impairment of retrieval mechanisms (Craik, 1968a). The literature on these points is fragmentary, however, and we shall not attempt a synthesis here (see several of the contributions to a book edited by Talland, 1968b, for a review of what research there is on aging).

Coding Analysis

The second of our analytic dimensions represents a fundamental shift in emphasis for the psychology of learning and memory. Prior to the middle 1960s the issue that preoccupied workers was *how* learning and memory worked, how information was registered, retained, and so on. Coding analysis has raised to equal status a second issue—what is it that gets learned? When a verbal item is presented to a subject, what aspects of that item are the ones that participate in the learning–retention–retrieval sequence?

This formulation implies that there are many attributes to the stimuli used by psychologists in learning experiments and that every attribute does not invariably get involved in every learning experience. When a telephone number is memorized it is unlikely that some aspects of the constituent digits play any role at all—for example, the fact that certain of the digits are prime numbers and others not. Likewise, it is unlikely that the number of syllables in a word has much effect in a situation where long lists of words are learned, as in the Tulving–Pearlstone experiment. The analytic responsibility is therefore to discover which codes, which selective representation of attributes, are the important ones in which situations.

Phonological coding in immediate memory.   One of the pioneering demonstrations of coding analysis in memory was a paper by Conrad in 1964. Conrad's work is covered in great detail in Chapter 4; here, we pause only to make the basic point. The question was how people retained, in the sense of what coding they employed, a list of six letters presented visually for immediate ordered recall. The items are presented briefly, read silently by the subjects, then recalled in order after the visual display has disappeared, without any intervening activity. Because the stimulus items occur visually, one may well expect that some form of visual coding is used in this situation, with subjects' remembering the visual forms of the items long enough to get them on paper.

What Conrad and others had shown informally in the early 1960s is that coding in this visual memory task is in fact in terms of the items' sounds. One piece of evidence had to do with substitution errors, when the correct letter for a given position was replaced with some incorrect letter. A very conspicuous type of substitution, or confusion error, was one in which the correct letter was replaced by another letter similar in sound to the former. For example, if the list to be remembered was BHKTCVR and the subject missed the fourth letter, T, he was greatly more likely to substitute another letter rhyming with T, such as P, than to substitute some letter than did not rhyme, such as F. This even though no sound ever occurred in the experimental room!

Conrad's 1964 paper is an elegant demonstration that errors of substitution in immediate memory are the same confusions as those found in listening to individual letters in noise. In other words, by knowing how likely subjects are to confuse two letters in a test of *listening acuity* one can predict confusions between those same letters in a test of *visual memory*. Furthermore, Conrad has shown that if a visual memory series has a high proportion of rhyming letters—such as BCTHVZ—the list is harder to recall than if the letters exclude most such rhyming clusters—HBKLMW.

These findings and the evidence in Chapter 4 point to a heavy involvement of the hearing–speech (phonological) system in immediate memory. The association of immediate memory with phonological coding, in turn, was a breakthrough with respect to the formulation of theories of short-term memory. For example, the evidence on phonological coding is consistent with a short-term memory mechanism the operation of which is tied to speech—the items are read from the screen, named internally, and then sounds of the names are remembered.

Other examples of coding analysis. Now let us consider a case where quite different forms of coding can arise from identical stimuli, dependent on how the subject processes the stimuli. Examine for several seconds the following stimulus sequence and then try to write it down on a piece of paper without looking back:

149162536496

This string of digits exceeds normal memory capacity by a large amount and, if learned as an arbitrary series, it is likely to take considerable effort. However, at some point you may have an insight about this particular series that makes it vastly easier to learn. The insight can be hastened by considering the same series presented in this fashion:

1 4 9 16 25 36

Presented this way most adult subjects would find the series trivially easy and could memorize any length string produced in the same way as long as they knew the squares of the successive integers. Likewise, one can affect the ease of learning this particular stimulus, which we owe to Katona (1940), by priming the subject with more obvious mathematical sequences first, such as 2 4 6 8 10 12. . . .

Here is another famous example (Lashley, 1951) of a stimulus that can be learned in two fundamentally different ways depending on how it is processed by the subject: This is a series of French words which make no sense in French (a French-speaking person should be consulted for their pronunciation and then the words should be memorized in series, preferably aloud):

PAS DE LIEUX RHONE QUE NOUS

Accepting for the moment the proposition that in an ideal experiment, on the right subjects, we can obtain a bimodal distribution of performance with these two memory stimuli, some finding them perplexingly hard and others laughably easy, we can see that to consider learning as a unitary process is seriously misleading. Radically different things are being acquired about these materials by those subjects who see the tricks than are being acquired by those who do not. These are admittedly far more dramatic cases than normally occur in memory experiments (except when such items creep in by accident) but the point applies quite generally. Subjects spend tremendous effort searching for meaning among meaningless materials presented to them. These efforts are not always successful and sometimes items seem to be learned by "sheer rote repetition" (see Underwood, 1964). However, the point is that quite different types of learning, quite different coding mechanisms, are involved in the contrasting situations. In one case a semantic, or meaning, system is central to the process, whereas in the other case a rote-learning system, which we shall later identify with speech, is involved.

Levels of coding. So far, our interest in coding has mainly been to demonstrate the variety of forms of representation that memory traces may assume. Recent ideas on coding (see especially Craik & Lockhart, 1972) have advanced a step further by relating the type of code employed in a task to the efficiency of performance. In other words, all codes are not equal in their usefulness. One generalization to emerge from this work is that codes involving the *semantic* properties of words (their meanings) are better than codes involving the structural properties of words.

This point is made in an experiment by Hyde and Jenkins (1969). Subjects in their experiment all heard the same list of 24 words and were all tested for recall of the words, in any order, following presentation. The seven groups of subjects were distinguished in terms of what they were told about the purpose of the experiment and by what they were told to do during the time they were listening to the list.

Some subjects were told that they would be tested for memory of the words, whereas other subjects were not. The latter groups, serving in what is called an *incidental-learning* situation, were given three tasks to perform during presentation of the words; these tasks appeared, therefore, to be the primary purpose of the experiment for them and any learning of the words that occurred was an uninstructed byproduct of the activities they were given to do. There were three such activities: First, some subjects were asked to rate the pleasantness of each word on a simple checklist. Second, others were asked to detect which of the words on the list contained the letter *e* and to keep a tally. Third, still other subjects were asked to estimate the number of letters in each word and to write it down in a space for each word. Notice that the pleasantness task involves the meaning of the word, whereas the other two involve processing structural features of the word. Corresponding to these three incidental learning groups (who, to repeat, were not under explicit instructions to learn the words) there were three additional groups who were asked to perform the same three tasks but who were warned that their memory for the words would be tested after presentation of the list. Finally, there was a single control group that was just told to listen to the words, with no explicit processing task, and to recall the words later.

Table 1.1 shows performance for each of the seven groups. We should consider first the six groups that have had some task to perform during presentation of the words. The findings can be summarized simply by saying that when the information-processing task during presentation has involved dealing with the meanings of the words recall is much better than when it has involved dealing with the structure of the words; however, whether the subjects are explicitly *trying* to learn makes almost no difference (there is only a slight advantage of intentionality with the number of letters task). The assumption is that the nature of the processing task has dictated the form of code that has been retained in memory. We may therefore say that processing on a deeper level,

TABLE 1.1
Mean Recall as a Function of
Learning Group and Task[a]

Group	Recall score (24 possible)
Incidental learning	
1. Pleasantness task	16.3
2. Presence of *e* task	9.4
3. Number of letters task	9.9
Intentional learning	
1. Pleasantness task	16.6
2. Presence of *e* task	10.4
3. Number of letters task	12.4
4. No task	16.1

[a]After Hyde and Jenkins (1969).

semantic rather than structural, leads to a more persistent form of coding. The final group, instructed only to learn the words, showed performance indistinguishable from the two groups that performed the semantic task. This leads to the conjecture that subjects have some implicit knowledge of these differences in coding persistence and that uninstructed subjects ordinarily try to establish a coding strategy based on meaning.

Again, it can be seen that coding analysis has provided a sort of breakthrough in the sense that the notion of separable codes must come before theoretical generalizations concerning levels of coding.

Coding as selection.   In most of the examples so far, alternate forms of coding have in common that they stand in one-to-one correspondence with the information to be learned: The same letters can in principle be equally well retained by visual or phonological codes and the same words by orthographic or semantic codes. In other cases, the coding format entails loss of information or actual augmentation. We consider the case where there is loss of information first.

In an experiment by Underwood, Ham, and Ekstrand (1962), subjects were given a paired-associate list to learn. The response terms were single digits and the stimulus terms were compound stimuli consisting of difficult three-letter units surrounded by a rectangle of some distinctive color. Representative items on the list are, for example, XYG–5, GVZ–9, XZG–4, and so on, with the three-letter units set in patches of such distinctive colors as red, green, and blue. The same stimulus compound for a pair was used on every trial; that is, if blue was surrounding ZYG on one trial it was also there on every other trial. As always in paired-associated learning, the subject's task was to provide the response term, a digit, in response to seeing the compound of the three-letter item in its distinctive color patch.

The hypothesis of interest to Underwood *et al.* (1962) was that subjects select information from the compound stimuli so as to make the task as easy as possible. In particular, the experiment was designed to encourage the subjects to encode stimulus terms in terms of their color component rather than in terms of their verbal component. Training was carried out until a point where each subject could correctly anticipate each of the seven responses on a single trial; the question was what selection, if any, went on among the stimulus components.

To evaluate stimulus selection a test of *transfer* was arranged by Underwood *et al.* (1962). Transfer experiments are designed to show what has been learned on one task by its effects on some second task. In this case subjects who had mastered the original list were divided into three groups. One group simply continued practicing the same pairings of digits with compound stimuli. A second group was transferred to a task in which the color was removed from each stimulus but otherwise the list remained the same. The third group was transferred to a task in which the three-letter verbal unit was removed from each item, leaving color—digit pairs. The outcome was that the group where the verbal stimuli were dropped was just as good on the second list as the control group, which received continued practice on the original list. This is consistent with the interpretation that they had been using only the color component of the compound stimuli all along, so disappearance of the verbal component was of no importance. In contrast, the group in which colors were dropped from the stimuli learned only very slowly, although they were not completely without positive transfer.

Selective coding is especially appropriate when the material presented contains more information than is necessary, as in the stimulus compounds discussed in the Underwood—Ham—Ekstrand experiment. Glanzer (1972) has shown a similar type of selection in an altogether different situation. The comparison is between remembering a list of random words for free recall and remembering a list of phrases, such as proverbs. Consider a list of items such as: A BIRD IN THE HAND IS WORTH TWO IN THE BUSH. A STITCH IN TIME SAVES NINE, PENNY WISE POUND FOOLISH, and so on. If the list is long it becomes an impossible job to process each word; however, by coding each proverb with a key word— BUSH, STITCH, PENNY, and so on—a selective code can be used that ought to be no harder than a straight list of unrelated words. We have no proof that subjects do employ such selective coding but because performance on proverbs is similar to performance on single words it is a plausible inference that they do.

Coding as elaboration. On other occasions the coding process consists of *adding to,* or elaborating, the presented stimulus rather than selecting information from it or simply translating it into a different format. It is reasonable to wonder why in the world subjects should voluntarily undertake greater memory loads by expanding stimuli through elaboration coding. The answer is that in a great many instances the burden on memory is reduced by elaboration rather than increased. This paradoxical economy is sometimes achieved through unification of diverse elements into a single memory trace.

A number of excellent examples of elaborative coding are covered in Chapter 5, which treats the use of visual imagery in detail. We shall anticipate this material with a simple experiment by Bower (1972a, p. 66) on paired-associate learning. The main variable in Bower's experiment was the type of instruction given a number of subjects before they all started learning the same lists of 20 noun pairs. Some subjects were given the so-called "standard" instruction, to learn each word pair such that given the lefthand item they could provide the righthand item. Other subjects were specifically instructed to use *visual imagery* in associating the words within a pair. All of the words were concrete nouns, denoting easily visualizable objects. The imagery group was asked to picture the two objects in some interacting scene in their "mind's eye." For example, if the two nouns to be learned were DOG and BICYCLE an obvious image to construct would be a dog riding a bicycle. If the words were PLANT and SHOE one might picture a houseplant growing from an ordinary shoe. The selection of what image to use was left entirely to the subject. Five seconds were given for a single trial with each pair in a 20-pair list. Each pair was then tested once, and another list presented for learning, until five successive lists had been learned and tested.

On a test for all 100 word pairs at the end of the experiment, subjects who had had the imagery instruction recalled about 80 pairs or words; subjects given only the standard paired-associate instructions recalled only around 50 of the pairs. Even though all subjects had the same amount of time to study the items, therefore, it turned out that directions to use visual imagery led to impressive gains in performance. (The experiment almost surely underestimated the effectiveness of visual imagery because many subjects in the control group—the standard instructions group—revealed later that they, too, had been trying to construct visual images.)

Construction of a visual image requires considerable elaboration of the information given: Besides whatever action may be inherent to the scene—the action of a dog riding a bicycle—there is also the necessity that any noun made in visualizable form must be a very specific instance of the noun class. The plant growing in the shoe cannot be some combined image of plants in general, it has to be broad leaved, sword shaped, palmate, or whatever. This type of elaborative coding, therefore, always goes beyond the information given. Why this coding technique should so greatly improve performance is one of the main issues of Chapter 5.

An experiment by Lindley (1963) illustrates elaborative coding in quite a different context. In his study interest was in *short-term memory* for three-consonant items. In short-term memory tests, a very short list or item, in this case only three consonant letters, such as BTL, is presented a single time and tested after a delay of about half a minute or less. Brown (1958) and Peterson and Peterson (1959) found that it was possible to measure forgetting with great precision over such short intervals of time provided the interval was filled with some distracting task, mental arithmetic, for example. The Brown–Peterson method, as it is called, is one of the most popular techniques for the study of human memory. Lindley's experiment used such stimulus items (called trigrams), as BTL, presented for just under 2 sec and followed immediately by a slide filled with numbers. The subject's task was to read the numbers as rapidly as possible in order that he be prevented from rehearsing the trigram during the retention interval. After 3, 13, or 39 sec of such number reading, memory for the three-letter trigram was tested.

The feature of the experiment that is of main interest here is that Lindley compared performance in this situation with and without elaborative coding cues for the trigrams. Elaborative coding cues consisted of a word context surrounding the item to be remembered. Whereas some subjects saw the item BTL standing alone, therefore, others saw the stimulus *douBTLess* presented on the screen. In the latter case the subjects knew by previous instructions that the upper-case letters were the ones to be remembered and that the lower-case letters were there as aids to memory. Other stimuli, with their associated contexts, were *eleCTRic, juDGMent,* and *eMPTy.*

At the termination of the number-reading task on each trial, memory for the trigram was tested in either of two ways. In one case, three asterisks (***) appeared as a signal for recall and in the other case the elaborative part of the context appeared, but not the item of course, for example, *dou---ess.* There are four possible conditions formed by the presence or absence of the word context at recall. Performance in these conditions is shown in Figure 1.3. The figure shows that performance gets worse with increasing retention intervals filled with the number-reading activity. However, the amount of this decline varied considerably among the four conditions, as follows.

The control condition, in which the word context was presented neither at acquisition nor at retrieval, was a good baseline against which to evaluate performance in the other conditions. In this control condition performance approached about 50% errors by the time 39 sec had elapsed. At the other extreme was performance in the group given a word context for the trigram at both acquisition and retrieval; here, scores declined by only about 10% in the same time period. The remaining two groups are the interesting ones, because they allow us to perform a stage analysis of the differences between the two extreme groups. Surely there must be some advantage purely to having a context cue at retrieval, independent of any coding that has occurred at the time of acquisition. Subjects who had never seen the original stimulus in the first place would have some chance of guessing letters from such a context cue as *co---ail.* In fact, a control experiment by Lindley showed this guessing rate to be about 30% for the materials he was using. Given both a fallible memory trace and also a strong context cue, a resourceful subject can reconstruct what the stimulus must have been. However, the Lindley experimental design includes exactly the

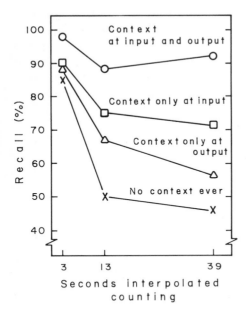

FIGURE 1.3 Recall of three-letter items as a function of retention interval and the presence of recoding and decoding contexts. (After Lindley, 1963.)

control we need for such reconstruction—the condition with a cue at retrieval but no cue at the time of acquisition. The amount by which this condition exceeds the control condition, with no cues ever, is an index of how much reconstruction goes on in the retrieval stage of this procedure.

Although such reconstruction clearly accounted for some of the facilitation seen in the condition with cues at both acquisition and retrieval, it can be concluded from the figure that much more of this facilitation derives from elaborative coding opportunities provided by the context at acquisition. From other work with the Brown–Peterson short-term memory method (Murdock, 1961a) it is known that memory for a single item, be it a word or a letter, is much better than performance on three such items. One way of describing the Lindley result is that the effect of context cues is to permit a reduction in the memory load from a string of three items (B, T, and L) to a single item (the word *doubtless*). Adding information actually reduces the memory burden with elaborative coding.

The term *decoding* is useful in the analysis of the Lindley experiment. What if the subject sees the trigram CKS in the context *baCKStop* but remembers only the word *backstop* during the number-reading period? When asked for recall, he may then be unable to decide whether it has been CKS he has seen or KST, both of which fit the context word and both of which follow the experimental selection criterion of three consecutive consonants embedded within a larger word. Conventional terminology for coding processes carries several distinctions that facilitate the description of these possibilities. The process of acquisition, which necessarily results in some kind of coded memory trace, is sometimes called *encoding*. Transforming a memory trace from one format or type of representation to another format is called *recoding*. In whatever form the memory trace survives in the retention phase there is also a process of *decoding* during the retrieval phase. The difficulty of the decoding process may vary considerably in different situations. Acquisition, retention, and even retrieval could all occur smoothly but performance could be impaired because of a decoding problem: In remembering proverbs, a subject might recode the one about early birds catching worms by means of a single word BIRD. He could well retain the word BIRD and retrieve it successfully only to find that he could not distinguish whether the proverb had been the correct one or rather the one about birds in the bush and in the hand.

Task Analysis

The third analytic dimension that should be a constant preoccupation in our study of human memory is task analysis. Certainly, the study of simple, elementary tasks can aid objective empirical work on underlying processes, but psychologists have been only partially successful in developing learning situations for the laboratory that are less complicated than those occurring in real life. Most laboratory tasks entail a subtle mixture of different components. What makes task analysis important is that experimental variables can have different, even opposite, effects on components of the overall task. Let us consider two examples.

Component analysis of paired-associate learning and transfer. One learning situation that has been popular with psychologist for generations is paired-associate learning, which we have considered in several earlier examples. A pair from such a list might be CUFFLINK–FRL. Naturally, a single pair of this sort would be mastered easily, but in a list of ten similar items, mastery of the same item would proceed slowly. A significant step forward occurred when Underwood and others, in the 1950s, had the idea of separating two or three logically distinct tasks the subject would have to accomplish in learning such pairs.

First, the subject must learn certain things with respect to the stimulus term—he must recognize its membership in the list and he must distinguish it reliably from the other stimulus items appearing on the same list. Second, the subject must learn, or integrate, the response term, which in our example is a list of three letters FRL, in order to make it a single unit that can enter into an association. Finally, the subject must attach the integrated response to the proper stimulus, in what has been called the associative or *hookup* phase.

In an experiment by McGuire (1961) these three aspects of paired-associate learning were neatly and independently operationalized as shown in Figure 1.4.

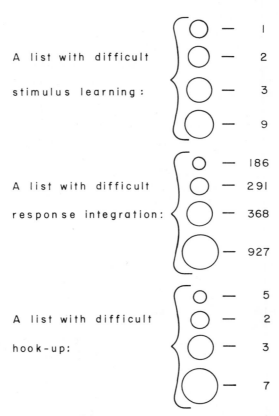

A list with difficult

stimulus learning:

A list with difficult

response integration:

A list with difficult

hook-up:

FIGURE 1.4 Paired-associate lists illustrating McGuire's (1961) experimental design for isolating three sources of difficulty.

The stimulus terms were always circles of varying diameter and the response terms were always numbers. The difficulty of the stimulus-learning phase was manipulated by selecting for the list a set of circles that had easily discriminable diameters or that had diameters so close together that it was difficult to tell which was which. The difficulty of the response-integration phase was manipulated by comparing single-digit response terms to three-digit response terms. The difficulty of the hookup phase was also manipulated by the relationship between circle diameter and the first, or single, digit of the response term—either larger circles went with higher digits in regular order, or the relation was random. McGuire found that these three separable aspects of difficulty had significant and largely independent effects on overall performance.

In itself this task analysis of paired-associate learning may seem fairly obvious, or even simple minded. We must remember, however, that intuitions have a convenient way of adjusting themselves to new insights, and most good ideas seem obvious after someone first achieves them. The payoff for task analysis in paired-associate learning has been that it permits making sense of experimental findings that have otherwise been perplexingly unlawful. This is particularly true in the field of verbal transfer (Martin, 1965). In experiments on verbal transfer (see also Chapter 8), subjects are asked to learn two paired-associate lists, one after the other. Of interest is the relation between the two lists in terms of what learning can be applied from the first to the second, or conversely, how the first list may interfere with the second. Stated differently, the objective of transfer research is to diagnose what has been learned on one list by the effect this first list has on the acquisition or retention of a second list.

Consider a first list of associations represented by the single pair, A—B. Using an alphabetic code, we can represent various transfer situations, or transfer paradigms, by a double pair, where the first pair, A—B, denotes the common first list and the second pair denotes the identity of the second list. For example, in the A—B, A—D paradigm the second list has the same stimulus items, A, as the first list, but a different response term, D; that is, one must learn to make a different response on the second list in the presence of a familiar stimulus. In the A—B, C—B paradigm, in contrast, one must make a familiar response in the presence of a new stimulus item. The A—B, C—D paradigm is often considered to be a baseline, or control, paradigm because there is no deliberate similarity relation between the two lists.

Much of the existing data on paired-associate transfer was summarized in 1949 by Osgood in his transfer and retroaction surface (the term "retroaction" refers to retroactive inhibition—the effect a second list can have in impairing retention of a first list—see Chapter 8). This three-dimensional graph, shown in Figure 1.5, is designed to display how much transfer there is between two lists as a function of how similar they are in terms of their stimulus items and also their response items. Assuming a constant first list, A—B, the various points on the graph show what happens with different second lists. For example, if the second list is identical to the first, a situation called the A—B, A—B paradigm, there will be high positive transfer, or facilitation, between the lists, as seen on the figure. If the stimulus terms remain the same and require entirely new responses, however, as is true of the A—B, A—D paradigm, confusion—negative transfer—results. It takes a moment to adjust to two horizontal axes, and also to assign decreasing similarity scales to them, but the Osgood surface has been important in crystallizing much of what was known at the time about transfer. One limitation of Osgood's analysis is that it is not analytic about the various components of paired-associated learning: It seems to assume that the associative, hookup phase is all that is going on when a person learns to associate two verbal items.

Martin's insight (Martin, 1965) was that we cannot speak in the abstract about the relative difficulty of the transfer arrangements shown in Figure 1.5. Their relative difficulties in any real situation are going to depend on how the overall paired-associate task represents a blend of the three components, stimulus

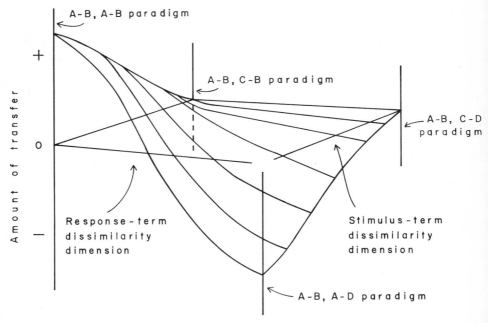

FIGURE 1.5 The Osgood transfer and retroaction surface. Note that the two horizontal axes are scales of decreasing similarity. (After Osgood, 1949.)

learning, response integration, and hookup. Consider, for example, the relative difficulties of the A–B, C–D paradigm and the A–B, C–B paradigm. If the response members of the list are all single digits, say, paired with common words, then it is known that learning the second list is approximately equal in difficulty for these two paradigms. That is, there is no transfer in the A–B, C–B paradigm, either positive or negative, relative to the A–B, C–D controls. (Positive transfer is indicated, of course, when the experimental group learns the second list faster than the A–B, C–D control and negative transfer when the experimental group learns more slowly.) Now, by way of contrast, consider an experiment that is logically equivalent but where the response terms are lists of five digits chosen randomly. So the list would resemble the following:

PEN–58396, HAT–94658, PIT–98627,

and so on. In this experiment it is reasonable to suppose that response learning presents a much larger proportion of overall task difficulty, as compared with the case where single digits are the response items. In this second case, we would expect strong positive transfer in the A–B, C–B paradigm as compared with the A–B, C–D paradigm because the former group of subjects could transfer their first-list (A–B) response learning in mastering the second list (C–B), whereas the second group could not.

The lesson here is that even with apparently simple tasks, such as paired-associate learning, we may not make blanket assertions about which transfer arrangements are positive and which negative. The relative difficulty of the various transfer paradigms depends critically on how the experimental materials used strike a balance among the different subcomponents of the overall task. Lumping together these subcomponents leads to a costly confusion of transfer results, whereas separating these subcomponents reveals an underlying orderliness.

Similarity in free and serial recall.   Consider another example of task analysis in the context of predicting which of the following two lists ought to be easier to learn:

List 1: TUB, CUB, BUT, CUD, BUCK, DUG, BUG, TUG, DUCK, PUP.

List 2: TUCK, BAG, BABE, POP, EAT, BET, TIED, DIG, GOAD, GAWK.

List 1 has greater similarity among its members than List 2, in this case similarity in terms of common sound (phonological similarity).

There is simply no answer to the question of which list is easier, in this case, because their relative difficulty depends entirely on the task set before the subject. If the task is to remember only which words have occurred on the list, independent of the order in which they have been presented, then the more similar List 1 gives better performance. However, if the task is one of reconstructing only the order of the items given, then List 1 gives poorer performance than List 2. For somewhat different materials, this relationship between free recall (recall in any order) and ordering of items has been shown experimentally by Horowitz (1961); similarity improves the former and impairs the latter measures.

Now in moving to a standard serial-recall task, in which the subject is held responsible both for the identity of the list items and for the order in which they have been presented, we see that performance depends jointly on two subcomponents: To recall a list of words in order one must not only know what the words from the list are (item information) but one must know also the order in which they have occurred (order information). The observed effect of similarity on serial recall therefore depends on the balance of the item and order components of the task. For the materials given in the examples above, Watkins, Watkins, and Crowder (1974) have demonstrated that with free recall, similarity improves performance but with ordered recall, similarity impairs performance. For lists of this type apparently the order component is dominant in serial recall: We know that for item information alone similarity is helpful, so if on a test of item plus order information, similarity yields a net harmful effect, then the item—information component must be outweighed by the order component.

In quite a different situation, Murdock and vom Saal (1967) obtained a similarity effect that went the opposite way in ordered recall. The main differences seem to be that their lists have been shorter and the dimension of similarity has been semantic rather than phonological or structural. We cannot digress to speculate on which of these differences accounts for the discrepancy in results from the study by Watkins *et al.* (1974).

What, therefore, is the effect of similarity on recall? It depends: It depends on the prevailing balance between item and order information for the particular task under study. Cases of this sort show that just because a single response measure is our index of performance, and just because the task seems simple, there is considerable danger in assuming that the underlying process is correspondingly unitary. It is probably the deceptive simplicity of many psychological laboratory tasks that makes task analysis so difficult; surely in complex skills, such as diving or tennis playing, the need for task analysis is obvious even to the layman.

Summary and Comment

The pedagogical approach in this chapter has been inductive. Principles of several sorts were introduced by concrete examples rather than by brute force assertion. In summary, it is appropriate to lay out some of the intended inferences in a more systematic fashion.

Methodology. At least half a dozen of the major experimental methods for studying human memory and learning have been described or mentioned here; these do not exhaust the supply of available techniques, and there are endless variations on them, but they are sufficient to provide a useful methodological overview.

It should be apparent from the examples used that the unit of analysis in this type of research is usually the verbal item—word, letter, or digit; these are the elements of performance that determine scores. Also, most of the time such items are presented in groups called *lists* for the subject to learn. Employment of lists of items rests on the fact that under most circumstances subjects perform uniformly well with a task of learning only three or four items. There are exceptions to this rule, however. With the Brown–Peterson task, which Lindley has used, a list of only three letters can yield substantial errors if attention is distracted immediately after presentation.

There are basically three ways a list of verbal items can be introduced to a subject for learning. The first is *free recall,* in which items are presented one after another and the subject must simply recall, later, which have been the items appearing on the list, without regard to the order in which they have occurred. Memory was tested by the method of free recall in the experiments by Hyde and Jenkins (1969) and by Tulving and Pearlstone (1966). If a *serial-recall* technique is used, the subject is asked to recall the items from a list in the order presented. Examples of serial recall were given in the sections on coding analysis (Conrad's immediate-memory tests for phonological confusions and the informal demonstration of memory for the series beginning, 1, 4, 9, 1, 6, . . .) and also in connection with the discussion of item and order information in the task-analysis section. The third major condition of presenting lists is the method of *paired associates,* in which the subject must learn to recall the response term shown the appropriate corresponding stimulus term. Experiments by Underwood (1964) on meaningfulness, by Bower (1972a) on visual imagery, and the research on transfer were all examples of paired-associate procedures.

The *cued-recall* procedure, used by Tulving and Pearlstone (1966) as a comparison with free recall, is clearly an intermediate case between paired associates and free recall; the subject receives the material item by item, without explicit pairing, but he is asked to recall the items in response to appropriate cues.

Given any of these basic tasks, an experimenter can choose between presenting the material to be learned only once and measuring performance on a single test, or presenting the material to be learned on repeated trials in order to measure the amount of time or number of repetitions required to achieve some criterion of mastery. It is conventional to denote the one-shot techniques as "free recall," "serial recall," and "paired-associate recall" (actually, "probe recall" is a more common term for this last task) and to denote the multiple-trial techniques as free-recall learning (sometimes, just "multitrial free recall"), serial learning, and paired-associate learning. From our consideration of stage analysis it should be obvious that these distinctions are somewhat arbitrary, for whether there is only a single test or many of them each must entail processes of acquisition, retention, and retrieval. When interest is in the rate of growth of performance over repeated trials on the same material, however, the term "learning" is most appropriate.

Another conventional distinction that is useful, although controversial, is that between short-term and long-term memory techniques. The term "short-term memory" is used when the subject is given relatively short periods of time between acquisition and retrieval. The distinction is sometimes one of degree: The *immediate-memory* task, a version of serial recall with short lists (lists near the length that the subject can just barely reproduce perfectly, often about eight items with college students), is usually grouped with short-term memory techniques because only a few seconds intervene between the acquisition and retrieval of any particular item in the list. However, a free-recall task with 30, 40, or more items is classed with long-term memory, mainly on the grounds that the time any particular item is in storage is more on the order of minutes than seconds. A long serial-recall list, for example, might also be classed with long-term memory. Finally, any of the multiple-trials methods, where interest is in the accumulation of learning over repeated experiences with the same materials, is clearly a long-term memory method.

One particular short-term memory method that has been covered earlier in the chapter should be singled out because of its widespread use and because it vividly illustrates the nature of the short-term memory methodology. This is the *Brown—Peterson distractor* task used by Lindley (1963) in connection with tests of recoding through verbal contexts. The essence of the Brown—Peterson task (a tool independently devised in England by John Brown, 1958, and in the United States by Lloyd & Margaret Peterson, 1959) is in presenting a very small number of items for the subject to learn and then distracting him from rehearsing the items at once, by requiring performance on some demanding distractor activity until recall is tested some seconds later. The Brown—Peterson method made it possible to examine forgetting losses over time periods an order of magnitude, a logarithmic unit, shorter than had been possible previously. We shall hear much of it and other short-term memory testing procedures in Chapters 6, 7, and 9.

Review of theoretical generalizations. Woven into illustrative experiments described in this chapter were several specific results with wide theoretical implications:

1. Although verbal materials that are high in meaningfulness are substantially easier to learn than materials low in meaningfulness, there is no difference in the rate at which they are lost from storage (Underwood, 1964).

2. Following exposure to a long list of categorically related words, there is much information available in storage that is not accessible to retrieval; such information shows up in cued recall but not in free recall (Tulving & Pearlstone, 1966).

3. Although short lists of letters can be presented visually and recalled in writing, they still produce errors in which subjects make substitutions based on sound, confusions that imply a phonological basis of coding (Conrad, 1964).

4. The intention to learn a word list has little or no effect on subsequent free recall compared to the effects of the information-processing task that must be carried out on the words. Tasks requiring some type of semantic decision lead to much better performance than tasks requiring attention to structural features (Hyde & Jenkins, 1969).

5. Instructions to form mental images in which two objects are visualized as interacting leads to better paired-associate performance than instruction simply to associate the two nouns denoting those objects (Bower, 1972a).

6. The expected interference or facilitation between two associative learning tasks may be summarized by the Osgood transfer and retroaction surface; however, the predictions shown on the surface may be altered by different balances among the separable components of paired-associate learning (Osgood, 1949; McGuire, 1961; and Martin, 1965).

7. In word lists, phonological similarity improves performance on free recall but it impairs performance on serial recall (Watkins, Watkins, & Crowder, 1974).

2
Iconic Memory

Between the two boundary episodes that allow public observation of information in memory—when at first the person receives the information to be stored and when later he overtly retrieves it—there is a complicated invisible history of transformation, abstraction, and elaboration. These operations are particularly dense in the first moments after presentation, during what is commonly called "perception." The scientific task, which is to recreate this invisible history, is made all the more difficult by the possibility that, unlike the unfolding of historical events in real time, these mental events are happening partly at the same time, that is, in parallel.

The event of categorization provides, fortunately, one logically necessary anchor point to help organize what must be occurring. At categorization, contact is made between incoming stimulus information and stable classifications in long-term memory, such as those that distinguish letters or words from one another. The term "categorization" shares meaning with the term "perception" but it is more appropriate to talk of categorization here because we are referring to the linguistic identification of units rather than, say, to detection of the fact that some unit has occurred. In short, such perceptual events as (1) detection that a stimulus has occurred, (2) classification of location, (3) classification by color, and (4) perhaps even full recognition of shapes without a common name (for example, @) all can occur prior to what we are calling categorization here; with true categorization a learned name is assigned to the stimulus input but not with these diverse examples. Precategorically, a linguistic character can be represented in the subject only as a collection of visual features, such as lines, angles, and curves, or of acoustic features, such as concentrations of sound pressure in a frequency—time frame. However, once categorization has taken place, very different responses can be assigned to such highly similar characters as O and Q, after visual presentation, or to /p/ and /b/, after vocal presentation.

Because the making contact of new stimulus energy with old category states must occur, on logical grounds, with adults receiving language symbols, and because, furthermore, it cannot occur instantly on entry of the energy into sense organs, categorization is used as a reference point to sort out mental events occurring between observable input and output.

The evidence examined in this and several of the chapters that follow indicates that humans have memory for information in precategorical form. Neisser (1967) has suggested the apt labels *iconic* and *echoic* for the visual and auditory precategorical stores, respectively. These are such excellent terms that they are used here even though the properties of echoic storage developed in Chapter 3 are discrepant with the echoic store Neisser has envisaged. Iconic and echoic memory are the logical starting points for the study of memory in general, or indeed of learning, although they have most often been considered a part of the psychology of perception or information processing. However, the operations used to study categorization and precategorical storage are not different from those which define the learning–memory experiment.

Sperling's Research on Iconic Memory

In a remarkable doctoral dissertation George Sperling (1960) both introduced to modern attention the idea of iconic memory and anticipated most of the research issues that emerged concerning it in the intervening years. He noted that if eight letters were flashed briefly on a tachistoscope screen people seemed able to report only about four or five correctly. Performance is furthermore relatively independent of how long the flash lasts, within the range of from 15 to 500 msec, and independent of how many letters there are on the screen, within limits of four to 12. In considering the fate of items not reported in such experiments Sperling faced the central dilemma of all memory failures. Were these missed letters simply never registered in the first place, were they registered but then lost before the time of report, or were they for some reason available but not accessible to report?

The subjects themselves claimed that for a brief period after the display was turned off all the letters were quite clearly available but that they faded rapidly during the slow, laborious process of identifying them one by one. The typical score of four or five letters correct would therefore represent not the amount of information in storage but rather the amount that could be rescued, so to speak, before the iconic representation had faded. Of course, this score could also logically represent a limit on rescuing information from the stimulus display itself if there were no such thing as an iconic store.

Sperling's major premise was that if there were an iconic trace available after the stimulus had physically disappeared, and if the trace contained more than four or five letters, then by asking the subject to report only a sample of the display it would be possible to get around the necessity for him to slowly identify all the letters as they were fading. The logic is quite similar to sampling of information in school examinations. If a student were given an hour to report exhaustively on his knowledge for an entire course, the score observed would have more to do with his rate of writing than his knowledge; however, an estimate of how much the student knows can be obtained by a limited number of carefully selected questions that sample his knowledge. The idea is that if he can answer 85% of these questions properly then he likely knows about 85% of the course material in general. Correspondingly, Sperling reasoned that if he instructed his subject to report only one row of a three-row display of letters then whatever percentage of correct performance he could achieve on that particular row should represent the percentage of the whole display available. Furthermore, the task was made dependent on memory by giving the indication of which part was to be reported only after the display had terminated. In this way, Sperling hoped to be sampling from the subjects' memories, just as examination questions posed after the course has ended likewise tap memory.

The subjects in Sperling's study saw two rows of three letters, two rows of four letters, three rows of three letters, or three rows of four letters. In the control conditions the subject was asked to report all of the letters he saw, whereas in other conditions a tone cue indicated which row was to be recalled in partial report. The pitch of the tone corresponded to the row probed; for example, in a three-row stimulus a high-pitched tone cued the upper row and so forth. Notice that the portion of the stimulus the subject actually had to identify and report, always three or four letters, lay well within the limit on items that could be grasped under conditions of whole report.

Consider for a moment now the possibility that there is no iconic storage and that coincident with the offset of the stimulus—a three-row array of 12 letters—a tone calls for report of one row. If there is no iconic storage the subject must rely in this situation on whatever information he has already been able to read off the display before it goes off. We know from the earlier research that this figure is around 4.5 letters from a display of this type. Therefore, if he can report 4.5 out of 12, or 37.5% from the entire display, we may expect he can report 37.5% of each row of four on the average, or 1.5 letters in the partial report situation. Of course some rows may enjoy better scores for purely visual reasons; we are now simplifying the situation by ignoring this complication. Working backward, if we conducted the partial-recall experiment and came up with an average figure of 1.5 letters per row we would estimate total storage capacity at the time the tone sounded as $1.5 \times 3 = 4.5$ letters, that is, the number reported per row times the number of rows that could have been cued. However, any excess of the score based on partial report over the figure achieved in whole report would be, by this line of argument, consistent with the persistence of iconic memory after stimulus offset.

In one of Sperling's (1960) experiments the display was exposed for 50 msec and a tone signaling report of one of three rows of four letters occurred, in separate series of tests, either 50 msec before stimulus onset, simultaneous with stimulus offset, or following delays of 150, 300, 500, or 1000 msec following offset. Figure 2.1 shows the outcome, in terms of estimated letters available, of these conditions as compared with typical whole-report data for a similar type of display. Recall that an estimate of six letters available in a condition indicates that the average partial report score for a single row must have been 2.0; six is half of 12, the total display size, and two is half of four, the row size. Why this partial report of a row of four letters is not perfect, when whole report gives 4.5 items, is considered shortly.

The results showed that subjects had about nine letters available "for rescue" if the tone indicating which row to report came right as the stimulus went off. That is, they could report three of the four letters from any row. However, partial report scores dropped to half this figure, almost exactly the level of whole report, if this cue tone was delayed by about half a second or more.

In a later study Sperling (1963) showed that the persistence of information in iconic memory depended on how bright or dark the visual fields just before and after the letter were. When the screen was dark just before and after the letters partial-report scores were higher and declined more slowly than when the screen was light just before and after the letters. This dependence of the partial-report performance on luminance of adjacent visual fields is quite consistent with the alleged sensory nature of iconic storage and it is quite inconsistent with other interpretations of Sperling's study, which are considered below.

Quite soon after Sperling's work was published Averbach and Coriell (1961) reported similar results from a study in which two rows of eight letters each were flashed and then a cue was given for only a single letter from the display.

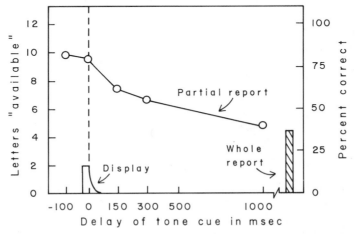

FIGURE 2.1 Performance in estimated letters available and in percent correct for whole report and for partial report as a function of delay of partial-report cue. (After Sperling, 1960.)

The cue was a mark appearing near the position where the letter to be reported had been on the array. With a cue following the display immediately these authors found an average of 75% accuracy with a single letter. This may be translated to an estimate of 12 out of 16 (75%) letters available. In their study, as in Sperling's, delay of the cue by more than 200 or 300 msec produced performance not superior to the ordinary whole-report score, roughly 30% accuracy.

Sperling and Averbach and Coriell were sensitive to the fact that these obtained estimates of storage capacities were *lower limits* on the amount of information subjects must have had available at the exact moment the post-stimulus cue occurred. Consider an extreme case where instead of presenting high, low, and medium tones to cue the three rows, the experimenter presented a number the cube root of which was related in a specified way to the location to be recalled; before the subject could interpret such a cue the trace would long since have decayed. Less obviously, the same thing must have been happening to Sperling's subjects, for interpretation of the cue is a form of mental transformation and no such process is absolutely instantaneous. When the cue occurs, therefore, the subject first must interpret its meaning and only then can he begin to carry out its instruction. Furthermore, by the time the information is gathered from the instructed row—by the time selective readout is complete—there must have been still more decay of the icon. In short, there is unavoidable delay, even with an "immediate" cue, in the partial-report situation.

Another complication in the partial-report experiment is the issue of *nonselective readout* prior to occurrence of the cue. This term refers to the fact that scores in partial report may be inflated by items the subjects have identified while awaiting the cue signaling which row is to be selected. After all, if by chance the subject should happen to read letters in the row that is then cued he has saved some work.

Averbach and Coriell (1961) have developed plausible ways of estimating the biases introduced both by (1) the fact that occurrence of the cue only initiates selective readout, and partial-report scores are therefore underestimates of capacity, and (2) the possibility that prior to occurrence of the cue there is nonselective readout, and partial-report scores therefore overestimate capacity. Although their exact results may apply only to the particular circumstances of their methodology, in particular, to situations with a blank white field before and after the stimulus array, Averbach and Coriell offer a well-justified estimate of 250 msec for the life of iconic storage.

Performance in these experiments is not completely passive on the part of the subject. For example, he has considerable latitude in what to do during the delay prior to onset of a poststimulus cue. Sperling (1960) and Dick (1971) have both made the point that the occurrence of nonselective readout—identification of items before the cue signaling which items are required—should depend on subjects' strategies and also on the experimental design used. Ideally what we want is a whole-report condition in which subjects begin immediately to read out or identify letters once the display occurs, and partial-report conditions in which the subject waits passively until the cue tells him where to look. Sperling called this passive approach the "equal-attention strategy," that is, a strategy of paying equal attention to each row prior to the cue. In a careful series of inferences, Sperling (1960) showed how the presence or absence of this strategy could be brought under experimental control. For present purposes we can go no further than to observe that an experiment of the Sperling type may or may not be indicative of iconic memory depending on rather subtle strategic variables. It seems to be the case that when partial-report performance declines steadily as a function of cue delay, the iconic store is being used in an equal-attention manner—that is, without contamination from nonselective read-out. This statement is supported by Sperling's observation that when subjects are induced not to wait for the signal before identifying stimulus items, their scores, although better overall than when only selective readout is used, are not a decreasing function of cue delay.

There are other interpretive problems associated with the simple fact that partial report is superior to whole report. It is a very general finding in memory research that the act of retrieving one item can have harmful effects on the recall of items not yet retrieved. This phenomenon has been termed *output interference* (Tulving & Arbuckle, 1963) to signify that output of one item may act as a source of retroactive interference with respect to other items. Does this factor cause the difference between partial and whole report in the Sperling experiment? It follows from output interference that there would be better performance, in terms of percent correct, when only four items are to be recalled than when all 12 are to be recalled (Dick, 1971). However, the advantage of partial report, if it depends only on a reduction in output interference, cannot be expected to vary with delay of partial-report cue. Reporting four items should be easier than reporting 12 whenever recall occurs. However, the data in most experiments show that partial-report scores converge, at long cue delays, on whole-report scores, despite the smaller influence of output interference on the former. Later in this chapter we shall review another source of evidence that output interference is not responsible for the Sperling partial-report advantage. Briefly, the crucial point will be that when the subject is excused from reporting part of the display on some postcategorical criterion there is no gain over whole report.

An advantage of partial-report scores over whole-report scores is therefore not sufficient to infer iconic memory unless the advantage disappears with longer cue delays; without this convergence output interference may be responsible. Likewise, the simple deterioration of performance over cue delays is not sufficient without a demonstrable advantage of partial report over whole report. The data pattern of Figure 2.1 needs to be complete; otherwise, straightforward interpretations, without recourse to iconic memory, can handle the elements of that pattern individually (see von Wright, 1972, for a discussion of these points).

Evolution of a Process Model for Visual Memory Tasks

Before we turn to further research on the nature of iconic storage, it is useful to consider a group of models successively elaborated by Sperling (1963, 1967, 1970) to account for behavior in the type of experiment we have just described. These theoretical statements in the form of diagrams are good examples of the information-processing approach to analyzing memory, an approach Broadbent first developed in his 1958 book, *Perception and Communication.* Also, the models themselves introduce much theoretical content that becomes indispensable in later sections of this book. The first and second models are shown in Figure 2.2. In these diagrams rectangles are meant to stand for memory stores and circles for processes that operate on them. Model I, at the top of Figure 2.2, states that light energy enters the organism, achieves storage in iconic memory, and is retrieved directly in visual form by a translation mechanism that produces the written answer. The only limitation on memory would be the duration of

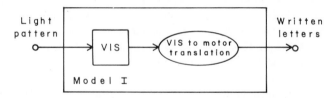

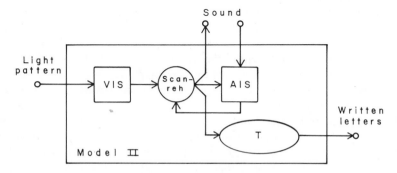

FIGURE 2.2   Sperling's Models I and II for visual memory tasks: VIS = visual information store, AIS = auditory information store, T = translation mechanism. (After Sperling, 1967.)

the icon; therefore, the whole-report score of 4.5 letters must indicate that while the subject is writing down the fourth or fifth letter the icon fades. This simple model can be rejected at once for we know that the writing responses are an order of magnitude slower than the life of the icon as revealed by the partial-report experiments—that is, it takes on the order of 3 sec to write a few letters whereas the icon is apparently gone on the order of .3 sec. For this reason and for a second reason Model II was developed.

The second reason for complicating the diagram beyond Model I was evidence Sperling found in his experiments that the memory items were translated into some type of acoustic or phonological form during performance of the task: (1) The subjects could be heard mumbling letters to themselves during a delayed-recall interval; and (2) when a letter was misrecalled, the letter substituted for the correct one was, more often than chance would allow, a letter that rhymed with it. For example, P might be reported when B would have been correct (recall Conrad's experiment from the last chapter).

According to the revised model, Model II, the contents of the icon are scanned by a speechlike internal naming mechanism with three possible outcomes. The first outcome is that the scan is carried out overtly by reading aloud, resulting in external sound as shown by the arrow exiting from the top portion of the diagram. The second possibility, which may coexist with the first, is a subvocal rehearsal that the subject remembers as an auditory image in echoic, or auditory, storage. The third possible outcome of a scan is translation to the written motor output. In the tachistoscopic experiment this model maintains that the information is first transiently held in iconic form but is then scanned and transformed into echoic form through naming. It is as if the subject hears himself scanning the names of the letters from the icon and then remembers the sound of his own voice. Of course if he scans the icon aloud he hears his voice directly, not some type of inner voice; but Sperling maintains in this model that the form of auditory or echoic storage is the same in either case.

The second feature of theoretical significance in Model II is the presence of a feedback loop. Note that the echoic store, AIS, has an arrow leading to the scan—rehearse process just as the iconic store, VIS, does. This represents the human's ability to scan and identify the contents of sensory stores both in vision and audition. Because the subject can thus essentially reperceive the contents of AIS, he can set up a chain of covert pronunciation and covert listening in order to recycle information indefinitely. For this model it makes no difference whether the looping is carried out overtly or covertly. With this feedback loop, we can now span the delay between the time of scanning iconic memory and the later time when the subject's pencil first begins to scrape across the paper. Model II, then, formalizes the position that the gathering of information from iconic memory is a naming operation where there are two overall limits on performance—the life of the icon and the life of the echoic store.

The objection to Model II is based entirely on considerations of timing. There are good data on how fast overt and covert naming can occur. Landauer (1962) reported that for well-known lists of characters subjects can typically recite aloud at the same rate they recite covertly, a rate of about six characters a second. This generalization has been confirmed recently by Lovelace, Powell, and Brooks (1973). This rate of speech is actually the maximum rate at which scanning can occur from a display in which the items and their order are previously unknown, because the Landauer method uses stimulus sequences that are highly overlearned. If the scan, identification, and naming operations are all occurring together as Model II supposes, then this rate of six per second must describe the maximum rate of gaining information from a visual display.

Now, however, consider results from another type of experiment, where the object is to measure the rate of reading out letters directly through precise control over the duration of displays within the visual system. Examining how fast the first few letters are grasped, before the limited echoic store holds performance down to a maximum of four or five, should give an independent estimate of the scan–rehearse operation.

It was Baxt (1871) who first contrived to limit availability of letter displays by cutting short the afterimage (which we might take here to be comparable to the icon) after specified intervals of time. He flashed a bright, distracting light shortly after exposing a display containing the letters to be reported and found a linear relation between how long the flash was delayed and how many letters were reported, up to about five letters. Sperling (1963) refined this technique by substituting a display of jumbled letter fragments for the flash; his subjects reported that when the interval between onset of the stimulus display and substitution of the letter jumble was varied it seemed that the second stimulus terminated availability of the first. Under these conditions Sperling obtained a result close to Baxt's, indicating the first four or five letters were extracted from the display at a rate of about 10 msec per character, or 100 characters per second. That is, as Sperling delayed the masking jumble of visual noise by each additional 10 msec the subjects were able to give another letter from the display.

We are therefore faced with an order of magnitude discrepancy between how fast people can name characters to themselves—at a maximum of about six a second—and how rapidly people can gain the first few characters from a time-limited display—about 100 a second for the first few characters. This discrepancy must mean that the initial information-gathering operation and the naming operation are not one and the same process, and to accommodate this conclusion Sperling (1967) proposed Model III, which is shown in Figure 2.3. The main change has been decomposition of the scan–rehearsal process into three separate components: (1) a rapid scan process, (2) a recognition memory buffer, and (3) a subsequent rehearsal operation. This separation allows rapid

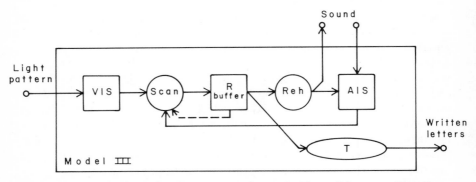

FIGURE 2.3   Sperling's Model III: same notation as in Figure 2.2 except R Buffer = recognition buffer–memory. (After Sperling, 1967.)

scanning (100 per second) to occur at a locus separate from the slow rehearsal (six per second).

In the new model information is first entered in the icon, VIS, and scanned rapidly, that is, at around 100 items per second. The scanning can be affected by biases defined by physical features, such as spatial location, but no contact has at this point been made between the input and categorical long-term memory traces. The products of the scanning are then fed into the recognition memory buffer, which is the locus of the categorical decision, or identification of the character in question. The input to the recognition buffer, that is, the product of the scanning, might be either a collection of visual features or a holistic form, depending on considerations beyond the scope of this discussion. The output of the recognition memory buffer is the consequence of contact occurring between the input from scanning and the stable linguistic response categories, such as letters and words. This consequence of categorization, occurring in the recognition memory buffer, is depicted by Sperling as a package of *motor commands* specifying how to pronounce the particular character, or item, in question. In other words, categorizing an item in the recognition memory buffer amounts to putting articulatory commands for that item into a state of readiness (Morton, 1969, makes a similar proposal). In computer terms, an item gets identified by identifying the address at which the motor subroutine is stored for producing that item. The important feature of this rather clumsy way of describing perception is that the states of motor readiness, or the packages of motor commands, can be activated very rapidly compared to the time necessary to actually execute these motor commands. This is a general idea that we shall meet elsewhere: that categorization results in mental events closely related to the production of items as speech.

Once an item has passed into this state of motor readiness in the recognition memory buffer, then its subsequent history is not different from that proposed in Model II. The interface of the fast scanning and the slow naming processes occurs in the recognition memory buffer, where category states are set up rapidly but acted on only slowly.

Model IV, shown.in Figure 2.4, is not fundamentally different from Model III except that certain considerations overlooked in the earlier version are added, considerations mainly of long-term memory requirements in information processing. The only other change is distinguishing the scan operation associated with VIS from the scan operation associated with AIS; it is certainly reasonable that one needs different scanning machinery for extracting visual features, say, than one needs for extracting acoustic or auditory features. For example, the auditory scanner must be able to bias the process according to such variables as pitch, which is not even a feature of visual displays, whereas visual scanning accepts position biases.

There are six aspects of memory, each given its own box in Sperling's model, that must be present on logical grounds in order for subjects to exhibit the variety of memory performances they do. Separating these requirements into compartments helps keep track of the separable functions being performed without necessarily commiting us to a theory of memory that holds for separate locations of these functions in the brain.

1. Visual long-term memory. In a later chapter we shall offer rigorous support for the notion that some long-lasting memories are kept in visual form without involvement of words. As an example, it is easy to remember having seen a face before, but this memory is probably not verbal in any way. One would be at a loss to describe a face in words such that a stranger would recognize a photograph of it.

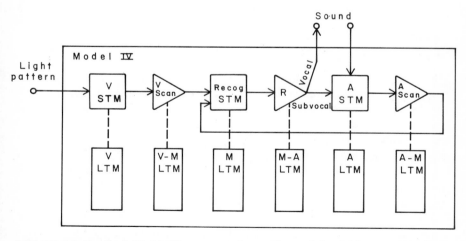

FIGURE 2.4   Sperling's Model IV: same notation as Figures 2.2 and 2.3 except V = visual, A = auditory, M = motor, R = rehearsal, STM = short-term memory, LTM = long-term memory. In this model written responding is not provided for. (After Sperling, 1970.)

2. Visual—motor long-term memory. This is the information used in categorization of visually presented stimuli. In the models we have been considering this memory holds statements of the form: "This set of visual features, or this pattern, goes with the item that has its articulation instructions stored at Location X in the motor long-term memory." This seems roundabout, but recall that a direct connection between the visual features and articulation has been ruled out by considerations of timing.

3. Motor long-term memory. Here are stored the actual packages of commands sufficient to articulate the various verbal categories that have been learned; the statements held in motor memory may include complicated sets of commands to muscles specifying coordinations the details of which need not preoccupy us here.

4. Motor—auditory long-term memory. Here statements of the following form are held: "Executing the routine for producing the letter X results in an auditory image that sounds like. . . ." This type of memory statement signals the importance of infantile babbling (F. Cooper, 1972). In babbling the relations between vocal output and the auditory images would become associated through repetition.

5. Auditory long-term memory. Just as some memories seem to be carried visually without necessary mediation through words, so also other memories are preserved in auditory form although less experimental evidence has been offered on this point. Examples that are persuasive include remembering the sound of a person's voice or remembering the timbre of a violoncello.

6. Auditory—motor long-term memory. In parallel with the visual categorization process described above, it is assumed here that recognizing speech involves a matching of auditory features with locations in which are stored commands for articulation of the item those features represent. These assumptions have been termed the "motor theory of speech perception" (Liberman, Cooper, Shankweiler, & Studdert-Kennedy, 1967).

In a way, this multiplication of memories can go on without end, as more complicated human information-processing situations are considered. However, the distinction between structure and function is never as exact as we sometimes wish. Either separate memory traces or separate types of attribute within single traces could be represented by the boxes. Furthermore, it is not critical that short- and long-term memories be given separate locations; one view of their relation is that short-term memory is activation of a certain subset of the long-term memory. One danger in flow diagrams, however, that needs to be balanced against their virtue in laying out the problems facing adequate theories in a systematic way, is that they may be making distinctions that turn out to be unnecessary. A second danger in these diagrams is that they suggest information flow to be occurring in real time and space, like a physical flow. That is, the temptation is to conceive of information as little bugs crawling from box to box in serial order (serial processing). Although it is true that some operations must logically occur before others, it is probably also true that many operations can at least overlap and at most occur simultaneously (parallel processing).

Properties of Iconic Memory

More on selection. The Sperling-type partial-report procedure quite nicely shows that subjects have some information about the display available after it terminates and that this information is in excess of their capacities for whole report. The evidence, it will be remembered, was that when the responsibility for recalling all display items was relaxed subjects could then achieve quite high scores on randomly-selected subsets of the display. By what right are we justified in calling this extra information visual? We have already mentioned one argument for this conclusion, in noting that Sperling has shown that a visual factor—brightness of the postexposure field—has a great effect on the duration of the extra information. If we were not dealing with a form of memory closely tied to the visual system, relative luminance should not have affected performance.

Sperling included another test of the precategorical nature of iconic storage in the 1960 report. In this case the strategy was to examine which different types of stimulus attribute could serve as the basis for selection. The original demonstrations used spatial discriminations as the basis for partial report—the subject was told where, in the fading icon, to direct his readout efforts. What would happen, Sperling asked, if the partial-report criterion were some postcategorical dimension? The condition he tried was one in which a tone directed either report of digits but not letters or letters but not digits from a stimulus display containing both types of characters mixed haphazardly. The finding was that under these conditions partial report yielded estimates of storage capacity no larger than whole report. An extreme example of the logic may help clarify the importance of this comparison. Imagine a display of digits and a poststimulus cue indicating to the subject he should report only those digits that are—or are not—prime numbers. Surely we can expect no advantage for partial report in this situation, for each symbol must first be identified in order to determine from long-term memory whether it is a prime. Likewise, in Sperling's study, each symbol had to be identified before it could be determined whether it was a letter or a digit.

There have been several more recent demonstrations of this point using a variety of precategorical and postcategorical cuing dimensions (Dick, 1969; von Wright, 1968). In a recent experiment by von Wright (1972) stimulus displays contained four consonant letters and four digits, mixed together and arranged into two rows of four characters, with half the characters colored red and half colored black. In addition to whole-report conditions, there were partial-report conditions in which a cue occurred either (1) 2 sec before the offset of a 200 msec display—that is, 1.8 sec before the onset of the display, (2) 5 msec after offset of the display, or (3) 500 msec after the offset of the display. The partial report cue dictated, in various conditions, selection by either spatial location, color, or linguistic class. The results from one part of the experiment, in which partial- and whole-report trials were not mixed together, are shown in Figure 2.5. The performance measure plotted in the figure is the difference in scores for partial and whole report, that is, the arithmetic advantage of partial report. A score of zero therefore means that partial report does not differ from the performance expectation for whole report. The main result is quite straightforward in showing an advantage for the two physical dimensions, color and location, but only a negligible advantage for class. Furthermore, after a delay of half a second, the differences approached zero.

The slight partial-report advantage for class is a bit of a puzzle, and as we shall see presently a similar finding has occurred in an analogous experimental situation in audition; however, there were only two subjects, out of eight, for whom the difference was statistically significant. It is possible that the factor of output interference was responsible for this small difference in two of the subjects.

Von Wright (1972) has also verified Sperling's contention that the occurrence of a pattern of results such as shown in Figure 2.5 depends partly on subjects' strategies. If (1) subjects are induced to outguess which poststimulus cue will occur, and (2) when partial- and whole-report conditions are mixed rather than given in separate experimental sessions, von Wright (1972) and Dick (1971) have shown that the pattern of Figure 2.5 does not occur. In these latter cases the partial report gains for precategorical selection criteria are smaller and they differ less from gains for postcategorical criteria.

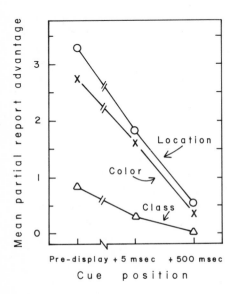

FIGURE 2.5 Advantage of partial report over whole report as a function of time of partial report cue for three-cue instructions. (After von Wright, 1972.)

Masking. There is a large body of research with the purpose of discovering properties of iconic memory, and of visual information processing in general, through the *backward masking* technique. In backward masking (see reviews by Neisser, 1967; Kahneman, 1968; Lefton, 1973) interest is in how a subsequent visual stimulus can impair performance based on a prior stimulus. The logic is indirect: If presentation of some kind of masking stimulus just after offset of a display of characters reduces performance on those characters, one possibility is that the subject is still extracting information from the icon set up by the original stimulus at the time the mask occurred. Variation in how long the mask is delayed after stimulus offset can then be instructive on how long the icon survives. In the next chapter we shall see this indirect logic applied to auditory memory.

There is quite good evidence now (Schiller, 1965; Turvey, 1973) that backward masking occurs at two basically different levels, peripheral and central. There are three main distinctions: (1) In peripheral masking a target display can be interfered with by any sufficiently bright visual stimulus mask, even a simple flash of light; in central masking, however, there must be some degree of similarity between the elements of the display and the patterning of visual features on the mask. (2) In peripheral masking the destructive effect of the mask is determined by a simple relation between target energy and the inter-stimulus interval (target offset to mask onset); in central masking, in contrast, the important relation between target and mask is the elapsed time between the onset of each, with little dependence on energic factors. (3) Finally, the conclusions in (1) and (2) correspond neatly with masking differences obtained in comparing monoptic masking (where target and mask are both delivered to the same eye) versus dichoptic masking (where target and mask are delivered to different eyes); clearly, the dichoptic masking effect must be more central than the monoptic effect.

The locus of iconic storage, in terms of the peripheral—central dichotomy we have just raised, is not known. It is possible that there is a level of iconic storage corresponding to both masking arrangements. However, the iconic store itself may be exclusively peripheral, say on the retina, with central masking reflecting stages of information processing that depend on the peripheral image but are themselves located much "deeper" into the central machinery. Naturally, we should be somewhat more comfortable using the term "memory" for an iconic store of central locus than for a store of peripheral locus, but the distinction is one of degree and the retina is, after all, classified as part of the brain in terms of cellular arrangements.

Summary

Categorization is the contact between incoming stimulus information and linguistic categories in memory; *iconic memory* is defined as storage at a level prior to this contact. The main demonstration of iconic memory is that subjects can selectively attend to physically defined subsets of a total display with greater accuracy than they can to the entire display provided the cue for selection occurs only after the display itself has terminated. By this criterion, iconic memory persists on the order of .25 sec.

An adequate model for performance in experiments on iconic memory includes components associated with scanning, recognition, rehearsal, and phonological recoding, as well as the long-term memory components necessary for these functions. Constraints on the properties of such an overall model include the striking discrepancy between the rate at which characters can be gained from a display (about 100 per second) and the rate at which subvocal rehearsal can occur (about six per second).

Two kinds of research that are particularly useful in elucidating properties of iconic memory, and of the system of which it is a part, are (1) studies showing selectivity from iconic memory to be possible only on the basis of precategorical, and not postcategorical, dimensions and (2) studies on peripheral and central masking.

Here is a memory system, therefore, in a rather limited sense of the term. Although probably an indispensible constituent of the process of reading, it has little to do with the common experience of memory. In miniature, however, it raises the major experimental strategies of stage, coding, and task analysis. The properties yielded by these analyses include decay with the passage of time, erasure by subsequent input, and perhaps unlimited capacity. It remains to be seen in later chapters whether other, postcategorical, memory systems show any of the same properties.

3
Echoic Memory

By convention, a sensory or precategorical memory carries information in a format faithful to its modality of arrival. In this respect a sensory memory resembles an image; however, an image, again by convention, is usually conceived as based on long-term memory and can therefore be aroused associatively without direct stimulation of the relevant modality. We can produce an image but not an icon in total darkness.

The sensory memory for audition has been called *echoic memory* by Neisser (1967). If anything, the need for an echoic memory is more acute than the need for an iconic memory, on logical grounds, but the evidence for it is less impressive. The reason a sensory store is more necessary for audition than for vision comes from inherent properties of these two modalities: Whereas meaningful visual patterns occur all at once, spread out in space, meaningful auditory patterns occur piecemeal, spread out in time. For an auditory event to be perceived as a unit the early portion of that event must be held while the later portions unfold. This assertion is most true for such auditory patterns as words, sentences, or melodies, but it can be argued with equal vigor for auditory patterns as simple as a sine wave.

DEMONSTRATIONS OF ECHOIC MEMORY

The main issue facing workers in this area has been not whether echoic storage exists but exactly how one goes about getting evidence for it. There are three main evidential approaches: recognition, sampling, and masking, and there are numerous subclasses.

45

Recognition Methods

If material is unattended, or uncategorizable, most theories hold that it resides briefly in the auditory system and then is lost. When a segment of information of this sort is repeated the subject can verify for us that the information has been stored and retained without his having to identify it. He can simply indicate that repetition has occurred; the time between original exposure and accurate detection of repetition gives an estimate of how long information has been retained.

The Guttman and Julesz experiment. In a famous but isolated experiment Guttman and Julesz (1963) applied the recognition technique to a message consisting of random broad-band noise, which sounds like a uniform hiss. Their strategy was to extract a section of this noise and repeat it end to end for an extended period. The independent variable was how long the repeating section lasted (that is, how often the same segment "started over") and the dependent variable was the subject's report of whether he heard repetition and its quality. Because there is no conceivable way for a subject to encode this random noise meaningfully it can be argued that detection of repetition must indicate echoic memory from one repetition loop to the next. The results showed that at fast repetition rates, when, for example, a 50-msec piece of noise was repeated 20 times a second, the perception was of a low tone. At slower repetition rates, down to a 250-msec segment repeated four times a second, a clear periodicity was heard, described by the authors as the sound of a motorboat. The slowest repetition rate at which periodicity was detected in this study was 1 sec. When one considers that detecting repetition of white noise segments is like recognizing two patches of waves to be identical while one is sailing across the ocean, it is quite remarkable that storage for as long as a second can be demonstrated. Other, more easily discriminated material should on these grounds last longer, even without attention.

Treisman's experiment. Such is the conclusion that can be drawn from a study by A. Treisman (1964), where subjects received coherent verbal messages in the two ears. The two messages were actually identical but one was delayed or lagged, a variable amount of time with respect to the other. The subject's main job was to shadow the input to one of his ears. Because shadowing—repeating aloud the contents of one message as soon as possible when it occurs—is supposed to occupy attention fully, then any knowledge the subject later possesses about the ignored information must have been encoded from a sensory trace at the time of the test rather than carried in some form of postcategorical memory. In other words, the shadowing task is assumed to prevent categorization of the nonshadowed words. In Treisman's study the independent variable was the time lag separating the first and second occurrences of the same message;

the main dependent variable was the time at which subjects noticed identity of the two messages, as the lag was gradually reduced. With a lag of several minutes we would expect no detection of repetition but with a lag of 1 or 2 msec we would expect perfect detection.

There are two situations of interest; in one, the channel with the first occurrence of the repeated message is the channel, left or right, to which the subject is instructed to pay attention and in the other situation the channel with the first occurrence of the repeated information comes on the ear to be ignored. The outcome was that when the message led on the ignored, nonshadowed channel the lag between occurrences had to be reduced to about 1.5 sec in order for the subject to notice the repetition. However, when the leading channel was to be attended the repetition was noticed at lags as long as about 4.5 sec. In other words, when only sensory memory could hold the first occurrence, until the arrival of the second occurrence, the two could not lag by nearly as much as when both sensory and postcategorical information would have been available from the first occurrence. It therefore makes sense that the critical lags were different depending on which version, leading or lagging, was ignored. The particular estimate of 1.5 sec when the leading channel was ignored is the estimate of echoic memory that can be derived from Treisman's study.

Sampling Methods

If a person receives some piece of linguistic information and does not categorize it right away then we should be able to gather evidence for precategorical storage by probing for the information at some later point in time. The recognition methods employed in the Guttman–Julesz and Treisman experiments sought to do this by repeating segments of the stimulus information, as the probe operation, with detection of repetition by the subjects as the recognition measure. Now we turn to methods in which a more direct probe operation is used to assess how much of the uncategorized information remains available to the subject. Obviously this type of probing, or sampling, is valid only if the information has not been identified (that is, categorized) in the first place.

Analogs to the Sperling (1960) experiment. There are two ways in which investigators have chosen to discourage immediate categorization of the stimulus items: One is by presenting much more information than the subject can categorize in the time given, and the second is by directing attention toward one source of information and away from a second but simultaneous source. It will be noted that the former strategy follows Sperling's example in visual memory: If the subjects indeed possess more sensory information than they can identify, then a suitable poststimulus cue should allow sampling of the extra information provided the cue comes soon enough after the stimulus.

The first convincing demonstration of effects similar to Sperling's, in audition, was an experiment reported by Moray, Bates, and Barnett (1965) on a preparation they called the "four-eared man." As in the visual studies, their subjects faced a dense rush of spatially-arrayed information that was then sampled with a partial-report cue. There were four messages of one or more characters, each presented at once, located in four separate apparent positions thanks to stereophonic mixing. Coincident with *stimulus offset* a light in one of four positions indicated which channel of the four to report. The results of these cued-recall tests were compared with a condition in which all four messages had to be reported on each trial, without regard for location. The finding was that estimates of storage capacity based on partial report exceeded estimates based on whole report, just as with Sperling's experiment.

However, Moray *et al.* (1965) failed, in a strict sense, to include those controls that are necessary to infer sensory memory: There was no variation in the delay of the poststimulus cue and therefore the advantage of partial over whole report could have arisen because of reduced output interference in partial report. As noted in Chapter 2, retrieval of information can act as interference with regard to information not yet retrieved; smaller output loads in partial report may therefore account for the advantage of partial over full report. Second, there is no comparison of partial report based on precategorical dimensions versus postcategorical dimensions; therefore, we do not know that the extra information, presumably gathered from auditory space in response to the poststimulus cue, has indeed been precategorical.

Darwin, Turvey, and Crowder (1972) extended the Moray *et al.* (1965) technique to cover these objections. They employed three auditory channels over which, respectively, three triplets of mixed digits and letters were delivered. The time from the onset of the first items to the offset of the third item, in each of the three simultaneous channels, was 1 sec. Within the space of 1 sec, therefore, the subject heard three short lists of three items each, each of these short lists coming over a different channel. In one condition the subject was required to recall as many items as he could, including information about when and where they had occurred. In other conditions partial report was probed by a visual signal—a bar occupying either the left, center, or right position on a screen—coming either coincidentally with offset of the auditory messages or following delays of 1, 2, or 4 sec.

The results are shown in Figure 3.1, plotted so as to correspond to Sperling's results (see Figure 2.1). Recall that a partial-report trial is like a multiple-choice examination, where the percentage correct on a subset of the material is taken to represent the percentage of all possible information known. If one of the three channels gives 67% correct recall, therefore, we assume that the subject knows 67% of the whole message at the time the cue has arrived, or six items. The results replicate the basic pattern of results from which Sperling has been able to infer iconic storage. There was an advantage of partial report over whole report,

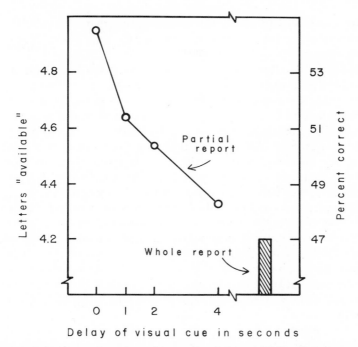

FIGURE 3.1 Performance in estimated letters (or digits) available and percentage correct for whole report and for partial report as a function of cue delay. (After Darwin, Turvey, & Crowder, 1972.)

just as Moray *et al.* (1965) had obtained. Furthermore, this advantage showed a regular decline as the partial-report cue was delayed, indicating the initial advantage could not be attributed to reduced output interference.

The next step is to be convinced that the information storage revealed by this probe technique is sensory in nature. Sperling, it will be recalled, felt justified in talking about a sensory store because (1) such visual factors as pre- and postexposure field brightness had substantial effects on the duration of the partial-report advantage, and (2) when such a nonvisual, postcategorical dimension as verbal class—letter or digit—was used as the partial-report selection criterion there was not a partial-report advantage over immediate memory span (whole report). Darwin *et al.* (1972) applied the second criterion in one of their experiments, using the same stimulus messages as used in the study represented in Figure 3.1 but telling subjects that the visual poststimulus cues, bars on the right versus left side of the screen, stood for required report of either only the digits from the nine-element display or of only the letters. To the consternation of the authors, there was some advantage of partial-report conditions over whole report, in this situation, which did disappear with the longer two delay conditions. However, this partial-report advantage at short delays was extremely small numerically and Darwin *et al.* (1972) concluded that physically organized dimensions were at least far more accessible in the echoic store than categorically defined ones.

In a study by M. Treisman and Rostron (1972) subjects heard six easily discriminable tones, each lasting 100 msec. The stimuli were presented in two volleys of three tones each, with the three tones occurring in three different apparent locations in auditory space. Two tones in succession therefore occurred in each of three locations. Following delays of 0–1.6 sec, a single tone was presented as a probe stimulus. The subjects were required to state whether or not the probe tone matched one of the six tones presented earlier. The results showed that compared to whole-report estimates of 2.6 tones, the probe gave estimates of nearly 3.5 items, an advantage that declined over increasing probe delays. Unless subjects in this study had absolute pitch or had assigned other types of verbal codes to the different stimulus tones, this pattern of results could be taken as supporting the finding of Darwin *et al.* in revealing properties of an echoic store lasting well over a second. (However, a limitation of this experiment is that the whole-report scores were based on recall tests and the partial-report scores on recognition.)

Naturally, a good deal more evidence of this type is needed before we may place much confidence in the view that the techniques used to sample from iconic and from echoic stores are truly comparable. Particularly necessary are experiments settling whether in the Moray *et al.* (1965) situation there can be sampling from postcategorical dimensions, as the results of Darwin *et al.* (1972) weakly suggest. If sampling by postcategorical dimensions works the inference that this method taps an echoic store must be correspondingly weakened; alternatively, the postcategorical organization of such an echoic store must be contemplated.

Sampling "ignored messages." Evidence from sampling methods about sensory storage is only as good as corresponding evidence that what is being sampled is information in raw, uncategorized form. The Sperling type of experiment that we have just examined relies mainly on the sheer rush of information to establish this important point; with nine items all occurring within a second, there is simply not time for the subject to encode all he hears. Information overload is also substantial in the original visual experiments by Sperling and Averbach and Coriell.

A second effort to guarantee the sampling of categorically unprocessed information is simply to instruct subjects to ignore one of two or more simultaneously arriving (as they are called, *dichotic*) messages. It has long been an article of faith, as noted above, that shadowing a rapid stream of speech precludes wandering of attention. There has been a controversy for many years about experiments with shadowing of one of two simultaneous dichotic messages, concerning exactly how much information "gets in" from the ignored message (see A. Treisman, 1969). It occurred to Norman (1969) that a problem in such experiments as they were usually performed was that to establish what the subject understood of the rejected messages required asking him about it at some later time. The delay this technique involves could have a lot to do with how much information is reported. For this reason, rather than to establish anything concerning echoic storage, Norman (1969) performed a study in which subjects were obliged to shadow the message (monosyllabic words at a rate of two per second) arriving over one ear. From time to time lists of six two-digit numbers occurred on the other, ignored ear at a rate of one two-digit number per second. At the end of the number lists Norman interrupted his subjects and tested recognition for items from the rejected ear. The finding was that the last two pairs of digits were recognized quite efficiently, but earlier items, more than 2 sec or so back, could not be. If subjects are to be credited with following instructions, they have not been categorizing the rejected message when it occurs on the ignored channel. We may therefore conclude that precategorical traces of the ignored information remained in useful form for on the order of 2 sec.

Glucksberg and Cowan (1970) replicated and expanded Norman's experiment by replacing the digits in the ignored message with a prose passage comparable to the one being shadowed. Into this they spliced a single digit at irregular intervals. The experiment consisted of interrupting the shadowing from time to time and requesting information on any digit that may have occurred on the rejected channel. The independent variable was the delay between the actual occurrence of the digit and the interruption for questioning. The results showed a systematic decay in scores on the information from the ignored channel as the query was progressively delayed. Furthermore, the subjects could not report that there had been a digit on the rejected channel unless they could identify it. In other words, they did not make errors of commission. This indicated that it was unlikely a categorizing response was occurring at the time the digit was heard; if they had been encoding the digit categorically, one might expect declining performance to consist of increasing confusion errors from short-term postcategorical memory—misidentifications of which digit had occurred.

The inferential problem in these experiments on recall of ostensibly unattended information is subtle. We are abruptly returned to one of the dilemmas introduced in Chapter 1, that of stage analysis. The subject must obviously make his response in the form of a categorized unit, but does he categorize it at the time of this retrieval response or has he done so automatically on hearing the item at acquisition? The first explanation, mainly supported by the authors of the experiments we have just reviewed, says that the unattended information lingers briefly in an echoic store and that if enough of it is left at the time the subject is queried about the unattended message, he can then perceive the item and report it to the experimenter. The alternative view, which Massaro (1972), for example, has espoused concerning these studies is that all items are categorically identified at input but only in a rudimentary way. Information coming over the attended channel is enriched by focal attention processes, such as rehearsal and comprehension, whereas that on the unattended channel is not, and therefore the latter appears to fade rapidly. A way to clarify the situation may be to combine, as it were, the Moray *et al.* (1965) technique with those used by Norman (1969) and others: There may be a single attended message, for which the subject is in some way responsible, and several unattended messages distributed spatially. Having several unattended messages in the company of a difficult shadowing task ought to preclude wanderings of attention and appropriate probe tests can then index the decay of echoic information concerning the rejected message.

An experiment by Eriksen and Johnson (1964) follows the logic of those we have been considering in this section—where a deliberately ignored message is sampled—but in this case the attended message is visual rather than auditory. Subjects were engaged in a primary task of reading a novel of their own choosing. From time to time, 28 times during a 2-hr session, a faint tone was sounded; the main response measure was simply whether the subject detected these tones. At intervals ranging from 0 sec to just over 10 sec following the occurrence of a tone, the reading light was turned out and subjects were asked to judge whether a tone had occurred during the last 10 or 15 sec. There were also occasions when the light was turned off for such a probe but in fact no signal had occurred. If we include occasions when the subject was uncertain in our analysis, the rate of false alarms, or the rate of saying there had been a tone on the catch trials when there had been none, was around 20%, whereas the rate of correct detections of tones when probed immediately after their occurrence was around 60%. However, the rate of correct detections fell off to about 50% as the time between the tone and the probe was increased to over 10 sec. This pattern of results is consistent with the notion that subjects examine a decaying echoic memory when stopped by the lights-off probe. However, it could also be that subjects were vaguely aware of the tone when it occurred but then forgot the fact that it occurred with elapsing time.

This latter possibility was tested in a second experiment in which the subjects were not interrupted from their primary reading task but were under instructions to report any spontaneous detections immediately. It was found that the rate of spontaneous detections was far below the probed detection rates, even when the probe was delayed to over 10 sec. Therefore, it is not likely subjects were aware of tones as they occurred and forgot about their occurrence during the delay before sampling in the first experiment. Instead, the data suggest that subjects examined the contents of echoic memory when the probe signal occurred. The roughly 10% decay in performance would then represent the fading echoic memory. The estimate of trace duration in the Eriksen—Johnson experiment is, on the argument presented above, somewhere beyond 10 sec. Although this figure is higher than those based on other methods, it should be kept in mind that the task of detection is inherently easier than identification or recognition; if echoic traces are subject to decay, therefore there may, after 10 sec, be sufficient information remaining to support detection performance but not to support recognition.

Masking Methods

A large body of research has been directed at the problem of echoic storage through methodologies involving one or another type of masking. In masking studies, generally, some distracting event follows stimulus presentation with the result that performance is poorer than without that event. Generally, also, if the distracting event is delayed there comes a point when performance is just as good as without masking.

It is difficult to draw valid conclusions about the form of storage on the basis of masking alone. The problem is illustrated, although in ludicrous form, by considering a new acquaintance to whom you have just told your name at a cocktail party. If you immediately pour your martini on his shoe, chances are he will not be able to subsequently retrieve your name; however, if you wait 5 min before pouring the martini, chances are he can retrieve it. Now, the essential result of many masking studies is simulated by this incident, but obviously there is no way to infer, from this data pattern, exactly in what form of coding the name has been stored, say, phonological or semantic coding. Yet this type of inference is just what investigators of masking try to draw. Obviously, therefore, the fact of masking is just the starting point and the surrounding conditions must provide the justification of the case that echoic memory is involved.

If the simple fact of masking is insufficient for reaching conclusions about the mode of information storage, however, the relation between the masking effect and the type of mask used can be the basis for powerful inferences. In the cocktail party example suppose we found that three treatments were equally distracting to the subject, by some such external criterion as a startle response, but not equally destructive of memory for the name: Suppose three treatments were the martini, a loud sound, and a sudden flash of light. If we observed that the auditory stimulus, but not the visual or liquid ones, destroyed memory for the name there would be a presumptive case for storage along some auditory-related dimension. If further research showed that following visual presentation of the stimulus to be remembered the relations among these interfering incidents and performance were reversed, then the argument would be further strength-ened. The lesson, to repeat, is that the observation of masking or interference is in itself the method, not the finding, that decides on the form of storage.

Masking of tones. Few sounds are simpler than single pure tones and therefore many investigators have used these as stimuli in hopes of tapping some of the most basic mechanisms of perception and retention in the auditory modality. In studies of backward masking with tones, a tone is presented and followed more or less quickly by some other auditory event. Performance decrements associated with the first, target tone are expected if masking occurs. Massaro (1972) has properly distinguished between studies of *detection masking* and of *recognition masking*. In detection masking the performance measure concerns whether the subject is aware the target tone has occurred at all or aware of its duration or intensity. In recognition masking the subject has learned to encode two or more tones differently and his discrimination of them is examined as a function of masking. In studies of forward masking the position of the target and mask are reversed; because it is with the possibility of echoic storage for the target that we are concerned, we shall consider only backward masking here.

Elliot (1962) presented 5- or 10-msec target tones of 1000 Hz followed by 50-msec bursts of 70 or 90 dB white noise. The measurement was how the noise affected thresholds for detecting the target tone as a function of the interval separating the target from the mask: 0, 1, 3, 5, 10, 15, 25, or 50 msec. The experiment was conducted under both monotic and dichotic conditions, which meant the target and mask were received, respectively, by the same ear or by opposite ears. The results showed considerable increases in thresholds, on the order of 20–50 dB, under backward monotic masking. Significant but smaller (around 10 dB) threshold increases were obtained under dichotic conditions. Because with threshold measurement the target tone is always faint relative to the strong masking noise, the interpretation of backward masking here is somewhat ambiguous. Elliott (1962) herself points out that perhaps the simplest explanation is that the mask actually overtakes the target and even arrives at higher neural centers first, for stronger signals are known to travel faster along the auditory system than weaker signals. Massaro (1972) has made the same case with regard to detection masking in general, concluding that there is no necessary reason for speaking of memory at all in these experiments.

In recognition masking, where the subject is obliged to evaluate the target on some previously established criterion, there is no such problem of the mask outrunning the target because both events can be delivered at the same amplitude. Massaro (1970) presented one of two pure tones, either 770 or 870 Hz, and his subjects were taught to identify these as the low and high tones, respectively. These target stimuli lasted for 20 msec and after silent delays of from 0 to 500 msec, a 500-msec masking tone, set at 820 Hz, was presented. All tones in the experiment were presented at 81 dB. The performance measure was the subject's ability to identify the target tone as high or low, as a function of the interval between the target and mask.

The results are given in the left panel of Figure 3.2, where performance of three subjects is shown individually. In the right-hand panel are the results of a similar study (Massaro, 1972) where 20-msec segments of the vowel sounds from HEAT and HIT were the targets (rather than high and low tones) and a jumbled mixture of the vowel sounds from PUT and PAT were used as a mask. Again, the measure of interest was the subject's ability to classify the vowel used as the

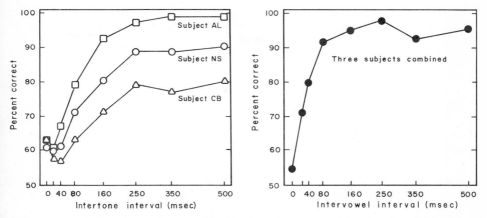

FIGURE 3.2 Percentage of correct identification of target sound as a function of delay of a similar masking sound: (left) tones masked by tones; (right) vowels masked by jumbled speech sounds. (After Massaro, 1970, 1972.)

target on each trial as a function of the delay after which the mask was presented. For both data sets, the important feature is a marked impairment when the mask comes quite rapidly after the target, within 100 msec of it, and a release from this masking with longer interstimulus intervals, between 100 and 250 msec.

Massaro (1972) maintains that results of this sort are sufficient to infer operation of a preperceptual auditory image system, or echoic memory:

> Given that the test tone lasted only 20 msec., some preperceptual image must have remained for perceptual processing necessary to improve recognition performance with increases in the silent intertone interval. This same result indicates that the masking tone terminated perceptual processing of the image. Since recognition performance levels off at about 250 msec. [in the tone experiment, shown on the left in Figure 3.2], the image probably decayed within this period. [Massaro, 1972, p. 129]

In other words, the tone was too brief a stimulus to be recognized during its actual presentation, Massaro says. Because increases in the poststimulus delay before presentation of the mask led to better and better recognition performance, there must have been some type of stimulus trace, an echoic memory, to be processed during the delay. Then, because performance was so closely related to the time between target and mask, the mask must have been terminating processing of the target. Finally, Massaro concludes that performance levels off at interstimulus intervals of about 250 msec because the echoic trace has decayed by this time.

At least two other rationalizations of these data are possible, however. First, it could be assumed that at short interstimulus intervals the target and masking tone were somehow combined or averaged. It would follow that if two otherwise discriminable stimuli were combined with the same mask, they would become less discriminable than before. The further separated the target and masks in time, the less likely this blending of the two would be.

Second, it could be maintained that the target and mask are both fully and independently processed whatever the interstimulus interval. As long as the subject never confuses which stimulus has been the target and which the mask there is no problem. If he does make such confusions, however, then the task becomes one of deciding which stimulus has led—a temporal order judgment. In Massaro's (1970) experiments with tones, for example, the mask was sometimes halfway between the high and low tones. As long as the subject kept track of the sequence high—low or low—high correctly, then he would not actually have to recognize the target. If there have been confusions between the target and mask, however, his score depends on his power of temporal order discrimination, which in turn depends on the interstimulus interval: If two events occur at widely separated times then their order is easy to perceive, whereas if they occur close together their order is more difficult to perceive (Hirsch, 1959). This reasoning suggests there may be a dependence between the function of masking versus interstimulus interval, on the one hand, and the similarity of the mask to the targets, on the other hand. There are some individual data showing relations of exactly this sort (Massaro, 1970, Experiment IV, Subjects HO and EB) but elsewhere (Experiment V), with other individuals, this pattern did not prove reliable. Further research with a wider variety of masking stimuli could help clarify the point.

Finally, the absence of masking beyond around 250 msec, in Massaro's data, does not necessarily indicate that the echoic trace has decayed at this time. An alternative explanation is that the subject has simply extracted all the useful information contained in the trace by this time.

The suffix effect. The other masking situation we shall examine deals with memory for lists of verbal items rather than identification of tones or single syllables. Dallett (1965) and Crowder (1967a) provided the first data on the suffix effect; however, it was not until publication of a paper by Crowder and Morton (1969) that an interpretation relevant to echoic memory was given it.

In a typical suffix experiment, a list of eight items is presented aurally at a rate of two items per second for immediate ordered recall. In the control condition there is either silence after the last memory item in the list or else some nonverbal cue, such as a tone or buzz, indicating the end of the list. In the experimental condition a spoken word, called a "stimulus suffix," is presented after the last memory item, in time with the prevailing rate of presentation. This extra verbal item is the same word over a substantial block of trials, in that it occurs on every trial at the same location following the last item, and the subject is therefore quite ready for it on every trial. In many studies the word "zero" has been used as the suffix item but any word works the same way. The subject is warned that this extra item is going to occur on every trial and that he need pay no attention to it. However, he is told that he may find the suffix convenient as a cue for when to begin recalling the memory series. The suffix word should therefore pose no additional memory load, just as a buzzer at the end of the list for the control condition should pose no additional memory load. However, as can be seen in Figure 3.3, the suffix causes subjects to commit more errors on the last serial positions than in the control condition. The two conditions are roughly the same over most of the list but the suffix condition gives depressed scores on the last portion of the function.

Crowder and Morton (1969) believed the suffix effect was consistent with a form of echoic memory they called "precategorical acoustic storage." Their theory stated that ordinarily in auditory presentation there is a separate sensory memory for the last item or for the last few items but that the verbal suffix displaces, or wipes out, this information. The precategorical acoustic storage system was said to be strictly limited in size, so that any new item would act to displace earlier items. It now appears that the capacity of this echoic-memory system is restricted to information concerning a single item. As the system is at a logical stage prior to identification, it does not matter whether the new item entering is a memory item or a redundant suffix item: the displacing effect on earlier echoic traces is the same.

It should be stressed that the main component of performance in such immediate-memory tasks is postcategorical memory, retrieval from a system where full identification has taken place. The contribution of precategorical acoustic storage is parallel and supplementary. It is parallel because information concerning the last item (or items) is assumed to be held simultaneously in

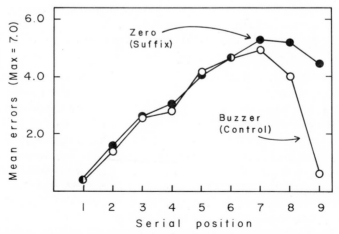

FIGURE 3.3   The effect of a verbal suffix (the word "zero") on the distribution of errors across serial positions in a nine-item immediate-memory test. In the control condition a buzzer was sounded in the same temporal position occupied by the suffix in the experimental condition. (After Crowder, 1972.)

ordinary postcategorical memory and also in the echoic store. It is supplementary in much the same sense—the subject has two types of information available concerning the last part of the list and he can correct any discrepancy by comparing the echoic information with the postcategorical, verbal information. It is erroneous to conceive of the last item, which is the locus of the suffix effect, as being "in" the echoic store at the time the suffix occurs; this last item is retained in the same postcategorical memory as the rest of the list, but there is an extra source of information about it that is present or absent depending on whether a suffix occurs.

When and how is the echoic information about the last item used? In the immediate-memory experiments under discussion here, the subject must recall the items in order and so there is a considerable delay between the presentation of the last item and the time it is retrieved. Although it is possible the information persists in sensory form during this delay, the more likely model is one that includes a process of covert rehearsal of the last few items immediately after they are presented. Indeed, intuitions suggest the subject always is covertly rehearsing the last few items presented, from the beginning of the list on. It is during the slight pause between presentation of the last item and initiation of overt recall that the subject may give a "onceover" to the last few items he has heard. Ordinarily, this is the moment when a comparison is made between his (verbal) memory of the last item and the still lingering echoic trace of the same item, using the latter to correct the former. When time comes for the public (written or spoken) recall effort, therefore, all performance is directly based on categorical information, with the last item having benefitted earlier from echoic memory. When the suffix occurs following the last item, readout of the echoic information from precategorical acoustic storage is prevented and the subject is left to rely on only the categorical information.

Research that can be found in Morton, Crowder, and Prussin (1971) and in Crowder (1972) has established the following properties of the suffix effect:

1. The suffix effect is larger, the sooner the suffix is delivered after the last item in the memory series. One of the main features of other types of masking situations (visual masking, masking of tones) is therefore reproduced with the suffix. Because there is no effect at all if between 2 and 5 sec elapse before presentation of the suffix we may be tempted to reason, as Massaro (1970) has, that the echoic trace must have decayed by this time. However, although this interpretation of the delay effect is possible it is also easy to handle the results by saying the delay measures how long it takes subjects to read out, or utilize, the information in the echoic trace. Therefore, perhaps after 2 sec the trace is still there but displacing it may not affect performance because the subject has already extracted all the information he can from it.

2. The suffix effect is independent of the meaning of the verbal item used as the suffix. It makes no difference in the result shown in Figure 3.3 whether the suffix item is a digit, a letter, a word, or even whether it is a categorizable character at all. One can get the same result with the words "zero," "rosy," and

"recall." The same result occurs when a meaningless grunt is used as the suffix or when a segment of backward speech is used. In terms of meaning, therefore, the similarity between the memory series and the suffix item is quite unimportant. Because the store is supposed to be precategorical, this is as it should be.

3. In contrast, the suffix effect is dependent on the similarity between the stimulus series and the suffix item when similarity is varied along physical dimensions. If the voice reading the memory series is different from the voice speaking the suffix, a significant effect of the form shown in Figure 3.3 is obtained, but it is a significantly smaller effect than occurs when the suffix voice and the stimulus voice match. The same is true when the stimulus list and the suffix are delivered from different apparent locations in auditory space—an effect is obtained when the suffix channel and the stimulus channel mismatch, but it is a smaller effect than when they match. This generalization is also consistent with notions of precategorical acoustic storage.

4. No suffix effect is obtained when the memory list is presented visually and the suffix is presented auditorily. This generalization represents the extreme case of a physical mismatch, such as considered above in Paragraph 3. However, this special case takes on considerable theoretical importance in view of the models sketched in Figure 3.4. On the left is a section of Sperling's Model III; the full model is shown in Figure 2.3. On the right is the type of model proposed by Crowder and Morton (1969). Notice that in Sperling's model there is a common fate—AIS—for both visual information that has been translated in the process of going through the recognition memory buffer, and for auditory information arriving from the environment through the ears. However, transformed visual information and auditory information do not meet until short-term memory in the model shown on the right. If, as Crowder and Morton claim, the suffix effect is occurring in precategorical acoustic storage, then an auditory suffix can not

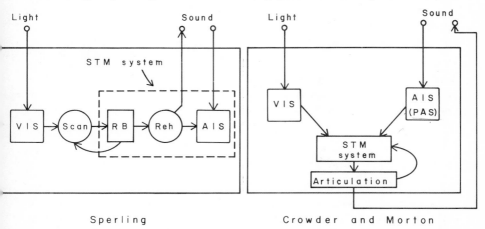

FIGURE 3.4 A comparison of the Sperling and the Crowder and Morton models with respect to acoustic input and rehearsal. The notation is the same as that in Chapter 2 except PAS = precategorical acoustic storage.

interact with a visual memory list. However, according to the Sperling model the suffix effect would have to occur in AIS in the auditory-only case. Because visual information, as well as auditory information, winds up in AIS, however, the prediction is that a cross-modality suffix effect should occur. The data show, on the contrary, that there is absolutely no suffix effect of an auditory item following visual input. A study by Morton and Holloway (1970) assures us that the auditory suffix in these cross-modality suffix studies is not ignored because in their experiment subjects must listen to the suffix in order to know whether to prefix their recall with a check mark or a cross.

5. The suffix effect depends on the type of speech sound being remembered. Crowder (1971) has shown that when subjects must remember strings of consonant—vowel syllables where the discriminable information is contained only in stop consonants, there is neither a recency effect in the control condition nor a suffix effect in the experimental condition. The stop consonants are the letters *b*, *d*, *g*, *p*, *t*, and *k*. To examine retention of information contained only within these letters, the subject may be presented with a series, such as *bah, dah, gah, gah, gah, bah, gah;* when such items occur on computer-produced synthetic speech, as has been the case in studies by Crowder (1971), we may be assured that the memory items differ only with regard to the initial stop consonant in each syllable. It has been determined that when vowels provide the information to be remembered, as with the series *gah, gee, gee, goo, gah, gah, goo,* there results a perfectly standard suffix effect of the type shown in Figure 3.3. Other speech sounds, such as the fricatives (*f, s, sh, v, z,* and so on) give intermediate results between the full suffix effect with vowels and the absence of one with stop consonants.

There is no a priori reason why the suffix effect should depend on the class of speech sounds to be remembered according to the Crowder and Morton theory of precategorical acoustic storage. The finding has led Crowder (1971) and others (especially Darwin & Baddeley, 1974) to suggest that echoic memory holds information about vowels better than it does information about stop consonants. As we shall see below, this is not quite so circular an inference as it seems.

Further Properties of Echoic Storage

On the basis of material presented so far, the suffix effect is only weak evidence favoring echoic storage; we have gone little beyond the martini on the foot level of analysis for it. However, the full argument tying the suffix effect to echoic storage was drawn from a broader empirical base.

The modality effect. If subjects are given memory-span lists (that is, lists of items at lengths of about seven or eight items—the amount of information that can just barely be recalled) under identical conditions of presentation, except that the mode of presentation is visual in one case and auditory in the other case, there is an advantage for auditory presentation that occurs only on the last part of the serial-position function. It makes little or no difference whether the source of the auditory presentation is an external voice, presented on recorded tape, or the subject's own voice, reading aloud from a visual display. What matters is whether or not the information has actually passed through the subject's ears. As a matter of fact, the comparison between visual and auditory presentation is probably best made between two visual-presentation conditions where in the first the subject is told to read the items silently to himself during presentation, and in the second he is asked to read them aloud. The results from such a comparison have been reported by Conrad and Hull (1968) in a simple experiment the result of which is shown in Figure 3.5; Corballis (1966) and Murray (1966) seem to deserve modern credit for the modality effect, although it was known a generation earlier (Washburn, 1916, p. 74).

The Conrad–Hull data show the large advantage of auditory presentation to be sharply restricted to the last part of the list, really to the last item, just as is the suffix effect in Figure 3.3. It was the claim of Crowder and Morton that the advantage of auditory presentation over visual owed to the presence of echoic memory and that this advantage could be removed by the stimulus suffix, restoring performance to what was found with visual presentation. An essential part of the argument is that echoic memory is larger than iconic memory, for otherwise there must be a sensory-memory contribution to visual presentation equalizing it with auditory presentation. According to the theory, therefore, it is precategorical acoustic storage, or echoic memory, that distinguishes the two

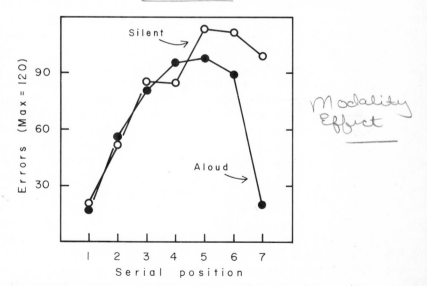

FIGURE 3.5 The modality effect in serial recall: errors as a function of serial position for visual presentation with vocalization silently or aloud. (After Conrad & Hull, 1968.)

serial position functions both in Figure 3.3 and in Figure 3.5—these data show a postcategorical memory process that is supplemented late in the list by an echoic store when presentation arrives through the ears. This echoic influence can be removed by the suffix.

The modality effect is quite prevalent in short-term memory tasks: It shows up in the recency portion of free recall for long word lists (Murdock & Walker, 1969); in tests of single items in the Brown–Peterson distractor situation (Grant & McCormack, 1969; Cooley & McNulty, 1967); and in short-term paired-associate tasks (Murdock, 1966a, 1967a).

Is the modality effect representative of the same echoic memory contribution alleged to occur in the suffix experiment? If it is, then we should expect to find that stimulus materials which fail to show recency and suffix effects should also fail to show the modality effect. This was confirmed by Crowder (1971, Experiment V) in an experiment with a technique similar to the Conrad and Hull study—uniform visual presentation of stimulus items under instructions for either covert, silent vocalization or overt vocalization. The stimulus materials were either stop consonants, *bah, dah,* etc., or vowels, *bah, bih,* etc., written out and exposed on a screen. There was a standard modality effect with vowels but none with stop consonants. This result has been confirmed by Darwin and Baddeley (1974) in immediate memory and by Watkins *et al.* (1974) in free recall of words. The significance of this dependence of the modality effect on stimulus class is that it greatly reinforces the Crowder–Morton contention that the modality and suffix effects depend on the same mechanism.

Implications of stop-consonant–vowel differences. There are several ways in which these data on speech classes can be used to discriminate among theories of both the modality and suffix effects. Kahneman (1973) has proposed the following alternative account of the suffix effect: The relevant parts of the system include only a verbal, postcategorical short-term memory and a selective attention system that can admit information selectively according to precategorical channel distinctions. There is no echoic store in this alternative theory. Subjects ordinarily break stimulus strings into smaller subgroups, which have an optimal size. The recency effect is caused by a particularly distinctive group anchored at the last item When the suffix is admitted into verbal short-term memory by selective attention, however, that is, when attention is not selective with respect to the suffix, then the recency group is overloaded. So thus, the suffix gets treated as an additional item insofar as the all-important grouping operation is concerned. If the suffix is admitted into postcategorical memory then the last item in the memory list is no longer the last item in the last group. However, when there is a delay before the suffix occurs (see Point 1 above), selective attention is able to guard against incorporation of the suffix into the recency group. Likewise, when there is a physical discrepancy separating the suffix from the memory series (see Points 2 and 3)—especially so strong a mismatch as visual versus auditory—selective attention can prevent entry of the suffix. This theory is adequate to cover the major features of the suffix effect without postulating any contribution from echoic memory.

The selective-attention-grouping hypothesis of Kahneman (1973) is all but ruled out by the negative results of the suffix and modality comparisons with stop consonants. There are two reasons: First, if the suffix effect occurs in postcategorical short-term memory, then because stimuli made up of stop consonants surely are entered into short-term memory (because they can be retrieved on test) there should be a suffix effect for them. That is, nothing known about either selective attention or about grouping suggests that stop consonants should be a deviant stimulus class. Second, the selective-attention-grouping hypothesis has nothing to say about the modality effect. Now, of course, there is no reason it necessarily should cover the modality effect; after all, the modality and suffix effects may be produced by entirely independent mechanisms. However, in light of the vowel—consonant data it becomes very unlikely that the modality and suffix effects are produced independently, for both phenomena depend in exactly the same way on speech class. Therefore, the failure of attentional hypotheses for the suffix effect to explain the modality effect can be considered very serious.

One additional hypothesis that has been proposed to account for the modality effect (Brelsford & Atkinson, 1968) is that auditory presentation forces more equal attention on items in a series than visual presentation does. This equalization of attention does not necessarily produce better overall performance, for unequal attention may be adaptive in forming efficient subjective codes—making meaningfully related groups in subsequences of the entire array. However, equal attention at least insures that each list item receives full uniform encoding. Tests of memory that tap short-term processes dependent on initial encoding may therefore show an auditory advantage, not because information has arrived through the ears but because encoding has been forced equally on all items. Because this theory should apply to any type of stimulus material—words, letters, digits, vowels, consonants—equally, we may rule it out on the basis of the evidence above showing absence of modality effects with stop consonants. Of course, this theory is also hard pressed to explain the differences obtained between mouthing, whispering, and soft vocalizing (Murray, 1967); these differences (mouthing worst and vocalizing best) are consistent with a theory stipulating importance for actual aural stimulation, but all of these procedures seem to equalize the distribution of attention.

Other hypotheses (see Watkins et al., 1974) about the modality effect are equally vexed by the consonant—vowel results. Included are (1) the assumption that short-term memory simply has a larger capacity for auditory than for visual information, and (2) the assumption that visual information suffers relative to auditory by having to undergo additional translation stages, such as implied by Sperling's model.

Echoic memory and speech. Naturally, most of these theories of the suffix effect and of the modality effect could be revised to include assumptions about different speech sounds. However, such revisions would seem very arbitrary. Consider the following: "Short-term memory has a larger capacity for auditory information than for visual information except when stop consonants are concerned, in which case the two capacities are equal."

Why is it not likewise arbitrary to make the assumption, offered above, that echoic memory holds vowel sounds better than stop consonants? The answer is that whereas the differing results for vowels and stops make no sense from the existing theories of short-term memory and attention, they make rather good sense from the point of view of speech perception research. A review of this argument is too digressive for the present context, but the essential points have been summarized by Crowder (1975) and by Darwin and Baddeley (1974). Briefly, there are a number of quite different techniques that have been used for studying the perception of speech in which differences between vowels and consonants have been reliably obtained; (1) the ABX discrimination task, where two different speech sounds are presented followed by a probe sound that is identical with either the first or the second (Liberman *et al.*, 1967); (2) direct same–different judgments, where the subject simply decides whether two speech sounds presented successively have been identical or not (Pisoni & Tash, 1974); (3) dichotic competition tasks where two different syllables are fed simultaneously into the two ears and accuracy scores are compared as a function of left–right differences (Darwin, 1971); (4) temporal order judgments (Day & Vigorito, 1973), where two sounds are lagged with respect to each other and the subject must decide which of the two has come first; and (5) the lag effect, where effects of a second syllable on perception of the first are studied as a function of lag and laterality (Studdert-Kennedy, Shankweiler, & Shulman, 1970).

In each of these divergent situations stop consonants show strikingly different results from vowels or other speech classes. The immediate memory differences we have been scrutinizing therefore fall into place alongside numerous results from speech perception. Because it is axiomatic that a sensory or precategorical memory system should display intimate relations with perception in the corresponding modality, it is not a gratuitous, extra assumption to propose that echoic memory is selective on speech signals. Indeed, arguments can be found in Darwin and Baddeley (1974), Crowder (1975), Fujisaki and Kawashima (1970), and Pisoni (1973) that the echoic memory difference between vowels and consonants is the major cause of the perception difference.

Summary and Comment

The main burden of this chapter has been to organize the various experimental methods that have been devised for studying echoic memory:

I. Recognition methods
   A. Broad-band noise repetition (Guttman & Julesz, 1963),
   B. Dichotic delayed speech (Triesman, 1964)
II. Sampling methods
   A. Partial report (Moray *et al.*, 1965; Darwin *et al.*, 1972)
   B. Sampling ignored messages (Norman, 1969; Glucksberg & Cowan, 1970; Eriksen & Johnson, 1964)
III. Masking methods
   A. Recognition masking of tones (Massaro, 1970)
   B. The suffix effect (Crowder & Morton, 1969)

Further properties of echoic memory have been elaborated through two additional areas of research: The modality effect (an advantage of auditory presentation over visual presentation) is important because it corresponds closely to the suffix effect in that (1) the modality effect appears only on the last few serial positions of a list, which is where the suffix effect occurs, and (2) the modality effect is absent when subjects are remembering lists of stop consonants, just as the suffix effect is absent under these conditions. The dependence of the modality and suffix effects on the class of speech sounds being remembered is important because it aligns these effects closely with what is known about the perception of speech, and also because these dependencies are foreign to models of postcategorical verbal memory, whereas the properties of a truly precategorical verbal memory system are expected to fit closely with perceptual phenomena.

Do the various experimental demonstrations of echoic memory all converge on a system with the same properties? On this critical question we must defer judgment until such time as transition experiments among the different experimental techniques become available. For example, if subjects in the auditory analog of Sperling's partial-report experiment (Moray *et al.*, 1965) are given stimulus arrays containing only distinctions among stop consonants, there should be no evidence for a partial-report advantage if this technique taps the same system as the suffix and modality effects. Given the fragmentary evidence from each of the six major methods, an intelligent guess about the duration of echoic memory is very difficult. However, except for the masking experiments by Massaro, none of the research efforts reviewed here pose objections to an estimate of about 2 sec.

Of what use would a 2-sec echoic memory be if it carried only information about the most recent vowel sound to occur in a speech stream? Certainly a high-fidelity tape recording of recent auditory events would seem to be a more useful capacity. It must be noted, however, that we do not know just how restricted the system is; it excludes the six stop consonants but perhaps information from most of the other phonemes, including but not limited to vowels, is admitted. Even if echoic memory were a mechanism specialized mainly for storing vowel sounds it would nonetheless have considerable functional significance. The *prosodic features* of speech—pitch, stress, intonation contours—are of obvious importance in human communication and they are encoded exclusively on the vowels; it is, for example, not possible to convey a rising pitch contour on the *ch* portion of the word "sandwich." In perceiving such prosodic features, which are changes over time, one needs simultaneous knowledge of events in the present and in the past: To know that the pitch of a word has risen at the end, one must simultaneously know where the pitch has terminated and where it has been at some previous point in time. Because verbal encoding of such variables as pitch is unlikely, this function is a natural feature of echoic storage.

4
Recoding by Speech in Short-Term Memory

All normal human beings know about their language initially through the medium of speech and even for those of us who manage to learn to read it is probably the case that language still remains somehow bound to phonology, to the process of talking and hearing. In this chapter we consider the possibility that speech is heavily involved in remembering linguistic elements, such as words or letters, even when they are not received by means of speech. For example, if a letter is traced on our back with a stylus, the process being considered is that of speaking that letter internally and then remembering some aspect of this internal speech. In connection with the information-processing models presented in Chapter 2 we have already faced these ideas (and Conrad's discovery of phonological recoding was covered in Chapter 1). Sperling's model holds that at the time of categorization visual information undergoes transformation that renders it into phonological form. We passed over this assumption at face value in Chapter 2 and now we need to build an empirical case for it. It should be understood that no claim is being made for an exclusive speech code in memory, nor even for an exclusive speech code in memory for language symbols. We shall see in later chapters unequivocal evidence that people bring a variety of coding strategies into memory experiments; however, for the moment our preoccupation is with speech coding alone.

The Concept of Recoding

Before we go on to examine speech recoding we should pause to consider the meaning of the term "recoding" itself, as this term is used in the analysis of memory. *Recoding* denotes a transformation on information that places it into a fundamentally different form of organization. In this sense recoding is quite different from *encipherment,* in which new symbols from the same vocabulary of characters are substituted for original ones on a one-to-one basis, or from *paraphrase,* where slightly different elements of a single-symbol system are used to describe the same informational situation. The following are two examples that vividly illustrate the recoding process in memory; both concern recoding as applied to a string of binary digits.

Binary-to-octal recoding. Faced with the task of remembering verbatim a list of binary digits, such as *000110101110,* there are several strategies that may occur to different people. One way, a poor way, would be to encode the list in the form given, as "oh, oh, oh, one, one, oh, one, oh, one, one, one, oh." This series can probably be repeated over and over until it becomes fixed, just as we seemingly remember a telephone number based on decimal digits by rote. If the binary string is grouped into triplets, however, another strategy can be applied, called a binary-to-octal conversion. The octal numerals are 0, 1, 2, 3, 4, 5, 6, and 7. They may be represented as three-place binary numbers according to a system illustrated in Table 4.1. In this system each octal number has a unique pattern of zeros and ones and vice versa. The value of the system is that the information in

TABLE 4.1
The Binary-to-Octal Conversion

Three-place binary numbers	Octal equivalents
0 0 0	0
0 0 1	1
0 1 0	2
0 1 1	3
1 0 0	4
1 0 1	5
1 1 0	6
1 1 1	7

Illustrations:

$$0\ 1\ 1 = 0 \times 2^2 + 1 \times 2^1 + 1 \times 2^0$$
$$= 0 \times 4 + 1 \times 2 + 1 \times 1$$
$$= 0 + 2 + 1 = 3$$

$$1\ 0\ 1 = 1 \times 2^2 + 0 \times 2^1 + 1 \times 2^0$$
$$= 1 \times 4 + 0 \times 2 + 1 \times 1$$
$$= 4 + 0 + 1 = 5$$

an original three-place number can now be carried in a single place. This system was first called to psychologists' attention by George Miller (1956) in an article where he observed that it seemed to be the number of bundles of information, or chunks, that limited how many things we could remember in a series rather than how rich these bundles were in information. Using the system shown in Table 4.1 the series *000110101110* can be recoded into 0–6–5–6; this gives four things to remember instead of 12, for the original 12-digit binary series. Therefore the conversion, or recoding strategy, is an efficient strategy. Because most college students can remember about eight digits after a single presentation it is possible for a user of this system to reproduce 24 binary symbols with very little strain if he is skilled at the recoding process.

The important point in this example is that the binary and octal versions of the same information are organized differently—they use different characters in their vocabularies and they have different numbers of these characters. There is no loss of information; from the octal *6* you can always get back to *110*.

The verbal-loop hypothesis. Conversion from binary to octal coding can occur equally well when stimulus presentation is in the auditory or visual modalities. Now we turn to a method that has been used mainly for simultaneous visual stimulus presentation, again, of binary series. The verbal-loop hypothesis was proposed by Glanzer and Clark (1963) to cover the following theoretical mechanisms: The person sees a string of binary elements and describes it to himself, then retains this verbalization until tested for recall. The hypothesis suggests that the recoding occurring here is fundamental, because the information put into memory is not a direct representation of the names of the elements themselves—"oh, oh, one, oh," and so on—but it is a set of phrases descriptive of the stimulus patterns, such as "three oh's, two one's, two oh-one pairs, three one's and oh." According to the verbal-loop hypothesis, therefore, the subject is not retaining the stimulus itself, or even some close neural correlate of it; instead he is retaining the words contained in his description of it.

Glanzer and Clark tested the verbal-loop hypothesis in an experiment with two independent parts. In one part of the experiment people saw eight-place binary numbers for .5 sec and then were asked to recall the items. Subjects in the other part of the study were not tested for memory at all; they simply looked at the same eight-place binary stimuli and were asked to write descriptions of them. The major finding was a strong negative correlation between accuracy in recall and the number of words used in describing the stimuli; that is, those stimuli that subjects described accurately with the fewest words were those that the other subjects were able to recall with the highest accuracy. As it happens, the stimulus we have used as an example above, *000110101110,* requires about 12 words to describe so not much gain is expected for this recoding over a literal element by element representation. However, other stimuli—*000111000111*— could be verbalized with greater economy. The very strong negative relation between accuracy and verbalization length attained by Glanzer and Clark with eight-place items is consistent with the hypothesis that subjects remembered their verbal descriptions in the memory part of the experiment. We know that longer lists of words should lead to more errors in memory; but if the stimuli are all remembered literally the verbalization length has been a constant eight items.

The merits of the binary-to-octal and verbal-loop strategies, and their universality, are not at stake here. They have been described only to make a point about the nature of recoding: Some of the time, perhaps most of the time with linguistic materials, we do not store and retain copies of the stimulus itself but some derivative of the stimulus that depends on a more or less active processing of it. The consequence of this recoding process is a fundamentally reorganized format in which stimulus elements do not stand in one-to-one relations with elements of the recoded product.

Recoding of Visual Stimuli through Speech

Consider a task requiring a person to read, silently, a group of consonant letters and then to reproduce them later in writing. It will be remembered that Sperling (1960) noted informally that subjects seemed to be using an auditory or phonological code—mumbling, whispering, mouthing the names of the letters—even though the task was visual with no sound occurring at all. He also noted that when an error was made it was likely to be a letter that rhymed with the letter that would have been correct.

Confusion among letters in immediate memory. On the basis of similar observations, Conrad (1964) undertook a systematic investigation of the relation between memory errors under visual presentation and the phonological similarity of the letters being remembered. Conrad's experiment, which was previewed in Chapter 1, had separate parts, one involving *auditory perception* of single letters and the other involving *immediate memory* for lists of letters under conditions of visual presentation. In the study of auditory perception, subjects heard single letters spoken against a background of white noise; their task was simply to respond with the letter presented. The level of white noise (which sounds like a steady hiss) was adjusted so that subjects quite often made errors. In the memory experiment different subjects saw lists of six letters and were required to write them down (in order) from memory immediately after presentation. In each experiment it was the nature of the errors rather than their frequency that was of interest.

In the listening experiment a confusion matrix was constructed, in which, for each letter presented, a record was made of the frequency with which each other letter was incorrectly used as a response. For example, in the case where the letters BCPTVFMNSX were the possible stimuli to be detected, when the correct item—the one actually presented against the auditory noise background—was V, the subjects most often confused it with B, next with C, and least with X. The data from the memory experiment were handled similarly. Only trials on which exactly one error occurred were considered for these purposes. (By only one error is meant that the subject has five of the six letters correct and in their correct positions but some sixth letter is incorrectly recalled.) Now, with these memory errors a similar confusion matrix was constructed, where, for each missed stimulus letter, the frequency with which all possible intrusions occurred was tallied. For example, in memory, when the subject should have recalled V but did not, the most common wrong letter was B, the next C, and the least common error was X, just the same pattern that occurred in the listening experiment.

When the two confusion matrices were placed side by side they were strikingly similar. The errors one makes in confusing certain particular letters with others in listening are the same errors of confusion one makes in visual memory. The correlation was +.64. Conrad and others termed the memory errors *acoustic confusions*, in recognition of the possibility that subjects remember the sound of some type of inner speech. More neutral terms, phonological or speech confusions, are used here.

The fact that confusions in visual memory tasks match confusions in auditory identification of letters is consistent with the view that visual items are recoded into a phonological, speech-based format for retention, just as binary strings in our examples above have been recoded into octal format or into verbal descriptions.

Conrad and Hull (1964) have demonstrated that when sets of letters having high phonological similarity are used in constructing strings of letters for immediate memory tests, performance is much worse than when sets of letters with low phonological similarity are used. Sperling and Speelman (1970) have extended this observation and constructed a mathematical model of a possible underlying mechanism in which phonemes are forgotten independently by an exponential decay process. According to the Sperling and Speelman model, and a less formal but similar proposal by Conrad (1965), the subject uses whatever phonemes he remembers from the stimulus to select a response from among the relevant subset of letters being used in the experiment. For example, if he remembers only that the item belonging at a particular location rhymes with "ee" he selects a letter from the set, B, C, D, E, G, P, T, V, Z, if all of those letters are being used in the experiment. If only one item from this confusable subset is being used in the experiment, say B, then by knowing the same partial information—that the item rhymes with "ee"—the subject can get credit for remembering the item. In this last case just as much forgetting has occurred as with the high-similarity vocabulary but because B is the only potential candidate for the item the result is a correct score rather than an error as the subject can eliminate all but one letter. By this view the confusion errors that occur are the consequence of forgetting rather than its cause. However, as we shall consider below there are also theoretical positions that maintain the opposite—that the presence of highly confusable items within a vocabulary produces forgetting.

Extensions of the confusion method. In Table 4.2 are summarized results of several experiments that extend the analysis of memory confusions in theoretically important ways (Conrad, 1972a). Each portion of the table is a collapsed confusion matrix in which columns stand for stimulus items and rows for response items. No correct responses are entered in these matrices. The matrices are all based on a vocabulary of nine letters: BCPTVFMNS. The full confusion matrix from this subset of nine letters has 9 × 9 = 81 cells, but here the letters are grouped by their rhyming class.

The chance matrix shows the frequency of errors of each type that can be expected if, when the subject misses a letter, the letter intruded in its place is randomly selected from the remaining eight letters. (Notice the response to "eh" letters is not evenly balanced because there were five "ee" letters and only four "eh" letters in the vocabulary.) The visual matrix shows the frequencies of errors that can be expected if immediate memory is based on visual shape. These estimates are derived by Conrad (1972a) from purely visual confusions collected by Thomasson (1970). The immediate-recall matrix recapitulates what we have already seen. When the subject makes a confusion error (a substitution error), in immediate visual memory tasks, the intrusion is a letter that is phonologically similar to the correct letter.

The delayed-recall matrix adds new and important information. In that condition subjects read lists of four letters and then were distracted for 7 sec by a

TABLE 4.2
Confusions among Consonants for Various Testing Situations[a]

Matrix source and rhyming class of response given	Rhyming class of stimulus presented	
	/i/ (BCPTV)	/ε/ (FMNS)
Chance matrix:		
/i/	50.0	62.5
/ε/	50.0	37.5
Visual matrix:		
/i/	35.6	79.1
/ε/	64.4	20.9
Immediate recall matrix:		
/i/	79.2	19.8
/ε/	20.8	80.2
Delayed recall matrix:		
/i/	58.2	58.1
/ε/	41.8	41.9
Suppression matrix:		
/i/	57.6	57.8
/ε/	42.4	42.2

[a]After Conrad (1972a).

digit-reading interpolated task before being allowed to recall. What is interesting about the delayed-recall data is not that performance is worse overall, although that is the case, but that the errors made tend to move in the direction of what is expected on a chance basis; when the subjects are prevented from rehearsing or recalling immediately by the interpolated digit-reading task the evidence for a speech code disappears, although performance does not drop to chance accuracy. So, either because of the passage of time or more likely because speech-based rehearsal of the series has been inhibited, subjects seem obliged to rely on some other form of coding.

The suppression matrix comes from an effort to deprive subjects of their normal, speech-based code in another fashion. In this condition subjects saw four-consonant stimuli as before but were required by the instructions to pronounce the word "the" repeatedly in unison with the appearance of each letter on the screen. The suppression technique was first used for this purpose by Murray (1967). It is evident that suppressing covert articulation eliminates the phonological confusion pattern. Although almost exactly two-thirds of the responses under this condition were correct, the information was apparently not being carried in a speech code. Because there is not any tendency for confusions to follow the pattern of visual similarity, however, we cannot assume that subjects have substituted representation in the visual mode for speech representations. Despite our ignorance of alternative codes, the suppression condition gives important information because it ties the phenomenon of memory confusions to events occurring in the mouth and vocal machinery. One may otherwise have proposed that B and P get confused in memory disproportionately only because they bear some other, more fundamental similarity to each other, and that it is this more basic relation that causes both the memory confusions between them and also, perhaps deep in the history of the language, causes the phonological relation between them. Direct evidence for a speech basis of the confusion effect is therefore provided by the suppression technique. A similar logic suggests looking at deaf subjects, among whom there is a chronic phonological deficit.

Conrad and Rush (1965) tested a number of deaf teenage children in a visual immediate memory situation and compared the confusion matrix they produced with one produced by comparable children with normal hearing. The evidence obtained was entirely negative in that there was clearly no pattern of confusions following phonological rules with the deaf children. However, there was not obvious evidence for coding based on visual shape either. The control subjects showed performance much like the adults' in Table 4.2. It was not that the deaf students chose confusion errors at random either, because when the group was divided on the basis of overall performance level it was found that the best and worst deaf subjects tended to make the same confusions of one letter for another. There was a rank correlation coefficient of +.49 between the two error matrices. The nature of the findings with this first experiment on deaf subjects is therefore similar to that with the suppression technique: The case is considerably strengthened for tying memory confusions to the speech system for normal subjects but the alternate code, used in the absence of speech, remains elusive.

Alternate memory coding in the deaf.   In a later experiment Conrad (1972b) has applied a different method to this issue of alternate coding among the deaf. In the 1972 study he relies on Conrad and Hull's (1964) observation that when phonological similarity is built into the vocabulary used in visual memory testing performance is dramatically lower than when it is not. Two subsets of letters, or vocabularies, were constructed for this more recent study, one with high phonological similarity, BCDPTV, and the other with high visual shape similarity, KNVXYZ. In ordered recall for sequences of from four to six letters, exclusively from one or the other of these vocabularies, Conrad found much worse performance for normal-hearing controls on the phonologically similar lists than on the visually similar lists; however, for the deaf subjects there was consistently worse performance on the visually similar than on the phonologically similar lists. This finding is consistent with the idea that compensatory visual coding is employed by the deaf subjects.

The analysis of how speech normally fits into memory function has been pushed still farther by Conrad (1972a) in a study of deaf children who varied in the degree to which they possessed some expressive speech skills. In a school for deaf children with great emphasis on training oral expression, Conrad found that he could distinguish two subgroups of subjects, all profoundly deaf since childhood. These subgroups were identified on the basis of confusions following a visual memory test of the type we have been reviewing here. One group gave few phonological confusions but abundant visual shape confusions and the other group gave few shape confusions but abundant phonological confusions. The assumption is that the latter group, whose memory errors resembled those obtained from hearing subjects, consisted of students whose speech training was advanced to the level that they employed speech encoding in memory.

To test for different memory-encoding strategies in these two groups, Conrad (1972a) compared the effects on them of an additional variable, vocalization at presentation in immediate memory. Just as in the Conrad and Hull (1968) experiment shown in Figure 3.5 of the last chapter, all subjects saw a series of letters on the screen, with half the subjects in each group being told to pronounce the letters aloud as they appeared and the other half told to remain silent at presentation. Now we already know what is likely to have occurred with hearing subjects in this comparison: The overt reading condition is likely to have led to better performance than the silent condition. Conrad (1972a) found that with the phonologically advanced, or articulatory deaf subjects (those who had yielded a pattern of memory confusions similar to the phonological confusions obtained with normal subjects), there was no difference between the silent and aloud presentation conditions. However, with the so-called nonarticulating subjects (those who had shown shape confusions rather than speech confusions) there was significantly worse performance in the overt vocalization condition than in the silent condition.

This outcome reported by Conrad (1972a) nicely illustrates several of the theoretical points made in this and in the last chapter. Normals do better with overt vocalization than with silent reading because of echoic memory. Naturally, the deaf subjects have no possibility of echoic storage, so we expect no positive factor enhancing scores when there has been aural information for them. The two groups of deaf subjects differ with respect to whether articulation is a natural mode of encoding; it is natural for the articulators but it is not for the nonarticulators, according to the independent evidence from analysis of confusion errors. When instructed to do what they would be doing anyway, therefore, the articulators showed no loss as a function of vocalization condition (but no gain because they did not hear). However, the nonarticulators are asked in the vocalization condition to perform laborious speech responses while they are encoding the stimuli. Because there is reason to believe these speech responses are unnatural for these particular subjects it should be no surprise that their performance is impaired, just as is likely if they had been asked to tap patterns with their feet.

Another important point from this study has to do with the nature of the speech code employed by normal subjects. Because items that have similar sounds also have similar articulatory programs, it is in principle quite difficult to separate acoustic from articulatory coding. However, the deaf articulators provide a critical test. They possess no possibility of acoustic imagery but they have at least some minimal production skills. The fact that they show data similar to that of normals—in memory confusions and, in a study not described here, in vocalization effects on reading—can therefore be taken to support an articulatory basis for the phonological or speech code.

Locke and Locke (1971) have provided converging evidence on alternate coding strategies in deaf subjects. They compared three groups on three versions of a paired-associate task. The groups were (1) hearing controls, (2) intelligible deaf, that is, deaf children whose speech was understandable in the judgment of their instructors, and (3) unintelligible deaf, whose speech efforts were not even minimally effective according to their instructors. The three paired-associate lists consisted of letter pairs designed to create three different conditions: (1) phonologically similar within pairs—B–V, F–X, P–T, . . . ; (2) visually similar—B–R, F–P, V–Y, . . .; or (3) dactylically similar, that is, similar with reference to finger-spelling gestures—B–Y, F–B, K–P. It was estimated that 93% of the intelligible deaf children and 68% of the unintelligible deaf children used speech in combination with manual language as their primary means of expression. The unintelligible deaf group was therefore "more dactylic" than the other deaf group.

The Lockes found that both recall accuracy and errors of confusion displayed a sensible pattern in light of coding predictions. In accuracy the controls scored higher than the deaf subjects on the list high in phonological similarity, whereas both deaf groups scored higher than the controls on the list high in dactylic similarity. The pattern was the same for confusion errors. In this study the role of visual coding was less apparent, with smaller between-group differences than those above and with accuracy giving a different picture than confusions. However, the main point is the clear demonstration of a dactylic alternative used among deaf subjects.

Development of speech encoding.   At what stage of development do children first begin to use speech to encode memory stimuli? Certainly one must know the names or labels of items to be remembered in order to employ a coding system based on speech, but is speech encoding automatic once these naming responses are possible? Conrad's (1972a) work with children suggests that the use of speech coding is not automatic even given the availability of a name code. In one experiment he tested children ranging in mental age from 3 to 11 years. The task was one where colored pictures of objects were presented for inspection and then subjects had to pick the objects presented from a set of eight possibilities on cards. The objects were common enough so that even the youngest subjects could easily supply their names. Furthermore, the experimenter named them overtly as he presented them during the inspection phase. There were two vocabularies, or sets, of eight pictures. One consisted of objects with homophonic names—cat, rat, bat, mat, hat, man, tap, bag—and the other consisted of objects with nonhomophonic names—fish, girl, bus, spoon, horse, train, clock, hand. Each child was given lists of such a length that, in the homophonic condition, he could achieve 50% correct responses on the average. Table 4.3 shows the results, including for each age group (1) the number of items presented on the average in order to achieve 50% accuracy with homophonic items, (2) the percentage of correct responding in the homophonic condition, and (3) the percentage of correct responding in the nonhomophonic condition. The first two rows should be no surprise because we know memory improves with age, even though the reason for this improvement is not clear, and

TABLE 4.3
The Development of Phonological Confusion[a]

	Mental ages (years)				
Stimulus type	3–5	5–6	6–7	7–8	8–11
Homophones	52.4[b]	52.0	51.9	52.1	52.4
	(3.2)	(3.8)	(4.1)	(4.4)	(5.9)
Nonhomophones	52.8	59.1	64.0	69.1	75.3

[a]After Conrad (1972a).

[b]The entries are percentage of correct responding. The figures in parentheses below the homophone data show the number of items that needed to be presented in order to obtain approximately 50% correct scores for the homophone condition at each age group.

because performance in the homophonic condition has been constrained by the procedure described. The important feature of the results is that at the earliest age there is no difference in performance between the phonologically similar and the phonologically dissimilar materials. Beginning around age 5 or 6 years, however, there was an increasing tendency for performance to be much better when the names of the memory pictures did not share phonological features.

Therefore, at an age when children clearly have the names of stimuli available, both because they are proved capable of naming the particular objects and because the experimenter has actually presented the names overtly, there is nonetheless apparently no efficient use of the names for purposes of short-term memory. This study gives no suggestion as to what type of coding supports recall of over three items in the case of the youngest age group, but something other than speech must be the agent. Having the capacity for a speech code and using that type of code seem to be two different things (see also Locke & Kutz, 1975). It is no coincidence (LaBerge, 1972) that the age range at which phonological similarity begins to make a difference in this study is near the age range where children seem to become ready to learn how to read. Prior to this age it is as if there is impaired contact between visual stimuli and the speech-based language system, even though the latter is fluent in the auditory—articulatory mode. LaBerge (1972) has remarked that children sometimes can read every word in a simple question but reach the end with neither memory for the sentence nor comprehension of it; however, when the same question is posed by voice they answer readily. So there is a more subtle step involved than simply learning to translate visual stimuli into names. Furthermore, speech is used not only in recoding visual stimuli but also in maintaining them through rehearsal. It may be this latter sense in which the younger subjects fail to enlist speech for memory.

Electromyographic evidence. One extension of an articulatory hypothesis for phonological memory coding is that it may be possible to pick up actual speech responses at the periphery during periods when visual information is being encoded or rehearsed in phonological form. The easiest application of this idea is the observation of actual whispering or lip moving during memory experiments, and indeed such observations have been made by Sperling and Conrad. However, the more interesting possibility, and a more difficult one to test, is that even in the absence of such overt activity there is covert articulatory activity. The issue then becomes how central this activity is. It would be possible to maintain a perfectly authentic speech code but at a level so deep into central symbolic representations—so far from the periphery, that is—that the articulatory machinery itself would not be involved.

Lock and Fehr (1970a) have tested the intermediate possibility, that much speech encoding in visual memory occurs far enough out into the periphery that the articulatory muscles are involved but not far enough out so that the movements are detectable in casual observation. Such *incipient* articulation can be measured with electromyographic techniques, in which a recording electrode is placed on the skin near a major muscle system; the electrode is sensitive to patterns of electrical activity driving from that muscle system. As Locke and Fehr have observed, such recordings are nowhere near detailed enough to permit evaluation of just what a person is (covertly) articulating; however, this capability can be approximated by careful selection of stimuli. Their idea was to capitalize on a gross articulatory feature, labial—nonlabial, with a very conspicuous muscular correlate. In labial phonemes such as /b, f, v, m p, w/ there is an obvious, sharp movement of the lower lip whereas in other phonemes, the nonlabials, there is not.

To measure covert speech during the memory experiment electrodes were pasted to the chin and to the lower lip, the latter just under the muscle most responsible for producing the labial phonemes. Electromyographic measures were taken continuously during the experiment. On memory tests lists of five two-syllable words were presented at a rate of about 1.5 sec per word; then there was a 10-sec blank interval that was terminated by a recall signal. The blank interval was included on the presumption that subjects would be rehearsing the five-word items prior to overt recall. All five stimulus words either included labial phonemes—BOMBER, WAFFLE, FAVOR—or contained none.

The labial and nonlabial stimuli did not differ in difficulty (3.95 versus 3.91 words recalled). However, peak amplitides of electrical activity at the lip site were consistently greater on trials with the labials than on trials with the nonlabials. This was true both during the presentation interval, when both perceptual and rehearsal activity would be occurring, and also during the blank interval, when only rehearsal would be occurring. This was the first evidence linking covert verbal activity to the actual content of what was being covertly verbalized; previously the ancient (Watson, 1919) concept of subvocal speech had been manifested only through the correlation of some electromuscular events with presumed activity or through inferences made from experimental operations, such as articulation suppression.

Locke and Fehr (1970b) subsequently applied their electromyographic method to children of chronological ages of 4 and 5 years. They found in this subject population that the pattern of activity was like that of adults during presentation of the words in that the labial words gave greater peak amplitudes then the nonlabials. However, during the blank rehearsal period there was no difference. This latter result reinforces the speculation from earlier in this chapter that young children do not use the speech code for improving memory even when there is independent evidence that the encoding process, in older children and adults, involves speech. This result particularly suggests that it is in verbal rehearsal that younger subjects are discrepant from adults and not in initial verbal encoding.

A somewhat different electromyographic technique has been reported by Glassman (1972). Rather than to diagnose the particular nature of covert articulation, his purpose was to use the electromyographic recording capability as a feedback source so that people could monitor the level of their own activity. This strategy actually extends the suppression technique used by Murray and Conrad. Whereas these latter investigators tried to minimize covert speech by keeping the articulation mechanisms busy producing some unrelated, redundant locution, Glassman tried to accomplish the same thing without adding any extraneous utterances. The specific idea is that people ordinarily may not be aware of the covert articulation in which they engage. To remedy this, a sensitive recording device, the electromyograph, hooked up to a salient signal source, a buzzer, was used to provide subjects with knowledge of the momentary amplitudes of electrical activity in their articulatory systems. This is an adaptation of the biofeedback principle, which psychologists apparently owe to Hardyck, Petrinovich, and Ellsworth (1967) from a study of silent reading that we shall consider below.

In Glassman's experiment, one group was pretrained to minimize articulatory activity. They were given a warmup session with various reading and recall tasks under conditions of continuous electromyographic monitoring. During this session a buzzer would sound whenever a certain amplitude was reached, the experimenter having control over this criterion level at all times. By adopting successively stricter criteria it was possible to train the subjects in the experimental group to inhibit their subvocal speech activity. The control subjects were hooked up to a similar recording device but no buzzer was used to provide feedback nor were they discouraged from using covert speech. In the memory task all subjects received after this training, the comparison was between three-word stimuli high in phonological similarity and three-word stimuli low in phonological similarity. The Brown–Peterson short-term memory task was used, with a distractor task involving figure analogies (visual reasoning) between presentation and recall of the stimuli. The design was therefore a two by two arrangement with vocalization training one factor and stimulus similarity the other.

There were no effects on recall of minimizing articulatory activity, although the phonological similarity of the stimuli had a strong overall effect. Therefore, the decrements in performance produced by the Murray type of suppression procedure—saying "the–the–the" in unison with stimulus input—may be contributing interference actively as well as removing some type of speech code. This deduction is based on the consideration that the Murray method sharply impairs recall, whereas the Glassman method seems not to; if the Murray method is only removing phonological coding it should have no more severe effect than the Glassman method. Of course, it is entirely possible that Glassman would have obtained a recall impairment if he had used more difficult memory stimuli. In a study we shall examine below, Hardyck and Petrinovich (1970) have been able to detect effects of a similar training procedure on a difficult task but not on a simpler one.

Glassman found that minimization training in his experiment had a strong influence on the nature of errors made, however. There were many more phonological confusions in the control group than in the pretrained, biofeedback group. These phonological confusions are the traditional primary source of evidence for phonological coding and their presence or absence is shown by this experiment to depend on the control of electrical activity in the speech-producing regions of the mouth.

The Glassman study has two important theoretical consequences. The first pertains to whether phonological coding in memory, as defined by confusions among rhyming letters, has an auditory or an articulatory basis. That is, do B and P get confused because they sound similar or because they are produced in ways that feel similar? From earlier discussions we already have two pieces of evidence: First, we would expect that if phonological coding were auditory it would share other features of known auditory memory systems; however, whereas two of the main auditory or echoic memory phenomena, the suffix and modality effects, occur only with aural stimulus presentation, phonological confusions are found with either aural or visual presentation. If the basis for phonological coding is auditory, therefore, it is a different system from the system that is used in echoic memory. The second point also favors an articulatory over an auditory explanation for the phonological code: We saw in Conrad's work on deafness that speech training for the severely deaf can produce patterns of confusions not fundamentally different from those used by normal subjects. This suggested that, because deafness of that severity precluded any auditory imagery, an articulatory rather than auditory phonological referent was the major one in normals. Now, in Glassman's study we see that a relatively peripheral control over articulatory activity produces very significant changes in patterns of speech confusions. This does not preclude auditory coding; for example, covert articulation may be necessary mainly to reach an auditory image, as Sperling's model implies. However, the fact is that this type of finding directly supports an articulatory hypothesis and it remains for an auditory hypothesis to show some need for another explanatory device.

The second major issue to which Glassman's study applies is somewhat digressive to the purpose of this chapter and so is mentioned only in passing. The contrasting view on what role similarity plays in forgetting, a causal role or a byproduct, have been mentioned above. When the level of forgetting and the frequency of speech-based confusions covary, either hypothesis can be shown to explain the data adequately. However, when the speech-based confusions vary drastically without corresponding changes in level of correct recall, as happens in Glassman's experiment, then the conclusion is supported that phonological effects are a consequence of partially forgotten traces and not the cause of the forgetting. Of course, there is always the possibility that some alternative code has been learned by Glassman's subjects and that errors have shown confusions appropriate to this new code; however, this view must rest on the implausible assumption that the new alternative code has happened by chance to be just exactly as efficient as the speech code.

Other lines of evidence.   There are several other experimental situations where a case has been advanced for speech coding in the handling of visual material. Eriksen, Pollack, and Montague (1970) wondered whether the speech complexity of verbal items, the number of syllables, affected only the time required for articulation of these items or also the time required to begin articulating them. If the latter is true then it suggests that some phonological representation is necessary very early in visual perception of linguistic items as well as in subsequent overt or covert pronunciation. To test this possibility they measured the time elapsing between appearance of a word on a screen and the first vocalization sound under instructions emphasizing overt naming of a word as soon as it could be read. They found that even when two words began identically, as do MAIN and MAINTENANCE it took appreciably longer to start pronouncing the word with more syllables.

With words such as these, however, the longer stimulus is also a wider stimulus in terms of visual angle; perhaps acuity differences account for the reaction-time advantage of short words. To test this Eriksen *et al.* (1970) replicated their experiment with two-digit numbers as stimuli. Some two-digit numbers have only two syllables, for example, 20, 14; some have three, for example 17, 39, and some have four, 97, 71; these items are not differentially discriminable visually as the short and long words may have been. Still, however, there was a latency advantage for the stimuli with fewer syllables. For the experiment as a whole each additional syllable cost 11 msec, on the average, in increased vocalization latency. The thing to notice about this figure is that it represents a process much too fast for internal speech. Actually, it corresponds closely to the estimate Sperling (1960) offered of 10 msec per item in visual scanning experiments in which a mask strictly limits processing time. In Sperling's experiments each letter is of course a syllable with regard to its name—"ef, el, wy,. . . ."

It can be argued that the Eriksen–Pollack–Montague demonstration applies to situations in which the word must ultimately be spoken overtly but that when reading words is for some other purpose there is no influence of speech complexity. Klapp (1971) has discounted this argument in a study in which under some conditions the subjects simply must decide whether two simultaneously-appearing words are the same or different. It took roughly 20 msec longer for each additional syllable in the items being judged. This was true both for two-digit numbers and for words. So apparently even if the task does not ever require reference to the name of verbal items, phonological complexity still sets a limit on reaction time. After all, the same–different task could be accomplished with words the phonological referent of which was unknown. It may be that reference to phonology is compulsory with verbal items, even when such reference is demonstrably maladaptive, much as reference to meaning seems to be compulsory in the Stroop test (Dyer, 1973; Stroop, 1935) under conditions where it is maladaptive. (In the Stroop test the subject tries to name the color of ink in which words, interfering color names themselves, are printed.)

Is the compulsory reference to speech so prevalent that it occurs in silent reading? This is an old question on which strongly partisan views keep resurfacing. One view (Goodman, 1968) is that early in learning to read the speech reference is indispensible but that later, with fluent readers, meaning gets extracted directly from the visual stimuli. The other position is that at some level the phonological correlate remains necessary. The problem in reaching a definitive answer is that fluent reading is usually too free wheeling and covert to measure, but then when reading tasks are devised that make measurement easier it can always be claimed that these factitious tasks have altered what normally occurs in reading. A study by Hardyck and Petrinovich (1970), which follows on the earlier study of Hardyck *et al.* (1967) that we have mentioned above, is freer of this objection than most. They used electromyographic recording to measure laryngeal muscle tension and amplified the resulting signals so as to provide external feedback to their subjects. The subjects were then trained to inhibit this speech activity during silent reading, using the biofeedback method later applied to short-term memory by Glassman. The measure of interest was how well subjects could answer questions about the passages they had read. On easier passages there was no reduction in comprehension with minimization training, just as Glassman had found in short-term memory. However, with more difficult passages the group trained to inhibit electromuscular responding from the speech apparatus could not answer questions on the passage as well as those not trained. From this we may conclude either that the speech reference is used only when the going gets tough in reading or, alternatively, that a difficult reading passage simply provides a more sensitive test of any experimental manipulation than the easy passage. One valuable feature of the Hardyck–Petrinovich study was inclusion of a control group that had training on inhibition of electromyographic activity in the forearm; these subjects did not experience more difficulty answering questions about the hard passages than about the easy passages, as the articulation inhibitors had. Other research (McGuigan, 1970) has measured the amount of electromyographic activity as a function of reading difficulty and established the same reciprocity, in that more covert speech appears in difficult reading tasks than in easy tasks.

Notice that, whereas the operations of the Hardyck and Petrinovich study parallel those of the Glassman study, the results do not. Glassman trained inhibition of covert speech without finding a performance impairment, whereas, at least in the difficult reading task, Hardyck and Petrinovich did. Of course Glassman might have found memory impairment with more difficult stimuli, as was noted above.

Corcoran (1966, 1967) has found evidence for speech mediation in several visual information-processing tasks that are related to reading. In one he had subjects inspect pages from *Punch* magazine crossing out all letter E's as rapidly as possible. The performance measure was the incidence of response omissions, where the person failed to cross out an E. The frequency of such omissions was roughly four times as great when the E was silent, or mute, in a word than when it was pronounced in a word—NOTE has a mute E and NET has a pronounced E. The occurrence of mute and pronounced E's is confounded with position within words, but the result has held up even when the analysis is position by position. In a second study Corcoran applied the same logic to proofreading, a task in which letters were systematically deleted and the subject's job was to mark where a new letter would have to be inserted. Here there were about three times as many failures to detect a missing mute E as there were failures to detect a missing pronounced E.

The experiments reviewed in this section—on naming latency as a function of syllable length, on reading comprehension as a function of learned inhibition of covert articulation, and on visual processing of prose as a function of the articulatory role of a letter within a word—all show the pervasiveness of speech representation in visual cognition. This is the major point being made in this chapter in order to suggest the large role played by speech coding in verbal short-term memory. The evidence reviewed is quite adequate for such a demonstration. The data reviewed are not adequate to settle two other important issues, however. The first of these is whether reading always has a speech referent. This question cannot be settled in the present context. To provide some perspective on the issue, however, it seems worthwhile to exhibit arguments against a compulsory speech referent. One of the most eloquent is an example cited by LaBerge (1972) of a sentence: "The bouy and the none tolled hymn they had scene and herd a pear of bear feat in the haul." Listening to this sentence would pose no problems but reading it does; there must be a visual contribution to the comprehension of meaning, therefore, beyond categorization in terms of speech. It is also frequently observed (Carroll, 1972; S. E. Martin, 1972) that some languages have written symbols that are not phonetic, namely ideographs, and so have no stable speech referent. Therefore speech cannot be a precondition to all reading. Even within our own language there are some symbols of this type: #, @, &, for example. A little thought, moreover, shows that our language is only partially phonetic—consider the words BOUGH, TOUGH, COUGH, THOUGH, THROUGH, for example.

Coding by sound or production: Acoustic versus articulatory representation. Another issue raised but not settled by the association of memory with speech concerns the exact nature of the code revealed by phonological confusions. It has been quite deliberate that we have used such terms as "phonological" and "speech-based" to describe this code because the fact of the association with speech is far more important than deciding what aspect of speech is involved. Now, however, we turn to the question of whether a substitution of B for P in visual memory is because B and P share a sound or rather because they share an articulatory gesture.

Hintzman (1967) undertook to answer this question with an extension of Conrad's original strategy of correlating listening errors with visual memory errors. He restricted this analysis to the set of six stop consonants shown in Table 4.4. The stop consonants can be arranged in a two-dimensional scheme according to whether they are voiced and according to their place of articulation in the mouth. In the voiced stops, B, D, and G, the onset of the voice tone is much sooner relative to the release of air pressure than in the unvoiced stops, P, T, and K. In the place dimension B and P are produced by releasing air pressure at the front of the mouth, D and T midways back, and G and K still farther back toward the throat. Hintzman's analysis depended on a previous finding that errors in the auditory perception of stops were not systematic with respect to place of articulation but that they were affected by voicing. G. A. Miller and Nicely (1955) showed that when subjects were listening to a single item in a noise background, confusions were governed by voicing such that B would be replaced by D or G and P would be replaced by T or K, but only rarely would B be confused with one of the unvoiced stops or P with one of the voiced ones. The auditory perception of these letters was not affected by place of articulation: If B were missed D was not a more likely substitute for it than G, even though D is closer to B in terms of place of articulation than G is. If B were replaced by an unvoiced stop, an unlikely event in the first place, P was no more likely a confusion than T or K, even though P matches B exactly in place of articulation.

Hintzman's reasoning was that when syllables using the stop consonants were being remembered in a visual task one would have only to determine whether place of articulation played a role in predicting confusions. If it plays no role then the memory code matches auditory perception. However, if place of articulation is predictive of memory errors then the memory code more closely matches the production, or articulatory, code because we know that articulatory locus defines similarity among these letters with regard to their production. In other words, place of articulation seems unimportant in listening to stop consonants embedded in syllables but it does play a role in articulation itself and so a simple determination should make it clear whether memory is like the listening pattern or like the articulation pattern.

The result was consistent with the articulatory interpretation. Subjects remembered lists of such items as "Bav, kaf, pav, daf, gaf, . . ." where only the initial consonant was scored in written recall. The data are given in Table 4.5. The

TABLE 4.4
The Stop Consonants

Voicing	Place of articulation		
	Front	Middle	Back
Voiced	B	D	G
Unvoiced	P	T	K

influence of voicing in this confusion matrix is easily verified by noting that, for example, when P is missed T or K are much more likely intrusions than D or G (118 versus 76 cases, respectively). The influence of place can be seen in two ways. First, notice again for errors to a presented P, that T is more likely than K (86 versus 32). Second, notice that when an error does violate the voicing feature there is nonetheless an effect of place; for example, D is a more likely confusion to P than G (48 versus 28). It therefore appears that place of articulation governs the occurrence of intrusion errors in short-term memory even though it does not, according to the Miller–Nicely data, govern the occurrence of confusions in perception. Therefore, by the logic of the study, the short-term memory code maintains articulatory features.

In a series of papers Wickelgren (1965, 1966) has gone even farther in relating memory errors to articulatory features. Wickelgren's studies have been conducted with auditory presentation, which makes them not entirely relevant to our present discussion of speech-based recoding in visual memory; however, he has had his subjects copy each item as it occurs in presentation, insuring an analysis of errors following only accurate perception. Wickelgren's analysis of consonant memory errors tested several systems for describing the letters in terms of distinctive features. He found that a system with four binary features worked best—voicing, nasality, openness of vocal tract, and place of articulation. Although this first approximation to a short-term memory coding system for English consonants clearly was based on articulatory gestures, Wickelgren was not willing to specify the production aspect of speech in memory coding. His reservations on this subject have since been spelled out in a separate paper (Wickelgren, 1969a): First, there is an intermediate possibility, between acoustic and articulatory coding that has been widely ignored. This intermediate possibility is that the memory code is basically abstract in its relation to speech, correlated with both perception and production but located, as it were, in neither.

TABLE 4.5
Memory Confusions among Stop Consonants[a]

Stimulus letter presented	Response letter (intrusion)					
	P	T	K	B	D	G
P	—	86	32	52	48	28
T	46	—	46	33	47	37
K	28	59	—	33	33	48
B	48	22	33	—	85	40
D	37	48	39	58	—	72
G	26	27	32	58	74	—

[a]After Hintzman (1967).

Second, he cautions that it is dangerous to accept the null finding of G. A. Miller and Nicely (1955) with regard to a place of articulation effect in listening. This danger derives partly from the way such listening confusions are collected. A source of noise must be added to the spoken signal in order to observe any errors at all, but this noise itself may not be neutral to the various discriminations occurring. A hissing sound might block discriminations of S from other letters more than it would damage perception of Q, for example. It is therefore difficult to be sure that an absence of place of articulation errors in hearing is general or specific to the testing situation. Finally, Wickelgren (1969a) has raised the theoretical point that certain ideas on speech perception make the opposition between articulatory and acoustic coding a false contrast. According to the motor theory of speech perception (Liberman *et al.*, 1967) speech sounds are perceived by reference to the way they are articulated; stated differently, behavior in recognizing speech sounds seems to correlate better with how those sounds are produced than with how they sound in terms of physical acoustic properties. Now if the motor theory of speech perception is true it can be seen easily that contrasting articulatory and acoustic coding in short-term memory is futile because acoustic or, better, auditory stimulus features themselves seem to be based on articulation.

These stipulations accepted, it is still the case that what evidential sources there are, and none is conclusive, support the articulatory position more than the acoustic position. These have been reviewed above and include (1) the articulatorily trained deaf subjects, (2) the clear association of peripheral articulatory effectors with memory through electromyography, and (3) the independent acoustic store established under the heading of echoic memory. To these we add the Hintzman–Wickelgren case that memory errors follow well systems based on articulatory gestures. These considerations converge on a presumptive case for an articulatory code. Even though the issue is not critical and we are probably best concerned with other problems, therefore, we may think of the memory code as articulatory until someone comes up with a corresponding list of arguments for an acoustic code.

There is one further point that has been mentioned before but merits repetition. The characteristic behavior of subjects in such memory situations as we have been considering includes both initial encoding of visual symbols into some other format, perhaps phonological, and a stage of covert rehearsal between acquisition and retrieval. The rehearsal stage is very likely to be phonological and it is very likely to be articulatory. We have no logic for choosing between the potential phonological influence at initial encoding and a potential phonological influence during subsequent rehearsal. The question is not, for present purposes, a burning one because the involvement of speech is securely established either way. However, in other contexts, including, for example, the developmental work of Locke and Conrad, the distinction may be an important one to maintain.

What is rather more important than the nature of the memory coding system based on speech is that it be clearly distinguished from echoic memory. As elaborated in the last chapter echoic memory must be set up by aural stimulation, whereas speech coding occurs with both visual and aural input, as we have here been at pains to show. Furthermore, there is evidence that the two codes, echoic and phonological, have different properties, as they should because echoic storage is organized precategorically, whereas the phonological code is postcategorical with respect to learned language categories. Cheng (1974) has shown that similarity in a visual–articulatory mode has effects at all positions of an immediate memory list but that the same similarity dimension in the acoustic mode affects only the last serial positions on the lists.

In Cheng's experiment, the subjects simultaneously pronounced internally and heard a list of seven consonant letters. The letters were either presented in a rhyming context, such as *kah, bah, rah,* or in a varied context, such as *kay, bee, are;* furthermore, this contrast between high phonological similarity (rhyming) and low phonological similarity (nonrhyming letter names) was independently controlled in the subvocal-pronunciation mode and in the aural mode. (Cheng's article should be checked for details on how this was done.) Generally, performance was better with low phonological similarity (nonrhyming contexts) than with high phonological similarity, but for the aural modality this was true only for the last three of seven positions, whereas for the articulatory modality it was true for all positions. The specificity of similarity effects in the acoustic (aural) mode to the end of the list fits exactly with the echoic-memory properties shown in the modality and suffix effects.

Summary

Recoding is the conversion of stimulus information from one storage format into another. The basic argument that visual characters are recoded into a speech or phonological format is that subjects make errors based on phonological similarity in memory situations that are totally visual in method. This pattern of phonological errors does not appear if there is a substantial filled delay before recall, if covert articulation is suppressed by some redundant locution, or with deaf subjects not specifically trained in speech. Comparative studies of the deaf and of developmental trends show some promise of uncovering alternate coding systems that are used in the absence of phonology.

Studies of electromyography of two kinds have been performed to provide converging support for phonological involvement in memory. In one, a correlation is revealed between muscle electrical potentials and specific verbal items being held in memory; in the other, suppression of such electrical activity is shown to affect evidence for phonological involvement. For visual cognition in general, rather than for memory specifically, three further techniques have been used to explore the involvement of phonological contributions: (1) the syllable effect on choice reaction times, (2) the effects of articulation suppression through biofeedback training, and (3) the effects of whether or not a letter is pronounced in a word on visual search for that letter.

The best evidence suggests that the form of coding revealed by phonological confusions is articulatory, although this conclusion must be qualified in several ways.

5
Nonverbal Memory

By and large people use words to communicate, to communicate across space with each other at a given moment in time or to communicate back and forth across history through oral and written chronicles. It is so impossible to imagine a nonverbal communication medium of sufficient complexity and flexibility to carry human experience that one is tempted to conclude that verbal communication is a criterion separating us from so-called lower forms of life. A further temptation is to generalize that just as words are central to social memory, permitting us to know about our ancestors and to leave messages for our descendants, so also are words central to our individual memory functioning. That is, we may as individuals know about the past by virtue of remembering the words we used to describe it at the time. We have seen in Chapter 2 that Sperling's model for iconic memory tasks includes just this idea insofar as the visual trace is translated by verbal naming and then held in the latter form. In another context Glanzer and Clark's (1963) verbal-loop hypothesis maintains similarly that certain types of nonverbal patterns are described on presentation and subsequent memory is carried through the words used in the initial description.

Of course, no one is likely to propose that preverbal infants have no enduring memories, or that memory for how a toothache feels is carried by an internal descriptive paragraph, or that a master violinist remembers nuances conveyed by his bow arm through words outlining various muscle groups and sequences. However, at least in those types of rational behavior often described as the "higher mental processes" the centrality of verbal language has been a foundation belief in experimental psychology for generations. The argument is that humans share with lower species numerous forms of processing, such as Pavlovian conditioning and instrumental training, but that what sets them apart are the complex mental operations that either depend on language or are highly correlated with language. For this reason the psychology of human learning and memory has largely been dominated by the tradition of verbal learning. Watson's (1919) belief that thinking is inner speech certainly implies that memory for mental events, at least, should depend on memory for the words involved in those events. Moreover, although Ebbinghaus gave very clear recognition to the existence of nonverbal memories (Ebbinghaus, 1964, p. 3, originally published 1885), his own research was so exclusively concerned with verbal memory and his influence on subsequent workers so gigantic that it is possible the preoccupation of later workers with verbal memory owes in part to him.

Still, as Paivio (1971a) exhaustively documents in his book *Imagery and Verbal Processes,* the alternative view that memory can persist in unlabeled sensory imagery never really died out completely. The Greek conception of memory as being like an impression made on a wax tablet was an early version of this view. Indeed, evidence has been accumulating rapidly that events can be stored in multiple codes, among which nonverbal imagery occupies a more or less coordinate role with verbal traces. In considering precategorical memory, of course, we saw that information persists in sensory form but for only severely limited periods of time, in vision. Moreover it was not clear that such sensory traces persisted after assignment of a verbal name to the input. Now in this chapter, by contrast, we turn to memory forms in which imagery, usually visual, persists for extended periods of time and coexists with retention of words covering the same events. It is something of a problem that different experimental techniques have tended to come up with memory systems having different properties; with some exceptions the situation can be characterized as one of "diverging operations." However, the quality of the evidence is impressive and so the various paradigms are considered one by one, even though in principle a textbook should probably not include large amounts of new and only partially digested research, especially when, as is the case now, considerable excitement has been attached to a new and fashionable research topic.

EIDETIC IMAGERY

If anything captures vividly the meaning of memory imagery it is the popular conception of photographic memory. We all dream of how life would be improved if we could scan the contents of a page—say, the conjugation of an irregular verb in a foreign language—and then effortlessly be able to call up any detail from that page later. This dream gives way to envy when we hear tales of people who actually possess such powers, usually someone's uncle or the brother of a roommate. The problem therefore becomes exactly how must one go about validating claims of this sort objectively. Hebb (1966, p. 43) offers suggestions for casual ways of evaluating the veridicality of images, such as comparing the speed of forward and backward reading for images of a page of text. Psychologists, however, have attempted to devise more easily standardized criteria for truly eidetic, or vivid, images. Sources for the early period of work on eidetic imagery, which occurred in Germany between about 1905 and 1930, are cited in R. S. Woodworth (1938, p. 45) along with a sketch of the typical research procedure. This early German work (Jaensch, 1930) established that once eidetic imagery was carefully distinguished from regular memories and from regular afterimages, from the former by its vividness and from the latter by its duration, it was found almost exclusively in preadolescent children and, curiously, it does not necessarily produce better recall of detail than noneidetic memory. These conclusions have generally withstood the scrutiny of modern investigators.

For nearly 35 years there was close to total silence on eidetic imagery in psychological journals. This period, beginning around 1930, corresponds to the heyday of puritanical behaviorism; imagery was a concept tainted with mentalism and introspection and psychologists were not inclined, or not clever enough, to objectify it. The silence was broken in 1964 by publication of an extensive study conducted by R. N. and R. B. Haber, as part of a program of normative, comparative, and cross-cultural research. A recent review by Gray and Gummerman (1975) is an excellent source for the newer work.

Haber and Haber (1964) examined 150 elementary school children in a standardized testing situation. The children were first shown examples of how to experience colored afterimages in order to accustom them to speaking about visual experience in the absence of stimuli, a type of behavior that is ordinarily discouraged in children on the basis of its being hallucinatory. They were then shown coherent pictures for 30 sec apiece and interviewed after each as they gazed at a blank field in the same location where the picture had appeared.

The subsequent question period was directed toward eight response measures, such as how long the image lasted, if there was one, whether it was colored positively, whether the child's descriptions of detail and color were accurate, and so forth. Somewhat over half the children (84) reported having an image following at least one of the stimulus pictures, but there was considerable spread with regard to the eight criterion scales indexing the overall quality of the image. What was of great interest and importance was that there was a small group of 12 children who were quite distinct from the other 72 who reported at least some imagery. They were distinct from the others in that they had seen for each of the four pictures an image that lasted 40 sec or longer, in that they tended to have high accuracy in describing the contents of the pictures, and in that they never used the past tense in describing the contents of the picture, always speaking instead as if the picture were still there. These 12 achieved positive-coloration scores of 90% as opposed to 34% for the others in the group reporting at least some imagery. They always scanned the blank screen with their eyes during the period they were describing their eidetic images, whereas the 72 subjects in the weaker imagery group scanned almost never—100% versus 2%, respectively.

It is quite important that these various criteria were discontinuous in their distribution across subjects for it is mainly when traits are distributed bimodally that individual differences should attract serious theoretical attention. One can always choose to speak of different "types" deriving from a unimodal distribution but such a description establishes nothing more than the commonplace fact of distribution about a mean.

Using the criterion of composite imagery scores that are set apart quantitatively and discontinuously to argue for a qualitative difference, the Habers' results indicate an incidence of just about 8% for eidetic imagery among school children. These individuals were not conspicuously different from their classmates in sex, race, or other standard classification variables, although a later report by Siipola and Hayden (1965) suggests an association with mental retardation. This later finding is provocative theoretically because it suggests that eidetic imagery may somehow be a stage of mental functioning through which people may all quite normally pass, perhaps prior to verbal fluency. The association with mental retardation suggests that some individuals either become fixated in some fashion or otherwise abnormally retain vestiges of this earlier stage on into subsequent modes of functioning. There is certainly an intuitive ring of truth to the assertion that preverbal memories are vivid visual representations.

The Siipola–Hayden report states that among retarded children the overall incidence of eidetic imagery, as measured by the criteria established in concert with the Habers, was 50%, between five and ten times the normal rate. Also, the occurrence of eidetic imagery in a retarded child turned out to be an accurate signal of organic, as opposed to familial, retardation. Although the organic versus familial distinction may be questionable on theoretical grounds—because it quite likely depends more on specialists' abilities to find an organic correlate than on whether there actually is one—still it does suggest the existence of some tangible physical substrate to this notoriously mentalistic phenomenon. It is frustrating that neither the Habers' original survey nor a followup to it (Leask, Haber, & Haber, 1969) turned up evidence for comparably dramatic traits distinguishing normal children who do and who do not possess eidetic imagery, beyond a somewhat higher incidence of eyeglasses among the eidetic group. Nor, unfortunately, have replications of this work on retardation been conclusive (Symmes, 1971) although the research ought to be procedurally straightforward.

In fact, the contradictions and false starts that are typical of the research following the Habers' restoration of the topic to modern attention leave us with very little to go on beyond the reality of the phenomenon and some idea of its prevalence. Paivio (1971a, p. 482) concludes that there is still no basis for other than highly speculative interpretations. As an example of an empirical contradiction in this field, there is the fact that sheer accuracy of report in picture-image experiments sometimes seems to be a positive correlate of eidetic imagery and other times not (Leask *et al.,* 1969). Doob's (1966) work on cross-cultural correlates of eidetic imagery is another example of a promising lead with a confusing outcome. An initial investigation showed rather high prevalence of eidetic imagery, defined with criteria comparable to those used by the Habers, among the preliterate Ibo of Northwest Africa. This interesting result fits with an analog to the individual developmental hypothesis considered above: Just as eidetic imagery may represent a vestige of primitive processing during the preverbal and preliterate stages of a child's growth, likewise whole societies may, in their preliterate stages, depend more heavily on imagery than societies having reached a higher level of literacy. Unfortunately, as Doob shows, tests of this reasoning, in which various groups differing in literacy were systematically compared, produced no sensible pattern of data. Degree of literacy was not, across either individuals or across groups, an inverse function of prevalence of eidetic behavior.

The fusion method. The most dramatic demonstration of eidetic imagery, dramatic for methodological rigor, for the almost unbelievable detail of the images involved, and for their duration, is found in a report of one subject by Stromeyer and Psotka (1970). These authors adapted a technique reintroduced to modern attention by Leask *et al.* (1969), in which two meaningless pictures are displayed successively. After the first picture has been removed, the second is displayed and the subject is told to maintain, or project, an image of the first superimposed on the second. Although each of the two pictures is meaningless when viewed alone, their superposition results in a recognizable object, and if the subject sees this object it is inferred that he must have had some visual memory for the first during presentation of the second.

Stromeyer and Psotka adapted random dot stereograms to this testing situation. A random dot stereogram (Julesz, 1964) is a pair of dot matrices, where, for example, each of 10,000 cells is randomly filled or empty with a probability of .50. A critical region of one of the two patterns has each dot systematically displaced but otherwise the two patterns are the same. Although this critical region corresponds to a familiar pattern it is totally impossible to see the pattern when viewing either matrix of dots separately. However, when the two matrices are combined stereoscopically the pattern is not only visible but, depending on the degree and nature of the transformation relating the two, emerges in depth. In testing their subject Stromeyer and Psotka simply showed one of the two dot patterns to one eye alone, waited for some period of time, and then showed the other pattern to the opposite eye, instructing the subject to superimpose her image of the first stimulus, which had since been removed. The test cannot be falsified because the patterns provide no coherent information individually and because memorization of such a random dot pattern other than visually would probably require months of work or even years. Still, this subject was able to see the stereoscopic pattern based on the combination of the second matrix with her eidetic image of the first. She spent about 3 min scanning the first pattern systematically, and was able to reveal an image of it after 24 hr. The sharpness she reported of the edges of the stereoscopic figure must indicate that the image was not even blurred during the time it was held in memory!

Summary comments on eidetic imagery.   The surest conclusions to be reached about eidetic imagery are existential (although Gray & Gummerman, 1975, demur even on this point); whereas all people seem to exhibit visual memories to some extent, as will be seen below, some individuals demonstrate a particular form of imagery that is sharply discontinuous with normal memory by virtue of its immediacy and its qualitative fidelity to the original stimulus. Quite unlike iconic storage, eidetic traces seem to depend on prior scanning of the display. This, and the fact that they last on the order of a minute rather than somewhat less than a second, strongly discourage the inference that eidetic images are an abnormal property of whatever visual system is responsible for iconic memory. Beyond a few additional demographic facts there is little known about eidetic imagery. Particularly missing are systematic efforts showing theoretically sensible relations of imagery to developmental, individual difference, and information-processing variables.

Eidetic imagery must be considered an abnormal condition of memory functioning because of its low incidence and its clear differentiation from normal process. It is a fascinating question for debate just how much there is to learn from normal process by considering abberations from it. On the one hand, one can point to advances in psychopathology, color vision, and cerebral lateralization, as cases where pathological states were tremendously valuable in advancing theory. On the other hand, although eidetic imagery has been cited as consistent with certain points of view concerning perception (Hebb, 1968), there is little theoretical mileage that has yet been based on it in the study of memory, per se.

There is no intended implication of these remarks that eidetic imagery represents the only type of exceptional memory that may be studied. In fact, precisely because there have been unambiguously noneidetic individuals with more startling powers than Habers' and others' eidetic subjects, we must be careful not to fall into the trap of attributing all supernormal memory, which seems "photographic," to eidetic imagery. Gray and Gummerman (1975) make this point effectively. They list nine thoroughly reliable cases that demonstrate such independence of extraordinary memory from eidetic imagery. One such case is the Russian mnemonist "S" whose detailed history is the subject of a fascinating book by Luria (1968); although S makes heavy use of visual imagery, just as normal subjects are shown to do later in this chapter, he does not possess eidetic imagery. Coltheart and Glick (1974) report a case study of a subject who could visualize verbal materials so vividly that she could rapidly spell backwards the letters in sentences as long as ten words; however, she had no unusually detailed images of nonverbal pictures and she could not perform exceptionally on tests of fusion. These and other cases are not anecdotal; they are reports of respected experimental psychologists using modern conceptual and experimental techniques (see also Hunt & Love, 1972). The point they make is that we need to be very careful to separate the criteria for eidetic imagery from other manifestations of abnormally powerful retrieval.

REPRODUCTION FROM MEMORY
OF FORMS

It was not without a small but persistent tradition of objection that the Ebbinghaus reliance on nonsense syllables for learning materials dominated the study of memory for about 75 years. One manifestation of this deviationist tradition is found in the long history of studies on the memorization and reproduction of visual forms. [Another is found in Bartlett's influential studies of memory for meaningful stories (Bartlett, 1932).] These are two excellent places to examine the literature on memory for form prior to 1960, when newer approaches began to emerge. One source is Woodworth (1938), which offers a lucid but warmly partisan summary of the field from the vantage of a controversy between Gestalt theorists and the dominant behaviorist–functionalist climate of American psychology at the time. The second source is a long review chapter by Riley (1962) from a broader perspective.

Basically, the Gestalt psychologists made two claims about memory for form, claims they conceived as being applicable, however, to memory generally. One was that the memory trace is nonverbal, or imaginal, and the other was that during the passage of time this trace undergoes automatic, "autochthonous", changes toward forms more in conformity with laws of organization than the originals. The theoretical alternative to the first assertion was that forms get encoded by their names, if they are meaningful, or by the names of natural objects they resemble, if they are nonsense forms. Woodworth (1938) advanced the *"schema with correction"* hypothesis to cover instances where a form could be encoded as some particular deviation from a familiar object. The alternative to the second assertion, that memory traces independently rearrange themselves to good figures in storage, is that details about the correction part of a schema with correction get lost during the course of forgetting with the consequence that remembered figures, especially when measured by the method of recall, are just simpler than the originals. For that reason, the reproduced forms tended to be better figures, in the Gestalt sense of the term, than the originals.

As will shortly become apparent there is now excellent evidence for the Gestalt theorists' first assertion, although such evidence has not been forthcoming until long after the controversy cooled. At the time, the proposition that forms could be remembered visually was effectively countered by Carmichael, Hogan, and Walters (1932) in a famous experiment. These authors presented ambiguous figures that were designed to resemble either of two familiar objects, such as a pair of circles joined with a crossbar so as to resemble either a pair of eyeglasses or a dumbbell (see Figure 5.1). All subjects saw the same ambiguous figures but different groups were given clues as to what each figure might look like at the time of learning. Later, in a test of reproduction it was found that verbal labels often had a strong effect on the way in which remembered figures departed from original figures; for example, there would have been a thickening of the crossbar in the sample described above for subjects told it looked like a dumbbell, and a curvature in the same crossbar for those told it looked like glasses, as illustrated in Figure 5.1. Therefore, Carmichael *et al.* (1932) have indeed shown that verbal labels can influence memory for visual forms; whether verbal labels always play this role, or even normally play this role, is a different matter, and we shall see presented that some visual memory seems to exist apart from any labeling.

The second assertion of the Gestalt theorists has not survived as well as the first. Baddeley (1968) performed an elegant test of this theory using stimuli consisting of circles with various sizes of gap; Hebb and Foord (1945) had used similar materials for the same purpose in an earlier study. According to the hypothesis that memorized figures tend to change during storage in conformity with Gestalt organizational principles, these gaps should "shrink in memory," or close up, as a consequence of the principle of closure. Recognition tests revealed, however, that gaps were remembered as larger, on a delayed-memory test, than they were in the original figure. This outcome is directly the opposite of a

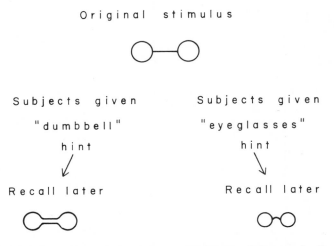

FIGURE 5.1 The effects of suggested encoding contexts on later reproduction of forms from memory. (After Carmichael, Hogan, & Walters, 1932.)

Gestalt prediction. It is, however, a result that conforms conveniently with the schema with correction notion of Woodworth (1938).

FUNCTIONAL CHARACTERISTICS OF IMAGES IN SHORT-TERM MEMORY

The case of the reality of visual imagery in human memory rests on three major bodies of evidence, and variants on them. Two of these, (1) studies of same— different reaction time and (2) studies of modality-specific interference, are covered in the present section under the heading of short-term memory because both of these research areas involve a relatively small amount of material to be remembered that is tested rather soon after acquisition. A third area of research that has been important in sustaining the reality of imagery is the area of mnemonic techniques in long-term memory; this is elaborated in a separate section.

Visual Imagery in Speeded Matching

The study of memory has been considerably enriched in recent years by a new dimension of response analysis—speed. In several notable methodological innovations investigators have been able to explore the structure and function of memory by asking not whether subjects can perform this or that act of retrieval from storage but rather how fast they can do it. One of the most important of these innovations concerns memory for form, a research program carried out by Posner and his collaborators.

The Posner and Keele experiment. Posner and Keele (1967) offered the first report of the visual matching technique. Their concern was with the trace laid down by a visually presented letter once it was recognized and named. According to such models as Sperling's, the name (categorical response for the item) is retained in some speech-related storage system and the visual information fades rapidly from iconic memory. The alternative of interest to Posner and Keele was that even after recognition and naming there might coexist knowledge about the letter's name and about its appearance.

The research logic begins with a simple two-choice reaction-time arrangement in which two familiar letters of the alphabet are presented side by side, with the subject instructed to respond as fast as possible with regard to whether the two stimuli represent the same letter. The special feature of the experiment is that a given letter may be represented either by an upper-case or lower-case symbol. Because the subjects' responses were to be based on the name identity of the letters rather than on their physical identity, presenting either *AA* or *Aa* signaled the response "same." The finding from this type of experiment is that when letters are physically identical as well as nominally equivalent (as with *AA*) reaction times are about 70 msec faster than when they are nominally equivalent but physically dissimilar—as with *Aa*.

Faster acknowledgement of nominal equivalence for physically identical characters than for nonidentical characters under simultaneous exposure is a result that follows quite naturally from theories of perception in which information is represented by increasingly sophisticated codes during input. Such theories maintain that knowledge of stimuli comes first in primitive forms, tied strictly to precategorical sensory processing systems, then achieves progressively higher levels of complexity as contact is made with more and more derivative, learned, classification systems. Paivio (1971a) captures this widespread viewpoint in his theory of meaning, which specifies progressive stages of (1) representational, (2) referential, and (3) associative meaning for familiar objects. These levels refer, respectively, to (1) the means by which stimuli evoke consistent images of themselves stored in long-term memory, (2) how these images are connected to verbal surrogates for them, and (3) how these entitites are elaborated in networks of denotative and connotative meaning. It may or may not be necessary to have a hierarchical system in that each of these levels of analysis must be completed before the others are achieved; however, it is for the moment adequate to state that the early or primitive forms of analysis are engaged before the more complicated forms of analysis. For example, a person knows about the physical appearance of a letter before he knows its name. Because if two letters have the same appearance they must also have the same name it is easy to see why there was a time advantage to the physical match (*AA* or *aa*) as compared to the name match (*aA* or *Aa*). The faster physical than name matches are interpreted to mean that information of a more primitive, and therefore more quickly achieved, format is being used in the former than in the latter.

Now what should happen if we separate, in time, the two letters the nominal identity of which is the decision criterion? In this new experiment the first stimulus is presented and then the subject must wait until a second is presented, holding the first somehow in memory, and compare the second stimulus with a memory trace of the first. Consider a limiting case when less than 1 msec separates offset of the first stimulus from presentation of the second. In this event the advantage of a physical match ought to be evident because visual sensory processes from the first stimulus would not have had time to fade. Another limiting case is to separate the two stimuli by several months. It seems reasonable, although not strictly required by prior knowledge, that in this time any vestiges of the first letter as a visual stimulus would have decayed and only the name would be remembered, making this case equivalent to a name match. Somewhere in between these two degenerate extremes, Posner and Keele reasoned, it would be possible to trace the decay of visual information from memory by noting at what duration, under conditions in which the interstimulus interval is varied, the physical and name matches produced equivalent reaction times.

In their study Posner and Keele (1967) always presented an upper-case letter (such as *A*) in the first stimulus position, and one of four possibilities was given as the second stimulus: the same nominal letter in the same case (*A*), the same nominal letter in a different case (*a*), or a different letter in either or lower case (*B* or *b*). The main result is given in Figure 5.2, which shows the advantage of a physical match over a name match, a difference score based on these two reaction times, as a function of the interstimulus interval separating the occurrence of the two letters. At the far left of the baseline we see the condition of simultaneity where the advantage is over 70 msec. This is the simple advantage of the simultaneous pair *AA* over the pair *Aa*, a finding we have already considered. On the extreme right of the baseline we see that by an interstimulus interval of 2 sec it has made no difference whether the second stimulus has been presented in the same case or in a different case, suggesting that latencies here are derived purely from knowledge of the letters' names and not what they look like. In between there is a regular decline in the difference score, which we may take to be indicative of decay of visual memory. The time scale of this decay is much longer than that reported in Chapter 2 for iconic memory and we shall see below that the memory tapped with this procedure has different properties than iconic storage.

Internal manipulation and generation of images.   Tversky (1969) has used the Posner–Keele method to good advantage in an experiment based on dual representation, verbal and pictorial, of experimentally developed materials. The importance of her investigation, apart from the charm of her stimuli, comes from her demonstration of internal transformations from one to the other form of representation. In Tversky's study the subjects were first obliged to learn the

FIGURE 5.2 The advantage of a match based on physical identity over a match based on nominal identity as a function of the time interval separating the two letters to be judged. (After Posner, Boies, Eichelman, & Taylor, 1969.)

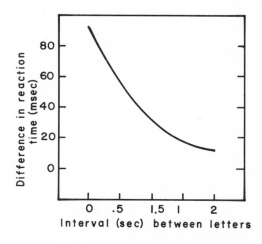

equivalences between pictures of faces and the names used to label them as shown in Figure 5.3. A little study will show these to be almost perversely difficult paired-associate materials, and indeed, subjects required about 4 hr of study before they were absolutely certain of all the pairings. We may think of a trained subject, however, as knowing each of the eight schematic "people" both by name and by picture.

The main experimental interest was in reaction-time trials in which two stimuli were shown separated, as in the Posner–Keele study, by a short time interval, subjects being timed on the speed of their decisions as to whether the two stimuli were representations of the same "person" from the set of eight. There are four basic arrangements for presenting the two stimuli: both pictorial, both verbal, first pictorial–second verbal, and first verbal–second pictorial. For each of these, further, the two stimuli can represent either the same or a different member of the set. We should expect performance to be faster when modalities match between the two stimuli than when there is a mismatch, at least for "same" responses.

However, Tversky's study included an additional variable concerned with the subject's *expectancy* for which version of stimulus two would be presented. Consider conditions in which the verbal version of a stimulus is presented first. In one condition, in which a given subject would be tested for a prolonged block of trials, the second presentation—either the same or a different member of the set of eight alternatives—was itself verbal also 79% of the time and pictorial 21% of the time. In another condition the first stimulus was also verbal, but the second 79% pictorial and 21% verbal. There were two additional conditions where the first-stimulus presentation was always pictorial, one in which the second was biased toward pictorial, and another in which the second was biased toward verbal representation. Therefore, whatever the first-stimulus modality, there was one condition in which the subject was expecting the second stimulus in the same modality and another condition in which the second stimulus was expected in the other modality. The first stimulus was displayed for 1 sec, there was then a pause of 1 sec, and reaction times were measured from the onset of the second stimulus, which continued for 4 sec.

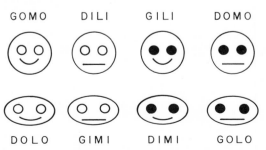

FIGURE 5.3 Schematic faces and associated nonsense names used by Tversky. (After Tversky, 1969.)

The results for the second half of the experimental session (when subjects were well practiced) are shown in Table 5.1. Consider cases where the first stimulus was presented in the form of a verbal name. Appropriate comparisons show that if the subject knew what to expect for the second stimulus, and his expectation was confirmed, as in V–V 79 or V–P 79, it made no appreciable difference whether there was a change in modalities or not (644 msec versus 641 msec). In contrast, if the second stimulus, following an initial verbal representation, was unexpected, as in conditions V–V 21 or V–P 21, there was a very substantial advantage to matching modalities (777 msec versus 860 msec). Finally, consider cases where the second stimulus was verbal, just as the subject had been led to expect, as in V–V 79 and P–V 79. Comparison of these two conditions permits the conclusion that if the second presentation is expected, it makes no difference whether the subject has been given a matching first stimulus, V–V 79, or a mismatched version that must be transformed in order to compare it with the second stimulus, P–V 79. Data from conditions of Tversky's experiment with *violated* expectations completely confirm the Posner–Keele result: If subjects have no predictive power for the second stimulus a physical match leads to considerably faster reaction times than a nominal match.

The conditions where expectations were confirmed (P–P 79, P–V 79, V–P 79, V–V 79) indicate that subjects can translate back and forth from one version to the other based on learned equivalences. Given the name GOLO a subject expecting the second stimulus to be pictorial can generate an internal image of a broad face with straight mouth and filled eyes, and he can generate an image in this way that is just as good as the one he would have derived from receiving the picture in the first place. Quite clearly, therefore, the imagery being measured with this reaction-time technique differs fundamentally from iconic imagery in that the latter is derived from some stimulus display, whereas the former can be

TABLE 5.1
Mean Reaction Time (msec) as a
Function of Stimulus Modality and
Expected Modality[a]

Condition			
S_1	S_2	Percent	Reaction time
V	V	79	644
V	V	21	777
V	P	79	641
V	P	21	860
P	V	79	636
P	V	21	785
P	P	79	634
P	P	21	768

[a]After Tversky (1969).

generated on the basis of a long-term memory. This type of evidence affords a rare glimpse of internal mental events at the level of what Paivio calls "referential processing," the level at which there is interaction between stored representations based on the names of things and representations based on their (visual) stimulus properties.

Posner, Boies, Eichelman, and Taylor (1969) have shown that transformations between an item's name and its visual image can occur on the basis of a spoken stimulus. In a portion of their research subjects were asked to decide whether the second of two successively presented letters had the same name as the first, just as in the earlier Posner–Keele experiment. Instructions indicated that the first letter might be presented in either of two ways, either an upper-case visual letter or the spoken name of that letter. The subjects were told to consider the spoken letter as equivalent to an upper-case visual letter. In one of their experiments the second letter was always upper case; so just as in Tversky's study, subjects knew what form to expect at the time they received the first stimulus. There were three interstimulus intervals, 0, .5, and 1.0 sec, separating the first stimulus, either spoken or upper-case-visual, from the second, which, as indicated above, was always upper case.

The comparison of interest is between correct latencies for the auditory and visual first-stimulus conditions. If the subject can transform the auditory input into an image of an upper-case letter that is just as good as the real thing, there should be no difference between the two modes, but if the transformation process is somehow limited, then the visual condition should show an advantage. It is certainly reasonable to expect the transformation process to take time and practice, however; one can not expect *instantaneous* translation of the auditory letter into an upper-case visual image. Likewise, subjects might improve with experience in this experimental situation.

Figure 5.4 shows confirmation of these expectations. Given in Figure 5.4 are difference scores representing the advantage in reaction time of having both stimuli in the visual modality, that is, the advantage of not being required to transform the auditory into a visual image. The data point of special interest is the one showing no advantage whatever when the interstimulus interval is a full second and when subjects have already served in the experiment for at least 2 days. Like the subjects in Tversky's study, these subjects, given time and practice, were able to treat a mismatched first stimulus in such a way as to enjoy the benefits of a physical match without having been given the nominal stimulus necessary for one. The dependence of this ability on practice and on the amount of time given for the transformation actually increases the reasonableness of the recoding explanation; it would be cause for some suspicion if the generation process had not depended on the time allowed for it.

A program of research by Shepard and his associates (L. Cooper & Shepard, 1973; Shepard, 1975) has provided impressive evidence on the internal transformations subjects can perform on visual information. In a typical study (Shepard

FIGURE 5.4 The advantage of visual over auditory presentation of the first of two occurrences of the same letter when the second is always visual. A positive difference means that it took longer to respond when the two modalities were different than when they were the same. (After Posner, Boies, Eichelman, & Taylor, 1969.)

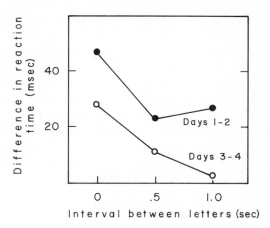

& Metzler, 1971) pictorial versions of three-dimensional arrays are presented side by side, each representing a stack of cubes articulated at several angles. The question is whether by rotating one of the two three-dimensional arrays it can be made to coincide with the other. (The reader can capture the flavor of this task by trying to decide whether the letter p or the letter q, when rotated appropriately, would coincide with the letter b.) The finding of importance from this research has been that the mental rotation necessary to perform the task goes on at a steady rate: It takes longer and longer to decide whether two representations of the same array coincide the more angular displacement separates them; furthermore, there is a linear relation between the amount of rotation necessary and reaction time. The mental rotation phenomenon is a persuasive one because of the staggering complexity of simulating it with purely verbal, or propositional, information processing. Indeed, Anderson and Bower (1973, p. 461) cite the Shepard and Metzler type of study as the single most uncomfortable result for computer simulations of cognition that eschew the concept of analog visual imagery.

Maintenance of imagery.   To this point it is clear that there is an advantage of physical matches over name matches, when the subject is under instructions to decide whether two temporally separated stimuli have the same name. This defines the presence of some form of visual memory. The same inference comes from evidence for an ability to use learned equivalences to transform a memory representation back and forth between an item's name and its appearance. Now we address another issue, whether a visual image can be maintained through some ostensibly voluntary process, just as a verbal memory can be maintained by vocal or by subvocal rehearsal.

There are two sources of evidence on this point in the research series of Posner *et al.* (1969). The first is an experiment in which the Posner–Keele technique was arranged to include variation in the subject's expectancy. The two stimuli were separated by interstimulus intervals of 0, .5, or 1.0 sec and the first stimulus was always an upper-case letter. The variable of interest was the set of possibilities for the second stimulus. In the pure condition the second stimulus was also always upper case, making all reactions possible on the basis of physical cues. In the mixed condition, the second stimulus was equally often upper and lower case. The idea here was that in the pure condition visual information is absolutely certain to be reliable as a basis for decision, whereas in the mixed condition it will be useful only half the time; therefore, if subjects are able voluntarily to maintain information in visual form they should do so in the pure condition. If they do maintain visual information more in the pure condition than in the mixed condition then the consequences should be evident in comparisons of physical matches, where both stimuli have indeed been upper case, for the pure versus the mixed situations. Specifically, if after a 1-sec interstimulus interval subjects have more visual information surviving in the pure than in the mixed condition because of some rehearsal process, then the reaction time to acknowledge identity should be faster there also.

This expectation was confirmed by the data. The two mixed conditions, one with physical matches and the other with name matches, yielded the original Posner–Keele result with a time advantage of about 85 msec at zero delay and very little advantage remaining after a full second. The consistently faster times for the pure condition, where all matches were physical, was supportive of the conclusion that subjects somehow maintain the visual format when it is to their advantage to do so. After 1 sec the time advantage of physical matches under the pure condition over name matches in the mixed condition was almost as strong as the advantage of physical matches under both conditions when there was no delay. This is exactly what can be expected of a subject with the ability to prevent dissipation of visual imagery through something like rehearsal.

The second general approach to studying the maintenance of visual imagery in memory used by Posner *et al.* (1969) is something of a backward strategy. They reasoned that one might learn what type of processing occured during a delay between the two stimuli in the same–different paradigm by determining what sorts of event would interfere with the advantage of physical over name matches. Stated differently, they wished to determine whether whatever memory trace supports the physical-match superiority is a form of central storage or a form of peripheral storage. The background logic includes certain established facts about interference with peripheral memory, such as storage in experiments on iconic memory. We know (Sperling, 1960, 1963) that exposure of jumbled letter fragments without meaning or systematic pattern can effectively mask, or terminate, the storage of the visual icon. However, more central demands on attention, such as having to remember verbal information, leave the usefulness and duration of visual icons intact (Turvey, 1966). Exactly the opposite is true of information held centrally in some form of verbal short-term memory.

Demands on attention during a retention interval, such as mental arithmetic, have strong interfering effects on verbal short-term memory (Brown, 1958; Peterson & Peterson, 1959; Posner & Rossman, 1965), whereas, although the experiment may not have been done, exposing the subject to visual "noise" is likely to have little effect on short-term verbal memory.

To assess whether the visual imagery used in the Posner and Keele technique is more central or more peripheral, by these definitions, one can simply interpolate either a visual disturbance, specifically a haphazardly filled checkerboard pattern, or an attentional disturbance, mental arithmetic, between the first and second stimuli of the paradigm under consideration here, as Posner *et al.* (1969) have done. Their result was that the superiority of physical over name matches was not affected, in comparison to blank-interval controls, by exposure to visual noise during the interstimulus interval but it was affected, indeed eliminated, by requiring the subject to perform an arithmetic problem. This result supports the inference that despite its genuinely visual nature, the memory trace that supports faster physical than name matches in this experimental situation has more in common with central, verbal short-term memory than with iconic visual storage. This does not at all mean that there is necessarily anything verbal about the trace itself, only that it seems to depend for survival on some central portion of the information-processing system in which our ability to carry out simultaneous tasks is limited. This conclusion, of course, is neatly consistent with the evidence that subjects can voluntarily maintain these visual memory traces and that they can voluntarily transform them to verbal referents when circumstances make this advantageous.

Modality-Specific Interference

With respect to the question: "How do we know that visual imagery in memory is a legitimately separate phenomenon from other forms of memory representation?" we have just considered one major line of evidence, the experimentation growing out of Posner and Keele's letter-matching experiment. We now turn to another major line of evidence aimed at fixing the reality of visual imagery operationally. The strategy in question is the old one that asks about the content or format of a memory by determining what events interfere with it. (The counterpart to this technique is the transfer method, where we ask what has been acquired in a task by determining what facilitation there is to some further behavior.) The assumption of the interference approach to visual imagery is that if one memory is held in visual form and another not, say in verbal form, then if there are two competing activities, one verbal and the other visual, there should be an interacting pattern of interference. Actually, the last of the Posner *et al.* (1969) studies covered in the previous section followed exactly this logic.

Bower (1972a) gave subjects pairs of words to associate under either instructions to use rote verbal repetition or to use an interacting visual image involving the two words in each pair. We shall examine such "imagery instructions" in detail in the next section; a subject under such instructions may try to learn the pair SCISSORS–WHEAT by picturing large shears harvesting grain in a field. Concurrently with the paired-associate learning task, there were two forms of a distractor task, pursuit tracking, with the finger, of a moving *visible* target or pursuit tracking, again with the finger, of an *invisible* tactually presented target. Figure 5.5 shows these two tasks schematically and Table 5.2 gives the results of the experiment in terms of proportion correct paired-associate responses. The finding of importance was a highly significant interaction between the instructions given subjects and the type of concurrent tracking task they had to perform. Under instructions calling for rote repetition of the pairs it made no difference whether the tactile or the visual task was used; however, under instructions for the formation of visual images linking words within a pair, the

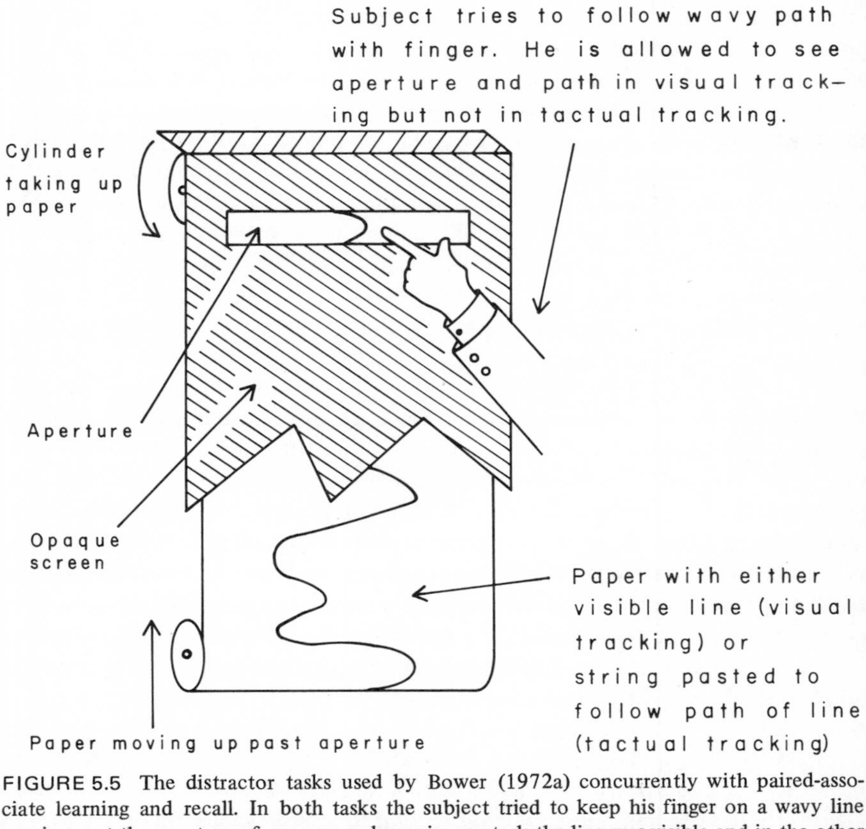

FIGURE 5.5 The distractor tasks used by Bower (1972a) concurrently with paired-associate learning and recall. In both tasks the subject tried to keep his finger on a wavy line moving past the aperture of a memory drum; in one task the line was visible and in the other it was invisible but could be felt tactually. (After Bower, 1972a.)

TABLE 5.2
Proportion of Correct Recall as a Function
of Instruction and Type of Distractor Task[a]

	Type of distraction	
Instruction	Visual	Tactual
Repetition	.28	.28
Imagery	.55	.66

[a]After Bower (1972a).

visual tracking task led to worse performance than the tactile version. We may be assured that the two tracking tasks were of equal difficulty because under rote repetition instructions they led to equal performance. Apparently, when subjects tried to learn the pairs by forming visual images involving the words to be remembered, concurrent use of the visual system, even for an unrelated task, was selectively distracting. This pattern of results is difficult to explain other than by the concession that the imagery instruction did indeed engage some genuinely visual process.

Brooks (1968) provided one of the first and best systematic exploitations of modality-specific interference in tying down the concept of visual imagery. His reasoning was also that if the visual system is occupied in some ongoing task it should interfere with manipulation or construction of visual imagery; however, in the experiment to be described here it was the overt visual task on which performance was measured rather than on the covert memory task in which imagery was allegedly playing a role. (In this respect the Brooks study complements Bower's.) In a clever experimental design Brooks managed to use the same stimuli for loading memory and for concurrent processing. Subjects were given either a sentence to remember, such as "The bird is in the bush," or a line drawing, such as a block letter F. For each type of stimulus there was a processing task based on the memory representation of that stimulus. With a sentence, the subject was required to classify each word as a noun or a nonnoun. With an outline of a letter, the subject was required to visualize each corner as an acute or open angle.

There were three modes of responding in these distractor tasks. In the vocal mode the subject responded to the successive elements of the stimulus with a series of yesses and noes. For the sentence given above, letting "yes" indicate the presence of a noun, the correct response sequence would be "no–yes–no–no–no–yes." For the outline F, starting at the extreme lower left and moving clockwise around the circumference of the polygon, the sequence, assuming "yes" means an open angle, would be "yes–yes–yes–yes–no–no–yes–

yes—no—yes." Selecting appropriate letters and sentences allows matching of the length of the response sequence, and the actual sequence of yesses and noes itself. The second mode of processing was pointing. Here a visual display with Y's and N's representing yes and no was placed in front of the subject, and he had to move down the display pointing to the appropriate letters in a specified order. The location of the letters was irregular so that constant visual attention was necessary. The third mode of response was tapping; left- or right-hand taps were assigned to the yes and no responses and a sequential series of taps was thus generated. One of two stimuli was therefore entered first in memory, either a sentence or a block letter; the idea was that the sentence would be held in some verbal form of coding and the letter drawing in a visual-imagery representation. Second, some sequential operation was performed on the contents of memory, using either a verbal, visual, or tapping response mode. The measure of interest was the amount of time required to complete the sequential classification task; memory for the stimuli would have been essentially perfect, if measured.

The results obtained by Brooks (1968) in one of his experiments are shown in Table 5.3. The interaction between the type of information entered in memory and the mode of classifying its properties was highly significant. When a sentence was in memory, the vocal mode of responding took longest; however, when a visual letter form was the stimulus in memory the pointing mode took longest. Again, we may be assured that overriding differences in difficulty between either representational form or response mode cannot account for the pattern of results. This outcome points with authority to the possibility of multiple codes in memory, each with a natural affinity for certain types of storage and information handling.

A final example, by den Heyer and Barrett (1971) using the Brown—Peterson method, will serve to complete the case for imagery based on modality specific interference. This experiment shows that different aspects of a single, unitary stimulus are held in memory through different representational systems. den Heyer and Barrett provided subjects with very brief flashes of stimuli, such as

TABLE 5.3
Time (sec) to Complete Classification Task as a
Function of Memory Load and Classification
Response Mode[a]

Memory load	Type of response		
	Pointing	Tapping	Speaking
Sentence	9.8	7.8	13.8
Diagram	28.2	14.1	11.3

[a]After Brooks (1968).

shown in Figure 5.6. After 10 sec of some interpolated task, the subjects were required to reproduce the stimulus on a blank grid with the same number of cells as the stimulus had. There were three interpolated tasks between acquisition and retrieval. In one, as shown in the figure, a visual similarity judgment was required, concerning which of three small grids had the same filled cells. In the second, there was a series of short mental-arithmetic problems, and in a third the interpolated interval was left blank. The special feature of the study was determination of two separate scores from reproductions of the original stimulus. The position score indexed the number of positions filled in the original stimulus that were also filled in recall, regardless of whether the latter were filled with the correct letters. The identity score indexed how many of the original letters were reproduced in recall, regardless of where they were placed in the grid.

In Figure 5.7 the results are given, in terms of percentage difference scores between the experimental and control conditions. The higher the score, the more a particular interpolated task disrupted a particular recall measure in comparison with the same score under conditions of no interpolated task. The finding indicates that separable aspects of the same stimulus in memory can be selectively disrupted by the verbal and visual forms of interpolated activity. It is difficult to imagine how this interaction, as well as the other similar ones shown in this section, can be accommodated by a theory that memory is a single unitary storage system devoid of coding distinctions. These results, however, are quite consistent with the view that some aspects of some memories are stored in the same cognitive system that is involved in active use of the visual system. With

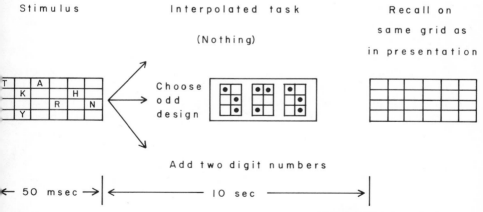

FIGURE 5.6   The task arrangement used by den Heyer and Barrett (1971). Subjects had to recall both the locations in which letters appeared and which letters had occurred, following either (1) no task, (2) a visual interpolated task, or (3) a verbal (mental arithmetic) interpolated task. (After den Heyer & Barrett, 1971.)

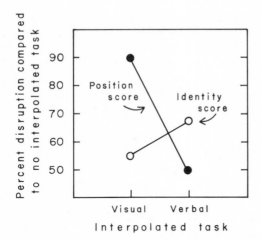

FIGURE 5.7 The amount of performance disruption, relative to control scores, caused by visual and verbal interpolated tasks. Position scoring measures whether the proper cells of the stimulus grid were filled in recall and identity scoring measures whether the correct letters were recalled, in whatever positions. (After den Heyer & Barrett, 1971.)

the other sources of evidence reviewed in this section, these data leave little doubt that visual imagery mediates some memories.

VISUAL IMAGERY IN LONG-TERM MEMORY

The case for nonverbal memory is, by now, a strong one. We have seen solid evidence for iconic memory, for eidetic imagery, and for short-term memory imagery systems involved in both speeded letter matching and in modality-specific interference. Each of these phenomena is of wide theoretical significance for our understanding of perception, reading, and information processing and the interrelations of these kinds of nonverbal storage are an urgent problem for a complete understanding of human memory.

However, it must be admitted that the demonstrations of imagery so far considered make little contact with what the layman regards as the psychology of memory. To the layman, awareness of memory centers on memory for events of the nonimmediate past, for words, for foreign equivalents, and for the names of familiar objects and faces. In other words, imagery is securely established in the intricate, fleeting, and complicated early moments of registration, but what pertinence does the concept of imagery have for long-term memory? When we speak of seeing things from the past "in our mind's eye" do we really mean remembering the words that those things originally elicited in us?

Memory for Pictures

One reason for an interest in the possibility of visual memory imagery is that storage capacity for pictures seems to be substantially higher than for words. If words could be transformed into pictorial images in the manner of generating images in the Tversky and Posner paradigm, people could possibly overcome limitations on verbal storage and actually improve their awareness of the past. There is strong evidence for high-capacity pictorial memory.

Recognition. Shepard (1967) allowed subjects free self-paced inspection of long series of words, sentences, or pictures of common objects taken from magazine advertisements and similar sources. In testing, 68 of these stimuli were presented one by one, each paired with a stimulus that had not been in the study series, for a forced-choice recognition test. In immediate testing 88.4% of the words were correctly chosen (chance being 50%), 89.0% of the sentences, and 96.0% of the pictures. Even a week later, pictures were still being remembered about as well, 87.0%, as words had been immediately.

Standing, Conezio, and Haber (1970) showed subjects a series of 2560 slides for 10 sec apiece. The slides were mostly colored scenes on vacation–family themes; many included people, some were city shots, both with and without vegetation. These slides were viewed in four daily sessions of 2 hr each, with 10 min of rest 1 hr after completing the inspection series. There was a forced-choice test consisting of 280 pairs of slides, one in each pair new and one from the previous study list. The three subjects achieved correct choices of 90%, 93%, and 85%, and two additional subjects, who had received a mere 1000 slides to study, got scores of 89 and 90%. On the basis of the former set of three subjects we can estimate that almost exactly 2000 pictures had been retained in memory until the time of the test, retained in at least enough detail to discriminate the correct pictures from similar incorrect ones. These three subjects chose the correct alternative an average of 89% of the time. We could estimate that for the whole population of 2560 stimuli they would have been right on 2278 (.89 × 2560) of the choices and wrong on the remaining 282. We might assume that on the latter 282 occasions the subjects did not recognize the correct alternative; otherwise it would have been selected. Assuming further that when the subjects have not recognized either alternative they have chosen arbitrarily (tossed a coin) between the two alternatives, we can deduce that there must have been another 282 occasions when the subjects have not recognized the correct alternative but have chosen it anyway (because the coin happens to land that way). In other words there must have been a total of 564 (2 × 282) cases of real recognition failure. Subtracting these recognition failures from the total stimulus set, therefore, we arrive at an estimate of 1996 (2560 − 564) retained pictures.

Impressive as these figures are in demonstrating the huge storage capacity of the human brain for organized visual information, Shepard's study has shown that recognition performance on single words is not far behind that for pictures, 88% versus 96%. Furthermore, it can be argued that recognition measures are not the best for testing retention of pictures as opposed to that of words. Pictures, the objection may go, contain many more different details than words and subjects may therefore have numerous independent chances of recognizing a picture, a recognition opportunity for each independent detail, but with unitary words there is only a single opportunity.

Recall. Because the greater detail inherent in pictures than in words allows recognition of the former to be based on multiple criteria (if any detail of the picture is recognized it must be an old picture), we need to consult experiments on *recall* for pictures and words. There are two ways to measure recall of pictures, recall of the name of the object pictured or recall (drawing) of the physical shape of the picture. Because the latter comparison places an undue premium on draftsmanship, the former comparison is the more valuable; however, it in turn requires experimental materials where each picture has an utterly unambiguous name.

Bevan and Steger (1971) have directly compared recall as a function of the abstractness with which objects are represented in presentation. In pretests a list of 21 common objects was developed to include not only very frequently encountered items but also to include only objects that could be reliably named by a group of fourth-grade students. The objects fitting these criteria were apple, book, bottle, coin, cup, eraser, flower, fork, key, lightbulb, match, matchbook, pencil, radio, ring, safety razor, scissors, shoe, soap, toothbrush, wallet. Three versions of each stimulus were then prepared: One was the physical object itself, another a black and white photograph of the object, and finally the printed word naming the object. Each subject received all 21 stimuli, seven as palpable objects, seven as pictures, and seven as words. The experiment was carefully balanced so that for one-third of the subjects each particular object, such as fork, was represented in each of the three possible ways. The subjects were either college students or fourth-grade students (ages of roughly 19 and 9 years, respectively) in order to check on whether the relation between recall and abstractness depended on age. Each stimulus was exposed for 5 sec on a sort of lazy-susan presentation device with 5 sec between stimuli. After presentation subjects were asked to list the names of the stimuli in any order they chose.

The results are shown in Figure 5.8, taken from Bevan and Steger (1971); scores from immediate and delayed tests are combined. Abstractness quite clearly affected memory for both children and adults, with performance improving from verbal to pictorial and further to actual representation of the stimuli. College students were better than children, although not reliably better in performance on objects. Paivio, Rogers, and Smythe (1968) have presented evidence that the difference between pictures and objects cannot be attributed to the presence of color in the objects; they compared colored with black and white pictures and found no advantage for color. These last authors also used a between-groups between-lists design, in which separate groups receive lists consisting entirely of one form of stimulus representation, a precaution that avoids the problem that one type of stimulus may be more interesting than another and thereby produce unequal attention within a list.

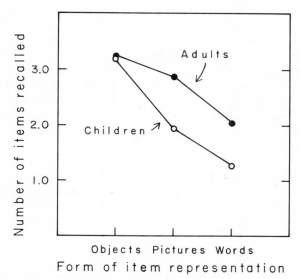

FIGURE 5.8 Recall performance of children and adults on items presented in the form of pictures, words, or as the objects themselves. The maximum score is seven. (After Bevan & Steger, 1971.)

The superiority of pictures to words in free recall is a well-documented result. In recent articles by Paivio and Csapo (1973) and by Paivio (1974) there are seven independent experiments showing the picture advantage. The average size of the effect is about .10 in terms of recall probability. It therefore seems that the exact form in which subjects receive stimulus information does make a difference in long-term memory, a difference that favors nonverbal presentation modes. This fact, and the dramatic storage capacities demonstrated by Shepard (1967) and by Standing *et al.* (1970), lead naturally to two issues: (1) how to "harness" this memorial power and (2) what theoretical sense can be made of the apparent influence of visual imagery in memory.

The Pegword Technique

An intriguing hypothesis can be advanced on the basis of conclusions reached in the preceding sections: Storing events in nonverbal, visual form is possible; furthermore, subjects can use learned equivalences between verbal and visual representational formats to transform information back and forth; finally, we know item for item storage capacity is greater for concrete pictorial material than for words, whether tested by recognition or by recall. The hypothesis these considerations invite is that people should be able to receive stimuli in verbal form, apply transformations between this verbal representation and corresponding visual representation, and thereby achieve improved memory.

In this section this reasoning will be established as correct. Visual imagery can be enlisted in the service of long-term memory with dramatic consequences. In fact, mediation of retention through imagery techniques is among the most powerful experimental effects that can be found in the psychology of memory, in terms of variance accounted for. Until very recently, however, these imagery techniques were either ignored or systematically played down within psychology. The Greeks used visual imagery as the foundation of mnemonic systems, which, in turn were an important part of the art of rhetoric. Later, such medieval scholars as the Mallorcan, Ramon Lull, employed visual forms of representation for complicated theological mnemonic schemes and for generating combinatorial relations among concepts (Paivio, 1971a, pp. 165–168). Entertainers in nightclubs and professional memory technicians today rely completely on such schemes, as do the popular paperback books on self-improvement that can be found in any drugstore bookshelf. The fascinating historical aspects of the applied psychology of memory have been sketched in Bower (1972a), Hunter (1964), and Paivio (1971a, Chapter 6); a richly detailed study of the subject has been published by Yates (1966).

In a chapter outlining a cybernetic approach to memory and learning G. A. Miller, Galanter, and Pribram (1960) described a rhyme to be used in memorizing lists of ten objects. This description of the so-called "pegword" technique seems to have been the first reappearance of imagery devices in modern experimental psychology. The pegword method is dependent on previously learning a simple rhyme in which a fixed list of concrete objects is memorized in order. The objects' names more or less rhyme with the integer names: ONE–BUN, TWO–SHOE, THREE–TREE, FOUR–DOOR, FIVE–HIVE, SIX–STICKS, SEVEN–HEAVEN, EIGHT–GATE, NINE–WINE, TEN–HEN. To use the system, take any ordered list and associate the members, one by one, with the concrete pegs in the rhyme. If a grocery list contains CARROTS, BEER, and BREAD as the first three items, visual images integrating a CARROT and a BUN, BEER and a SHOE, and BREAD and a TREE would be formed. A partly opened hot dog bun with a raw carrot lying inside, for example, rather than a hot dog, would serve as the first image, a large shoe used as a beermug would be servicable as the second, and a tree with slices of bread instead of leaves could be the third. Naturally, longer lists of pegwords permit memorization of longer collections of items. (The reader is encouraged to try learning lists in this manner; many people find the effectiveness of the system a revelation and, following Dale Carnegie, use it to improve the quality of their daily lives.)

Clearly the pegword technique transforms simple free recall or serial learning into a paired-associate scheme, in which the accessibility of the stimulus members is guaranteed by previous training. Bugelski, Kidd, and Segman (1968) provided the first modern experimentally controlled demonstration of the pegword method, using a one-trial, paired-associate task in which the digits 1 through 10 were the stimuli and common nouns were the responses. In their study there were two variables of main interest, instructions and study time. These were combined factorially into a 3 X 3 experimental design, with matched groups of ten subjects in each of the resulting nine conditions. Experimental subjects were taught the pegword jingle and given instructions on how to use it in memorizing lists of ten items. A rhyme control group was given exactly the same training on the jingle but the subjects were not told how to use it. The third group was not given any training in the jingle or in the use of visual imagery. Each of the ten pairs in the list was presented only once, for 2, 4, or 8 sec, for different groups, within each instruction condition. Later, there was a single test of recall in which the digits were presented alone and 4 sec allowed for anticipation of the response words. In addition, each subject was tested in a comparable practice word list before administration of the three instructional sets.

Table 5.4 shows the results. On the practice list, before the pegword method had been introduced, the three instructional groups are seen to be satisfactorily matched in performance, and there is also an appreciable effect of study time on recall. On the second list the advantage of using the pegword technique can be seen quite clearly in scores of the experimental group, but only at the two longer study times. The performance of the experimental group at the slowest presentation rate actually gives only a minimum estimate of how effective the pegword system is because performance (19.4) was limited by a ceiling of 20.0 words; essentially, these subjects remembered the list perfectly.

There was a striking anecdotal coincidence in the Bugelski *et al.* (1968) investigation. One of the subjects in the experimental group turned out to have

TABLE 5.4
Paired-Associate Recall as a
Function of Learning Instruction[a]

Group	Time per pair (sec)		
	2	4	8
Experimental	8.9	15.9	19.4
	(9.5)[b]	(10.7)	(13.0)
Rhyme control	7.8	11.7	12.3
	(9.6)	(11.1)	(13.7)
Control	8.6	12.5	14.6
	(9.5)	(11.1)	(12.6)

[a]After Bugelski, Kidd, and Segmen (1968).
[b]The scores in parentheses are from a practice list learned prior to the instructional manipulation.

been a professional nightclub performer part of whose act was a memory demonstration in which she commonly learned 40-item lists. Far from biasing the results in the direction of obtained differences, however, this subject had been in the condition with only 2 sec study time per item and she actually got a worse score than the mean for her group! So, just as in the work of Posner *et al.* (1969) above, the generation of images takes time. Of course all psychological processes take time, Helmholtz having effectively disproved in 1850 Müller's contention that some mental operations are effectively instantaneous (see Woodworth, 1938, p. 299), but the time required for generation and manipulation of visual images (see also Shepard & Metzler, 1971) is on the order of seconds. Besides the practical limitations imposed by this plodding slowness of imaginal processing, it makes the use of imagery accessible to conscious awareness, unlike many of the processes discussed in Chapter 2, for example, where fabulous processing rates on the order of 100 items per second have been proposed. It was perhaps this possibility of introspection about imagery that caused its neglect during the austere period of philosophical behaviorism and also the same accessibility of imagery to consciousness that makes the pegword-type techniques so easy to master.

Extensions of the pegword method. Subsequent research on the pegword method has clarified some aspects of its operation and left others in doubt. Apparently, whether or not the images used are bizarre makes no difference, contrary to the overwhelming belief of ancient and modern nonscientific experts that bizarre images are better retained than common ones (for example, Lorayne & Lucas, 1974, p. 9). However, it is quite important that the two objects being associated through imagery be pictured imaginally as interacting, rather than, say, standing side by side independently. Both of these generalizations have emerged from a two by two experiment by Wollen, Weber, and Lowry (1972) in which the experimenter suggested specific pictorial content to stimulate images mediating a list of word pairs. That is, if the pair to be learned was BUN–CARROT, the subject would be shown a drawing with a bun and a carrot. In two conditions the drawings represented bizarre versions of the objects pictured and in the other two the objects were presented normally. In orthogonal conditions, the two objects were either somehow joined in an interactive way or pictured independently. These conditions are shown in Figure 5.9. The results indicated that bizarreness made no difference but that interaction did. Experiments by Wood (1967) and others (Paivio, 1971a, p. 348) have generally replicated the negative results with bizarreness and experiments by Bower (1972a) confirm the beneficial effects of constructing interactive images. A study by Collyer, Jonides, and Bevan (1972) actually shows an inhibitory effect of bizarreness, although it can be argued that the control condition in this study was inappropriate. There is probably a good reason why people have so long believed, apparently incorrectly, that images should be bizarre in order to be useful: Imagery systems tend to be used when the two objects to be associated

Noninteracting, nonbizarre

Noninteracting, bizarre

3.50
Correct

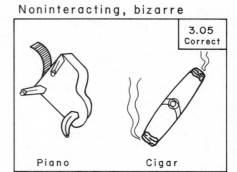

3.05
Correct

Interacting, nonbizarre

Interacting, bizarre

6.60
Correct

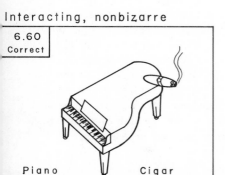

6.67
Correct

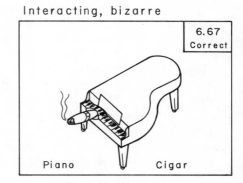

FIGURE 5.9 Illustrations of suggested encodings for the pair PIANO–CIGAR. The encodings vary in bizarreness and in whether the two items are pictured as interacting. The inserts give the recall scores. (After Wollen, Weber, & Lowry, 1972.)

are not otherwise strongly related; for example, no special mnemonic is needed for the pair TABLE–CHAIR. Given that the two items are not otherwise strongly related, on sampling grounds alone any composite image is likely to be bizarre. The number of concrete objects represented by common words in the language is very large and the chances of an arbitrarily selected pair's fitting conveniently into a commonplace visualization is quite small. The reader can try to construct nonbizarre images involving such pairs as SHOE–SAXOPHONE, EARRING–AUDITORIUM, or TEACUP–LOCOMOTIVE. It has probably been mainly on superstitious grounds, therefore, that bizarre imagery has been prescribed.

Interference in the pegword system. It is quite natural to expect repeated reuse of the pegword technique to lead to interference among lists successively attached to the same objects. It does, although there is some doubt concerning whether the amount of such interference is reduced compared to other learning methods (Paivio, 1971a, p. 336). An experiment by Bower and Reitman (1972) seems to have identified the crucial variable. In their study subjects learned five lists of 20 words each in a single experimental session, with testing of each list immediately following its acquisition, testing at the end of the entire session, and testing 1 week later. The question was whether the five lists would show differential interference as a function of the following three previously learned mnemonic systems.

In the single-item condition subjects learned a 20-word version of the ONE–BUN rhyme and were told to form completely new images for each of the five lists, not thinking of earlier images during formation of new ones. In the progressive elaboration condition the same pegword scheme was learned, but subjects were told that as each peg got reused in a new list they should introduce the new image into a compound of previous images associated with that peg. For example, then, by the time the fourth list was acquired, each of the 20 pegwords would participate in an image including the peg itself—say, TREE—plus four list items—say, a tree with a WINDOW in the trunk, through which a PUPPY was jumping, and a ROPE dangling from the upper branches with a pair of SCIS-SORS tied to it, given that WINDOW, PUPPY, ROPE, and SCISSORS were the words occupying the third serial position of the four successive lists. In their third condition, Bower and Reitman introduced the most ancient of the mne-monic strategies, the method of loci, where a fixed layout of geographical positions, such as the houses on a familiar street, are used instead of peg objects; each item in the memory list is imagined successively at each of the locations in the imaginary itinerary. Bower and Reitman suggested to their subjects that their typical route through the Stanford campus on a Wednesday be used as the sequential source of locations in which to imagine objects from the list. In addition, this group was told to use the method of progressive elaboration. In all conditions the items were presented aloud at a 10-sec rate.

The results are given in Figure 5.10, where the three learning methods are compared as a function of the five lists; subjects were asked to give the positions each item had occupied in the list of 20, as well as to recall the items themselves. The results are shown separately for the test after the learning session had just finished and for the test a week later. Immediate recall was around 87% and did not vary with instruction condition or list position.

The main message of the end of session test is that when the single-item strategy was used, each list learned independently, there was indeed interference among lists. This can be supported by the overall inferiority of the single-item condition and especially by the inverse relation between recall and the number of lists, for that group, intervening since acquisition. When progressive elabora-tion was used, in contrast, recall was uniformly better and performance on the first lists did not suffer with interpolation of successive lists. Comparing the end of session tests with performance a week later, and keeping in mind the uniform but not perfect immediate-recall scores in the high 80s, it can further be concluded that the elaboration method reduces the rate at which items are

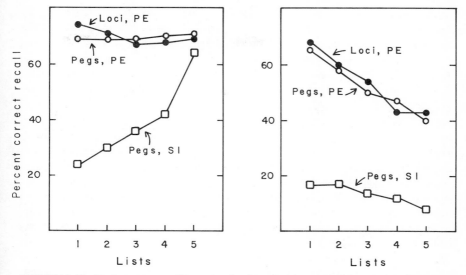

FIGURE 5.10   Performance on five successive lists as a function of mnemonic technique: PE is progressive elaboration, SI is single item. The left panel gives recall at the end of the experimental session and right panel gives recall a week later. (After Bower & Reitman, 1972.)

forgotten. Finally, there was no difference between the rhyming pegword method and the method of loci, although the latter incorporates only sequential, and not absolute, positional information.

Strictly speaking we are not permitted to conclude that it has been the establishment of composite images that has benefited the progressive elaboration groups rather than the possibility that they have rehearsed each previous list during acquisition of each concurrent one, thus providing many more repetitions of the early ones than they otherwise would have received. However, through whichever mechanism, the instructional package does successfully eliminate interference. It should be added that the five lists in this experiment were massed together in the same session. The dangers of interlist confusion may be substantially reduced when more separation in time and space occurs between reuses of the mnemonic techniques, provided this separation does not increase forgetting. The alternative conclusion (to there being reduced interference with separated lists) is at least shocking and at most absurd—that a devoted user of the technique would cumulate lists on the same peg through a lifetime, compounding grocery lists, lecture notes, and rosters of friends' names into gigantic compound tableaux with scores on scores of elements. There is an obvious limit to progressive elaboration.

Stage analysis.   The elaboration strategy used in conjunction with imagery clearly had a beneficial effect on retention, as well as on acquisition in the Bower and Reitman experiment. The third list was retained at 89% immediately after acquisition of all three instructional groups. Later, performance for the single-item pegword subjects declined to about 35% and 15% at end of session recall tests and week-later recall tests, respectively. For the progressive elaboration pegword subjects, performance decrements over the same period were only to levels of 70% and 50% at the end of session and week-later tests. Here, however, the use of imagery has been confounded with the elaboration method and we do not know whether the use of visual mnemonics, per se, has effects beyond ease of acquisition and ease of retrieval.

When conditions of acquisition and retrieval are held constant, with time in storage alone varying, so as to allow inferences about retention, the evidence is mixed. Groninger (1971) showed a slower rate of forgetting between 1 and 5 weeks for subjects who had learned using the method of loci; however, in a study by Olten (1969) there was no residual effect on the retention phase caused by verbal sentence-mediation mnemonics when degree of acquisition was controlled. A study by Lowry (1974) showed equal forgetting losses for materials learned by (1) visual imagery, (2) sentence mediation, and (3) rote repetition. There is no consistent evidence, therefore, that imagery or other mnemonic techniques have any effect on forgetting as such.

PAIVIO'S DUAL-TRACE THEORY

Why is visual imagery important to the study of memory? One possibility is that it simply shows that there are multiple coding options and that some, particularly visual coding, are better than others. By this view, there are excellent evidential arguments for imagery and for the assistance it provides in memorizing, but the real theoretical foundations of learning and memory must still be sought in verbal processes. Paivio has offered the most systematic rejoinder to this attitude, which states that imagery is an isolated curiosity. Paivio's (1971a) dual-trace hypothesis is a comprehensive statement about the relation of verbal and nonverbal factors in cognition. His position is that imagery is complementary to verbal representation in memory and thought, and that the balance between these modes is a function of concreteness–abstractness of the materials dealt with and of the type of task in question. A long and careful research program conducted by Paivio and his associates has resulted in evidence from several different experimental situations converging on this dual-coding hypothesis; it is summarized in detail by Paivio (1971a) in his book and integrated into a number of wider problem areas, such as language. We cannot begin to build here the elegant inferential structure Paivio has but only to give the flavor and some of the substance of his efforts.

Paired-associate learning. Paivio's view of such techniques as the rhyming pegword method is that the jingle provides reliable concrete images on which to base effective retrieval plans, or effective access to the associated information. It will be recalled from the discussion of McGuire's analysis of paired-associate learning in Chapter 1 that stimulus and response terms do not have symmetrical roles in associative learning: The stimulus term must, above all, be distinguishable from other potential stimuli, and, once so distinguished, it must be recognized in order to lead toward the associated response. That response, however, must be an integrated unit, capable of reproduction, but it need not be especially assured of recognition on its own. In short, the stimulus term has a special role in providing access to the association in retrieval. Paivio's view is that the pegword system works so well because the jingle provides an utterly foolproof set of distinct and recognizable access routes to the new associations that may have been formed in its use.

When we turn to ordinary paired-associate learning, where the subject must accept the stimulus terms given him by the experimenter rather than rely on his own permanent set of pegword stimuli, the same principles apply. Stimulus terms that lead to a stable, discriminable, recognizable representation should be better than stimuli that do not. Because the response term carries no such responsibility for gaining access to the association, these qualities are less important for it. It follows that stimulus-term concreteness should be positively correlated with paired-associate learning, as found by Wimer and Lambert (1959) in a study comparing concrete objects with words representing those objects as stimuli for nonsense-syllable responses. It follows also that when pairs involve one noun and one adjective (Lambert & Paivio, 1956) the noun–adjective order should be easier to learn than the adjective–noun order, which is the case. This is on the reasonable assumption that such nouns as KETTLEDRUM lead more reliably to a stable, discriminable, and recognizable representation than such adjectives as GREEN, even though the compound of these two terms is quite readily integrated into a single association. Starting from GREEN there is a much more diverse fanning out of possible representations than from KETTLEDRUM and therefore access to the correct one is less likely. Concrete items are therefore well suited to the access function of stimulus terms in paired-associate learning.

From the proposition that concrete stimulus terms provide more reliable access routes to associative compounds than abstract stimulus terms (Lambert & Paivio, 1956) it is a reasonable step to the additional suggestion that visual imagery should be the important attribute underlying concreteness. Because imagery potential and concreteness of words are so highly correlated we shall not be careful to distinguish the terms here.

In experiments with nouns as both stimuli and responses in paired-associate learning, Paivio relied initially on ratings of concreteness–abstractness gathered on the spot. Published norms of Paivio, Yuille, and Madigan (1968) now make it possible for workers to obtain materials at specified levels of concreteness, as well as of other attributes, such as meaningfulness. The basic finding in studies with orthogonal variation in stimulus and response concreteness (producing high–high, high–low, low–high, and low–low conditions) has been (Paivio, 1965) that pairs where both terms are highly concrete (HOUSE–SHOE) are learned better than high–low pairs (HOUSE–TRUTH), which, in turn, are better than low–high pairs (TRUTH–HOUSE), with low–low pairs (TRUTH–SKILL) worst of all. The significant difference between the high–low and low–high pairs, favoring the former, permits the conclusion that stimulus concreteness is more important than response concreteness, as predicted by the hypothesis that a special advantage in *eliciting* associations should occur with concrete, easily visualizable terms.

Note that the observation of greater stimulus than response effects of concreteness is exactly the opposite to effects of meaningfulness in paired-associate learning, where, with great consistency, the response effects are greater than the stimulus effects (Sheffield, 1946). In light of the different responsibilities for stimulus and response members of paired-associates, however, this ought not to be surprising: Whereas meaningfulness (or its close correlate, familiarity) must surely correlate with ease of integration and emission as a response there is no reason why concreteness should. For example, TRUTH should be a better integrated response than VERACITY, but there is no reason why BUNGALOW should be a more effective elicitor than HOUSE.

An experiment reported by Bower (1972a) suggests that, as Paivio maintains, the effects of stimulus concreteness occur at the retrieval stage in paired-associate learning as well as in acquisition. A concrete–abstract pair and an abstract–concrete pair ought to be equally easy for the purposes of constructing some mediating, compound image initially but because the concrete term should more easily elicit its corresponding visualization in recall the compound image should be more accessible when the term presented in testing is the concrete one. In Bower's experiment subjects received one trial on a paired-associate list including high–low, low–high, and high–high pairs with respect to imagery concreteness. After a single forward test, subjects were tested a second time in either the forward or the backward direction. For a pair with a left-hand member high in concreteness and a right-hand member low in concreteness, a retrieval hypothesis would predict better forward than backward recall, whereas the opposite should be true of a low–high pair. The high–high pairs should give a way of estimating whether there were forward–backward differences in this situation independent of imagery effects.

The results are given in Table 5.5. The pattern shown there indicates both acquisition and retrieval effects. The evidence for a concreteness effect in acquisition is that, whatever the retrieval direction, performance was lower when a pair involved some abstract, low-imagery item than when it did not; for example, when a forward test was made with a high-imagery term the high–high pairs were somewhat better recalled than the high–low pairs. The evidence for retrieval factors is found in the interaction of recall direction and type of pair in the high–low and low–high conditions. For pairs with mixed imagery value it

TABLE 5.5
Paired-Associate Recall as a Function of
Stimulus and Response Imagery and Direction
of Testing[a]

	Recall direction	
Type of pair (imagery)	Forward (S-?) (%)	Backward (R-?) (%)
High–low	81	70
Low–high	56	71
High–high	85	85

[a]After Bower (1972a).

was better to be given the high-imagery term in testing whatever the condition of acquisition. (It must be remembered in this study that because all pairs have been once tested in the forward direction there has been differential strengthening for the high–low and high–high pairs.)

Converging evidence from other tasks. Paivio's dual-representation theory is quite like Posner's general view. Stimulus attributes may be grouped into classes in memory according to the item's name or what it looks like. The balance between these representational systems differs, Paivio says, according to whether a concept is abstract or concrete. A concrete item, such as HOUSE, whether it is presented in verbal or in pictorial form, leads both to a visual image and to a verbal code. An abstract item, such as TRUTH, leads easily to verbal coding but only with difficulty to an imaginal code. The meaning of a term, such as HOUSE, then derives from its dual representations in that it easily elicits both related images and related words, whereas the meaning of an abstract term such as TRUTH, is primarily interverbal, according to Paivio. Of course, an abstract word can always be made concrete by additional mediation, such as TRUTH–POLITICS–WATERGATE–JAIL but such extra operations ought to take time.

Appropriately, because some imaginal processes should be time consuming, one arm of Paivio's research program has been experimentation on response latency. This research depends on subjective reports, as does much of the imagery work; however, as we shall see the results are subtly tied to stimulus properties and therefore unlikely to result from disingenuous subjects. In one study subjects were asked to learn pairs of nouns under instructions either to mediate learning by visual images or by verbal strings. For such a pair as HOUSE–ROPE a visual mediator would be an image of a house with an enormous coiled rope thrown across its roof, whereas a verbal mediator would be a phrase, such as "The old HOUSE had doors hinged with ROPE." The measure of performance in this study (Yuille & Paivio, 1967) was how long it took subjects to report that they had discovered such a mediator. The noun pairs were either concrete–concrete, concrete–abstract, abstract–concrete, or abstract–abstract. The results, as given in Figure 5.11, are consistent with the dual-trace hypothesis. Subjects trying to discover an interverbal link between the paired words did so with approximately the same latency whether the stimulus term was abstract or concrete. When an image was the required mediator, in contrast, it took much longer if the stimulus item was abstract than if it was concrete. The interaction supports the independence of these two processes.

Paivio, Smythe, and Yuille (1968) have reported another quite different method for tying subjective reports into a systematic inferential pattern based on stimulus attributes. They had subjects learn lists in which there was separate variation of stimulus and response imagery, meaningfulness, or both. Ordinarily, imagery and meaningfulness are strongly correlated. Therefore the authors were obliged to select their materials carefully in order to keep these variables orthogonal in this study.

The subjects' reports of using three learning strategies were examined as a function of list type. The three possibilities were visual imagery, verbal mediation, and rote repetition. There was a high dependence of reported visual imagery on concreteness of items, particularly on stimulus concreteness, but verbal mediation was unrelated to concreteness and imagery reports were unrelated to meaningfulness. Again, an interaction with stimulus type supports independent parallel-storage systems. Also supported by this and the previous pattern of results is the idea that all types of stimuli are readily represented verbally, whatever their concreteness, but that the main variation is in the presence or absence or, more properly stated, the accessibility of imaginal representations.

The dual-trace hypothesis includes statements on the differences between the verbal and visual forms of meaning, which are not conceived as being interchangeable in function. Just as information in visual space is present simultaneously—the eye registering a vast amount of detail in a single glimpse—and

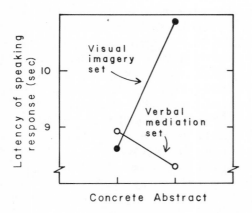

FIGURE 5.11 Latency of discovering a mediator for word pairs as a function of abstractness of the words in the pair and instructional set. (After Yuille & Paivio, 1967.)

information in the verbal-speech system successively—language being spread out in time rather than space—Paivio has hypothesized that the verbal and imaginal modes are specialized for serial and parallel information processing, respectively. (In his book Paivio has aligned this distinction with current research controversies in perception and language as well as memory.) One important result of recognizing that visual and verbal memory coding are parts of systems specialized for different functions is that imagery should not be expected to be facilitating in every memory situation.

To this point we have been looking largely at the implications of the ancient pegword system, at experiments either employing that system or at paired-associate learning experiments where the task is functionally similar. If visual imagery is specialized for spatial, parallel representation, then such tasks should show large effects of imagery because they all depend on integrating two items initially separated in time and space, the stimulus and response, such that they are fused into a single entity, one part of which can be elicited by the other. Other tasks, where some temporal distinction is necessary, such as serial ordering, may not show benefits of imagery. This general line of reasoning was tested in a set of conditions by Paivio and Csapo (1969). Their study crossed stimulus and task variables so as to produce interactions predicted by what we may call the "specialized dual-trace hypothesis." The stimulus variable was covered by using three types of stimuli: (1) pictures of objects, (2) concrete nouns, or (3) abstract nouns. The underlying reasoning was that accessibility of visual imagery should be greatest for pictures, intermediate for concrete nouns, and least for abstract nouns. Verbal representation, in contrast, should be equal for abstract and concrete nouns and possibly reduced for pictures, because there would be cases where there was some ambiguity in naming pictures. These three materials were tested in four memory tasks, each conducted under two rates of presentation. The four tasks included two where seriality was important—immediate memory and serial learning—and two where seriality mattered less—recognition memory and free-recall learning. The reasoning here was that imagery should be more beneficial when seriality does not matter than when it does. Finally, fast (5.3 per second) and slow (2 per second) rates for each task were included to test the proposition that beneficial effects of imagery should occur only when there is sufficient time for the arousal of images. (Recall the findings of Bugelski et al., 1968, on this point.)

There is not space to do even summary justice to the patterns of findings obtained by Paivio and Csapo; however, generally the results conform to predictions that can be generated on the basis of the above logic. Figure 5.12 shows the main trends. Note, for example, that pictures facilitated greatly when the rate of presentation was slow, but only for the "parallel" tasks, where memory for order was not important. Also, memory for abstract nouns was least affected by the rate of presentation, consistent with the dependence of these items solely on verbal coding.

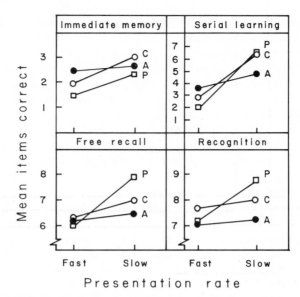

FIGURE 5.12 Performance on four memory tasks as a function of presentation rate and type of stimulus materials: C is concrete words, A is abstract words, P is pictures. (After Paivio & Csapo, 1969.)

N. Frost (1972) has shown that subjects' expectations for the method in which they are to be tested can affect the occurrence of visual coding (see also Tversky, 1973). She presented pictures that could be organized according to orthogonal semantic and visual categories. In free recall, as we shall see in a later chapter, people reveal organizational properties of lists that are salient to them by *clustering,* that is, by recalling items from the same category in adjacent positions. Frost's stimuli permitted observation of whether subjects utilized organization based on visual form, on semantic category, or both. When subjects had been led to expect a test of recognition for the pictures presented as stimuli, but when they were actually tested by free recall, there was evidence for both types of organization; if one item had just been recalled, it was statistically likely that the next item called would be from the same visual or semantic category. If two items shared both visual and semantic similarity—as pictures of a belt and shoestring would, for example—it was especially likely that they would be recalled together. Frost concluded that items were cross-classified when they were encoded.

That such double encoding was not automatic, however, was shown in a second condition where subjects were treated identically except that they had been led to expect a recall test rather than a recognition test. Here, in recall, there was no tendency to cluster according to visual shape and items sharing both visual and semantic features were no more likely to be recalled together than items sharing only semantic features. This all suggests that subjects have control over the balance of verbal and imaginal coding used in memory tasks: Depending on expectations for the mode of testing, they either encode information about visual shape (when expecting recognition tests) or not (when expecting recall tests). The pattern is consistent with Paivio's hypothesis that recognition benefits more than recall from pictoral encoding and it shows that subjects are, in some sense, aware of this fact.

THE QUALITATIVE NATURE OF IMAGES

A persistent difficulty with the concept of imagery has been the problem of defining what images "really are." With memory images, as with memory in general, there is an almost irresistible tendency to rely on metaphors. As Paivio (in press) has observed the exact metaphor chosen has varied through history but it has always depended on whatever technology has been currently popular for recording visual experience. We can therefore trace an evolution from the wax tablets of the Greeks, through photography, motionpicture photography, and, recently, to holography (Pribram, Nuwer, & Baron, 1974). Adherents to the nonvisual metaphor of the digital computer as a model of the mind and of memory have been vigorous critics of the evidence and reasoning reviewed in this chapter (Anderson & Bower, 1973; Pylyshyn, 1973).

Much of Pylyshyn's (1973) critique depends on the point that imagery, if it exists, must be photographic. He argues (Pylyshyn, 1973, pp. 8 and 9), for example, that if a retrieved image is to be useful in retention, there must be an internal eye to perceive and process the material contained on the image, just as we need to perceive freshly a photographic recording of a scene. As it turns out, there is evidence that may be offered on this point.

Mental snapshots? There has actually been little research on the visual nature of the images used in these experiments. An exception is a study by Neisser and Kerr (1973). They contrast two views of how real objects are perceived in their proper spatial arrangement. The Helmholtz position, endorsed by most perceptual psychologists, is that the brain receives from the retina a two-dimensional mosaic and that inferences are made about spatial relations on the basis of the same cues we use in perceiving relative location in a photograph, a process called unconscious inference. The contrasting view, advanced by J. J. Gibson, is that we perceive the layout of objects in the world somehow directly. According to this view there is information reaching the visual system that conveys the relative locations of objects without an additional step of inferring how these objects must be arranged for the current retinal mosaic to obtain. By the Gibson position we can perceive that one object is hidden by another, whereas by the Helmholtz position we cannot. Gibson's view is that as objects disappear from view and emerge from behind one another we continue to perceive their layout in space directly; Helmholtz would maintain that a hidden object is known only through memory. As Neisser and Kerr point out, we can simply ask people whether they are truly perceiving a hidden object, such as a coin in a pocket, but their answer depends too much on their own preconceptions and semantic refinements to help us.

Neisser and Kerr's (1973) insight was to test the proposition by comparing the *mnemonic effectiveness* of images based on hidden objects versus images based on objects not hidden. We know that when subjects are asked to learn the pair PIANO–CIGAR performance is likely to be improved if they think of, or image, a piano with a cigar sitting at the edge of the music rack. Now the question is whether the same benefit to memory occurs when subjects think of a piano with a cigar *hidden from view* down below the strings. If imagery is a mental snapshot then there should be facilitation only when both objects are "mentally visible" and not when one of them is concealed. If imagery corresponds to a Gibsonian percept, a knowledge of spatial layout, however, then the concealed element should be an effective mnemonic element.

The task used by Neisser and Kerr consisted in reading sentences with two major concrete objects represented; we may think of these objects as the two terms of a paired-associate item. Subjects were not told they would later have to remember the pairs but were instructed only to rate the vividness of each sentence at the time of its presentation. The three conditions differed in the type of images implied by the sentences. In the pictorial condition, the two objects were portrayed in an interacting scene; in the separate condition, the same objects were not spatially close; in the concealed condition, one of the objects was somehow hidden by the other. In Table 5.6 are examples of each of the three types of sentence subjects received.

After reading and rating these materials for the vividness of the imagery they evoked, subjects were given a surprise memory test in which they were required to respond, in terms of our examples, with the response STATUE OF LIBERTY given the stimulus HARP. Table 5.6 shows that recall in the concealed images condition is just as good as in the pictorial condition. In other words, as long as the image suggested to the subject involved the objects to be associated in close proximity, it made no difference whether the imagined scene would, in the real visual world, have allowed both items to be seen or whether one of the two would have been hidden. Imagining a harp inside the statue's torch is just as good as imagining it balanced on top of the torch, insofar as setting up an enduring statue–torch association. However in the separate condition, with images in which the objects to be associated were deliberately placed in remote spatial positions, performance was impaired. This conforms exactly to the finding by Wollen *et al.* (1972), who also noted that the objects pictured in a visual image must be interacting somehow for a mnemonic advantage to occur. Neisser and Kerr performed a second experiment with methodological refine-

TABLE 5.6
Mean Recall and Vividness Ratings as a Function of Imagery Conditions[a]

Condition	Example sentence	Experiment I		Experiment II	
		Recall	Vividness	Recall	Vividness
Concealed	A harp is hidden inside the torch held by the Statue of Liberty.	4.83[b]	3.38[c]	4.12[b]	3.19[c]
Pictorial	A harp is sitting on top of the torch held by the Statue of Liberty.	5.21	2.82	4.12	2.63
Separate	Looking from one window you see the Statue of Liberty; from a window on another wall you see a harp.	3.96	3.17	2.92	3.13

← most vivid

[a]After Neisser and Kerr (1973).
[b]Maximum possible recall = 6.
[c]Most vivid = 1; least vivid = 7.

ments and obtained just the same pattern of results. This second study is also shown in Table 5.6.

It is of very special interest that the pictorial condition led to significantly more vivid images than either of the other two conditions and that these latter did not differ from one another. Across conditions, that is to say, there was a lack of correlation between vividness of images and their helpfulness in facilitating memory. This independence of vividness and mnemonic effectiveness is a direct violation of the snapshot metaphor: The pictorial and separate conditions are quite an adequate manipulation for producing mental pictures of different vividness, yet they do not produce different amounts of memory facilitation; therefore, the memory facilitation must not be a product of the photographic clarity of images.

Neisser and Kerr showed, in further support of this conclusion, that for any given subject, considered separately, his more vividly rated sentences were not the ones he recalled best. Across subjects, moreover, those who generally reported getting vivid images did not perform better in memory than those subjects who reported less vivid images. A final crucial point: Vividness was significantly correlated with the latency of forming images (a negative correlation). Therefore, we can rule out the possibility that vividness ratings are simply unreliable and incapable of correlating with any other variable.

In summary, it seems from these data that images elicited by verbal materials are not like mental snapshots. Objects that would be invisible on a snapshot nonetheless received the full memorial advantage of imagery instructions. Furthermore, there is no relationship between vividness of imagery and its memorial effectiveness. In terms of the recurrent issue we have been facing in this section and previously, the Neisser–Kerr experiment suggests a somewhat less peripheral and more central concept of visual imagery in memory than some of the initial reports implied. If Gibson is correct about perception in general, however, then these data support the exact parallel between concurrent visual experience and visual experience in memory.

The Neisser and Kerr finding places objections to the concept of imagery on the part of artificial-intelligence workers (Anderson & Bower, 1973, pp. 449–461; Pylyshyn, 1973) in rather a different light. These critics, especially Pylyshyn, object that the photographic metaphor is a fatal weakness of the concept of imagery; yet here we find that on both theoretical (Paivio, in press) and experimental grounds (Neisser & Kerr, 1973) the photographic metaphor may be rejected anyway, and has been, by exactly those who are most committed to a separate role of imagery in memory. The real issue of contention, once we have dismissed the snapshot metaphor along with the wax-tablet metaphor, is whether or not information maps into two fundamentally different representation systems, one propositional–verbal and one somehow imaginal. As Anderson and Bower concede, the data on modality-specific interference give especially strong support to the dual-trace notion. Other lines of evidence are equally persuasive (Kosslyn, 1975; Paivio, in press) but have somewhat less to do with the topics of learning and memory than the material covered here.

Finally, a startling piece of evidence against the mental snapshot metaphor comes from a study by Jonides, Kahn, and Rozin (1975). These authors compared performance of normal college students with that of totally (and congenitally) blind college students in a Paivio-type experimental design involving manipulation of word concreteness and of imagery instructions (see also Paivio, 1971a, pp. 518–520). The results showed no effect of blindness— the facilitation from concrete words and the facilitation from instructions to form mental images were just as great for blind subjects as for normals. Because the blind subjects tested in this study have never had any visual experience, whereas they show essentially normal patterns of facilitation in memory, the lesson of Neisser and Kerr is confirmed and extended by the Jonides et al. (1975) result. These authors had no special insights as to what the coding processes involved in the memory facilitation were for their blind subjects but, as they mentioned, the possibility would be strengthened that something similar to an abstract *spatial* mode of cognition was being tapped. Neisser (1972) has been the foremost spokesman for this view, that the distinction being groped for among workers in imagery is between the verbal and spatial modes rather than between the verbal and visual. Blind subjects would certainly need some modality for dealing with objects in space and for imagining such objects in the absence of direct sensory experience. The suggestion is that it is this spatial modality that underlies the mnemonic effect.

SUMMARY

Eidetic imagery is an important expression of memory organized along visual, nonverbal dimensions. Beyond its existence, its rarity, and its apparent association with early or abnormal cognitive development, there is little of theoretical substance that can be said of it, however, and therefore the place of eidetic imagery in the theory of memory depends on further development. An early literature on the reproduction of visual forms was inconclusive with regard to the issue of nonverbal memory storage, despite claims made about the literature by Gestalt theorists.

Among modern demonstrations of normal visual imagery in memory, studies of same—different judgments on pairs of stimuli separated in time are important (Posner & Keele, 1967; Tversky, 1969). These reaction-time experiments have revealed that visual imagery is under the control of subjects in that they can voluntarily perform transformations on imaginal representations and generate them from verbal representations.

In research on modality-specific interference it is shown that two aspects of memory, one presumably imaginal and the other verbal, are differentially affected by some distracting tasks, which themselves are devised to involve specialized visual or verbal cognitive functions. Such interactions between memories and interfering events (a pattern of results sometimes termed *double dissociation*) is extremely difficult to accommodate with a unitary view of the memory-representation system.

In long-term memory tasks, both recognition and recall are better for pictures than for words denoting the pictured objects. Furthermore, in associative learning, words that are readily evocative of pictorial representations (concrete rather than abstract words) are at an advantage. In the pegword mnemonic system, this phenomenon is exploited to particularly dramatic effect through a consistently applied set of highly visualizable and accessible stimulus terms that may be used to form associations with new material.

On the basis of most of this evidence, and on other demonstrations as well, Paivio has articulated the dual-trace hypothesis, suggesting two fundamentally distinct modes of cognition, one spatial—visual and the other temporal—verbal.

6

Primary Memory

If one accepts, in any sense whatever, the concept of conscious awareness, then it is a useful problem to consider what it is that occupies consciousness. Whether the contents of consciousness are visual images, words, or something far more abstract than either, one thing is sure: Consciousness holds some span of information that is broader, in time, than the instantaneous present. People are simply not aware of the smallest, irreducible, units of changing energy in the world. Instead, consciousness contains some span of time that we define as "the present" but that includes information from the very recent past.

It is bound to be true, on logical grounds, that any span of consciousness that is not instantaneous implies a form of memory, for, in that case, something that has happened in the chronological past is a part of the psychological present. It is in this sense that James used the term *primary memory:*

> But an object of primary memory is not thus brought back; it never was lost; its date was never cut off in consciousness from that of the immediately present moment. In fact, it comes to us as belonging to the rearward portion of the present space of time, and not to the genuine past. [James, 1950, pp. 646–647, originally published, 1890].

Such a definition of primary memory as part of the psychological present makes our commitment to stage analysis difficult: As James points out in the passage above, there is no question of *retrieving* primary memory information for it is already in a state of retrieval. A compelling intuitive feel for this concept comes from listening to a lengthening series of random digits; at any moment it seems as though there are several elements in a state of effortless access, but other, earlier items can be had only at the expense of effort.

These statements hardly do service to our usual standards of rigor and evidential test. However, they are intended to convey the flavor of the memory phenomenon under study in this chapter and the rest of the chapter is an evaluation of how 15 years of intense research have improved on James' approach. First, however, we should dispose of some terminological points. The terms *short-term memory* and *long-term memory* denote task situations in which humans are tested for their memory of previous events. In short-term memory tasks it is usual for subjects to receive relatively small amounts of information to learn, with testing occurring within a half-minute or so. In long-term memory tasks, considerably more information is usually given, with testing occurring after minutes, hours, days, or longer.

PROCESS DUALISM IN MEMORY

We shall see that a good deal of theory surrounds the question of whether there are distinct memory systems, in humans, roughly corresponding to short- and long-term memory tasks. Those who maintain that there are two such distinct memory systems recognize, however, that most actual testing situations involve some mixture of them, so different terms have been advanced to cover the possible dual nature of memory. There are two popular terminological distinctions: *Short-term storage* versus *long-term storage* and *primary memory* versus *secondary memory*. It would be proper to say, therefore: "Short-term memory, as measured by the distractor technique, entails greater use of long-term storage (or secondary memory) than short-term storage (or primary memory.)" However, it would be inappropriate to speak of a short-term memory contribution to short-term storage. Out of deference to James, and to avoid the confusing common locution, "short-term," we shall hereafter refer to the process distinction in terms of primary and secondary memory.

Historical Background on Process Dualism

When the first reports of short-term memory experiments, at least in modern times, reached the journals in the late 1950s (Brown, 1958; Peterson & Peterson, 1959) it was generally accepted that the laws covering short-term memory were different from those established for the familiar long-term memory tasks. This acceptance of process dualism was understandable in view of the vast differences that separated experimental procedures in the two cases: In the short-term memory experiments only a few letters were presented and these were forgotten within a few seconds if the subjects were distracted from rehearsal by some interpolated activity, such as mental arithmetic. Brown (1958) and Broadbent (1958) proposed that such once-presented information decayed autonomously with time unless supported by an active rehearsal process, the function of which was to postpone decay and, gradually, to support a buildup of permanent storage. The Petersons' view of their own experiment was similar; they saw little possibility of interference from either earlier or later experiences as a cause of forgetting with their method. Yet they found that a single three-letter syllable deteriorated to about 10% correct recall after only 18 sec of mental arithmetic. [Recall that we discussed the Brown–Peterson method in connection with Lindley's (1963) experiment in Chapter 1.]

In contrast to these findings stood the massive, then very active, tradition of verbal learning—acquisition, unlearning, transfer, and competition among long serial and paired-associate lists, with retention measured after hours, and even days. Although the Petersons were careful to suggest that their research on individual items might have applications to the understanding of what happened to a *particular pair* during list acquisition, most workers were content to see the paradigms as measuring different things. Broadbent's (1958) influential book, which was the first major statement within the field of cognitive psychology as it is now understood, included a thoughtful treatment of Brown's theory and experiments.

Hebb (1961) saw the new short-term memory experiments as confirming principles based on his own dual-trace theory of memory, in which a transient reverberatory process, perseveration, might support short-term retention, whereas long-term memory would depend on structural changes in the brain, consolidation. Hebb proposed and conducted a test of this view, based on the idea that immediate retention of a digit list similar to a telephone number would be dependent solely on the short-term reverberatory process. If this were so, memories used to repeat back a digit series immediately would not survive the next trial, on which a new series of digits occurred. Hebb found, however, that when a particular nine-digit stimulus was repeated on every third trial during a series of tests, there was a gradual improvement in performance on it. He was forced to conclude that, maladaptive as it seems, a long-term trace is laid down for even such transient memory tasks as immediate recall.

It was a paper by Melton (1963a) that made the case for a functional continuity between short- and long-term memory situations. Melton's paper assembled evidence from a number of sources showing that the same experimental variables that play a decisive role in long-term memory also operate, and in the same fashion, in short-term memory. He showed that the repetition effect in Hebb's experiment was a lawful function of the number of intervening nonrepeated memory-span stimuli between repetitions of the critical item, just as one would expect from a continuous incremental theory of associative strength. He showed that in the Brown–Peterson situation, the rate of short-term forgetting was systematically greater the longer the list of consonants (varied from one to five) being retained, just as list length had been one of the standard determinants of difficulty in traditional verbal learning. Data from Hellyer (1962) were displayed to make the point that as the number of repetitions of nonsense trigrams was increased from one to eight there was a progressively smaller decrement in short-term memory caused by an interpolated task. At that time, there was no substantial evidence on the factor of similarity in short-term memory, one way or another. Melton's influential conclusion in 1963 was that because the same laws applied to the two situations, we would be best advised to assume they represent different points on a task continuum. However, in Melton's view, the short-term memory techniques presented opportunities for studying these common theoretical principles with greater precision than with the more cumbersome list-learning procedures.

The Waugh and Norman theory. Waugh and Norman (1965) accepted the evidence Melton had offered but challenged his conclusion that we needed but a single memory system. Their theory proposed a distinction between primary memory and secondary memory together with a model for how these two systems interact. Perceived information is first represented in a limited-capacity primary-memory system. From primary memory, some information is lost but other information is rehearsed. Rehearsal not only prevents the displacement by new information, but also causes transfer to the secondary memory system, which has an unlimited capacity. The model is shown in the left-hand portion of Figure 6.1. The special feature of this model is that in any particular experimental situation, recall can be based on information about a particular item either from primary memory or from secondary memory, or from both. This follows from the assumptions of the theory that whenever rehearsal occurs there is transfer to secondary memory as well as maintenance in primary memory. However, the primary memory system is limited in the number of items it can hold, so a certain point is eventually reached where new input displaces the old input and the subject is left dependent on secondary memory alone.

One effort reported in the Waugh–Norman paper is the direct measurement of primary memory. To do this, they relied on a situation in which rehearsal was discouraged by instruction, in hopes the transfer would thus be blocked, leaving complete reliance on primary memory. They presented lists of 16 digits to

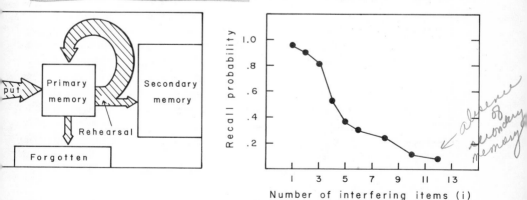

FIGURE 6.1   The Waugh and Norman model (left) and the result of their probe experiment (right). The results from the 4-per-second and 1-per-second presentation rates are combined. (After Waugh & Norman, 1965.)

subjects at either a fast (four per second) or slow (one per second) rate. After the series was over a single item from the series, called a *probe,* was presented again with the task being to emit whatever digit had followed the probe digit in the series. The results obtained by Waugh and Norman are shown in Figure 6.1 to the right of the flow diagram There was only a small inconsistent effect of presentation rate, which encouraged them in the belief that the important commodity was indeed the number of interfering items placed between input and output of an individual item, rather than the passage of time. Also, performance seemed to approach a zero asymptote at long intervals between input and the probe test, which reinforced their belief that nonrehearsal instructions had eliminated secondary memory from the situation.

Was this allegedly pure primary memory curve shown in Figure 6.1 the same component found in other tasks in which primary and secondary memory both would make contributions? Waugh and Norman argued that it was; however, to verify this claim it was necessary to extract the secondary-memory contribution from mixed situations. Just as the zero asymptote, in their probe experiment, was taken to indicate the absence of secondary memory, Waugh and Norman assumed that a nonzero asymptote, in the Brown–Peterson situation for example, would indicate the presence of, and amount of, secondary memory accumulated through rehearsal during the item's residence in primary memory. Above, for example, we noted that Peterson and Peterson (1959) found performance on three-letter stimuli to level off at about 10% correct after 18 sec of mental arithmetic. Because secondary memory is permanent, by definition in the model, there is no reason to assume that the apparent asymptotic value of performance ever declines, whatever the retention interval. So all one needs do is to estimate the value of the asymptote from a Brown–Peterson experiment in order to find what the probability of recall based on secondary memory is.

There is an intimate relation between the concept of primary memory and the free-recall technique. When subjects are presented with a list of words and asked to recall them immediately after presentation, without regard for their order in the sequence, performance is strongly related to serial position. The most conspicuous feature of the free-recall serial-position effect is a large *recency* effect (see Figure 6.3, for example)—performance is often almost perfect on the very last serial position and it declines sharply over the half-dozen or so items prior to the end of the list. With long lists there is then a flat middle range of serial positions, giving way to a primacy effect (advantage of early serial positions) that is of smaller magnitude than the recency effect. It is the recency effect that has been attributed to primary memory; when the list ends, the argument goes, the last few items are still retained in a fragile state of conscious accessibility and they may be emitted, therefore, as long as nothing else comes along to displace them.

Now, how may we derive numerical estimates of primary and secondary memory from the free-recall paradigm? The assumptions are quite similar to those made in the componential analysis of the Brown–Peterson task. As we said, with long lists there is a flat region of the serial-position function covering items from the central portion of the list. It is assumed that this performance level reflects a constant contribution of secondary memory to performance at all serial positions. By analogy with the Brown–Peterson logic, this flat segment of the serial-position function is called the "asymptote."

The Waugh–Norman model assumes that the two sources of information, primary and secondary memory, combine independently to determine ultimate performance. This independence is represented by the formula

$$p(R_i) = p(PM_i) + p(SM) - p(PM_i)p(SM)$$

where $p(R_i)$ denotes the probability of recalling an item correctly after i intervening events, $p(PM_i)$ denotes the probability of recalling an item from primary memory after i events, and $p(SM)$ denotes the probability of recalling an item from secondary memory, assumed not to vary with i. The terms of the formula can be rearranged to solve for $p(PM_i)$,

$$p(PM_i) = \frac{P(R_i) - p(SM)}{1 - p(SM)} .$$

Application of this logic, with a known asymptote, to a Brown–Peterson experiment and to free recall is illustrated in Figure 6.2.

With this method, Waugh and Norman extracted numerical estimates of primary memory from a number of experiments in short-term memory and free recall. These derived primary-memory scores were then compared with the "pure" primary-memory functions obtained from their own probe experiment, with good general agreement. In view of this good agreement, they concluded that primary memory is a stable mode of storage affected only by the number of intervening items and that dependence of short-term memory tasks on the variables discussed by Melton reflects only a varying contribution from secondary memory.

Modern Arguments for Process Dualism in Memory

The Waugh and Norman paper was very important because it provided a specific model for interaction between primary and secondary memory, because it specified the nature of primary memory more completely than previous workers had—Waugh and Norman suggested the term *echo box* on the basis of their subjects' introspections—and finally, because it showed that a dualistic theory would fit the data on repetition, list length, proactive inhibition, and so on just as well as Melton's monistic theory. However, showing that either a monistic or a dualistic theory can fit various data is not the same as demonstrating the necessity for a dualistic theory. Subsequent research has more adequately made the case for a two-process theory on the basis of the following type of argument:

(a)

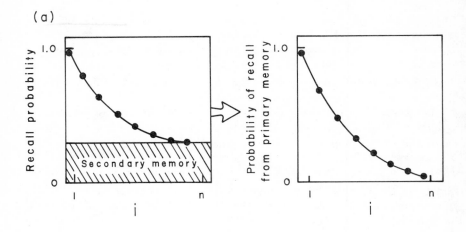

(b)

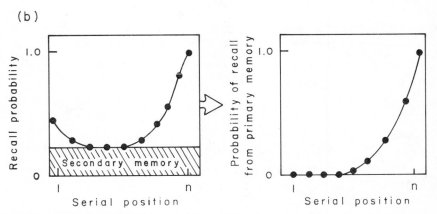

FIGURE 6.2   Application of the Waugh and Norman model to data from (a) the Brown-Peterson distractor task and from (b) free recall. The term *i* stands for the number of events intervening between input and output of the item in question.

First, we must isolate situations in which the major component of memory is probably either primary or secondary memory. Next, we examine the effects of several different independent variables. If some of these variables affect only the putative primary-memory task, then our original assumed distinctions between two kinds of memory is supported. (Actually, we shall see somewhat later in the chapter that an even stronger case is possible when variables affect the two components in the opposite direction.) This general research strategy may be termed *functional dissociation* and it has appeared in several different forms in this literature.

Coding. Baddeley and Dale (1966) studied the effect of semantic similarity on paired-associate retention in both short-term and long-term memory tasks. Their materials were pairs of adjectives. In the long-term memory task subjects learned lists of eight pairs for eight trials, then a second list of eight pairs, and then finally were tested on the first list. The variable of interest was the similarity between the lists. In the control condition there was no particular relation between the adjectives used in the two lists, whereas in the experimental condition the two lists had highly similar stimulus terms. For example, if ANXIOUS–NOISY had been on the first list, the experimental group might have had to learn the pair AFRAID–SUBTLE on the second list. As would be expected from well-known laws of verbal interference (Chapter 8), the control group did better on the first-list recall than the experimental group. With highly similar stimuli and different responses, interference is high, as the Osgood model in Chapter 1 shows.

In the short-term memory part of the experiment by Baddeley and Dale, a procedure introduced by Murdock (1961b) was used. With this method a short, two- or three-item list of paired-associates is presented a single time and one or more pairs are then tested only a few seconds later by presenting the stimulus term alone. In experimental tests, Baddeley and Dale gave lists that included two pairs with similar stimulus terms, conforming to the same pattern of similarity (ANXIOUS–NOISY then AFRAID–SUBTLE) used in the other task, whereas on control trials there were no built-in similarity relations. In two variations of this basic procedure there was very little evidence for any similarity effect. The control group did outperform the experimental group by a tiny margin under all conditions but that was what we would expect from the fact that a secondary-memory component might well show up even in brief short-term memory tasks. The overall pattern of similarity effects was quite clear: Similarity on a semantic dimension had a tremendous effect in long-term memory and little or none in short-term memory.

The other part of this argument for functional dissociation is that *phonological similarity* has, in turn, a very substantial effect on short-term memory but little or no effect on long-term memory. Baddeley (1966) showed that when a ten-item list, high in either phonological or semantic similarity, was presented for *immediate* recall, there was a strong harmful effect of phonological similarity but none of semantic similarity. When the same lists were learned under the same conditions, except with an interpolated number-copying task occupying about half a minute before recall of the word lists, it was semantic similarity that affected performance and not phonological similarity. This fits well with the model in that once primary-memory items are removed by some distractor activity one is left with the long-term secondary-memory component.

Together, these demonstrations were taken to show that primary memory was phonologically coded and secondary memory semantically coded.

Functional dissociation in the free-recall serial-position curve. Glanzer (1972) and his associates (especially Glanzer & Cunitz, 1966) have worked within the free-recall paradigm making much the same point as Baddeley. In free recall, it will be remembered, the Waugh and Norman theory suggests a stable asymptotic contribution from secondary memory and a transient contribution from primary memory that causes the recency effect. (The primacy effect is ignored in these analyses.) When some variable is applied to free recall, therefore, we look to see whether the effect is on the recency portion of the serial-position curve, on the asymptotic middle portion, or both. The evidence that is especially important for the dualistic memory hypothesis is that many variables affect only the asymptotic region and not the recency portion, whereas a few others show the opposite relation.

Several examples of variables that influence only the prerecency portion of the serial position curve are shown in Figure 6.3. We see in Figure 6.3a that slower presentation rates lead to better performance than faster presentation rates, in free recall, but only for the first 15 or so items out of a list of 20 (Glanzer & Cunitz, 1966; see also Bernbach, 1975). In Figure 6.3b is shown the effect of word frequency on single-trial free recall (Sumby, 1963); the familiar words are recalled better than low-frequency words but only at the early serial positions. In Figure 6.3c are data from Murdock's (1962) experiment on list length and free recall; longer lists lead to poorer recall for any given item, but not at the last few serial positions of the lists. Finally, in Figure 6.3d are data from quite a different type of experiment (Belmont & Butterfield, 1971); in this task a series of elements is displayed visually in different spatial locations. At the end of the list a probe element, which has occurred in the list, is presented alone and the subject's job is to indicate in which spatial location the probe has occurred. What the figure shows is that performance in the primacy portion of the serial-position function—where we mean by position the temporal order of the items—is greatly affected by mental retardation, whereas performance on the last couple of items is independent of this variable. All four of these potent variables in Figure 6.3 selectively affect all positions in the list but the last few. (Actually, the simplest application of the Waugh and Norman model suggests some effect of these variables on the last positions, too, but a smaller effect than that observed in earlier positions. See Bernbach, 1975, for a discussion of this point.)

A complementary situation occurs in free recall when an interpolated task is interposed between presentation and recall. Postman and Phillips (1965) and Glanzer and Cunitz (1966) have required subjects to wait several seconds before recalling word lists, with the delay filled by some arithmetic or counting task. In Figure 6.4 are the data from Glanzer and Cunitz. Performance is independent of conditions across the first dozen or so positions but on the last few serial positions the presence and duration of a distractor task have a large effect on recall. The presumption here is that in this case only the primary-memory component is being affected and not the secondary-memory of recall. Gardiner,

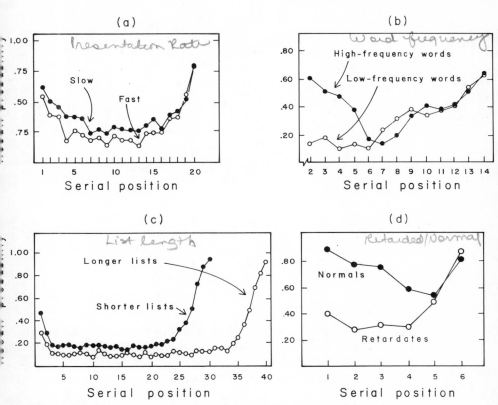

FIGURE 6.3 The effects of four independent variables on the serial position function. (a) Performance as a function of persentation rate, either three or nine seconds per item (after Glanzer & Cunitz, 1966). (b) The effect of word frequency (after Sumby, 1963). (c) The effect of list length, 30 versus 40 items (after Murdock, 1962). (d) An experiment on probe memory for position with normal and mentally retarded subjects (after Belmont & Butterfield, 1971).

Thompson, and Maskarinec (1974) have demonstrated that if the distractor task is difficult and long enough, in this type of experiment, there is a reversal of the recency effect, such that performance on the last item is worse than performance on the next to last item and so on (see also Roediger & Crowder, 1975).

Negative recency. The reversal of recency obtained by Gardiner *et al.* (1974) was first discovered, in a somewhat different situation, by Craik (1970). Instead of postponing initial recall of the list by some distractor task, Craik had subjects recall the list immediately, yielding the conventional serial position effect with a large recency advantage. After a number of such lists, just before being excused from the laboratory, Craik's subjects were unexpectedly asked to recall all of the words presented during the entire session. Between the presentation of the

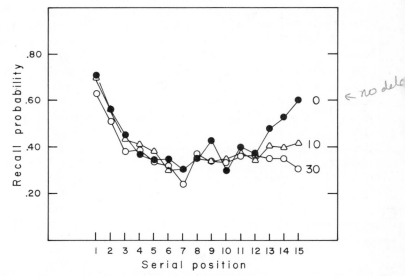

FIGURE 6.4 Serial position functions for three periods of delay between presentation and recall of free-recall lists, 0, 10, or 30 sec. (After Glanzer & Cunitz, 1966.)

average list and its recall during this final recall test, therefore, there were several presentations and recalls of other intervening lists. Craik's data showed a normal primacy effect in the final recall test; however, there was a decline in recall over the last few serial positions, a phenomonon he named *negative recency*.

Madigan and McCabe (1971) have shown negative recency in a short-term paired-associate situation. Subjects were given five pairs, with immediate testing of one pair by presentation of its stimulus term. After the experiment, in which 50 such trials were conducted, items from the whole session were tested again. For the first two positions there was only about a 15% decrement between the immediate test and the final free-recall test, from around 35% correct to around 20% correct. For the last item in each list of five, however, there was a drop, between tests, of from 100% to 0% correct recall!

According to models of the Waugh–Norman variety, negative recency is just what we should predict: When primary memory is removed either by a distractor task or by intervening memory tests there is only secondary memory left, which, according to the model, depends on the amount of rehearsal during initial primary-memory storage. As we have seen, this amount of secondary memory is ordinarily equated with the stable asymptote. Strictly speaking, however, there ought to be less secondary memory for the final few than for earlier items, because the very last items were in primary memory for so little time in the first place. The very last item itself for example, could not have been rehearsed very long at all because testing began just after it was presented.

In support of this interpretation is evidence from the technique developed by Rundus (1971), in which subjects are asked to think aloud during presentation of a list of words. Tallies are kept of how often the subject reports thinking of the word in each serial position. The result is given in Figure 6.5, where Craik's (1970) negative recency effect is also displayed for comparison. There is an obvious, strong correlation between the probability that the particular position is rehearsed and the probability that it is recalled in final recall. This correlation, of course, does not establish that the rehearsal *causes* the ultimate level of recall. In fact, we shall see later in this chapter (Craik & Watkins, 1973; Watkins & Watkins, 1974; Woodward, Bjork, & Jongeward, 1973) that there are some situations in which the amount of rehearsal is not correlated with the ultimate recall level.

The most important point about negative recency, for the moment, is that recall in the earlier parts of the list suffers only slightly by imposition of a delay, whereas recall for the last few recency items suffers enormously. This is true with either the distractor-task paradigm or the double-testing paradigm of Craik, with words tested once after presentation and once again in a final-recall measure. A second point about negative recency is that it makes possible the following type of statement: There is a variable that has opposite effects on performance depending on whether one looks at performance based mainly on primary memory or performance based mainly on secondary memory. This variable is serial position. For the recency items, recall is a positive function of serial position in immediate recall; however, for the same items in delayed-recall, performance is an inverse function of serial position. When the same variable has opposite performance consequences in short-term and long-term memory tasks,

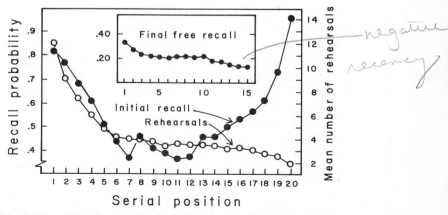

FIGURE 6.5 Serial position function for initial free recall and corresponding data on the number of rehearsals given items at each position during list presentation (after Rundus, 1971). The insert shows the negative recency effect in final free recall (after Craik, 1970).

it becomes almost impossible to maintain that a single, common, theoretical mechanism underlies the two cases.

Arousal and memory. Because a negative correlation between initial and delayed recall, when the correlation is computed across some variable other than subjects, is so important for the issue of dualistic theories of memory, we shall consider additional reports of such a finding. Kleinsmith and Kaplan (1963) measured skin resistance during the single acquisition trial they gave subjects for a list of eight word–number pairs. Their purpose was to trace memory for words learned under either conditions of high physiological arousal or low physiological arousal, as defined by changes in skin resistance during acquisition. The finding was that at a 2-min retention interval there was an advantage in recall for the words learned under low arousal (about 47% versus 8%). However, at a 20-min retention interval there was no difference, and at intervals of 45 min, 1 day, and 1 week, there was a significant advantage of high-arousal materials (about 43% versus 1% after 1 week). For whatever reason, therefore, arousal seems to hurt recall at early retention intervals but to favor recall at later retention intervals (see also Kleinsmith & Kaplan, 1964; Levonian, 1968, McLean, 1969; Walker & Tarte, 1963). As before, a single-factor theory of memory would be at pains to explain this pattern of results.

Brain damage and functional dissociation. One final approach to dualistic processing in memory is found in studies of human brain-injury cases. As we have noted in the section on eidetic imagery in Chapter 5, we should remain open to the possibility that studying pathological functioning can reveal aspects of normal functioning. Such revelations have been of value, apparently, in the fields of color vision, hemispheric specialization, and psychopathology. If individuals who have suffered one or another brain injury show general, across the board deficiencies in memory, then nothing has been learned about normal processing. However, if such individuals show specific deficiencies in what we have elsewhere learned are chiefly primary or chiefly secondary memory tests, then the distinction between these types of memory is supported.

Shallice and Warrington (1970) report several experimental tests on a subject, K. F., who had suffered a left parietooccipital fracture some years previously. His verbal IQ was somewhat below normal although his nonverbal IQ was normal. However, his digit span, the number of digits he could reliably report back, was only one! In one series of tests, Shallice and Warrington examined free recall for lists of ten high-frequency words. Thirty different lists were presented; his percentages of correct recall across the ten presentation serial positions were, respectively, 50, 33, 23, 23, 23, 33, 40, 30, 30, 83. The one-position recency effect he gave is to be contrasted with the usual recency effect in lists of ten items, which extends back approximately five items (Murdock, 1962). However, the one-position recency effect is perfectly consistent with K. F.'s digit span of one. His performance on other parts of the list is somewhat lower but not greatly lower than what one expects from normal subjects.

In a Brown–Peterson task, Shallice and Warrington found essentially normal performance for K. F. with regard to asymptotic levels of correct items—about 45% words correct after 10 or 15 sec of interpolated counting. However, performance at 0 or 5 sec was hardly any better than this asymptotic level, with the result that he produced a nearly level retention function. In short, K. F. behaved like a man with very sharply impaired primary memory but essentially normal secondary memory. Although this fact is consistent with the distinction between primary and secondary memory, note that it poses difficulties for the transfer model of how primary and secondary memory are related: If secondary memory receives its input from primary memory, how can a severely damaged primary memory nonetheless feed perfectly normal quantities of information into the next stage? (To this difficulty we shall return later.)

Wickelgren (1968) has tested a man named H.M., whose temporal lobes were partly removed to help control epilepsy. This individual contrasts vividly with K.F. in that with H.M. the deficit is entirely in the formation of new secondary-memory traces. H.M. has an apparently normal digit span, and performs normally on IQ tests. Wickelgren carried out a number of tests in which a list of items, digits, or tones was presented for study, following which, after a delay, a single item from the list was presented for a yes–no recognition decision. In normal subjects Wickelgren had found it necessary to assume some permanent-memory component in order to describe performance on this task with a mathematical model, just as Waugh and Norman found it necessary to assume a stable secondary-memory component to accommodate Brown–Peterson data. In the case of H.M., however, when he was tested on the same tasks, Wickelgren found that there was no need to assume anything beyond a primary-memory component. He was, as it were, a chronic case of nontransfer to secondary memory such as Waugh and Norman had tried to simulate in their probe-digit experiment.

Together, K.F. and H.M. provide the sort of evidence we have been claiming supports some type of process dualism in memory. One shows no effect of an injury on primary memory but a large effect on secondary memory, whereas the other shows the opposite relationship. On the assumption their performance would not have been different prior to their injuries, we might draw an analogy between their different brain afflictions and two experimental manipulations. The specificity of consequences for the brain damage matches the properties of theoretically defined memory systems and thereby supports the distinction between them.

Wickelgren (1973) has written a forceful critique of the evidence and logic that we have reviewed in this section on process dualism. His conclusion is that some few of the sources we have described here are valid evidence for the functional distinction between primary and secondary memory but that many others of them are not valid. It would be disproportionate to the scope of this chapter for us to take Wickelgren's points up one by one. However, it can be observed that the conclusion being advanced in this chapter is somewhat weaker than the establishment of two memory systems with different functional properties. We have here been arguing for process dualism, for a distinction between two operating principles, rather than insisting on two separate memory stores, as such. To decide that a two-process theory is necessary is an easier step than deciding exactly on the nature of the two processes being distinguished. The data on functional dissociation speak more to the question of whether a two-process theory is necessary than to the properties of either of the two processes themselves. For example, functional dissociation is compatible with either the assumption of two retrieval processes (Watkins, 1974a) or of two codes (Wickelgren, 1973) as well as with the assumption that there are two separate memory stores.

The Measurement of Primary Memory

If we choose to assume, with most workers in the field, however, that primary memory is indeed a separate memory system, and given that it is independent of a large number of variables, what is the actual capacity of the system? Immediately a prior question comes up: What is the unit of analysis in which the capacity of primary memory should be defined? Fortunately, much the same property of invariance that has served to establish primary memory as a functional entity serves also to suggest that the proper unit of measurement in it is the word, or verbal item. A number of studies (Craik, 1968b; Glanzer & Razel, 1974; Watkins, 1972) demonstrate that estimates of primary memory are invariant with such properties of words as their frequency, their syllable length, and their morphemic length (number of meaning units). This is just as we should expect in a postcategorical memory store, where category states correspond to available verbal response units (Sperling, 1970; Morton, 1969). There are four different methods for estimating how many verbal units can be held in primary memory. Our survey of them closely follows the treatment of Watkins (1974a), although there are a number of subtle points in his paper that cannot be covered here.

The Waugh and Norman method. We have already seen that from the assumption that total recall includes independent retrieval from primary and secondary memory, Waugh and Norman (1965) have offered the following equation for estimating the probability that an item has been retrieved from primary memory after the passage of i intervening events:

$$p(PM_i) = \frac{p(R_i) - p(SM)}{1 - p(SM)}.$$

The capacity of primary memory is then evaluated by applying the formula

$$Cap = \sum_{i=1}^{L} p(PM_i),$$

where L is the list length. There are some assumptions that go into estimating i, the number of intervening events, but they are not central to the theory. Therefore, if for a free-recall experiment we had an asymptotic performance level of .40 and scores on the last five positions of .40, .45, .60, .80, and .95, the $p(PM_i)$ values, respectively, would be .000, .083, .333, .667, and .917 and the total capacity would be estimated at very close to two words. Craik (1971) has summarized the results of many applications of this method showing total primary-memory capacities of about 2.5 items (see also Glanzer & Razel, 1974).

The problem with this method is best seen in connection with free recall. Although the middle portion of the free-recall serial-position curve shows an asymptote that is extremely stable (see figures in this chapter) the negative-recency phenomenon tells us that secondary memory is probably not really constant across the last few serial positions. Indeed, the model of Waugh and Norman predicts such instability, as we commented above, because little rehearsal can ever be afforded the last items. The probability of retrieving items from secondary memory therefore could be quite a bit lower for the last several of the recency items than for interior list positions. If so, one may systematically overcorrect for secondary memory in late positions by applying the Waugh–Norman equations, which assume a stable asymptote.

The Raymond method. Raymond (1969) proposed a way around this problem which uses different estimates of secondary-memory retrieval at each individual position in free recall. Application of this method depends on doing two experiments, one on immediate free recall and the other on free recall when retrieval is postponed by a distractor task, the purpose of which is to remove primary memory (see Figure 6.4). The equation looks just like the Waugh and Norman equation except $p(SM)$ is subscripted as $p(SM_i)$ to reflect the fact that separate estimates of $p(SM)$ are now being used for each position or each level of number of intervening items.

The problem with Raymond's method is that a distractor task may have effects of different magnitudes, depending on its difficulty and duration (Gardiner et al., 1974; Roediger & Crowder, 1975). A short, easy distractor task leads to a removal of the recency effect but not a reversal of it, whereas a long, difficult task produces the reversal (Glanzer & Cunitz, 1966; Postman & Phillips, 1965). A short, easy task has little effect on early serial positions, whereas a long, difficult task reduces recall in the early serial positions as well as in the recency positions. On the assumption that the longest, most difficult interpolated tasks that have been studied are presentation and recall of half a dozen or so additional free-recall lists, as in the Craik (1970) negative-recency experiment, we obtain ludicrously generous estimates of primary-memory capacity, extending all the way back to the early list positions, using the Raymond method. However, when relatively innocuous distractor-interpolation activities are used, this method yields estimates of capacity of about 2.5 words.

The Murdock method.   Murdock (1967b) and Craik (1968) have applied an empirical law first described by Murdock (1960b) to develop a third method for estimating the capacity of primary memory. Murdock observed that when free-recall lists of varying length are given with a constant time per item, the number of words recalled is a linear function of the number of words presented,

$$R = kL + m$$

where R is the total number of words recalled, L is list length, and m and k are constants. The constant k indexes the amount of additional recall that is obtained for every additional item added to the list. The other constant, m, which is of interest here indexes the amount of recall that is independent of list length. The value of m is therefore a sort of guaranteed perfect-recall package and corresponds to the general, Jamesian definition of primary memory. Values of 3.2 to 4.1 have been reported for m. Provided one does not present lists shorter than m items (one could hardly expect to find recall of 3.2 words when only two are presented in the first place) and subject to another minor reservation raised by Watkins (1974a), this method is not seriously flawed; it provides convergence on estimates derived from the other methods.

The Tulving and Colatla method.   The simplest method for calculating primary-memory capacity is to count the number of items in a list for which it is true that no more than seven events—either presentations of subsequent words or prior recalls—intervene between presentation and retrieval (Tulving & Colatla, 1970). This method gives results comparable to those achieved with other procedures. Craik (1971) has found primary memory capacities of 3.6 items with the seven-events definition of Tulving and Colatla and 3.3 items with a more stringent six-item definition.

Watkins (1974a) has noted that the Tulving and Colatla Method seems rather arbitrary and that it is subject to some of the same problems we noted with the other methods. For example, it, as well as the other three techniques, is likely to give quite undependable results with short lists: If the seven-event criterion were used for *verbatim* serial recall of a seven item list, it would yield a capacity of 7.0 items but verbatim recall of an eight item list would yield a capacity of zero!

Watkins (1974a) proposed a more rational method of choosing from among these four measurement approaches: Recall that our chief reason for accepting the primary—secondary memory distinction in the first place was the differential effects of some variables on the recency and prerecency portions of the free-recall serial-position curve. The question in measuring primary memory is how to translate the relative size of this recency effect into a sensible number. Watkins has proposed that we should take some experiment in which one of these discriminating variables is a factor—say, presentation rate, which affects recall probability everywhere except in the recency segment—and see which measure of primary memory yields the biggest interaction term of that variable with serial position. In other words, we take several means of deriving numerical estimates for primary and secondary memory; then, for each, a 2 × 2 table is constructed with memory component (primary versus secondary) as one dimension, presentation rate (fast versus slow) as the other, and performance entered in the body of the table. For each of these, we know that the general pattern is a large difference favoring slow presentation for the secondary-memory component but little or no effect of rate on the primary-memory component. The question is, for which means of dividing primary and secondary memory is this differential effect, this interaction, larger. (The Raymond method could not be compared with the other three because data on immediate versus delayed recall were not available for the experiment Watkins analyzed for these purposes. Also, we are streamlining the statistical test he used somewhat, although without any distortion of his logic.)

Watkins (1974a) found that the Tulving and Colatla method was the best by the criterion we have just established; the F ratio for the interaction associated with Tulving and Colatla's method was larger than those associated with the other methods. Furthermore, the Murdock method seemed to give a somewhat lower interaction than the Waugh–Norman method, which was intermediate. When we seek to measure primary memory in free recall, therefore, the Tulving and Colatla procedure seems to be the method of choice. As it happens, it is also the easiest.

Comment on the measurement problem   There are two significant points to be made about the measurement of primary-memory capacity. First, it is important that each of these methods produces estimates of between two and three items, or slightly larger, even though the third and fourth methods are quite different from each other and from the first two. In a survey of 32 independent studies, Glanzer and Razel (1974) reported a mean estimate of 2.2 words, with a standard deviation of .64 words. Of course, we cannot know how much consistency there should be, but the agreement found is not likely to turn out much smaller than the reliabilities of the measures themselves.

Second, the absolute size of the primary memory system is important. The estimate of two or three items is less than half the so-called "span of immediate memory." The span of immediate memory is measured by noting the length of series, usually digits, that the subject can reproduce accurately most of the time, or sometimes the length that he can reproduce 50% of the time; typical values of the memory span are seven or eight items. This discrepancy is probably caused by the presence, in the memory-span situation, of both secondary- and primary-memory components. Craik (1971) has strengthened this interpretation by reporting that the correlation, across subjects, between memory-span and secondary-memory estimates from free recall is +.72, higher than the correlation between memory-span and derived primary memory estimates, which is +.49. Furthermore, many variables, such as IQ and meaningfulness, affect memory span but do not affect primary memory scores. So, although memory span has traditionally been considered a measure of immediate, that is, nonmediated retention, it is very probably loaded with a large secondary-memory component.

In this connection, Crowder (1969) found that recency was the same, in memory for eight-digit numbers, whether or not the subject knew how long a stimulus list to expect; however, the size of the primacy effect was strongly influenced by this knowledge. Performance was overall much poorer in the unknown length condition, with accuracy closer to three items than to seven items. Furthermore, Crowder (1969) found that under the condition of unknown list length—where we can guess that only primary memory was at work—there was no relationship between subjects' overall scores and the size of their primacy effect. However, when the list length could be anticipated during presentation the better subjects had larger primacy scores than the poorer subjects.

Individual Differences and Primary Memory

We have already seen strong suggestions that primary memory is not a function of several variables with powerful effects elsewhere in verbal learning. Now we shall look at a few studies that have directly applied the two-store notion (primary versus secondary memory) to well-known sources of individual differences.

Age (Thurm & Glanzer, 1971). In childhood, memory gets better with increasing age. This empirical relationship is so lawful that Binet saw fit to define mental age partly in terms of growth in the memory span. There are now grounds for suspecting that the change in memory with age has nothing to do with primary memory, at least beyond 5 years. Glanzer and Thurm tested 5 or 6 year olds on free recall for a pictorial series of familiar objects. Accuracy as a function of list length, age, and serial position is shown in Figure 6.6. It is quite clear from the figure that the substantial differences between these two age groups are restricted to the early portions of the serial position curve and that the recency effects, the primary-memory components, are equal. Craik (1968a) has applied the same type of two-store analysis to the other end of the age continuum. He found that there was indeed a decline in memory performance between ages 22 and 65 years; however, the change was entirely in the secondary-memory component.

Intelligence (Ellis, 1970). Using a somewhat different task, Ellis has discovered much the same pattern of results when comparing normal college subjects with mental retardates of comparable chronological age. Note that this

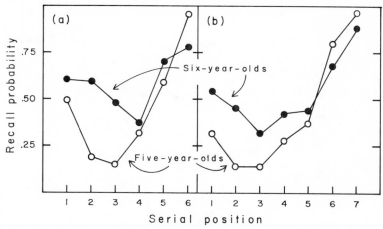

FIGURE 6.6 Serial position functions for five- and six-year old children (a) on six-item lists and (b) on seven-item lists. (After Thurm & Glanzer, 1971.)

is not just a comparison of minimally different subject populations but of normal subjects against individuals who require institutionalization. Therefore, finding them equivalent, as Ellis did, on some measure of mental functioning is a striking result. It was also the case that the retardates did not profit, as did normals, from a slowing down of the presentation rate.

Mnemonic ability (Raymond, 1969). Even in a homogeneous group, such as one finds in college, some subjects do better than others in such a task as free recall. Raymond compared immediate and delayed recall for subjects with overall high scores and those with overall low scores. The results are shown in Figure 6.7 (taken from Glanzer, 1972). It is quite easily seen that these two groups are much more different in their asymptotes than in the recency segments of their serial-position curves. When Raymond corrected for secondary memory she found that primary-memory scores of the better and poorer subjects were not different.

Primary memory is by itself almost a boring topic, therefore. Whatever experimental factor or individual difference we consider, the capacity remains fixed at two or three items. Only the interpolation of additional verbal materials between acquisition and retrieval of material seems to damage the primary-memory component of recall.

THE NATURE OF PRIMARY MEMORY

We shall now move to a survey of efforts to characterize the nature of primary memory and its relation to secondary memory, having agreed that some two-factor approach to memory is necessitated by the evidence contained in the first

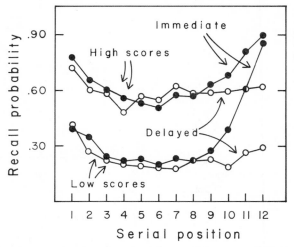

FIGURE 6.7 Serial position functions for subjects with high and low overall scores in Raymond's (1969) experiment in immediate and delayed recall. (After Glanzer, 1972.)

section of this chapter. First, there will be a review of the relation between primary memory and coding, then a critical discussion of the concept of transfer from primary to secondary memory, and finally a section presenting some recent alternatives to the basic Waugh and Norman approach to primary memory.

Is Primary Memory Phonological?

Now that we have the tools for measuring primary memory we can return to the question of coding in long- and short-term memory tasks, an issue we introduced above in order to defend the necessity for some type of dualistic theory. Kintsch and Buschke (1969) performed two experiments using the Waugh and Norman probe technique. Lists of 16 words were presented, followed by repetition of one word from the list, called the probe; instructions were to recall the word that had immediately followed the probe word. In one experiment there were two conditions, one with a list of 16 unrelated words, and the other with eight pairs of synonyms scattered throughout the list. The results are given in Figure 6.8, on the left. The synonyms created confusion and led to worse performance than found with the unrelated words. However, as the primary-memory analysis for these data shows, this effect is entirely on the prerecency asymptote, with no consequence for primary memory at all. A second experiment in the Kintsch and Buschke report contrasted lists of unrelated words and lists with eight pairs of homonyms, rather than synonyms. In this case, as the figure shows, there is no effect on the asymptote but a large effect on the derived primary-memory scores.

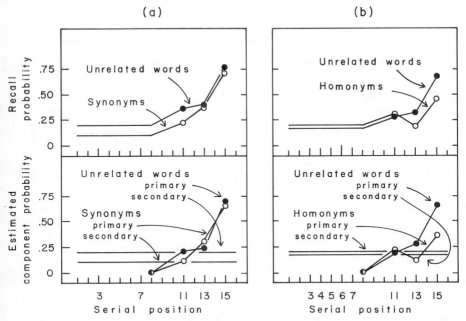

FIGURE 6.8 Performance in probed recall from lists of 16 words. (a) Recall probability (upper functions) for lists of unrelated words versus lists with pairs of synonyms and the analysis of these data (lower functions) into primary-memory and secondary-memory components. (b) The same type of data and the same analysis for the comparison of unrelated words with homonym pairs. The serial positions that were actually tested in the experiment are given numerals on the horizontal axis. (After Kintsch & Buschke, 1969.)

The Kintsch and Buschke study is consistent with a view that primary and secondary memory are organized according to different codes, a phonological code for primary memory and a semantic code for secondary memory. In terms of the Waugh and Norman transfer model, this means that while items are in primary memory it is not strictly a copying process that transfers them to secondary memory but rather a phonological-to-semantic recoding.

An experiment by Tell (1972) has established a similar pattern for the Brown–Peterson short-term memory task. In Tell's experiment there were either 2.7 or 10.8 sec of distractor activity between presentation and recall of a three-consonant trigram. The experiment was a two by two design in which the meaningfulness and phonological similarity of the trigrams were varied. Figure 6.9 gives examples of stimulus trigrams resulting from orthogonal variation of these factors. The results, shown in the same figure, are quite straightforward empirically: both factors have affected performance at both time intervals. However, there was an interaction such that meaningfulness was more influential at the longer interval and phonological similarity at the short interval.

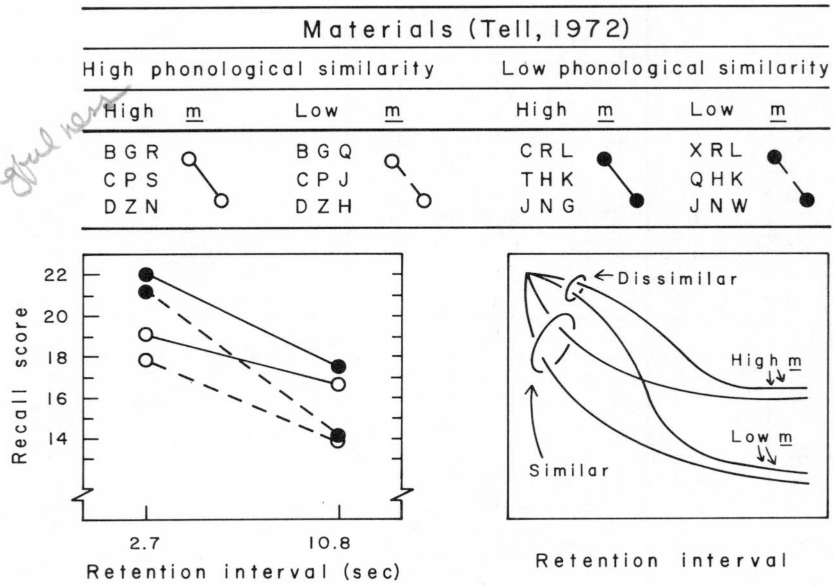

Materials (Tell, 1972)

High phonological similarity				Low phonological similarity			
High	m	Low	m	High	m	Low	m
B G R		B G Q		C R L		X R L	
C P S		C P J		T H K		Q H K	
D Z N		D Z H		J N G		J N W	

M = meaningful

FIGURE 6.9   Materials from the Tell (1972) experiment (top) and results (bottom, left). (Lower right) Theoretical expectations for complete functions when one variable affects only primary memory and another affects only secondary memory. (After Tell, 1972.)

The curve on the lower right of Figure 6.9 shows the theoretical form of the distinction between primary- and secondary-memory effects in the Brown–Peterson paradigm as applied to Tell's findings. Notice that what we really need to make this distinction is not only two different asymptotes, which is rather an easy pattern to demonstrate, but also two different rates of approaching the asymptote, independent of the value of the asymptote itself. This latter requirement is much more difficult to establish. For example, if performance is constrained by the ceiling at the shortest retention interval the initial rate of loss appears more gradual than it is.

Leaving these reservations aside, however, the pattern of results in Tell's data and in Kintsch and Buschke's data inclined many workers to view the coding distinction, phonological versus semantic, as isomorphic with the component distinction, primary versus secondary. This generalization has been useful in imposing a rough organization on the field of short-term memory but it may be wrong.

In the first place, the association of phonological coding with primary memory comes entirely from experiments with short-term memory tasks (such as those used by Kintsch and Buschke and by Tell) and not from free recall; but it is from the free-recall technique that much of the rest of our knowledge of primary memory comes. Worse, moreover, when we look at the effects of phonological similarity on free recall a puzzling pattern of results emerges: The recency portion of the serial position curve is relatively unaffected by similarity and the prerecency portion is facilitated by similarity. These findings are shown in Figure 6.10, where we see part of the results of a study by Watkins *et al.* (1974). This study was mentioned in Chapter 1, and it is the subject of more discussion in the next chapter. For the moment, we note the absence of any appreciable effect of phonological similarity on that very recency effect that has been a defining manifestation of primary memory.

Second, to restrict primary memory to information coded phonologically makes it hard to maintain the James definition of primary memory unless one wants to claim that consciousness can be only verbal. Yet few of us would be willing to so restrict the nature of consciousness. The skilled violinist in furious concentration over the phrasing of a difficult musical passage does not, by any stretch of the imagination, have a "blank mind"; yet he is not talking to himself. Likewise, a subject required to perform spatial operations on three-dimensional geometric figures such as those alluded to in Chapter 5 (Shepard & Metzler, 1971) is absorbed in nonverbal information processing. Now, of course, there is no compulsion for us to remain faithful to the William James criterion of primary memory. However, retaining it, with the implication that primary memory can, on occasions, be filled with nonverbal content, pays off in other ways, as follows.

Recall from Chapter 5 that Posner and his associates demonstrated a form of visual storage that was distinct from iconic storage because in their research it (1) lasted on the order of seconds rather than fractions of a second; (2) was disrupted by interpolated information processing in the verbal mode, mental arithmetic, rather than by visual noise; and (3) could be established by a generation process from auditory input. If we relax the identification of primary

FIGURE 6.10 Free recall probability as a function of serial position and of phonological similarity. The auditory and visual presentation conditions are combined. (After Watkins, Watkins, & Crowder, 1974.)

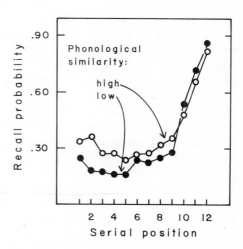

memory with phonological coding, it makes excellent sense that visual storage should be impaired by mental arithmetic; both are competing for the same limited space in primary memory. On the other side of the coin, a verbal memory load should be more disrupted by a verbal interpolated task than by a visual one and there is evidence for that interaction also in Chapter 5. The fact that dissimilar tasks interfere with one another (verbal task versus visual memory), therefore, shows that there is some convergence of information processing on a single attention channel; the fact that interference is more severe when two tasks share the same coding system (visual storage less impaired by verbal distractor than verbal storage) tells us that at some level there are multiple channels. In Chapter 5 we were anxious to stress the latter point and right now we are stressing the former.

The disruption in verbal short-term memory caused by nonverbal interpolated tasks in the Brown–Peterson paradigm is also compatible with the view that primary memory holds whatever type of information a human is operating on, or in some direct sense, experiencing. Crowder (1967b) showed that memory for words was impaired by a serial key-pressing task in which ten lights, arrayed from left to right, had to be extinguished by pressing a corresponding array of ten keys. When the key-pressing task was made more difficult by destroying the one-to-one correspondence between lights and keys based on left-to-right position, the disruption of memory storage for words was markedly greater. However, it was not likely that Crowder's subjects depended on verbal mediation for their key-pressing activity. Watkins, Watkins, Craik, and Mazuryk (1973) have shown disruption of verbal memory by nonverbal tasks in other situations. (In the next chapter we shall deal more fully with the issue of what, about nonverbal tasks, leads to their effect on verbal memory. The main factor seems to be their difficulty.)

Atkinson and Shiffrin (1968) formalized these considerations of coding in their model. They divided the short-term store, their term for the primary-memory component, into several substores distinguished by their mode of coding. They felt the auditory–verbal–linquistic mode, basically phonological, was probably the most important mode in verbal memory experiments, but separate space was left for such other modes as kinesthetic and visual.

This expanded view of primary memory allows us to characterize it, following Posner (1973) and others, as *operating memory*—the mental process whereby a small amount of information can be held in a highly accessible state for transformation, rehearsal, recombination, or other operations. Most memory experiments employ verbal stimuli and so are extremely likely to place a premium on verbal processing operations, and thus on phonological coding. However, now that we acknowledge other modes of processing to share in the same limited-capacity attentional system it is possible for us to embrace James' concept of primary memory as a part of the phenomenal present and also to accommodate discrepancies between phonological similarity effects in free recall and in short-term memory.

Transfer between Primary and Secondary Memory

It was a basic part of the Waugh and Norman model (Fig. 6.1) that information was first stored in primary memory and then, through a process of rehearsal, transferred to secondary memory. In effect, this assumption gives us a new vocabulary in which to talk about the process of learning. It is not acquiring information, as such, that constitutes learning; instead, it is the transfer of information from a temporary to a permanent form of storage. Because the search for a useful way to talk about learning has been a central occupation of philosophy and psychology straight through their histories, we shall deal with the transfer notion and recent critiques of it in some detail.

The Atkinson and Shiffrin theory. This is an excellent place to review the memory theory of Atkinson and Shiffrin (1968) because it is more explicit than other theories about both the transfer process and also about the interrelationships among the various other subsystems of memory. The most basic distinction in the Atkinson and Shiffrin theory is between *structural features* of memory and *control processes* applied to the memory system voluntarily. The structural features include, but are not limited to, physical constraints in the portion of the brain responsible for memory. Limitations on capacity that are outside our control can also be classed as structural properties of memory. Control processes, in contrast, are voluntary adjustments made within the constraints set by the structural system. The decay characteristic of an iconic image would be a structural feature; however, control processes would be enlisted following an instruction to read out a certain portion of the icon. Consider a comparable distinction in physiology: There are anatomical factors that constrain what the knee joint of a human being can do; however, within those constraints we are constantly exerting a great deal of voluntary control over the knee. Psychologists have not always been comfortable, in the middle of this century, with the idea of voluntary control over mental events. One contribution of the Atkinson and Shiffrin position was to reject this reluctance stemming from our behaviorist heritage. Because the "mentalistic" control processes they described can be stated in mathematical terms or built into a digital computer program, there is not the same loss of rigor that accompanies irresponsible mentalism.

The major structural features of the memory system built by Atkinson and Shiffrin are three memory stores, rules governing decay from them, and channels of transfer among them. These features are illustrated in Figure 6.11. Information arriving at the sense organs is first represented in the *sensory register,* a set of modality-specific memories having the properties of iconic and echoic stores (see Chapters 2 and 3). Passing through a long-term memory

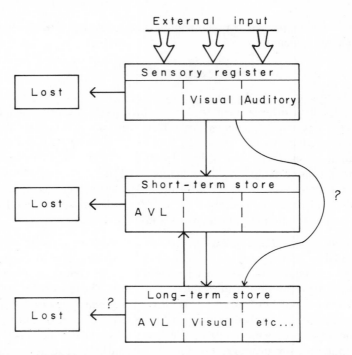

FIGURE 6.11 The memory system of Atkinson and Shiffrin (1968): AVL is auditory–verbal–linguistic. The question marks indicate uncertain transfer operations. (After Atkinson & Shiffrin, 1968.)

search, which eventuates in recognition, the information is next held in a *short-term store,* which lasts on the order of seconds. The recognition process is not well indicated on the figure, but it is conceived as a search of long-term storage sufficient to retrieve the name of the linguistic symbol presented but not other information about it. Reserving the possibility that there may be numerous modality-specific short-term stores, Atkinson and Shiffrin chose to concentrate on what they called the *auditory–verbal–linguistic* component of short-term storage. This corresponds to the outcome of the type of phonological recoding discussed in Chapter 4. The *long-term store* holds information that has been transferred from short-term storage. Information that reaches the long-term store is relatively permanent, in contrast to the sensory register and short-term store, where decay rates are rapid. Like Sperling's Model IV, the Atkinson–Shiffrin model recognizes that there are several different long-term memories specific to different modalities. Although long-term imagery is thus included in the model, however, Atkinson and Shiffrin have little to say about it.

One of the main functions of the control processes is the general regulation of information flow among the three memory stores. The possibilities for such flow are built-in structural features: For example, there can be no transfer from long-term store to the sensory register, no matter how hard the subject tries. Likewise, no matter how much the subject wants to, he cannot rehearse subvocally at a rate of 100 words a second. Within constraints imposed structurally, however, there is an impressive range of options. In the sensory register, control processes dictate the investment of attention in one or another sensory modality. Within any modality, there is a comparable investment of attention to various information sources—selection among spatial sources in vision and audition, color coding in vision, frequency coding in audition, and so on.

In the short-term store the most important voluntary process is rehearsal, saying the information to be retained over and over covertly. The two purposes served by rehearsal, according to Atkinson and Shiffrin, are (1) simply maintaining information for direct, immediate use and (2) keeping information in a state of access pending coding operations for long-term storage. The first of these functions of rehearsal is conspicuous when we rehearse a telephone number on the way to the telephone. The second function is illustrated by saying a paired-associate item over and over while attempting to generate a visual image in the context of a pegword technique. A very specific set of assumptions has been made by Atkinson and Shiffrin about the properties of *a rehearsal buffer,* which subjects voluntarily set up under certain circumstances. It is from this buffer model that predictions for repetition effects are derived and so we shall return to it in Chapter 9.

Whereas transfer between the short- and long-term store occurs inevitably, as a structural feature, there is considerable control possible over the form of the transfer. When rote repetition is the dominant process, long-term information is built up about an item but only slowly. However, an active effort at recoding, such as through visual images, results in much more permanent long-term representation. The distinction between these two forms of transfer is of more than passing interest. When attention is diverted from rehearsal by elaborate imagery or other recoding operations, long-term storage is very stable for the item recoded but at any one moment only that single item is in the accessible rehearsal state. When many items are being rehearsed in a relatively mechanical way, however, there is quite excellent short-term recall because so many items are in the accessible rehearsal state yet no one of these items benefits from the sophisticated recoding.

Within the long-term store the main control operation is retrieval, as directed by a search procedure. These search routines are especially intuitive if one introspects about the task of recalling names for the capitols of states. The contrast between recognition and recall tests is often considered crucial for understanding of the search process in long-term storage.

As we shall see in Chapter 9, the buffer model of Atkinson and Shiffrin is quite explicit in detail and for this reason, possibly, writers in the area of learning and memory have not sufficiently distinguished it from the overall memory theory of which it is a subsection. From the specification of control processes covering the transfer from primary to secondary memory, however, we may infer that Atkinson and Shiffrin have a two-factor theory of learning—a slow accumulation of strength in the permanent store when rote repetition occurs and a rapid transfer of information to the permanent store when some recoding strategy is employed.

Difficulties with the transfer model. The model of Waugh and Norman, Figure 6.1, specifies the interrelationship of primary and secondary memory as well as their distinctness. Recent evidence has raised grave difficulties with this simple concept of transfer of information from primary to secondary memory.

There is an initial logical problem that in primary memory the items are postcategorical in the sense that their names (the phonological or other stable representations of words, letters, or whatever) have already been achieved. However, these names, together with routines for matching them with precategorical sensory input, are themselves necessarily in the permanent store. The model seems to maintain that access to secondary memory does not occur until after the items have been categorized, an impossible situation logically. As we just saw, Atkinson and Shiffrin assumed that the only portion secondary memory made contact with initially was the section containing names.

The problem is less serious than it seems. Tulving's (1972) distinction between *episodic* and *semantic* memory is useful in clarifying the matter. In an experimental test of memory we often speak quite loosely about whether information is in memory or not. For example, if the word ELECTRICIAN occurs on a list but is not retained later, we sometimes speak of its not being learned, or being learned but not retained. Of course this is silly: The word ELECTRICIAN has been a part of our subject's memory store long before the experiment, and surely nothing that has happened in the experiment has erased it. What we mean is that there was not acquisition or retention of the fact that the word ELECTRICIAN has occurred in that particular time and place where the experiment has been conducted, on such and such particular list. Virtually all of the study of memory, until recently, has been concerned with memory for such occurrence information, or in Tulving's terms, for episodic memory. Episodic memory deals with events that are defined by experiences in specific temporal and spatial locations. Semantic memory, in contrast, contains information without any specification according to the exact circumstances of acquisition. Knowledge in semantic memory permits deductive inferences, such as that vultures have wings, and also such dictionary information as how words are spelled and with what other words they are associated. When we restrict our attention to episodic memory, it is still useful to consider that although a word in primary memory has gone through a semantic-memory categorization machine, it has not yet, as an episode, made contact with long-term coding.

A far more serious problem with the Waugh–Norman transfer model and with similar models based on the same idea (Glanzer, 1972) is raised sharply in a report from Smith, Barresi, and Gross (1971). These investigators presented a list of 13 paired nouns for study and tested one of these pairs later. One item occurred every 4 sec under two different instructions, given to separate groups. One group, the imagery group, was told to form a visual image connecting the two nouns given in each pair. The other group, the repetition group, was told to read each pair aloud, slowly, twice in a row while it was being presented.

The imagery instruction, as we should suspect from the information in Chapter 5, was by and large superior to the repetition instruction; however, this difference was most pronounced on the asymptotic portion of the list rather than on the final two items. The estimated asymptotic recall probability for the imagery group was .66 and for the repetition group was .45. Application of the Waugh–Norman equation, however, using these asymptotic figures as secondary-memory contributions, gave higher primary-memory scores for the repetition group than for the imagery group. Therefore, we have here another example of a negative correlation between recall from primary and secondary memory.

The theoretical difficulty posed by opposite effects of imagery instructions on recall from primary and from secondary memory is that secondary memory is supposed to depend for its input on the current contents of primary memory, according to the transfer model of Waugh and Norman. Therefore, conditions leading to good representation in primary memory ought to lead to good secondary-memory representation, as sort of a side effect. Conditions that curtail representation in primary memory, in contrast, ought to restrict the time during which information can be transferred to secondary memory. However, here in the Smith et al. (1971) study we have better primary memory giving way to worse secondary memory in the repetition condition as compared with the imagery condition. Similar difficulties for the Waugh and Norman transfer model come from evidence we have considered earlier that (1) a brain injury can adversely affect primary memory but leave secondary memory intact (Shallice & Warrington, 1970) and (2) high autonomic arousal can impair short-term recall but facilitate delayed recall of the same information (Kleinsmith & Kaplan, 1963). These latter two results have been encouraging to the separation of primary and secondary memory but they are not compatible with the simple transfer notion relating the two memory stores.

Obviously, there needs to be some adjustment of the simple transfer concept of the relationship between two stores. The suggestion of Smith et al. is the *direct contact hypothesis,* which holds that information feeds in parallel, following categorization, into primary and secondary memory. Because of limited capacity to process information, there is some reciprocity in setting up these two forms of storage; an instruction that tends to emphasize one of them, therefore, as imagery instructions may emphasize secondary-memory semantic coding, works to the disadvantage of the other. Conversely, the repetition instruction would facilitate primary-memory coding, which often would be phonological, at the expense of the secondary-memory coding. We shall return to the idea of reciprocity, rather than transfer, as the basic relation between the stores after looking at some other grounds for concern with the transfer conception.

Maintenance rehearsal. Both the Waugh–Norman model and the Atkinson–Shiffrin *buffer model*—but not the Atkinson–Shiffrin general theory—specify rehearsal as the means for building up permanent memory. We have just shown, with the Smith *et al.* (1971) experiment, that negative correlations between primary and secondary memory make the idea of transfer unlikely. There are now reasons for doubting that the process of rehearsal can serve as the sole mode of transfer anyway.

Craik and Watkins (1973) report two experiments making the point that the amount of time for which an item is rehearsed does not, under some circumstances, affect its probability of retrieval from long-term, or secondary, storage. In their first experiment, Craik and Watkins employed an incidental-learning task, that is, a task in which subjects had not been led to expect any subsequent test of memory at the time they were exposed to the stimulus items. The subjects received lists of words with different initial letters. Before presentation of the list the subjects were told that words beginning with a certain initial letter were critical, and that at any time they should be prepared to report whatever had been the last instance of a word beginning with the specified critical letter. If, for example, *B* were the critical letter, subjects might receive a list comprised of DOG, BAT, CLOCK, DESK, WINDOW, PAPER, BOMB, WOOD, LEAF. The correct answer, following LEAF, would be BOMB.

Assuming that the subjects held words beginning with the critical letter by a rehearsal process, we may estimate differential amounts of rehearsal for the words BAT and BOMB, in our example; BAT would have been rehearsed during four words, whereas BOMB would have been rehearsed only during two words. If the surprise test of memory for the whole list were held just after the word LEAF, the results would be indeterminate because of a heavy primary-memory contribution. However, in a test of recall held at the end of the session we should expect to see only recall based on secondary memory. According to the Waugh and Norman model BAT should be recalled better than BOMB because it has been held longer by rehearsal. As an additional manipulation, Craik and Watkins varied the rate of presentation, so that not only the number of items during which a critical word was rehearsed but also how long it was rehearsed could be examined in relation to ultimate levels of recall. The findings showed an effect of presentation rate, with items recalled more often from the slow presentation condition than from the fast presentation condition. However, when performance was compared as a function of the number of intervening items for which an item remained in the presumed rehearsal state, there was no effect on recall. Percent final recall for items held during 2, 4, 8, and 12 intervening items was 19.5, 21.0, 18.5, and 19.0, respectively. Therefore, what has been termed *maintenance rehearsal* serves to keep information accessible without increasing its accessibility to free recall from secondary memory.

In a second experiment Craik and Watkins (1973) addressed the negative recency phenomenon. According to the Waugh and Norman position on negative recency it is because the last few items have decreasing opportunities for rehearsal that so little transfer of them to secondary memory takes place, and, consequently, that so little final recall of them is seen. Recall the data of Rundus (1971) in Figure 6.5, showing that indeed the last few recency items in the list do receive progressively less and less rehearsal. Craik and Watkins have argued that if inadequate rehearsal is responsible for negative recency then any operation that insures compensatory rehearsal for the last few items ought to eliminate the negative recency effect.

In this study, subjects' rehearsal behavior was tape recorded during presentation, in the fashion of Rundus, as well as during recall itself. There were two conditions under which lists of 12 words were studied. In both, there were three measurements of interest—the number of rehearsals accorded words in each position, the level of initial recall, and the level of final free recall at the end of the session. In one of the two main conditions the conventional free-recall procedure was followed, with recall immediately after presentation, except that subjects were told to pay special attention to the last few words. In the second condition, they were given the same instructions but a 20-sec delay was imposed between the last item in the list and initial recall. Because the delay was unfilled and because they had been told to emphasize the last few words, it was expected that subjects would spend the 20 sec rehearsing the last few words, a circumstance that should have eliminated negative recency, if it were true that negative recency is caused by a rehearsal deficit.

The results are shown in Figure 6.12. First of all, we can see from the left-hand panel that instructions for emphasis of the final items has caused even the control—immediate initial recall—group to rehearse these words more than has been the case in the Rundus experiment. Furthermore, the delayed-recall group, as expected, has accomplished a really exaggerated amount of rehearsal for these final items. If we take the rehearsal—transfer notion literally, then we should expect final recall for the four recency items to be better than for the first four primacy items in the delayed-recall condition because the recency items have enjoyed more rehearsals. In the middle panel of Figure 6.12 we see that initial recall for these critical recency items was nearly perfect in both conditions. However, the right-hand panel has the important information. There, it is seen that there has been no long-term gain whatever from the extra 20 sec of rehearsal invested by the delayed group in the final four items. There was no negative recency in either case, actually, but at least there was a dramatic variation in rehearsal rate that failed to produce any variation in recall.

Woodward, Bjork, and Jongeward (1973) have demonstrated a similar ineffectiveness of rehearsal in a different situation. They presented individual words to subjects in the context of a directed forgetting experiment. Following each word in the list was a signal (green or red mark) instructing the subject that he could either forget the item that had just occurred or that he should try hard to

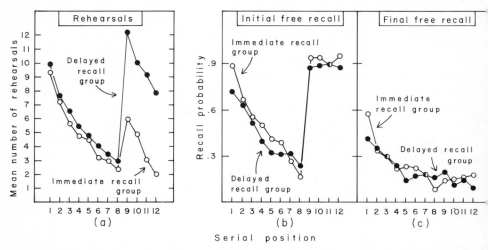

FIGURE 6.12   Serial position functions for immediate and delayed (20-sec) recall groups in terms of (a) the number of rehearsals given items (b) the level of initial recall, and (c) the level of final, end-of-session, recall. (After Craik & Watkins, 1973.)

remember that item in anticipation of a monetary reward for recalling it. The variable of interest was whether the cue signaling which type of word each particular item was (to be retained or forgotten) occurred right after appearance of the word or at some delay. In conditions with a delay imposed between presentation of the critical word and the signal (to retain or forget it) we can make the assumption that the word is being held in a rehearsal state; the subject cannot afford to lose it until he knows whether it is one of the rewarded ones.

The delay between occurrence of a word and the signal was varied between 0 and 12 sec. A check indicated that subjects were indeed retaining the word throughout this period because when asked for the previous word at the end of its "rehearsal period" subjects were quite good at providing it. However, in a test of final free recall at the end of the experimental session, there was no advantage of increasing time in rehearsal: Performance was no better, in three replications of the study, for items with a long delay before announcement of whether or not the item was to be retained, than for the items with only a short delay. Because the subjects demonstrably are keeping the items accessible during this period, this is another demonstration that rehearsal need not lay the groundwork for effective registration in secondary memory.

There are two further matters for comment in the studies by Woodward *et al.* (1973). Even though the amount of rehearsal time had no effect on final-recall probability, there was a large effect of whether the signal provided at the end of the rehearsal time stipulated that the item in question should be retained or forgotten. Recall was much better in the former case than in the latter. This could indicate that much of the important processing of a word goes on after the next word in the list has occurred, for until the next word in the list has occurred (actually until just before it) there is no difference in the treatment of words to be forgotten or to be retained.

The second point is that Woodward *et al.* (1973) show an improvement in performance as a function of rehearsal interval when memory is tested by *recognition,* after the final free-recall test, which showed no effect. The authors' interpretation of this finding is important: They say that although maintenance rehearsal has no effect on free recall, it is nonetheless contributing some kind of useful information to secondary memory, information that supports recognition. They go on to conjecture that maintenance rehearsal may provide more and more associations between an item and the context in which it occurs, whereas the type of information processing that supports final free recall consists of association among the various words on the list (interitem associations). It is not that rote rehearsal is ineffective inherently, therefore; it is rather that it is a different learning process than the process that is most beneficial to free recall. These ideas will be introduced again in Chapter 11 in connection with the retrieval theory of Anderson and Bower (1972).

The independence of rehearsal and final free recall in the studies by Craik and Watkins and by Woodward *et al.* tells us that whereas rehearsal may be a necessary condition for making items accessible to free recall from secondary memory it is not a sufficient condition.

Alternatives to Transfer

Recently, such studies as those reviewed in the last section have led to revised conceptualizations of the relation between primary and secondary memory. These views have much in common but they are organized here around their various sources.

Atkinson and Shiffrin.   In emphasizing the nature of their rehearsal buffer as a control process rather than an invariant part of the memory structure, Atkinson and Shiffrin (1968) presented what amounted to an alternative to the transfer notion regarding how primary and secondary memory are organized. They stressed that it is processing capacity that is limited in short-term memory, not, as Waugh and Norman had assumed, a fixed storage capacity. A limitation on processing capacity means there can be varying amounts of storage space ' available in primary memory depending on how busy the subject is doing other, demanding mental operations. If the subject is engaged in complex encoding operations, Atkinson and Shiffrin state, he is likely to have a smaller primary-memory capacity, in terms of items, than if he is simply rehearsing as many items as possible at a time. However, this reduced primary-memory capacity is only the price paid, in terms of short-term retention, for a high level of registration in secondary memory. They specifically use the example of visual imagery as a control process that can work simultaneously to the disadvantage of primary memory and to the advantage of secondary memory. [This is of course just what Smith *et al.* (1971) found.]

> In our view, the maintenance and use of the [rehearsal] buffer is a process entirely under the control of the subject. Presumably a buffer is set up and used in an attempt to maximize performance in certain situations. In setting up a maximal-sized buffer, however, the subject is devoting all his effort to rehearsal and not engaging in other processes such as coding and hypothesis testing. In situations, therefore, where coding, long-term search, hypothesis testing, and other mechanisms appreciably improve performance, it is likely that a trade-off will occur in which the buffer size will be reduced and rehearsal may even become somewhat random while coding and other strategies increase [Atkinson & Shiffrin, 1968, p. 113].

Although Atkinson and Shiffrin thus embraced the view that encoding for primary and secondary memory could be reciprocally related, the idea was not used in their development of mathematical models. As we shall see in Chapter 9, they chose a task, continuous paired-associate learning, that would emphasize reliance on primary memory and discourage encoding for secondary memory.

Shulman. H. Shulman (1971) has advanced a similar proposition, which he called the *time-dependent encoding hypothesis.* According to this view, rehearsal in the phonological code and recoding into semantic format are time-dependent processes that must be traded off against one another or shared at the same time. Furthermore, the phonological code is more rapidly achieved than the semantic code. When the task demands large-capacity short-term retention the subjects do not trade off rehearsal capacity against more difficult semantic encoding but when the task demands semantic encoding that option exists. Shulman argued that given these two types of encoding it would be unnecessary further to assume two different memory stores; he proposed that either phonological or semantic encoding could exist in either primary or secondary memory and that therefore the distinction between these two stores was superfluous.

H. Shulman (1970) put these ideas to test in a situation similar to one that had been used by Bregman (1968). Subjects received a list of ten words and then a yes—no question concerning one of these ten words. If, after receiving the list, the subject saw the letter *I* he was to respond on the basis of whether or not a probe word was *identical* to one of the list words. If he saw the letter *H* he was to decide whether or not the probe word was a *homonym* of one of the list words. If he saw the letter *S,* he was to decide whether or not the probe word was a *synonym* of one of the list words. The idea was to show that subjects had these three types of information available, identity information, phonological information, and semantic information, even in a short-term memory probe task. Furthermore, the rate of presentation was varied between .35 and 1.4 sec per word; according to the time-dependent hypothesis there ought to be better encoding of semantic information with slow rates of presentation.

Shulman's main results are given in Figure 6.13. In the left panel are the proportions of correct responding, for all rates of presentation combined, as a function of serial position and type of test. In the right panel are the latencies of correct responses for the same conditions. Shulman argued that his data supported a role for semantic information in primary memory. Despite the lower accuracy and longer latencies of responses to semantic probes in the synonym condition, the shape of the serial-position curve was similar to that obtained with the other probe types. Because the shape of the serial-position function, particularly recency, defines primary memory, there must be semantic information involved in it. If there were not semantic encoding in primary memory we should have found the synonym serial-position curve to be flatter in the last positions than the other two curves. Also, Shulman found that slower rates of presentation improved accuracy in semantic tests but not in the other two types of test.

Baddeley (1972) has challenged Shulman's conclusions on the grounds that the subject may not be using semantic information even when performing the synonym test. The alternative possibility is that the subject uses the probe word to generate a candidate for membership in the list and then compares a phonological representation of the list against this newly generated probe. So, if the word SUBPOENA appeared on the list, the subject's ability to say "yes" to the probe SUMMONS might not mean he had stored the meaning of the word SUBPOENA; rather, it could mean only that he had generated SUBPOENA from

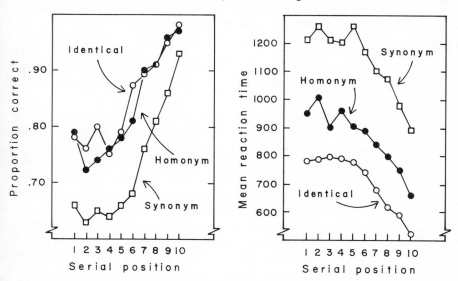

FIGURE 6.13 Probe test performance as a function of serial position and relation of probe to target item: (a) proportion correct; (b) reaction time. (After Shulman, 1970.)

SUMMONS at the time the probe was presented and tested SUBPOENA against the contents of a phonological store. Therefore, this particular experimental task may not be completely conclusive, although Shulman has pointed out that Baddeley's mechanism requires an unrealistically fast semantic-generation process.

Craik and Lockhart. We have been at pains to emphasize, earlier in this chapter, that the evidence for two-process theory in memory demands we have two of something, but it does not specify what. It is largely a matter of taste whether to propose two different memory stores, on the one hand, or a single store with two different codes, phonological and semantic, on the other hand. Craik and Lockhart (1972), recognizing this, have suggested the idea of two separate stores has outlived its usefulness. They propose instead that we view memory as a byproduct of perceptual information processing. The important aspect of perceptual processing is that it occurs at numerous levels of complexity—sensory, phonological, and semantic, for example. Whatever the chronological order in which various types of encoding occur, we may speak of some kinds of processing as *deep* and others as *shallow,* with reference to semantic content. For example, processing visual features would be shallow by this criterion, whereas generation of a verbal associate to an item, or integrating it into a meaningful visual image, would be deep. Craik and Lockhart propose that, as a general rule, the deeper the type of processing, the more persistent the memory trace that is a byproduct of that processing. The experiment on incidental learning by Hyde and Jenkins (1969), which is described in Chapter 1, is a good empirical framework for this concept. As Craik and Lockhart concede, these ideas are formally equivalent to assuming a different memory store associated with each type of coding. However, they maintain that one is led to ask different, more provocative, questions about memory with the "depth of processing" view.

Craik and Lockhart (1972) propose that information can be recirculated within one level of processing, as well as advanced toward deeper levels. Although they consider that this rehearsal can occur at any level in principle, it is at the phonological level that they suggest such maintenance is easiest, presumably because of the association of speech with that level. The term *primary memory* is applied to this type of rehearsal and the assumption is made that it ". . . merely prolongs an item's high accessibility without leading to formation of a more permanent memory trace" (Craik & Lockhart, 1972, p. 676). Once attention is diverted from information undergoing this maintenance rehearsal, it is assumed to be lost at a rate depending on how far the analysis has proceeded toward semantic depth. Therefore, the amount of time spent in shallow, maintenance processing should have no effect on registration of information in permanent memory. This is, of course, exactly what Craik and Watkins and Woodward *et al.* observed in the studies we have described above.

Like Atkinson and Shiffrin and like Shulman, Craik and Lockhart conceive of a reciprocity between maintenance processing, which is fine so long as there is no diversion of attention, and what they call elaborative processing, in which deeper levels are achieved and in which there are therefore slower long-range decay rates. When rehearsal or processing leads to deeper analysis in terms of meaning, then additional processing time should enhance recall.

With the Craik–Lockhart hypothesis the theoretical distinction is between maintaining the same level of processing or advancing toward deeper levels. The distinction between maintenance and elaboration is the same whatever level we are considering. One would presumably have the option, therefore, when at the level of denotative meaning, of maintaining that code or advancing toward connotative meaning. In this sense the maintenance–elaboration distinction is independent of the actual code system. This makes the Craik–Lockhart position somewhat more abstract than the Shulman position, according to which the essential distinction is between coding in semantic versus phonological form. In the Atkinson–Shiffrin theory, the distinction is between codes, also, but the codes are found in fundamentally separate memory stores. The common features of these three sets of ideas are that they recognize the necessity for some process dualism in memory processing, and that they maintain that subjects voluntarily use the two subsystems differentially according to demands of the task at hand and limited processing capacity.

The conceptual distinction between maintenance and elaborative rehearsal is important but it does not rule out the possibility that in many situations the two types of processing covary with one another. Information that is not still present in physical form must somehow be held in a state of accessibility during the search for a good elaborative coding scheme. For example, while seeking a good visual image linking the words MELODY and CONSPIRACY, the subject needs somehow to prevent the decay or displacement of these words from primary memory and even though such maintenance of them does not directly affect their long-range recallability it does permit them to be encoded in an effective mnemonic. Therefore, maintenance rehearsal should not be maligned as an inferior mental operation for two reasons. First, as the recognition results of Woodward et al. (1973) showed, rote repetition can directly facilitate long-term recognition without facilitating long-term recall. Second, maintenance rehearsal serves to provide the occasion for elaborative encoding by preventing decay or displacement of information during the search for an elaborative code. In some situations we should expect a complementary relation between the two types of processing rather than a reciprocal one, even though it was very important to have had the demonstration we have just received that maintenance and elaborative rehearsal are separable.

The major point, however, is that reciprocity between maintenance and elaborative processing allows a ready explanation of the phenomenon of functional dissociation when primary and secondary components seem to be negatively correlated. For example, the data on arousal and memory (Kleinsmith & Kaplan, 1963) are less puzzling in this light: Certain items are more likely to receive elaborative processing than others in presentation. These items are subject to poor recall immediately, relative to words that receive maintenance processing, but to better recall at longer intervals. The high arousal elicited by presentation of these words is either the cause or the byproduct of this elaborative processing. In either case, associating high-arousal words with elaborative processing brings this phenomenon into line with those we have been discussing in this section.

More on the Recency Effect in Free Recall

To an extraordinary degree the concept of primary memory has been tied to the recency effect in free recall. We close the chapter with two recent experiments on this phenomenon. One of these ties together the negative-recency effect of Craik with the distinction between maintenance and elaborative rehearsal. The other provides a mild degree of discord, lest we allow ourselves too complacent an attitude on the "complete understanding" of the recency effect.

The Craik and Lockhart framework suggests that subjects may employ certain strategies, during presentation of a free-recall list, to maximize performance by means of distributing efforts between maintenance and elaborative rehearsal. If the subject knows when the end of the list is coming, it is possible that he increasingly abandons efforts at elaborative coding in favor of maintenance rehearsal. This strategy would pay off for the last few items in immediate recall, but the toll of nonelaboration would be evident in final recall. Watkins and Watkins (1974) have put this reasoning to test. They manipulated whether or not the subject could accurately gauge how soon the end of the list was to occur. In one condition, subjects checked off cells arranged in columns as each word in the list was presented. There were the same number of cells as there were words in the list, so subjects knew exactly when the last word would occur. In the other condition there was a column of cells also but there were always more cells than list items. The idea was that with known list length the subject would adopt a recency strategy of shallow or maintenance processing, which would lead to good immediate recall of the recency items and poor final recall of them. However, the subjects who were ignorant of list length would persist in an elaborative strategy until the end.

The hypothesis was verified impressively. With known list length immediate recall of recency items was enhanced but final recall of recency items was inhibited relative to performance in the condition with unknown list length. This is just as would be expected on the basis of a tradeoff between elaboration and maintenance under voluntary control. Notice that the Watkins' data provide us with another example of a negative correlation between initial and delayed recall.

A long-term recency effect in free recall. It is tempting to conclude this chapter on the harmonious note sounded by the Watkins' experiment. Their study ties together many of the themes stressed here, including the association of the recency effect with a limited-capacity rehearsal buffer, the dissociation of primary and secondary memory through the phenomenon of negative recency, and the distinction between maintenance and elaborative rehearsal. There is, however, one final experimental finding that needs to be added in order to convey an accurate outline of what is known about the recency effect and this finding poses something of a problem for virtually all of the views presented earlier in the chapter. Without doubt the long-term recency effect discovered by R. A. Bjork and Whitten (1974) will ultimately be shown to be consistent with our current concept of primary memory, both taking their places as parts of some more general explanatory scheme. In the meantime, we are forced to treat it is an isolated but important finding with mildly troublesome implications for the concept of primary memory.

R. A. Bjork and Whitten (1974) were interested in a condition with periods of mental arithmetic interpolated within a free-recall list. The usual comparison (Glanzer & Cunitz, 1966) is between a condition with words presented for immediate free recall versus a condition with the words followed by a period of mental arithmetic and then the free-recall test. This last comparison produces the result, which Bjork and Whitten have replicated in one of their experiments, that interpolation of arithmetic after the last memory item reduces or eliminates the recency effect. The interpretation is, of course, that the mental arithmetic displaces the contents of primary memory, leaving the subject with only second-ary memory.

In the two conditions of main interest here, Bjork and Whitten inserted a period of 12 sec of mental arithmetic between each of 13 pairs of words (the words were presented in pairs only for convenience and the subjects were under free-recall instructions). In what we may call these two *spaced presentation* conditions, there was one with an additional period of 30 sec of mental arithmetic before recall and another with immediate recall. The major finding was a substantial recency effect in the spaced presentation conditions, not as large a recency effect as that obtained with no interpolated arithmetic but unmistakable and of equivalent size in the immediate-recall and in the delayed-recall groups. The most interesting comparison is between the two conditions where there are 30 sec of mental arithmetic just before recall. In one the words were presented without interruption and in the other they were presented with the 12-sec distractor task between every other word. Because the same amount of distraction occurred between the last pair of items and recall in these two conditions, there should have been no influence of primary memory on either. Indeed, if primary-memory capacity is larger than two words, the condition with spaced presentation should have been even more depleted of primary memory because all but the last pair of words would have been cleared by the inter-presentation distractor periods.

Yet, there was a clear and sizeable recency effect in the condition with spacing of items during presentation, even though that same condition had enough distractor activity after presentation of all the words to remove the recency effect obtained with conventional (massed) presentation. The result has been replicated by Tzeng (1973a) and by Wilkinson (1975). The important logical sequence to keep in mind is this: with conventional presentation of a free-recall list, recency is destroyed by adding a period of distractor activity. The recency effect can then be restored by adding additional distractor activity to the intervals between words in presentation.

One manner for an adherent to the primary-memory explanation of recency to escape the anomalous finding of a long-term recency effect is to deny that these two recency effects are in fact caused by the same mechanism. It is possible that by spacing the interpresentation intervals with periods of a distractor task, Bjork and Whitten are introducing some totally new factor into the situation. This new factor happens to produce a recency effect but by no means the same recency effect as that supplied by the primary memory mechanism. For example, surrounding the last item in a visually presented series with a colored background might well enhance recall of the last item even were primary memory removed by an interpolated distractor task.

Bjork and Whitten chose to provide an alternative theory of the recency effect in general, one that could account both for the previous results supporting the concept of primary memory and also for their own demonstration of a long-term recency effect. Their model is described in Chapter 12 in some detail. In brief, they suggest that recency occurs to the extent items in a series form a distinc-tively ordered array. Whether an item is distinct from nearby items depends, they suggest, on some type of Weber–Fechner ratio expressing its age relative to the ages of the neighboring items. In a conventional procedure with testing of free recall immediately after the last word is presented, the relative age of the last item to the next to last is quite small. However, if the time of recall is delayed by a distractor task, then the relative ages of these two items become similar. (Imagine a distractor task of 1 hr in order to see the ratio of the last item's age relative to the age of its predecessor becoming vanishingly small.) Now, when the relative ages of items in the recency segment have been more nearly equalized by such a period of postpresentation distractor activity, the distinctiveness may again be restored by additional spacing of the memory items from one another during presentation by the distractor activity. This is therefore a convenient way in which to rationalize the original recency effect with conventional procedures, the removal of this effect by a distractor task after the last item and its restoration by the Bjork and Whitten manipulation.

The Bjork–Whitten model of temporal discriminability has the disadvantage of making contact only poorly with the rest of the literature on primary memory. However, it should be noted that it finds excellent independent support elsewhere in the literature on serial-position effects (see Chapter 12). Both the model and the finding on which it is based pose significant challenges for future workers in this area.

SUMMARY

Once the study of short-term memory was enabled by methodological developments, it was of interest to know whether the same principles applied to it as to long-term memory. Actually, it is now widely appreciated that both long-term memory tasks and short-term memory tasks are interdependent expressions of primary and secondary memory. This is easiest to see in the free-recall task, with its recency segment generally attributed to primary memory and its asymptote attributed to secondary memory. In the Brown–Peterson short-term memory task there is a similar attribution of the slope of the forgetting function to primary memory and of the asymptote to secondary memory.

The arguments that primary and secondary memory should be considered as separate memory systems are actually instances of a more general proposition that there is a need for a two-factor theory of memory in order to deal with what we have been calling "functional dissociation." Functional dissociation refers to our ability as experimenters to affect components of the whole recall process independently in such situations as, but not limited to, those mentioned in the preceding paragraph. When functional dissociation extends to the demonstration of variables with opposite effects on the two components, it provides negative evidence for the simple transfer model relating primary and secondary memory proposed by Waugh and Norman.

The measurement of primary memory capacity is difficult because no measurement technique is theoretically neutral; yet at the same time it is reassuring, because the estimates of capacity usually turn out to be about the same (2.5 words or so) whatever method is used. The stability of primary memory capacity across measurement techniques and across different populations of subjects argues that it is quite a fundamental structural feature of human information processing.

Despite widespread early belief to the contrary, primary memory is probably not inherently phonological. The importance of speech to much of information processing and especially to most laboratory memory tasks makes it common for there to be a heavy phonological component, but the equation of primary memory with conscious attention makes it clear that the capacity can be invested in other forms of coding besides verbal. This notion that primary memory is less a *place* and more a *process* is consistent with evolving ideas on the relation between primary memory and more permanent modes of storage. The simple transfer notion has given way to the distinction between maintenance rehearsal, which serves to keep relatively large amounts of information accessible, and elaborative rehearsal, which handles quantitatively less information but results in more lasting storage.

This same sense of primary memory as a process instead of a memory store has been leading workers in the area more and more into what we may term the psychology of learning rather than the psychology of memory (given the rather arbitrary separation of the acquisition stage into the learning domain with retention and retrieval classed together in the memory domain). In the next chapter we shall direct our attention specifically to the problem of retention in the context of the short-term memory situation.

7
Forgetting in
Short-Term Memory

In this chapter we withdraw somewhat from the abstractions of primary and secondary memory in order to examine a more tangible problem for theoretical analysis: A subject who has demonstrably learned a small message can under some conditions forget it within less than a minute if he is prevented from rehearsal by a distractor task. Why? Short-term memory tasks of this sort have offered persuasive evidence for choosing from among conflicting theories of forgetting and the data are relevant to forgetting from both primary and secondary memory.

THEORIES OF FORGETTING

There are three major theoretical approaches to the loss of information in short-term memory, *decay, displacement,* and *interference,* and there is more than one way of organizing these three approaches. According to decay theory, the only function of a distractor task in the Brown–Peterson paradigm (the main situation of concern in this chapter) is to prevent the subject from thinking about the memory stimulus; the material processed in the distractor task makes no contribution of its own to forgetting. The displacement and interference positions, however, although not belittling the facilitation that can result from rehearsal, maintain that the contents of the distractor task are crucial in producing the loss, either (1) through displacing relevant information from a fixed-capacity store or (2) by producing some type of confusion between similar traces. On this criterion the displacement and interference theories, together, oppose decay theory. In another sense, however, it is the decay and displacement approaches that are similar to one another and in conflict with the interference approach. Both the decay and displacement theories attribute forgetting to the structural properties of the memory system, its spatial capacity (displacement) or temporal limits (decay), rather than to the information placed in the system. The interference theory, in contrast, attaches great importance to the nature of the particular items that are placed in storage together.

We shall first look at efforts to choose between the decay approach and displacement—interference approaches; that is, our first concern is whether there is an active contribution to forgetting on the part of the distractor task. Then, there are described several experiments that discriminate among theoretical positions on the role of *similarity* in short-term memory for the purpose of comparing the displacement and interference theories. Finally, these ideas are focused on the empirical laws of forgetting that have been generated from the Brown—Peterson task. In the course of explaining each theory the one or two experiments that are most crucial in supporting or refuting it are presented concurrently.

Decay Theory

Brown (1958) proposed that short-term retention is governed by a principle of decay with the passage of time but that rehearsal of information can postpone the onset of this decay. The simplest prediction that can be derived from Brown's "rehearsal and fading trace" theory is that a period of overt rehearsal between input and the distractor task should have no effect on the slope of the forgetting function once the distractor task starts. Hellyer (1962) reported data that seemed to violate this expectation in showing a regular family of curves with decreasing slopes as a function of the amount of overt rehearsal given items before onset of the interpolated task (see Figure 7.1a). It therefore appeared that allowing rehearsal retarded the loss of information during the retention interval. However, if we add to the rehearsal—decay theory a distinction between primary and secondary memory, with the stipulation that our interest is in primary-memory forgetting mechanisms, then the Hellyer data pose no problem—the effect of repetitions may be occurring entirely on the asymptotic (secondary-memory) portion of the retention curves. If the effects of repeated exposure on short-term memory were entirely a primary-memory effect, we would have a family of functions approaching the same asymptote at different rates, as shown in Figure 7.1b. Needless to say, it takes a large and careful experiment to distinguish these three possibilities. However, because we know (from other experimental tasks) that repetition affects secondary memory and because the data of Figure 7.1a show little in the way of differential slopes approaching asymptotic performance, the conservative conclusion is that repetition affects only the secondary-memory component. In this respect the Hellyer experiment is an important one in showing how thoroughly blended primary- and secondary-memory processes become in the short-term memory task.

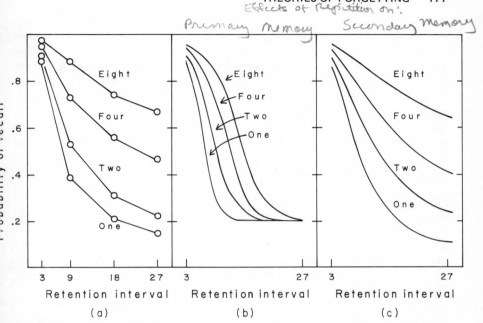

FIGURE 7.1 (a) Recall probability as a function of retention interval and number of presentations (1, 2, 4, and 8). (b) and (c) show, respectively, the ideal data pattern if the effects of repetition were entirely on primary memory or entirely on secondary memory. (After Hellyer, 1962.)

Actually, whether rehearsal strengthens the memory trace or not is an independent issue from whether decay is a plausible hypothesis for forgetting. More crucial data come from experiments in which a constant amount of information is differently arranged across the passage of time. If decay theory is to be believed then the fewer seconds there are separating input and output of a given element the better performance ought to be. There are numerous experiments on immediate memory where the rate of presentation has been varied (Posner, 1963) but their interpretation is troublesome for two reasons. First, the results are quite inconsistent, with fast rates leading sometimes to better performance than slow rates, sometimes the other way around, and sometimes no difference. Second, the supposed advantage of fast presentation rates, that information has to be held in memory for less time than with slow rates, is balanced by a second factor. This second factor is a combined process of higher-order organization, grouping, and rehearsal, which serves to improve recall and which is easier at slow presentation rates than at fast presentation rates. Therefore, immediate-memory presentation rate is not a critical variable for testing decay.

The Waugh and Norman (1965) experiment, detailed in Chapter 6, was designed to be a better test of decay in that, through instruction, the subjects were led not to rehearse during presentation. The list of digits was read at either a four per second rate or a one per second rate prior to presentation of the probe digit. If decay were the only factor responsible for forgetting then there should have been a fourfold advantage to the fast rate. However, the results showed almost no difference. Waugh and Norman concluded that primary memory loses information because of displacement from subsequent input and prior output rather than because of the passage of time. Correspondingly, if experiments on free recall are examined separately for primary and secondary memory, it is found that presentation rate has its effect on secondary memory exclusively (Bernbach, 1975; Glanzer, 1972).

The Wingfield–Byrnes experiment. The best evidence favoring a role for decay with time is found in a recent report by Wingfield and Byrnes (1972). Indeed, this report contains what seems to be the only indication in the literature that real time, time on a wristwatch, is directly related to forgetting. These authors used a technique invented by Broadbent (1954) in which the subject receives two simultaneous messages of three digits each, one message in each of two channels, rather than a single list of six digits. In Broadbent's experiment the two lists of three digits each were fed into the two ears, with a left–right pair occurring at a rate of two pairs per second. Broadbent's interest was in the order of report as well as accuracy. He found that subjects tended to recall first the entire message from one channel and then the message from the other channel rather than recalling in the order of arrival, that is, first left–right pair, second left–right pair, and then third left–right pair. The subjects reported everything that had occurred on the left side before turning to the right-side message or vice versa. Broadbent concluded that the other strategy, recalling pair by pair on the basis of the order of arrival, was difficult because it required switching back and forth between channels. His explanation for the favored ear by ear strategy was that subjects attended to one channel while holding the contents of the other in a buffer memory.

Wingfield and Byrnes (1972) adopted the Broadbent method to their purposes with three modifications. They used channels separated by voice quality, a male versus female recording voice, rather than by spatial separation. Also, they measured the exact times at which subjects recalled each list item. Finally, they dictated to their subjects which recall system to employ; some recalled channel by channel, male first then female or vice versa, and others recalled the first pair of digits, then the second, and then the third. Figure 7.2a shows the results of the study for the two groups separately. On each panel is the relation between *recall latency,* the time between recall of an element and presentation of the last pair of digits, and *recall accuracy,* with six bars in each figure corresponding to the six output positions. We see first of all that the channel by channel strategy is superior to the pair by pair strategy both with respect to overall accuracy (look at the height of each bar) and with respect to latency (look at how far

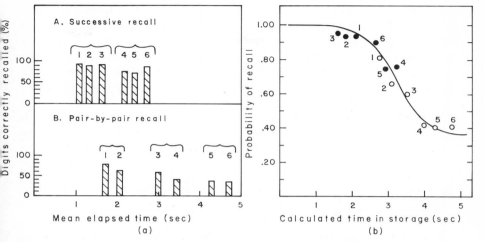

FIGURE 7.2   Results of the Wingfield and Byrnes (1972) study: The filled circles represent the successive recall mode and the open circles represent the pair-by-pair recall mode. (a) Recall latency since the last input digits (on the horizontal axis) and accuracy (on the vertical axis) separately for each item in the two recall mode conditions. (b) Both recall conditions plotted on the same function relating accuracy in recalling a digit to the estimated time it spent in storage. (After Wingfield & Byrnes, 1972.)

each bar is to the right along the horizontal axis). Within each graph, there is also a decreasing accuracy across the six output positions.

Now what is the relation between the latency advantage and the accuracy advantage for the channel by channel order of recall? Wingfield and Byrnes reasoned that according to the decay theory the pair by pair order might show up as worse simply because it occured later, after traces had decayed further, than the channel strategy. They were in a position to examine this relation because, unlike previous workers, they had recorded recall latencies for this task. In Figure 7.2b is a plotting of recall accuracy for both conditions, digit by digit according to output order from one to six, as a function of the total time in memory. The total time in memory is found through knowledge of both the presentation rate and the latency of emission. Notice that because under the channel strategy subjects recalled the items faster than they had been presented, the third item recalled was stored for less time than the first recalled.

The significance of the composite curve in Figure 7.2b is that all the data, from both recall conditions, are reasonably well fit by a single continuous decay function. Moreover, it is properly a decay function because chronological time is the correlate of accuracy and not the number of intervening events. The suggestion is that information in both conditions undergoes the same history of temporal decay, but for some unspecified reason the pair by pair strategy leads to later recall and therefore more decay. We do not in one sense have a complete picture of why the pair by pair strategy is worse than the channel by channel strategy; that requires some idea of why there is a difference in response latencies in the two situations. However, there is the correlation, in the Wingfield—Byrnes study, between performance and time with number of intervening events held constant and that correlation is uniquely consistent with the decay theory of memory.

In terms of a componential analysis, however, the assignment of decay to primary memory is more problematic than the assertion that decay occurs. The trouble is that performance in the Wingfield and Byrnes study may include a memory component from the echoic system (see Chapter 3). Great care is needed to associate an obtained decay effect with primary memory exclusively; in this case it may be useful to replicate the experiment under conditions of visual presentation, in which there is probably no contribution from sensory memory.

There are not many other comparative tests of decay theory in terms of experimental predictions. Norman and Rumelhart (1970), however, have performed another type of comparison. They constructed a comprehensive model of human memory with explicit mathematical assumptions for initial perception, storage, and different modes of retrieval. They devised two alternative submodels for the loss of information in short-term memory, the time-dependent decay model and the item-dependent decay model, corresponding to what we have been calling the "decay" and "displacement" theories, respectively. These two versions of the overall model were then applied to data of Murdock (1962) from free recall with varying presentation rates (Fig. 6.3). They found that the data were fit better by the time-decay model than by the item-decay, or displacement, model. This is a second comparison, therefore, where a time-dependent process seems favored. However, Norman and Rumelhart were quite guarded in generalizing from this result. They observed that there might be a dependence between the comparison of the two submodels and the nature of the overall model in which the submodels were integrated. As they point out, their result stands in contradiction to the finding that with varied presentation rate in the probe task (Waugh & Norman, 1965) it seems to be the number of intervening items that most directly affects performance.

The Reitman technique. Reitman (1971) introduced a novel experimental test for choosing between decay and displacement or interference ideas. As she pointed out, most distractor tasks have two potential effects during the retention interval of a Brown—Peterson task: They prevent rehearsal and they also contribute agents of displacement to the store. To separate out these different effects it would be important to find a task that effectively prevented rehearsal but had no content of its own—a mental vacuum. One may propose that sleep is such a state, but we cannot induce sleep for punctate intervals of 30 sec or less during an ongoing experiment and, furthermore, there is always the problem of dreaming.

Reitman attempted to operationalize the mental-vacuum state with a *tonal detection task* in which, during a retention interval, the subject was required to listen intently for a faint tone. The tone occurred fairly rarely and was so faint that subjects ordinarily could detect it only half the time even if they were doing nothing else. The idea was that the subject would be in a state of straining to hear tones but otherwise unoccupied mentally. This tonal detection task was compared with another detection task in which a stream of syllables was presented at a two per second rate. The syllable was always "doh" except occasionally the syllable "toh" would occur and it was the subject's job to detect the occurrence of "toh" against the background of "doh." This task was adjusted such that on the average performance was equivalent, at around 50%, to performance in detecting tones against a background of noise. The tonal detection task and the syllable detection tasks are therefore about equally difficult but only the syllable task can be said to include any content that may displace or interfere with memory information.

A group of three four-letter words are presented on the screen first, followed by a 15-sec period of detection, either syllabic or tonal, and then a signal to recall the words in order. The main result of the experiment was extremely high memory performance following a retention interval filled with the tonal detection task: The mean score after tonal detection was 92% correct and the median was 100% correct (13 of the 18 subjects had perfect scores and five had scores ranging from 67 to 89%). However, when the syllabic distractor task was used, there was more forgetting—77% or 70% correct depending on whether or not a vocal detection response was used. Detection performance itself was roughly equal in the tonal and syllabic tasks so we could not argue that the poorer memory performance with syllables was caused by a more difficult distractor task. Rather, it would seem that the presence of verbal content in the syllabic task and the absence of verbal content in the tonal task were responsible for the memory difference. If decay were operating there should have been losses with both distractor tasks.

However, what about the possibility that subjects were able to rehearse the memory words better in the tonal task than in the syllabic task? Reitman concluded originally (1971) that rehearsal was not a factor in her experiment because (1) subjects' introspective reports indicated they had not been able to rehearse during the tonal detection task, and (2) measurement of detection in the absence of a memory load showed equivalent scores to those obtained when detection occurred in the presence of a memory load. The case against decay theory, of course, rests on the assumption that tonal detection is indeed a mental vacuum, with neither a contribution from new interfering materials nor a compensatory process of rehearsal.

Unfortunately, a more recent look at the problem of rehearsal has forced Reitman (1974) to reverse her earlier claim that subjects do not rehearse the memory stimulus during tonal detection. The missing part of the earlier argument (Reitman, 1971) was that rehearsal, if it were occurring, would in fact impair performance on the detection task; otherwise, there would be no reason to attach any importance to the observation that detection during memory was just as good as detection alone. In other words, if rehearsal and tonal detection did not depend on the same limited-capacity mechanism then it would be no surprise that detection did not suffer when subjects had words to keep in mind and possibly to rehearse. Of course, if subjects were rehearsing in the Reitman situation, moreover, then it is no surprise, in turn, that there is no evidence for decay of traces during the detection task.

In the 1974 study Reitman encouraged subjects to engage in covert rehearsal during the time they were engaged in tonal detection. (She also increased the size of the memory items from three words to five words, in order to avoid possible ceiling effects in recall.) The results showed that *condoned* covert rehearsal could indeed be inferred from decrements in tonal detection; when subjects were asked to rehearse the relevant memory item during tonal detection they were poorer at detecting the signal tones than when they were told not to rehearse. So far so good: This observation essentially upholds the validity of the method (see Shiffrin, 1973, Experiment 2, for a related study).

However, Reitman's next step was to use detection-task scores with new analytic criteria in order to identify subjects who were covertly rehearsing when instructed not to. Briefly, she identified as rehearsers those subjects whose detection in fact suffered when there was a memory load as opposed to when there was not (even though in the earlier study, for all subjects taken together, there had not been a significant decrement in detection). When such "rehearsers" were identified and discarded, the remaining "nonrehearsers" showed a reliable and substantial memory loss during the time they were trying to detect tones. In other words, Reitman's newer study shows that there is reciprocity between tonal detection and covert rehearsal. When this reciprocity is used to identify surreptitious rehearsers, the remaining subjects, for whom the term "mental vacuum" is more appropriate, showed evidence of decay. Reitman (1974) concluded that in her earlier study there had either been a ceiling effect on memory performance or the subjects had been covertly rehearsing but the experiment was not powerful enough to detect it.

To the extent one is willing to buy the proposition that tonal detection approximates conditions of a mental vacuum, then, the Reitman situation tends to support the decay theory. At least, this research (especially with the clarification of Reitman, 1974) places the burden on displacement or interference theories to explain how detection provides a source of interfering material to short-term memory for words.

Displacement and Interference

This concludes our discussion of the principle of decay, as such; the acid bath theory of Posner, to be discussed presently, has some properties of a decay theory but not others. I have presented what are perhaps the only serious pieces of evidence for an unadorned decay principle despite the very widespread informal acceptance of decay and the predisposition of many theorists favoring it. It is natural that this should be so, because a decay principle is essentially an admission of ignorance—ignorance as to what observable antecedent conditions may produce forgetting. The form evidence must take in order to support decay is often a demonstration that such other factors as we know about are unlikely to operate in a situation in which there is nonetheless forgetting. This is the argument behind Reitman's technique. The trouble is, however, that it is difficult to assert with any conviction that all other possible causes of forgetting have been removed, such as, for example, daydreaming during tonal detection in Reitman's study. The great bulk of evidence collected so far with the various short-term memory techniques has favored the deleterious contributions of the interpolated materal as being the causative factor in forgetting, through either displacement or interference. It is now time to consider the difference between these two positions.

The choice between displacement and interference turns mainly on the role that similarity plays in short-term memory. A pure displacement theory, such as those of Waugh and Norman (1965) and Atkinson and Shiffrin (1968), does not include statements covering the degree of similarity between what is being retained and what is being interpolated in order to displace it. For example, Waugh and Norman assigned exactly the same interfering role to digits in the interpolated backward-counting task of Peterson and Peterson (1959) as they did to words coming between input and output of a particular item in the free-recall task. However, digits are obviously not nearly as similar to three-letter stimuli as words are to other words. Therefore, a displacement position is a structural hypothesis about forgetting: If there are only n slots in the primary-memory system then the process of displacement begins once $n + 1$ items have arrived and it makes little or no difference what these items are.

Despite the attractive simplicity of such a pure displacement theory, even its original advocates probably do not take seriously its extreme implications. For example, would interpolated music or calisthenics operate on verbal memory in the same way as interpolated counting? Waugh and Norman (1968) showed that the interpolation of predictable events had a reliably smaller effect on short-term retention than the interpolation of unpredictable events. Because no theorist has seemed inclined to insist that similarity makes absolutely no difference in the displacement process, therefore, and because a displacement theory must take on the character of an interference theory if it is modified to accommodate similarity factors, we shall turn to interference theories. It should be kept in mind, however, that some similarity effects in short-term memory may turn out to be attributable to the secondary-memory component rather than to primary memory. Only Waugh and Norman (1968), of those that have considered the problem, have taken measures they consider adequate to assign the effects of interpolated-task materials (of predictability in their case) to primary memory.

The general nature of interference theories is to provide a way of rationalizing the effects of similarity in memory. There are three principal versions of interference theory, which are in fact three very different hypotheses. The first, an application to short-term retention of the classical interference theory of long-term memory, to be described in more detail in Chapter 8, is discussed later when we take up the data on proactive inhibition. The other two interference positions, Posner's "acid bath" theory and Estes' "associative coding" theory, are taken up now.

Acid bath and the locus of similarity effects. The acid bath formulation (Posner & Konick, 1966) is a response to the problem of similarity in short-term memory, particularly in terms of a stage analysis of performance. Similarity effects seem to pose a serious difficulty for a decay theory in that similarity is defined by relations among elements, which, according to the basic decay principle, should not matter. However, the presence of similarity-based confusions in recall is handled by a more elaborated decay theory (Conrad, 1965, 1967) with the argument that it is only after forgetting has occurred that similarity comes into the picture. We want to consider the decay theory's position on similarity in detail, now, because the acid bath theory makes sense only in contrast to it and the interference theory.

Conrad's (1965, 1967) position is that memory traces fade with the passage of time, until, at the moment of retrieval, the subject is up against the requirement to emit a response. He then examines his partially decayed traces and selects some response that matches whatever features of the stimulus remain. If only the vowel sound /i/ ("ee") is left, in a letter-memory study, then the subject may be equally likely to choose B, C, D, or some other rhyming letter. However, according to Conrad (1965), the subject selects only from among items that are available in the current memory store, so if the vocabulary includes only B and D from the letters of the alphabet in that particular rhyming set then the choice does not result in other letters, such as C. It follows from these general lines of argument that performance ought to be worse with a similar vocabulary than with a heterogeneous one: Say the subject receives B and remembers only the phoneme /i/, from it, later. If B is the only letter in the vocabulary with the /i/ phoneme, then the subject may appear to have remembered the letter, although in fact he has only reconstructed that it must have been B. However, if the vocabulary has included four letters from this set, then his chances are only 25% of being correct on the basis of the phonemic information that /i/ has been the vowel sound. So Conrad's theory predicts worse performance when there is high phonological similarity in an experimental vocabulary than when there is not, as was found by Conrad and Hull (1964). The main point for now is that the similarity effect occurs at the *retrieval stage* according to this form of decay theory.

According to a version of interference theory based on either McGeoch's original formulation of response competition or based on the more complicated unlearning–spontaneous-recovery mechanisms (see Chapter 8), similarity inhibits performance through competition at the time of retrieval: because the letters B and P are similar, their associations to other letters in the string entail more competitive relationships than if they were more distinct. The interference and decay views clearly differ in that decay theory says similarity effects are the consequence of forgetting, whereas the interference theory says similarity causes the forgetting. However, as Posner and Konick (1966) have pointed out, they are similar, these two theories, in placing the locus of similarity effects in the retrieval stage rather than in storage or acquisition.

In contrast, the acid bath theory holds that traces decay interactively during the retention interval, the rate of spontaneous decay being higher if there are similar items stored together than if not. By analogy, the number of items all in store at the same time is like the amount of acid into which memory traces are plunged and the similarity among them is like the concentration of acid. So when a memory stimulus is high in phonological similarity, the elements within it should be lost at a greater rate during the retention interval than when the item contains elements low in phonological similarity. Here, obviously, the effect of similarity is occurring at storage rather than at retrieval.

The test of the acid bath hypothesis conducted by Posner and Konick was based on the proposition that the size of a phonological similarity effect should be a function only of how long information had been in storage and not a function of other variables known to have an influence on performance. Their experiment included variation in length of the retention interval and in the difficulty of an interpolated task. For present purposes, the major dependent variable was not just the level of performance but, more importantly, the degree of effect of phonological similarity, that is, how much performance was hurt by similarity. According to the decay and interference theories, which hold that similarity has its effect at retrieval, the size of the similarity effect should depend on how strong the correct trace is relative to potentially competing, or confusing, incorrect traces. It ought not to matter whether the correct trace is relatively weakened by a long period of time in storage or by a shorter period of time in storage but accompanied by a difficult distractor task. In other words, there ought to be a tradeoff between storage time and interpolated-task difficulty according to the decay and interference theories.

According to the acid bath theory, however, the size of the similarity effect should depend only on the time in storage and not on the difficulty of the interpolated task. Take an extreme example: Imagine that normally the memory trace is weakened to a level of 17% after a 20-sec interpolated period of relatively easy mental arithmetic. Now, consider an interpolated task that is so difficult that performance drops to 17% in only 1 sec. For the decay and interference theories, there should be the same influence of similarity in these two cases because the amount of impairment by similarity depends on the strength of the correct memory, 17%. However, according to the acid bath view, there should be no effect of similarity to speak of in the 1-sec difficult-task condition because 1 sec is not long enough for a greater rate of time decay to have its effect.

To test this reasoning Posner and Konick (1966, Experiments III and IV) had subjects remember three-consonant stimuli in a Brown–Peterson situation, with 0, 5, 10, or 20 sec of either an easy or a hard distractor task. The stimulus vocabulary used to construct the memory items was either high or low in phonological confusability–B, C, D, P, T, V, Z, or H, J, L, N, Q, R, X, Y. The results are shown in Figure 7.3c; above are idealized predictions based on the acid bath theory (Figure 7.3b) and the decay or interference theories (Figure 7.3a).

Consider the predictions first. According to the acid bath prediction, there ought to be no interaction between phonological similarity and interpolated-task difficulty; however, there should be an interaction between phonological similarity and retention interval, with larger similarity effects at long retention intervals where differential decay rates have had a chance to show up. This prediction was borne out by the data: The amount of decrement in performance caused by going from low similarity to high similarity was the same for the easy and hard tasks, but it was greater at long retention intervals than at short retention intervals. Figure 7.3c shows the effectiveness of similarity in changing performance—scores on the high-similarity items minus scores on the low-similarity items—as a function of both task difficulty and retention interval. There was no tendency for the size of the similarity effect to depend on task difficulty, but it did depend on retention interval. These findings are consistent with the view that similarity is having its effect during the retention interval and inconsistent with either the decay account of similarity or the traditional interference account.

We have presented the acid bath theory at some length because it is an ingenious hypothesis, strikingly different from competing theoretical positions in the field of short-term memory, and because the associated experiments by Posner and Konick are models of subtle derivation linking hypothesis and test. Unfortunately, the Posner and Konick (1966) research is nearly the only positive evidential base for the theory (however, see a related study by Reicher, Ligon, & Conrad, 1969). We must not entertain any longer a theoretical position that is supported by only a single test, however brilliant that test is.

Besides, there are other grounds for rejecting the acid bath theory as a general position on forgetting. The basis for this statement is seen in an experiment by

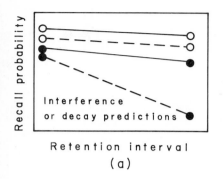

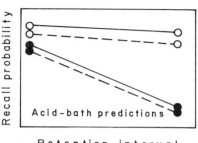

Task	Interval (sec)			
	0	5	10	20
Easy	3.6[a]	14.7	12.6	20.0
Hard	4.9	14.7	11.8	15.0

[a] Entries are difference scores directly related to the size of the obtained phonological similarity effect.

(c)

FIGURE 7.3 Predicted and obtained relationships among short-term memory performance, phonological similarity of stimuli, and difficulty of interpolated task: solid lines represent easy task, dotted lines represent hard task; filled circles represent high phonological similarity, open circles represent low phonological similarity. (a) An interaction between the second and third factors as predicted by either interference or decay theory. (b) The prediction of the acid-bath theory. (c) Results given in terms of difference scores, in errors, between high and low similarity conditions.

Watkins, *et al.* (1974). In their experiment words very high in phonological similarity—BAT, CAB, BACK, TAB, TACK—or words lower in phonological similarity— BOUGHT, COB, BUCK, TUBE, TACK—were compared as a function of two recall conditions, serial recall versus free recall. As Figure 7.4b shows, serial-recall procedures gave the Conrad-type result, where similarity impaired recall. However, under free-recall conditions similarity actually improved recall as seen in Figure 7.4a. Watkins *et al.* (1974) were able to discount the possibility that subjects simply encoded the prevailing vowel sound in high-similarity lists and then spewed out the whole set of words that could be produced with this vowel, using the consonant sounds that appeared in the experiment, B, D, G, P, T, and K. They left at least two words, acceptable by this definition of the memory set, out of the list actually used, giving a means of estimating

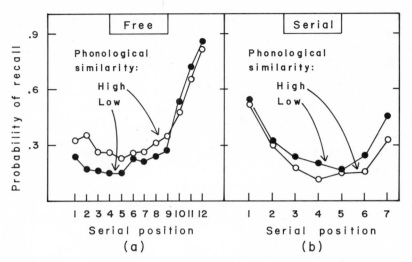

FIGURE 7.4 Free recall (a) and serial recall (b) as a function of serial position and phonological similarity of the to-be-remembered word lists. The auditory and visual conditions are combined. (After Watkins, Watkins, & Crowder, 1974.)

fabrication by subjects from the vowel sound plus knowledge of the consonant vocabulary. Because there were few cases where these excluded words intruded into recall, it was concluded that phonological similarity did not have its beneficial effect by allowing fabrication without memory of the actual list items.

The facilitation of free recall by high similarity poses a fundamental problem for the acid bath theory, of course, because high similarity should have caused the items to decay faster than normal before the recall process has even begun. It should not have mattered how memory for the list was subsequently tested; the high-similarity lists should always have been lost faster than the low-similarity lists. Other cases where similarity aids free recall (for example, Horowitz, 1961) are equally damaging to the acid bath theory.

Because of the Posner and Konick findings showing similarity effects occurring during storage rather than at retrieval, we were led to reject an unembellished decay theory and also a response-competition version of interference theory. (Later, we shall have other grounds for rejecting the unlearning–recovery version of interference theory in the short-term memory situation.) Now, because of facilitation in free recall by similarity, we are rejecting the acid bath theory (an embellished decay theory) as well. There is a new theory of forgetting by Estes (1972) that is capable of handling most of the results we have offered as being crucial so far.

Estes' associative coding theory.   The starting point for the associative coding theory was Estes' dissatisfaction with existing conceptualizations of the distinction between item and order information. We have not been careful to make this distinction thus far, so a brief digression is necessary now.

The first question is whether memory for what has happened needs to be distinguished at all from memory for the order in which events have happened. By either of our two classical approaches, decay theory or interference theory, the distinction is not necessary. Conrad (1965) has suggested that errors of order, such as transpositions where two items from a stimulus are exchanged with respect to position, are really caused by loss of item information. For example, if the series ABCDE is recalled ADCBE one might suspect that only the relative ordering of B and D had been lost from memory. However, according to Conrad's analysis, the following may have happened instead: The subject recalls A and then faces the problem that the next item has decayed. Either B or D fits with the retained phoneme /i/ so on some proportion, say 50%, of the trials he says D. He then comes to the fourth position, after recalling C without incident. He thinks D belongs in the fourth position but he also remembers having just recalled it. Knowing that the stimuli ordinarily do not contain repeated letters, he responds with the next most likely unused candidate, B. This combination of circumstances makes it seem as though order has been forgotten but actually only item information has decayed. To support this view Conrad has shown that the same letters that are likely to lead to phonological confusions are likely to lead to order errors.

The interference theory, which can be extrapolated from traditional verbal learning to short-term memory, also maintains that order and item information are inseparable. The reason is that memory for a series, such as ABCDE, is contained in item-to-item associations, A–B, B–C, and so on. Therefore, the sense in which the subject remembers an item is exactly with respect to its order of occurrence in the series.

Estes (1972) says that the chief problem with these views that unify item and order information is that there are certain cases where item and order information display different relationships with experimental operations, a functional dissociation such as that described in Chapter 6. One such operation is the length of the retention interval. In a modified Brown–Peterson situation Estes reports that there is a preponderance of order errors at early intervals, relative to errors based on phonological similarity, as compared with later retention intervals. E. J. Bjork and Healy (1974) have made a similar point, that order and item information can be dissociated by different relations to the temporal course of forgetting. Second, Healy (1974) has shown that the relation between order errors and serial position is different from the relation of item errors to serial position: Order errors, that is, transpositions, show both a primacy and recency effect, whereas item errors, intrusions and response omissions, show mainly a primacy effect. As a third example of differential effects of variables on item and order errors, there is a study by Wickelgren (1967) on immediate memory for lists of digits as a function of instructions to group in subgroups of various size. The best size of a rehearsal group turned out to be three. However, this was true mainly of order information, for there was little effect of rehearsal-group size on item information.

Estes has concluded that we need a new theory of how item and order information are related. His theory is associative in the sense that it is based on connections between mental representations established under conditions of temporal contiguity. However, unlike most (but not all, see Chapter 12) previous associative theories, the associative coding theory is hierarchical. Elements of an ordered chain are not associated with each other; instead they are connected to higher-order nodes, called *control elements*; the control elements divide the sequence into chunks. For example, in the series ABCDE a traditional associative theory proposes associations between A and B, between B and C, and so on. However, the associative coding theory proposes that A, B, and C are each individually attached to some control element and, perhaps, D and E to another. There are no direct connections among these five list elements.

The principle of hierarchical coding is applied simultaneously at several levels. Each letter, for example, may be thought of as being composed of more than one phoneme and the letter name as a control element for this pair of phonemic elements. The name "b," for example, would control the phonemes /b/ and /i/. A three-level hierarchy is shown in Figure 7.5. The letter M signifies Estes' view of retrieval as being initiated by some motivational source, such as the command "recall."

Now what about order information in the system? Estes has proposed that elements undergo a repetitive recycling process, a reverberatory loop, in connection with their particular control elements. This recycling between a lower-order element and its control element occurs at a rate determined by the refractory phase of the elements involved. On the average, therefore, because the elements attached to a control element start the looping at different times, order is preserved by the sequential activation and rhythmic reactivation. This reverberatory process is the equivalent, in Estes' theory, of primary memory. It is assumed that the reverberatory process between elements and their associated control elements is occurring simultaneously at each level of the hierarchical structure. The mechanism is used by a comparison process wherein the order in which higher-level representations occur is checked against the corresponding order of lower-level representations. For example if the letter names B and C are recycling in that order, a comparison is made against the phonemic level to verify that the phonemic features /b/, /i/, /c/, and /i/ are ordered the same way. The reactivation process might die out at different times for different types of representation, for example, to accommodate the transience of visual iconic coding.

This is, so far, a system for predicting perfect performance. To allow for error, Estes advances the idea that individual recycling events are subject to random error with respect to timing. This means that at a certain level, when time has passed since establishment of the loops, they can become perturbed with regard to order. So, at the level of letter names, from the principle of random error in recycling times, item B may be recycled unusually slowly on some occasion at

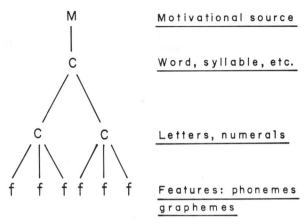

FIGURE 7.5   The hierarchical memory structure proposed by Estes. (After Estes, 1972.)

the same time that item C goes through the loop unusually fast, leaving the subject with the incorrect order ACBDE. Because these perturbations are random, exchanges of order among elements increase over time. That is, because exchanging B and C depends both on the recycling time for B being slow and also on the time for C being fast, an unfortunate coincidence so to speak, then the probability of both timing errors occurring in adjacent time frames gradually increases with time.

At this point the objection may be raised that many errors other than transpositions occur in this type of experiment; sometimes the subject recalls an element that has not been in the string and sometimes he leaves a space blank. Estes' theory provides two mechanisms for such item errors. In tasks such as the Brown–Peterson situation, where the materials to be remembered are followed by some distractor task, the very last piece of information in the stimulus stands in temporal adjacency to the first piece of information in the distractor task. Having the stimulus material back to back with intervening material sets the stage for order exchanges between the two types of item. When this happens the nature of the error actually made depends on the relation of the materials. If a series of letters is followed by a series of digits as the distractor materials, then the subject may arrive at the retrieval test with a series such as ABCD4. Because he knows the experiment is one involving memory for letters of the alphabet, and not digits, he then simply states that he does not know the last item in the series, producing an error of omission. If the stimulus material and the distractor material are from the same class, however, then the result may be an intrusion from outside the list, ABCDX.

Another means of producing item errors in this system is seen when one considers the level of features of letters, such as phonemes. Consider a higher-order control element superordinate to a chunk of two letters, F and G. These letter names, in turn, are control elements for the pairs of features, $/\varepsilon/$ $/f/$, and $/d\mathfrak{z}/$ $/i/$, respectively. If, of these four phoneme features, the inside two exchange because of perturbations of timing, the subject is left with a sequence $/\varepsilon/$ $/d\mathfrak{z}/$ and $/f/$ $/i/$. Because neither of these pairs combines to make the name of a letter of the alphabet, and because the subject knows the experiment concerns letters, these nonacceptable combinations are not emitted. Indeed, Estes has assumed that when unacceptable combinations of this sort are produced, the corresponding items are lost from memory.

There are two accounts for loss of item information, therefore, but they are both dependent in a fundamental way on loss of order information. In this sense the theory resembles classical associative theories, by making item information derivative from order information. In its hierarchical, multilevel approach, however, the theory has the character of organizational, information-processing models.

One of the most transparent predictions of Estes' theory concerns the differential serial-position functions for item and order errors in the Brown–Peterson task. Transpositions, the prototype of order errors, result from exchanges between adjacent stimulus items. In a four-item stimulus, ABCD, the first and last items have only one neighbor, within the stimulus, with which exchanges can occur; however, the second and third items have two adjacent neighbors. Therefore, there ought to be more transpositions involving the inner serial positions than the outer serial positions. Item errors, however, either omissions or intrusions from outside the list, occur at least partly because of exchanges between the stimulus and the distractor materials. Because only the end of the stimulus is in temporal contiguity with the distractor material, the theory predicts increasingly more item errors toward the end of the stimulus item. Healy (1974) has verified these predictions. When the task contains a mixture of item and order information, as Brown–Peterson tasks ordinarily do, she found different serial-position curves for scoring criteria based on a free-recall standard as opposed to transpositions. Transpositions showed a bow-shaped, symmetrical relation to serial position, whereas item errors increased steadily with serial position. In separate experiments that isolated the order and item requirements experimentally—one task requiring only item information and the other requiring only order information—Healy confirmed these generalizations.

One reason we have rejected the acid bath theory is that similarity has a beneficial effect on free recall, whereas in serial recall the effect is inhibitory (Watkins et al., 1974). This pattern of findings can be handled by the Estes theory. In free recall, although memory for order is not required, the hierarchical organization and recycling processes are assumed to be the same as in serial recall. At the level of items, in this case words, exchanges of order would therefore have no consequence in free recall for either high- or low-similarity conditions—BAT, CAB, TAB, or BOUGHT, COB, BUCK, respectively; in other words free recall would not penalize transpositions of whole items. However, at the level of phonemic features, there would be a differential consequence of order perturbations: With high similarity, it would make no difference whether vowels in adjacent items exchanged because the vowel sounds would be constant through the whole list. With low similarity, however, the exchange of vowels from adjacent items would lead to item errors. If COB and BUCK exchanged vowels, the resulting performance would be an intrusion—CUB—and a likely omission, because BOCK is not commonly considered an English word. It is assumed, of course, that the extent to which consonant phonemes undergo exchanges of order is the same for the two conditions. The variety in vowels would therefore work to the disadvantage of low similarity in free recall.

The same type of argument explains the high-similarity disadvantage in serial recall. Assume again that the contribution of consonant phonemes and their ordering is the same for the high- and the low-similarity conditions. Memory for serial order is preserved by differential recycling times for constituent phonemes of the items. In the case of low similarity the vowel elements, as well as the consonant elements, are reliable cues for order; however, in the case of high similarity, there are only consonant cues for order because the vowel is the same in every item. In other words, there is simply more reliable order information when an item has more discriminable elements looping with their control elements than when an item has fewer discriminable elements.

It is important to note that this inhibitory effect of similarity on serial recall (because with high similarity there are fewer reliable order cues than with low similarity) depends on the process of random perturbation over time of the reverberatory mechanism. Therefore, according to the Estes model the similarity effects are caused by events occurring during the retention interval, rather than at the time of retrieval. This model is therefore consistent with evidence amassed in favor of the acid bath theory (Posner & Konick, 1966). The Estes theory is preferable, however, because it readily accommodates the advantage of similarity in free recall, whereas the acid bath theory does not.

A comment on order information. We observed that the Estes model was motivated in part by a consideration of the distinction between item and order information. It is not clear how profound that distinction is: On the one hand, there is absolutely no doubt that errors on a particular short-term memory trial fall into two classes with different properties and that theoretical positions ignoring this fact are overlooking part of the phenomenon to be explained.

On the other hand, the concept of item information is at least incomplete and at best unsound. In experiments with familiar symbols comprising the learning task, there is no question that the subject knows them and knows them perfectly, as items, both before and after the experimental appointment. What, then, do we mean by item information? We mean the information recording the occurrence of a particular item on a particular trial—as it were, an association between the item in question and a representation of (absolute or relative) time.

However, if item information reduces to a matter of knowing when an item has occurred, then how is it different from order information? The main difference is apparently one of the time scale against which the occurrence of items is being measured; the convention seems to be that we speak of item information when it is a matter of locating the item in one trial versus another and we speak of order information when it is a matter of locating an item in one position or another of a multielement unit presented within a trial. In this light, item and order information are revealed to be fundamentally the same but directed at different levels of organization. Clearly, a theory such as that of Estes is admirably designed to handle the requirement of such different levels of organization.

The argument thus far. In most situations the passage of time is less correlated with performance in short-term memory than is the occurrence of interpolated events (Waugh & Norman, 1965); the Wingfield and Byrnes study has been highlighted here because it is a notable exception. The upshot of the Reitman experiments is inconclusive: If tonal detection really is a mental vacuum then, because performance declines during tonal detection, a decay principle is supported indirectly. If any mental content were able to "leak in" during tonal detection, however, then such an inference would not be permissable. Because the decay theory of forgetting is not heuristic (in the sense it leads one to do only experiments that attempt to rule out other factors), furthermore, we decided to make a provisional assignment of forgetting to the interpolated task (but see the section on proactive inhibition below). Our next issue is therefore a question of how the interpolated task produces loss of the stimulus material.

The choice between a pure displacement theory and some form of interference theory hinges on the role of similarity. It is possible that the primary-memory component of short-term memory is indifferent to similarity and that observed similarity effects stem from secondary memory processes. Unfortunately, there are not experiments available at this time that permit this conclusion to be accepted or rejected. Taking the short-term memory situation as a whole, therefore, the importance of similarity leads us to seek some version of interference theory. The acid bath theory has received strong support from evidence (Posner & Konick, 1966) that similarity has its effect during the retention interval rather than at the time of retrieval. However, the acid bath theory was not able to comprehend the entire pattern of similarity effects in free and serial recall as well as Estes' associative coding theory does.

Most of our concern thus far has been with the interference from similar materials within the stimulus item. We now turn to the two other logically separable sources of interference in Brown–Peterson tasks—interference from the interpolated materials and interference from prior trials. These two sources of interference are denoted by the terms "retroactive" and "proactive" inhibition, respectively, but it should be understood that these two terms are in no way explanations for information loss. They are shorthand terms for the results of experimental operations.

THE BROWN–PETERSON TASK

Having reviewed some of the major theoretical alternatives for forgetting in short-term memory, we are now in a position to give systematic consideration to the Brown–Peterson task. Investigators have not always been careful to provide data allowing estimation of asymptotic forgetting levels; therefore it is not always possible to separate out the primary- and secondary-memory components of performance. However, we shall venture the distinction when it seems possible. It is convenient to divide work on the Brown–Peterson task into experiments with primary concern for the effects of the interpolated task on forgetting of an item (retroactive inhibition) and experiments with primary concern with the effects of prior trials on forgetting of an item (proactive inhibition).

Retroactive Inhibition in Short-Term Memory

Because retroactive inhibition is a name for an experimental result and not a theoretical principle we shall include under it a wide range of experimental operations that have in common the observation that changing the nature of what happens during the retention interval affects the subsequent level of recall. The two main operations have to do with the difficulty of the interpolated task and with the similarity of the interpolated material to the memory stimulus.

Rehearsal again. The harder the task intervening between presentation and recall the worse the recall. As we saw in Chapter 6, Crowder (1967b) had subjects remember groups of five English words during a key-pressing interpolated task; each of ten keys was associated with a light from a corresponding spatial array of ten lights. The subjects were required under all conditions to perform at their maximum rate on the key-pressing task, which was self-paced so that each time a response was made a new stimulus occurred. One variable was the relationship between the ten lights and the ten keys. In the easier condition the relationship was direct, with the leftmost light matching the leftmost key and so on across the array. In the harder condition the spatial array of lights was related to the array of keys by a random assignment. Even though subjects in both conditions professed to be performing as fast as possible there was more forgetting of the words with the hard task than with the easy task. Posner and Rossman (1965) showed a similar result with varying degrees of difficulty of a numerical-manipulation task. The interpretation of these demonstrations of a relation between recall and interpolated-task difficulty is based on the logic that the subjects must divide his attention between rehearsal of the memory stimulus and performance on the interpolated task (see also Peterson, 1969). Dillon and Reid (1969) expanded our information on interpolated-task difficulty in an important way. They were interested in a Brown–Peterson situation in which each retention interval included both a period of easy interpolated activity and a period of difficult interpolated activity. Following the procedures of Posner and Rossman (1965) their subjects always received digit pairs during the retention interval, and they had either simply to read the pair aloud within 1 sec (easy task) or they had to add the two digits together and classify their sum as odd or even (difficult task). Dillon and Reid found that when a retention interval included periods of both easy and difficult digit processing it was better, other things equal, to have the easy task occur early in the interval and the difficult task occur later. Generally, it made little difference which task occupied the last 5 or 10 sec of a 15-sec interval but it made a large difference what happened during the first 5 or 10 sec. Further comparisons led Dillon and Reid to conclude that their study supported a componential analysis with primary memory effectively blocked by the difficult but not by the easy task and secondary memory actually enhanced by the easy task; they proposed that when the easy task follows immediately upon presentation there is an effective lengthening of the presentation time.

The studies we have reviewed on reciprocity between rehearsal and interpolated activity all lend face validity to the Jamesian conceptualization of primary memory as being the temporal extent of conscious awareness, particularly if one is willing to grant that the contents of a rehearsal loop roughly coincide with conscious awareness. Leaving consciousness aside, we are led by these experiments to consider the possibility that rehearsal does not simply maintain items "in" primary memory but rather that rehearsal "is" primary memory! The Dillon and Reid paper is particularly suggestive in this regard inasmuch as it makes clear the status of postpresentation rehearsal (as allowed by their easy task) as a continuation of the presentation interval. By this view, then, the function of a difficult interpolated task is essentially to terminate the presentation episode. We now turn to studies that emphasize the content of the interpolated task rather than its difficulty.

Similarity of interpolated materials. A study in which different interpolated-task conditions probably did not permit differential rehearsal was reported by Corman and Wickens (1968). This stipulation is important because difficulty is likely to be an unwelcome covariate with many manipulations of the interpolated task. The design of the Corman and Wickens study is shown in Table 7.1. The subject was told that he would hear a stream of characters most of which would be digits. However, every stream would include consonant letters in the fourth, fifth, and sixth positions and these three letters would be the targets of a memory query at the end of the total stream of 20 characters. In the control condition the three letters from Positions 4, 5, and 6 were the only letters in the

TABLE 7.1
The Corman and Wickens Study[a]

		Results		
Condition name	Construction of condition	Percent correct	Omission errors	Intrusion errors[a,b]
Control	NNN CCC NNN NNN NNN NNN NN	61.1	28	–
Experimental early	NNN CCC NNC CNN NNN NNN NN	42.4	38	45
Experimental late	NNN CCC NNN NNN NNN NCC NN	49.4	33	35

[a]From Corman and Wickens (1968).
[b]Counts errors of intrusion from the two interference letters only.

series; however, in the experimental conditions two of the interpolated digits (the digits occupying Positions 7 through 20) were replaced by letters. The two experimental conditions were distinguished only by where this pair of letters occurred within the stream of interfering digits. In the experimental–early condition the letters were in Positions 9 and 10 and in the experimental–late condition they were in 17 and 18. In all conditions, the subject had to shadow the successive elements as he heard them and the presentation rate (2/3 sec per item) was designed to make this a demanding procedure. There were two issues: Would a single pair of interpolated letters (different from the letters being remembered) lead to more forgetting than a uniform stream of digits? Second, if so, would the location of this specific "dose" of similarity-based interference be of any importance?

First of all, then, the Corman and Wickens study clearly revealed a retroactive inhibition effect based on class similarity. As Table 7.1 shows, both experimental conditions were substantially worse than the control condition. This is the most reliable and important finding in the study—that conceptual (postcategorical) similarity of a successive pair of elements from among a list of 12 elements significantly impairs recall. (We must assume here that phonological similarity between the stimulus letters and the interference letters was not greater than between the stimulus letters and the digits, in order really to be sure that it was *conceptual* similarity; however, the specificity of similarity of whatever type to this small-scale manipulation is impressive anyway). It is quite unlikely that this pattern can be "explained" by an appeal to rehearsal, to say that more rehearsal is allowed by repeating 12 items when none is a consonant than when two are consonants.

The experiment by Corman and Wickens is quite provocative, theoretically, in the comparison between the early and late letter interpolation conditions. Unfortunately, however, the evidence is rather weaker in the case of this comparison than it is in the case of the comparison between the control condition, with no letters in the stream of digits, and the two experimental conditions, which included letters. What the data showed was that there was a disadvantage to having the interfering letters come early in the distractor period as opposed to late; however, the difference was not reliable statistically. We shall see shortly that a good deal of theoretical mileage depends on this result and, fortunately, a study by Landauer (1974) makes it clear that the Corman–Wickens result (early versus late similarity) was not a matter of experimental error but rather a nonsignificant manifestation of a real phenomenon.

Landauer (1974) employed a continuous paired-associate task in which subjects studied pairs consisting of nonsense syllables and single digits (DOB–8, for example) on a single presentation and were later tested for the association through exposure to the stimulus term alone. In the studies that are most relevant here (Experiments II and III) the variation in similarity was based on structural–phonological properties of the nonsense-syllable stimulus terms. If a critical item were DOB–8, for example, the pairs presented between original study of this critical item and its test were both similar to it (BOP–6, TOD–5, POB–9) and dissimilar from it (SIM–6, NIM–5, LIN–9). In all conditions there were items from both the similar set and the dissimilar set intervening between presentation and testing of the critical pair; that is, there was no control, such as that of Corman and Wickens, in which the distractor materials were all from the dissimilar set. However, in the Landauer study the variable of interest was whether the similar distractor pairs were placed early or late within the constant interval between presentation and testing of the critical pair. In both Experiments II and III, Landauer (1974) found that when a fixed presentation-to-test interval was filled with some items that were structurally similar to the target pair and with other items that were not structurally similar, it was better to have the dissimilar items early in the sequence and the similar items late than the other way around. We might conclude from the Corman and Wickens study that best of all would be to have no similar items at all in the sequence of events between presentation and recall of the critical item, even though Landauer himself was not interested in this condition.

Note how discriminative this result is (that a specific application of similarity-based interference is more harmful to performance if it follows soon after acquisition of the target material than if it follows later in a retention interval): It is inconsistent with a decay theory of the type proposed by Conrad (1965), which says that faded items are replaced at retrieval by whatever accessible items there are that share surviving features with the correct trace. The Conrad theory would predict more errors when interference occurred late in the retention interval because then there would tend to be more strong viable alternatives to the correct trace still accessible than when the potential interference occurred early in the retention interval and, therefore, it (the similar material) too, might be in a degraded state by the time of test. The McGeoch (1942) type of interference theory based on response competition at recall would seem not to make any prediction for the early and late comparison. However, a more recent version of the interference theory of forgetting, called the "response-set suppression" hypothesis (see Chapter 8), must maintain that interference is more effective the closer it is to recall, which is indeed the case in paired-associate list experiments (Newton & Wickens, 1956).

The Landauer result is consistent with the acid bath theory: The sooner similar items are added to the memory items the longer there is for the differential decay rates to operate; recall that the more similar items there are in storage at the time the faster they all decay. Finally, it should be no surprise that as the Estes associative coding theory and the acid bath theory seem to share predictions about the locus of similarity effects in the retention phase, Estes' theory predicts the greater effectiveness of early than of late interference.

Wickelgren (1965) examined retroactive inhibition based on phonological similarity in the Brown–Peterson paradigm. In his experiment, a memory list of four letters was presented at a two per second rate, followed by a tone, the purpose of which was to demarcate the stimulus item from the letters occurring during a retention interval of 4 sec, wherein another eight letters were presented. Attention to the interpolated letters, those coming after the tone, was insured by having the subject copy them down on a piece of paper. A tone terminated presentation of the eight interference letters, and the subject then had to recall the original four stimulus letters. A variety of conditions was studied with the major variable being the phonological relation between the memory letters and the interpolated letters. Consider cases where the four stimulus letters all came from a set of six letters with the phoneme /ɛ/–F, L, M, N, S, and X. In one condition the eight interference letters were equally divided between the remaining two letters from this set of six and letters from a contrasting phonological set–B, C, D, G, P, T, V, and Z. In another condition there were two similar letters and six contrasting letters in the interference set and in a third condition there were only contrasting letters in the interpolated set. The finding was that performance was an inverse function of the number of items in the interpolated string that were similar to the letters in the stimulus string: With four similar and four different, correct recall was 49.8%; with two similar and six different recall was 60.5%; and with all eight interpolated letters different it was 68.4%. By a free-recall criterion the result was the same (72.1, 77.2, and 86.2% correct, respectively) so the retroactive similarity effect was not restricted to order information. Wickelgren's study included numerous other comparisons of this sort and they all showed the same pattern of highly specific interference based on phonological similarity.

As does the Corman and Wickens experiment, the Wickelgren experiment establishes unambiguously that retroactive inhibition is a significant source of forgetting in short-term memory and that the amount of interference is responsive to similarity. What these studies do not permit is alignment of the retroactive inhibition result with a component analysis of short-term memory into primary and secondary memory. The experiments to extend our analysis in this way are straightforward but they have not been performed. Therefore, as elsewhere in this chapter, here we must content ourselves with the more empirical issue of the factors responsible for information loss in short-term memory tasks.

In this connection it is useful to review a result we discussed in Chapter 4—Conrad's (1967) finding on the relation between phonological confusions and retention interval in the Brown—Peterson task. Conrad presented four-consonant units from the vocabulary B, C, P, T, V, F, S, X, M, N; the stimulus was followed immediately by a stream of digits and the subject had to shadow all materials, letters and digits, as they were presented. There were either six or 18 interfering digits separating the stimulus from recall, which, at a presentation rate of 150 characters a minute, represented retention intervals of 2.4 and 7.2 sec, respectively. Correct performance dropped from 62% to 38% between these two intervals, but Conrad's main interest was in the nature of errors made. At the short interval errors were well predicted by phonological similarity, whereas at the longer interval they were not. This result is consistent with theories that place the effects of similarity during the storage phase but inconsistent with theories that place the locus at retrieval. Conrad's finding that phonology predicts errors only at brief retention intervals therefore reinforces the acid bath position or the associative coding position. Furthermore, if the phonological similarity effects, in this case confusions, are a property of secondary memory then they should be showing up in asymptotic performance as well as in immediate performance; therefore this evidence provides a hint that similarity can operate within primary memory.

Proactive Inhibition in Short-Term Memory

In the first years following introduction of the Brown—Peterson technique, the paramount issue was whether it would be possible to apply the same theoretical principles to short-term memory as had been current in verbal learning; we reviewed much of this controversy in the last chapter. Peterson (1963) rejected the proposition that proactive inhibition was important in short-term memory because when he broke down performance according to the first, middle, and late stages of an experimental session (Trials 3–8, 9–14, and 45–50) there was no evidence for deteriorating performance. If anything there was a practice effect. Melton (1963b) thought Peterson's argument was inconclusive because the deterioration caused by proactive inhibition might be occurring very rapidly. Because Peterson had disregarded practice trials, the analysis he performed, starting on Trial 3, might have missed the major buildup of interference.

At about the same time, Keppel and Underwood (1962) showed that Melton was right. In their experiment three-consonant items were tested after either 3 or 18 sec of an interpolated task. The experiment was designed to permit comparison of performance as a function of trials. Their data are shown in Figure

7.6. A useful measure of the amount of forgetting in this situation is the difference between performance at the 3-sec interval and at the 18-sec interval. By this criterion there was no forgetting on the first trial, but there was progressively more on each succeeding trial. Loess (1964) showed that if Keppel and Underwood had extended their experiment beyond six trials there would probably have been little additional increase in forgetting: In the Loess experiment, the sudden buildup of proactive inhibition was apparently complete between three and six trials, or, alternatively, it may have continued beyond that point but was swamped by a practice effect working in the opposite direction.

An extensive experiment by Noyd (1965; reported in some detail in Fuchs & Melton, 1974) provides considerable clarification on the occurrence of proactive inhibition: In Noyd's study lists of two, three, or five words were presented in the Brown–Peterson situation under conditions permitting the observation of proactive inhibition and its accumulation across initial trials. With no proactive inhibition at all, that is, on the very first trial, scores for two-word stimuli were 2.00, 1.96, and 2.00, respectively, for retention intervals of 4, 8, and 24 sec of interpolated activity. Corresponding scores for three-word stimuli were 2.78, 2.78, and 2.78 and corresponding scores for five-word stimuli were 3.38, 3.15, and 3.19. On the first trial, therefore, there was no loss after 4 sec, although if one wants to assume that scores would have been perfect without any interpolated activity, there was some loss between 0 and 4 sec for the three- and five-word condition. Houston (1965) has verified this last conjecture; he showed that for five- and six-word stimuli there is a rapid loss between an immediate test (0 sec interpolated activity) and retention intervals of up to 6 sec.

Now consider performance in the Noyd experiment on later trials, in which there is a potential influence of proactive inhibition. For the same three retention intervals of 4, 8, and 24 sec, scores for two-word items were 1.86,

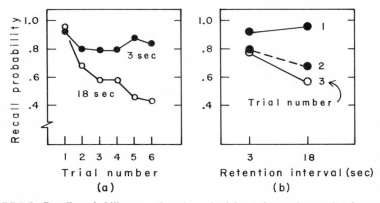

FIGURE 7.6 Recall probability as a function of trial number and retention interval. (a) and (b). Data from the first three trials are plotted in two ways. (After Keppel & Underwood, 1962.)

1.74, and 1.60; scores for three-word items were 2.49, 2.14, and 1.79; whereas scores for five-word items were 2.75, 2.20, and 1.46. Therefore, although without proactive inhibition the retention functions are completely flat after 4 sec, with proactive inhibition added to the picture there is substantial forgetting between 4 and 24 sec.

At the empirical level, the Noyd (Fuchs & Melton, 1974) data oblige us to qualify somewhat the statement based on Keppel and Underwood (1962) that there is "no forgetting" on the first trial of a Brown–Peterson experiment. Although this is the conclusion permitted by Figure 7.6 for three-letter stimuli, the Noyd evidence forces us to acknowledge a loss for three- and five-word stimuli between 0 sec (where performance would be close to perfect) and 4 sec. At the theoretical level, Fuchs and Melton are willing to assign the loss prior to 4 sec of interpolated activity to a process of displacement from primary memory, much in the spirit of our comments above on the Dillon and Reid (1969) experiment: In the early part of the retention interval there is tendency to rehearse the stimulus items which competes with the performance of the interpolated activity; this rehearsal is essentially the same thing as primary memory and the most important factor affecting it is the difficulty of the interpolated task. By using up the limited processing capacity available to a subject, a difficult interpolated task displaces the contents of primary memory. Naturally, the more words there are in the stimulus string, the more vulnerable they are to such displacement, and so we can account for the differential loss of two-, three-, and five-word items in Noyd's experiment.

That leaves the secondary-memory component of short-term memory as the locus of proactive inhibition, according to Fuchs and Melton, because the process of displacement ought to be the same on the first trial as on subsequent trials. The flat asymptotic data from Noyd, between 4 and 24 sec, show that on the first trial there is no progressive loss from secondary memory. However, on later trials, the comparison of performance at 4 and 24 sec shows that when proactive inhibition is at work there are progressive losses within secondary memory.

However, there is simply not yet enough evidence to be confident about the attribution of proactive inhibition to secondary memory, even though it seems plausible and has empirical support. Craik and Birtwistle (1971) examined proactive inhibition across successive free-recall lists and found perfectly unambiguous evidence for the conclusion that the primary-memory component (defined by them as the recency effect in accordance with the practice described in Chapter 6) was quite stable over successive lists whereas the asymptotic (secondary memory) part of the free-recall serial-position curve showed a progressive decline. Clear as this evidence is, one may advance the complaint that progressive losses in single-trial free recall over the first few lists do not necessarily represent the same mechanisms as progressive losses in the Brown–Peterson situation over the first few trials.

The most straightforward research plan to settle this issue is to remain within the Brown—Peterson task, to collect enough data points to allow separate estimates of slope and asymptote, and to examine the effects on these parameters of variables known to influence the degree of proactive inhibition. Turvey and Weeks (1975) have done exactly this and have turned in conclusions directly opposite to those we have just been entertaining! They interpret their componential analysis to suggest that proactive inhibition selectively affects the primary-memory contribution to total performance. Although the point needs to be settled, we are fortunately not constrained to await the solution to this problem before going on to construct a theory for how proactive inhibition operates in the Brown—Peterson situation.

The role of similarity in proactive inhibition.   There is evidence that not only is the presence of prior learning necessary for progressive losses with longer and longer retention intervals in the Brown—Peterson task, but also that the similarity of this prior learning is crucial. Wickens, Born and Allen (1963) demonstrated this point in an experiment on the release from proactive inhibition. In their study a control group was tested on four successive trials of a Brown—Peterson paradigm with the same stimulus material, say three-consonant items, on each of the four trials. The experimental group had three trials with another class of stimulus materials, say three-digit items, and was then shifted on the fourth trial to consonants. On the critical fourth trial, therefore, both groups received the same stimulus material under the same conditions and both had had three prior trials in the task; however, for the control group these prior trials employed the same stimulus vocabulary as the critical trial, whereas for the experimental group the previous experience was with dissimilar items. The result is shown in Figure 7.7. The shift in materials for the experimental group has been the occasion for a release from inhibition, in that performance on the fourth trial has been restored nearly to the initial level. So apparently the buildup of proactive inhibition occurs not just because there have been prior trials, but because these prior trials share some characteristics of the current trial.

Fuchs and Melton (1974) have reported data of their own, and earlier data of Noyd, showing that the interference between the current stimulus and prior ones is specific to certain structural features of the stimuli. In Noyd's study the stimuli varied in length (either two, three, or five words) and he found that intrusions from an earlier trial were more likely when the earlier trial and the current trial matched in length than when they did not.

Fuchs and Melton, in their own study, showed that there was a relation between the position into which some word from a prior trial intruded and the position which the intruding word had occupied on the prior trial. If the subject made an error on the third position of a three-word item and if this error were an intrusion of a word that would have been correct on an earlier trial in the

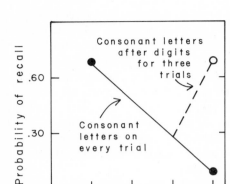

FIGURE 7.7 Recall probability as a function of trial number. The data are for a group receiving consonant letter stimuli on each of four trials and for a group receiving digit stimuli on the first three trials and then letters on the fourth trial. Only the fourth-trial performance of the latter, experimental, group is shown; however, the dashed line connects this performance of the fourth trial with earlier performance on the control group in order to convey the idea of a release. (After Wickens, Born, & Allen, 1963.)

experiment, then it was much more likely than would be expected on the basis of chance that the source of the intrusion was also the third position of the item from the prior trial.

In Noyd's experiment, there was a striking relationship between the occurrence of intrusion errors and how far back in the experimental sequence these intruding words had originally occurred. On 69% of the occasions when there was an intrusion from a prior trial it was the immediately prior trial that was the source; on 12% of the occasions it was from two trials back; on 5% of the occasions it was from three back, with decreasing frequencies for more remote sources. Therefore, it is not only across broad classes of similarity relations that proactive inhibition is selective on prior trials, as the Wickens *et al.* (1963) study may have suggested, but also the effect is selective on the recency of, and the exact structural properties of, prior trials.

Wickens (1972) has made an extensive analysis of exactly which stimulus dimensions lead to a release from proactive inhibition when there is a shift from one level to another of the dimension during a series of Brown–Peterson trials. The logic behind this effort is Wickens' supposition that when a particular type of shift affects performance, then subjects, in some sense, must have been using that dimension to encode the stimuli. In Wickens' experiments the experimental and control group are treated identically for the first three trials but on the fourth trial the experimental group is shifted to a different stimulus vocabulary. If performance on the fourth trial is identical for the two groups, we conclude that the stimulus dimension along which we shifted materials was not an important one. Take an extreme case: Both groups are given three-digit stimuli for four trials. The experimental but not the control group is shifted on the last trial to a three-digit number evenly divisible by 7. No significant release from proactive inhibition should occur under these conditions, because subjects just do not encode three-place numbers by reference to their divisibility by 7.

However, when we find some type of shift that produces a large release then we are left to conclude that the shifted stimulus property is quite important with respect to encoding in the Brown–Peterson situation. For example, a shift in category membership, say, from articles of furniture to food items, produces around a 75% return to initial performance levels, after three trials of buildup; from this we infer that subjects use category membership when they encode items.

Wickens and his associates (Wickens, 1972) have generated a massive amount of data on how various types of shift affect the release from proactive inhibition. These data are somewhat digressive to our present objective because they pertain to issues of encoding at acquisition rather than to the cause of forgetting. However, we cannot deny an intimate relation between these two questions, so an outline summary is appropriate. Wickens has found that dimensions he calls *semantic* usually produce a large release from inhibition when subjects are shifted from one level to another on the fourth trial. In addition to the example of taxonomic category we have cited above—furniture to foods—there are less intuitive cases where the shift is from one end to another along a dimension of *connotative meaning*. A discussion of connotative meaning is beyond the scope of this section; however, one type of connotation words have (see Osgood, Suci, & Tannenbaum 1957) is evaluative, good or bad. Although subjects do not have the impression that they think of whether words in a Brown–Peterson task are pleasant or unpleasant, shifting from such words as KILL, FIRE, HATE to such words as MOTHER, WISE, ABLE, produces a release from proactive inhibition almost as large as shifting among denotative categories. It is a provocative finding that these derived, almost unconscious, aspects of words affect performance nearly as much as utterly straightforward aspects. A systematic integration of this issue with equally provocative ideas about the role of meaning in the initial perception of words can be found in Wickens (1972).

Certain ostensibly obvious shifts among word stimuli produce almost no release from proactive inhibition. Shifting from verbs to adjectives, from verbs to nouns, from present to past tense of verbs, and from singular to plural nouns, all result in essentially no change on the fourth trial. Other dimensions, especially phonological ones, seem to produce an intermediate release. In one particularly clever experiment Wickens tested phonological coding against other possibilities. In a sequence of trials where the stimuli were sometimes three-letter items and sometimes three-word items, there was a sequence of three adjacent trials that were all composed of three-letter stimuli—JXP, BTR, and XJC. Two groups differed on the type of stimulus occurring immediately after these three "build-up" items. The control group saw next a stimulus, such as JRC, and as we should expect their performance was just as bad on JRC as it had been on the immediately prior stimulus XJC. The experimental group saw the three-element stimulus JAY ARE SEA on the trial after XJC. If all coding were phonological this second group should have been equivalent to the group receiving JRC;

however, there was a large release, a large improvement, for the group where the critical item was spelled out in the form of words. This, of course, is not inconsistent with Conrad's evidence that phonological coding is evident only in the first few seconds after presentation because the interval between presentation and test was always 20 sec in Wickens' experiment.

An important feature of the interference effect of prior items on the recall of current items is its dependence on timing relations in the experiment. For an earlier item to affect performance it obviously must remain in memory. If 30 years elapse between one item and the next there is little possibility of the first's affecting the second. Loess and Waugh (1967) have made this point with somewhat shorter intervals. In a Brown–Peterson task they set the retention interval at a constant 9 sec but varied whether the interval between adjacent trials was 0, 15, 30, or 60 sec. Over six trials, there was absolutely better performance with longer intertrial intervals and a slower decrement from trial to trial than with shorter intervals. With intervals of over 2 min, they showed in their Experiment II that there was essentially no buildup of proactive inhibition. Kincaid and Wickens (1970) held the interval constant for the first three trials but varied the interval before the fourth trial from 0 to 120 sec; the more separated in time the fourth trial was, the better performance on it, up to the point that after 2 min the fourth trial was about as good as the first.

Summary thus far. The evidence up to this point indicates the following empirical rules governing forgetting in a Brown–Peterson situation when the nature of the interpolated task is held constant: For any forgetting to occur there must be some prior experience with the task—first-trial performance is generally perfect (unless somewhat longer stimuli than three items are used, in which case there is a loss over the first few seconds and then stable performance). Second, this prior experience must involve stimuli that are in some respects similar to the current material—shifting stimulus vocabulary produces a release from proactive effects. Finally, the prior, similar material must have occurred recently. This last point follows from the studies of Loess and Waugh and of Kincaid and Wickens. It also follows from the Noyd evidence that most intrusions in recall of the current item come from the immediately previous item. Bennett (1971, 1975) has made the same point with a technique employing a recognition measure. On each trial the subject was faced with a two-choice decision between the stimulus that actually had occurred on that trial versus a previous stimulus; the finding was that performance was increasingly poor as the distance from which the incorrect alternative came was shortened (see below for a fuller description of the Bennett study).

Hypotheses for Proactive Inhibition

Now what theoretical principles are consistent with these findings? There are no fewer than five ideas that may be identified.

Spontaneous recovery. Keppel and Underwood (1962) incorporated the phenomenon of proactive inhibition in short-term memory with the then dominant process account of forgetting in long-term memory, the unlearning and spontaneous-recovery hypothesis. We shall have occasion in the next chapter to deal with this and related ideas in very great detail; however, for the moment it is nonetheless essential to convey the bare bones of this hypothesis.

The starting point is the stimulus–response framework and its associated faith that learning in any circumstances can be reduced to a matter of linking a stimulus term, A, to a response term B. The hypothesis is defined by the statements it makes about what happens when there are two response terms learned successively in association with the same stimulus term. This transfer aspect of the theory is based on the assumption that forgetting is primarily a matter of having the same stimulus attached to more than one response with the consequence that the two responses compete for expression.

The unlearning hypothesis says that when an association of the sort $A–B$ has already been learned and the subject is required to learn a second association, $A–D$, there is a process, akin to experimental extinction, that weakens the $A–B$ association. The idea is that when learning $A–D$, the subject is faced with his familiar stimulus term, A, and quite naturally he is likely to make the old familiar response B to it, at least implicitly. However, because B is not the correct response there should be extinction, or unlearning, of A.

The special feature of the unlearning mechanism that is relevant to proactive inhibition is spontaneous recovery. We know from experiments on conditioning in lower animals that if a response is extinguished, it can nonetheless recover in strength following a lapse of time in which there is no further training of any kind. After learning $A–B$, for example, the subject is given the task $A–D$. This leads to unlearning of the $A–B$ association. Later, however, we should expect the strength of $A–B$ to recover spontaneously. Now because the subject cannot both make the original response, B, and the interpolated response, D, at the same time, if the B term is recovering in strength it must be working to the detriment of the D term. This expectation is confirmed in the phenomenon of proactive inhibition: An earlier association has been unlearned through formation of the association in question; the earlier association begins to recover following acquisition of the second association; and to the extent this recovery occurs it impairs ability to recall the more recent association.

Keppel and Underwood (1962) have adapted the unlearning–recovery mechanism to the Brown–Peterson task: On a particular trial, the acquisition of a stimulus item (such as a three-letter trigram) necessitates unlearning of material from a previous trial. At the outset of the retention interval, therefore, the newly acquired trigram (three-consonant stimulus) is strong and potentially competing associations from earlier in the experiment have been weakened through unlearning. However, as the interpolated period lengthens, there is spontaneous recovery of the prior materials, causing increasing competition in the recall of the target materials. By this view, the only reason performance declines during a lengthening period of interpolated activity is spontaneous recovery.

There are two possibilities for exactly what the associations are that undergo this unlearning and recovery. It could be a matter of associating each stimulus item with the experimental context—the room in which the session occurs, the presentation machinery, the experimenter, and further unspecified external and internal cues. This context would remain fairly stable from trial to trial, whereas the stimulus itself would change from trial to trial, setting up the $A-B$, $A-D$ conflict. The second possibility is that some symbolic stimuli are used by the subject on each trial to provide access to the target item. For example, the three items in a stimulus to be remembered could be associated with abstract *positional cues,* such as "first," "second," "third" (see Chapter 12). A more extreme example would be the use of a mnemonic device over and over: The method of loci, for example, could be employed with three-word stimuli, placing an image aroused by the first word in one familiar location from a childhood neighborhood, the second item in an adjacent location, and so on. Reuse of any such system would require unlearning of previous associations.

Direct evidence for competition between the target on a particular trial and prior trials may come from overt intrusions, cases in which the subject incorrectly produces an item that has occurred on an earlier trial. If the unlearning—recovery conception of proactive inhibition is correct, there should be direct evidence that such intrusions from prior trials increase in frequency during the retention interval, matching the assumed recovery of traces from those prior trials. In several Brown—Peterson experiments conducted by the author (for example, a study by Melton, Crowder, & Wulff, cited in Melton, 1963a) no such relation was obtained; instead, intrusions from prior trials were rare at short intervals, frequent at intermediate intervals, and again rare at longer intervals. Because errors of any type are quite rare at the shortest intervals usually tested in experiments of this sort, the overall relation between intrusions and retention interval is one of a declining proportion of all errors attributable to intrusions. However, this pattern was not repeated in the Fuchs and Melton (1974) experiment, where intrusions increased relative to other errors as the retention interval was lengthened. The occurrence of intrusions as a function of retention interval is a relevant source of evidence but it is complicated by the consideration that any factor working to produce large rates of response omissions would tend to drive down the rates of intrusions. If subjects at long retention intervals had low expectations for recall, for example, they might withhold responding altogether more often than at short retention intervals, where they are used to being correct. At best, therefore, the intrusion evidence offers little support for the unlearning—recovery theory. Because this theory has had no evident heuristic value within the field of short-term memory and because its position within the field of long-term memory is troubled (see Chapter 8) we shall dismiss it pending some possible future rehabilitation.

The seesaw hypothesis. In situations where a list of materials must be learned on each of several trials, the relation between performance and serial position changes over trials. At first there is relatively more primacy and relatively less recency than later in practice. This is true in short-term paired-associate tasks (Murdock, 1966b) and also in free recall (Dallett, 1963; Maskarinec & Brown, 1974). Murdock (1966b) suggested a relation between this phenomenon and proactive inhibition in short-term memory. If the whole trial, including the stimulus item and the distractor materials, is considered as a long list, then the stimulus item is the "primacy" portion of that list. If lists show less primacy during later stages of practice than during earlier stages, the build-up of proactive inhibition would then be, in a sense, explained. Note that this is the type of explanation that does not attach an underlying mechanism to a finding but shows that phenomenon to be a special case of a more general phenomenon.

The important feature of this hypothesis is that it suggests a limited capacity that gets invested differently as practice goes on—first the primacy items are stressed and then later the recency items are, but total capacity does not change. This seesaw hypothesis has the testable implication that if only one could measure the interpolated task, which is analogous to the later serial positions in the overall "list," there should be an improvement going on at the same time proactive inhibition is building up. Although Murdock (1966b) reported some rather weak evidence favoring this prediction, other experiments quite clearly show no change, even on some occasions, an improvement, in interpolated-task performance as a function of trials (Crowder, 1968a; R. R. Frost & Jahnke, 1968). This hypothesis can therefore be rejected.

Attention. An uninteresting account (uninteresting in terms of providing new insights) of proactive inhibition departs from the proposition that subjects get bored during a sequence of Brown–Peterson trials and consequently pay increasingly less attention to items at acquisition. The freshness and challenge of the test situation quickly fades over the first handful of trials, and the subject degenerates to only halfhearted attempts to encode the stimulus in a form that can survive the interpolated task. However, if some change punctuates the experimental routine, such as a different type of stimulus material or a long intertrial delay, then the subject is restored to a more alert state, and correspondingly, his performance is restored to its former level also.

It is admittedly difficult to rationalize why some changes are, in this sense, refreshing and others are not. For example, why should a change in connotative meaning be as effective as a shift from letters to digits? Likewise, it is a stretch to imagine that an intertrial interval of a minute should prove capable of restoring subjects' attention. However, a little reflection confirms that the attention hypothesis as stated here is in fact a special case of a general class of hypotheses that focuses on the acquisition phase of the memory episode.

Two very similar recent experiments seem to allow us to dismiss this hypothesis quite unequivocally (Loftus & Patterson, 1975; Watkins & Watkins, 1975). In both studies, the special feature of the design was a final free-recall test for all of the words presented during prior Brown–Peterson trials. The question was whether words that had originally been presented on the first trial would be recalled better, at the end of the session, than words from the second trial, and so on, in parallel to the known decrements in recall of these items on their original short-term memory tests. However, the very fact that initial short-term retention of a Trial-1 item is larger than of a Trial-3 item poses a potential methodological problem: Because the subject was likely to have recalled the former but not the latter, the processing that occurred at the time of recall might well work to the advantage of earlier items. In both the Loftus and Patterson and the Wakins and Watkins studies, this problem was circumvented by not testing some items at all on the initial Brown–Peterson phase. The important final-recall data came from only these, the nontested items. Also, both experiments used taxonomic categories to produce releases from proactive inhibition; there would be a series of three buildup trials with one category, then three with another category, and so on.

The results of both experiments were quite clear. Within a category, there was a significant decrement caused by proactive inhibition over the three trials, on tested items. On items not tested initially but tested later in the final free-recall measure, performance was constant across trials within a category. We may therefore infer that the reason the second trial of a Brown–Peterson trial sequence shows lower recall initially than the first is not because it is less well processed in the acquisition phase. If it were indeed less well learned than the first item, then in final free recall it would be at a disadvantage as well as in initial recall. We must therefore look to the other two phases, retention and retrieval for the locus of proactive inhibition effects in short-term memory.

Acid bath.   Although we dismissed the acid bath theory earlier as a comprehensive theory of memory on the basis of the Watkins *et al.* (1974) study, it could still be a useful concept in particular situations. It is well suited to the facts of proactive inhibition. The assumption that memory traces decay at a rate set by the amount of similar information in storage is perfectly consistent with the buildup of proactive inhibition over the first few trials. When materials are shifted along some similarity dimension, it follows from the acid bath hypothesis that performance should improve (although perhaps we need some more careful specifications before feeling comfortable with data on what kinds of shift produce a release, and on how large this release is). Because the acid bath theory is one of the few theories remaining in the field of memory that assign a role to the passage of real time, the data on relief from proactive inhibition with increased intertrial spacing are particularly congenial to it. Note that with the acid bath theory the crucial predictions for proactive inhibition stem from assumptions about the storage phase.

Retrieval discriminability. The last hypothesis about the source of proactive inhibition in short-term memory is the one that seems, at the time this is being written, most adequate. It focuses on mechanisms that operate at the time of retrieval, assuming that there is no relation between the accumulation of proactive inhibition over trials and the level of acquisition or the degree of retention for items. The hypothesis has the character of interference theory (Chapter 8) but it avoids the unlearning–recovery assumption.

The subject normally faces one principal problem at retrieval: He has learned a number of items in the context of the experiment yet he must distinguish the correct one from among all of them. On the first trial of the experiment, of course, there is really only one item associated with the experimental context, so performance is excellent. After several trials have passed by, however, then the only criterion for selecting the correct memory is a *recency rule:* The item corresponding to the most recent memory trace is the correct one. The task therefore amounts to a case of temporal discrimination (see Chapter 9) or at least the retrieval component of the whole task does.

Using an analogy with depth perception, and recalling the similar argument made in Chapter 6 to understand the data of Bjork and Whitten (1974), we see why performance deteriorates during the retention interval of any particular trial in the Brown–Peterson situation: When the stimulus has just been presented (that is, at an early retention interval) its own age in storage is just a tiny fraction of the ages of traces from other, previous items; there is a big differential in time between the correct item and potential interfering items, enhancing their temporal discriminability. However, after some time spent performing the distractor activity the various traces, correct and incorrect, have all receded toward the past and have become less distinct, just as objects in different spatial locations become less distinct as they all recede into the distance.

It follows from this general perspective (which is obviously not presented here in rigorous form) that if an especially long intertrial interval is inserted into the trial sequence, performance should improve on the trial just following the long gap, just as having an extra space between railroad ties allows each of the single ties to remain distinct at longer distances than otherwise. The data on release from proactive inhibition with shifts in stimulus dimensions are handled with equal ease: The emphasis on temporal discrimination in accounting for proactive inhibition owes to the fact that ordinarily there is no other basis for identifying the correct memory trace. If there is a change in the stimulus material, however, then this fact can itself become the distinguishing feature at recall. To follow our initial analogy with depth perception, it is as if the nearest object in a relatively distant array were uniquely colored, obviating the need for relying on only the fallible cues to depth. On the trial of a shift in stimulus materials, there is the unique new category (or new response class, or whatever) obviating the need for relying on only the fallible cues to temporal discrimination. Following a comment, we shall observe a rather direct experimental simulation of this process by Gardiner, Craik, and Birtwistle (1972).

We have seen that there are five hypotheses that have been advanced in order to account for the phenomenon of proactive inhibition in short-term retention. These ideas distribute themselves in a balanced way among the three components of our stage analysis, acquisition, retention, and retrieval. The unlearning–recovery hypothesis, first of all, is a hybrid in that the recovery process occurs during retention but its effects are manifested in response competition at the time of recall. The attention hypothesis speaks to the acquisition stage, the acid bath hypothesis speaks to the retention stage, retrieval discriminability obviously speaks to retrieval, and the seesaw hypothesis is neutral.

The Gardiner *et al.* (1972) experiment is decisive on the matter in that it allows dismissal of all but one hypothesis. All subjects in this experiment received exactly the same materials over a block of four trials. The first three of these four trials were for the purpose of building up proactive inhibition and the major interest of the experiment was in whether or not there would be a release from this proactive inhibition on the fourth trial. For all subjects there was a semantic distinction between the first three trials and the fourth trial but it was a subtle one: In one set of materials the shift was from a set of flower names denoting garden flowers (ROSE, PANSY, TULIP, CARNATION, ORCHID) to a set of flower names denoting wild flowers (POPPY, DAISY, DANDELION). In the other set of materials subjects saw games played indoors on the first three trials and were shifted to games played outdoors on the critical, fourth trial.

It was essential to the logic of the experiment that control subjects, who simply went through the four trials without special instructions, did not show a release from proactive inhibition on the fourth trial. This was the case; uninstructed subjects apparently do not encode games and flowers in such a way that they benefit from a category change with the particular semantic distinctions built in to the Gardiner *et al.* (1972) design. There were two experimental groups to be contrasted with this control group, whose members, we have just seen, showed a progressive accumulation of proactive inhibition and no release on the fourth trial. Both of the two experimental groups were informed explicitly during the fourth trial that the materials had been shifted to a new subcategory of the overall category from which they had been receiving materials (garden flowers to wild flowers). The instructions at presentation group was given this information just prior to receiving the fourth-trial stimuli; they were therefore aware at the time of encoding that there had been a shift. The instructions at recall group was told, but only at the time of recall, that the fourth trial contained items distinguishable from those presented on the other three trials. During acquisition and during the interpolated task the instructions at recall subjects were treated just like the controls.

The results are shown in Figure 7.8. We start with the control group, which reveals a steady deterioration over trials and no release. Next the instructions at

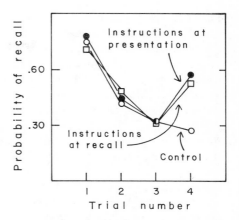

FIGURE 7.8 Recall probability as a function of trial number and instructions concerning category membership of items. (After Gardiner, Craik, & Birtwistle, 1972.)

presentation group should be examined. They, it will be observed from the figure, show a substantial release from proactive inhibition. Once a subject is alerted to the subtle distinctions between wild flowers and garden flowers (or between indoor and outdoor games), therefore, he shows the release. The question is what the source of this release is. It could occur at acquisition, retention, or retrieval. To decide this, the instructions at recall group is necessary. These subjects were treated identically to the control subjects up through the moment of testing. Because the control group did not show the release, the instruction at recall group should not do so, either, if the release is produced by events at either acquisition or at retention. However, if the release is produced at the time of retrieval, then the instructions at recall group should resemble the instructions at presentation group.

As the figure shows, the critical instructions at recall group performed indistinguishably from the instructions at presentation group; it made no difference whether subjects were alerted to the distinguishing criterion for Trial-4 stimuli just prior to acquiring them or just prior to recalling them. Therefore, we may infer that the release from proactive inhibition is caused by events occurring during the retrieval process. This result fits neatly with the retrieval discriminability hypothesis and with the evidence that we have used to reject, one by one, the other four hypotheses: As the subject scans his memory traces from the experimental context, during retrieval, he must ordinarily distinguish traces only on the basis of their age. However, if he also knows that the most recent item has other distinguishing features from all other traces then he may use these other features, in this case a taxonomic feature too subtle to have been noticed at acquisition. It would not matter, moreover, whether the information about this distinguishing criterion were gained at acquisition or at retrieval.

Bennett's (1971, 1975) analysis of proactive inhibition is favorable to a retrieval discrimination, or as he calls it, a trace confusability interpretation, too. His point of departure is the relation between the occurrence of intrusions in recall of a particular item and the distance back to the trial, which may be termed the *source* of the intrusion. Noyd (1965) showed that this *source lag* is usually a single trial or two. From the trace confusability hypothesis this relation is understandable: The immediately previous trial is closest to the correct item in time and therefore most likely to be confused with it, the next to last item is next most confusable with the correct item, and so on. However, there is another interpretation. Maybe earlier trials have simply deteriorated so far they are incapable of providing interference. This second notion is quite different from the first, for it says that earlier items provide competition not by virtue of when they have occurred but by virtue of their strength in relation to the correct item.

Bennett used a recognition situation to test these ideas, in a study to which we have already made passing reference. On each retrieval test the item actually presented on that trial was presented again in company with an item that had occurred on a previous trial. The lag between times of occurrence of the current item and the incorrect item was varied between one and 12 trials. Control data were provided by a choice between the current item and some completely new item, which had never occurred in the experiment. The results are shown in Figure 7.9, which shows the overall relation of performance to lag. Recognition was clearly better the longer the elapsed time between the current trial and the source of the incorrect alternative. However, because the incorrect item has in all cases been presented intact, in undecayed form, Bennett argues that it must be something other than just the similarity and availability of a prior item that makes it interfere with a current item. Prior items presented as recognition decoys are available in the Bennett experiment independently of the lag after which they are brought in to serve as decoys. Their similarity to the correct item is also independent of this lag. Given that the recognition task may be used validly to simulate mechanisms occurring in the Brown–Peterson short-term

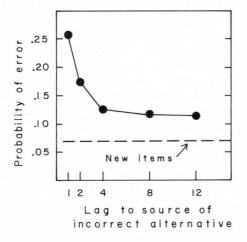

FIGURE 7.9 The probability of selecting an incorrect recognition alternative as a function of the lag separating the source of that incorrect alternative on an earlier trial from the time of testing. (After Bennett, 1975.)

memory task (see also Gorfein & Jacobson, 1973), this result suggests that traces of experimental events must be compared, in retrieval, with respect to some criterion such as their age. We know from the Loftus–Patterson and the Watkins–Watkins studies of 1975 that the traces from trials at different stages in the buildup of proactive inhibition are equally available in the sense of showing equal recall at the end of the session. What must change, then, with the accumulation of proactive inhibition, is the temporal distinctiveness of those traces. The Bennett experiment brings this temporal discrimination problem to the surface by equating the correct and incorrect traces in all respects but their time of occurrence.

CONCLUSIONS

There are two major loose ends that we must acknowledge in closing this chapter. The first has been mentioned on several occasions already: We badly need a comprehensive and authoritative statement on whether such variables as interpolated-task difficulty, retroactive similarity, and proactive inhibition have their effects on the primary-memory or the secondary-memory components of short-term memory. There are partial answers to this matter, but not nearly enough studies with a sufficient sampling of retention intervals to allow separation of slope and asymptote effects.

The second major issue for further research concerns the locus of forgetting sources in the Brown–Peterson method. There are three logical possibilities for the source of interference acting to produce forgetting on a given trial (we are discounting autonomous decay): First, there is the possibility that interference from within the "item" itself is the cause of some forgetting. Fuchs and Melton (1974) have identified this source as *intraunit interference* and they point to the relatively poor performance subjects in their study show on five-word items, even in the absence of proactive inhibition, as a likely manifestation of intraunit interference. We have only to conjecture the results to be obtained with eight-word units in the Brown–Peterson situation to imagine that with neither proactive inhibition nor any appreciable interpolated activity is there likely to be less than perfect performance.

Forgetting can also be shown to be caused by information from prior trials, of course, as our extended discussion of proactive inhibition has shown. Finally, the interpolated task during the retention interval is a third source of performance decrements, as we have seen in the material on Estes' associative coding theory and the acid bath theory of Posner. The problem is that rather different experimental operations and theoretical language have been focused on these three sources of forgetting.

For example, the heroes of the chapter were probably Estes' theory of timing perturbations in rehearsal and the retrieval discriminability hypothesis for proactive inhibition. However, these two propositions seem to have little in common. It is to be hoped that some more advanced theoretical language, able to demonstrate that the two are at least consistent, will emerge.

In another context this chapter has been an excellent data base on which to test the usefulness of the analytic strategies and distinctions advanced in the first chapter. Coding analysis was applied with instructive results to the studies involving phonological similarity (Conrad, 1965; Wickelgren, 1965; Watkins, Watkins, & Crowder, 1974) and to the encoding of various semantic and structural attributes in Wickens' proactive-inhibition—release paradigm. Of course, the concept of stage analysis was absolutely crucial in untangling the various hypotheses for proactive inhibition and in the testing, by Posner and Konick, of the acid bath theory. Task analysis played an important role in two separate efforts to identify the different properties of item information and order information, one effort by Estes (1972) within the Brown—Peterson context and another by Watkins et al., (1974) in the comparison of similarity effects in free and serial recall. Finally, the distinction between primary- and secondary-memory components has obviously been another concept that has figured importantly into this material.

Turvey and Weeks (1975) correctly observe that the Brown—Peterson method of studying memory is hardly new in view of such early work as that of W. G. Smith (1895); instead, the method is a rediscovery. What is new, however, is the application to the technique of such analytic machinery as that identified in the preceding paragraph. This is surely one of those areas of research and theory to which students of memory may point with some satisfaction.

8

The Interference Theory
of Forgetting
in Long-Term Memory

It is widely agreed that the large set of evolving propositions and principles known as *interference theory* is the most comprehensive theoretical system in the field of human learning and memory; the relevant objective analyses would probably show it to be one of the two or three most extensive theoretical efforts within all of experimental psychology. Interference theory was originally directed at the problem of forgetting but it soon became the framework for process theories of human learning as well.

At this point in the book we are turning from chapters on coding analysis (visual and auditory sensory memories, speech coding, and visual imagery) and on short-term memory processing (primary memory, forgetting of individual items) to chapters concerning long-term learning and memory processing (forgetting theory, effects of repetition, and organizational processes). The choice has been to begin this coverage with the chronologically earliest research tradition. A considerably longer historical perspective on the study of learning and memory is offered in Chapter 12.

Historically, three periods in the development of interference theory may be distinguished and they serve to organize the present coverage. The first period, beginning around 1900, was marked mainly by the influence of McGeoch (1942) and saw the articulation of a theory of forgetting based on competition, at the time of retrieval, between responses associated with a common stimulus. In 1940 Melton and Irwin proposed a dynamic factor in forgetting analogous to experimental extinction, unlearning, and the next 20 years were largely devoted to elaborating and verifying implications of this hypothesis; this second period may be said to have culminated with an important review paper by Postman in 1961 called "The Present Status of Interference Theory." The third period began shortly thereafter, and has been characterized by increasing doubts concerning the centrally important unlearning hypothesis and by the proposal of additional factors.

EARLY EVOLUTION
OF INTERFERENCE THEORY

Intuitively, the most obvious aspect of forgetting is that we recall more and more poorly with the passage of time. It is quite natural in light of this intuition to suppose that memories fade because of the lapse of time since learning. Thorndike (1914) formalized this reasoning in his "law of use," which maintained that although the use of habits leads to strengthening of them, the passage of time without practice, that is, disuse, weakened them. McGeoch (1932) is generally credited with having buried the law of disuse, or *decay theory*, as the same idea is often called.

The case against decay of memory through sheer disuse. McGeoch (1932) argued on several grounds that the supposition that memories fade because of the passage of time is theoretically sterile as well as wrong. For one thing, performance sometimes can be shown to increase rather than decrease during a period of disuse, as with the phenomenon of reminiscence, in which there is a brief period of improvement following practice, before forgetting is seen to take over (Ward, 1937; Hovland, 1938). Correspondingly, as noted above, the procedures of experimental extinction constitute a case in which performance deteriorates with (unreinforced) practice, further contradicting a simple interpretation of the law of use. McGeoch stated that time per se was a totally unsatisfactory theoretical mechanism. It is not time that causes rust, for example, although rust is ordinarily correlated with time, but rather the process of oxidation; the disuse principle encourages us to mistake a correlation with time for a causation by time. In addition, McGeoch showed how, with the amount of time since learning held constant, it was possible experimentally to vary the amount of forgetting over a huge range by manipulating what went on during that time, such as requiring or not requiring the interpolated learning of other materials. This ability to tie forgetting to operations independent of time was his strongest argument for seeking a theory of forgetting through those operations themselves.

A close relative of the disuse theory is the proposition that some organic correlate of learning, physical changes in brain cells for example, deteriorates with the passage of time. Although he did not quite deny that such deterioration occurred, McGeoch argued against it as a general theory of forgetting because it lacked direct evidence, it seemed to be untestable, and because in natural life, often the oldest memories of older people would be those that seemed the strongest, rather than the "fresher" memories.

Whereas there has recently emerged a related proposition that memory traces deteriorate autonomously with the passage of time in certain restricted situations, namely, short-term memory (see Chapters 6 and 7), little support for disuse as a general theory of memory has been voiced since McGeoch's (1932) paper.

At the time, the only serious alternative to disuse theory was considered to be some theory based on *retroactive inhibition*. The reasoning surely was that if the time interval itself did not cause the forgetting then something occurring during that interval would necessarily be responsible. The prototype retroactive inhibition experimental design was used initially by Müller and Pilzecker (1900). There were two experimental groups, each learning and later recalling an original list of verbal items. The control group was allowed to rest during the interval between acquisition and retrieval, whereas the experimental group was obliged to learn a different list of items, called the interpolated list, before recall. The obtained advantage of the control group over the experimental group in retrieving information from the original list defines the phenomenon of retroactive inhibition. Suitable choice of materials makes it possible to show nearly complete retention by the control group and nearly complete forgetting by the experimental group, at least with some retrieval measures, making the theory of why retroactive inhibition occurs tantamount, in the eyes of McGeoch, to a theory of why forgetting occurs.

Consolidation Theory

One of the two major views on the operation of retroactive inhibition was offered by Müller and Pilzecker (1900) themselves (see Woodworth, 1938, p. 227). The essence of their *consolidation theory* is that learning is not really complete at the time practice is discontinued. Instead, there is some period of time during which the consequences of learning *perseverate*, that is, remain active in some sense, following practice. During this period of perseveration the memory trace becomes more securely fixated, or *consolidated*, leading to better performance on a later memory test than that possible without this activity. The theory really has two assumptions—that there is an active perseveration following practice and that this perseveration promotes a stronger memory trace than is possible without perseveration. The application of perseveration—consolidation theory to retroactive inhibition is straightforward in that the interpolated task is seen as destroying or interrupting the perseveration process with the consequence of preventing consolidation. The experimental group performs more poorly than the control group, in retroaction experiments, because the original task that both groups learned has never been completely fixated owing to disruptive action of the interpolated list given experimental subjects.

Consolidation theory was consistent with some types of intuition and with experimental facts as well. Müller and Pilzecker reported that subjects often spoke of involuntarily reviewing, or more accurately, rehearing, contents of a list previously memorized, especially in the period immediately following learning. The hypothesis is consonant also with the phenomenon of posttraumatic retrograde amnesia, in which some sudden and intense injury, particularly an injury to the head, results in memory losses for what has happened just before the shock; the idea is that trauma can literally jar loose the coordinated pattern of perseveration occurring at the time and impair consolidation.

A distinction between perseveration and consolidation. Müller and Pilzecker (1900) were quite clear in stating that the consolidation of learning occurred because of perseverating neural activity following overt practice. More recently, Hebb (1949) has been equally explicit on the same point by citing the principle of *neurobiotaxis*, the idea that with repeated reverberatory firing, the first of two cells grows new or enlarged synaptic knobs in proximity with the second (Hebb, 1949, pp. 62–63). However, there is no necessary dependence of a consolidatory process on actual repeated neural perseveration: There may be time-dependent biochemical changes of some other sort that can promote enhanced learning without entailing repeated cell discharge. As we shall see, most of the evidence for consolidation theory comes from behavioral preparations in which no effort is made to measure perseveration independently; that is, research efforts have gone into demonstrating the presumed consequences of perseveration (consolidation) rather than into showing evidence for the perseveration itself.

In view of these considerations the term "consolidation" is seen to be more abstract than the term "perseveration" and although they are often used interchangeably, we shall favor the former term, leaving open the exact nature of what postacquisition events are the crucial ones.

Early evidential arguments for consolidation. Early experimental evidence thought to favor consolidation theory included a set of experiments on retention as a function of whether sleep or wakefulness filled the retention interval (see McGeoch, 1942, pp. 474–477). In 1885, Ebbinghaus (1964, p. 77) considered the possibility that forgetting was retarded by sleep on the basis of evidence that performance on 24-hr retention tests was not as poor as earlier segments of the forgetting function would have predicted. The first and best-known experiment on sleep and memory was that of J. G. Jenkins and Dallenbach (1924), with two subjects who actually lived for a while in the laboratory, learning lists of nonsense syllables at various times of day such that they could be tested after 1, 2, 4, or 8 hr following learning, and such that these intervals would be filled largely with sleep or wakefulness. There were impressive differences favoring sleep for each of the two subjects. Moreover, although the Jenkins–Dallenbach study is not up to modern standards, methodologically, recent studies (Ekstrand, 1967) have replicated the basic finding. The evidence favors consolidation theory in that a period of mental inactivity such as sleep was thought more conducive to perseveration and consolidation than a period of waking activity. Other studies, such as that of Minami and Dallenbach (1946) with insects as subjects, established the advantage of a postlearning quiescent period; in the Minami and Dallenbach study, cockroaches learned an avoidance habit and were then either placed in a dark immobilizing environment—a matchbox filled with tissue paper—or allowed normal activity. The results showed better retention following the quiescent than the waking state.

As we shall see presently an alternative theory of retroactive inhibition is that the subject learns something during the interpolated period that overtly or covertly enters into competition with the original material. Specifically, this competition, or interference, position denies that the interpolated task interacts with some lingering aftereffect of learning the first task. Because periods of sleep or inactivity tend to protect subjects from potentially competing material, the sorts of evidence just reviewed are inconclusive.

For this reason and for several others McGeoch (1942, pp. 487–488) discounted consolidation as a realistic possibility for the general case. He had observed that no one had proposed periods for perseveration lasting more than a few minutes but that in retroactive inhibition experiments it was possible to wait 6 weeks before giving subjects an interpolated list and to observe significant interference as compared with control groups receiving no interpolation. This last fact would have to mean that organized patterns of reverberatory activity last 6 weeks, or longer, for everything we learn. Also the consolidation theory generally leads to predictions that the intensity of a task should directly relate to how much it disrupts previous learning. The evidence (McGeoch, 1942, p. 487), on the contrary, indicates that very intense but nonverbal tasks have almost no effect on verbal learning traces. The degree of retroactive inhibition, in contrast, is very closely related to the similarity, on several dimensions, between original and interpolated learning, a finding that receives no obvious rationalization in consolidation theory.

Finally, there is the phenomenon of *proactive inhibition*. In proactive inhibition the experimental and control groups both learn some material at the same time and are later tested for it under identical conditions; the experimental group, however, previously learns some other list of materials, whereas the control group rests before learning the single, critical, list. The decrement in memory for the critical list resulting from prior learning could not be caused by disruption of perseveration—consolidation because performance on the second list, the performance of interest, followed a consistently favorable period for consolidation for all subjects.

Modern status of consolidation theory. Good ideas die hard and the idea that memories are incomplete at the instant practice terminates, and that events occurring just then may impair later retention of what has been learned, are elegant notions. The clinical literature on traumatic retrograde amnesia has steadfastly been based on the assumption of some consolidatory process, although as M. Williams (1969) observes, head-injury types of amnesia have long been separated theoretically from normal forgetting on a number of criteria. Hebb's neuropsychological theory (Hebb, 1949) depended fundamentally on his dual-trace hypothesis, which was a major statement of consolidation theory. According to the dual-trace hypothesis, experience is first recorded in the form of reverberating organized patterns of neurons, which, if allowed to be active long enough, lead to formation of structural changes in the nervous system that carry more permanent memory:

> ... some memories are both instantaneously established and permanent. To account for the permanence, some structural change seems necessary, but a structural growth presumably would require an appreciable time. If some way can be found of supposing that a reverberatory trace might cooperate with the structural change, and *carry the memory until the growth change is made*, we should be able to recognize the theoretical value of the trace which is an activity only, without having to ascribe all memory to it. The conception of a transient, unstable reverberatory trace is therefore useful, if it is possible to suppose also that some more permanent structural change reinforces it. There is no reason to think that a choice must be made between the two conceptions; there may be traces of both kinds, and memories which are dependent on both [p. 62].

The virtue of the dual-trace mechanism as proposed by Hebb is that it explicitly recognizes that there may be two sets of laws for learning and memory. Consolidation theory is thus absolved of responsibility for explaining retroaction after 6 weeks, but it can seek evidence for trace disruption following shorter periods.

Major empirical and theoretical implications of the dual-trace hypothesis have occurred in several widely separated fields. In human memory, the revival of interest in short-term memory, roughly corresponding to publication in 1958 of Broadbent's book *Perception and Communication*, was one example. As we observed in Chapters 6 and 7 the separation of memory into primary and secondary memory components quite nicely fits a consolidation position, although consolidation is only one of several bases that have been proposed to cover the relation between the two systems.

Second, there has been a slow but steady continuing interest in the factor of sleep as an influence on retention of previously learned material. Much of this literature is reviewed by Ekstrand (1972) and so it is not surveyed again here. We can generalize that without any doubt memory is better following a retention interval containing sleep than one not containing sleep (see also Hockey, Davies, & Gray, 1972). However, Melton (personal communication, 1975) has observed that this phenomenon may not mean what it appears to: When subjects sleep during a retention interval they must have gone through a period of "going to sleep" which control subjects have not. The possibility is strong that trying to fall off into sleep entails a mental state almost irresistably conducive to overt rehearsal of the material to be remembered, especially when, as in some cases, the subjects have been asked to go to sleep immediately after learning. However, Ekstrand (1972, pp. 73–74) cites evidence that memory is a reliable function of whether or not, during a sleep period, there has been extensive rapid eye movement activity (a presumptive indicator, during deep sleep, of dreaming); performance is better following periods of sleep without such rapid eye movement than with such movement. This latter observation is less equivocal than the straight sleep versus nonsleep evidence; however, it is still possible that the content of dreams during rapid eye movement sleep has entered into competition with the memory materials according to interference principles that are elaborated later in this chapter.

The third modern research area that owes to the dual-trace mechanism is in the field of animal learning, in which some disruptor of trace consolidation is commonly introduced experimentally in order to observe amnesia (as opposed to waiting for the animal to undergo some accidental head injury). The basic idea is that there are electrical or pharmaceutical agents that ought efficiently to block organized neural activity in the brain and its resulting consolidation. If such agents are delivered soon enough after acquisition of some habit, then the effects of blocking consolidation should be observable. Indeed, by research with variation in the delay between learning and administration of the trace-disruption agent we may follow the time course of consolidation. There are three rather distinct phases in this research history:

1. Duncan (1949) taught rats a simple habit under distributed practice. After each trial, some rats received electroconvulsive shock at sufficient levels to induce convulsions and presumably to destroy any organized brain activity, especially in higher centers. The delay between each trial and the subsequent shock was varied parametrically from 20 sec to 14 hr. The results showed that if electroconvulsive shock occurred within 15 min to 1 hr after a trial, the rate of learning was seriously impaired, and the more so the shorter the interval was. If 1 hr or more elapsed following a trial, however, the results of that trial had apparently been consolidated into what Hebb would call the structural trace, for learning with such delays was not worse than that of control animals receiving no shock. As Coons and Miller (1960) have pointed out, however, there is no logical basis for attributing these results to amnesia. If the electroconvulsive shock were punishing to the animals, they would have learned to avoid responses that were closely associated with punishment, and the same results would have occurred. That is, the Duncan experiment does not allow choice between an amnesia and a punishment interpretation of performance decrements.

2. Other experimental situations can be used, however, that overcome the Coons–Miller objection (McGaugh, 1966). The feature of these situations is that the punishing or amnesic effects of electroconvulsive shock, given either has occurred, lead to opposite results. To use a sadistic example, imagine the following sequence of events: First, candy is offered a child, but he is punished severely when he takes the candy. Then, on top of the punishment an electroconvulsive shock is delivered. Now next time around, what happens depends on whether the electroconvulsive shock has been punishing or has been an amnesic agent. If it has been punishing then the child should have two reasons not to take the candy, the regular punishment and also the electroconvulsive shock. If

the electroconvulsive shock destroys recent memories, however, then the child should cheerfully take the candy, having "forgotten" that this action has led to punishment last time. By delaying the time elapsing between the punishment and the electroconvulsive shock we can trace the course of consolidation. Evidence from experiments with this logical design has sharply reduced the time intervals over which electroconvulsive shock is effective from Duncan's estimate of an hour, down to a matter of minutes, and sometimes seconds (Chorover & Schiller, 1965; McGaugh & Gold, 1974).

3. Even these experimental results have been called into question recently, by evidence that memories affected by electroconvulsive shock delivered just after learning can, under some circumstances, be recovered. Clinical observations of posttraumatic retrograde amnesia have anticipated this result: The period over which injured humans cannot retrieve information has been known to "shrink" as time passes since the injury. For example, a football player hit hard on a particular play is at first amnesic with regard to the several plays preceding his injury but days or weeks later, perhaps, can recall all but the last few seconds during the critical play. This recovery is of extreme importance theoretically, because it indicates that memories of the recovered period have been "there all along," and therefore have been fully consolidated, but the retrieval of them has been somehow blocked. That is, whereas consolidation theory depends on traumas that prevent memories from ever getting permanently laid down in the first place, recovery from amnesia suggests that it is only *access* to the memories that is blocked.

This type of stage analysis of experiments on consolidation has been summarized recently in a theoretical review by R. Miller and Springer (1973). They conclude that the evidence of spontaneous and prompted recovery for events preceding anticonsolidation agents is quite abundant and that whatever true consolidation exists—and they believe with Hebb there must be some activity preceding structural trace formation—is probably over in a brief fraction of a second. (A more guarded evaluation of some of this same evidence is reached by McGaugh & Gold, 1974.) If this is the case generally then functional theories of memory can essentially overlook, without danger, the consolidation process, although the machinery of consolidation theories (Landauer, 1969) may be important. The Miller–Springer article can be extended to imply that this importance relates to the process of retrieval. That is, there may be an active short-term process that supports a passive long-term process, but instead of referring to the laying down of memory traces these may refer to establishment of retrieval systems for that information.

McGeoch's Response-Competition Theory

McGeoch (1942) put together the basic outlines of a major alternative to consolidation theory in what he called a "transfer or competition of response theory." The ideas had been anticipated, as is usually the case, by others, notably Webb (1917), but the early evidence for it and the systematic, program-matic statement of interference theory would be properly assigned to McGeoch.

The most important feature of McGeoch's theory, or of any interference theory of forgetting, is the hypothesis that retrieval failures occur because some unwanted memories are retrieved instead of the information to be remembered. In terms of our stage analysis logic from Chapter 1, the basic idea is that forgetting is not a loss in retention or availability but is a blockage of retrieval (accessibility) caused by competing information. The term "transfer" suggests the cause of this competition: On the basis of similarity among stimulus situations, inappropriate responses are transferred into the critical test. Without the learning of any potentially competing responses, or without the occasion for their transfer into the test for the information in which we are interested, there can be no forgetting.

Looking back on McGeoch's original formulation from the viewpoint of Osgood's (1949) subsequent analysis of transfer in terms of paired-associate similarity relations (see Chapter 1), we can see that the $A-B$, $A-D$ paradigm is proposed as the basic condition of forgetting: Two different responses, B and D, are learned in association with the same stimulus situation, A, and when that common stimulus situation recurs the two responses consequently compete with one another for emission. In retroactive inhibition experiments the reason the original list cannot be recalled as well following some interpolated list as it can following a period of rest is that the interpolated and original lists compete at the time the subject is trying to retrieve only the original list. The occurrence of overt intrusions in recall—interpolated-list items mistakenly recalled during the effort to recall only the original list—was taken by McGeoch to be strong direct evidence for the transfer-competition mechanism.

However, overt outcroppings, or intrusions, of interpolated learning into recall of original learning are not nearly frequent enough to account for the entire decrement attributable to the interpolated task. The theory as articulated by McGeoch (1942, p. 494) held that inhibition could occur through one response system's blocking another response system, dominating it, as he put it, without overt transfer of individual responses. The one clear stipulation of McGeoch's position that became central to later developments in the theory was that the original and the interpolated materials were learned independently. Although having learned a prior list makes it more difficult to learn a similar second list than otherwise, a phenomenon known as negative transfer or associative inhibi-tion, still, once the second list has been learned it exists in memory concurrently with the first. Most importantly, learning the second list does not weaken the first, according to the *independence hypothesis* of McGeoch. Martin (1971) observed that McGeoch really had what may be termed an *independence–dominance hypothesis:* Two habit systems were acquired independently, with one dominating at the time of recall.

In terms of stage analysis, the consolidation and interference theories could not have been more different in their explanations of retroactive inhibition.

Consolidation theory holds that the original list has never really been thoroughly acquired in the first place, whereas interference theory holds that the original list has not only been adequately learned but also retained intact until the time of testing, at which point retrieval failures arise through competition from similar materials learned during the interpolated period.

So far, then, the theoretical evaluation has gone through stages somewhat as follows. Memories do not just fade with the passage of time under conditions of disuse. Instead, performance decreases with time because of something that occurs during the elapsing retention interval. This means that theories of retroactive inhibition are tantamount to theories of forgetting. Of the two major explanations, consolidation and interference, McGeoch's interference theory based on transfer of responses between similar situations and competition dominance at the time of recall is the most adequate. It follows that the principal experimental task for students of memory is to find out about transfer, for transfer is the necessary prior condition to observed forgetting.

Although it was apparent to early workers that retroactive inhibition and transfer should somehow have varied as a function of the similarity between original and interpolated learning, it was by no means clear what the form of the relation should have been. Intuitively, the maximum similarity between original and interpolated materials is *identity,* a situation that does not produce inhibition at all. At the other extreme, where the two tasks are unrelated and minimally similar, one can expect some inhibition but less than may occur at some intermediate degree of similarity. These expectations produce a U-shaped function between performance on an original list and the similarity of that original list to what has been learned during interpolated learning. Worst performance was predicted for conditions with "enough" similarity to produce transfer and competition but "not so much" similarity as to produce near identity of the tasks (as, for example, would occur with a list carrying words synonymous to those on another list). The U-shaped prediction was termed the Skaggs–Robinson law (Robinson, 1927; Skaggs, 1925); efforts at verifying the Skaggs–Robinson law within a single experiment were largely frustrated (see McGeoch, 1942, p. 461–466).

The important refinement in the concept of similarity and its relation to retroactive inhibition came with the widespread adoption, during the 1930s of the paired-associate methodology (serial learning and the memory-span technique having previously enjoyed greatest popularity). The importance of paired-associate learning was that it permitted separate and independent control over stimulus similarity and response similarity. With the paired-associate method it became possible to put into experimental practice such crucial theoretical conceptualizations as interference between two lists with the same stimuli and different responses, the $A-B, A-D$ paradigm. The natural consequence of applying stimulus and response similarity to paired-associate learning was the Osgood transfer and retroaction surface (Osgood, 1949; see Chapter 1). In fact, Osgood introduced his formulation as a resolution of the similarity paradox, that is, of the confusion that had theretofore surrounded the effects of similarity in transfer and retroactive inhibition. Notice that the interchangeability of the terms *transfer* and *retroaction* in the label of the surface reveals Osgood to have subscribed to the prevailing attitude from McGeoch, that transfer = retroactive inhibition (through competition) = (implicitly) forgetting.

McGeoch's three-factor theory of forgetting. It is not widely recognized that McGeoch had a three-factor theory of forgetting. The first factor was interference by intervening activities, which we just considered in some detail. This first factor was by far of most interest to McGeoch, moreover, because it was the one obviously capable of experimental evaluation. In summary, interference from intervening (interpolated) activities was thought to arise when some original and interpolated materials shared stimulus elements but had different responses prescribed as symbolized in the $A-B$, $A-D$, transfer relation. These two habits were acquired independently of each other; that is, following interpolated learning, the same stimulus term A had two strong response terms B and D associated with it at the same time. Performance decrements occurred when, at recall, one response system dominated another, as evidenced by overt intrusions. Implicit in these notions is that the memory trace is permanent: When it seems that we have forgotten something the memory is still there but retrieval of it is blocked by other memories.

The second of McGeoch's three factors was altered stimulating conditions:

> Everything learned is learned in response to stimulating or antecedent conditions which are a part of the learning situation and specific to it. It is learned also in a complex context of environing conditions not specific to it . . . alteration produces a decrement in retention, if as a result of it (a) the stimuli necessary to elicit the originally learned acts are not effectively present or (b) new stimuli are introduced which evoke competing responses in sufficient strength to block the originally learned ones [McGeoch, 1942, p. 501].

Here, McGeoch is asserting the proposition that what is intended to be "the stimulus" within a learning experiment, called the *nominal* stimulus, is actually only a portion of the entire *functional* stimulus that enters into association with a response. Besides the nominal stimulus, the functional stimulus includes stimulus events that are nonspecific to the particular association. For example, the association between two words would include associations involving such stimulus events as incidental cues around the external environment (lights, chair, sounds, etc.) and internal environment (gastric sensations, daydreaming, etc.). These stimulus cues would not help the subject in mastering the list because their occurrence would not be reliably correlated with correct pairings; however, the absence of these cues, later, would weaken the tendency of the nominal stimuli to evoke the response. Such incidental, contextual cues are quite likely to change as a function of time. For example, the bird stops singing outside the window between learning and recall of a list or the itching of a bite subsides. It follows that, if contextual cues change with time, performance can indicate forgetting, without necessarily any factor serving specifically to weaken or compete with any individual association.

The analysis of stimuli into component elements is inherent in the learning theories of Guthrie (1935) and Estes (1955), who elaborate the notion formally to include the assumption of an automatic stimulus change, called "stimulus fluctuation," occurring with time. The same idea has sometimes been called *stimulus generalization decrement* by those in other areas of learning. More recently Bower (1972b) has summarized these notions, applying them to a variety of problems in memory, including the animal literature on electroconvulsive shock. We shall have a close look at the Estes theory in the next chapter in connection with the concept of *encoding variability*.

It is hard to imagine how one can be a determinist, philosophically, without accepting stimulus change as a cause of forgetting. A determinist is bound to believe that behavior is caused by the universe of antecedent conditions active at every instant and that subsequent reinstatement of this universe leads to identical behavior as has occurred originally. By the same token, incomplete reinstatement of all antecedent conditions would not be expected to elicit exactly the same behavioral consequence. Some forgetting appears to be inevitable almost on a priori grounds.

McGeoch (1942, pp. 501–505) found support for stimulus change as a factor in forgetting from such studies as Abernathy's (1940); Abernathy showed that college students scored more poorly on examinations when classroom learning was tested in a different room or when the proctor for the examination was different from the original instructor than when these factors remained constant. (Scores were lowest when both the room and proctor were changed.) Related research has been performed more recently by Bilodeau and Schlosberg (1951) and by Greenspoon and Ranyard (1957). Experiments on contrived stimulus change (such as, in the case of the Bilodeau and Schlosberg study, a shift in rooms) have not always yielded positive results (Strand, 1970); however, the outcome of such procedures depends on experimenters' being lucky enough to guess which contextual stimuli may be unusually salient ones and also on the level of attention to such cues permitted or encouraged by the ease of the task and boredom of the subjects.

The third of McGeoch's three factors has received little attention experimentally: inadequate set at the time of measuring retention. What he had in mind, although the concept was not worked out very carefully, was the importance of approaching acquisition and retention from the same motivating and orienting conditions, especially when recall is viewed as a problem-solving sort of activity. In a trivial sense this principle covers the case where a completely unmotivated person does not exhibit retention. In a more sophisticated sense, and one that clearly anticipates the concept of control processes introduced to modern attention by Atkinson and Shiffrin (1968), McGeoch means to include cases of search through memory where the wrong set is being searched, as when we systematically go through dormitory mates in the effort to place a familiar face which, in fact, comes from a classmate rather than a dormitory mate. Finer analysis suggests the possibility that this third factor in actuality reduces to various special cases of the second factor, stimulus change.

THE UNLEARNING HYPOTHESIS
AND SPONTANEOUS RECOVERY

The second major stage in the history of interference theory was based on the rejection of McGeoch's independence hypothesis in favor of the alternative view that learning of some interpolated material weakens the traces left by the original material. This *unlearning hypothesis* was derived from an experiment by Melton and Irwin (1940) on retroactive inhibition as a function of the degree of interpolated learning. Subjects first learned serial lists of 18 nonsense syllables for a constant five trials of original learning. The major variable was how many trials occurred with an interpolated list—5, 10, 20, or 40—the purpose initially being to verify that with high degrees of interpolated learning there was a slight reduction in retroactive inhibition as compared with moderate degrees (which was true). After interpolated learning, all subjects relearned the original list, and the amount of inhibition was defined as the difference in recall between a particular group and controls who simply rested in the interval between training and relearning the original list. As so often has happened in the field of memory, the major contribution came as a direct result of a novel means of data analysis, in this case one in which errors were classified at each level of interpolated learning as to whether or not they were intrusions from the interpolated list.

The overall result of the study by Melton and Irwin (1940) is shown by the top, solid line of Figure 8.1, which gives the total amount of retroactive inhibition obtained. The figure also shows, for each degree of interpolated learning, how many intrusions from the interpolated list into recall of the original list occurred. Whereas total retroactive inhibition continued to grow and then level off as the amount of interpolated learning increased, the incidence of intrusions from the interpolated list first increased but then declined; with the highest number of interpolated trials, moreover, where the interpolated materials should have been strongest, they hardly ever intruded into efforts at retrieving the original list. This lack of correlation between inhibition and intrusions seemed difficult for McGeoch's theory that retroactive inhibition results only from competition and dominance at recall. This difficulty stems from the assumption that intrusions ought to be a direct (although not exhaustive) measure of the amount of response competition going on. In other words, from the McGeoch point of view, one symptom of response competition, retroactive inhibition, grew monotonically with interpolated trials, whereas another symp-

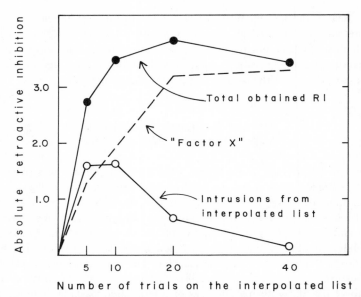

FIGURE 8.1   Retroactive inhibition as a function of degree of interpolated learning: RI is retroactive inhibition. The absolute retroactive inhibition is the arithmetic difference in recall between a rest control group and experimental groups learning the interpolated list. The total decrement is separated into a component that can be assigned to overt response competition (intrusions) and a component that cannot ("factor x"). (After Melton & Irwin, 1940.)

tom, overt intrusions, did not. This led Melton and Irwin to propose that a second factor was operating to determine the total level of retroactive inhibition; they evaluated the relative strengh of this second factor as the arithmetic difference between total retroactive inhibition and that amount of retroactive inhibition that could be directly indexed by intrusions, a quantity which they then drew on the figure labeled as "Factor X." With low degrees of interpolated learning, intrusions account for most retroaction, whereas with high degrees of interpolated learning Factor X played the larger role.

Melton and Irwin (1940) gave a very tentative identification of Factor X as *unlearning*, of weakening, or originally learned traces (List 1) during interpolated learning. According to the unlearning hypothesis, the original responses intrude explicitly or implicitly during interpolated learning, as can be expected by a transfer theory; because they are incorrect with respect to the task at hand (List 2) these original-list intrusions are not reinforced or are even punished, and accordingly they tend to get extinguished. The longer interpolated learning lasts, the more such extinction ought to occur, with the result that at high degrees of List-2 practice nearly all retroactive inhibition results from the weakening of original learning and not from competition between it and interpolated learning.

This two-factor theory of retroactive inhibition implies that when retroactive and proactive inhibition are compared just after acquisition of the second of two lists, retroactive inhibition ought to be more severe than proactive inhibition, because both involve response competition, but only the retroactive paradigm involves unlearning of the list the retention of which is being measured. This line of reasoning was confirmed by Melton and Von Lackum (1941).

The next major development in the theory was an extension of the analogy between unlearning, as measured in retroactive inhibition studies, and experimental extinction, as studied in animal conditioning. The extension, by Underwood, follows the reasoning that if original-list responses are really extinguished during the course of interpolated learning, then they ought to exhibit *spontaneous recovery* during a blank interval following the interpolation, just as extinguished conditioned responses recover strength following the extinction session. Recovery would be indexed by an improvement in performance on the original list after increasing time in a retention interval; as it were, backward forgetting. This counterintuitive prediction was confirmed by Underwood (1948a, b) and also by Briggs (1954), although the numerical magnitude of the recovery obtained was not always impressive. Briggs also interrupted subjects during the interpolated-learning stage of an *A—B, A—D* paradigm, that is during *A—D* learning, and asked them to recall either of the two terms that had been paired with the stimulus, *A*. He found, as the unlearning theory required, that the frequency of *B* responses during interpolated learning steadily decreased as practice continued and Briggs interpreted this decline as an "extinction curve."

However, the procedure of providing the stimulus term (*A*) and asking subjects for either response term (*B* or *D*) is not sufficient for demonstrating changes in the underlying strengths of the two response systems because this method, invented and called "modified free recall" by Underwood (1948b), indicates only which of the two responses is stronger at a given moment in time relatively, not absolutely. The problem is illustrated in Figure 8.2, where two representations of underlying strength for the two responses are shown. If we assume that the probability of giving a response is proportional to the ratio of its strength to the strength of the competing response, and if we recognize that the modified free-recall method allows only one response to be given, it is clear that either of the two panels on the left can result in apparent unlearning as shown on the right, although only in the lower of the two left panels is there any actual decline in *A—B* strength. This is an expression of the learning–performance distinction, or, in the language we have set up in Chapter 1, of the distinction between availability and accessibility. Declining ability to provide first-list responses during interpolated learning means either that these responses are being weakened by unlearning or that acquisition of the second-list responses increasingly causes competition and displacement of the first-line responses, although the latter maintain their strength. What makes it impossible to distinguish learning from performance effects in the modified free-recall situation is the fact

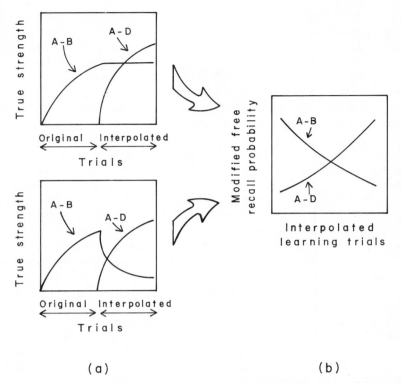

(a)   (b)

FIGURE 8.2   Two theoretical rationales (a) for the obtained (b) frequencies of first- (*A–B*) and second-list (*A–D*) responses in modified free recall during the course of interpolated learning. In the upper portion of (a) there is no loss in first-list strength during interpolated learning, whereas in the lower portion of (a) there is.

that the subject can provide only one response term; only the outcome of competition ever sees the light of day, not the relative strengths of the competitors.

The term "strength" is being used in this chapter in a very noncommittal way to refer to some underlying property of the memory trace. In the next chapter we shall consider with some care, and then reject, what is called the "strength theory of memory," which maintains that there is a single commodity of familiarity (or strength) associated with each verbal item to a varying degree, depending on its normative and situational frequency.

The Barnes and Underwood experiment.   Barnes and Underwood (1959) contrived to solve this problem by devising an altered testing method, called "modified modified free recall" (MMFR), where the subject was given the stimulus term common to the two lists, *A,* and asked to provide either or both response terms and furthermore was given generous time to do so. Relaxation of the timing limits and allowing for both terms to be emitted would theoretically eliminate response competition from the situation, so Barnes and Underwood reasoned that if $A-B$ response frequencies declined significantly during the course of $A-D$ learning, they could attribute this to a decline in availability, or in underlying strength. They did observe this. Their lists contained eight paired-associate items, with the original list and the interpolated lists learned in immediate succession; the main variable was the number of trials of the inter-polated $(A-D)$ list. Following one trial of interpolated learning, subjects were able to retrieve 6.7 first-list responses, but this frequency declined over conditions with 5, 10, and 20 trials, respectively, to 5.4, 5.0, and 4.1 responses. Naturally, performance on the second list showed huge gains over these conditions because subjects were receiving direct practice on it. Postman (1962) replicated the unlearning effect with modified modified free recall in a study with a mixed-list design, in which the same second list contained both $A-D$ pairs and $C-D$ pairs. Nearly 20 years after the proposal of unlearning, therefore, the Barnes and Underwood study provided secure experimental support for it, and the two-factor—competition, unlearning—theory of retroactive inhibition was in excellent shape. Recall, moreover, that because retroactive inhibition was assumed to be the prototype for all forgetting this meant the theory of memory was in correspondingly excellent shape.

Proactive inhibition reevaluated. This simple picture was complicated by a paper by Underwood in 1957 called "Interference and Forgetting." Underwood set for himself the theoretical problem of accounting for losses over 24 hr in retention of a single list of verbal items. A search of the literature for studies in which serial lists of items were learned to a criterion of one perfect recitation and then recalled 1 day later showed that one might expect about a 75% loss in scores. The question was why. According to the dominant view of the time, this loss, like virtually all forgetting, could be attributed to retroactive inhibition from experiences occurring between acquisition and retrieval. Underwood argued that it is simply implausible that a college sophomore, in the space of 1 day, would come in contact with information sufficiently similar to serial lists of nonsense syllables to cause this much interference. Indeed, as we saw in connection with the factor of "altered stimulation conditions," several studies were available showing that even slight alterations in the experimental context could limit the interference of otherwise comparable sets of materials:

> . . . it seems to me an incredible stretch of an interference hypothesis to hold that this 75% was caused by something which the subjects learned outside the laboratory during the 24-hour interval. Even if we agree with some educators that much of what we teach our students in college is nonsense, it does not seem to be the kind of learning that would interfere with nonsense syllables. [Underwood, 1957, p. 51]

In contrast, Underwood argued, the common practice of testing all subjects in all conditions of an experiment made it possible that *proactive inhibition* was supplying interference sufficient to account for the 75% loss. That is, even though the interval between learning and retention was unfilled in the studies being surveyed, it was usually the case that the subject had previously learned many quite similar lists under precisely the same experimental conditions as the list in question. (This use of experimental designs in which all subjects served under all conditions was quite deliberate and was intended to provide greater statistical power.) Underwood advanced two types of evidential support for his position. He first displayed data from previous experiments in which 24-hr retention had been measured after unfilled intervals with serial lists, but with separate performance scores available as a function of the amount of learning the subject had previously undergone.

In one such study (Greenberg & Underwood, 1950) the subject was required to learn four lists on each of four successive days, recalling the previous day's list before learning each new one. When there had been no prior learning, on the first day, the list was retained with 69% accuracy 24 hr later, but this level steadily declined over days until, when there had been three prior lists, scores had dropped to the figure we saw above -25% retention (75% loss).

The second evidential argument for a proactive hypothesis was based on a selective survey of experiments on 24-hr retention in which two figures were developed for each—first, the mean level of recall performance for the experiment as a whole, and second, the mean number of prior lists a subject participating in that study had learned. (This second line of argument is, of course, really a cross-experiment version of the first.) For example, if a counterbalanced experimental design involved five conditions, each subject serving in each, and two practice lists, then the overall average number of prior lists for that experiment would be four. The result of this extensive tabulation and search of the literature is the composite graph shown in Figure 8.3. As this figure demonstrates, when there has been no prior learning subjects can be expected to retain in the neighborhood of 70 or 80% of the material after an unfilled 24-hr interval. When prior learning accumulates, however, the performance levels drop sharply and after five or six lists the expectation is more on the order of 20 or 30% retained (rank-order correlation of $-.91$). On the basis of considering prior learning, therefore, we must revise the answer to our original question: Unless the subject has previously learned similar lists in the same laboratory, about 25% of a single list is forgotten, not the 75% previously considered. There is "less forgetting" to be explained than it first seemed, and Underwood has presented technical reasons for suspecting even this revised figure to be an overestimate of normal forgetting.

Now, how are we to account for this 25% loss, Underwood asks. If the alternative hypotheses are retroactive and proactive inhibition, the source of interference can come either from the 24 hr intervening between learning and recall or from the 15 years or so of verbal experience most college-age subjects have lived through before walking into the laboratory. Underwood suggests that it is much more likely that the previous learning is responsible. This rationale

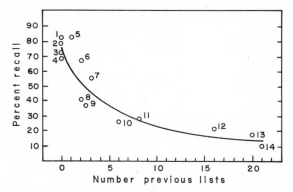

FIGURE 8.3   The recall of serial lists as a function of number of previous lists. Each point represents one of the following studies: 1, Weiss and Margolius (1954); 2, Gibson (1942); 3, Belmont and Birch (1951); 4, Underwood and Richardson (1956); 5, 6, Williams (1950); 7, Johnson (1939); 8, Underwood (1952, 1953a, b, c); 9, Lester (1932); 10, Kreuger (1929); 11, Cheng (1929); 12, Hovland (1940); 13, Luh (1922); 14, Youtz (1941). (After Underwood, 1957.)

gained added plausibility in light of the demonstrated potency of proactive effects shown in the composite graph.

Finally, Underwood provided an explicit mechanism for the operation of proactive inhibition in single-list situations. The special feature of this mechanism was its integration of verbal learning in the laboratory with humans' everyday use of the natural language. Consider the necessity of a naive subject learning the nonsense syllable GYT in some task or other. If we provisionally accept the possibility that somehow a series G–Y–T is what is acquired—a sort of miniature serial list—then an interfering relationship exists between this new task and the subjects' prior language habits such as would represent the English word GYP. In order to acquire the GYT habit, it would be necessary to unlearn the GYP sequence in some sense, just as in the traditional two-list retroactive inhibition situation acquisition of the second-list $A–D$ habit would require unlearning of the first-list $A–B$ habit. So, in the single-list case, Underwood is saying that just the same associative relationships obtain as in the two-list retroactive inhibition paradigm, except that the two conflicting habits are in one case from inside the laboratory and the second case from outside the laboratory.

Of course, if the prior natural language habit GYP is unlearned, then after an interval it should exhibit spontaneous recovery, according to the theory; indeed, it must be this spontaneous recovery that accounts for the loss of retention for the new learning over time, along with such factors as stimulus change. As the previous habits recover from their extinction they come more and more into competition with the experimentally prescribed response system and lead to worse performance. In our example, GYP would recover during the 24-hr interval and compete with GYT at the time of attempted retrieval. It is important to realize that this recovery mechanism is central to the account of time-dependent forgetting in the proactive paradigm, because the unlearning factor favors the experimental list and because competition alone does not change over time.

In summary, Underwood's 1957 paper made at least four important contributions, as follows,

1. It showed how, in previous research on verbal learning, the use of counterbalanced experimental designs, in which all subjects served in all conditions, had led to seriously distorted estimates of how much people forgot during an unfilled interval. The realization that only about 25% of a single list is lost overnight brings verbal-learning retention more into line with the generally good retention obtained with motor skills and with the generally good retention obtained with conditioned responses.

2. It revealed the great destructive power of cumulative, between-session proactive inhibition, which for the historical reasons explored above had been very widely neglected in comparison with retroactive inhibition. The occurrence of proactive inhibition within an experimental session was well known; as noted above, Melton and Von Lackum (1941) measured the extent of proactive inhibition and compared it with retroactive inhibition in order to verify a deduction of the unlearning hypothesis.

3. It provided a balanced view of the theoretical connection between verbal learning and the natural language. The dream of Ebbinghaus (1964, originally published in 1885), had been to invent truly meaningless stimulus materials, his nonsense syllables, in order to examine fresh learning in a *tabula rasa* organism, an organism with a mind like a clean slate ready to receive new associations. By 1928, however, when Glaze showed measurable differences in the meaningfulness of nonsense syllables, workers appreciated that subjects benefited from the natural language through positive transfer. What Underwood pointed out was the likelihood that the effects of the natural language were not all positive in relation to laboratory learning, that with nonword stimuli the subjects needed to overcome strong natural-language tendencies in order to a acquire those demanded by the experiment.

4. It placed a crucial central burden on the theoretical mechanism of spontaneous recovery. Recall that to explain the erosion of memory traces over time in proactive situations, there is only the competition provided by recovering prior traces. This means that for the first time, a theory of retroactive inhibition cannot be considered as tantamount to a theory of forgetting, and that the dual mechanisms of unlearning and competition cannot any longer be considered to constitute a complete theory of forgetting. To be exact, we should point out that in single-list experiments, stimulus change can account for retention losses over time. However, if proactive inhibition is defined (as it should be) as the differential loss over time caused by the occurrence of a prior list, compared

with a no prior list control, then recovery is indeed the only possible forgetting mechanism.

THE THIRD STAGE:
DEVELOPMENTS SINCE 1961

In 1961 Postman published a paper called "The Present Status of Interference Theory" in which were summarized the views presented so far and evidence favoring them. This paper is a landmark in that it represents the furthest evolution of the McGeoch–Melton–Underwood theory at the point in time just before the picture becomes very considerably clouded. There is not space here to do justice to the great investment in research designed to evaluate the interference theory since its 1961 statement. We shall be content with showing two things, (1) the variety of tests for the theory that have been derived and (2) the fact that the 1961 form of the theory has been revised and even abandoned in certain central respects. Before summarizing a number of research programs testing predictions of interference theory there is a more general, logical point to consider.

Logical difficulty with the recovery postulate. As used in interference theory spontaneous recovery has the status of an undefined primitive concept, not requiring explanation itself. However, because only recovery can account for the increase in proactive inhibition over time, it is the pivotal hypothesis in the theory. This is a result of the centrality assigned by Underwood (1957) to proactive inhibition in the theory.

This central concept, spontaneous recovery, however, has just the same theoretical status that McGeoch so objected to in decay theory—it is something occurring more or less autonomously in time! Worse, serious problems arise when one tries to construct a theory of spontaneous recovery that is faithful to other aspects of interference theories generally. One proposition that appears from time to time in the literature (Koppenaal, 1963; Liberman, 1944; N. Miller & Stevenson, 1936) is based on the reasoning that extinction occurs because extinction procedures promote acquisition of some new, but difficult to specify, habits that are incompatible with performance of the trained response (see also Estes, 1955; Guthrie, 1935; Konorski, 1967; Wendt, 1936). As this new response system is learned during extinction training there appears to be a diminution'in performance of the original response just as in the retroaction paradigm the original list seems to be lost during acquisition of the interpolated list. Extinction, after all, fits the customary definition of learning as a change in performance occurring under conditions of training.

Objections to this "interference theory of extinction" have often been listed (Hall, 1966, p. 278 ff.; Hilgard & Marquis, 1940, p. 116 ff.; Osgood, 1953, p.

344 ff.) but for some reason have been seldom examined with the critical scrutiny reserved for more fashionable theoretical issues. A great advantage of the interference theory of extinction that has appealed particularly to Miller and Stevenson and Liberman, is the handy derivation it offers for spontaneous recovery. If one is willing to assume that following training forgetting occurs for both the original training and also for the product of extinction, and if one further assumes that, following Ebbinghaus, the course of such forgetting is negatively accelerated, then the relative gains in strength of the original response are easily explained. As N. Miller and Stevenson (1936) put it: "... older habits, set up during rewarded training, would be on a relatively flat portion of their forgetting curve, while the newer habits, established during nonrewarded training and responsible for slower running, would be on a relatively steep part of their forgetting curve [p. 222]."

The argument is represented graphically in Figure 8.4. Note that there is no assumption that acquisition of the extinction response system itself directly weakens the original habit. The problem for our present purposes with this conceptual package is that it bases an explanation of recovery on assumptions about forgetting. Of course, the theory outlined in the previous section does just the opposite—it bases an explanation of forgetting on assumptions about recovery.

Verification of the Spontaneous Recovery Hypothesis

The first clear responsibility was to show the spontaneous recovery mechanism on the same terms as the unlearning mechanism had been shown by Barnes and Underwood, that is, with MMFR tests. It was necessary to find evidence for recovery of first-list acquisition because of the very great emphasis shifted to proactive inhibition in the theory and the dependence of time changes in proactive inhibition on recovery. Therefore, a number of studies were conducted in the early 1960s in which subjects learned two lists in succession, conforming to the A–B, A–D paradigm, with testing at varying periods following termination of A–D practice. The crucial feature of these studies was the use of the MMFR procedure, specifying unpaced recall of both responses that had been paired with the given stimulus (Abra, 1969; Birnbaum, 1965; Koppenaal, 1963). These and other studies are reviewed by Postman, Stark, and Fraser (1968) and the outcomes are almost universally negative. Occasionally a recovery effect would be reported but typically only at one of several delay retention intervals. Typically the amount of recovery obtained was numerically small, and sometimes it was observed only under very special circumstances, as for example in the study by Silverstein (1967), with exaggerated degrees of overlearning on the first list.

The criterion for demonstrating spontaneous recovery was ambiguous--the theory seemed to require an absolute increase in first-list availability but, as a

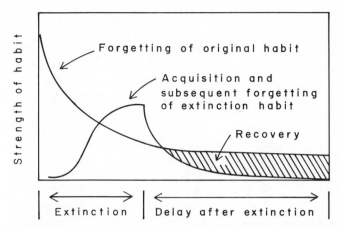

FIGURE 8.4 Explanation of spontaneous recovery based on negative acceleration of forgetting functions for the original and extinction habits. (The same principle operates if the two habits are learned to the same strength; however, in that case it must be assumed that the resultant response is a probabalistic rather than deterministic function of the two underlying strengths.) (After N. E. Miller & Stevenson, 1936.)

number of investigators observed, the more proper control was a single list, the hope being to show this single list forgotten at a faster rate than the "recovering" first of two lists that had been learned in succession.

Postman *et al.* (1968) presented an extensive empirical analysis of the experimental conditions under which recovery had been obtained in previous studies. They were able to demonstrate spontaneous recovery in their own laboratory, by following the procedures that had been used in these other studies; however, the dependence of recovery on the specific conditions of testing led them to a drastic revision of the theory of how interference changes over time. They observe that where first-list responses recover between early and late MMFR tests, conditions tend to favor reinstatement of second-list responses at the time of testing. For example, at an immediate MMFR test performance on the second list is often nearly perfect; therefore, the subject is trying to remember first-list responses in the context of plenty of easily recalled second-list terms. If these second-list response terms remind the subject of a strategy he has followed during acquisition of the second list, trying to avoid thinking of the first-list responses, then, even under MMFR, the first list may seem weaker in memory than it really is.

Postman *et al.* (1968) called this strategy *response-set suppression.* The idea is that when a subject faces acquisition of a second list under conditions of negative transfer, such as can be expected with the *A–B, A–D* paradigm, he develops a strategy of avoiding the first-list responses as a class, not on an individual stimulus–response basis. An example that is simple almost to the point of degeneracy is when the first list contains words as responses and the second list contains numbers; even when the stimulus terms are common to the two lists, it is quite intuitive that the subject can rapidly instruct himself to avoid thinking of words once he appreciates that numbers are the prescribed response class in the second list. When the first and second lists employ the same response type, the response-set suppression strategy is more difficult and more important. It is more important when the two lists have the same kind of responses than when they have different kinds of responses because the tendency of first-list response terms to intrude during interpolated learning is not controllable with a prior selection criterion. For the same reason, moreover, the strategy is more difficult with uniform response types because only the criterion of list membership can be used to support selection.

Response-set suppression was not a completely new idea for Postman *et al.* (1968): Newton and Wickens (1956) had previously advanced the concept of *generalized response competition* and a *selector mechanism* was also assigned a related function by Underwood and Schulz (1960). We cannot pause to trace the empirical logic that lies behind these two earlier notions, but the special usefulness of the idea of response-set suppression, the uniquely new assumptions added by Postman, Stark, and Fraser, has to do with the strength of suppression strategies as a function of time of testing. Right after the completion of second-list acquisition the suppression strategy would be maximally active, they said, especially if the method of testing somehow maintained the context of second-list acquisition. In other words, the suppression strategy has a property of inertia. With passing time after second-list acquisition, however, it is reasonable that the tendency to suppress dissipates, leading to apparent recovery of the first-list responses; the recovery may therefore have been caused by the dissipation of response-set suppression.

The notion of generalized suppression of first-list response terms obviously depends on the subject's ability to discriminate list membership of the two response classes, B and D in $A-B$, $A-D$ transfer. As we observed in our degenerate example (see also Postman, Keppel, & Stark, 1965) this would be quite easy if the two sets were from different linguistic or lexical categories. However, we also know (Postman & Underwood, 1973, p. 27) that even with a single response type the ability to distinguish list membership is quite good immediately after both of the lists have been acquired and deteriorates with time. This list discrimination skill is intuitively plausible: Today we can remember whether events have occurred on Monday or Tuesday of this week much better than we shall be able to do so a year from now, even if we remember the events themselves. Therefore, suppression of the first-list responses depends on being able to distinguish them from the second-list responses. Even if the strategy of suppressing first-list responses does not dissipate with time since second-list acquisition, the ability to do so may decline because suppression usually depends on list discrimination. This theoretical language is obviously in sharp contrast to the pairwise extinction—recovery hypothesis.

Tests of the Response-Set Suppression Hypothesis

The Postman, Stark, and Fraser hypothesis of response-set suppression was proposed as an alternative to the unlearning–recovery theory summarized in Postman's (1961) paper, "The Present Status of Interference Theory." A number of experimental situations have been examined with a view to discovering which hypothesis fares better under conditions where they seem to yield opposed predictions for performance. We shall now review several of these experimental situations because they exhibit some of the more careful and thoughtful work being done on forgetting theory currently. However, it should be kept in mind that the facts of the matter may indicate that both the pairwise unlearning–recovery mechanism and some mechanism of response suppression are involved in double-list interference experiments.

Modified MMFR. The response-set suppression idea was tested in an experiment by Postman, Stark, and Fraser (Experiment III of their 1968 paper). Three methods of testing recall were employed to assess first-list $(A-B)$ response strength at two intervals following second-list $(A-D)$ acquisition. In the conventional MMFR condition, the subject was provided with the common stimulus term, A, and asked to recall both of the associated response terms, with plenty of time allowed by an unpaced testing sequence. In a second version of the MMFR tests, which we shall call "MMFR with D term provided," the experimenter tested for retention of the $A-B$ association by providing not only the A term, but also the potentially interfering D term, from the second list. This second condition was intended to remind the subject of his second-list strategy (suppression of first-list responses) by providing him with the items from the second list. MMFR with D term provided should therefore produce a higher degree of inertia in the selection strategy on immediate tests than the usual MMFR condition, in which the second-list terms may or may not crop up in recall to maintain the anti-List-1 bias. With more inertia to start with, in the MMFR with D term provided than in the conventional MMFR condition, there would be more opportunity for the selection bias to dissipate with the passage of time and consequently more apparent recovery. In a third recall condition, unpaced list recall, the subject was asked to retrieve only items from the first, $A-B$, list; an immediate test under this condition was expected to produce very little maintenance of the "suppression of first list" strategy on an immediate test (that is, very little inertia) and consequently little apparent recovery between the immediate and the delayed test.

In summary, the predictions from response-set suppression were for most recovery in MMFR with D term provided, next most in conventional MMFR, and least in unpaced list recall. The logic was that these three conditions would entail, respectively, decreasing tendencies of the "suppression of first list" strategy to carry over from second-list learning, where it was appropriate, to an immediate test, where it was inappropriate. Finally, the less inertia, or carryover, entailed in an immediate test, the less improvement in first-list performance could be expected through dissipation of a suppression of first list strategy. This predicted outcome was exactly the one obtained by Postman *et al.* (1968).

Multiple-choice testing. Several other lines of evidence have been considered to be of crucial importance for the Postman–Stark–Fraser suppression theory, among them the observation that the occurrence of retroactive inhibition is nearly eliminated when a multiple-choice recognition method of testing is used, rather than the usual recall-anticipation method (Garskof, 1968; Postman & Stark, 1969). In the multiple-choice method of testing the stimulus term is exposed on each trial in conjunction with several of the response terms from the current list, including the correct one; the subject's job is to select the correct response from among the others, and his choice is either confirmed or corrected by exposure of the correct pairing after each choice.

In an experiment reported by Postman and Stark (1969), this new method was contrasted with the conventional method in which the stimulus term is presented alone and the subject has to recall the response. Furthermore, the method of acquisition was the same as the testing method: For both groups, study trials alternated with test trials during acquisition but these trial-to-trial tests were recall (given the A term only) for groups later to be tested by recall and multiple-choice recognition (distractor items all from current list) for subjects later to be tested by recognition. The conventional recall procedures gave 9.7 out of 10 first-list items for a control group that learned only a single list. When two lists were learned, recall performance on the first list was 9.0 for the $A-B$, $C-D$ control paradigm and 4.7 for the $A-B$, $A-D$ paradigm. Corrected recognition scores for the multiple-choice subjects were 9.6, 9.6, and 8.9 for the same three conditions, respectively. In short, whereas the usual pattern was seen with recall, the three groups were about equal with recognition. One might worry that the near equality of performance in all conditions for the multiple-choice groups was caused by a ceiling effect, because these scores were all near 100%; however, a similar study by Anderson and Watts (1971) showed much the same pattern.

If retroactive inhibition is a matter of unlearning individual stimulus–response associations, in conjunction with competition, there is no reason why it should occur only with recall and not with recognition methods. Therefore this evidence falsifies that portion of the 1961 theory which describes competition and unlearning in pairwise units of analysis. By the same token, this absence of retroaction under recognition conditions is consistent with the response-set suppression theory. If, on every test event, the responses provided all come from the current list, there ought to be no necessity for suppression of responses from other lists. Anderson and Watts (1971) showed that when multiple-choice tests in the two-list situation included incorrect alternatives from both of the lists, there was significant retroactive inhibition. This seems to indicate that when competition between response sets on the two lists is built into the recognition situation performance suffers, and Postman and Underwood (1973) cite this result approvingly as evidence favoring the response-set suppression hypothesis.

However, the evidence is not yet conclusive on the matching or multiple-choice experiment. There is some empirical uncertainty on the matter. First, the direction of differences between $A-B$, $A-D$ experimental and $A-B$, $C-D$ control groups consistently tends to favor the latter, even when these differences fail to achieve statistical significance (see especially Experiment IV from the Postman *et al.*, 1968, article). Second, statistically significant retroactive inhibition has been obtained in the $A-B$, $A-B$r interference paradigm, in which the second list has the same response terms as the first, but each is repaired with a different stimulus (Postman & Stark, 1969). Because there is no way for the response-set suppression hypothesis to accommodate this result (with multiple-choice testing in the $A-B$, $A-B$r situation) Postman and Stark conclude that both specific associative unlearning and also response-set suppression are valid mechanisms but that the former gets enlisted only under conditions in which the latter cannot. Even in the paper that marks the introduction of the new response-set suppression hypothesis (Postman *et al.*, 1968, p. 689) it is conceded that this result with the $A-B$, $A-B$r paradigm is conclusive support for specific unlearning in some situations. Merryman (1971) applied a type of task analysis to this situation in which he suggested that even after interpolated $A-D$ learning, there were surviving, intact, backward $B-A$ associations. In a matching test, the subject sees several potential backward associations, that is, several response terms paired with the relevant stimulus, and matches them one by one against his list of retained first-list backward associations, easily choosing the correct one. So, although the subject cannot get from the A term to its relevant B term and thus suffers retroaction on the recall test, he can get from the B term back to the A term and has no trouble with the recognition test. This interesting possibility was tested in a situation where Merryman sometimes "extinguished" both the forward and backward associations of $A-B$ pairs, a paradigm he called the $A-B$, $A-D$ plus $B-E$ arrangement. Under this paradigm there was significant retroactive inhibition, as compared with $A-B$, $C-D$ controls, even though in the same experiment the straight $A-B$, $A-D$ arrangement yielded no interference. The idea was that in the case where forward and backward associations were both destroyed—$A-B$, $A-D$ plus $B-E$—the basis for matching in the Postman–Stark (1969) recognition situation was also destroyed. However, as Postman and Underwood (1973) point out, the Merryman procedure does introduce a new term, E, into the situation, and its effects are unknown; they also emphasize that it was only a small amount of retroactive inhibition that occurred after $A-B$, $A-D$, $B-E$ interpolation.

The absence of retroactive inhibition with multiple-choice testing is consistent with an altered version of two-factor theory, as Postman (1969) has commented.

This extension of the 1961 theory depends on a task analysis applied by McGovern (1964) to paired-associate interference experiments. She maintained that in addition to forward associations and backward associations and response integration, associations were formed also between the response terms and the "experimental context." As we commented in an earlier discussion of stimulus change as a factor in forgetting, the stimulus functions of contextual associations are hard to specify, but they are considered to include aspects of the testing situation that are formally unrelated to the task, including subjective moods, the physical layout of the testing room, the visual or auditory presentation device, and so forth. Because these stimuli remain constant during the first and second lists of an interference experiment, it follows from the programmatic approach of interference theory that acquisition of the second list ought to require unlearning contextual associations to the first-list response terms.

If the major source of unlearning is unlearning of the first-list contextual associations it makes sense that no decrement is observed in multiple-choice tasks: The subject is always presented with whatever response term he needs and never has to produce it from scratch. In a broader perspective, both the contextual-association hypothesis and the response-set suppression hypothesis hold that ordinarily there is a problem connected with the first-list response terms, independent of the stimuli they go with. According to the former position the context cannot elicit these responses in order for the subject to select, and according to the latter position the subject is still operating under an inhibition against emitting them. Providing the responses in multiple-choice testing ought to obviate the difficulty according to either hypothesis. However, Postman (1969) points out that the contextual-association hypothesis encounters other difficulties when directed at the multiple-choice situation. Because there is little or no retroaction with this recognition technique, it means we must attribute most of the retroaction found with regular recall to the unlearning of contextual associations. (Otherwise, because opportunities for pairwise, stimulus–response unlearning are the same with either recognition or recall there can be no accounting for why some specific unlearning does not occur with recognition.) However, then there occurs the theoretical puzzle of why contextual associations undergo unlearning but direct stimulus–response associations do not! Although either position accounts for the results, Postman argues that the response-set suppression hypothesis does so without raising new difficulties.

The main reason for proposing contextual associations in the first place (McGovern, 1964) has been the fact that some considerable unlearning is obtained in the $A-B$, $C-D$ paradigm when it is compared against a control that learns only a single list. Because there was no pairwise association to provide competition in the $A-B$, $C-D$ paradigm it had to be assumed the context was providing the common stimulus function. This consideration sets the stage for the next test of the response-set suppression idea.

Pair-specific interference.   It was Melton (1961) who suggested that important evidence for the nature of unlearning could be gathered from mixed-list experiments with some pairs conforming to the *A–B, A–D* paradigm and others in the same list conforming to the *A–B, C–D* paradigm. Both specific forward and contextual associations would operate on the *A–D* second-list pairs, whereas only general contextual factors would operate on the *C–D* pairs. Furthermore, with pairs of each type mixed in the same list, so that both *A–D* and *C–D* pairs were being learned at the same time in the second list, there would be no prediction of differential interference possible with the response-set interference notion: If the first-list responses are suppressed during second-list acquisition it should be equally true of the *A–D* and *C–D* pairs. However, the results show that there are pair-specific effects in this experiment (Delprato, 1971; Wichawut & Martin, 1971). An *A–B* pair is retained more poorly if the subject has learned a conflicting association based on the same stimulus term than if an entirely fresh pair has been interpolated, even though both conditions are mixed in the same interpolated list. Furthermore, Delprato (1971) showed that the size of the difference is directly related to the number of trials on which the *A–D* repairing occurs. It should be added that pair-specific effects, by this definition, have not always turned up (Birnbaum, 1970).

Postman and Underwood (1973) concede that the pair-specific interference phenomenon is a contradiction of the response-set suppression notion. They add, however, that the hypothesis can be amplified to cover pair-specific interference. Given that during second-list acquisition the subject has the ability to identify pairs where the same stimulus term has been repaired, *A–D,* and to distinguish such repaired items from entirely new items, *C–D,* then it is reasonable that he should selectively suppress first-list responses for only the repaired items. There is independent evidence (Postman, 1966) that consistent differentiation of repaired items from control items can occur in these mixed-list experiments, and therefore it is sensible to assume suppression is selective. Therefore, at the expense of an epicycle (a small subhypothesis tacked on to a larger hypothesis in order to account for some unwelcome evidence) the Postman–Stark–Fraser notion can be seen as accommodating pair-specific interference. In fact, however, this epicycle is a rather large price to pay in order to rationalize the phenomenon of pair-specific interference: In the absence of other criteria for selection (such as relative recency or formal class) the subject is portrayed as adopting a criterion (whether or not a particular pair gets the repairing treatment) that is identical to the Melton and Irwin criterion for specific unlearning—common stimulus terms.

List-determined clustering.   Martin (1971) has argued that the response-set suppression hypothesis, because it depends critically on the formation of effective list-discrimination habits, makes the prediction that when subjects are asked for free recall of all responses after a double-list training experience they should exhibit clustering according to list membership. (By clustering, as we shall see in Chapter 10, we mean the tendency to recall items from the same category in adjacent positions in free recall. If a list of words has several animal names scattered in it, subjects tend to recall these together more often than can be expected on a chance basis.) The idea is that the formation of selection or suppression biases presupposes an important list-membership habit tantamount to a form of categorical organization; there is no way to suppress a list unless it can be distinguished from other items. However, the evidence (Martin & McKay, 1970; Merryman, 1971) suggests that, on the contrary, clustering tends to follow common stimulus terms rather than common lists. Specifically, the result is that response terms from the first list, or from the second list, do not appear in adjacent recall positions but instead the two response terms, B and D, paired with the same stimulus term, A, appear together. This result is also embarrassing to the 1961 theory just as it is to the response-suppression view, because pair-specific response competition is hardly compatible with the two supposedly antagonistic responses appearing together in recall. Actually, the common-stimulus clustering observed by Martin and McKay is probably more inconsistent with the 1961 theory than with response-set suppression, because the latter just requires some common-list organization without prohibiting common-stimulus organization. Finally, either hypothesis can be modified to allow the common-stimulus term to mediate recall of the responses. The clustering result is therefore not particularly useful in distinguishing the hypotheses.

In summary, of the four types of evidence aligned with the response-set suppression hypothesis of Postman et al., (1968), the first (dependence of recovery on MMFR testing method) is favorable, the second (occurrence of retroactive inhibition with recognition testing) is empirically mixed and therefore inconclusive, the third (pair-specific effects in the mixed-list $A–B$, $A–D$ + $A–B$, $C–D$ paradigm) is unfavorable, and the fourth (list-determined clustering) is not really discriminative. Perhaps the wisest conclusion is that of Postman and Underwood (1973, p. 37), that neither specific associative unlearning nor response-set suppression should be abandoned at this time, because there is at least some support for both mechanisms.

Verification of the Single-List Proactive-Inhibition Mechanism

The use of the $A–B$, $A–D$ interference paradigm in this research probably owes to an analogy with real life more than to the supposition that the laboratory situation itself is representative; seldom are two incompatible habits successively acquired in the same stimulus situation. The more representative problem for forgetting theory, as Underwood recognized in the 1957 paper, is acquisition of a single habit or series of habits against some background of prior learning, and then subsequent test. It is only the underlying assumption that forgetting of such singly acquired habits is ultimately a result of the influence of conflicting associations that justifies bringing the conflict into exaggerated focus with retroactive- and proactive-inhibition experiments. As we saw, the interference theory account for single-list situations was an important aspect of the 1961 theory, for besides its greater fidelity to real life forgetting than contrived two-list situations, the dependence of single-list interference theory on natural language habits for the first time (except for earlier work on meaningfulness) allowed contact between the experimental psychology of forgetting and psycholinguistics, albeit a highly sterilized contact.

A single list is retained with about 20 or 25% loss after 1 day, provided there had been no deliberate prior or interpolated learning. This loss is assumed to come from the interference between the criterion laboratory materials and language habits the subject exercises in everyday life. It is assumed further that the direction of this interference is largely or exclusively proactive—that the conflict exists between laboratory learning and learning that has occurred before the experimental session, rather than with learning occurring during the interpolated retention interval—because, among other reasons, there is almost incalculably more opportunity to learn something that can interfere with the laboratory experience in 15—20 years antecedent to the experiment than in the 24 hr or so after it. The form of this proaction, according to the theory summarized by Postman in 1961, is as follows: During acquisition of the criterion list, prior natural language habits intrude erroneously and gradually get unlearned. During the retention interval they recover in strength, however, and at the time of retrieval they inhibit emission of the correct response.

Underwood and Postman (1960) elaborated this hypothesis to include two potential sources of such *extraexperimental interference, letter-sequence interference,* and *unit-sequence interference.* Letter-sequence interference is expected to occur when the items are encoded as lists of letters and when these letters do not obey rules of letter sequences in the natural language, for example as in the item QJH where the usual restriction on U after Q is violated. Unit sequence interference occurs when items approach real words, but where the artificial ordering (in a serial list), or pairing (in paired-associate learning), imposed by the experimental task on these words, or wordlike stimuli, violates word-order rules in the language, as with the pair WHP—SNK, which may elicit word encodings of WHIP and SINK and consequently violate the semantic environments in which these two words ordinarily occur.

Underwood and Postman proposed that the amount of extraexperimental interference should be a function of the meaningfulness of verbal items, but in opposite directions for the two classes of interference. Letter-sequence interference should vary inversely with meaningfulness because the more meaningful the items, that is, the closer to words, the less violation there should be of language letter-sequence habits. Unit-sequence interference, however, should be a direct function of meaningfulness because the more meaningful the items, the more likely they are to suggest words with anomalous semantic relations to the arbitrarily selected associations.

To test the letter-sequence interference hypothesis, high- and low-frequency letter sequences are compared, with expectations for better performance on the high-frequency sequences. As Postman (1969) has stated the results of numerous tests have been consistently negative. The only variable that seems to affect the degree of forgetting observed over intervals of even weeks, when a single list has been learned, is the amount of original learning on that list. When lists differing in meaningfulness are equated for original learning, their retention is equally good subsequently. As we have observed in Chapter 1, this fact flies in the face of folk psychology, which says that meaningful things are easier to retain, and it disconfirms the less intuitive derivations of Underwood and Postman (1960) from interference theory.

Underwood and Ekstrand (1966) set out to discover why proactive inhibition is so massively evident in the laboratory when successive lists are learned, yet is so difficult to show when one of the response systems comes from outside the laboratory, as in the single-list studies. They reasoned that there are two very significant differences between prior laboratory learning and prior language habits, as sources of interference. First, the prior language habits are much better learned than prior laboratory learning. Second, the language habits are typically learned by distributed practice, over a period of years, whereas the prior laboratory associations are generally acquired in a single sitting. Underwood and Ekstrand undertook to simulate these two features of natural language habits independently of one another. In an $A-B$, $A-D$ paradigm, all subjects learned the second $A-D$ list to one perfect recitation and then recalled it 24 hr later. There was a two-factor design covering the conditions of the first-list, $A-B$, learning, with the degree of learning as one factor—either 12, 32, 48, or 80 trials—and distribution of practice the other—$A-B$ learning trials were either distributed equally across 4 days or concentrated on a single day.

The results are shown in Figure 8.5, which gives recall for the second, $A-D$, list as a joint function of $A-B$ practice and distribution. For a given degree of prior learning, distributed practice led to much less interference with the critical $A-D$ list than massed practice. Furthermore, when prior learning was by distributed practice the amount of interference was independent of the degree of prior learning. This is to say that it seems to make no difference how well a potentially competing prior association has been learned so long as it has been learned over an appreciable span of time. Indeed, by an indirect argument, Underwood and Ekstrand argued that there was no proactive inhibition at all in the conditions involving distributed prior learning. In answer to the original question, therefore, it appears that prior language habits and experimentally acquired lists fail to interfere as the 1961 theory specifies because the prior language habits had been learned under conditions of distributed practice, and

FIGURE 8.5 Performance on recall of a second list (*A–D*) as a
function of distribution and
degree of first-list (*A–B*) practice.
The percentage of retention
scores are reciprocal loss scores
taking into account the degree of
original learning of the list under
test. (After Underwood &
Ekstrand, 1966.)

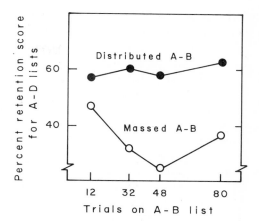

not because they had been so heavily overlearned. Besides leaving the single-list
forgetting estimates of 20–25% unexplained, this conclusion raises the subsequent question of why prior habits acquired with distributed practice do not
compete with new learning. In research since the Underwood and Ekstrand
paper, Underwood and his students have focused their effort on this question
and on the factor of list differentiation.

List-differentiation hypothesis. The hypothesis to which this research program has most consistently generated encouragement is that proactive inhibition
depends mainly on failures of *list differentiation*. The task in the proactive-inhibition experiment is to recall items that have occurred on the most recent of at
least two successive lists. In contrast with the unlearning–recovery hypothesis,
which says that unlearned prior habits are recovering to compete with the most
recent habits, the list-differentiation hypothesis says that all items are, and were,
equally available but that with the passage of time since acquisition it becomes
more and more difficult to discriminate which items are the most recent. The
list-differentiation hypothesis was proposed quite early and was elaborated in
Underwood's dissertation, on proactive inhibition (Underwood, 1945), but the
unlearning–recovery mechanism played the dominant theoretical role in the
meantime.

Recall the necessary relationship between the Postman *et al.* (1968) response-
set suppression ideas and the present list-differentiation hypothesis: List differentiation is a necessary condition for the operation of any suppression or bias
against first-list responses to develop during interpolated learning. That is, there
must be a process whereby the subject learns to identify list membership before
he can hope to select among lists when emitting and editing responses, unless of
course there are other criteria distinguishing the two response classes (such as the
difference between letters and digits). Therefore, list differentiation seems to be
a precondition for response-set suppression.

To explain the course of proactive inhibition over time one can hold a simple, pure list-differentiation hypothesis. Right after acquisition of the second list, differentiation is high and so there is no competition. However, as time passes the two lists are increasingly more poorly differentiated and, at recall, the first-list responses start cropping up. Everything has been available right from the start; there is no unlearning or recovery; it is just that right after second-list acquisition intrusions from the first list can easily be rejected by means of their inappropriate list membership.

Although when two lists are easily differentiated there is little specific competition by way of intrusions, as suggested in the preceding paragraph, there is likely to be strong effective generalized competition, or response-set suppression. That is, for the same reason that first-list responses can easily be rejected when they intrude, the subject is in an excellent position to suppress them as a class. It seems to be necessary that a list-differentiation hypothesis be supplemented with some version of generalized competition, or set suppression, in order to account for the time changes in retroactive inhibition, specifically the improving performance on List-1 items with time.

Underwood and Ekstrand (1967; see also Underwood & Freund, 1968) have reasoned that retention of a list is protected against interference from a prior list acquired under distributed practice because that prior list is easily differentiable from the list in question on a temporal basis. If so, it should be possible to reintroduce interference by artificially weakening the basis of the differentiation. They tried to do this by repeating some of the prior-list responses, which had been learned under distributed practice, in the second list. The idea was that time is ordinarily a sufficient basis for distinguishing old from new responses but that mixing old and new items on the second list should destroy this temporal basis for recalling only appropriate, second-list items. Underwood and Ekstrand measured performance only on new items as a function of whether or not items from the prior distributed-practice list were mingled with these new items. They found, in accordance with their hypothesis, that the advantage of prior distributed practice was almost eliminated when such repetition between lists occurred. Note that the logic behind this experiment demands the unit of analysis be the list rather than the individual association. Stated differently, this study supported the conclusion that proactive inhibition occurred only when there was some basis for confusing old and new items—either confusion based on a similar time of learning or confusion based on item repetition.

We can restate the hypotheses and experimental results in this section in terms of a concrete example: Imagine that a student starting a new foreign language learns a list of English–Spanish word equivalences. The student had previously learned German well and the question is why the German words do not interfere more than they do with retention of the new Spanish lesson. (In this example the German language is playing the role of prior learning and the Spanish language is playing the role of the new associations from the laboratory.) Underwood and Ekstrand (1966) reply to this question that because the German has been acquired over a long period of distributed practice, it is easily temporally distinguishable from the current Spanish words. Specifically, any potential competition from German could be rejected on the basis of its temporal associations; possibly, also, the subject could limit his search for Spanish words to the portion of his memory carrying only recent memories. The contribution of the Underwood and Ekstrand (1967) experiment was to show that if the temporal discriminability were broken apart by giving the student a lesson containing a mixture of some English–Spanish items but also some English–German items, then the new Spanish items would indeed show interference.

List-differentiation theory is a special case of an important set of ideas about memory, the thrust of which is that retrieval of information is mainly a matter of matching available memories with particular contexts (Anderson & Bower, 1972, 1974; Tulving, 1972). It is after all naive, as we have observed earlier, to conceive of a "raw acquisition" process in verbal learning experiments when the items used are usually a part of subjects' stable language systems long before their service in a psychology experiment. The list-differentiation hypothesis is faithful to a much more realistic concept of what happens in verbal learning: The subject learns that a particular item occurred in some particular contextual setting. The idea that time is an important constituent of the contextual setting is, furthermore, one that appears useful in several places in this book. It should perhaps be no surprise that the list-differentiation theory being elaborated here for proactive inhibition in paired-associate list experiments is fundamentally the same as the hypothesis advanced for proactive inhibition in short-term memory by Bennett (1975) and by Gardiner et al. (1972) in research covered in Chapter 7. In Chapter 12 we shall examine with approval the same idea in connection with the recency portion of the serial position curve, as anticipated in the discussion of Bjork and Whitten's (1974) experiment in Chapter 6. In all of these discussions the major idea is that information in a relatively close temporal location is easier to retrieve than information from temporally distant locations.

Locus of Interference
at the Level of the Individual Association

Thus far, we have dealt with two major avenues for testing the 1961 theory. First, there was the effort to verify directly the spontaneous recovery postulate. This effort led to the response-set suppression theory. Second, there was a set of derivations and tests based on interference expected from prior language habits; this effort led to the list-differentiation theory of proactive inhibition. In the course of discussing these developments we have at the same time been discussing another fundamental and testable aspect of the 1961 version of the theory— that interference occurs at the level of the stimulus–response pair rather than at the level of list organization.

In commenting on Postman's (1961) paper, "The Present Status of Interference Theory," Melton (1961) recognized how essential location of interference at the level of the pair was, for the theory, and also how little evidence there was at the time permitting such a location. He suggested that it would be valuable to observe the overt intrusions made by subjects in the course of second-list learning; it would then be a great triumph for the theory if these actual first-list items turned out to be the items showing up as unlearned on a subsequent MMFR test. However, Runquist (1957) and Keppel and Rauch (1966) failed to produce such a direct correlation.

Keppel and Rauch (1966) further tested this idea, which we may call the *elicitation hypothesis,* by employing instructions designed to produce different rates of intrusions from the first list during the second list acquisition phase. They hoped that groups that had been led by these instructions to make large numbers of overt intrusion errors would show large amounts of unlearning. Although this result did not occur, it could always be claimed (Postman, 1969) that subjects simply adjusted their balance between covert and overt intrusions in accordance with the instructions but overall intrusion rates remained constant.

Goggin (1967) tested the elicitation hypothesis in a particularly clever way. She compared retroaction in paired-associate learning with two presentation methods—prompting and confirmation. In the prompting method each pair is first exposed for study and then the stimulus term is presented alone for drill. In the confirmation, or anticipation, method the order of these two events is exactly reversed. The subject is essentially never wrong on tests during acquisition with the prompting method because he has always just received the correct response item only a second or two earlier. Also, understandably, the subject is unlikely to make intrusions during second-list acquisition under the prompting method. As the elicitation hypothesis would predict there was less unlearning with the prompting method than with the confirmation method. This positive evidence is one of the few relatively uncomplicated verifications from predictions based on the Postman (1961) theory. However, the positive evidence was from gross comparisons and not from individual pairs.

In all, three approaches to testing the pairwise-interference notion have been covered at different points in this chapter. First there was the comparison of retroaction in mixed-list $A-B$, $A-D$ versus $A-B$, $C-D$ paradigms. The evidence generally favored pairwise associations, at the expense of response-set suppression. However, the latter hypothesis can be adjusted through an epicycle to accommodate the result. Second, there was the absence of retroaction with multiple-choice testing; this evidence went against a pairwise position, but considering backward associations might provide a way out. Third is the evidence considered in the present section, where the outcome can be termed only mixed.

Independent Retrieval

A novel approach to testing interference theory has come from examination of the microstructure of retrieval in $A-B$, $A-D$ experiments. This approach was discovered by DaPolito (1966) and was extended by Greeno, James, and DaPolito (1971) and Martin (1971). Consider the MMFR recall test in an $A-B$, $A-D$ paired-associate experiment. There are four possible outcomes when a particular stimulus term, A, is presented: The two appropriate responses may both be recalled, neither may be recalled, or one but not the other may be recalled. Represent these by the set $(BD\ B\overline{D}\ \overline{B}D\ \overline{B}\overline{D})$, where B means a correct response on the first list, $\overline{B}$ means incorrect, and D and $\overline{D}$ have the same meaning for the second list. If it is true that responses compete on the basis of common stimuli and that acquisition of $A-D$ leads to unlearning of $A-B$ then certain predictions follow concerning the relative frequencies of the four specified outcomes. These may be stated in terms of dependencies among probabilities of the various events. As an example consider the probabilities $p(B|D)$ and $p(B|\overline{D})$, which are, respectively, the probabilities of correctly retrieving the first-list response given correct retrieval of the corresponding second-list response or given incorrect retrieval of the corresponding second-list response. In the fictitious table shown in Table 8.1, $p(B|D)$ is $2/3 = .67$ and the $p(B|\overline{D}) = 4/6 = .67$ also. In words, these are the probabilities of getting the first-list response in the presence of correct second-list responding or in the absence of correct second-list responding, respectively. The theory specifies dependencies of the sort that correct second-list performance ought to be associated with incorrect first-list performance because the second-list response is supposed to block the first-list responses. It should therefore be true that $p(B|D) < p(B|\overline{D})$. Another prediction concerns the relation between conditional and unconditional probabilities—for example, the probability of correctly providing the first-list response conditionalized on the second-list response $p(B|D)$. If the unlearning—competition theory is true there ought to be an inequality, $p(B) > p(B|D)$: In the example, $p(B) = 6/9 = .67$ and $p(B|D) = 2/3 = .67$ also. There are a number of comparable predictions. DaPolito has shown that where interference theory predicts inequalities the actual data from a number of experiments show independence. An example of data analyzed this way comes from a 1969 experiment by Abra, cited by Martin (1971). In this study two lists of the $A-B$, $A-D$ paradigm were learned, ten pairs on each. Recall was measured either at the termination of interpolated learning or after 24 hr. The data are given in Table 8.2. Note first that there is absolute

TABLE 8.1
Hypothetical Recall Frequencies
in MMFR Following $A-B$, $A-D$
Acquisition Lists

Recall B?	Recall D?		
	Yes (D)	No ($\overline{D}$)	
Yes (B)	2	4	(6)
No ($\overline{B}$)	1	2	(3)
	(3)	(6)	(9)

TABLE 8.2
Response Probabilities and Independence Predictions for
the Abra Experiment[a]

Response	Immediate MMFR			24-hr MMFR		
	D	$\bar{D}$		D	$\bar{D}$	
B	.43	.11	(.54)	.42	.35	(.77)
$\bar{B}$	.38	.08	(.46)	.14	.09	(.23)
	(.81)	(.19)		(.56)	(.44)	

	Results	
Predictions	Immediate MMFR	24-hr MMFR
$p(B \& D) <$ $p(B)p(D)$ $p(B\vert D) <$ $p(B)$	$p(B \& D) = .43$ $p(B)p(D) = .44$ $p(B\vert D) = .53$ $p(B) = .54$	$p(B \& D) = .42$ $p(B)p(D) = .43$ $p(B\vert D) = .75$ $p(B) = .77$

[a]Data from Abra (1969).

spontaneous recovery in the subjects' abilities to provide the first-list response term, B; $p(B)$ at immediate testing is .54, whereas at 24 hr it has risen to .77. Likewise, there is proactive inhibition in that the level of second-list responding, $p(D)$, goes down from .81 to .56. So what might be called *gross reciprocity* occurred. According to the standard version of interference theory (Postman, 1961) these changes are correlated in the sense that specific first-list responses recover to inhibit retrieval of second-list responses. However, despite the correlation between increasing first-list recall and decreasing second-list recall there is independence in both data sets. Below the table are listed several conditional and unconditional probabilities and their predicted dependencies. The microstructure fails to reflect these predicted dependencies to any convincing degree. For a particular stimulus the occurrence of correct first-list retrieval is independent of the occurrence of second-list retrieval.

Hintzman (1972) and Postman and Underwood (1973) have pointed out that the independent retrieval phenomenon may not indicate what it seems to. The major problem is that the entries into contingency tables such as we have been considering are combinations of subjects and items drawn from a large sample and that the subjects can be expected to differ in ability and the items in difficulty. What makes for independence in these tables is "too frequent" occurrence of joint recall (BD) or joint failure ($\overline{BD}$) of recall, relative to recall of one but not the other. Apart from considerations of interference, however, we expect high frequencies in these cells (BD or $\overline{BD}$) whenever there has been pooling of subjects or materials with variable performance. For example, a high frequency of $\overline{BD}$ entries would occur if all items were tremendously difficult or tested after a 25-year retention interval, and likewise a high frequency of BD entries would occur if the task were inappropriately easy. Now it may be that if the predicted dependencies actually exist in data such as those of Table 8.2 they may still not be apparent because at the same time the BD and $\overline{BD}$ cells are being inflated by subject—item difficulty artifacts such that the outcome balances to independence. That is, opposed types of dependencies could mask each other completely. This possibility is illustrated in Table 8.3, where performance on a hypothetical pool of 90 subject—item combinations is decomposed into good subjects, who rarely miss both B and D, and poor subjects, who rarely get both B and D correct. In each of the component matrices there is the sort of retrieval dependency predicted by interference theory, $p(B|D) < p(B)$; however, in the composite table for exactly these same data, on the right, there is complete independence. Exactly the same tables could be used to illustrate easy and hard stimulus terms in the A—B, A—D paradigm, for a uniform set of subjects. In reply to Hintzman (1972), Martin and Greeno (1972) concede the problem and demonstrate, by stratifying subjects on the basis of overall scores, that independence holds for all levels of subject ability. In a separate analysis they have shown the same thing when stratification is on the basis of item difficulty. Finally, they took joint classifications of subject ability and item difficulty and showed that for each such breakdown there was the same retrieval independence.

Even that is not quite enough, however, for there may be interactions between subjects and items such that some items are easy for some subjects but not others. Consider an extreme case where the subjects each spoke one of three languages and where items from each of the three languages were mixed for all subjects in the experimental materials. Combining and stratifying on the basis of overall difficulty level would clearly be insensitive in such a case and sources of artifacts would be the same as shown in Table 8.3.

TABLE 8.3
Hypothetical Recall Frequencies in MMFR

	Good subjects			Poor subjects			All subjects together		
	D	$\overline{D}$		D	$\overline{D}$		D	$\overline{D}$	
B	20	20	(40)	0	20	(20)	20	40	(60)
$\overline{B}$	5	0	(5)	5	20	(25)	10	20	(30)
	(25)	(20)	(45)	(5)	(40)	(45)	(30)	(60)	(90)
$p(B|D) = .80$				$p(B|D) = 0$			$p(B|D) = .67$		
$p(B) = .89$				$p(B) = .44$			$p(B) = .67$		

Martin and Greeno (1972) conclude that if the artifacts can be discounted, the interference theory prediction is clearly disconfirmed but that, at worst, if there remain masked sources of artifact then the theory is simply untestable. Postman and Underwood (1973) reply that the theory is perfectly testable, but not with the DaPolito type of retrieval-dependency analysis.

There is a further complication to the independent retrieval phenomenon. Postman and Underwood (1973) maintain that the pair-specific interference theory never predicted retrieval dependencies in the first place! Their argument is that a proper interpretation of the elicitation hypothesis leads one to expect strong $A-B$ associations to accompany strong $A-D$ associations in a subsequent test. The basis for this prediction is that if $A-D$ is strong, which ought to mean it was acquired rapidly, then there was not sufficient occasion for the $A-B$ pairing to get unlearned. It is when $A-D$ is weak, having required laborious repetitions during acquisition of the transfer list, that we can expect, according to the elicitation hypothesis, $A-B$ to have been repeatedly intruded and consequently unlearned.

Stimulus-Encoding Theory

Martin (1971) has observed that the gross reciprocity between $A-B$ and $A-D-$ the increase in recall of the former over time and the decrease in recall of the latter over time—seems not to be handled by the pairwise-interference theory of 1961 because of the independent retrieval phenomenon. Furthermore, he concluded, the idea of response-set suppression is insufficient on the grounds that there is no list-based clustering in free recall of the response terms.

We have seen at some length that although the Postman (1961) theory is without doubt in considerable disarray, still, Martin's absolute assertion of bankruptcy is perhaps premature. However, the value of Martin's contribution is less dependent on the outcome of the many-sided debate that we have been reviewing here than it is on the new lines of evidence he has tried to introduce and his effort to formulate an alternative theory of reciprocity between $A-B$ and $A-D$ stated in terms of *stimulus encoding.*

Martin's theory stems from the distinction between nominal and functional stimuli (Underwood, 1963), that is, between the stimulus as defined by the experimenter and those aspects of that experience the subject actually uses in learning the pair. This distinction is quite explicit in the multicomponent analysis of paired-associate learning we have spoken of in Chapter 1. McGuire (1961) has laid this reasoning out in stimulus–response terms as follows:

$$S-r-s-R_1 R_2 \ldots R_n,$$

where the upper-case S stands for the physical, nominal stimulus, and the upper-case Rs stand for elements of the overt response, such as individual letters in a verbal item. Between these observables stands the lower-case r, representing an internal encoding response made to the overt stimulus, and lower-case s, representing the fact that this internal response can serve as an elicitor of responses. Martin's interest is in the encoding link, $S-r$, where the subject hits on some aspect of the stimulus, as presented, to use in forming an association.

According to Martin there is not a single inevitable link but rather a family of possible encodings,

$$S- \begin{cases} r_1 \\ r_2 \\ r_3 \\ . \\ . \\ . \\ r_n \end{cases}$$

from which the subject can choose. Consider the nonsense syllable ZAT, to be paired with some number, say 41. This stimulus item could suggest encoding of *Sat, Zap, Zorro, Fat,* or simply *Z*. In associating the stimulus with the response 41, Martin suggests that the subject settles on one of these encodings and then attaches 41 to it: ZAT–(sat–sat)–41. (The encoded response *sat* is listed twice merely to satisfy the stimulus–response language used above. It would be simpler to consider *sat* simply a mental event with both properties of a stimulus and of a response.)

In transfer, the subject in our example might have to learn the pair ZAT–78. In Martin's theory this second association to the same stimulus requires selecting a new encoding of the nominal stimulus, say ZAT–(fat–fat)–78. The nominal stimulus therefore inherently leads to some variety of encoding possibilities and the subject capitalizes on this variety in dealing with a transfer situation. What gets retrieved in recall, say, in MMFR, depends on which encodings of the nominal stimulus get sampled at the time; the associations between functional stimuli and responses remain intact and stable. That is, the subject leaves our example with both the (sat–41) and also the (fat–78) links; which response occurs in MMFR depends on which of the encoding responses (ZAT–sat or ZAT–fat) occurs at the time the nominal stimulus, ZAT, is given.

To explain the reciprocity and time dependence of retrieving from $A-B$ and $A-D$ lists, Martin proposed that the sampling distribution across encodings shifts during an interpolated list and thereafter gradually drifts back toward some initial sampling distribution. This assumption allows the time courses of retroaction and proaction to be predicted. To allow for the independent retrieval phenomenon Martin has the sampling of encodings at any point in time independent of each other. In other words thinking of *sat* or *fat* in response to ZAT should be determined as follows: Using *sat* may be twice as likely as using *fat* at one time and equally likely at some later time; however, at either time, the sampling of *fat* is independent of whether *sat* is also sampled. If the probability of ever sampling *sat* is .45 at the time of some test, it is also .45 given that *fat* is also sampled.

A significant property of the Martin theory is that there is no limit on the size of sample of encodings. If the subject were allowed only two encodings per test, for example, then the retrieval dependencies would return. However, this is a model of MMFR, where time is relatively unlimited, so such a restriction should not be considered a drawback of the system.

Several important questions arise from the Martin theory. They are issues that are not likely to have arisen otherwise, and because they seem to be issues of general importance for human learning, their articulation must be considered one of the accomplishments of the model. Three of these issues are treated briefly here:

1. How does the subject break with his first-list encoding when undertaking acquisition of the second list? It would seem that having just developed a stable encoding, *ZAT–sat,* there would be great resistance, suddenly, to a different encoding *ZAT–fat*. Although acknowledging this as a problem for the theory, Martin (1971) observes that a proposal by Greeno (1970a) provides the type of mechanism necessary. Greeno has proposed rather a revolutionary revision in the stage analysis of human learning discussed in Chapter 1. It will be recalled that traditionally two important stages have been identified (besides stimulus learning), response integration and associative hookup. It has been generally agreed that responses must come into the subject's active repertoire before they can be attached to stimuli. Based on an empirical method of stage analysis, wherein the sensitivity of learning phases to various stimulus and response variables is assessed, Greeno has identified two stages himself, but quite different ones. In a nutshell, the first stage consists of entering into storage the stimulus–response pair as a unit, or *gestalt,* and the second stage consists of discovering a retrieval plan such that given the stimulus, retrieval of the response is possible. Postman and Underwood (1973) have criticized this as a general theory of human learning, but for the moment the essential point is that Greeno's first stage portrays the stimulus and response as an interacting unit where each term affects the encoding of the other. To take an extreme example, when the pair WHITE–HOUSE is entered into memory a very different content occurs than the sum of encodings for the two words independently (see Chapter 11). Martin uses this concept to his advantage in negative transfer by suggesting that when the same old nominal stimulus occurs with a new response term that new response term facilitates, or indeed dictates, a different encoding of the stimulus. In our example it is partly because of the new response, 78, that the encoding of ZAT switches from *sat* to *fat*.

2. Given a mechanism for switching encodings from the first to the second list, what is the evidence that subjects actually do so? Unfortunately for the theory, the evidence is rather weak. The most direct method of testing the encoding shift hypothesis is the sort of experiment reported by Goggin and Martin (1970). In their study three groups learned two lists conforming to the $A-B$, $A-D$ paradigm. The experimental conditions were defined by extra cues presented along with the stimulus terms. These extra cues were sometimes relevant and sometimes irrelevant. In the stay condition, for example, the stimulus terms were forms; on the first list, these forms were paired with digits. There was variation in the color in which the forms appeared, but these colors were not correlated in any way with the responses. When the second list came, the same forms had to be associated with different digits and again, it was irrelevant to the task what colors were used. This condition is called the "stay" condition to represent the subject's obligation to remain with the same encoding attribute, form, during the second list that he had used during the first list. In the second condition, called the "switch" condition, if form were the relevant variable in the first list, color would be the relevant variable in the second list. In other words, in moving to the second list the subject would now have to ignore the form of the stimuli and pay attention only to the colors in which the forms were printed. The free condition used second lists where there was a perfect correlation between color and form—that is, a triangle would consistently be presented in red and a square consistently in blue. The prediction from stimulus-encoding theory is that these subjects ought to switch. Just as our example has called for switching from the *sat* to the *fat* interpretation of ZAT, so also in this experiment subjects who have been selectively attending to form should now find it to their advantage to attend to color. However, the finding was that the free subjects behaved indistinguishably from the stay subjects. Both the free and stay subjects suffered significantly more retroactive inhibition than the switch subjects. Therefore, the free subjects would have been better off if they had followed the reasoning behind Martin's stimulus-encoding theory and behaved as the switch subjects but for some reason they did not. Related studies with similar outcomes have been reported by Williams and Underwood (1970) and by Weaver, McCann, and Wehr (1970). Although this type of experiment is probably the most direct test of the encoding-shift hypothesis, there are other kinds of data that are somewhat more positive (see Martin, 1972, pp. 71–75).

3. How can separate encodings of the same nominal stimulus be independent if one encoding is associated with another? A third issue raised by Martin's theory of stimulus encoding in negative transfer concerns the independence of stimulus components from each other. Clearly, if there are four possible encodings of a nominal stimulus, and if two of them are tied, respectively, to the $A-D$ list responses and the $A-B$ list responses, then if these encodings are

themselves associated, a retrieval test is likely to show exactly the dependency not observed in the DaPolito-type analyses. That is, if the encoding of ZAT learned in the first list—sat—were associated with the encoding learned in the second list—fat—then if either were retrieved at recall there would be some facilitation in retrieval of the other. An important assertion of the theory, therefore, is that the stimulus components do not become associated with each other although each can be associated individually with the response. To bring such independence to the surface Wichawut and Martin (1971) presented word triads associated with additional single words as responses, all in a paired-associate setting. In testing, single words from the stimulus triads were presented and subjects were asked to produce all other words belonging in that item, both other stimulus words and the response words. The major finding was that if the subject was able to emit the response term, then he could also produce other stimulus terms. However, if a stimulus component did not lead to the response, there was no probability of its leading to another stimulus component. Although it is possible to conclude that the subject never saw (functionally) stimulus components that led neither to a response nor to other stimulus components, it would be possible to interpret these data as consistent with stimulus-component independence. Martin obviously prefers the latter view, whereas Postman and Underwood (1973) present arguments and evidence favoring the former view.

It is likely to be some years before the viability of stimulus-encoding theory can be assessed with any confidence, as indeed the viability of interference theory can hardly be said to have been established even now after 30 years. One great virtue of the stimulus-encoding theory is that it reinstates into the psychology of memory the stimulus problem—that is, it provides machinery for the crucial step wherein a physical stimulus gets attached to a perceptual response. This neglected aspect of associative learning has been termed the Hoffding problem, after the gestalt psychologist who emphasized it (Rock, 1962).

CONCLUSIONS

In this section we shall try to do two things: (1) review the highlights of interference theory and its evolution and (2) offer some perspective on the status of the theory today.

Chapter Summary

The main feature of any version of interference theory is the location of observed forgetting decrements at the retrieval stage: Retained responses from similar stimulus situations are aroused in testing and somehow inhibit one another through competition. The major historical competitors to interference theory assign forgetting (that is, observed performance losses) to different stages. The decay theory attributes forgetting to an actual weakening of the memory trace during the retention stage and the consolidation theory attributes forgetting to disruption of a lingering covert after effect of the acquisition stage. For a variety of reasons decay and consolidation are no longer considered viable *general* theories of forgetting and almost all experimental attention in the last few decades has been devoted to what version of interference theory is most adequate to account for the evidence.

Although McGeoch's (1942) three-factor theory of forgetting included statements of *stimulus change* (generalization decrement) and *inadequate set,* all of his experimental and theoretical energy went into an exploration of transfer and competition as factors in retroactive inhibition. The first major revision of McGeoch's ideas on retroactive inhibition came with the Melton and Irwin (1940) *unlearning hypothesis* that original associations underwent experimental extinction during interpolated learning; a corollary was that the unlearned associations would display *spontaneous recovery* with the passage of time since interpolated learning. The spontaneous-recovery corollary assumed great importance when Underwood (1957) made the case that proactive inhibition was more influential a source of observed forgetting than retroactive inhibition, the increasing time course of proactive inhibition being attributed to recovery of prior associations.

The Postman (1961) statment, "The Present Status of Interference Theory," incorporated the unlearning–recovery machinery with then-available evidence on retroactive and proactive inhibition and the entire package was both internally consistent and largely in harmony with the data. However, since 1961, interference theory has been greatly complicated by disappointments in the laboratory and by alternative or supplemental hypotheses that have been offered in response. There have been three major empirical disappointments: (1) little or no evidence for spontaneous recovery has been obtained in MMFR testing; (2) predictions based on the interaction of single lists from the laboratory with prior natural-language habits have consistently failed to work out; and (3) evidence on the pairwise specificity of interference and competition has been mixed at best (for example, the DaPolito independence phenomenon and the reduction in retroactive inhibition with multiple-choice testing). These findings have led to such revised notions about interference as the *list-differentiation hypothesis* of Underwood, the *response-set suppression hypothesis* of Postman, and the *stimulus-encoding hypothesis* of Martin.

Interference Theory Today

How should we evaluate the confused theoretical state that has been unfolding recently? There are basically two approaches and choosing between them is largely a matter of conceptual style on the part of the scientist. One possibility is to cling to the principle of parsimony and hope that one reasonably simple mechanism can play the unifying role of unlearning and recovery in the 1961 theory. In certain places in their writings, Martin (1971) and Postman *et al.* (1968) seem to be trying for such comprehensiveness with their stimulus-encoding and response-set suppression theories, respectively. A second approach is to abandon parsimony to some degree and to embrace each new hypothesis as a supplement to the overall theory when data demand such a supplemental hypothesis. This second approach is defended on the grounds that it was foolish ever to have expected a simple explanation to be adequate given the great complexity of the target behavior.

The answer is far from clear as to which of these approaches is better. In connection with the first, we saw that the two most serious alternatives to unlearning and recovery, response-set suppression and stimulus encoding, stumble almost immediately on experimental disconfirmation, the former somewhat more than the latter. The second strategy, adding on new assumptions as they become necessary, is of course, not likely to be disconfirmed but precisely that fact is its chief weakness.

According to Kuhn (1962) scientific revolutions begin with a gradual process of accumulation of major and minor inconsistencies. However, until a totally new way of asking questions, a truly revolutionary conceptualization, occurs, we live with the old system for want of an alternative, appreciating that it is a somewhat damaged structure. It now seems that the interference approach to forgetting and human learning is now in such a stage of development. With such concepts as unlearning, response competition, list differentiation, generalized competition, the selector mechanism, forward associations, contextual associations, backward associations, response integration, and more, there are few individual findings that cannot somehow be accommodated. However, accommodating much of the evidence reviewed in the last section of this chapter is at the expense of more and more epicycles and, furthermore, the point has been reached where it is not clear exactly what type of evidence is sufficient to falsify the theory.

In closing, we should cite the reservations held about the theory by Postman and Underwood (1973) themselves. The major problem, as they see it, is the failure of the present theory, even with its various epicycles, to handle proactive inhibition with any economy. The problem is that any version of unlearning or suppression hypothesis has nothing to say about the process of interference from prior learning. Therefore, the concept of response competition must be used. However, it has been repeatedly demonstrated (Koppenaal, 1963) that proactive inhibition occurs and shows reliable increases with time when testing is by MMFR; that is, the second of two lists in an $A-B$, $A-D$ situation is forgotten more rapidly than a single list, even when tested under conditions believed to eliminate competition, specific or generalized, among responses.

Somehow, therefore, it must be assumed that MMFR does not eliminate competition. This strikes Postman and Underwood as possible, but unattractive. They suggest an alternative possibility, which holds that in $A-B$ acquisition the subject "uses up" the good mediators, or stimulus encodings, leaving only less stable bases for formation of $A-D$ associations in the second list. We shall not examine the mechanisms of this hypothesis, but clearly it is formulated in a language totally foreign to earlier assumptions of interference theory.

9
The Effects of Repetition on Memory

If any generalization is basic to the field of learning it is that an experience that occurs twice is more likely to be remembered than a single experience. In this chapter we consider the conditions under which this generalization holds true and theories about why it is true.

THE APPARENT GRADUALNESS OF LEARNING

That perfection through practice is fundamentally a gradual process is so compelling an intuition that few laymen, and few psychologists until recently, would pause to question it. As Ebbinghaus (1964, originally published 1885) put it:

> These relations can be described figuratively by speaking of the series as being more or less deeply engraved on some mental substratum. To carry out this figure: as the number of repetitions increases, the series are engraved more and more deeply and indelibly; if the number of repetitions is small, the inscription is but surface deep and only fleeting glimpses of the tracery can be caught; with a somewhat greater number the inscription can, at least for a time, be read at will; as the number of repetitions is still further increased, the deeply cut picture of the series fades out only after longer intervals [pp. 52–53].

For Ebbinghaus the job was not to question these self-evident truths but to discover the mathematical form of the relationship; for example, he speculated, and later demonstrated empirically, that the rate of learning is at first more rapid than it is later, a property called _negative acceleration_. In the tradition of Ebbinghaus there was considerable early work on the ideal form of the learning curve: Is negative acceleration universal? Is the underlying form, rather, S shaped? Is the learning curve a different shape for different subpopulations of subjects? This research tradition is summarized in Chapter III of McGeoch's book (McGeoch, 1942; see also McGeoch & Irion, 1952).

As plausible as the intuition of gradual learning is, however, an equally plausible intuition in the field of *problem solving* is that acquisition comes through a sudden process of insight, at least some of the time. Köhler (1925) was not the first to subscribe to insight as a sudden mode of performance change (see Yerkes, 1916) but he provided what, for many, was a vivid image on which to peg the concept—the chimpanzee Sultan reaching from between the bars of her cage with a contrived tool of two sticks in order to reach a banana. In the field of animal discrimination learning the controversy between gradual strengthening and sudden insight was debated with clever experimentation and warm polemics in the 1930s and 1940s (Krechevsky, 1938; Spence, 1945). For all intents and purposes, Harlow (1949) resolved much of the controversy by showing that inexperienced monkeys solve perceptual-discrimination problems with slow step by step gains in performance, whereas subjects who have had experience with hundreds of such problems previously solve them in a sudden insightful manner, often after a single trial.

All-or-None Memorization

The logical steps necessary to connect the apparently gradual progress in learning with the apparently sudden progress in problem solving are to assume that (1) the learning process involves insight and (2) the gradual appearance of learning curves is caused by an artifact. Rock (1957) made this connection explicitly, and along with Estes (1960) opened the gradual versus sudden controversy again within the field of human verbal learning.

The first part of Rock's argument was that subjects face individual pairs on a paired-associate list as individual problems the solution for which entails hitting on a *dependable mnemonic,* much in the manner of image formation, which has been studied more recently in experiments on visual imagery (see Chapter 5). There is nothing cumulative about such discovery of a mediating device; it occurs all at once.

The demonstration that gradual acquisition curves may be artifactual is simple: Even if the underlying acquisition process is sudden insight, this insight can be expected to occur on different trials for different items on a list of, say, a dozen paired associates. Rock asserted that on a given trial through the list, the subject only paid attention to a few of the pairs, succeeding, perhaps, on only some of these. What seems for an individual subject to be the growth of mastery on a list of items, therefore, is in fact a mixture of perfect learning on those items for which an adequate mnemonic has been found and complete ignorance on those items for which an adequate mnemonic has not been found. This general position soon came to be known as the "all-or-none" theory of learning and has been contrasted with "incremental" learning.

The gross analysis of learning curves.   Even if we disregard differences in time of learning for different items on the list, we may still not make any safe inferences about the sudden or gradual nature of learning from group acquisition curves. The problem is that different subjects are expected to learn at different rates because of differences in ability, motivation, and so forth. The top half of Figure 9.1 illustrates the problem: On the left part of the top panel we see an average learning curve representing the combined performance of a number of different subjects. The right portion of the top panel shows how this group curve may be the average of subjects all of whom have either learned in gradual increments or all of whom have learned by sudden transitions from zero to perfect performance on a single trial.

Can we then examine individual protocols of single subjects for single items and determine whether these show sudden or gradual acquisition? Yes, but even the result of this inspection is inconclusive, as the lower panel in Figure 9.1 shows: First of all, the result of a single-subject—single-item acquisition curve necessarily tends to resemble the sudden curve on the left-hand side for many situations, because there is often no response the subject can emit that is only partially correct. (If the response term is a single digit, how can it be given partially correct?) However, even though the all-or-none performance shown in Figure 9.1 is consistent with an all-or-none acquisition process, it is also consistent with a gradual, incremental theory of acquisition that includes the concept of a response threshold. This assumption is that even though strength may be accumulating through gradual increments over trials, this strength must exceed some critical threshold value before it is expressed in performance. Therefore, the gross characteristics of acquisition curves are irrelevant to the controversy and we must examine experimental situations of a more analytic nature. There are three such experimental situations, representing contributions of Rock (1957), Estes (1960), and Bower (1962).

Rock's dropout experiment.   Let us consider an item that, in the course of learning a list, has not yet been responded to correctly. According to the all-or-none theory this item is still at zero strength but according to the incremental theory it is at some intermediate, subthreshold strength. Rock's (1957) idea was to compare these contrasting assessments of a not yet recalled item by dropping it out and replacing it with a completely new item. If the incremental theory were true, then by throwing away a partially learned but not yet correctly recalled item we would delay ultimate mastery of the list. If the all-or-none theory were true then throwing away such items would not make any difference because, until they are learned, such items might as well not have even been there.

Rock used the recall method of paired-associate learning, in which study trials through the list alternated with test trials. Following each test trial for the experimental group, Rock removed items that had not been given a correct

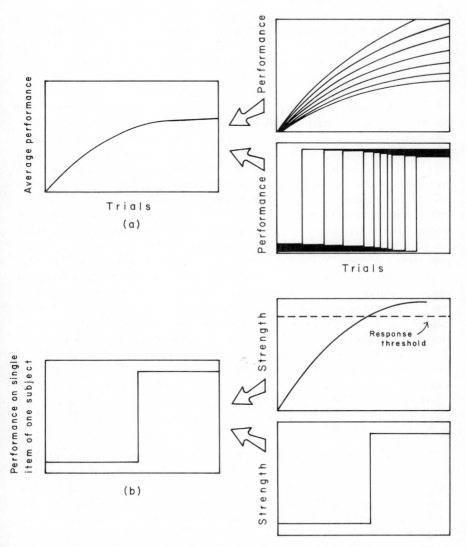

FIGURE 9.1 The impossibility of establishing all-or-none or incremental learning (a) from group performance curves or (b) from individual performance curves. In each panel the observed curves on the left could have resulted from either of the two underlying representations of strength on the right.

response on that particular trial and replaced them, prior to the study trial that followed immediately, with completely new items the subject had never seen. The materials in this study were pairs with single or double letters as stimuli and two-digit numbers as responses. In the control group, subjects simply practiced the same unchanging list until they learned it; in fact, both groups continued alternating study and test trials until they reached the criterion of one perfect recitation. To repeat, the logic of the study is that according to an incremental model the control group should reach criterion faster than the experimental group because the former gets the benefit of any subthreshold learning that occurs on a trial whereas the experimental group does not.

The result, in two separate replications reported by Rock (1957) was identical performance for the control and experimental groups, in support of the all-or-none prediction. In the discussion section of his results Rock observed the possibility of an artifact inherent with his procedure, however. The artifact was a consequence of the fact that within the entire pool of possible paired associates from which items were sampled, some would necessarily be more difficult than others. The experimental group, furthermore, would be expected to miss difficult items disproportionately. This meant the experimental group would be having difficult items dropping out from trial to trial and would eventually wind up with an easier list than the control subjects, who were "stuck with" whichever pairs had been selected for them on the first trial. Although Rock discounted the potential importance of this artifact in his article, subsequent research (Williams, 1961) indicated that it was a decisively important consideration: When a control-group subject is asked to learn whatever particular list of items someone in the experimental (dropout) group has wound up with at the time he has reached criterion, the control subject has a significant advantage on the average. Therefore, although Rock's study served the important function of rearousing interest in the nature of the acquisition process among workers in verbal learning (a matter often left for students of learning in birds, rats, and monkeys in those days), and although he anticipated more modern attitudes about mediation and problem solving in paired-associate learning (Postman & Underwood, 1973), his experiment was, strictly speaking, irrelevant.

The Estes RTT experiment.   Estes (1960) had the idea that evidence pertinent to the all-or-none controversy might come from examination of the microstructure of paired-associate learning trials. Accordingly he invented several types of "miniature experiment" designed to answer specific questions about performance on pairs as a function of their reinforcement and performance histories. In the best known of these, called the RTT paradigm after the sequence, repetition–test–test, Estes contrasted the incremental and all-or-none theories in a provocative manner: Assume a list of paired associates is presented to a group of subjects for a single study trial and then each item is tested a single time by presenting the stimulus terms alone in a different order than their original sequence. For this set of items and subjects the result is a certain probability of correct recall, say, .50. What exactly does this figure mean? If we ignore, for the moment, differences in item difficulty, in subject ability, and guessing, quite different interpretations can be derived from the incremental and the all-or-none theories. According to the incremental theory the .50 success rate means that all the items, for all subjects, have been hovering at around the same intermediate strength of 50% and, because of some oscillation principle or random error, this strength has resulted in correct recall half the time. The all-or-none view is that half the items are fully learned and half are not at all learned.

These two notions lead to quite different predictions for the outcome of a second test trial without intervening study. The incremental theory holds that all subject–item combinations are at an equal strength of .50 (still ignoring any prior familiarity or difficulty factors), both those which on the first test have eventuated in success and also those which on the first test have eventuated in failure. Independent of first-test outcome, therefore, the probability of correct recall ought to be .50 on the second test also. The all-or-none view holds that first-test successes (particular items that have been reported correctly by a given subject) represent cases of perfect learning and therefore should be correct on a second test with a probability of 1.00; items missed by particular subjects on the first test are just like items never presented, that is, they have zero strength, and therefore probability of recalling them on a second test ought to be 0.00 or at a level of guessing. Actually, we would not expect perfect second-test performance on items correct on the first test because subjects might forget learned pairs in between the two tests. However, the other prediction, that performance be at chance on a second test of items that were incorrect initially, holds.

Estes found that the probability of correct recall on the first test was .49. A subsequent test of these items, the ones correctly recalled, gave a probability of .71 correct; this is less than 1.00, but we are allowing for forgetting so this poses no disconfirmation. A second test of items missed on the first test gave a recall probability of .09; this is greater than 0.00 but the recall probability would have been .125 if subjects were simply guessing, so, in effect, the obtained .09 means zero acquired strength. This result is reliable (see also Estes, Hopkins, & Crothers, 1960) and it seems an elegant demonstration of all-or-none learning. However, it is not without its own potential artifacts.

One of these is discussed by Estes (1960) himself, the problem that items are not equally difficult and that those items missed on the first test may have been much harder than those correctly recalled on the first test. If those items missed on the first test were the difficult items we should not expect them to be at .49 on the second test. Estes provided what he considered to be a control against this problem but, on this and other scores, proponents of incremental learning were not convinced (Underwood & Keppel, 1962).

Bower's two-state all-or-none model.   Bower's approach to all-or-none learning was to teach subjects a list of paired-associate items and compare their sequences of successes and failures on individual items with detailed predictions from a simple model. We can do no better than to quote Bower's (1962) own description of this model:

> Considering a single item, it can be in either of two states at the beginning of each trial: conditioned to its correct response or not conditioned. If the item is conditioned at the beginning of a trial, then the correct response occurs. If the item is not conditioned, then the probability of a correct response depends somewhat on the experimental procedure. In experiments by the writer, the subjects were told the N responses (Integers 1, 2, ..., N) available to them and were told to respond on every trial regardless of whether they knew the correct answer. If the N numbers occur equally often as the to-be-learned responses to the items, then the probability that the subject will guess correctly on an unlearned item is $1/N$ on the simplest assumptions; correspondingly, his probablity of guessing incorrectly is $(1 - 1/N)$ [p. 35].

Given these assumptions, we cannot always determine from knowledge of the subject's performance on a particular item on a particular trial whether that item was then in the learned or the unlearned state. In particular, if it was counted as correct, that outcome could have arisen either through a lucky guess or through learning. However, if there has been an error then we know for sure that the item has not yet been learned.

Bower's model has only two parameters c and N: The rate constant c is the probability that an unlearned item becomes learned during a trial. The probability of guessing correctly on an unlearned item is $1/N$, where N is the number of equally likely response alternatives. Prior to learning, an item should show a constant average probability of correct response of $1/N$ and, once learning has occurred, it should show a constant probability of 1.00.

The extreme simplicity of this model allows predictions to be generated with great ease. For example, what is the probability of an item's receiving an incorrect response on Trial n? Following Bower (1962) we shall call this probability q_n. In order to have an error on Trial n, it must have been true that the item was not learned on any of the preceding $n - 1$ trials. The probability of an item's not being learned is $1 - c$ on any trial. By the conventional rules for combining probabilities of independent events, the probability that, trial after trial for $n - 1$ trials, the item has consistently escaped being learned is $(1 - c)^{n-1}$. Because we are interested in the case where an error is made on Trial n, however, we must exclude the possibility that a lucky guess occurs on this trial, $1/N$. So, two things must happen: (1) The item must still be unlearned prior to Trial n, an event with probability $(1 - c)^{n-1}$, and (2) on Trial n the subject must guess wrong, an event with probability $1 - 1/N$. Altogether, the probability of both these necessary events occurring is then $(1 - 1/N)(1 - c)^{n-1}$, the expression we want for q_n. The accuracy of this expression and other more interesting issues, such as the independence of the parameters c and N, can then be evaluated from the data. For a number of such tests, Bower found the observed experimental data corresponded closely with predictions from the model and corresponded very poorly with predictions from an incremental model. In Kintsch (1970, pp. 61–80) and in Greeno (1968, pp. 152–164) there are careful step by step expositions of this type of model and how predictions are derived from it; these are not mathematically difficult treatments and the interested reader is urged to follow them through. A more complete treatment is available in Atkinson, Bower, and Crothers (1965).

The main criterion for evaluating the all-or-none learning model has been the property of *stationarity*. According to the model, performance on an item prior to the last error must arise from nothing but guessing. Say there have been eight trials prior to the last error; if nothing but guessing is producing occasional correct responses during that period then the success rate should be no greater on Trials 5–8 than on Trials 1–4. However, if performance before the last error reflects at least some incremental growth in strength, then we should expect trials just before the last error to show up somewhat better than trials at the very beginning of practice. Stationarity then is the property of a constant success probability across the period up to the trial of last error.

As Kintsch (1970, p. 79) explains, the simple two-state all-or-none model of Bower survives these and other tests beautifully but only under a restricted set of experimental conditions, in which lists of moderate length are used with two response alternatives that are well known to the subject. Once these stipulations are violated, such properties as stationarity do not hold. Binford and Gettys (1965) gave subjects more than two response alternatives and also included the innovation of asking subjects for a second guess following every error. Whereas the all-or-none model clearly requires only chance performance on a second guess, the observed performance was considerably more successful and improved steadily across trials before the last error.

Analytic Value of All-or-None Processes

Recall from Chapter 1 that *task analysis* is the isolation and separation of more elementary subprocesses from a global task. In paired-associate learning the distinction between response learning and associative hookup (Underwood & Schulz, 1960; McGuire, 1961) allows a more analytic application of the all-or-none idea than is possible when these subprocesses are lumped together.

In particular, the failure of Bower's model to fit data from experiments with more than two response alternatives can be rationalized by the assumption that the associative hookup stage is all-or-none and that the response-learning stage is a separate all-or-none process (Kintsch, 1963, 1970, p. 80). This amounts to a three-state all-or-none model: From an initial state of total ignorance an item jumps suddenly to a state wherein the response alternatives are known themselves but not associated with appropriate stimuli and then, finally, another sudden jump to the learned state. This model fits data from experiments where $N > 2$: The nonstationarity observed by earlier workers with such experiments is now predicted, because before the trial of the last error there ought to be a transition between the initial state and the response-learning state and this transition ought to be associated with an improvement in performance. Kintsch (1963) was able to estimate the period during which an item was in the intermediate state and to show that, for this span of trials, stationarity held.

Kintsch (1963) applied the three-state model to Rock's (1957) situation, with the dropout procedure. He found that a model assuming all-or-none processes for both response learning and hookup stages yielded numerically accurate predictions and performance in the experimental group, using parameters estimated only from the control group.

Another task-analytic approach has been to consider the paired-associate task from the viewpoint of forgetting (Bernbach, 1965; see also Restle, 1965). These models take off from the idea that because a particular pair can always be recalled correctly right after its presentation, learning must occur perfectly on every trial, even the very first (see Tulving, 1964, for related ideas about memory processes in trial-to-trial learning tasks). The issue is then whether the association is forgotten or not before the time of the next trial and whether the forgetting is all-or-none.

The issue of gradual versus sudden learning has been set in perspective by a review by Restle (1965). Restle details the variety of assumptions that are often indiscriminately grouped under these labels, isolating four separable versions of all-or-none theory and three versions of incremental theory that produce data resembling those predicted on all-or-none assumptions. In view of the models that compound several all-or-none processes to cover task-analytic stages of learning, Restle concludes that greatly refined statements are needed about what, exactly, is the controversial issue.

> Logically, there are several versions of all-or-none hypothesis, including: (a) All learning is all-or-none; (b) There exists at least one task that is learned all-or-none; (c) A single item of a paired-associate list is learned all-or-none; (d) A single item of a paired-associate list, provided the list includes no stimulus confusion, response integration, etc., may be learned all-or-none; (e) Concept formation, discrimination learning, and certain other tasks are learned all-or-none; (f) Any learning task that involves only one difficulty is learned all-or-none. [Restle, 1965, pp. 323–324.]

From our discussion up to this point we may conclude that (a) and (c) are false on the basis of studies with more than two response alternatives. Hypotheses (b) and (d) are true, depending on what additional factors one wishes to list with the term "etc." in (d). Because a two-alternative paired-associate task is in some respects similar to certain concept-formation tasks (Atkinson *et al.,* 1965; Trabasso & Bower, 1968), there is at least partial support for hypothesis (e), although perhaps not for its inclusive implication that all concept formation is all-or-none. Restle observes that hypothesis (f) is really the most interesting of the set and, although we are not in a position to know exactly how to remove all but one source of difficulty from a task, still, the application of separable all-or-none processes to multiple-state models has proved instructive. In a similar vein Kintsch (1970) concludes:

The question posed initially, whether learning is all-or-none or incremental thus turns out to be badly put. The true problem seems to be: under what conditions should learning be represented as an all-or-none process, under what conditions can it be represented as the sum of several all-or-none processes, and under what conditions is a genuine incremental model appropriate? [p. 85]

The most conservative conclusion is perhaps that the almost axiomatic belief of Ebbinghaus that repetition strengthens a unitary memory trace has been shaken by a new body of sharply analytic and skeptical research. It is against this background that several new experimental and theoretical programs for conceiving of the nature of repetition have emerged in the last decade; to these we now turn.

EFFECTS ON RECALL OF SPACING REPETITIONS OF INDIVIDUAL ITEMS

So far in this chapter our interest has been in tracing the consequences for performance of different numbers of presentations as manifested in practice curves. Now we shall put the problem in a more subtle context: Given the same number of presentations what are factors that affect the recallability of repeated items? The particular factor isolated for study in this section is the amount of spacing, or lag, that intervenes between two occurrences of a repeated item. In gross terms, it has been found that a repetition is more effective if the two occurrences of the repeated item are spaced widely apart, in a sequence of other items to be remembered, than if they are massed closely. This phenomenon is the point of departure for numerous theories of why it is that repeating an experience improves its memorability in the first place. Obviously, therefore, the material to be reviewed in this section is perfectly central to theories of learning.

There are three main experimental methodologies in which repetition spacing has been studied extensively: free recall, continuous paired-associate learning, and the short-term memory distractor method. A number of distinguishable theoretical notions have been offered to cover data in these situations. Because the theoretical notions are most easily described within the experimental context from which they have arisen, we shall adopt a methodological organization for the remainder of the chapter. However, it is to be hoped that the generality of the problem and, more important, the generality of its solution, will not be lost because of this organizational scheme. For a somewhat different organization of this material, the reader can consult a recent review of spacing effects by Hintzman (1974). Another source of information about spacing effects is a group of papers given at the Midwestern Psychological Association meetings in May, 1969, and subsequently published together in the *Journal of Verbal Learning and Verbal Behavior,* Volume 9, Number 5 (1970).

Spacing of Repetitions in Free Recall

A reference experiment for the influence of repeating items within a free-recall list has been reported by Melton (1967) and the major result of his experiment is shown in Figure 9.2. [The data of Figure 9.2 actually come from a close replication of Melton's (1967) study reported by Madigan (1969); Melton's reference is only a preliminary report.] Forty-eight different words were presented visually at a rate of 1.5 sec per word. Some words occurred once on the list; however, other words occurred twice. For the latter, the main variable of interest was the number of events (presentations of other words) intervening between the two occurrences of the repeated item, the *lag* at which the item was repeated. In Figure 9.2 the probability of recall is given as a function of whether or not items were repeated, and if so, at what lag. The obvious chief findings were that performance on twice-presented items was better than on singly presented items and that this advantage was a systematically increasing function of lag. Melton (1970) has shown that the lag effect in free recall is independent of rate of presentation (between 1.3 and 4.3 sec per word) and occurs with either visual or auditory presentation. A number of remarks on this important empirical relationship are necessary before we go on to survey the various theories that have been proposed to cover it.

Control over positions of occurrence within the list.   Given only the data from Figure 9.2, the alert reader should become suspicious of an artifact. From Chapter 6 we are well aware that performance on free-recall lists is a function of the serial position occupied by a particular item, with a special advantage in recall to items occurring near either the beginning or near the end of the list. The problem for the interpretation of the data in Figure 9.2 is that items repeated at

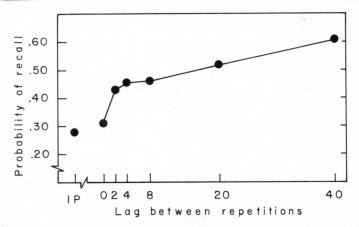

FIGURE 9.2   Recall probability as a function of repetition and the lag between occurrences of repeated items: 1P is one presentation. (After Madigan, 1969.)

long lags have necessarily been presented closer to the advantageous early and late list positions than items repeated at shorter lags. For example, if there were only 50 presentation positions within some hypothetical list, an item repeated at a lag of 48 would have to occur in Positions 1 and 50 and one would not know whether performance on that item was excellent because it was repeated at a long lag or because it occurred in the last (and in this case first) serial position, where recall would be excellent anyway. In contrast, an item repeated at a lag of five or ten could easily have been located anywhere in the list, without getting near the primacy and recency ranges. In other words, the increasing function relating recall probability to lag may simply reflect the increasing likelihood that, at longer and longer lags, occurrences of repeated items get "pushed out" toward regions of the list where performance is uniformly good.

Concerning Melton's experiment there are two replies to this potentially dangerous artifact. The list contained, as we have said, 48 different words, four words each at the six values of lag tested and eight items presented only once. That makes a total of $(4 \times 6) + 8 = 32$ words (and 56 presentation events) thus far. In addition, Melton's subjects saw eight items at the very beginning and eight items at the very of the list that were "buffers," producing a total list length of 72 events. These 16 items in the buffer zones were indistinguishable from the other items on the list to the subjects. However, the main data tabulations and analysis completely ignored these primacy and recency buffers; they were only there to absorb, as it were, the bulk of the primacy and recency effects, so that the observations of interest would come from a relatively flat part of the serial-position function.

Second, if one remains suspicious that these buffers may not have removed all of the primacy and recency effects, one can examine particular repeated items according to the exact locations of their repetitions. The relevant question would then be: "For a repeated item the last occurrence of which was exactly at position 63, was performance higher if the first occurrence were at a long lag (say of 40) than if it were at a shorter lag (say of 8)?" An analysis of data from a comparable study by Glenberg (1974) summarizing the results of such an inquiry is given in Figure 9.3. We note from the figure, first, that indeed there is an extended recency effect, even when items from the eight-position recency buffer are thrown out. However, the figure shows also that for a given list position there is an independent contribution of lag to performance. That is, although it is true that having its second occurrence within the last dozen positions helps any repeated item, still performance for such an item is better if the first occurrence has been spaced at a larger lag than if it has been spaced at a smaller lag.

Terminology. There are actually several different phenomena in the data of Figure 9.2 and they ought to be distinguished carefully. A *repetition* effect refers to the fact that all conditions in which a word has been presented two

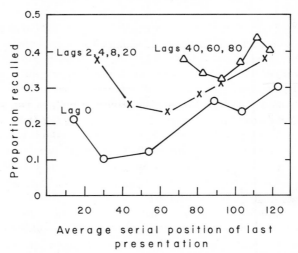

FIGURE 9.3   Recall probability for repeated words with varying lags between repetitions as a function of the serial position of the last occurrence of the item. (After Glenberg, 1974.)

times show much better recall than those in which a word has been presented only once. A *distribution* effect refers to the fact that performance is better when at least some other items separate the two occurrences of a repeated word, than when these repetitions occur back to back, at a lag of zero. Finally, it is the case that when at least some other items separate the repetition, performance steadily improves as a function of how many intervening items there are, a pattern of results we may call the *lag effect.* (Some writers have also termed this latter result the "Melton effect" in deference to its discoverer.) Some empirical controversy has surrounded the distribution and lag effects, although not the repetition effect; why apparently comparable experimental procedures have not always produced consistent results is discussed in detail by Melton (1970) but it should not detain us here.

Violation of the total time law. The third remark about the findings of Figure 9.2 is that they violate an otherwise useful principle in human memory called the "total time law" (Bugelski, 1962; Cooper & Pantle, 1967). This empirical generalization states that, within certain limits, the degree to which an item can be recalled is a direct function of the total study time afforded it independently of how that study time is distributed among short, frequent exposures or long, infrequent exposures. For example, five 2-sec study opportunities ought to lead to performance comparable to ten 1-sec opportunities. Whereas this law does indeed apply to numerous diverse situations, it is very clearly denied by both the distribution and the lag effects, because in those two cases exactly the same study time is simply occurring at different points in time.

The independence baseline. Waugh (1963) pointed out that rational expectations for recall of repeated items could be derived from performance on once-presented items. If the subject remembered two totally independent experiences on the two occasions in which the nominally identical item occurred, he would receive the same score for recalling either the first of these two memories, the second, or both. Take the single-presentation recall probability from the Melton–Madigan study, .28, as an overall estimate of memory for single presentation events. The probablity of recalling either or both of two such independent events is then $p_1 + p_2 - p_1 p_2 = .28 + .28 - (.28)(.28) = .48$, where p_1 and p_2 stand for probabilities of recalling the first and second events. Using this independence baseline as our estimate of what recall should be for repeated words, we see that in Figure 9.2 recall is below expectations for a lag of zero and somewhat above it for long lags. Massed practice is worse than independence, as it were, and distributed practice is better.

Notice in Figure 9.3, however, that there is an extended recency effect stretching back across the list in this kind of experiment, even when we discard performance on items from the primacy and recency buffers. Because our single-presentation estimate of .28 has been taken from all serial positions except for the buffer zones, there may be some contamination from serial position of the comparison between single-presentation performance and performance at long lags. What we need are estimates of single-presentation performance taken specifically from the two serial positions at which our repeated items are to occur. For example, if we were interested in whether repetition at positions 34 and 54 were better or worse than the independence baseline, we would proceed as follows: First, we would examine performance on nonrepeated items at these two positions, say .25 and .30. Then, we would determine the independent-events probability of getting either or both of these positions correct, $.25 + .30 - (.25)(.30) = .475$. This, finally, is the estimate against which to examine actual performance when the same item is repeated in those two locations. Glanzer (1969, Experiment II) has performed the equivalent of this procedure and reports that with increasing lags performance on twice-repeated items approaches and meets the independence baseline but does not exceed it significantly.

The proper summary of the matter therefore seems to be that at short lags performance on repeated items is poorer than is expected from two independent memory traces but that it converges on this expectation at longer lags. This generalization is not just a passing curiosity; it has been interpreted and expanded to particularly good theoretical advantage by Paivio (1974), as we shall see in a later section.

Theoretical Alternatives for Distribution and Lag Effects

Figure 9.2 presents a theoretical problem of the very first importance for learning and memory: Why and under what circumstances does repetition of an event improve its memorability? There is no theory of learning that does not embrace the fact that repetition leads to enhanced performance; the explanatory puzzle here is why this improvement is dependent on spacing of repetitions. We now survey very briefly the range of theoretical views on this issue.

Strength. The central premise of explanatory devices based on the concept of strength is that there is a single memory trace corresponding to an event, such as a word, and that repetitions increase the strength of that single trace in a monotonic manner. In Figure 9.4 is shown the application of the strength hypothesis to repetition. Presentation of an item causes an abrupt increment in strength, which is then lost during intervening delays. The effect of repetition is to cause an equal increment in strength to that caused by the first presentation, with a constant forgetting slope afterwards. That is, the rate of loss is the same after the second presentation as after the first, but the starting point is higher.

This theory is included here mainly because it figures prominently in a research problem initiated by Morton (1968) that is considered later in this chapter. It is obviously not useful here, for it predicts that massed practice ought to be superior to distributed practice, which is contrary to the fact.

Inattention. Waugh (1970), Greeno (1970b), and Underwood (1970) have suggested that the distribution and lag effects should not be described as an enhancement of performance at widely spaced lag intervals but rather as a

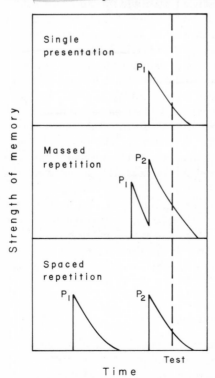

FIGURE 9.4 The strength theory of memory as applied to repetition-spacing effects: P1 is first presentation; P2 is second presentation.

depression in performance at massed lags. Furthermore, they specify that the inhibitory mechanism at short spacing intervals has to do with more or less voluntary disengagement of some active acquisition process caused by boredom. The proposition is, first of all, that recall is really in principle determined by total study time, setting the theoretical recall value for twice-presented items, perhaps, at what we have described above as the independence baseline. Second, however, the subject is assumed not to get (or take) the full benefit of total study time under conditions of massed practice. According to some adherents to the inattention theory (but not Greeno, 1970b) the subject reinvests whatever capacity is detracted from the second occurrence of the repeated item, in massed repetition, in some other processing activity, possibly the encoding of other items in nearby list positions. Note that the locus of the spacing effect for inattention theories is clearly at the second rather than the first occurrence of the repeated item.

Glanzer (1969) and Greeno (1970b) have advanced a variation on the inattention theory that entails a special role for primary memory. From Waugh and Norman (1965) the assumption is accepted that secondary-memory strength is proportional to the time information resides in primary memory. Additionally, the two-store inattention theory suggests that the rate of transfer from primary to secondary memory is somewhat under the control of the subject, perhaps through the degree of effort applied to rehearsal or to some elaborative encoding process. The critical assumption is that when an item arrives that is already represented in primary memory there is a reduction in the transfer rate: When a completely fresh item occurs, the subject devotes a full measure of effort into a secondary-memory transfer; however, when an item occurs that the subject already seems to know, because it is still held in primary memory, it is given less effort. Note that the item need not have actually been promoted to secondary memory: Its presence in primary memory simply gives what may be a false sense of security, as it were. If, finally, the first occurrence of a double-presentation item has completely passed from primary memory at the time of the second occurrence, then the repeated item can be expected to benefit from the amount of processing appropriate to two independent items.

We should not pass from this preliminary sketch without commenting that, as it stands, the two-store inattention notion is incapable of handling the lag effect that Melton has obtained over extended lags. The reason is clear: The probability of the repeated item's first occurrence still residing in primary memory should have dropped to zero by the time about three additional items have been presented and therefore full processing should be occurring uniformly at all lags wider than this. The difficulty is that to explain an advantage of extended lags the two-store theory has to maintain that even after a lag of 20 items there is still some probability of primary-memory representation of the first presentation, otherwise there is no reason for finding better performance with a still wider lag.

Consolidation.   In another context we have seen that Hebb's dual-trace mechanism is the ancestor of current notions that experience is first represented in labile reverberatory form and then promoted into a permanent form of storage later. Landauer (1967) has worked out an articulation of consolidation theory that allows a direct application to the free-recall studies being covered here. The main assumption is that the first process, neural reverberation (in Hebb's language the activity trace) decays steadily and that the amount of consolidation into long-term, permanent memory is proportional to the integral of the decay curve—the area under the curve showing short-term decay. This reasoning is illustrated in Figure 9.5 and is applied there to short and long lags. Although the momentary strength of consolidation is the same whatever the spacing interval, adding a second presentation merely restores the process to the same maximum. That is, whenever the second presentation occurs it simply resets the consolidation process as if the first presentation has never occurred. This being the case, there is more total consolidation activity for distributed than for massed repetition. However, note here that the effects of the second occurrence of the repeated item are constant, independent of lag, and that it is the differential

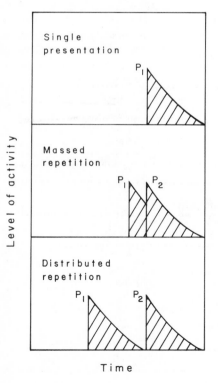

FIGURE 9.5   The consolidation theory of memory as applied to repetition-spacing effects. The amount of permanent memory is proportional to the shaded areas of the three panels.

effectiveness of the first occurrence that determines the lag effect, exactly opposite to what is held by the inattention theories.

The *rehearsal* hypothesis of Atkinson and Shiffrin (1968; see below) has the same logical structure as the consolidation hypothesis. Their notion is that when the interpresentation lag is long there is more total rehearsal for a repeated item than when the interpresentation lag is short. The overt-rehearsal technique of Rundus (1971), which we introduced in Chapter 6, provides direct support for this assertion. When Rundus asked subjects to supply a continuous running vocalization of their rehearsals during a slow-paced free-recall experiment with variation in interpresentation lags of repeated items, he found that short-lag items had less total rehearsal than long-lag items and that the difference could be attributed to differential rehearsal during the lag itself. Like the consolidation hypothesis, therefore, the Atkinson–Shiffrin rehearsal hypothesis maintains that the differential processing favoring long lags occurs in response to the first rather than to the second presentation of the repeated item. Also, like the consolidation hypothesis, the rehearsal hypothesis emphasizes the relation between total processing and some single commodity, long-term storage strength. The two hypotheses differ in that consolidation is conceived by most to be an involuntary, perhaps unconscious, process, whereas rehearsal is conceived by most to be a voluntary, conscious process. The structure of the explanation is therefore the same in a logical sense, and how much of a distinction one wants to draw on the basis of the voluntary–involuntary opposition is at least partly a matter of taste (see Hintzman, 1974).

Encoding variability. Melton (1970) and Madigan (1969) have endorsed hypotheses for the lag and distribution effects that rely on variability in encoding. Figure 9.6 gives the flavor of encoding variability notions. This theory recognizes quite explicitly that the memory representation of a word—how it gets encoded—depends on the cognitive context in which it occurs. For example (see Thomson, 1972), the item IRON is going to be encoded differently when neighboring list items are COPPER, ZINC, and BRASS, than when the neighboring items are CLOTHES and STARCH. This is an extreme example, of course, and it serves only to make the point that all words are somewhat ambiguous semantically and that they always occur in one type of conceptual framework or another. What becomes crucial is the context operating at the time of retrieval, in particular whether the subject can recreate some or all of the contextual cues available during list presentation. Assuming that ordinarily he cannot recreate all the context that has prevailed at presentation, then an item stands a higher chance of retrieval if it has occurred in two contexts—two conceptual neighborhoods—than if it has occurred in only one. As Figure 9.6 illustrates, massed repetitions tend to restrict a word to one encoding context, whereas spaced repetitions tend to diversify the encoding context used and therefore enhance recall in the long run. The usefulness of multiple encodings may come from

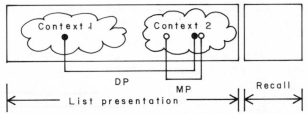

FIGURE 9.6 The encoding-variability theory of repetition and spacing effects: DP is distributed practice; MP is massed practice.

having two memory traces per se, or, as Melton (1970) suggests, from having two retrieval routes directed at the same memory trace. We shall distinguish these two alternatives below.

Experimental Tests of the Alternative Theoretical Explanations

At the time of writing there is no single clear favorite among the several theoretical notions that have been advanced to explain the free-recall spacing data. However, some agreement has been reached on the types of experimental techniques that are capable of permitting inference on the matter and we shall outline these now.

The locus of the effect.   One important difference between the consolidation theory and the inattention theory is that variation in recall as a function of lag is caused by variation in registration of the first occurrence of the repeated item, according to the consolidation theory, and by variation in the registration of the second occurrence, according to the inattention theory. If we could only determine which of the two occurrences suffered at short lag intervals, we could exclude one of these classes of explanation. (The encoding variability theory is not explicit as to which occurrence should vary most because, with this theory, it is the multiplicity of encoding contexts that makes a difference and not their order.)

Hintzman, Block, and Summers (1973) capitalized on the phenomenon of *modality tagging* to help settle this point. Modality tagging is the process whereby subjects are able to report on the particular format in which an item has been presented in a long list, not just on whether or not it has been presented. In one experiment on modality tagging, these authors presented a list of 80 words, some auditory, some visual, some occurring once and some occurring twice; of those items occurring twice, some were in the same modality on each occurrence, and some were given in two modalities, either auditory–visual or visual–auditory. The main finding of this experiment (Hintzman *et al.*, 1973, Experiment I) was very simple: People were quite good at recalling the modality or modalities in which a word had been presented. Given a word, for example, that had been presented twice, first auditorily and second visually, the

mean judgment that exactly that order of mixed-mode presentations had occurred was 35%; on only 15% of the occasions did people think such a word had
been visually presented first and auditorily second (4 and 6%, respectively, of
the responses were for the auditory–auditory and visual–visual alternatives). The
accuracy of modality tagging has several theoretical implications but an immediate methodological implication is that by varying the lag between mixed-
modality repetitions one can determine which tag, that associated with the first
or with the second occurrence, is the one to suffer from closely massed
repetitions.

Hintzman *et al.* (1973, Experiment II) gave their subjects a list of 120
presentation events, including second occurrences of words presented twice; the
items were distributed among several conditions of repetition and modality.
Single-presentation items were presented in either the visual or the auditory
modality. Repeated items were presented in four modality arrangements, visual–visual, visual–auditory, auditory–visual, and auditory–auditory, each represented at four spacing intervals—lags of 0, 1, 5, and 15 intervening items. In
testing the subject was given a list with words from all input conditions mixed
together with words that had not occurred. The task was to make a frequency
judgment as to whether each word on the test list occurred zero, one, or
two times and, if it had occurred, in what modality or modalities it had
occurred. The measure of performance for this study is not whether an item can
or cannot be retrieved, therefore, but whether its frequency and circumstances
of occurrence can be remembered. (We shall deal in more detail with the
frequency-judgment task later in this chapter.)

The data analysis for this experiment is somewhat complex but we can
summarize its argument without going into detail: Take one of the two mixed-
mode repetition conditions, say visual–auditory. Now, for this condition the
subject would sometimes correctly judge that items had, in fact, occurred under
the visual–auditory arrangement. When the subject is in error about such an
item, however, then what does he say? Would he think both presentations were
auditory or that both presentations were visual? (We can forget, for present
purposes, about auditory–visual choices.) If he thinks both have been visual, or
that there has been only a single presentation that has been visual, then this
subject is telling us that the first presentation of this (visual–auditory) item is
more salient to him than the second. Otherwise, if the second occurrence were
better remembered than the first, he would err in the direction of overestimating
auditory frequency, either by choosing the auditory–auditory response category
or by assigning his memory of a single presentation to the auditory category. In
this way we can determine whether one modality or the other is the more salient
memory.

A spacing effect was found in this study. With higher lags subjects reported
frequency estimates closer to 2.0 than with lower lags. The crucial question is,
for the two-modality repetition conditions: Which modality, the first or the

second, accounts for the increase in accurately judged frequency associated with long lags? For the visual–auditory condition, our example, the finding was an increase in the judgment that some auditory event had occurred that accounted for the overall increase in frequency-judgment accuracy. In other words, for this visual–auditory condition, the subjects are telling us that, as the lag between the two events is increased, they become more and more certain that somehow the word in question has occurred in the auditory mode and yet they are not becoming more certain that it has occurred in the visual mode. This must mean that at longer lags the integrity of the second occurrence is increasing or, alternatively, that the second occurrence has been short changed at conditions of massed repetition. Because the inattention theory suggests exactly that, that through boredom or the presence of the first repetition in primary memory the subject does not devote a full measure of attention to the second occurrence, Hintzman *et al.* (1973) have concluded in favor of the inattention class of theory and against consolidation theory, which attributes the lag effect to differential processing of the first occurrence.

For other reasons that we cannot pause to consider here Hintzman (1974, pp. 88–89) has chosen a slightly different version of inattention theory than those we have explained above [that is, inattention to the second occurrence (1) caused by boredom with a repeated item at close lags or (2) caused by the presence of the first occurrence in primary memory]. His notion, called the *habituation* hypothesis, is like the inattention notion in that it attributes poor performance at short lags to insufficient processing of the second occurrence. However, unlike the other versions of this notion he assumes the process is involuntary. (The term "habituation" refers to a diminution in some unlearned response tendency with repeated exposure to the appropriate stimulus; one of its properties is recovery with time since exposure.)

Another source of indirect evidence that subjects do not take full advantage of items repeated at short lags is a study by Shaughnessy, Zimmerman, and Underwood (1972, Experiment III). These authors allowed subjects to pace themselves through a long list of words that included both massed repetitions (lag = 0) and spaced repetitions (lag > 0). The items were on slides and the subjects were simply given control over the slide-changing mechanism. The average time for studying an item, overall, was just over 5 sec; however, the main interest was in comparing study times for items repeated under massed versus distributed practice. The results showed a consistent tendency to take less time inspecting repeated items that had just occurred (lag = 0) than inspecting other repeated items that had occurred earlier in the series. In recall, the results revealed the same advantage to distributed repetition over massed repetition that we have seen elsewhere. The Shaughnessy *et al.* (1972) experiment therefore supports the conclusion reached by Hintzman *et al.* (1973) that the locus of the performance decrement on immediately repeated items is in processing of the second occurrence. The Shaughnessy *et al.* (1972) study also provides prima facie evidence that a simple inattention mechanism may be at work. Of course, from comparisons of subjects' voluntary study times under self-paced conditions we cannot strictly generalize to their behavior under the usual rhythmically paced presentation conditions; however, the patterns of recall have not been altered by the self-pacing feature and the burden of proof probably belongs with those who maintain that a generalization between self-pacing and forced pacing should not be made.

Further tests of the inattention hypothesis. If massed repetitions lead to much poorer performance than that expected from the independence baseline because the second occurrence of an item gets less than a full share of attention, what happens to the attentional capacity released in this manner? One strategy for testing the inattention theory has been the examination of performance on items presented adjacent to repeated items. If repetition effects operate through more or less expenditure of effort on critical items then there may be compensatory facilitation in performance on nearby noncritical items, specifically on such noncritical items as the one immediately following the massed repetition. Although Potts (1972) failed to confirm an extension of this reasoning in a paired-associate experiment, Elmes, Greener, and Wilkinson (1972) obtained more positive results in a free-recall situation. These authors examined recall for the item immediately following the second occurrence of a word when the first occurrence of that word had been set at lag intervals of zero, three, or ten intervening words. First of all, they found that performance on the repeated word itself varied from 12 to 21 to 23% correct, respectively, as a function of lags of zero, three, and ten, in conformance with Figure 9.2. Performance on the word just following the second repetition of the critical word was the mirror image of these scores, however, just as the inattention theory would require—38%, 25%, and 18% correct for lags of zero, three, and ten. These results of Elmes *et al.* (1972) seem sharply inconsistent with the consolidation hypothesis for the same reason as the studies reviewed in the last section do, inasmuch as the findings by Elmes *et al.* (1972) implicate the second occurrence as the locus of differential processing in repetition rather than the first occurrence. However, the results are quite consistent with the notion that the subject at least partly ignores the second occurrence of massed repetitions. As the authors observe, furthermore, encoding variability theory need be modified only slightly in order to accommodate the Elmes *et al.* (1972) result: It may be assumed that the discovery of a new encoding for a repeated word has an inhibitory effect on learning the next word in the list. To evaluate this suggestion fully, we would need to know about recall of critical items following the occurrence of a single-presentation control; this observation is missing in the Elmes *et al.* (1972) report, yet whether or not their obtained reciprocity between recall of repeated items and recall of the following items reflects facilitation or inhibition depends on knowing the outcome of this control condition.

Several studies have tested the inattention hypothesis by contriving artificially to keep attention fully sustained to all occurrences of items. If the allocation of attention is voluntary and if the experimental operations insure uniform allocation, then the spacing effect ought to disappear under these conditions. Given the validity of these assumptions, evidence on this point is considerably less favorable to the inattention hypothesis than the evidence we have been reviewing so far. D'Agostino and DeRemer (1973) required subjects to recall object phrases from a long list of sentences. To control the processing time invested in each sentence, the authors asked subjects to read each sentence aloud, to form a visual image of the content of the sentence, and then to spend the remainder of a 10-sec study period describing the visual image to the experimenter. Recall of the object phrases was tested either by cuing with the subjects of the sentences or by noncued free recall. The result depended on the manner of testing: With free recall, a distribution effect (between lags of zero and five) was obtained but in cued recall it was not. Therefore, at least the free-recall findings are difficult to explain by a pure inattention theory. Given that the experimental procedure precluded differential attention to massed and distributed sentences, there should have been no difference in performance on them.

In conceptually similar experiments, Hintzman and Summers (reported by Hintzman, 1974, p. 88) and Elmes, Sanders, and Dovel (1973) tried to insure attention to the second occurrences of items regardless of spacing. Hintzman and Summers accomplished this by monetary incentives for recall of critically selected items and Elmes *et al.* (1973) presented some items in a highly distinctive format (distinctive voice or distinctive typestyle) in order to bring about the same consequence. In both of these experiments, there was no attenuation of the effects of spacing.

As Hintzman (1974) has commented none of these three experiments is conclusive, nor are they conclusive in the aggregate, but they at least fail to confirm a very obvious deduction from a pure inattention theory. The problem may be, however, that even though these three studies have tried to equate the amount of processing expended on second occurrences, they nonetheless have failed to equate the type of processing. As we have seen in Chapter 6, current views on secondary memory assign little lasting importance to sheer maintenance rehearsal. Instead, it is elaborative processing that produces good performance in the long run. The interesting point is that once this distinction between shallow maintenance processing and deeper, elaborative processing, is made the differences between the inattention hypothesis and the variable encoding hypothesis begin to evaporate.

"Forced" encoding variability.   Madigan (1969) performed the first of a group of experiments designed to verify the encoding variability hypothesis by direct control over the encoding process itself. The target words were nouns, but each was presented with another noun serving as a cue word designed to bias the semantic interpretation placed on the target noun. Some items were presented only once and others twice. There were two conditions of repetition, each tested at a number of interrepetition lags: One condition retained the identical cue word with the repeated word on each of its two occurrences, whereas the other repetition condition involved two different cues presented with the same repeated noun. For example, the target word CHILL might occur twice in a list, separated by a lag of four intervening items. In the different condition, the word *fever* would be presented beside CHILL on its first occurrence and the word *snow* beside it five words later; in the same condition the cue on both occurrences would be *fever*. Madigan found that providing different cues improved performance on twice-presented items significantly over the condition with the same adjective cue used each time. More importantly, this improvement seemed to be located chiefly at the short item lags, particularly at zero. This makes excellent theoretical sense from the point of view of encoding variability. The reason, according to this theory, for enhanced performance at long lags is that the subject is inclined to give a different semantic interpretation, or retrieval route, to the item at each of its two occurrences. Now, the Madigan experiment seems to indicate, if we force the subject to use two different encodings, even at short lags or adjacent repetitions, we can simulate the advantage of a long lag. Therefore, it is not the elapsed time that is important in long-lag conditions, as the consolidation theory holds, but the correlation of a long lag with enhanced possibilities for multiple encoding.

Thios (1972) performed a comparable experiment with sentence materials. Subjects saw sentences on the form: "The high-powered DRILL entered the masonry BLOCKS" and following the study phase were asked to recall the object word BLOCKS given the subject word DRILL. There were three conditions defined by the form in which some sentences were repeated twice during the input list: same (The high-powered DRILL entered the masonry BLOCKS), similar (The electrical DRILL pierced the stone BLOCKS), and different (The fire DRILL cleared the city's BLOCKS). The major findings of the Thios study were that (1) the similar condition led to best overall performance on repeated subject—object pairs but (2) the lag effect was eliminated for the different condition, just as in the Madigan study. A fascinating outcome of the Thios experiment, and something of a puzzle for theory, was that the similar condition was better than the other two at all lags, and by a substantial amount.

Finally, Gartman and Johnson (1973) applied the same logic to homographs, which are words with more than one meaning, such as FOOT or MATCH. These words were located as individual items in free recall lists, but their encoding was biased by the immediately preceding word; for example, the word FOOT could occur just after INCH or, alternatively, just after LEG. Under two conditions of repetition such homographic words were repeated, (1) with either different contexts on each of the presentations, or (2) with the same context on both presentations. In a control condition, nonhomographs were repeated with no context at either occurrence. The results are given in Figure 9.7. Using the control condition, without any context, as a baseline, we see that with identical forced encodings of repeated items, recall is held down to the level of massed repetition regardless of the actual lag between presentations; likewise, with built-in different encodings on the two occurrences of repeated items, recall is elevated to the level of widely distributed lag intervals, regardless of the actual lag.

Variability in context versus variability in semantic interpretation. These experiments by Madigan (1969), Thios (1972), and Gartman and Johnson (1972), as well as by others whose procedure and results were similar (D'Agostino & DeRemer, 1973; Johnston, Coots, & Flickinger, 1972), all operationalize encoding variability under the same guiding assumption that it is variability in how a semantically ambiguous word is interpreted that captures what ordinarily occurs in free-recall experiments with increasing lags between two presentations of an item. This operationalization of encoding variability is quite compatible

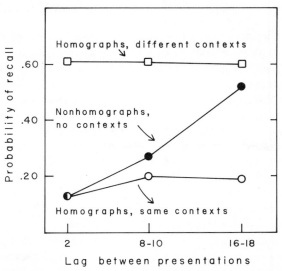

FIGURE 9.7 Recall probability as a function of lag between presentations of repeated items with variation in whether contexts are provided and in whether these contexts are the same on both occurrences of repeated items. (After Gartman & Johnson, 1972.)

with Martin's theory, which we have reviewed in Chapter 8; in both cases there is selection from among alternative interpretations of a fixed nominal stimulus. Although encoding in the sense of assigning a meaning to a word is clearly relevant to the hypothesis, there are other senses in which encoding variability may be used (Glenberg, 1974; Hintzman, 1974, p. 94). No serious theory of learning maintains that an individual item is learned in a vacuum. Strict stimulus–response associative theories maintain that a response is learned only in the context of some adequate stimulus. More recent theories based on the notion of organization (Chapter 10) maintain that an item is learned as part of a higher-order unit, a subjectively organized cluster of word concepts. One recent theory of retrieval (Anderson & Bower, 1972, 1974) has stressed that individual items get learned against a background of flowing contextual events, the daydreams, distractions, interoceptive and exteroceptive cues, and task-relevant thought that occurs during input of a list. Whether the stimulus or cue function is conceived to be a unitary event or a constellation of elements, and whether the cue events are task-irrelevant context or subjective units from among the target items, any theory of this type provides a second source of encoding variability. The critical word can be assigned the same meaning on the two occasions of its repetition, but it may be integrated with a more or less different context. The target LOCOMOTIVE can hardly receive two independent semantic interpretations but it can easily be integrated with a subjective group of "large things" (BUILDING, BOULDER, . . .) on one occasion and with a subjective group of "things with wheels" (SEWING MACHINE, TURNTABLE, . . .) on another occasion later in the list.

Hintzman (1974) has voiced several objections to a theory of encoding variability that depends on variety in the *semantic interpretation* of repeated words. As he observes, the homograph ought to be most variably encoded when the two occurrences lead to totally independent semantic analyses and this independence ought to occur when there is no recognition of the item as having been repeated on the occasion of its second occurrence. To the extent there is a recognition response at the time of the second occurrence then there is overlap between the two encoding responses. However, there is evidence (Madigan, 1969; Melton, personal communication, 1975) that not only can subjects recognize repeated words over long lags, but it is only for words actually recognized in this way that the lag effect is true! At recall, only words judged as having been repeated show the lag effect. It may be said, in other words, that recognition of repetition at the time of the second occurrence and subsequent memory for that repetition are necessary conditions for the Melton lag effect. This must then mean that words are given essentially the same meaning on their two appearances and that variability in their encoding must refer to variability in the contexts, either word-to-word context or extratask context, with which the target word gets associated. Hintzman (1974) concludes that this latter view of encoding variability, the one that Melton originally had in mind, although not the one that the series of homograph studies suggests, is a perfectly viable theoretical account of the experimental literature on spacing effects.

In a series of experiments involving memory for concrete nouns and/or for line drawings of the objects these nouns represent, Paivio (1974) has offered an interesting variant on the Madigan procedure. These studies further clarify what the "variability" in encoding variability may be. In Paivio's studies, subjects received long lists of mixed verbal and pictorial items, some occurring only once and some occurring twice. For items occurring twice, there was a variation in the lag between presentations and also in the format in which the repeated items was presented—verbal—verbal, pictorial—pictorial, verbal—pictorial, or pictorial—verbal. In all cases free recall was verbal. Furthermore, subjects were given either standard free-recall instructions or, alternatively, they were given an incidental-learning cover task (before each presentation they were to guess whether a word or a picture was going to occur).

The aspect of Paivio's findings that resembles those from the Madigan paradigm is recall from intentional-learning conditions: When an item was presented twice in the same modality (verbal—verbal or pictorial—pictorial) performance was well below the independence baseline for massed repetition and roughly approximated the independence baseline for spaced repetition (lag = 48 events). When the item was presented in mixed modalities (either verbal—pictorial or pictorial—verbal), however, its recall was at the level predictable from independent memory traces even with a lag of zero. In Paivio's view, these results conform poorly with an hypothesis of the distribution—lag effect based on variable contextual retrieval cues; presumably the context changes little between massed presentations but if such massed presentations have occurred in different modalities then it is as if two independent memory traces have been formed but they are not necessarily independent semantically. That is, in accord with Paivio's dual-trace hypothesis concerning separate verbal and imaginal codes (see Chapter 5), he is suggesting that mixed-modality repetition sets up independent memories, not multiple retrieval routes to a single memory. Because the unmixed repetition conditions approach the same independence baseline with distributed repetition it is reasonable to interpret the lag function as representing increasingly independent traces also, unless one wishes to have one theory for the mixed-modality conditions and another for the unmixed conditions.

Paivio found that under incidental learning conditions the lag effect was eliminated and that performance conformed rather to the independence base-line. This outcome is not entirely consistent between the two experiments reported in Paivio's article; however, if it is true, independence of traces in incidental learning supports the inattention hypothesis. The reasoning here is that in incidental learning attention is spread by the orienting, cover task uniformly across all items presented. Processing capacity is being invested in the orienting task rather than in such devices as elaborative coding. With intentional learning under standard instructions, however, there is attentional capacity being invested in coding for memory and consequently differential allocation of this attentional capacity becomes a real possibility. In blunt terms, the subject is just not paying out attention to memory coding under incidental instructions and therefore he cannot be short-changing items repeated at short lags.

Summary of inferences thus far. We started this section by displaying the basic phenomenon first reported by Melton (1967) in Figure 9.2 and by offering several clarifying remarks. We were then able to dismiss the strength hypothesis out of hand because it failed even to allow the Melton lag effect. The consolidation hypothesis and its variant, the rehearsal theory, were discounted with somewhat less finality, mainly on evidence from Hintzman *et al.* (1973) that the locus of the lag effect is in the second rather than the first occurrence of the repeated item. The data of Elmes *et al.* (1972) showing variation in recall of the neighbor of a repeated item also indicated the locus of the lag effect being at the second presentation, contrary to the consolidation hypothesis. The inattention hypothesis has received support from the Shaughnessy *et al.* (1972) result that subjects who are adjusting their own study times tend to short-change the second of two massed repetitions. The Elmes *et al.* (1972) study also is consistent with the inattention hypothesis. Studies aimed at forcibly sustaining attention equally to all items were not successful in confirming the inattention hypothesis, however.

Experiments using Madigan's (1969) forced encoding paradigm with semantically ambiguous items have favored a general encoding variability position; however, a similar pattern of results reported by Paivio (1974) for nonhomographic items presented in mixed modalities shows that semantic ambiguity is not a necessary interpretation of variable encoding. Because the lag effect occurs only when particular items were recognized as having been repeated (Madigan, 1969) we must dismiss the possibility that the beneficial effect of encoding variability is in the establishment of two totally independent memory traces. We may further discriminate the various hypotheses by turning, now, to other tasks.

Cued Recall in Continuous Paired-Associate Learning

Consider a task in which pairs of items are presented in a more or less continuous stream, with the occurrence of new items interspersed with tests of old items. The interval between the presentation of a particular pair and its test can be controlled easily and, of special interest now, an item can be presented twice before testing, with variation in the lag between the two presentations and in the lag, or retention interval, between the second presentation and the test. Figure 9.8 illustrates a sequence of events in such a task, sometimes called *continuous paired-associate learning.* Results with such a task reported by Peterson, Saltzman, Hillner, and Land (1962) and by Peterson, Wampler,

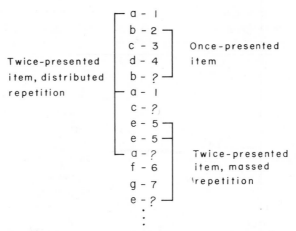

FIGURE 9.8   The sequence of events in a typical continuous paired-associate learning task.

Kirkpatrick, and Saltzman (1963) provide the occasion for considering two subtle aspects of repetition effects on recall and also for introducing two major theoretical arguments, the *stimulus sampling theory* of Estes (1955) and the *buffer model* of Atkinson and Shiffrin (1968). Therefore, although not nearly as much research on repetition has been done with the continuous paired-associate method as with other tasks, the payoff is quite large in terms of theory.

A short-term advantage of massed practice. In free-recall tasks there are no data showing an advantage of massed repetition over distributed repetition. However, Peterson *et al.* (1963) have shown that with the continuous task massed practice is better if the test comes very soon after the second presentation but distributed practice is better if the test comes after any appreciable delay. Peterson *et al.* (1963) presented short words paired with numbers from the set, 1, 2, . . . , 15. Some pairs were shown only once before being tested, whereas other pairs were shown twice before testing. The independent variables of interest were the lags between presentation and testing for single-presentation items and the lags between the first and second presentations and between the second presentation and testing for double-presentation items. In addition two presentation rates, 2 sec or 4 sec per paired-associate event, were tested. The results from Experiment III of the Peterson *et al.* (1963) report are shown in Table 9.1. For both data sets there is a sharp decline in performance as a function of retention interval just prior to the test and also an overall advantage of two presentations over a single presentation. However, it is the interaction between lag and retention interval that is important in this study. This interaction shows that when memory is tested early, at 2 or 4 sec following the second presentation, massed repetition produces better scores than spaced repetition but that when memory is tested after a longer delay, then spaced re-

TABLE 9.1

Recall Probability as a Function of Distribution
of Repetition and Testing[a,b]

Presentation rate	P1–P2 lag	P2–Test lag	
		2 sec	8 sec
2 sec	0 (massed)	.87	.26
	8 (distributed)	.79	.29
	Single presentation control	.79	.14
4 sec	0 (massed)	.78	.26
	16 (distributed)	.75	.45
	Single-presentation control	.67	.23

[a]After Peterson, Wampler, Kirkpatrick, and Saltzman, (1963).

[b]P1 = first presentation, P2 is second presentation. P2–Test lag is the retention interval between the second presentation and the test.

petition is better than massed. Sperber (1974) has reported the same interaction in a study of comparable conditions. (Sperber's data show a fascinating dependence of this outcome on intelligence.)

Does this pattern of data contradict what we know about repetition effects in free recall, where the advantage seems always to favor spacing? It does not, in fact, contradict results from free recall, once it is realized that there is typically a large retention interval between the second occurrence of an item and its subsequent free recall. That is, free-recall data, in these types of experiment, are always collected under conditions of a long retention interval. The retention interval is long partly because investigators have wanted to avoid contamination of experimental comparisons by the steep recency component of the serial-position curve and therefore they have included a so-called "recency buffer" of noncritical items. Given this recency buffer and also subjects' tendencies to recall the last few items first, we may estimate that something on the order of 20 or 30 sec is the minimum separation of presentation and recall for repeated items in free-recall studies with conventional presentation conditions. Perhaps if instances of repetition were deliberately placed in the recency range and were then recalled first by subjects, an advantage of massed repetition in free recall could be found.

By their choice of lag intervals between repetitions Peterson et al. (1963) have not allowed us to distinguish between distribution effects and lag effects. (Distribution effects, it will be recalled, show that having some separation between occurrences of a repeated item is better than having no separation at all, whereas lag effects show that, given at least some separation, a long lag is better than a short one.) The problem arises here because Peterson *et al.* (1963) have compared a relatively wide distribution interval (four intervening items) against no distribution at all (zero lag), instead of considering the comparison of two distributed conditions with unequal nonzero lags. In some of the discussion to follow, therefore, we shall be lumping the distribution and lag effects together. It may be misleading to assume that a lag of ten differs from a lag of one or two intervening items in the same way that the latter differ from a lag of zero; Glenberg (1974) is quite explicit in rejecting this continuity. However, as a parsimonious first approximation, this strategy seems preferable to the assumption that different principles apply to different ranges of the total repetition-lag dimension.

The problem posed by the result of Peterson *et al.* (1963) is how to rationalize the short-term advantage of massed repetition in view of all the hypotheses offered in the previous section to account for the opposite effect. Given the surplus of such hypotheses, what we clearly do not need is some additional unrelated hypothesis brought in specifically for the short-term massed-practice advantage. Instead, we need a single framework that is predictive of the interaction itself (that is, the interaction shown in Table 9.1). Estes' (1955, 1959) stimulus fluctuation theory serves this purpose. As will become apparent, Estes' model is a special case of the encoding variability hypothesis.

It bears passing comment that Estes' stimulus fluctuation theory was developed many years prior to any interest in spacing effects and that it was developed to cover time-dependent response patterns in conditioning studies with lower animals. Its power to accommodate findings in the spacing literature is therefore all the more impressive, because most of the other notions we have been dealing with here have been developed specifically to explain spacing effects.

Estes' stimulus fluctuation model. In this simplified version of the theory (Estes, 1955, 1959) we assume that temporal contiguity is the only condition necessary for a stimulus and a response to become associated. However, the concept of the stimulus is quite special in Estes' theory: Instead of being a unitary stimulus, such as a sound, or a word, the stimulus is portrayed as a population of elements, each a tiny fragment of the universe and, ideally, each of potentially equal importance. Now the set of all possible stimulus elements can be divided into two important subsets, the ones that are actually available or capable of being "sampled" at a given moment and the ones that are unavailable to the subject at that moment. It is assumed that individual elements wander in and out of the available set on a random basis that is dependent on time. At one moment, some detail in the visual periphery or some occasional sound may be a part of the sampled set of elements but for various reasons it may not be the next moment. In general, given a brief interval of time very little exchange among the available and unavailable subsets occurs; but given an arbitrarily long interval there can be full exchange in the sense that whether an element has been available at one point in time is not predictive of whether it is at another point in time. The ebb and flow of sampling with time is called *stimulus fluctuation*.

Now, we want to consider what happens when a pattern of stimulus elements, which may include a word, occurs in temporal contiguity with some response, such as the internal representation of a number. We know that certain elements of the stimulus universe are available for sampling and others not. The particular version of the theory that we are examining assumes that, of the available stimulus elements, a certain proportion, θ, get attached, or conditioned, to the ongoing response; this process is called "stimulus sampling." Immediately after a learning trial, therefore, we may classify all stimulus elements in a two-dimensional partition: Some elements are available for sampling and others unavailable; second, some have just been sampled and are therefore conditioned and others are not conditioned. Right at the moment of learning on the first trial all of the conditioned elements are in the available set, by definition, but as time passes the process of stimulus fluctuation leads to exchanges between the potentially available and potentially unavailable sets with the result, for conditioned elements, that some "wander" into the unavailable set. With unlimited time the densities of conditioned elements would equalize in the available and unavailable sets. Therefore, at any time after learning our four-way partition includes four types of stimulus element, unavailable–unconditioned, unavailable–conditioned, available–unconditioned, and available–conditioned. The performance observed on testing is assumed to be directly proportional to the fraction of conditioned elements in the available set relative to all elements in the available set.

The Estes prediction for spacing effects takes the following form: When practice is massed little fluctuation occurs between the two presentations and therefore elements in the (relatively unchanging) available set are very thoroughly conditioned, because independent random samples of size θ from the available set are taken twice in a row without much fluctuation intervening. If testing occurs at a time when there has still been very little fluctuation, performance exceeds that in conditions in which more total elements have been conditioned, such as is the case with distributed repetition, but in which fewer of the elements available in the testing context are conditioned. When a great deal of fluctuation occurs between the second presentation and testing, however, what counts is that a maximum number of different elements have been conditioned and that occurs under distributed practice, in which fluctuation has occurred between the two presentations. The short-run advantage is therefore a long-run deficit.

Figure 9.9 illustrates how the theory works numerically, for the special case where (1) there are a total of 100 stimulus elements in the universe, (2) exactly half of these are available for sampling at any moment in time, (3) 80% of

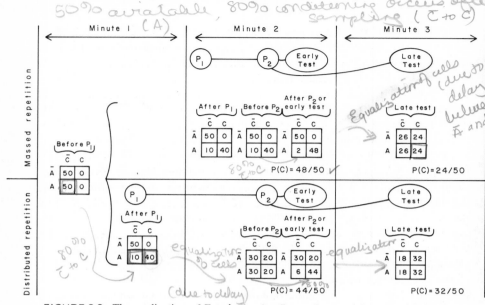

FIGURE 9.9   The application of Estes' stimulus fluctuation model to repetition and spacing effects: P1, P2 are first and second presentations, respectively; A is currently available set of stimulus elements; $\bar{A}$ is currently unavailable set of stimulus elements; C is conditioned stimulus elements; $\bar{C}$ is unconditioned stimulus elements; $p(C)$ is probability of a correct response.

available elements become conditioned through sampling (that is, $\theta = .80$), and (4) there is no fluctuation during a period of 1 min but complete fluctuation between minutes. This last assumption violates the continuous nature of stimulus fluctuation, of course, but it does not distort the basic picture of how the theory works. The illustration assumes that there are three epochs, 3 min, during which the presentation and testing episodes occur. With massed practice the two presentations and also the "early" test (short retention interval following the second occurrence of the critical item) all occur within a single minute and so there is no fluctuation whatever. Because there is no fluctuation in the case of massed practice, in our example, there are two opportunities to sample, or condition, the 50 available elements; on the first, 40 are sampled (.80 X 50) and on the second repetition eight more are sampled (.80 X 10). Therefore, by the time of the early retention test, with still no fluctuation, 48 of the 50 available stimulus elements are attached to the correct response, giving a probability of correct recall of 48/50, or .96.

Below, in the lower panel of Figure 9.9, we can follow the case of distributed repetition in a corresponding manner. Although the outcome of the first presentation is identical, there is fluctuation during the interval between the two presentations. This interpresentation exchange equalizes the densities of conditioned elements in the available and unavailable sets, at 20 apiece. Of the 30 available, so far unconditioned elements, 24 are conditioned on the second occurrence (.80 × 30). These new 24 elements join the 20 conditioned elements from the first occurrence that have not settled in the unavailable set for a net response probability of 44/50 = .88. Clearly the model anticipates better performance following massed repetition than following spaced if the test is soon enough to escape (much) fluctuation. Note, however, that whereas only 48 elements ever get conditioned in the massed condition, a total of 64 eventually get conditioned in the distributed condition. In the long run, with a delayed retention test, this produces a net advantage for the distributed condition.

Another way of describing this result is to observe that forgetting is much more rapid following massed than following distributed practice. From discussions in Chapter 1 we know that the proper definition of forgetting includes simply the comparison of two different retention intervals following identical training circumstances. In Figure 9.9 we may compare predictions for the early and late retention intervals to estimate forgetting. In the example, the loss is 50%, from correct-response probabilities of .96 to .48, for the massed condition, and only 27%, from .88 to .64, for the distributed condition.

How does the use of molecular stimulus elements in Estes' theory translate to the language of stimulus-encoding variability as we have been using it in connection with Martin's theory in Chapter 8 and in connection with the Melton–Madigan notions considered earlier in this chapter? It is surely not profitable to think of the nominal stimulus, say, an individual word, as being fractionated into an almost infinite number of elementary components, fading in and out of consciousness.

Bower (1972b) has provided a resolution of the notion of encoding variability that incorporates ideas from stimulus sampling theory. Bower's theory departs from the assumptions that each nominal stimulus has the potential for providing several different functionally distinct experiences and that these are the "stimulus elements" corresponding to stimulus sampling-fluctuation theory. Each of the stimulus elements, or encodings, gets associated in an all-or-none fashion to responses or other mental events. The key new feature of Bower's theory is the ←
contextual determination of encoding. Figure 9.10 presents Bower's schematic representation of stimulus encoding and sampling. The nominal stimulus XQH can be encoded in any of N ways, as enumerated by the operators 1 through N. The sense of the term "operator," in this context, includes a deliberate stimulus selection process, such as encoding a particular meaning of a word. Each of the operators used in encoding has consequences that Bower calls "stimulus elements"; these correspond to the internal representations that result from different encoding operations. To these stimulus elements the responses are attached. For our purposes the major point is the effect of context on the sampling probabilities of various encodings. It is this contextual influence that provides a framework in which Estes' process of stimulus fluctuation can occur naturally.

As we have suggested before, the context itself includes a variety of interoceptive and exteroceptive background events occurring during presentation of nominal stimuli. Not only gastric cues and occasional sensory messages, but also

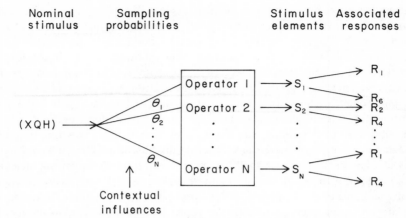

FIGURE 9.10 The process of stimulus encoding and sampling according to Bower's theory: XQH is the stimulus presented; θ_i is the probability that a particular encoding operator is active, S_i is the stimulus as encoded by a particular operator. (After Bower, 1972b.)

streams of cognitive episodes and strategic decision making are included. Bower imagines two ways in which there can be changes in context. *Systematic contextual changes* are abrupt (and usually deliberate on the part of the experimenter) shifts in the sampling distribution of encoding operations. Changing from one experimental room to another would be one example, as discussed in Chapter 8. Another example provided by Bower is the extreme biasing of encoding found with homographs in the studies of Madigan (1969) and those who have later adopted his procedure. These brute-force contextual manipulations of encoding are contrasted with *random contextual drift:*

> ... it is reasonable to suppose further that there is a slow drift or gradual change in the prevailing context as other items or events occur during a lapse of time. The change in context presumably grows progressively over elapsed time. As the context changes, so does the setting of the encoding operators, thus making active a somewhat different set of s of the N possible operators. Thus change in context is rarely total; states of the mind recur many times over. . . . Nonetheless, the average overlap between contexts at times t and $t + k$ will decrease to some asymptotic proportion as k increases [Bower, 1972b, pp. 93–94].

This discussion makes it clear that although contextual stimuli can enter directly into associations with verbal response terms, as Estes has implied, the solution preferred by Bower is to have context influencing the likelihoods that different encoding operations can produce any of several functional stimulus elements. Our problem is therefore resolved: The Madigan type of experiment, with biased encoding of homographs, is a special case of how context operates in general. The Estes ideas about stimulus fluctuation, which are so crucial for a consistent theoretical account of differences between massed and distributed practice, are applicable to cases in which such drastic systematic contextual changes do not occur, leaving the more subtle process of random contextual drift to manifest itself.

Distribution that is excessive. Note that in the Estes model as we have sketched it there is no forgetting, in the sense that all fluctuations are from the available to the unavailable states, and vice versa, but not from the conditioned to the unconditioned states. Data exist to suggest, however, that under some circumstances in repetition experiments, there is forgetting between the two presentations. Peterson, Wampler, Kirkpatrick, and Saltzman (1963) reported an experiment where the same materials used to produce the data of Table 9.1 were presented with a constant interval of 16 sec between the second presentation and testing. The interval between the two presentations or repeated items was 0, 2, 4, 8, 16, or 32 sec. The proportion of correct recall for these spacing intervals, respectively, was .39, .43, .47, .50, .51, and .45. Although the downturn at the longest spacing interval was not statistically significant, essentially identical data were obtained by J. L. Young (1966) in a study of similar design with many more data points. As we shall see presently, the same result has been reported by Atkinson and Shiffrin (1968) and by Glenberg (1974); there can be little doubt, therefore, that at least under some conditions spaced repetitions can be "too distributed" even when plenty of time elapses between the second occurrence of the item and testing.

Glenberg (1974) has shown that the inflection point on spacing functions for continuous paired-associate learning depends on the retention interval separating the test from the second presentation. In his experiment, lags of 0, 1, 4, 8, 20, or 40 events intervened between presentations of critical items, with retention intervals of 2, 8, 32, or 64 events separating the second occurrence from testing. The main result is shown in the left panel of Figure 9.11. With short retention intervals prior to testing (two or eight events) the function relating performance to interpresentation lag was clearly an inverted U but with longer retention intervals (32 or 64 events) there was a steady improvement with increased lag, just as Melton (1967) obtained for free recall.

From Peterson *et al.* (1963) we have the additional information that with zero or one event coming between the second presentation and the test, performance is better at a lag of zero events than at a lag of four events. Putting all of these continuous paired-associate learning experiments together (J. L. Young, 1966; Glenberg, 1974; Peterson *et al.*, 1963) we may tentatively construct the family of curves shown in the right panel of Figure 9.11. We shall establish presently that data from a similar situation by Atkinson and Shiffrin (1968) fit the same empirical generalization.

Glenberg's own account of these functions is a hybrid of encoding variability and stimulus fluctuation theories: Like Estes he assumes that at short

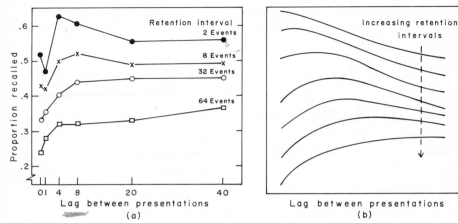

FIGURE 9.11   The relation between recall probability and lag separating two presentations of an item as a function of the retention interval between the second presentation and the test. (a) Data from Glenberg (1974). (b) An idealized family of curves incorporating an absolute superiority of massed practice when testing is almost immediate.

interpresentation lags relatively few different context elements participate in the encoding of the nominal stimulus, whereas with longer lags the encoding is more diverse. That is, in terms of the Bower (1972b) formulation, at long lags there is a greater variety of context elements that lead to the correct encoding of the stimulus than at short lags. This handles the increasing lag function for longer retention intervals: When a premium is on recapturing the context that prevailed during encoding, the more different contexts there were the better the chance of a match at retrieval.

Now, however, what about the opposite functions obtained at short retention intervals, that is, the decreasing performance as a function of lag obtained when testing is soon after the second presentation? Here, Glenberg's assumption is that the context at the time of testing is generally bound to match the context at the time of the second presentation for the simple reason that little or no time has elapsed between the second presentation and the test. Given that a relevant retrieval route is, so to speak, guaranteed with these short retention intervals, what is the good of even having a first presentation? The answer is that a first occurrence ought to be no good whatever if it is totally independent of the second occurrence in terms of context. This independence of contexts is likely to be approached with long lags between presentations. With short lags, in contrast, the two contexts are more likely to overlap to some extent, providing a means of facilitation. If the context of the second occurrence is not sufficient, on some occasions, to determine the correct encoding but if it can lead to a partially independent context deriving from the first occurrence, then together the two contexts stand a better chance of eliciting the proper encoding (which, in turn, leads to the response) than either does alone. This machinery is conceptually equivalent to Estes' (1959) account of why massed practice surpasses distributed for short retention intervals, although it is a more specific formulation as regards process.

However, we have still not yet achieved an explanation for the nonmonotonic curves in Figure 9.11. The assumptions we have just been attributing to Glenberg are sufficient only to produce a family of *monotonic* lag functions, descending functions for short retention intervals and ascending functions for long retention intervals. Some additional factor needs to be introduced in order to produce the inverted U shapes that seem to be the rule. In graphic terms, what we need is some variable that can do either of two things—selectively depress performance at short lags or selectively depress performance at long lags. The situation is shown in Figure 9.12.

The basic underlying lag functions predicted by the Estes–Glenberg logic are shown in the left panel and they are monotonic. To produce nonmonotonicity we may either add a decremental factor at short lags, as in the center panel, or at long lags, as in the right panel. The figure makes it apparent, schematically, that somewhat different consequences result from the two options inasmuch as the higher performance curves become nonmonotonic through application of a short-lag decremental factor and the lower performance curves become non-monotonic through application of a long-lag decremental factor; however, the quality of the data do not permit a clear choice on this basis and we shall not consider it further.

There is a simple, plausible candidate for both of these two possible decremental factors. The decremental factor operating at short lags may be inattention,

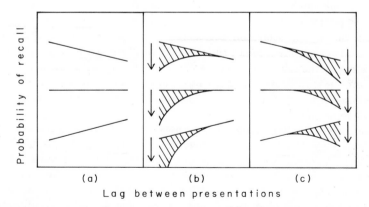

FIGURE 9.12 Theoretical representations of the relation between recall and lag between presentations of a repeated item. (a) Shows the interaction implied by the Estes model. (b) and (c) show, respectively, the consequences of adding a decremental factor operating at short and long lags.

driving performance down for just the reasons proposed by Underwood (1970) and others. The idea, it will be recalled, is that at short lags the subject recognizes the second occurrence as a repetition and slights it in terms of processing. Alternatively, the decremental factor at long lags could be forgetting of the item to be repeated before its second occurrence. It is intuitive that if the first occurrence of the repeated item is somehow lost before the item is repeated, the subject is recalling only the second occurrence at testing and performance should be no better than in single-presentation controls. This forgetting would therefore be working in an opposite direction as a function of lag from encoding variability. More formally, the Estes model can easily be modified to include the possibility that, with time, elements not only fluctuate in and out of the potentially availables state, but also these elements become associated with new responses that are unrelated to the critical item. This is what is called "counterconditioning" in conditioning theory.

Either inattention at short lags or forgetting at long lags could be responsible for the nonmonotonicity observed in the data of Glenberg and others. Glenberg himself seems to opt for the inattention theory by assuming that at lags of zero the second occurrence adds nothing to the first. Of course, it is entirely possible that both factors are involved.

Before we leave the relationships in Figures 9.11 and 9.12, we should note that Glenberg (1974) has offered converging evidence for his interpretation of the basic difference between massed and distributed repetition, that is, the difference shown in the left panel of Figure 9.12. Glenberg's idea is that when the second encoding context is guaranteed to be salient at recall by a minimal retention interval between the second occurrence and testing, then the first repetition serves a supporting function by being associated both with the correct encoding and with the context of the second occurrence, a function that becomes progressively less likely as the lag between presentations increases because the two encoding contexts then become more independent. With longer retention intervals prior to the test, in contrast, the main problem is in having at least some overlap between the testing context and the context prevailing at either of the two presentations, an increasingly likely proposition if the two presentations occurred in different contexts, as would be the case with distributed repetition.

Glenberg's notion, therefore, is that short retention intervals give a descending lag function because the context of the test overlaps highly with the context of the second presentation. Experimentally, he reasoned, one might be able to simulate the effects of a short retention interval by comparing noncued with cued recall. If the subject is supplied with retrieval cues that are likely to reinstate the context of the second occurrence, then the results ought to resemble those for short retention intervals, even if the actual time between the second presentation and testing is substantial. This prediction was confirmed in separate experiments involving both the Brown–Peterson distractor paradigm and the free-recall paradigm.

There is independent support, therefore, for the explanation Glenberg offers for why the effects of distributed practice interact with retention interval. We have reviewed earlier in the chapter the evidence favoring inattention as a decremental factor operating at short lags. Now we turn to the model of Atkinson and Shiffrin, as it applies to the issues at hand, for this model provides a different perspective on repetition, including the notion of forgetting between presentations as a decremental factor at long lags.

The Atkinson–Shiffrin buffer model. Having outlined in Chapter 6 the overall structure of the memory system proposed by Atkinson and Shiffrin (1968), we shall now concentrate on their specialized buffer model for certain short-term memory tasks. It should be held in mind that this buffer model is proposed by them only as a special case of short-term memory processes, applying to conditions with very limited opportunities for application of sophisticated, "elaborative" coding mechanisms.

Atkinson and Shiffrin assume a rehearsal buffer with a fixed number of slots for information, each slot handling chunks the size of verbal units. Occupancy of slots is all or none in the sense that an item is either entered with full strength in the buffer or absent from it. During the time an item is in the buffer it is assumed that the strength in long-term storage is being incremented continuously. Entry of a new item into the buffer displaces some current item; however, the subject has some control over whether or not to enter a new item. These general assumptions have been applied specifically to the continuous paired-associate task. In the version of continuous paired-associate task used by Atkinson and Shiffrin, a fixed number of stimulus items keep recurring during an experimental session, constantly getting repaired with new responses; the task is to keep track of the current status, as it were, of a fixed number of such stimuli, on the order of half a dozen. This task was designed specially to test the buffer model because it discourages efforts to build up much long-term storage—the subject would be foolish to develop an elaborate mnemonic to remember that 46 goes with the letter Y when in a matter of seconds the same number could be repaired with the letter B.

The task under consideration is therefore similar to that outlined in Figure 9.8 with the exception that a fixed number of stimulus items is used over and over again, either four, six, or eight. The stimulus terms in the experimental work of Atkinson and Shiffrin were two-digit numbers and the responses were the letters A through Z. The attractive feature of their model is that it permits very precise quantitative tests once clear assumptions have been made about the operation of the system. Although we have already conveyed the flavor of the theory, therefore, it is worth continuing to its application. To do so, our assumptions must be made even more explicitly:

1. The rehearsal buffer has a fixed capacity r and information entered in it includes the order of arrival.

2. What is rehearsed is ordinarily the pair of items, not just the response term.

3. Long-term storage strength builds up at a rate represented by the parameter θ during the residence of a pair in the buffer.

4. Once out of the buffer the long-term storage strength corresponding to a pair decays at a rate represented by the parameter τ.

5. Entry of pairs into the buffer is governed by rules based on a distinction between two types of items. O (for old) items are those the stimulus term of which is already in the buffer, albeit perhaps paired with some other response term. N (for new) items are those the stimulus member of which is not in the buffer. It is assumed that O items are always entered into the buffer; that is, when a stimulus in the buffer gets repaired with a new response the subject always rehearses the new response. (Otherwise the subject would sometimes be left rehearsing the old incorrect responses.) It is assumed that N items enter the buffer with probability α and that some current occupant of the buffer is knocked out at random. That is, when a completely fresh stimulus occurs the subject rehearses it with some fixed probability.

6. Any item currently in the buffer is recalled perfectly when tested.

7. If an item is not in the buffer, when tested, a search of long-term storage is made. The outcome of this search depends on how long the item has been in the buffer initially and also on how long it has been since the item has left the buffer.

8. At lag of zero between presentation and test, the probability of correct recall is unity even if the item is not in the buffer. This assumption makes explicit the distinction between short-term storage (primary memory) and the rehearsal buffer; Short-term storage is a memory structure that may or may not include a rehearsal buffer, the operation of which is optional.

Let us consider some applications of this detailed theory to experimental data. In Figure 9.13 are shown data from a simple experiment in which the variables are (1) lag between a single presentation and test and (2) the number of stimulus items for which the subject is responsible. If the stimulus set included only four items then for the entire session these four two-digit numbers were presented, tested, and repaired, in haphazard order, with letters of the alphabet. With stimulus set size of six there were six such stimuli, and so forth. The predictions of the theory are that the smaller the stimulus set the better the performance because with small stimulus sets more items are O items than with large stimulus sets and O items always enter the buffer with priority. Figure 9.13 (caption) also shows the numerical values of the four parameters for which the best fit between data and theory is obtained. Notice in the context of our treatment of primary memory (Chapter 6) that the size of the buffer turns out to be two pairs.

Another simple prediction of the theory concerns how a given presentation–test lag is filled with O and N items. If a certain length of lag is filled with repeated reuses of the same stimuli there should be better performance than when that same lag is filled with many new different stimulus items, given that

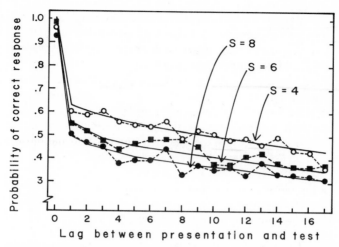

FIGURE 9.13 Recall probability as a function of the lag between presentation and testing of continuous paired associates. The parameter *s* is the number of different stimulus terms for which responses had to be learned and remembered. The solid lines are predictions of the buffer model of Atkinson and Shiffrin. The following best-fitting values were obtained for the parameters of the model: r (buffer size) = 2; α (buffer entry probability) = .39; θ (buildup of long-term storage) = .40; τ (long-term storage decay rate) = .93. (After Atkinson & Shiffrin, 1968.)

the size of the overall stimulus set is fixed. Atkinson and Shiffrin found this to be true—it is better to have a single stimulus term getting repeatedly repaired, during the retention interval for some other, critical item, than to have a variety of different associations presented and tested during that same interval.

For purposes of this chapter the extension of their model made by Atkinson and Shiffrin to multiple presentation is especially crucial. The extension was quite direct in that the same parameters θ and τ covering input and decay rates for long-term storage were assumed. Furthermore, the same entry rule for O items to the buffer was retained. The additional assumptions covering repetition were all concerned with the handling of N items, items the stimulus terms of which were not in the buffer. Whereas in the single-presentation situation these items would very seldom be correctly responded to on the basis of long-term memory, in the case of multiple presentations it would be quite possible that an N item had been in the buffer previously for some appreciable time and that therefore the subject could give the correct response entirely on the basis of accumulated long-term storage strength. Atkinson and Shiffrin decided for this reason to include in the rule for N items that if they were already well known when presented for study they would not be entered in the buffer. This assumption of course is a form of "two store inattention" hypothesis, as this hypothesis was presented above. Note, however, that here the criterion for differential processing of the second occurrence is whether or not there is a trace in long-term storage of the first occurrence, not whether there is such a trace in short-term storage. The new theory is represented schematically in Figure 9.14.

Now, considering the lag occurring between two presentations of the same pair, it can be seen that prediction of a nonmonotonic function comes from the properties of the long-term system. With massed practice the second presentation of a repeated pair makes it an *O* item and it has no effect on the buffer. Because there has been almost no time for long-term storage strength to build up, moreover, this massed repetition approaches single-presentation performance. With moderate distribution the first presentation has been producing

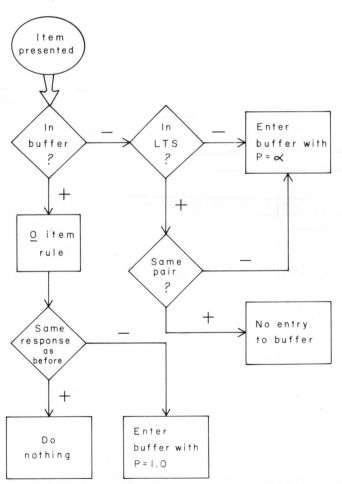

FIGURE 9.14   Flow chart representing the major assumptions of Atkinson and Shiffrin's buffer model as applied to multiple presentation of items.

buildup in long-term storage for some time when the second presentation occurs and this enhances performance. With extremely widely spaced repetition, how-ever, the decay assumption (from long-term storage) comes into play; in the extreme case no trace of the first presentation exists when the second occurs, and performance then approaches the single-presentation level again. For this situation, therefore, the full distribution of practice function represents, accord-ing to the Atkinson and Shiffrin theory, a constant contribution of the second presentation to performance coming from the rehearsal buffer plus, at increasing intermediate levels of spacing between repetitions, the waxing and waning of a contribution to performance from long-term storage. Atkinson and Shiffrin verified with a computer simulation that this inverted U-shaped function was indeed a consequence of the assumptions listed.

Figure 9.15 shows a family of obtained performance curves relating recall of a pair to the interpresentation lag in a double-presentation situation. The param-eter is the lag between the second presentation and testing, called "lag b" to distinguish it from the lag between presentations. We see, first, that when there is no lag between the second presentation and testing is makes no difference whether practice has been spaced or massed and that when there is a long lag before testing, also, it makes no difference; these two findings are the results of ceiling and floor effects, respectively. However, at intermediate levels of spacing between the second presentation and testing, there is the inverted U-shaped function predicted from the buffer model.

The buffer model does not predict an interaction between the lag separating presentations and the lag between the second presentation and testing. Its accomplishment here is rather to account for the initial rise in the spacing function and then for the falloff at long interpresentation lags obtained first by Peterson *et al.* (1962) and by Young (1966). If the interaction between

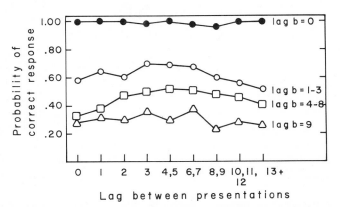

FIGURE 9.15 The relation between correct recall probability and lag between presenta-tions: the parameter *lag b* is the "testing lag" or the number of items intervening between the second of two presentations and testing. (After Atkinson & Shiffrin, 1968.)

interpresentation and testing lags were part of the model, we would have expected to find a declining function in Figure 9.15 for short lags between the second occurrence and testing with an ascending function for long ones—both of these superimposed on the inverted U that results from their model. This would show, in other words, short interpresentation lags to be beneficial at short testing lags but harmful at long testing lags, just as Estes' theory predicts and as Glenberg (1974) found. The ironic thing is that although unexpected by their model such a trend is evident in the Atkinson and Shiffrin data! This is easily observed by sighting down imaginary lines from the first to the last points on each of the two middle functions on Figure 9.15; this line runs down for short testing lags and runs up for longer testing lags.

Summary of spacing effects in continuous paired-associate learning. We have a neatly consistent picture of the empirical laws governing situations in which the same nominal pairing is studied on two occasions and tested on a third. The basic function relating performance to the spacing of the two presentations is an inverted U; the optimal spacing is somewhere intermediate between extreme massing of repetition and extreme distribution. However the exact location of the optimal interval is determined by the delay between the second presentation and testing. If this testing delay is short, then massed repetition is favored but if this delay is longer then more distributed schedules of repetition are favored.

Theoretically there are two options for embracing the whole pattern. One could accept the Atkinson and Shiffrin model for the inverted U and then include mechanisms to predict the interaction between interpresentation lag and testing lag. Alternatively, one could accept the Estes model of why interpresentation lag interacts with testing lag and include either or both of the two decremental factors identified above, inattention or interpresentation forgetting, to predict the U-shaped lag function. Partly, it is a matter of taste which of these options one chooses. The Atkinson and Shiffrin model has been somewhat more widely used in the field of human memory than Estes' theory has, but alternatively, precisely what adjustment one would need to make in the Atkinson and Shiffrin model to allow the critical interaction to emerge has not been worked out. As we saw, the extension of the Estes model is quite natural. Furthermore, there is the fact that the Atkinson and Shiffrin model places the locus of the spacing effect at the first presentation of the repeated item (the waxing and waning of long-term storage occurs for the first presentation during the interval between presentations), and we saw in the section on free recall that available evidence establishes the locus rather at the second presentation. All things considered, adoption of the Estes account seems the more parsimonious alternative.

Practically, our rather complete empirical understanding of distribution effects in associative learning has attractive implications for optimization of the education process, particularly in such easily mechanized and highly controllable situations as the acquisition of vocabulary in a foreign language or the memorization of arithmetic tables. Atkinson (1972) has been actively investigating these applied areas from a theoretical position similar to the models discussed here. He has demonstrated an interaction between testing delay and training method—with lists of German words—such that the method with the worst short-term success rate is best in the long run, and vice versa.

Single-Item Short-Term Memory Techniques

As we have seen, many theories of repetition effects in memory depend on hypotheses about what happens during intervals of time between two presentations of some item and intervals between such presentations and subsequent testing. In free-recall experiments, as in continuous paired-associate experiments, the events with which these time intervals are filled are, by the nature of the task, occurrences of new items and/or testing of old items from the same set as the critical items. For some purposes we need better control over what happens during interpresentation and retention intervals and for such control we may turn to the Brown–Peterson task. Here, single items are presented once or twice and later tested with some distractor task, such as mental arithmetic, filling intervals between presentations and prior to the test.

Consider the following experiment reported by R. A. Bjork and Allen (1970): A three-word unit, such as ARCH–NEWS–BANK is presented twice, several seconds apart, and then tested later. A moderately difficult interpolated task always separates the second presentation from the test. The independent variable is the difficulty of the interpolated task separating the two occurrences of the trigram on study trials—one task is harder than the task occurring after the second presentation and the other task is easier than the task occurring after the second presentation. Which should lead to better performance on the test, an easy task in the interpresentation interval or a hard task in the interpresentation interval?

The experiment was designed as a test of consolidation theory. Consolidation theory suggests that the amount of consolidation during the interpresentation interval of constant length should be greater with an easy task than with a hard task. The logic for this prediction is explained in Figure 9.16. Recall from earlier discussion that the total eventual memory strength is supposed to be proportional to the integral, over time, of both consolidation episodes, that is, in graphic terms, to the shaded areas in Figures 9.5 and 9.16. The shaded area resulting from the second presentation, P_2, is assumed to be uniform and independent of the interpresentation task. However, the amount of consolidation resulting from the first presentation and taking place prior to the second presentation should be greater with an easy filler task during the interpresentation

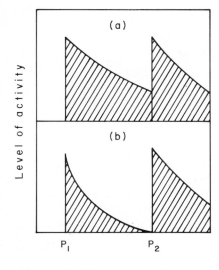

FIGURE 9.16 Predictions of consolidation theory for the R. A. Bjork and Allen (1970) experiment. Shaded area represents the total amount of permanent (long-term) memory resulting from the two presentations P_1 and P_2. In (a) the task between P_1 and P_2 is easy, resulting in more total consolidatory activity than in (b) when the interpresentation task is difficult. The task following P_2 is always of moderate difficulty.

lag than with a difficult one. The underlying assumption is that even though consolidation is unconscious it requires "cognitive space" in a way that would be reciprocal to the performance of some unrelated task concurrently.

A theory based on encoding variability, formalized in terms of any of several specific models, would hold the important thing to be that the subject was in a *different state* when the second repetition occurred than he was when the item was originally presented. It is a natural assumption that a difficult task is more likely to move him into this different state, in a constant amount of time, than an easy task.

In the experiment by R. A. Bjork and Allen (1970) the interval between the two occurrences of a three-word item was either 4.5 sec or 18 sec. The task during this interpresentation interval was either shadowing digits (repeating them after a prerecorded voice) at the rate of three every 1.5 sec or at the rate of five every 1.5 sec, the easy and hard conditions, respectively. Between the second presentation and the test of recall there was an interval of either 12 sec or 30 sec always filled with digit shadowing at an intermediate rate of four every 1.5 sec. The results are shown in Table 9.2. The left portion of this table shows a control experiment designed to demonstrate that the hard and easy tasks really did differ in difficulty. In this control experiment there was only a single presentation followed by a test after either the easy or hard shadowing condition. As we see, scores are substantially lower after the hard task than after the easy task, both conditions also showing a decline with time. We may therefore be assured that when the second presentation has occurred in the real experiment, the one

TABLE 9.2
Percentage of Correct Responses as a Function
of Distribution of Presentations,
Task Difficulty, and Retention Interval[a]

Control experiment			Main experiment		
	P_1–Test interval			P_2–Test interval	
P_1–Test task	4.5 sec	18 sec	P_1–P_2 task	12 sec	30 sec
			Easy 4.5 sec	73	61
Easy	54	45	Hard 4.5 sec	75	63
Hard	39	32	Easy 18 sec	82	70
			Hard 18 sec	84	77

[a]After Bjork and Allen (1970).

on the right, more about the first presentation has been forgotten in the hard condition than in the easy condition.

From this point of view, the results in the right portion of Table 9.2 are counterintuitive: For each combination of interpresentation interval and retention interval it has been the hard task in the interpresentation interval that has led to better performance than the easy task. (Notice that there is also an overall advantage of distributed practice).

In a way this outcome is akin to the Madigan-type experiment described above. The starting point is an advantage of a long interpresentation interval over a short one (unless there is very early testing). Madigan showed that one could simulate a long interpresentation interval by building in different encodings for an item. Gartman and Johnson showed the same thing and also that one could simulate the effects of a short interval by ensuring the same encoding at two temporally distributed intervals. Now, the experiment by Bjork and Allen (1970) shows another way of simulating the effect of a long interpresentation interval—keep the subject extremely busy during a shorter interval. This result is sharply inconsistent with consolidation theory. It is also inconsistent with the rehearsal-buffer theory of Atkinson and Shiffrin, for according to that theory more transfer to the long-term store should occur under the easy interpresentation task than under the hard interpresentation task. The Bjork–Allen findings are consistent, however, with the Estes stimulus fluctuation model or with other versions of variable-encoding theory. It is quite reasonable that in order to encode a nominally identical item differently on a second presentation than it has been on the first, it is better to have forgotten the first encoding than to still remember it.

Because of its great theoretical value we should be unusually careful in evaluating the quality of the data in the Bjork–Allen study. There are two problems: The first is the extremely small numerical differences obtained by Bjork and Allen and the fact that no statistical tests are reported in defense of the generalization that performance under the hard interpresentation task condi-tion is better than under the easy task. However, Tzeng (1973b) has replicated the experiment under conditions only slightly different from the original ones and he has obtained a large and statistically significant advantage of the hard interpresentation task over the easy task extending over a wide range of spacing intervals.

The second problem with the experiment by Bjork and Allen (1970) is less easily dismissed. It is possible that not only the absolute difficulty of an interpolated task determines performance but also the relative difficulty. If so, it is further possible that the same task is differentially perceived as difficult as a function of the task that has occured just before. Specifically it may be that shadowing by four's seems easier after shadowing by fives than it does after shadowing by three's. The conclusion would be that performance on the ulti-mate test was better for a hard interpresentation task not because of the interpresentation task itself but because in this condition the subject found the constant, moderate difficulty task preceding recall much easier than when the interpresentation task had been easy. There is quite a simple test for this possibility and it is left to the reader to discover.

Fortunately there is an experiment by Robbins and Wise (1972) that, although not excluding a perceived-difficulty mechanism, renders it somewhat less likely. Theirs was a continuous paired-associate task where items were presented either once or twice before testing. The independent variable was the imagery value of the noun pairs used as stimuli. The critical items were always medium-imagery noun pairs. In single presentation conditions these were followed immediately either by high-imagery noun pairs or by low-imagery noun pairs.

Because there is a substantial effect of noun imagery on this kind of task, Robbins and Wise reasoned that the high-imagery materials could be considered easy relative to the low-imagery materials. Indeed in the single-presentation condition, the medium-imagery pairs followed by high-imagery pairs were re-called better than those followed by low-imagery pairs (74% versus 65% correct recall).

In a pair of double-presentation conditions the two occurrences of critical, medium-imagery pairs were separated by other pairs the imagery of which was either low or high, that is, hard or easy, respectively. Just as in the Bjork and Allen (1970) study, conditions that led to worse performance following single presentation led to better performance when interpolated between two occur-rences in double-presentation conditions; when the high (easy) pairs came between the two presentations of critical medium-imagery pairs, recall on testing was 64% correct, whereas it was 76% correct when the low-imagery materials were used to separate the two presentations of the critical items. Now, of course, it is possible that there are contrast effects in the perception of the difficulty of interpolated learning tasks—that the medium pairs seem harder to learn after high-imagery pairs, for example—and that perceived learning difficulty is potent as well as actual learning difficulty; however, that interpretation seems rather forced. In other words, the Robbins and Wise experiment has obtained just the same result as the Bjork—Allen—Tzeng data and as it comes from quite a different testing situation we may be reassured against the possibility of some task artifact with the distractor method.

Although it is tempting to leave the Bjork and Allen (1970) experiment on this conclusive note, it must be mentioned that there are, after all, known boundary conditions on its generality. Roediger and Crowder (1975) performed an experiment similar in design to Bjork and Allen's but with an entire free-recall list as the unit to be repeated after varying delays filled with tasks of varying difficulties (as opposed to having single items as the unit of repetition). The finding was opposite to that of Bjork and Allen (1970); recall of a list was better if two repetitions of that list were separated by an easy task (or none at all) than if separated by a difficult task. Roediger and Crowder (1975) conclude that their study does not constitute a failure of replication but that it rather serves to isolate the type of learning process to which the Bjork and Allen finding applies and to distinguish that process from others to which it does not apply. In an argument too detailed to summarize here, they assign these two learning processes to the two factors in retrieval proposed by Anderson and Bower (1972, 1974; see Chapter 11 of this book).

Intraserial Repetition in Immediate-Memory Span

For completeness, it should be added in passing that repetition of items within a series has quite different consequences for ordered recall in the memory-span situation than it does within the free-recall paradigm. At the empirical level, it seems to be a fair generalization (Crowder, 1968b; Jahnke, 1969) that massed repetition within an immediate-memory list (say, eight items presented at two per second with no delay before recall) produces an enhancement in recall of the repeated item, whereas spaced repetition produces a decrement. In both cases we are referring to a scoring based on the recall of an item in its correct serial position. The decremental effect of intraserial repetition when several other items intervene between occurrences of the repeated item is termed the "Ranschburg phenomenon," after the German investigator who first reported it in the early 1900s. Papers by Jahnke (1972) and by Hinrichs, Mewaldt, and Redding (1973) provide access to the modern literature on the Ranschburg phenomenon. These two papers also offer interesting suggestions as to the source of the effect. However, at present, ideas on the Ranschburg phenomenon make little or no contact with ideas on the general problems of repetition as understood elsewhere in this chapter. For this reason, we shall not emphasize it here.

Summary of Repetition Effects on Recall

If we are willing to make the assumption that spacing effects in different task situations (free recall, continuous paired-associate learning, Brown–Peterson distractor task) are all related at the level of underlying theory, an assumption Hintzman (1974) does not share, then the evidence reviewed in this section permits considerable narrowing of the viable alternatives. Of the hypotheses broadly consistent with an advantage of distributed over massed practice, the consolidation notion can be rejected on the basis of the Bjork and Allen study, as can the Atkinson and Shiffrin rehearsal hypothesis. Both of these viewpoints stressed, in different ways, the variable effects of the first presentation in a direction opposite to that required by the Bjork and Allen study. Furthermore, Hintzman *et al.* (1973) showed that assuming the locus of spacing effects to be in the first presentation was untenable for other reasons as a general proposition.

The various versions of inattention and stimulus-encoding variability hypotheses are therefore left as major contenders. These two classes of notion may be complementary rather than antagonistic: When the context of encoding closely matches on two presentations it is reasonable that less encoding activity should be elicited by the second than when the two contexts differ. As we have seen, the Estes stimulus fluctuation model (elaborated by Bower's notion of varying retrieval cues) is capable of handling much of what we know about repetition, especially when the concept of inattention at short lags is added in order to accommodate nonmonotonic lag functions. Although this solution may seem overly pluralistic to some, it is possible that the encoding variability and inattention mechanisms refer to different levels of the same basic principle.

THE EFFECTS OF REPETITION ON JUDGMENTS
OF RECENCY AND FREQUENCY

Quite naturally experiments on memory for verbal items tend to emphasize retrieval or recall as the performance criterion; however, it is often instructive to ask whether the subject can respond to other types of interrogation about information he has just experienced. For example, judgments of when or how often items occurred in a list could cast light on the same theoretical issues as efforts to recall the items themselves. It turns out that the theoretical alternatives covering recency and frequency judgments in lists with repeated items closely resemble some of the theories we have just been considering for repetition effects in recall. There are basically two positions, strength theory and multitrace theory. Strength theory maintains that subjects judge how recently or frequently an item has occurred by judging how strong the memory trace is along a single dimension. To use a homely example, we could estimate when a loaf of bread had been purchased by observing how stale it is.

Multitrace theory maintains that two occurrences of an item lead to partially distinct memory traces. There are two ways of conceiving this distinction between multiple memory traces of the same nominal event: Time tagging theory (Yntema & Trask, 1963) suggests that some representation of absolute or relative time is part of the memory representation stored when an item occurs; for example, our loaf of bread could be marked "Tuesday." Context tagging theory (Anderson & Bower, 1972, 1974) suggests that events become associated with other events that have been occurring contiguously in time; because the contextual panorama is constantly changing the same item will be associated with different outside events if it occurs at two separated times. To exemplify the last of these hypotheses, we could estimate, the age of a loaf of bread by noting that it was damaged in a fall resulting from icy sidewalk conditions, which we remember obtained last Tuesday.

Testing strength theory.   A simple, elegant test of the strength hypothesis was conceived by Morton (1968). Consider a task where the subject received a list of digits and afterwards is asked about whether a specific two digits in the list have occurred in one or another order: 6 1 3 6 9 5 1 4 8 2 5 3 . . . "Did 9 or 2 occur later in the list?" According to strength theory the subject responds by measuring the strength of the two memory traces and calling the stronger one the more recent. We now complicate the experiment slightly by asking sometimes about items that have occurred twice in the list according to one of the schedules of repetition shown in the left panel of Figure 9.17. By comparison with the control condition, the condition called "After" should clearly be at an advantage according to strength theory—the usual edge in strength of the more recent item is exaggerated by its having occurred twice. According to the multiple-trace theory also, the after condition should be easier than the control condition, because there have in the former case been two opportunities to associate the more recent item to a "late" time tag or to a "late" contextual event. The interest in the experiment is focused on the before condition, where strength and multitrace theories advance different predictions. The right-hand panel of Figure 9.17 shows the strength conceptualization of the before condition as compared with the single, control condition. Because the earlier item was repeated in the before condition it has a combined strength that exceeds that of the later item, and therefore the earlier item should show some tendency to be judged as having actually occurred later, given the subject is using a decision rule specifying that the stronger of the two items is to be called the more recent. Subject to a qualification we shall see below, the multiple-trace theory yields the prediction that prior repetition, in the before condition, ought to facilitate, again because two occurrences have given the repeated item twice the opportunity to become associated with a reliable time or contextual tag. From the viewpoint of strength theory, therefore, the before condition ought to be harder than the control because the usual correlation between strength and recency has

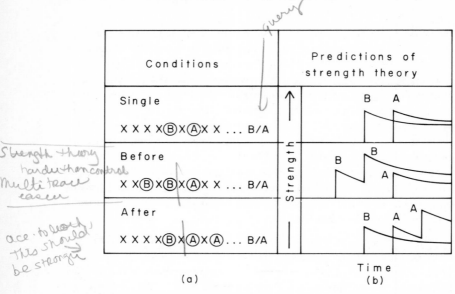

query

Strength theory
harder than control
multitrace
easier

ace. to recency
this should
be stronger

FIGURE 9.17   The logic of Morton's experiment on judgments of recency. The critical items are *A* and *B*, with the *X*'s representing filler items. *B/A* stands for the query to the subject after presentation of the list, "Was *A* or *B* first?" (b) shows hypothetical strength values for *A* and *B*; according to the strength theory the subject decides that whichever trace is the stronger one is also the most recent. (After Morton, 1968.)

been tampered with. From the viewpoint of multitrace theory it should be easier because the two traces accruing to the repeated item should enhance the changes an accurate positional tag has been learned.

Morton's results (1968) favored the strength theory in that the before condition led to poorer accuracy (.467 correct) than occurred in the control condition (.517 correct). As expected on either basis, the after condition was best of all (.620 correct). Apparently making the earlier of two items appear stronger through repetition makes it also appear more recent.

This result is quite consistent with the unidimensional strength theory of item repetition. Theories of that type, however, were found totally inadequate in our survey of repetition effects on recall; it seemed instead that multiple-trace hypotheses, such as the encoding variability notion, could better handle the evidence on recall. Flexser and Bower (1974) have had an important insight that could resolve this discrepancy in favor of multiple-trace theory. They demonstrate that the result we have been examining—a decrement in performance on the before condition as compared with the single condition—is not, after all, uniquely supportive of the strength hypothesis.

In their first experiment, Flexser and Bower dispose of two uninteresting objections that could be made to the Morton demonstration. First, one might reject Morton's result because he used strings of digits, stimulus material so devoid of variety or meaning that the subject was left with nothing but strength as a basis for his judgment. More pointed is the objection that if the subject completely fails to recognize one of the two items presented for comparative recency judgment, then he is likely to choose the other item as having been the more recent. Because repeating an item may enhance the probability that it is recognized as having occurred on the list it may be through this indirect process that a repeated item gets judged as being more recent. In Flexser and Bower's study (Experiment I) comparative recency judgments were made only on occasions when the subject was sure that he had received each of the two items on the list. Furthermore, the items were meaningful words rather than digits. Under these two modifications, the Morton result still occurred: The before condition led to poorer accuracy (.479 correct) than the single condition (.700 correct).

Therefore, the disadvantage in recency judgments of the repetition before condition (BBA) over the single-occurrence control condition (BA) may not be dismissed as an artifact. However, Flexser and Bower (1974) have gone on to show that at least one plausible version of multitrace theory can easily accommodate the phenomenon. The gist of their argument (which, in the paper, is spelled out as an explicit mathematical model) is that each event in the series gets associated, in a fallible way, with accurate contextual tags; because the tagging is fallible, there is some probability that the order of events from the list is perturbed in memory. On some occasions, therefore, the order BA is remembered as AB through normal error. In double-presentation conditions each of the three critical events, call them B_1, B_2, and A, are likewise associated in a probabilistic way to contextual tags. It is assumed that the exchange of B_2 and A, leading to a representation of BAB in memory for the true sequence BBA, is equally likely as the simple exchange of AB for BA in the single-presentation control condition. However, in the BBA condition, there is also some probability of an exchange between B_1 and A, which leads to an error through the memory representation ABB (exchange of B_1 and B_2 does not, of course, produce an error). This means that the control (BA) and repetition (BBA) conditions are equated for one source of error but that the repetition condition has two opportunities for error instead of just one. To paraphrase the authors, the subject in the single-presentation condition has only to realize that A has occurred after B but the subject in the before condition must realize that A has occurred after each of the two Bs.

In their second experiment, Flexser and Bower derive opposite predictions for performance in a variety of conditions from the unidimensional strength theory and from their own multitrace theory. The results were generally consistent with the latter and not with the former. For that reason, and because of further evidence favoring a multitrace view that is taken up immediately below, we may dismiss the strength theory of recency judgment with just as much confidence as we have dismissed the strength theory of repetition in recall.

More evidence for multiple-trace theory. The hypothesis that repeating a nominally identical item results in separate memory traces is supported by other evidence besides that obtained from the Morton task. Hintzman and Block (1971 Experiment II) performed an elaborate experiment on position judgments in which words occurred either once or twice in a long list with 50 events (called "events" rather than "items" because there were repeated items). The list was divided into four successive zones, which we might call *A, B, C,* and *D.* After receiving the list, subjects were given a piece of paper with the words listed one by one. Next to each they were to indicate in which tenth of the list they thought the word had occurred. Also, they were told to record two locations, two tenths, for words they thought had occurred twice. Singly presented words in fact occurred in either zone *A, B, C,* or *D,* whereas doubly occurring items occurred in either *A* and *C, A* and *D, B* and *C,* or *B* and *D.*

The results are presented in Table 9.3. Notice first that only in the upper-left and lower-right quadrants are there correct frequency judgments, that is, only in the quadrants where subjects have given one judgment of position for singly occurring items and two judgments for doubly occurring items. The main result of the experiment, for present purposes, was that subjects seemed able to judge where one occurrence of a repeated item had occurred independently of where the other occurrence had occurred. When the first occurrence was in Zone *A,* therefore, it made little difference whether the second was in *C* or in *D* (2.2

TABLE 9.3
Judged Frequency as a Function of Actual Frequency
and Distribution of Repetition[a,b]

Location of actual occurrence	One occurrence	Two occurrences	
		First	Second
A	3.6	2.9	6.9
B	5.2	2.6	7.6
C	5.7	3.7	6.5
D	7.2	2.0	7.0
A and *C*	4.2	2.2	7.2
A and *D*	4.6	2.4	8.0
B and *C*	5.6	3.5	7.5
B and *D*	4.9	3.1	8.1

[a]After Hintzman and Block (1971).
[b]The entries are judged locations, in tenths of list length. The correct frequency judgments are in the upper left and lower right quadrants.

FIGURE 9.18 Mean frequency judgments as a function of number of occurrences in each of two lists presented in succession. The first digit of each label represents the number of occurrences on List 1 and the second digit represents the number of occurrences on List 2. The frequency judgments were collected separately for the two lists (see the label on the horizontal axis). (After Hintzman & Block, 1971.)

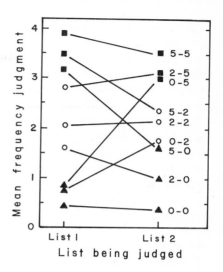

versus 2.4) with regard to locating accurately the first occurrence, although the second occurrence itself was accurately placed (7.2 versus 8.0).

This demonstrated capacity to judge the position of two occurrences of a repeated item independently makes no sense from the single-dimensional strength viewpoint. However, it is consistent with a multiple-trace, or time-tagging, hypothesis. In an even more persuasive study, Hintzman and Block (1971, Experiment III) presented two lists separated by 5 min of performing some interpolated activity. Each list had over 100 events and some words were repeated many times. In fact there were nine conditions, which can be represented by a two-digit code where the first digit refers to the frequency of an item in the first list and the second digit represents the frequency in the second list: For example, in condition 0–2 a word has occurred twice in the second list but not at all in the first. In condition 5–2 a word occurred five times in the first list and twice in the second, and so on. The complete list of conditions was 0–0, 0–2, 0–5, 2–0, 2–2, 2–5, 5–0, 5–2, and 5–5.

The subject's job was to judge the local frequency of each word that had occurred on the list. Opposite each word appearing on the test there were two spaces, one to record the judged frequency of the word on the first list and one to record the judged frequency on the second list. The results are shown in Figure 9.18. Again, the main lesson to be drawn from the data is that subjects generally do very well. Judgment of first-list frequency is not completely independent of second-list frequency—note that, for example, the first-list frequency is judged higher in Condition 2–2 than in Condition 2–0. However, these "spillover" effects were small compared with the accuracy of direct judgements. About 90% of the variance in List-1 judgments of frequency was explained by actual List-1 frequency, whereas only about 10% was explained by List-2 frequency. It is just unimaginable that such precise estimates of local density of repeated words can have come from a memory presentation in which the nine conditions are distinguished only by the amount of strength remaining for a single memory trace. Comparable results have been reported by Anderson and Bower (1972). They repeated words across four lists according to all 16 possible patterns of occurrence and nonoccurrence on four independent selections. They found, as in the experiment by Hintzman and Block (1971), that subjects were quite good at identifying local occurrences. Their subjects, for example, could correctly assign a doubly occurring word to Lists 1 and 4 rather than Lists 2 and 3 even though a strength theory would almost necessarily maintain these two patterns would have similar amounts of strength.

In summary, research on judged frequency and recency supports the multiple-trace notion. It is always possible that the strength of an individual item can have some effect on performance in other tasks we have not considered yet; however, to this point there is some question whether the concept of strength itself is at all necessary.

SUMMARY

In the initial section of this chapter our interest was in the dynamics of learning with particular regard to whether the process was one of gradual strengthening or of sudden insight. We concluded that simple models of all-or-none learning and many of the experiments originally advanced to support them were not adequate. The choice is then between two alternatives. One can breathe a sigh of relief and return to the traditional notion of a gradually strengthening memory trace, much as intuition and early theorists in learning always presumed. The second alternative is to advance theories in which several all-or-none processes contribute as components to total scores. This choice is partly a matter of personal style, because there are seldom diverging predictions for these two attitudes. However, in an indirect way, the material from the later sections of this chapter gives some guidance about what to do: The consistent failure of a unidimensional strength position to predict repetition effects, both in recall and in recency–frequency judgments, should probably be taken to signify that the long-range usefulness of strength theory in other problem areas is limited.

Most of the work on the effects of within-list repetition on recall has been done with the free-recall paradigm, where Melton has observed the classic rising pattern of recall as a function of lag between the two presentations of a repeated item. Several distinguishable hypotheses are adequate to cover this simple result, including variants on three major classes of idea: (1) inattention, proposing a decrement in the processing of the second occurrence when it comes just after the first occurrence; (2) consolidation (and rehearsal), proposing that more total processing accrues to the first occurrence when plenty of time is allowed before the second occurrence; and (3) encoding variability, proposing that spaced repetition is more likely to lead to two different encoding contexts for an item, and consequently to better recall, than massed repetition.

Experiments on the locus of the spacing effect at either the first or at the second occurrence of the repeated item and on the variability in encoding of repeated items tend to favor the encoding variability hypothesis, although not necessarily to the exclusion of the inattention hypothesis. In continuous paired-associate learning, the basic pattern of results that is important is that under conditions with testing immediately after the second occurrence (or where, in some other manner, an adequate retrieval cue is provided) the relation between interpresentation lag and performance is changed. The generalization seems to be that massed practice is either absolutely or relatively better than distributed practice if testing is early, whereas distributed practice is superior in the long run. This interaction is well handled by variants on Estes' stimulus fluctuation model; however, an additional factor must be added in order to account for the nonmonotonicity in lag functions that seems to be the rule with continuous paired-associate learning.

The experiment of Bjork and Allen, using the Brown–Peterson distractor paradigm, provides a refutation of the consolidation–rehearsal explanations for the lag effect, at least for the experimental conditions where the lag effect is usually examined.

In judgments of frequency and recency, apparent support for strength theory from the Morton (1968) paradigm gives way before a more complex multiple-trace model by Flexser and Bower (1974) and studies of position judgments by Hintzman and his associates.

The consolidation mechanism shares with what has been called strength theory the assumption that an item's representation in memory varies in some single dimension. Therefore, the rejection of consolidation theory for repetition–recall situations is quite compatible with a corresponding rejection of strength theory in experiments on judged frequency and recency.

From all of these areas comes the generalization that the repetition of nominally identical events leads to partially independent memory traces, the more so if the repetitions are spaced, and that it is through this multiplexing process, rather than through the steady growth of a single commodity, that practice makes perfect.

10
The Organization
of Memory in Free Recall

Two indisputable facts motivate the argument of this chapter: We all know huge, organized fields of information—such as the names of Major League baseball players or the contributors to English literature over the centuries—yet from a single experience with a fresh set of such names, or other items, we can extract miserably few memories, even immediately afterwards. The free-recall task seems to capture this paradox in a single experimental setting. A single trial with a list of unrelated words gives a span of immediate free-recall memory that is slightly poorer than with letters or digits, but during subsequent trials with the same materials the subject can accumulate the ability to retrieve dozens of items. What is it that happens on repeated efforts to learn that allows us to overcome the sharp limitations of immediate memory? This question is obviously a variant on the main issue in the last chapter and at some point in the future we may have a common theoretical frame for studies of intralist repetitions and studies of free-recall organization; for the present, separate treatment is most convenient.

We need initially to clarify the sense in which this type of experiment is about learning. Naturally, every item on a list of common words has long since been learned, stored, and repeatedly retrieved before the subject walks into a psychology laboratory. The words are well known before the first trial. However, in the experiment only a small subset of the subject's verbal repertoire is chosen for joint study by the subject and the experimenter. It is this choice that is the object of learning and not the words themselves. Tulving (1972) has illuminated this point by a distinction between semantic memory and episodic memory, a distinction already introduced in Chapter 6 but worth repeating here. Semantic memory contains knowledge that has become rather independent of the situation in which it has been acquired, such as mathematical rules and the properties of objects. Episodic memory contains records of experiences that are relatively fixed with respect to time and space, traces that such and such occurred in a specified context. For example, we can remember the word NUTSHELL in that we know how to pronounce it, spell it, and generate its denotation and connotation, but we may forget that it was one of 20 words read in a list 30 sec ago. This book is about episodic memory, but in the present chapter we shall constantly be in view of mutual influences and interactions between the two systems.

The early two-store models, such as that of Waugh and Norman (1965), have a ready answer for how subjects break free of the limitation on immediate memory in order to learn good-sized lists: Each time an item is presented on successive trials it resides at least for awhile in primary memory and therefore it stands a better chance of getting copied or transferred to secondary memory with repetition. We now know from Chapter 6 that such a view is seriously weakened by newer ideas on the relation between primary and secondary memory; mere residence in primary memory carries no guarantee of growth in secondary memory (Craik & Watkins, 1973) but instead it is the depth or quality of initial processing that relates to permanent storage.

In the earlier chapter we were content to observe that some type of semantic processing appears to be the key to secondary memory registration (Walsh & Jenkins, 1973). It is now our job to ponder the nature of the semantic processing that is effective.

From numerous otherwise opposing points of view there has emerged agreement that the crucial semantic processing arises from, or perhaps results in, relations among list items rather than elaboration of items in isolation. Profound rumination on the deeper significance of the word WATERFALL is not what does the job so much as remarking on the presence of the word RAINBOW earlier in the list. Mandler (1967) is particularly explicit on this point in his use of the concept of recoding, or chunking, from G. A. Miller (1956). Miller had observed that memory span seemed limited not by the nature of the material being recalled but by the number of items; therefore, any technique that could result in a mapping of many items onto few items, such as the binary-to-octal recoding scheme we discussed in Chapter 4, would increase the total amount of information carried in immediate memory. Mandler's view is that the same type of thing goes on in free-recall experiments with words: As the subject thinks about the list he discovers, or invents, relations among the items based on their meaning. Items that get related in this way organize themselves into economical packages of information, or chunks, allowing more room in memory for additional items. In an almost trivial case, the words NORTH, SOUTH, EAST, WEST could be recoded into a higher-order unit DIRECTIONS, which would compress four pieces of information into the space of one.

There are three main methods that have been proposed for manifesting organization people use in learning long lists of words. We shall deal first with these and then take up some research that has had the purpose of testing the nature of organization.

Measurement of Organization in Free Recall

Probably all memory is organized, but it is no accident that theory on the organization of episodic memory has come largely from the free-recall method. The reason is that most ideas on organization have departed not from the fact of recall per se but instead from careful attention to the order in which items are recalled. Because order of recall is totally constrained in the serial and paired-associate learning methods the popularity of these methods waned somewhat starting in the early 1960s, when organization theory began receiving wide attention. [However, we should not fail to observe that the serial and paired-associate tasks may well operate on the same organizational *principles* as studied in free recall (Postman, 1971); all we have said is that limitations on measurement techniques have married organization theory to the free-recall task.] More than anything, it was the discovery of clustering in free recall that launched organization theory and its basis in recall order.

Clustering. When a list of words includes two or more members of a semantic category, such as animals, there is a tendency for these related words to be recalled together even though they may have been presented in different regions of the list altogether. This is the phenomenon of clustering and it was discovered by W. A. Bousfield (1953). We pause to place the discovery of clustering in context before elaborating the conditions of Bousfield's experiment.

What is interesting about Bousfield's discovery is that it almost surely was not an outgrowth of the currently accepted psychology of human learning and memory. More likely the impetus came from an extraordinarily innovative study reported previously by Bousfield and Sedgewick (1944) on a topic we would now call retrieval from semantic memory. In the study by Bousfield and Sedgewick (1944) subjects were required to recall instances of various taxonomic categories—animals, makes of automobile—relying on knowledge they had gained before they had entered the laboratory. The speed with which they retrieved these items from semantic memory was recorded and the result was that people often seemed to emit bursts of closely related items followed by a pause, then more bursts, and so on. It was natural to wonder whether comparable category effects might occur for materials learned in the laboratory:

> The purpose of this paper is to describe the results of the use of a technique for quantifying clustering as here defined. The theoretical significance of this undertaking derives in part from the assumption that clustering is a consequence of organization in thinking and recall. If clustering can be quantified, we are provided with means for obtaining additional information on the nature of organization as it operates in the higher mental processes [Bousfield, 1953, p. 229].

The subjects received a list of 60 words comprised of 15 instances from each of four categories—animals, names, professions, and vegetables. The list order was assembled by random sampling without replacement so that the category members were mixed; the first few items were MUSKRAT, BLACKSMITH, PANTHER, BAKER, WILDCAT, HOWARD, JASON, PRINTER, CHEMIST, RADISH, MUSHROOM, OTTO. . . . The measurement problem of interest was to show that the occurrence of category mates in adjacent recall positions was greater than would be expected by chance. To establish the chance baseline a manual simulation technique was devised: For each subject, an artificial subject was contrived by drawing tokens randomly from an urn stocked with 60 tokens, each labeled with one of four category designations. Each artificial subject was paired with a real subject such that the number of random draws for the artificial subject equalled the number of words actually recalled by the real subject. By three different measures of category adjacency there was significantly more clustering in the recall of real subjects than in the artificial group.

To explain the clustering phenomenon Bousfield distinguished between two sources of strength for an item, one deriving from its isolated occurrence on the list and the second—called the "relatedness increment"—deriving from a "parasitic" spread of strength from a category instance to other members of the category. Bousfield seems to have subscribed to the position that clustering occurs during output; he states that at any point in the recall sequence all items have comparable individual strengths but items from the same category as the item the subject has just produced are favored by the relatedness increment. For example, the process of retrieving PANTHER from the list above adds an increment to the term WILDCAT, making it more probable than some extracategory term, for instance MARVIN.

The major controversy that motivated work on clustering in the years immediately following Bousfield's report was whether it was necessary to assume a role for the category as a higher-level organizational unit or whether simple word-to-word associative principles could handle the facts. An extreme form of the hierarchical hypothesis came up a few pages ago when we considered that the items NORTH, SOUTH, EAST, WEST could be compressed into and remembered as individual elements of a larger unit, DIRECTIONS. The occurrence of clustering is a natural consequence of this model because at retrieval the chunk DIRECTIONS can be unpacked all at once.

The word-to-word associative viewpoint discounts the importance of category membership in favor of preexisting strong normative associations among words. Therefore, the claim would be, NORTH and SOUTH are likely to occur together in recall because there is a strong connection between them, not because they are both members of the same category. So, for example, other strong associates, such as BLUE and SKY, are likely to occur also in recall clusters even though they have no common category relationship.

Although Bousfield's theory was in a subtle way intermediate between these extremes, the report by J. J. Jenkins and Russell (1952) of *associative clustering* was quite explicitly nonhierarchical. J. J. Jenkins and Russell (who were, incidentally, aware of Bousfield's discovery even though their own study was in print before his) gave their subjects a list of 48 words. The 48 words were chosen from word-association norms such that there were 24 pairs of highly associated words, such as BLACK–WHITE, HIGH–LOW, TABLE–CHAIR, ... The words were jumbled and checked to see that no two words belonging to the same pair occurred adjacently in presentation. In free recall, however, members of the same pair frequently were produced together. The overall mean recall was about 24 words and roughly half of these were recalled in normatively strong pairs. In a later study from the same laboratory (Jenkins, Mink, & Russell, 1958) it was shown that total recall from such lists of 24 pairs was higher the stronger the normative associative strength of the pairs; furthermore, the advantage of strongly related pairs seemed to occur entirely in increased clustering.

Meanwhile, Bousfield and Cohen (1953) had extended the idea of the relatedness increment to an explicitly hierarchical theory based on the general notions of Hebb (1949). In this theory the relevant mental organization for lists with categorized instances includes subordinate structures corresponding to the word presented, superordinate structures corresponding to the category names, and connections between the subordinate and superordinate structures. The occurrence of clustering and the facilitating effect clustering exerted on total recall were seen as consequences of strengthening bonds between the higher and lower structures during learning as well as increments to each alone. For example, recalling PANTHER initiates connections established during list acquisition to the superordinate ANIMAL and from that back down to the instance WILD-CAT. The Hebbian structure is shown in Figure 10.1 and contrasted with a word-to-word associative structure.

The role of the superordinate. Deese (1959) extended the word-to-word associative approach to larger collections of words than the pairs used by Jenkins and his associates. His suggestion was that with a sizeable list the total number of strong pairwise associations might be the critical determinant of both the number of items recalled and of the extent of clustering. His measure of the totality of pairwise associations that interconnect items in a restricted list was called *interitem associative strength.* Interitem associative strength is measured in a straightforward manner with free-association norms: For a given collection of words one simply observes the frequency with which each one elicits one of the others. These relative frequencies are then averaged for the list as a whole. The following list, all words suggested by the word BUTTERFLY, has an interitem associative strength of 28.3—that is, the average relative frequency of mutual elicitation in free association is 28.3%: MOTH, INSECT, WING, BIRD, FLY, YELLOW, NET, PRETTY, FLOWER, BUG, COCOON, COLOR, STOMACH, BLUE, BEES.

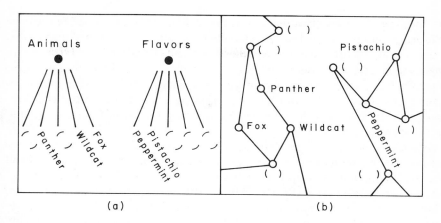

FIGURE 10.1 Contrasting theories of memory representations for the phenomenon of categorical clustering: (a) hierarchical and (b) word-to-word associative.

Deese found that total recall from a list of this sort was much higher than from a list of words with lower interitem associative strength. Furthermore, it made no difference whether the superordinate BUTTERFLY was presented to subjects during learning or not. Deese reasoned that if category effects were based on bonds between instances and the superordinate then there should have been some facilitation from presenting a suitable superordinate. If word-to-word associations were responsible for such findings as clustering, however, then one ought not to have expected any role for the category name, as was the case. Deese's account is that the subject initiates recall from a small core of words held in immediate memory. From these words he follows his free associations through what we now call semantic memory. In deciding whether to recall words on which he stumbles in this manner the subject employs a rule that when two or more list words converge through free associations on the same item that item should be recalled. Because lists with low interitem associative strength seldom produce this convergence, performance depends on how tightly the list is organized. From this model Deese was able to derive predictions for the occurrence of intrusions, nonlist words emitted in recall. Specifically, it follows that with high interitem associative strength intrusions should be fairly rare—because most converging free associates are actually on the list—and should show high communality across subjects; but with low interitem associative strength there should be more intrusions per subject—because high associates to list items are not being counted as hits—and with less communality among subjects. Both predictions were supported by the data.

One could argue, however, that although Deese's experiment showed no role for the category label over and above the influence of interitem associative strength, still, with only a single category on the list one could hardly generalize to the type of organization that results in clustering. Of what use to the subjects can it be to organize the list into subunits if all items wind up belonging to the same chunk? What might be called, after Mandler and Miller, the *adaptive significance* of organization—releasing us from the limits of immediate memory by reducing the effective number of list items—could not be served any more by putting all items into the same category as by putting each item into a different category. Even a list without any deliberate categories could be given a gratuitous superordinate, WORDS.

A doctoral dissertation by Marshall (1967; see also Cofer, 1965) was useful in teasing apart interitem associations and category membership as organizational factors. He noted that whereas some highly associated words are members of the same category, such as TABLE–CHAIR, others are just as highly associated but not members of any common category, such as SIT–CHAIR. This circumstance makes it possible in principle to dissociate words' interassociative relationship from their common category membership. Marshall tested six groups in a four-trial free-recall situation. Each group received a single list of 24 words, developed somewhat in the fashion of Jenkins and Russell (1952), from 12 pairs of related words. One variable in the experiment was the strength of the free-association relationship between the two words in each pair, as measured by a specially devised index proportional to the amount of overlap among all associates to a word. There were six levels of within-pair relatedness, corresponding to the six groups in the experiment. Additionally, however, each list of 24 words contained six pairs with uncategorized members—BED–SLEEP, MOUNTAIN–HIGH. So although each of the six lists, given to the six different groups, had its own, constant level of within-pair associative strength, half of the pairs in each list were categorized and half were not. Each list was presented for four trials, each following a different randomized order of words.

The performance measure of most interest was the amount of clustering, which Marshall measured by the *repetition ratio*—the proportion of words recalled that were recalled in clusters (the size of a cluster for this study is two). Figure 10.2 shows the main findings. In the left-hand panel we see that the higher the relatedness of the two members of a pair the greater the tendency to recall those two items together. This result confirmed what Jenkins *et al.* (1958) had shown earlier. In the center panel the data are broken down according to halves of each list, the pairs with both members common category members versus the pairs with members just as strongly related but not category mates. There was very clearly a larger tendency to a cluster when the two items were from the same category, as the hypothesis based on a superordinate–subordinate memory organization would have predicted. A strict word-to-word associative hypothesis, in contrast, would have expected only the amount of within-pair relatedness to influence organization, without any extra facilitation from category membership.

Before leaving the Marshall experiment we should note, in the right-hand panel, that whereas each of the two main factors—relatedness and category

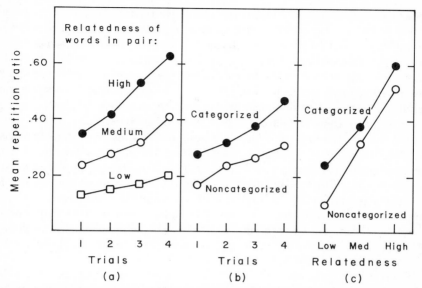

FIGURE 10.2 Clustering scores (repetition ratio) (a) as a function of trials and associative relatedness of word pairs in the list, (b) as a function of trials and whether or not the word pairs were from a common category with relatedness held constant, and (c) as a function of relatedness and categorical membership. (Data from Marshall, 1967; figures after Cofer, 1965.)

membership—affected clustering significantly, there was also an interaction between the two factors, with the category effect stronger with relatively unrelated words than with strongly related words. Apparently, as Cofer (1965) suggests, subjects use any basis for organization they can find and category relations are attractive in the absence of strong associative bonds.

What clustering is good for. Somewhat earlier we accepted too uncritically the rough argument: organization helps, clustering represents organization, therefore clustering helps. Why not make quite a different argument, in which organization is seen as the consequence or byproduct of good retention and not the cause of it? Perhaps the student who hands in a neat examination paper in elegant calligraphy does so because he has found the questions easy and has had extra time to lavish on surface cosmetics, not because the neatness has helped him remember the material.

Most workers in the field are quite skeptical of this sort of argument. Unfortunately, however, there is little evidence either way. Puff (1970) has reported an experiment that is pertinent, but the generality of the results seems to be in doubt. Puff gave 40 subjects a list of 30 ostensibly unrelated words and another larger group, 76 subjects, a list of comparable words with ten items each from three taxonomic categories. The lists were presented for 60 sec of study, all words simultaneously visible. The subjects who received the 30 unrelated words remembered fewer words (13.20) than those who received the categorized list (16.66). The most interesting finding resulted from breaking down the categorized-list group into those who showed a statistically significant tendency to cluster (35 subjects) and those who did not show clustering (41 subjects). The clusterers remembered 17.00 words and the nonclusterers remembered 16.26 words, a small and nonsignificant difference. The suggestion of this result is that having a categorized list improves performance for some reason but that clustering is only an inconsequential byproduct, not the reason itself.

Evidence for the same conclusion comes from a study by Cofer, Bruce and Reicher (1966), showing that with categorized lists, *blocked presentation,* in which all common category instances are presented together rather than randomized throughout the whole list, improves clustering scores as compared to random presentation but, at least under some conditions, it does not improve the amount of recall. Note that we have faced a similar inferential issue in immediate memory, when trying to decide whether phonological similarity effects are representative of the agent for memory, the fundamental code, or are the symptom of partially forgotten traces.

However, the generality of the Puff experiment has been challenged by Thompson, Hamlin, and Roenker (1972) who have found a positive relationship between clustering level and total recall for subgroups of subjects. The main differences between their study and Puff's seem to be (1) a three-trial assessment of individual differences in clustering rather than a single-trial assessment, (2) using subjects only with extremes in clustering scores rather than splitting the total group in half, (3) using a list with four categories of 12 items rather than three categories of ten, and (4) using item by item presentation rather than whole-list presentation. Whichever of these factors has been responsible for the discrepant outcomes it is obviously premature to conclude that clustering is unrelated to total recall. However, we should not be too smug about the causative role of clustering in good recall until considerably more data of this type have been reported.

A more positive approach to clustering's beneficial effects was taken by Cohen (1963). Cohen departed from the G. A. Miller (1956) orientation, that hierarchical recoding during presentation of a list effectively reduces its length and therefore permits a larger proportion of the list items to be stored. A possibility suggested by this orientation is that a category name, serving as a higher-order chunk, ought to be as easy to remember as a word; for example, if a subject can recall n words from a list of unrelated items, perhaps he can also recall n categories from a list of words organized into categories. Now, of course, given the subject has recalled the presence of a category, say *animals*, from a list, he still needs to recover which particular animals have occurred on the list. Cohen treated this decoding problem as a relatively separate aspect of total recall and manipulated it by varying the degree to which category members were exhaustively sampled; for example, if NORTH, SOUTH, EAST, and WEST were all presented, then *directions* would have been presented as an exhaustive category, whereas presenting LINCOLN, POLK, NIXON, and TAFT would not exhaustively sample the category *presidents*.

In Cohen's experiment there were nine main conditions: In three of these conditions, subjects received either 10, 15, or 20 ostensibly unrelated words. In another three conditions there were either 10, 15, or 20 *categories* in which each category contained either three or four words that completely exhausted the category (NORTH, SOUTH, EAST, WEST; ADDITION, SUBTRACTION, MULTIPLICATION, DIVISION; BLONDE, BRUNETTE, REDHEAD; KNIFE, FORK, SPOON). In the final three conditions there were again either 10, 15, or 20 categories of three of four words each, but the categories nonexhaustive (ENGLAND, FRANCE, GERMANY, RUSSIA; SAXOPHONE, TRUMPET, CLARINET, OBOE; WILLOW, OAK, MAPLE; MINUTE, WEEK, YEAR). Therefore, a list with 20 categories would contain a total of 70 words—ten three-word categories and ten four-word categories. The words were presented in haphazard order with the restriction that no category mates could appear in adjacent positions.

There were no surprises in the data for recall of words in that the expected positive relation between list length and number of recalled words occurred as did an advantage for exhaustive categories. With unrelated words the mean scores were 7.5, 9.1, and 9.5 from list lengths of 10, 15, and 20, respectively.

The main interest of the experiment lies in the number of chunks recalled—the number of categories presented on the list from which at least one member has occurred in recall. This measure is given in Figure 10.3 for the nine main conditions. For the conditions with unrelated words, these scores match the ones given in the last paragraph, but for the other six conditions this measure of chunks recalled gives no credit beyond the first category member recalled. The data do not show the expected invariance of chunk recall across conditions. The exhaustive categories show an edge over nonexhaustive categories and, more seriously, the categorized lists diverge widely from the lists of words at the longest length. With a list of 20 words subjects recalled about 9.5 but with 20 categories subjects recalled at least one member from about 12.5 of the categories.

However, Cohen noted a confounding between the unit of analysis (word versus category) and study time. When we are considering success in getting out some representative of the category in recall we should count study time with the category, whereas when the word is the chunk of interest it should be the time spent with a word. Because words have been presented at a constant 3-sec rate in all conditions, this makes the comparison in Figure 10.3 unfair, as a category with four members has had a total study time of 12 sec and a category with three members has had 9 sec; the average category has therefore been presented for 10.5 sec. To remedy this Cohen (1963) did another experiment. In one control condition of the new study Cohen presented a list of 20 unrelated words

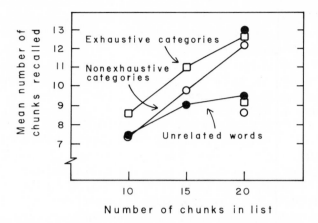

FIGURE 10.3 The relation between number of chunks (unrelated words or categories) on a list and the number of chunks represented in recall (by recall of a word or by recall of at least one category member) as a function of whether or not the list contains categories and, if so, whether these categories were exhaustive or nonexhaustive. The unconnected points for 20-chunk lists are from a control experiment the conditions of which are described in the text. (After Cohen, 1963.)

with each word appearing for 10.5 sec, the average category study time from the first experiment. In this new condition there was a mean recall of 13 words, quite comparable with chunk recall in the 20-category categorized lists (about 12.5). In the other new control conditions words within exhaustive or non-exhaustive categorized lists were presented at a 1-sec rate. Here, recall for chunks was even slightly worse than recall for unrelated words shown in Figure 10.3 (around nine chunks). The generalization from Cohen's study is quite consistent with the recoding hypothesis: When total study time is held constant, a category behaves about like a word, at least with regard to the relation between list length and recall.

The influence of study time per chunk is further emphasized by a parenthetical observation: Note that in categorized lists there have equally often been three-word and four-word categories. If the time per category is an important variable, then category recall should be greater with the four-item than with the three-item categories, because the subject has 33% more time with the former. This prediction also was confirmed by the data.

Although it is not impossible for an advocate of associative, or nonsuperordinate, clustering to accommodate these findings (Cofer, 1967), they are more nearly consistent with a theory in which the superordinate plays a crucial role. However, what about recalling the words within a category, given that the subject has recalled at least one exemplar of it? Cohen found a surprisingly simple rule covering retrieval of items within a category: Once the subject had recalled at least one item from a category, he would recall 63% of the items within that category for nonexhaustive categories and 85% of the items within the category for exahustive categories. This rule held for different list lengths and different category sizes. The picture that emerges is of a two-stage recall process, in which access to higher-order categories is first accomplished and then access to words within the category. We shall see the separability of these two stages again below.

Subjective organization.   One question of importance is whether such a two-stage model holds true for lists of words that are not organized neatly into categories. Tulving's work on the measurement of *subjective organization* (Tulving, 1962) was intended to suggest that, even when the experimenter has not arranged the list into obvious categories, the subject nonetheless organizes the material into superordinates, which, for him, are conceptually coherent. Imposing organization on ostensibly unrelated words is a creative, constructive process, and because such private thought processes are ordinarily the very hardest mechanism for a psychologist to study, Tulving's proposal of an objective way to measure subjective organization was eventually received with great enthusiasm. There had always been the implicit faith that clustering experiments simply brought to the surface organizational processes that were of great generality; the problem was to devise a measurement strategy to show that clustering-like behavior occurred when categorical organization was not, as it were, forced down subjects' throats.

Tulving's (1962) basic idea for measuring subjective organization was that when the same items were being learned over several trials, under free-recall instructions, then items belonging to the same subjective category should tend to be recalled together. How are we to know, however, whether two items recalled together on a particular trial are members of a subjective category or not? The answer is that if two items are recalled in adjacent positions on a number of different trials, then they probably have been organized together by the subject. The order in which the items are presented is changed on every trial, so that no items keep occurring together in input; if they occur consistently together in output Tulving's proposal is that they are members of a single subjective unit. The observation of growth in recall adjacencies over trials of learning (subjective organization) provides a way out of the circular reasoning implied by most prior ideas on learning: performance (recall scores) improves because of associations, the presence of which can be inferred only from that same performance. With his measure of recall order, Tulving expected to be able to assess the growth of episodic memory structures in a logically independent way with respect to the growth in recall per se.

To describe the amount of such organization occurring over the whole list, for a certain number of trials, Tulving proposed a measure based on information theory; the measure was a numerical answer to the question: "Given that the subject has just recalled a particular word on a particular trial, how uncertain are we as to what he will recall next, as compared to how uncertain we would be without knowing what he just recalled?" The details of the original subjective organization measure are not particularly important now: It varied between 0 and 1.0, the former score occurring if recall order on two adjacent trials has been totally independent and the later score occurring if the recall order (of the same items) on two adjacent trials has been perfectly correlated. Other ways of expressing this correlation have been devised (A.K. Bousfield & Bousfield, 1966; S. Ehrlich, 1970; Pellegrino, 1971; see especially R. Sternberg & Tulving, 1974, for a general review of the measurement problem); however, most of them are based on the number or proportion of pairs of words recalled in adjacent output positions on successive trials. The measure of choice (Sternberg & Tulving, 1974) seems to be *pair frequency,* the observed number of item pairs recalled together (without regard to order inversions within the pair) on successive trials minus the number of such repeated item pairs to be expected by chance; because this measure is no more difficult to compute than most of the other alternatives, including Tulving's original formulation, and because it meets criteria of reliability and validity better than other measures, it should probably be accepted as standard.

In the experiment that illustrated the subjective organization concept, Tulving (1962) presented lists of 16 words for 16 trials, each trial a different ordering of the words, with instructions for free recall after each presentation. The words were unrelated in that they had been selected from a larger pool haphazardly, although, as we all know, human cognitive ingenuity would make a list of truly unrelated words a practical impossibility. In this experiment there was, of course, a steady improvement in the number of words recalled over the 16 trials. At the same time, the subjective organization scores increased monotonically. However, subjective organization scores for artificial subjects (recall outputs from real subjects with the order of emission deliberately randomized) showed essentially no gains across trials.

There is increasing consistency in the order in which words are recalled, therefore, as learning of a free-recall list progresses. We must be aware that this basic result is essentially a simple correlation between two behavioral measures and that a correlation does not provide logical grounds for defending an argument that one type of behavior (organization) causes the other (recall); as with measures of clustering, there is always the possibility that increasing mastery of the list permits, somehow, an increasing tendency to recall related words in close proximity.

Converging operations in support of subjective organization. Tulving (1964) undertook to relate the concept of subjective organization to the microstructure of *individual items'* histories from trial to trial in free-recall learning. His point of departure in this analysis was the proposition that the then-current controversy about whether items were learned gradually or suddenly (see Chapter 9) was, in fact, a misguided issue. All items, in any type of verbal-learning situation, are perfectly well learned the first time they are presented; the proof of this is that at any point in the presentation episode the subject can be asked to retrieve the very most recent item and he does this without error. All items are always learned, therefore, and the question for theory is under what circumstances they are remembered until the time of testing or until the next trial (Bernbach, 1965). In multitrial free recall Tulving suggested two relevant classes of forgetting: First, an item presented on a trial may be forgotten even before the test following that same presentation trial. This Tulving called "intratrial forgetting"; on the first trial of an experiment in multitrial free recall, all but those items correctly recalled have by definition suffered intratrial forgetting. The second class of forgetting in multitrial free recall covers the case where an item is learned during presentation, remembered long enough to be correctly recalled in the test phase of that trial, but then forgotten before its attempted recall on the next trial, despite its occurrence on the study list on that next trial. This second class of forgetting is called "intertrial forgetting"; its definition includes items that were correct on one test trial—indicating intratrial retention—but then incorrect on the next trial.

There are four possible histories of being correct and incorrect that a particular item can have across a pair of adjacent trials: It can be recalled correctly on both trials (CC); it can be recalled on the first trial of the pair but not on the second (CN); it can be recalled on the second trial but not the first (NC); or, finally, it can be omitted from recall on either trial (NN). Tulving identified these four outcomes with the two classes of forgetting and the corresponding classes of retention—intertrial and intratrial—as follows: Items in the NN category were lost twice to intratrial forgetting; items in the CN category were lost to intertrial forgetting; items in the NC category were retained through intratrial retention; and items in the CC category were retained thorugh intertrial retention. These identifications are not airtight. For example, the CC items could have been retained twice through intratrial retention, once on each trial, although forgotten between trials. However, no one can claim that the CC, CN, NC, NN classification is not strongly related to the underlying theoretical partition of intra- and intertrial retention.

The ultimate validation of these distinctions is in the evidence produced with them. In Figure 10.4 are shown the trial by trial changes in CC, CN, NC, and NN frequencies for a multitrial free-recall experiment. The main message from this figure is that there is little change in the number of new items recalled on each trial (NC). It is the CC component, items recalled on both of two adjacent trials, that grows. The assertion is that subjective organization may be identified with intertrial retention (CC)—items that are carried from one trial to the next are carried in an organized package the contents of which tend to be recalled in adjacent positions. The correlation between mean intertrial retention (CC) scores over successive trials was +.99. The correlation between these two measures, as individual differences variables, with data pooled over trials, was +.58. In

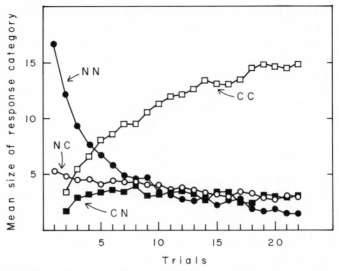

FIGURE 10.4 Changes in types of correct and incorrect response sequences across trials in multitrial free recall learning: CC is correct on Trial n and correct on Trial $n + 1$; NC is incorrect on Trial n and correct on Trial $n + 1$; CN is correct on Trial n and incorrect on Trial $n + 1$; NN is incorrect on both Trials n and $n + 1$. (After Tulving, 1964.)

contrast, the correlation between subjective organization and intratrial retention (NC) was essentially zero, −.07. These correlations suggest that the identification of subjective organization with CC histories is a valid first hypothesis.

Buschke (1974) has recently proposed a new way to track the growth of consistent organization within multitrial free-recall lists. The approach is based on an alteration in the usual presentation technique—instead of presenting each item in the list on every trial, Buschke has explored conditions where on every trial subjects see only those items they have earlier failed to recall. In one version of the technique, called "selective reminding," only those items are presented on a trial that have not been recalled on the immediately preceding trial (Buschke, 1973) and in another version only those items are presented on a trial that have never previously been recalled on any trial (Buschke, 1974). With either variant, Buschke has been able to identify a group of items that are consistently recalled, without further presentation, on every subsequent trial of the experiment. The number of items in this category increases steadily throughout learning and it seems to be a good converging measure of stable intertrial retention with presumably strong subjective organization (see also M. E. Ehrlich, 1972).

The central argument in Tulving's thesis (Tulving, 1962, 1964) is that repetition affects performance indirectly, by permitting the growth of organization, and does not per se lead to good recall. This position is difficult to prove or disprove, partly because much of the evidence on organization is correlational.

However, Tulving (1966) has reported two types of demonstration that repetition alone is insufficient for learning in multitrial free recall. It does not follow from such demonstrations that, therefore, subjective organization is what makes the difference; but failing to discredit the role of sheer repetition in free-recall learning would make one suspicious that any such fancy concept as subjective organization is necessary.

The first of the two approaches followed by Tulving (1966) was closely related to the class of experiments on incidental learning (See Chapters 1 and 6). Two groups were given an identical list of 22 words to learn over a dozen free-recall trials. Previously, one group had been given six trials with the same 22 words, used as the left-hand members of pairs of items where two-digit numbers were the right-hand members, under some pretext that each pair had to be read aloud. A control group had six trials of reading verbal pairs also, but the items in these pairs were all different from those on the free-recall list they were subsequently required to learn. The results showed no difference between the two groups even though one group had seen each of the items to be learned six times previously in the same experimental context. By any simple theory that merely experiencing a word strengthens it independently of other items on the list, the experimental group should have been well on the way to learning the entire ensemble.

The second demonstration experiment in Tulving (1966) has attracted greatly more attention than the incidental learning study, but it now appears that this second method does not show quite what it seemed to originally, so we shall deal with it summarily. Like the study we have just seen, it was a transfer experiment. This time, however, there was a special relation between the materials on the two tasks—the second list included the entire first list. Both the experimental and control groups learned the same list of 36 words under multitrial free-recall conditions. The groups differed in respect to a prior task. The control group learned a list of 18 words different from those on the second list. The experimental group, however, learned an 18-word list that contained exactly half of the same words later to appear on their 36-word list. The experimental paradigm is therefore called *part—whole transfer.*

If words are learned independently through sheer repetition then the experimental group should have an immense advantage over the control group because, for them, half the list would already have been learned. However, Tulving pointed out that if it were organization that supported learning, rather than repetition, the finding of transfer between the two lists for the experimental group would depend on whether the organizational scheme developed for the first list were appropriate, or even useful, in learning the second list. That is, the sublist of 18 words learned by the experimental group could be organized in a manner that conflicted with the optimal organization of the total list of 18 words. Because the control group would have no prior tendency to organize the words on the second list in any way, they should be able to hit on the optimal system right away.

The finding was that although the experimental group started out somewhat ahead of the control group on the second list, it was later outstripped by the control group and wound up at a distinct disadvantage. In contrast to the first demonstration, therefore, where prior repetition of words on the critical list was entirely neutral with respect to ultimate learning of the critical list, here the finding was that prior experience with materials from the second list actually inhibited learning of the second list. The hypothesized explanation was that in dealing with the part list of 18 words, the experimental group formed subjective organization patterns that conflicted with what would have been the most appropriate organization of the second list. R. J. Sternberg and Bower (1974) have recently reviewed the large literature on this experimental problem, identifying several boundary conditions on part-whole negative transfer, among them: (1) subjects who are informed of the relation between the two lists (that the entire first list is included in the second) show not negative transfer, but positive transfer (Wood & Clark, 1969); (2) subjects who are encouraged to guess in recalling the second list also do not show negative transfer (Slamecka, Moore, & Carey, 1972).

R. J. Sternberg and Bower (1974) have been able to rationalize the entire pattern of results—the negative transfer obtained by Tulving, the absence of negative transfer with informed subjects, and the disappearance of negative transfer with encouragement of guessing—in terms of a single consistent hypothesis. They adopt the concept of *list tags* (markers) from the theory of Anderson and Bower (1972; see Chapter 11 of this book); this idea holds that a word can be recalled as having been a member of a particular list only if there is some tag on the memory representation of that word designating its occurrence on the list in question. For all subjects in the Tulving paradigm, each item on the first list receives a tag for that list. For experimental subjects, however, the assignment of tags to the second list is more complicated than for the control subjects. The control subjects have entirely new words on the second list and therefore no problem. However, the experimental subjects have a second list that includes items from the first, items already tagged as having occurred on the first list. Assignment of two different list tags to the same items conforms to the $A–B$, $A–D$ paradigm of negative transfer, the letter A standing for the word and the letters B and D standing for the two different list tags. For control subjects the transfer paradigm is the easier $A–B$, $C–D$ arrangement. Now if the experimental subjects have unusual difficulty assigning second-list markers to first-list words we should expect some *untagged items* on the second list, items that keep occurring on second-list trials but that the subject still has identified only as first-list items. These items are not recalled because to the best of the subjects' knowledge, in the experimental group, they are not relevant. It is as if the subject says to himself: "Yes indeed, I saw METHODIST but it was on the first list, not the second."

R. J. Sternberg and Bower performed an experiment in which experimental subjects were asked to recall, during second-list learning, all items from both lists and to identify as best they could, the particular list from which each item came. From a detailed analysis of the results they were able to find strong support for their hypothesis that negative transfer occurs because the double-list items cannot readily be tagged as occurring on the second list. Naturally, if subjects are aware of the experimental design the problem does not arise; they recall all words from both lists. Also, if they are encouraged to guess we should expect the improperly tagged items to be recalled anyway.

Postman (1971) has performed related experiments on transfer in order to test the proposition that interitem dependencies (either units of subjective organization or pairwise association) are formed in the normal course of multitrial free recall with unrelated words. The basic idea was to train subjects on a free-recall list and then transfer them to a derived paired-associate list in which the pairs, both stimulus and response members, came from the free-recall list. If subjective units had been formed originally, then they would tend to be broken up in transfer to the new, arbitrary pairings, and paired-associate performance ought to suffer as compared with controls, whose paired-associate list was unrelated to the prior free-recall items. The results of several versions of the basic experiment showed consistent negative transfer in the experimental condition. This phenomenon rules out the possibility that acquisition in multitrial free recall depends on the isolated strengthening, through sheer repetition, of individual items. Less certain are the precise properties of the interitem dependencies that cause the negative transfer. However, M. K. Johnson (1972) showed that if the derived paired-associate items were chosen such that pairmates in transfer learning came from apparent subjective units in prior free-recall learning (chosen on the basis of recall adjacencies) then the negative transfer was eliminated and weak positive transfer resulted.

Mandler's sorting method.   One frustrating aspect of the subjective organization measure devised by Tulving is that one cannot easily identify the particular organizational. units employed. Some workers, Tulving himself for one, have responded to this problem by returning to categorized lists in which the organization is under the control of the investigator, having made the point that ostensibly unrelated lists get treated by subjects as if they are subdivided into categories. (However, see Postman, 1972, for a rejoinder that obviously categorized lists and ostensibly unrelated lists may be organized by subjects according to different principles.) Another response to the problem of covert subjective organization has been to remain with unrelated words but to make the process of subjective organization explicit. Mandler and his associates have followed this path, operationally separating the organization process from the recall process.

The starting point was an experiment by Mandler and Pearlstone (1966) on the behavior of subjects in sorting a collection of words into categories. There were two groups, each given a deck of 52 cards with a word written on each card. The words were not obviously related to one another. The "free" group was instructed to sort the 52 words into categories of their own choosing, anywhere from two to seven categories in all. They were told that practice in sorting the same words into the same categories would continue until a criterion of sorting consistency, near-identical sorts on two successive trials, was reached. The yoked control group received the same words, but each of these subjects was paired with a counterpart in the free group and was required to sort the cards into the categories his partner had produced. After criterion was reached all subjects were asked to recall the words. Not surprisingly, the free group required many fewer trials to reach criterion (3.5) than the yoked group (7.5). However, despite about twice as many exposures to each word on the part of the yoked subjects, mean recall of the words from the two groups was the same. For subjects there was a correlation of .96 between the number of groups used in sorting and the mean recall; when the number of trials to achieve the sorting criterion was eliminated as a factor, through partial correlation, the relation dropped only negligibly, to .94. These correlations were of primary interest to Mandler, as we shall see presently.

The thrust of the experiment by Mandler and Pearlstone (1966) was that, as Tulving had suggested, the effect of repetition on recall was not direct; instead, repetition provided the occasion for organization to occur and organization was what supported good recall. Mandler (1967) extended this reasoning in an incidental learning experiment with a two by two design: In each of four groups, subjects were either asked to sort 52 words into categories of their own choosing, or not; and they were either told that following five presentation trials they would be asked for recall of the words, or not. All subjects received the same presentation sequence, sorting subjects told to write the words in columns representing their categories and nonsorting subjects told simply to copy the words down in presentation order. The results are shown in Table 10.1. An additional group, which received the same words paired with digits and was told to keep a running count of digit occurrence, recalled only 10.9 words. The main result of the experiment was that all cells of the design were equal except the cell representing subjects told neither to categorize the words nor that they would be responsible for recall later.

TABLE 10.1
Mean Recall of Words as a Function
of Instructions[a]

Categorizing instructions	Recall instructions	
	Present	Absent
Present	31.4	32.9
Absent	32.8	23.5

[a]After Mandler (1967).

In other words, instructions to recall make no difference if subjects are told to categorize the words just as in the Hyde and Jenkins (1969) study described in Chapter 1. Likewise, instructions to categorize make no difference if subjects are told they will have to recall the words. Instructions to recall are therefore tantamount to instructions for organization, and vice versa. In effect it seems as though the internal processes resulting from organization of the material are equivalent to the internal processes activated by learning instructions: consequent recall scores are about the same. For both of the groups asked to categorize the words, there was a significant positive correlation between the number of categories formed in sorting and the number of words subsequently recalled; for the intentional group this correlation was .64 and for the incidental group it was .53.

Mandler attaches great importance to the positive correlation between number of sorting groups and recall: If memory is ordinarily limited to a fixed span of around five items then by forming groups the subject can adopt groups as the unit and remember five groups, each containing several items. Optimal use of this strategy would suggest that in the range allowed, two to seven, the more categories the better. Subjects choosing to sort into only two or three groups would be underusing their capacities. In a set of six experiments comparing sorting organization and subsequent free recall, Mandler found consistently large positive relations between number of categories and free recall. However, the correlation between trials of sorting (indexing number of exposures to the words) and recall was zero. In these experiments, the mean number of categories used was 4.5 and the number of words recalled was usually between 25 and 30. This suggests a hierarchical organization in which approximately five higher-order units are constructed with somewhat under five words subordinated in each. Put differently, the slope of the regression line relating number of words recalled to sorting categories was, for the experiments together, 3.9 items; that is, a typical subject gained nearly four items in free recall for every additional category he decided to employ in sorting.

Two restrictions Mandler (1967) imposed on his subjects were explored by Adler (1969). As we mentioned above, subjects in Mandler's studies were obliged to sort using between two and seven categories. What would happen if subjects were allowed to use more than seven categories? The limiting case, of course, is when 52 categories are used for the 52 words; because this extreme is indistinguishable from no categories at all, we should expect the overall relation to be curved, with a maximum falling somewhere around seven categories but performance falling off after this optimal number of groups is reached. Second, Mandler excluded from experiment any subject who chose other than a conceptual basis for sorting, such as word length, initial letter, or whatever. Adler wanted to see whether these subjects, too, would show the positive relation between number of sorting groups and recall.

Adler (1969) was able to identify two distinct groups on the basis of their sorting strategy. A group who had obviously used a structural sorting criterion—

alphabetic distinctions, part of speech, length—showed no correlation whatever between the number of groups used and recall ($r = .06$) even though there was sufficient variability in the number of groups used by these structural sorters for correlation with some other variable to be possible. However, the remaining subjects, presumably using a semantic basis for sorting, showed the usual high correlation ($r = .70$). In addition, for these semantic sorters there was a significant curvilinear component in the correlation beyond seven groups; in other words, the positive relation between groups and recall began to call off after the optimal figure of seven groups. Adler's analysis of the situation fits very nicely with the Craik and Lockhart (1972) view. She maintains that subjects undertaking the sorting task face a choice between two antagonistic requirements—sorting in order to reach criterion rapidly and be out of the experiment sooner, as opposed to sorting in order to lay the groundwork for good recall afterwards. In return for the easier sorting associated with the shallow, structural level of analysis, the result was poorer recall.

Therefore, in Mandler's work we see the same common themes that appeared elsewhere in this survey of research on organization in memory—the adaptive significance of organization in overcoming a limited memory span, the uselessness of simple repetition in promoting recall, and emergence of higher-order units than the single word. The usefulness of these ideas seems to be amply demonstrated by the Bousfield, Tulving, and Mandler research programs. However, as we have also seen, each individual approach does leave the same ambiguity that always attaches to correlational research. For example, in the Mandler studies the correlation between number of sorting categories and recall could come about through the heavy role of memory in the sorting task itself. That is, the sorting task can be considered a paired-associate situation with as many different response terms as there are sorting categories; reaching criterion on this sorting task therefore requires substantial memory for how each word has been classified from trial to trial. Subjects who have excellent general memory ability find themselves both able to cope with larger numbers of categories in sorting and able to recall more words at the end of the experimental session, but subjects with poorer memories must be content with fewer sorting categories and with fewer recalled items. These two observations do not have to be related in a causal manner. Perhaps for this reason the two by two experiment by Mandler, portrayed in Table 10.1, is among the most significant pieces of evidence after all because it suggests instructions to recall and instructions to organize are functionally equivalent in their effects on recall.

Slamecka's Independent Trace Storage Hypothesis

The most interesting and provocative recent set of ideas and experiments about organization in free recall is an outgrowth of some data reported by Slamecka in 1968. Prior to that report, the issue for theory had been mainly whether retrieval dependencies in free recall could be accommodated by an item-to-item associative model or whether it was necessary to invoke the more exotic notions of higher-order units and subjective categories. We saw several instances in which these approaches seemed to yield different conclusions (see Postman, 1972, for a recent look at the matter), but in one important respect they actually were in agreement—that the memory store was organized into units larger than the single item, either pairwise associations linking items into a network or, alternatively, familylike groups of items gathered under higher-order unit representations.

Slamecka (1968) has proposed a truly radical alternative, that items are stored independently of one another; SADISM and MASOCHISM, by this notion, are no more closely related in memory than are SADISM and CHICKADEE. Immediately one is led to ask why, in that case, is there clustering in free recall of categorized lists? Slamecka proposes that although the memory store is totally unorganized the process of retrieval is itself organized. The subject forms a plan, during input, for exactly how he is going to retrieve the items. This plan is sensitive to categorical aspects of the items used; therefore, if the subject notes during input that there are three obvious categories, animals, professions, and flowers, on the list he may decide to try recalling all the professions first, and then the other categories. He is all the while flinging the items randomly into storage but carrying an evolving plan for organized retrieval. This would account for clustering and for subjective organization.

Although Slamecka was not clear on why such organized retrieval would be adaptive for the subject, we might conjecture that systematic retrieval would help the subject refrain from recalling items more than one time. We can picture books thrown into random locations in a library: The subject wanders through this chaotic store looking for items marked as having occurred on the list. He would be expected to cross and recross his path numerous times, which would result in repeated recalls of the same items unless he had a plan for systematically retrieving one type of item before another, and so on. (There is a hidden assumption in this realization of Slamecka's hypothesis—that whereas occurrence on a list leaves a tag or trace, occurrence in prior recall does not leave such a trace; although it becomes a bit contrived, this proposition can actually be derived from what we know about proactive inhibition in list identification.)

Slamecka reasoned that many of the Mandler and Tulving results could be accommodated well by assuming that the effectiveness of a retrieval plan would vary as a function of different experimental conditions. For example, the relation between number of sorting categories and subsequent free recall can be handled by the proposition that the subject develops a more efficient retrieval plan than when only a few categories are used. Likewise, cuing effects, such as found in the Tulving and Pearlstone (1966) experiment (see Chapter 1), may be handled by the assumption that providing category names simply reminds the subject of the retrieval plan he is likely to have developed in the course of hearing a categorized list.

The importance of Slamecka's 1968 article was not in the strength of his hypothesis about retrieval plans; indeed this was not very carefully spelled out. Instead, it was the elegance of the test he proposed for organized, either associative or hierarchical, storage: If items are connected in either of these two fashions in storage, then giving the subject one item at the time of recall should help him get to others. If items are stored independently of one another, in contrast, then getting free access to one does not necessarily help in retrieving others. The experimental procedure is therefore beautifully simple: Give two groups of subjects the same list to study. Afterwards, allow the control group to recall all the items it can but give the experimental group one or more of the list items as cues for the remainder. The two groups are then compared in recall only for the items for which both groups have been responsible—the critical items.

In the first study in the 1968 article, Slamecka gave subjects two presentations of a 30-word list at a two words per second rate. The lists were either low-frequency words, high-frequency words, or the well-known "butterfly" list (see above, this chapter). The experimental groups received 15 of the words from one of these lists and were asked to write in the remaining 15 words, whereas the control groups were simply given a sheet of blank paper. The finding was that on the critical words, the experimental groups were significantly worse than the control groups, for each list. Because all results need replication but negative results absolutely demand it, Slamecka continued. In the second experiment, three lists of rare words were used and the experimental groups received either 5, 15, or 25 of the 30-word lists as cues. The control groups were significantly better in each case. In the third experiment the maximum possible cuing was provided—the list had 30 words and 29 of these were presented to the experimental group as cues; still, there was a significant advantage of the control group in recall for the single word not seen as a cue by the experimental group. In the fourth experiment, the lists were categorized, five categories with six instances in each. Experimental groups received at recall either one word from each category, three words from each category, or five of the six words from each category (either 5, 15, or 25 cue words, in total), the task, again, being to recall the remainder. Here, too, however, there was a highly significant advantage for the control group, which received no cuing. In a later study (Slamecka, 1969) it was shown that even when subjects were given three successive study–recall trials with the same list, there was no advantage of cued recall over free.

These results present three puzzles, which can be addressed separately. First, and most striking, why was the experimental group actually worse than the control group in study after study? There were ample reasons, as we saw, for predicting superiority of the experimental group and failure of these predictions would have been troubling enough to a believer in dependent storage. Part of the solution to this first puzzle is straightforward: There turns out to be an artifact in the experiments we have covered so far—the experimental group has been required to spend the first few seconds, or more, of the recall time reading the words presented as cues, thus depriving them of the quick burst of recall for the primary-memory items at the end of the list available to the control group. There are two ways to go about correcting this inequity. First, one could deprive the control group, also, of their primary-memory recall by imposing a distractor task of backward counting between the list and recall; this would leave the control group and the experimental group both without any benefit from primary memory. The second way of equating the control and experimental groups for primary memory would be to allow both groups to retrieve freely for an initial period after list presentation, only later giving experimental subjects their cue words from the list. Slamecka carried out both of these controls in his first series of experiments (1968) and found in both cases that the differences between groups reduced to zero.

The second puzzle from the Slamecka (1968) article is found in the fourth experiment, the only study in the series in which a categorized list was used. It will be recalled that for a list of 30 words, divided into five categories of six members each, the experimental groups received either one, three, or five of the six words in each category as cues. As in the other studies, there was no positive cuing effect. This result is a problem because it seems to contradict an earlier experiment by Tulving and Pearlstone (1966); the results of that study can be reviewed by consulting Figure 1.2. Subjects in the study by Tulving and Pearlstone received lists of varying length with words divided into blocks of items from the same category, the category name being presented just prior to each block. The main finding was a large advantage of cued recall over free recall, when cues consisting of the names of the categories were used. Here are two experiments with categorized lists, therefore: In one, the category names are used as retrieval cues and produce a large advantage; in the other, however, category instances—items from the list to be recalled—are used as cues and there is no advantage. The problem is that subjects should surely have been able to think of the category names suggested by cue words in the Slamecka study and, if they have, then they are effectively in the same experimental situation as the subjects of Tulving and Pearlstone.

The apparent conflict between the Slamecka result and the Tulving–Pearlstone result presupposes the analysis of recall into two components—recall for higher-order units and recall for the words nested within these higher-order units (see our discussion above of Cohen, 1963). The limitations on recall, according to this view, can come either from forgetting of higher-order units or from inability to exhaust those high-order units of their contents, once retrieved. One supposes that cuing by category names helped the Tulving–Pearlstone subjects because there were too many higher-order units in the list for them to remember unaided; indeed, it was when the number of categories was largest that there was the greatest cuing effect. However, Slamecka's categorized list contained only five categories. Because five is ordinarily well within the memory span, we may suppose that subjects had no particular difficulty remembering what the higher-order units were anyway, and therefore that cues identifying the categories would have been redundant.

This line of reasoning was tested in the obvious way by Hudson and Austin (1970). These authors used a list of 30 words just as Slamecka did, but unlike him they overloaded their subjects with more categories than they were likely to be able to recall on their own, without cues. The list contained ten categories with three words nested within each. There were three conditions following uniform input of the list: free recall; cued recall in the manner of Tulving and Pearlstone, with category names; and, finally, cued recall in the manner of Slamecka, with instances from the categories. The result was that both cued-recall groups had better recall than the free-recall control group; however, there was no difference between cuing with category labels or cuing with list instances representing the categories.

This result, incidentally, brings us to an empirical generalization: List items serving as retrieval cues aid recall when they provide access to higher-order units that the subject has been unable to contact without cues, but otherwise they do not. The first part of this statement is the resolution of the second puzzling aspect of the Slamecka experiment. The third puzzle is raised by the final part of our empirical generalization, the failure of list items to facilitate recall of each other given that access to higher-order units is no problem. Slamecka's conclusion was that items were stored independently. Indeed, the most explicit model of free recall based on an associative network (Anderson, 1972), a computer program called Free-Recall Associative Network, clearly failed to predict the Slamecka result.

It seems possible for us to conclude from the first part of the empirical generalization, however, that items are not stored independently of the higher-order units within which they are grouped. Therefore, the independence that exists seems to be among items connected vertically to a superset. Roediger (1973) has shown most conclusively that once access to the higher-order unit is guaranteed there is no facilitation by list items—to the contrary, items inhibit each other. In Roediger's experiment subjects were always given the category label of the items they were trying to recall. The experimental manipulation was whether, in addition to the category label, they were given instances from the category. In one set of conditions categories of six or seven items were tested. In the condition where only the relevant category name was given, the probability of recall was .63. When either one, three, or five category instances from the list were presented along with the category name, the recall probabilities were, respectively, .62, .56, and .52. In short, recall declined with increased cuing from the list under conditions where there was uniform access to the category label. Rundus (1973) and Slamecka (1972) have reported similar evidence for inhibition. The empirical generalization covering cuing effects from list items can therefore be expanded to more explicit form: List items serving as retrieval cues facilitate recall to the extent they allow access to higher-order units with which the subject has otherwise been unable to make contact; however, these cues inhibit recall of items within a higher-order unit.

Inhibition from list-item cues.   Now how can we rationalize the second half of this new generalization? Slamecka's original purpose was to show an absence of facilitation, thus supporting his independent-storage proposition, but he did not anticipate a genuine inhibition. Roediger (1973, 1974) proposed that the inhibitory influence of retrieval cues from the target list, under conditions where higher-order units were accessible, could be understood with reference to the phenomenon of *output interference*. Output interference is the name of the very pervasive finding in memory that the process of retrieving some items has a damaging effect on the retrieval of other items; other things equal, the earlier in the retrieval sequence an item is tested, the better it is recalled. One reference experiment for output interference in long-term memory is a study by A. D. Smith (1971). In his study a list of categorized items was presented and the order of recall was controlled by using category names as retrieval cues. The finding was a steady decline in the probability of recalling the contents of a category as the retrieval of that category was progressively moved later into the recall series. In short-term memory, the effects of output interference are much more pronounced (Tulving & Arbuckle, 1963); however, the Smith study reassures us that the effect occurs in long-term memory situations.

Roediger's (1974) hypothesis is that receiving list items as cues, within accessible categories, forces involuntary retrieval of them and this retrieval effectively pushes the attempted retrieval of other items farther out along a gradient of output interference than if the cues were never presented. Let us examine this proposition step by step: The first part is that, regardless of whether or not the subject is able to recall a list item on his own, seeing it written down in front of him produces a recognition type of retrieval response. Second, this retrieval is presumed to have the same inhibitory effect on unrecalled items as a normal retrieval. In this way Roediger provides a mechanism for the second factor in the two-part empirical generalization. There are some subtleties to this application of this output interference which are too digressive for us to pursue now, particularly the relation between output interference within a higher-order unit and among higher order units; however, we can press further with our analysis of what types of theory of list organization are consistent and what types are inconsistent with the picture of cuing as it has emerged thus far.

The fact that cues, category names or instances, are beneficial when they provide access to otherwise inaccessible category units is an affirmation of some organizational structure where items are connected to a higher-order representation, the type of system to which Bousfield was originally drawn by his clustering observations. Figure 10.1 shows such a structure in the left panel. Now the simple fact of facilitation through access to higher-order units also can logically be taken as support of at least some types of associative structures, where no higher-order representations, such as category names, are used but where items are organized in distinct bundles of associations, as shown in the right-hand panel of Figure 10.1. However, because these bundles are held together by item-to-item associations, it is very difficult to see how the structures on the right-hand side of Figure 10.1 can ever accommodate the inhibition finding.

Note that the type of structure pictured on the left of Figure 10.1 is essentially the same as E. Martin (1971) has proposed based on entirely different experimental operations. In Martin's studies on stimulus component independence (see Chapter 8) there were three stimulus words to be learned with a single paired response term. Testing by providing one of these four terms gave evidence that the subject could get from one stimulus term to another only if he remembered the associated response; that is, only by virtue of something one might wish to call a higher-order association, and not directly, was it possible for one of the stimulus items to lead to another. If one makes the assumption that a response term in the Martin situation serves the same function as a category representation, or higher-order unit, in these recall experiments, therefore, the theoretical conclusion is very similar. Likewise, it will be recalled that the Estes (1972) account of associative structures in short-term memory (see Chapter 7) fits just the same family of theories. Estes' model is particularly well suited to the handling of order information and we shall deal with it in some detail in Chapter 12. After pausing for a summary, we shall return to a somewhat similar model by Shiffrin (1970) and Rundus (1973) that provides an explicit account of how the inhibitory consequences of output come about.

Slamecka has therefore proposed a simple procedure for finding out whether items are stored in a dependent manner, cuing with list items. When primary-memory artifacts are removed from the procedure, it turns out that these list cues help recall only when they remind the subject of a higher-order unit representation he otherwise is likely to have missed. When access to a high-order unit is guaranteed, in contrast, the presence of list-item cues has a demonstrably inhibitory effect on the recall of other items from that higher-order unit. This pattern of results is most consistent with an organizational theory in which items are connected not to each other but only to a higher-order control element. This leaves the question of the source of the inhibition. Roediger has suggested it obeys the same principles as the phenomenon of output interference—implicit retrieval of the cue items is tantamount to explicit retrieval. Now our final question is how, exactly, the output interference works and it is about this issue that the model of Rundus (1973) is relevant.

The Shiffrin–Rundus model. Before we explain the Rundus (1973) model, we should acknowledge that it is an amplification of similar ideas expressed by Shiffrin (1970, pp. 385–386), even with respect to the nested hierarchical memory structure (pp. 376–379); but the explicit application to Slamecka's situation is best found in Rundus (1973).

In Figure 10.5 is shown a portion of a list organized in terms of the Shiffrin–Rundus notions. The superordinate of all items is ultimately the designation LIST, but intermediate nodes, labeled with the letters RQ, for retrieval cue, are the immediate control elements for individual list items and conform roughly to category names. The model is not concerned with the learning of a structure such as this, but with retrieval of items from it. The retrieval process is

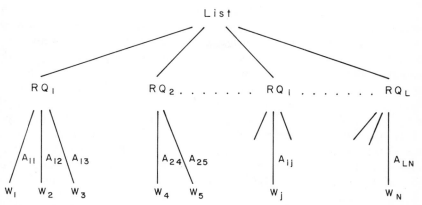

FIGURE 10.5 Hypothetical organization of items (W) and retrieval cues (RQ) following study of a free-recall list. The terms A_{ij}, stand for the strength with which RQ_i is connected to item W_j. (After Rundus, 1973.)

assumed to initiate at the highest level, LIST, and to follow paths down to the RQ nodes, and then from the RQ nodes to individual items. The important parts of the model concern the rules for selecting the various pathways and, notably, the rules for stopping, or giving up, when a particular retrieval route is not being productive.

One assumption is that the link between each item and its superordinate RQ is a link with a certain strength, denoted by the letter A. There might be various reasons why some items would be more strongly connected to their super-ordinates than others—taxonomic frequency, degree of learning on the list, presence of implicit associations in acquisition, and so on. These variable-strength measures play a role both in the decision as to which RQ gets consulted first and also in the decision as to which words get retrieved once the process is under the control of a particular RQ. First, the retrieval process selects one of the RQ nodes. Each RQ is connected to the LIST node by a strength that is simply the sum of the strengths by which each item is connected to the RQ in question. That is, if the words in one category are connected to the category name more strongly than the words in a second category, then there will also be a stronger connection between the LIST designation and the category name with the more strongly attached instances. Now, how does the strength of the connection between LIST and RQ determine which RQ is consulted first? The rule is that the probability of choosing a particular RQ is equal to the relative strength of that LIST–RQ connection as a proportion of all the LIST–RQ connections that there are. In our example we have shown only three RQ's; to find the probability of choosing any individual one, we can take its strength and divide it by the sum of all three strengths.

Now, once an RQ has been selected, what happens? The process is quite analogous. Once within a category, that is, under the control of a particular RQ, a process of retrieving items is set in motion. Which item is retrieved first depends on the strengths connecting each item to the RQ. The probability of a particular item being selected for retrieval is equal to the strength of that item's connection to the RQ divided by the sum of all the connections from that particular RQ to items. If the word reached by this process has not yet been recalled, then it is recalled at that point. If it has been recalled already, however, then the process returns to the RQ and starts again, selecting items by the proportionality rule (that is, by dividing the strength of a particular item by all those attached to the same RQ). Early in recall there is little chance that an item has already been recalled; however, as time goes on there should be more and more occasions where the subject comes up with an item he has already emitted. The model includes a rule (Shiffrin, 1970, p. 385) that when a certain criterion number of successive failures occurs—when a certain number of previously recalled items is reached—then the RQ in control is abandoned and another RQ is selected. This is how recall stops: Higher-order units and items under the control of a particular higher-order unit are sampled with replacement. When there are too many failures to come up with a new unit or item, another unit from the next higher level is selected. Eventually, there ceases to be any fresh higher-order units either, and the whole process stops.

Output interference can be explained as a special case of the sampling with replacement feature: The more items have already been recalled, the higher the probability that an already recalled item is selected and the lower the probability that a remaining item is. The more already recalled items selected in a row, the higher is the chance of exceeding the criterion number of failures to recall a new item and hence the larger the chance of giving up prematurely (that is, before the whole store is searched thoroughly). By Roediger's reasoning, presenting list items as cues adds them to the category of already recalled, or useless, items and increases the chance that these items are selected and therefore that the retrieval process stops before getting to some other unrecalled item. It is easy to see this process operate by considering an extreme case, such as the experiment of Slamecka in which the control group has had to remember 30 unrelated words and the experimental group has had 29 of these words presented as cues for the single target item. The experimental group had almost nothing but "already recalled" list items in their pool and therefore they would have been obliged by the assumptions of the Shiffrin—Rundus model to give up quite soon, whereas the control group had a good chance that the critical item would be selected before nearly that much previous recall would have built up.

Rundus (1973) made an additional assumption for output interference, that recalling an item strengthens its connection to the relevant RQ. This assumption is not unreasonable, and it may prove useful in some other setting; however, it is not necessary for the prediction of output interference or list cuing effects. (I thank Jim Antognini for convincing me that this is true.)

So we conclude with a simple explanation for why retrieving some items inhibits retrieval of others, and this explanation is meant to apply equally to implicit retrieval of items presented as cues in the Slamecka paradigm: the retrieval of some items increases the proportion of all possible items that have already been retrieved, making it increasingly likely for a criterion run of previously retrieved items to occur, shutting off the recall process altogether. The unretrieved items need not necessarily be any the weaker, it is just that getting to them involves unacceptably many retrievals of useless prior retrievals. Apparently a model of the type Shiffrin and Rundus have proposed can accommodate the major findings of list-item cuing experiments, at least the inhibition observed in such experiments. It could be expanded to encompass the facilitation from access to higher-order nodes by adding assumptions about failures of LIST-to-RQ associations. It is also notable that this type of retrieval rule fits well with many intuitive accounts of recall failure, when one association seems to block others in the sense that repeated efforts at retrieving a target lead only to the same unwanted item. Finally, the idea of sampling with replacement might be expanded to a more general theory of verbal interference and could eventually provide an alternative way of conceptualizing first- and second-list dominance relations in the $A-B$, $A-D$ type of experiment (see Chapter 8). In fact, the account offered by Anderson and Bower (1973) of retroactive inhibition carries much of this flavor.

Summary

We began this chapter with the issue of how to characterize the organization that is observed with free recall of once-presented words. The main theoretical opposition that emerged from such clustering experiments was between a nested-hierarchy memory structure and a pairwise-associative structure. Although there was evidence for both types of process, this theoretical issue informed our treatment of most of the other experimental situations covered later in the chapter.

The examination of subjective organization in the recall of unrelated words expands the clustering observation in three directions. First, it releases the concept of organization from a restriction to units previously arranged in common by the experimenter to units developed idiosyncratically by the subject. Second, it directs attention to the role of organization in the learning process, from trial to trial, rather than concentrating on static memory structures. Third, the material on subjective organization leads us to question the role of sheer frequency in this acquisition process.

The concept of dependent storage and the cuing technique of Slamecka have added a still more analytic approach to the organization of memory. There are two main results. First, it is clear that cuing with one target aids the recall of another only indirectly if the former helps in gaining access to the latter through an otherwise inaccessible higher-order unit; this generalization clearly supports the nested-hierarchy organizational principle rather than the interitem associative principle. The second general result has been the uncovering of inhibitory tendencies within the recall process. The inhibitory influence of one target's recall on the recall of another, in turn, merits our attention for two reasons: First, it leads naturally to an explicit model for output interference, based on the concept of repeated sampling of previously recalled items; this model is welcome in that it addresses the largely neglected issue of when and how recall stops. Second, the inhibitory relationship among list items in conjunction with the assumption of excitatory connections to a higher-order unit is just the theoretical structure proposed by Estes (1972) for serial order information in short- and long-term memory; it is lamentably infrequent that theoretical developments in two quite different experimental paradigms converge on the same theoretical structure and so we shall, in Chapter 12, be especially serious in our consideration of the Estes model.

11
Retrieval

Few students have escaped the experience of hitting on the correct answer to an exam question on the way out of the testing room. Few musicians and actors have not been seized by the panic of a so-called memory slip during public performances. And few of us have not had the embarassment of blocking on a friend's name when introducing a group of people in quick succession to a newcomer. These distressing experiences all point to the principle that learning and remembering are a waste of time unless there is appropriate access to the stored material at the moment of truth. The ideas to be covered in this chapter all represent ways of dealing with this important problem of retrieval from memory.

We must start with the regrettable, although not arbitrary, exclusion of semantic memory from our discussion. When people retrieve facts—such as their grandmothers' maiden names or whether flounder have scales—they are without doubt exercising the retrieval process that is of greatest ultimate importance. However, we shall be concentrating on episodic memory here, as in the rest of this book (see Chapters 6 and 10 for Tulving's distinction between semantic and episodic memory). One possibility is that retrieval from the two systems obeys the same laws and at least one experiment (Anderson & Lewis, 1974) supports this view. Anderson showed that latencies to verify a fact from semantic memory (Napoleon was French) were lengthened if subjects had previously learned related information of an episodic nature (Napoleon drove a Chevrolet).

Overview of retrieval. In principle we should be responsible for dealing with retrieval separately for each type of memory we postulate. It is likely that most workers in the field would agree that four basic memory systems have been isolated: *sensory* (iconic and echoic) *memory, primary memory, secondary memory,* and *semantic memory,* where it is understood that the first three systems are episodic in Tulving's sense. Having already rather highhandedly dismissed retrieval from semantic memory on grounds of space limitations, we are left with three potential retrieval situations to examine.

Retrieval from sensory memory may be a pseudoproblem in that sensory memory could itself be simply an aspect of pattern perception. We must not take time here to review the messages of Chapters 2 and 3, or to sketch current views of pattern perception; however, it is a fair possibility that retrieval from sensory memory is just the same process, repeated, that eventuates in perception in the first place. That is to say, using echoic memory to rehear the last item from a list of digits is a form of retrieval from memory because some time has elapsed since the information occurred; however, the process of encoding the persistent sensory information probably does not differ from the process of encoding the information originally. Pattern perception is of course a crucial problem for theory, and identifying retrieval from sensory memory as being the same as pattern perception does not solve the conceptual problem. For reasons of scope, however, we must leave these issues to others.

That leaves primary and secondary memory. In Chapter 6 we all but dismissed retrieval from primary memory as a necessary process by our loose definition of primary memory as being the conscious, immediate present. If James was right that information in primary memory has never really left consciousness, then retrieving it, getting it back into consciousness, is a misnomer at best. As earlier evidence has shown, however, we have no powerful way to determine that any particular item is in primary memory at any particular time, except for determinations that are circular with respect to the present issue (such as deciding that items with perfect immediate recall are in primary memory). Given this indeterminacy we must fall back to the weaker distinction between short- and long-term memory tasks. The first section of this chapter deals with retrieval from short-term memory; it will be useful to keep in mind the puzzle of whether or not primary memory is the dominant system in this task and what conclusions result from that issue for James' definition of primary memory.

STERNBERG'S MEMORY-SCANNING PARADIGM

As our preliminary discussion of stage analysis has revealed, one of the major problems in the study of memory is that in order to scrutinize one of the three stages—acquisition, storage, or retrieval—one is obliged to take the other two into account somehow. One approach to the difficulty that the staged nature of memory poses for the study of retrieval has been to arrange conditions where acquisition and storage are perfect, allowing observation of retrieval uncomplicated by failures from the previous stages. To insure perfect acquisition and storage, S. Sternberg (1966) contrived a task where subjects were given an immediate test on material comprised of only a short list of digits, from one to six in length, clearly within the memory span of college students. Now, naturally there is a problem with short lists of that sort in that the accuracy of recall or recognition is almost invariably perfect. So Sternberg tested his subjects not on whether they could retrieve items from the list but rather on how fast they could do so. The unique experimental situation designed by Sternberg and the experiments he and others have performed with it (S. Sternberg, 1969a, 1975) have led to a comprehensive and influential theory of retrieval from short-term memory.

The job of Sternberg's subjects was simple: They were given a short list to memorize, say, the digits 2–3–5–8 and then, after a pause of a second or two, a test digit was flashed on the screen. This probe digit, called the test stimulus, was either a member of the list just memorized, called the positive set, or it was not (in which case it belonged to the negative set). If the test stimulus matched one of the items from the positive set the subject had to make one response (a "yes" indicator) but if it did not match he had to make another. The measure of the performance was how rapidly the subject responded to the test stimulus. For example, if the probe were the digit 6, the subject would make the response (lever pulling) corresponding to "no" if he had memorized the list given above. The instructions called for responding as rapidly as possible without any substantial levels of errors. In fact, the subjects were able to comply with this request for careful, fast responding as is shown by mean error rates of less than 5%.

Some Explicit Models of Retrieval

Before we turn to the results Sternberg obtained in his original experiment (Sternberg, 1966) with this task, we pause to survey some of the possible mechanisms that people could logically employ to arrive at a response and what implications these mechanisms have for latency measurements. One thing is certain: at some point there must be a comparison of the test stimulus with members of the positive set (the list of characters presented initially). Unless this comparison occurs the subject is obviously unable to decide whether to say yes or no. There are two broad approaches to thinking about this comparison process, serial processing and parallel processing, and several different specific versions of each.

Parallel-processing models. In models based on the idea of parallel processing, different mental operations are allowed to occur at the same time. In the memory task under consideration here this means that the test stimulus is compared with each individual item in the positive set simultaneously. One specific version of the parallel-processing approach says, furthermore, that all comparisons start at the same time and finish at the same time; that is, this version states that there is an identical comparison time for each of the items in the positive set. If the subject makes his response after the comparisons are all finished, then his reaction time in deciding whether the test stimulus had been in the positive set should include the comparison time, plus various other processes, such as encoding the target, deciding on a response, and executing the response. Furthermore, the duration of the comparison process should be the same however many items there have been in the positive set, just as the duration of a horserace is the same regardless of how many horses are running, if all horses start at the same time and run at the same speed.

A second version of the parallel-processing model states that although all comparisons are initiated simultaneously, some are slower than others in being completed. This variance in comparison times could occur for many reasons, such as, for example, inherently lower discriminability of some letters as compared with others. So although all comparisons may start at the same time, they are achieved at different times. Now what should be the effect of the number of items in the memory set on overall reaction time in this case? First, it depends on the decision rule the subject employs. One possibility is to postpone any decision, the selection of a positive or negative response, until after all comparisons have been completed. This is called an "exhaustive" rule. If an exhaustive parallel comparison is used, we should expect the reaction times on the average to increase with increases in the number of elements in the positive set. (If there are ten horses that can be chosen to race and two or three of them are notoriously slow there is a chance, if only a few horses are selected to be in the race, that no slow horse will be included and that all will come in early; however, if all ten horses, or nearly all of them are chosen to race, then there is bound to be a wait for one of the slow ones to finish.)

To choose between the model with no variation in comparison times and the model with variable comparison times, the main criterion is whether reaction times increase as the size of the positive set increases. As it happens Sternberg (1966) has found that it takes longer to respond with a larger memory set than with a smaller memory set, so that the no-variance parallel model is ruled out (except for an improbable version which we shall mention below). The variable finish-time parallel model is not proved by this outcome, however, because there is a class of *serial-processing models* that predict the increase in latency with set size.

Serial-processing models. The term "serial processing" reflects the view that only one mental operation is carried out at a time. The general implication for the Sternberg task is that subjects compare the test stimulus one by one with the members of the positive set. Here the prediction is perfectly obvious that the more items there are in the positive set the longer it should take to complete this serial comparison. However, the details of this relation depend on the particular version of serial-processing model adopted.

The simplest form of serial-processing model is one that seems rather far-fetched on an intuitive basis. According to the *exhaustive serial model* the subject always compares the test stimulus to each item in the positive set, before making a response. What seems implausible about this model is that on positive trials the subject will be making logically unnecessary comparisons. He will, for example, sometimes perform comparisons of the test stimulus with the second and third positive-set members after there had been a match between the test stimulus and the first positive-set member.

A more plausible serial comparison model holds that each item in the positive set is compared with the test stimulus unless and until there is a match. That is, when the subject, as it were, finds the test item in the positive set he stops making comparisons and emits the positive response but if he fails to find it then he emits the negative response. This is called the *self-terminating serial comparison model*. The self-terminating and exhaustive serial comparison models both predict that decision times should get longer the more items are included in the positive set. How can we differentiate their predictions?

The crucial observation for distinguishing these models has to do with the difference between latencies of positive and negative responses, trials in which the correct answer is "yes" (where the test stimulus really was in the positive set) and trials where the correct response is "no." According to the exhaustive model the subject always compares, on either type of trial, the test stimulus with each positive-set member. If so, then each time the size of the positive set is increased by one item exactly one more comparison is added, whatever the response.

However, the self-terminating model holds that the comparisons on positive trials usually stop part way through the total list of positive-set members; on the average the number of comparisons to be made on positive trials is $(s + 1)/2$, where s stands for the number of items in the positive set. This means that for positive trials each additional item added to the positive set costs the subject only about one-half an additional comparison, on the average. On negative trials, in contrast, the subject must always complete comparisons of all the positive set items to the test stimulus; on negative trials, therefore, there must always be s comparisons. So to decide the issue all one need do is examine the positive responses separately from the negative responses. If adding more items to the positive set has an effect on negative responses that is about twice as large as on positive responses, then the self-terminating model is sustained. However, if the growth of positive and negative latencies is about equal as the positive set is enlarged then the exhaustive model is sustained.

Notice that the crucial prediction is not that positive responses be faster than negative responses in general. There can be many reasons for an overall difference: If the correct answer is positive more often than negative, that reduces times for positives. If, for some reason, people enter a trial with some type of readiness to respond positively, that, too, is the same however many items in the positive set. What we are interested in is the growth in response time as the set is enlarged.

There are several other interesting versions of memory-comparison models; however, we have covered enough by now to look at the actual results of Sternberg's experiment.

Sternberg's Original Experiment

In the first published report of the memory-retrieval task S. Sternberg (1966) described two experiments. In the first he presented from one to six digits as the positive set for subjects to memorize, and then after a 2-sec delay, he presented the test stimulus, which on half the trials matched one of the members of the positive set and on the other half of the trials did not. Times from the onset of the test stimulus on a screen until completion of a lever-pulling response were recorded automatically. A new list of digits was presented as the positive set on each trial.

The results are shown graphically in Figure 11.1. The response times are plotted as a function of the size of the positive set. The rate of errors was extremely low—1.3% in this study. First, note that the functional relation between set size and response time is linear rather than curved. The larger the set, the longer the reaction time, and each additional item in the memory set caused the same increment of time. That is, each new item to be processed cost the same amount; going from five to six items in the positive set added the same amount of time to the response as going from two to three items. The amount added by each new item in this study was 38 msec, the slope of the best-fitting linear function. Of course there could be a serial process with a curved relation-

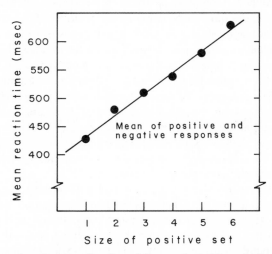

FIGURE 11.1   Reaction time as a function of the number of items in the positive set. The points give the mean of positive and negative trials and the line gives the least-squares regression line. (After Sternberg, 1966.)

ship, as would occur if subjects either speeded up or slowed down as they went through the memory set items. However, the findings of constant slope across the whole function is particularly supporting of an item by item, methodical, scanning process.

There is, however, at least one form of parallel comparison model that is compatible with the relation observed in Figure 11.1 (Corcoran, 1971). According to this model all comparisons begin at the same time but the speed with which they are completed depends on how many comparisons there are to be made. This assumption makes sense if one thinks of a system with limited power that can be spread out across many simultaneous operations or concentrated in one or a few operations. (A student in one of my graduate classes, Jim Pomerantz, suggested several years ago the analogy with an elevator, which can carry many people at once but, being weak, raises them more and more slowly the larger the number of people aboard.) In order to accommodate the linear relationship between set size and latency, this limited-power, parallel-processing model must make the further assumption, that the loss in power occasioned by each additional unit to handle is a constant. To some this may seem too much of a coincidence—it certainly casts doubt on the elevator analogy—but there is no clear reason for ruling it out on the basis of Sternberg's evidence. Townsend (1971) has placed this and other alternative models in the context of the broader issue of whether or not we could ever conclusively decide between serial and parallel processes.

The same linear function in Figure 11.1 has been fitted to both the positive and negative responses. Following the reasoning from the previous section, Sternberg concluded from this fact that the serial scanning he had proposed for the comparison process was exhaustive rather than self-terminating. It happened that the absolute times of positive and negative responses were equal, but, as we noted above, it is the equality of slopes, the cost of adding new items to the positive set, that is crucial. Sternberg found also that there were flat serial-position functions for the positive responses; subjects were no more rapid at saying "yes" to the first item in the memory set than to the last item in the memory set, as one might have expected based on one particular version of a self-terminating comparison model.

In a companion experiment S. Sternberg (1966) reported results of a closely similar procedure in which the same positive set was used for over 100 trials in succession rather than a different set on each trial. Although one might have expected different results on the basis of a vastly greater degree of learning with the fixed-set procedure as opposed to the varied-set procedure, the outcome was almost exactly the same! In the first study, with the varied-set procedure, the best-fitting linear function relating set size and reaction time was

$$\overline{RT} = 397.2 + 37.9s,$$

where $\overline{RT}$ stands for mean reaction time and s for set size. This can be read to mean that reactions took 397.2 msec whatever the type of set used plus an additional 37.9 msec for each member of the set. In the fixed-set experiment, where the same list was used for a long series of trials, the equation was

$$\overline{RT} = 369.4 + 38.3s.$$

The important conclusion is that, although there has been a lower intercept (369.4 versus 397.2), the rate of serial scanning is nearly identical. Repeated experience with a particular positive set did not in the least allow faster scanning of its individual elements.

The near-identical estimates of scanning rates for the fixed-set and varied-set procedures, about 26 characters per second (1.00/.038), are pertinent to the issue of whether this memory-scanning paradigm taps primary memory, secondary memory, or both. With any major involvement of secondary memory we would expect to find better performance with high degrees of overlearning than after a single fleeting presentation of a memory list. If responding is being based on primary memory in some Jamesian sense, however, then it should make little difference whether there is also a strong memory trace in secondary storage. Independence of scanning rate from degree of learning therefore supports a functional role for primary memory in this task.

Our ability to represent Sternberg's data by a straight line function relating reaction time to positive-set size suggests two classes of information processing contributing to overall response times. Those contributions that occur only once on each trial are grouped together and represented in the equation by the intercept. Those contributions to total response time that occur once for each member of the memory set are of course represented by the slope. Can we partition these various subprocesses in such a way as to rationalize the seemingly irrational strategy of exhaustive search?

Most modern attitudes toward latency measurement in information processing conceive of several independent serial stages intervening between stimulus presentation and completion of the overt response (see particularly E. E. Smith, 1968; S. Sternberg, 1969a). For example, some theorists propose four stages: (1) stimulus encoding—the target is perceived and rendered into a form suitable for comparison with memory representations of the memory set; (2) serial comparisons—carrying out of the postulated scanning operations with few or many items to scan, depending on s; (3) response selection—depending on the outcome of the scanning stage, a positive or negative response is selected; and (4) response execution—translation of the decision outcome into overt action. Notice that an additional assumption is necessary when the scanning is exhaustive: How does the information that a match has occurred get retained until the time of decision making? (If scanning is self-terminating, a decision is always made on the spot, right after each comparison.) To account for this logically necessary memory process, S. Sternberg (1969a) included the concept of the *match register*, which can be thought of as a binary switch that is set during the comparison process if a match occurs and remains set until the next trial. The match register holds, presumably without additional processing time or effort, the information that the test stimulus has matched, say, the third positive set item until all s comparisons have been completed.

The response selection process, deciding on the basis of the outcome of scanning whether a positive or a negative response should occur, is crucial to the understanding of the difference between self-terminating and exhaustive comparisons process and also to the rationalization for why an exhaustive process may actually be the superior mechanism. If the decision about whether to make a positive or a negative response is very slow, then there may be an advantage to doing it only once per trial rather than once for each item scanned, as must occur with a self-terminating process. With an exhaustive scan, the decision making occurs only once, but of course it is at the expense of an additional memory store, the match register, to retain information on matches until the serial comparisons are all completed.

A second remark on Sternberg's 1966 report concerns the absolute speed of the serial comparisons, 38 msec per item or 26 items per second. As we saw in Chapter 2, the rate at which we can talk to ourselves is roughly six items per second. The scanning rate implied by Sternberg's data is so much faster than this figure that it clearly rules out subvocal speech as the vehicle for comparisons. Apparently, people do not encode the probe item and then compare by rehearsing the memory set to themselves. This conclusion has several ramifications. For one thing it raises the question of coding with respect to the Sternberg task, an issue we shall be considering in the next section. Also, the rapid scanning rate is consistent with the fact that people have no useful introspections about how they perform the item recognition task. They usually state, when pressed, that they either perform an instantaneous parallel match or that they perform a self-terminating serial search—both models ruled out by the data, but the latter plausible as a conscious strategy. However, this unconscious nature of the mechanisms involved in this task raises again the issue of whether the form of memory involved is primary memory, which according to James is consciousness per se. We cannot dwell further on these puzzles, which must remain unresolved.

The Code of Comparisons

In some form, the test stimulus gets carried through some type of memory store, according to the serial-scanning model which we are provisionally accepting. In one of Sternberg's experiments (Sternberg, 1969a, Experiment III) an effort was made to discriminate various possibilities for the code in which the test stimulus is compared against the positive set. The main operation in this study was the form in which the test stimulus was presented to the subject—either intact or degraded. The intact probe was a clearly legible display just the same as used in the other experiments. The degraded form of the probe item was the same except that a grid of dots was superimposed on it, with the effect of reducing legibility considerably. The fixed-set procedure was used, in which the same positive set was used, trial after trial, for a long session.

The question is how the degraded test stimulus affects performance. Assuming there is some impairment, the interesting possibilities are defined by whether the increase in time occurs only in the intercept, only in the slope, or both. Our prediction depends on our hypothesis for what gets carried through memory in the comparison stage. If relatively little cognitive processing goes on in stimulus encoding, it may be that a replica of the test stimulus as it appears on the screen gets taken to the memory store, type style, smudge marks from the screen, and, in this case, the masking grid superimposed on the test character. If this were the case, then it would be reasonable for comparison to take somewhat longer in the degraded condition than in the intact condition, because in the degraded condition the illegibility would hamper each comparison. The consequence of this would be an increase in the slope of the set-size latency function for the degraded condition: Each new item would cost more time but the operations occurring only once, such as encoding, response selection, and response execution would be unaffected.

A second possibility is that the stimulus-encoding stage involves a cleaning up of visual input such that the outcome of encoding is some type of normalized, essential, character representation. Because encoding of the probe occurs only once on each trial, the effect in this case is seen entirely on the intercept. It takes longer to clean up a degraded test stimulus than an intact one, but once the normalized product of encoding is taken into memory, each comparison should be the same in the two conditions. The results of this study showed a substantial increase in the intercept caused by degradation of the probe item; the intercept effect occurred both early and late in practice. In the first session only there was an increase in the slope as well as this intercept effect. In the second session, therefore, with well-practiced subjects it appears that the encoding stage includes operations to normalize or tidy up the probe before consultation of the memory store but that the memory comparisons themselves are just as fast with the probes that have required more tidying up as with those that have required less. In the first session, however, with less well-trained subjects, there seemed to be a residual effect on the comparison stage as well as the large effect on the intercept. This pattern of data is consistent with the view that efficient encoding requires practice and that subjects in the first session have not yet gotten the hang of it. The main result to remember is the large intercept difference and, for well-practiced subjects, the lack of a slope difference. This pattern of findings has been replicated in a similar study by Bracey (1969).

Although the encoding stage is far and away the most likely locus for an intercept difference, there is also the logical possibility that subjects consult memory with the degraded test stimulus, compare it at the same rate as an intact probe to the positive set, but then require longer to decide whether or not a match has occurred than they do with an intact probe. Because this decision occurs only once on each trial, lengthening it, too, affects performance by a constant amount independent of the set size.

Generality of the exhaustive scanning model. The reader may well object, at this point, that this account of memory scanning in recognition is perhaps accurate for such sterile stimulus domains as digits, but that stimuli richer in meaning would not be handled in the same way. A. Treisman and Sternberg (reported in Sternberg, 1969a) have reported a study in which three very different populations of visual stimuli were compared in the Sternberg task situation. The method was similar to that of Sternberg (1966) and, in one of the three conditions, the stimuli were digits, just as in the original study. In the two other conditions the stimuli were photographs of faces and nonsense forms, respectively. In these latter two conditions, following the varied-set procedure, subjects would inspect lists of varying length (one to six) containing faces or forms and then receive a probe. The main point is that digits, faces, and forms differ drastically in the extent to which they can be represented in memory verbally; if the results show equivalent performance in all three conditions a visual model is supported.

The main result of this study was that *roughly comparable* performance was obtained on these three stimulus types despite their greatly different complexity and meaningfulness. For digits, the best-fitting straight line relating size of the positive set to reaction time was $\overline{RT} = 378 + 36s$; for forms and faces, respectively, the equations were $\overline{RT} = 369 + 45s$ and $\overline{RT} = 404 + 56s$. Although faces were scanned somewhat more slowly than the other types of stimuli, still all three scanning rates were in the same ballpark (20 or 30 per second) and nowhere near the rate of subvocal speech (six per second). The exhaustiveness of scanning, as manifested in equal slopes for positive and negative responses, remained the same across the different stimulus classes and the linearity of the functions also remained the same. We may suppose from these findings that the result of serial exhaustive scanning is not at all limited to the use of familiar characters; they are simply convenient stimuli. It is certainly not permissable to reach any firm conclusion about the mode of memory involved in the Sternberg task from this single result. However, the result is consistent with a form of visual representation and it is inconsistent with a verbal representation. Further evidence comes from a study by Chase and Calfee (1969) in which the mode of presentation—visual or auditory—for the memory set was varied orthogonally with the mode of presentation of the probe item. These authors found that scanning estimates were faster when the modalities of the memory set and probe items matched than when the two were presented in different modalities (see Sternberg, 1975, pp. 18–20).

With respect to the issue of how general is the exhaustive scanning model, therefore, we have concluded that across different types of stimulus material it is widely applicable as long as the task remains the same. Now, by contrast, Sternberg (1969a) has shown that the model is not necessarily applicable to variations in the nature of the task, even seemingly small variations. In one experiment, the subjects memorized a short list of digits but were tested rather differently than in the original study. In this new experimental task, the probe item was always an item taken from the memory set and the subject's job was to recall the item that had followed the test stimulus in the serial presentation of the positive set. For example, if the list presented were 2–5–7–4–8, there would be a pause and, say, the digit 7 would flash on the screen—the subject would then respond "four." The measure of interest was again latency and, as before, errors were reasonably infrequent, although higher than in the yes–no recognition task. The results, which are not enumerated here, show evidence for a serial-scanning process with two very important differences from the pattern we have seen above. First, the scanning in the recall experiment, the one now under consideration, seemed to be self-terminating rather than exhaustive; that is, subjects apparently scanned the memory set until they reached the probe item and then recalled its successor, but they did not always scan the whole list. Second, the rate of scanning was inferred to be much slower than in the earlier studies. The best estimate was about four items a second in the new experiment, whereas we recall that it was about 26 items a second in Sternberg's original experiment. These two exceptions fit together neatly (see Sternberg, 1975, pp. 22–23). If scanning is going slowly, at a rate commensurate with subvocal speech, it stands to reason that subjects will have the entire process under conscious control and thus will display the "rational" strategy of only searching until a match is found—all the more so, because there are no negative trials in this particular experiment and so a match is guaranteed.

Boundary Conditions on Sternberg's Model

The serial exhaustive scanning model derived from Sternberg's experiments is a specific theory of retrieval in this recognition situation. More important than this specific model, however, is the *conceptual domain,* which includes such theoretical distinctions and machinery as serial versus parallel; terminating versus exhaustive; high-speed scanning, separation of encoding, comparison, decision, and response stages in recognition; and the additive-factors method of analysis (which we have not discussed here—see S. Sternberg, 1969b). This is the more lasting contribution to theory in memory and it constitutes a minor but authentic, scientific paradigm in the sense of Kuhn (1962).

Very little has occurred in recent years to question the value of Sternberg's paradigmatic contribution seriously, although there have been numerous challenges to various of the specific aspects of his theory. As an example of the latter, there have been several reports that in situations close to Sternberg's original study systematic serial-position effects occur (Corcoran, 1971; Raeburn,

1974); that is, the speed of positive responses has been a function of the location of the probe within the order of presentation of the positive set. This important observation is of course incompatible with the exhaustive model. However, the present point is that authors have not questioned Sternberg's contentions about how one goes about deciding between exhaustive and terminating scanning operations based on the latency data. To conclude this section, we shall survey a few of the more interesting boundary conditions that have been discovered in this field.

Semantic category effects in word lists. Naus (1974) and Naus, Glucksberg, and Ornstein (1972) have demonstrated that a self-terminating strategy can be induced by memory sets that include categorized word lists. Their subjects received lists of two, four, six, or eight words. For each list length there was one condition in which two semantic categories were represented and another condition in which there was only one category. The categorized lists had both girls' names and animals, whereas uniform lists had only one of these. Given that categorization improves performance, Naus *et al.* (1972) have considered two explicit models for how this improvement may occur. One possibility is the *directed entry* strategy, in which subjects determine category membership of the probe on its presentation and then search only the relevant portion of the memory set; this strategy is likely to be employed only when there is a two-category memory set, of course. In comparison to results obtained with the single-category positive sets, this model would predict a raised intercept, to reflect the extra time in encoding consumed by having to retrieve the category of the probe item. However, in return for the extra encoding time required for categorizing the probe, the subject could restrict his search to the relevant category, reducing by one-half the number of instances to be tested. This model carries the prediction, therefore, that the two-category conditions differ from the one-category conditions in two ways—a higher (slower) intercept but a slope only half as steep (because each nominal increment of two items in the size of the memory set increases the number searched by only one).

Naus *et al.* (1972) considered the *random entry* model, or strategy, as an alternative to directed entry. This model holds that in the two-category conditions the entire memory set is organized into two parts and an exhaustive search begins in one of these two categories by a random process. But if the first category searched is the same category as the probe then the second category is not considered at all. This is a self-terminating process with respect to categories but exhaustive within categories. That is, decision and response selection operate after each categorical search, but that categorical search itself is exhaustive. In contrast to the one-category conditions, the random entry model predicts that the two-category conditions would show unchanged intercept values because there is no obligation in this model to decide what category the probe belongs to on its presentation. However, the slopes ought to be different for the one- and two-category conditions. If the first category entered is the same as the category of the probe, then only half the items in the total positive set need to be inspected; however, if the subject does not happen on this lucky coincidence then all *s* items need to be inspected. Therefore, because these two outcomes are equally likely, by the nature of the experimental design, the average number of items searched will be the average of ½ *s* and *s*, or ¾ *s*. In their experiment Naus *et al.* (1972) found that going from the single- to the double-category conditions led to a slope that was 76% as steep, remarkably close to the value of 75% predicted from the random entry model. There are two major conclusions. First, an exhaustive search of the entire memory set is not inevitable in these experiments. Second, and almost more interesting, the partition of the memory set can occur on a semantic basis, even though the rate of search has remained about as rapid as in Sternberg's first study.

Serial-position effects. We have mentioned already that Sternberg (1966) reported flat serial-position functions for positive trials (in varied-set conditions, of course, where the serial position of an element changes as the new memory set gets presented on each trial), whereas other investigators, to the contrary, seem to have obtained such effects in ostensibly comparable experiments. On closer examination there are two explanations for such position effects—which are usually a matter of the last serial position being faster than the earlier ones (Kirsner & Craik, 1971). One explanation is that when the probe is from the last serial position of the memory set just presented, it is easier to process sensorily, to encode, but that the entire memory set is exhaustively scanned just the same. The other possibility is that the advantage of the last serial position reflects a self-terminating rule where the last item is checked, and a decision made, before the subject goes on to check other members of the positive set. This second explanation, of course, directly contradicts the exhaustiveness assumption. However, it predicts the serial positions showing fast responses (e.g., the last item) also to have shallow slopes; if the subject compared the probe consistently to the last item before it is compared to other items, and if a response choice or decision is made just after checking the last item, then on trials where the last item is indeed presented there will be fewer items searched than on trials where one of the other, non-favored items is presented. Technically, it should make no difference how many items are in the positive set, when the last position is the test stimulus, according to this model.

This is what Raeburn (1974) observed. In an experiment with digits, she found the slope (across set sizes of from three to six items) for all but the last position to be 37 msec per item but for the last item itself, it was only 8 msec.

Raeburn's interpretation of the serial-position slope effect is that, in general, certain items from a positive set are given a high-priority status by the subject. These high-priority items are consistently scanned before other items and decisions are reached after the high-priority subset is scanned but before low-priority items are scanned. This self-terminating model, so far, naturally predicts a steeper slope for negative responses than for positive responses. However, Raeburn has postulated also that the subject forms a high-priority subset of negative items, which are scanned before some of the positive items are. A negative item could receive this high-priority status by virtue of frequent repetition in an experimental session, among other ways. There is not space to review Raeburn's research here, but she has obtained evidence favorable to the high-priority idea, including evidence that subjects make comparisons of the probe to negative items, to items that have not occurred in the memory set. A similar model has been proposed by Theios, Smith, Haviland, Traupmann, and Moy (1973).

The Atkinson and Juola model.   Atkinson and Juola (1973, 1974) have made a major extension of Sternberg's model by adding machinery that permits accommodation of recognition from long-term memory and also makes suggestions about the course of perceptual learning. In this extended model there are two successive types of memory comparison: First, the *subjective familiarity* of a probe item is evaluated against a double criterion. The idea of subjective familiarity in this context is our first encounter with the strength theory of recognition, and so we should pause, here, to explain it carefully.

The assumption is that corresponding to each verbal unit there is some location in semantic memory. This location, according to the strength theory, may accumulate (and lose) some commodity or energy in proportion to the frequency and recency with which the corresponding item occurs. For example, of two words with equal frequencies in the language, there would be more strength for one that had occurred in the last hour than for one that had not occurred in several days. The amount of strength corresponding to units is quite variable even when none has recently occurred—for example the representation in semantic memory of such a word as BOOK has more of this commodity than the representation of a such word as CRANKSHAFT, at least for many of us. However, when a word occurs in some context, as in the middle of a psychology experiment, there is a temporary change in the amount of energy at its location such that having just heard CRANKSHAFT, a person's semantic memory might have more strength at its location than at the location for BOOK, provided the latter has not been presented.

As we were saying, the first of the two memory-comparison processes in the Atkinson and Juola (1973, 1974) model is an evaluation of a probe item's familiarity, or strength. If a subject has just heard a positive memory set on the first trial of a recognition experiment, we can assume that the presented items (the positive set) have high familiarity in comparison to all other items, which have not been presented. Items that have never been presented in the experimental context have extremely low familiarity compared to items that have been presented. The Atkinson–Juola theory says that a double criterion is applied in that the subject makes a fast positive response whenever the location of the probe item has a very high familiarity and that he makes a fast negative response if the location of the probe has very low familiarity. In the intermediate case, where the familiarity or strength value of the probe item in semantic memory is neither extremely high nor extremely low, the second process is engaged. This second operation is just the same as Sternberg's proposed serial search—the items in memory are checked one by one against the probe. These assumptions are portrayed in Figure 11.2

Therefore, the theory says that there are two types of memory comparison, an initial fast familiarity check and a slower, methodical scanning process. If the familiarity check is decisive—by virtue of the probe's being either very familiar or very unfamiliar—the second, slow process can be avoided altogether. The second type of comparison is sensitive to the size of the memory set but the first

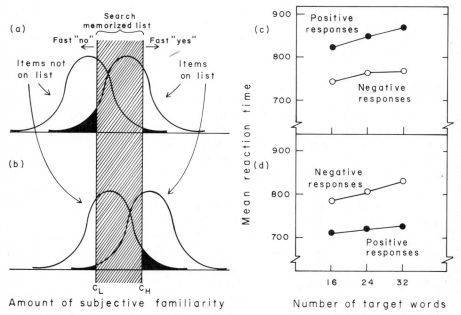

FIGURE 11.2 The Atkinson and Juola model (a & b) and results from one of their experiments (c & d). The overlapping distributions in (a) and (b) show theoretical means and variances in subjective familiarity for test items that had not been on the study list (left distribution) and for items that had been on the study list (right distribution). If a test item has a familiarity value greater than the low criterion, C_l, but lower than the high criterion, C_h, the subject undertakes a serial search of the positive set. If a test item falls outside these two criteria there is a fast response without search. (a) shows the distributions at the start of the experimental session and (b) shows the situation later in the session when all items' familiarities have been increased relative to the criteria. The occurrence of errors is represented by the dark areas under the distributions. (c) and (d) show mean reaction times as a function of the size of the positive set for positive and negative responses separately, early and late in the experimental session, respectively. (After Atkinson & Juola, 1973.)

not. This model includes an explicit functional distinction between semantic and episodic memory: The initial familiarity check occurs in the semantic memory store, where, as we have seen, words reside on an enduring basis with some measure of associated familiarity. However, the second recognition operation, a serial search that is resorted to when the familiarity check is inconclusive, is carried out in an episodic memory store established specifically by the presentation of the positive set.

Let us informally consider some implications of this theory. Take Raeburn's finding that there is a much smaller effect of memory-set size on latencies for the last serial position (in varied-set procedures) than on latencies for all other positions. This can be handled neatly by the Atkinson—Juola theory on the assumption that there is always an abnormally high familiarity index for the most recently presented item. That is, if the last item in the just-presented memory set is in a high state of familiarity, by virtue of having been the last item, it follows from the model that the number of other items in the memory set should make little difference, because the serial search need not occur.

Now consider an experiment in which relatively long lists of words are used as the memory sets. At the beginning of the experimental session we would expect that for one reason or another, some but not all of the positive-set items would have sufficient familiarity to allow a fast "yes" response and that some, but not all, of the negative set items would have sufficient unfamiliarity to merit a fast "no." Now what would happen as the session continues and both the positive and negatives get used again and again? Generally, all items, both positive and negative, should become more familiar. This would mean that as practice continued more and more of the positive items would be qualifying for the fast decision mode (providing the criteria remained the same) but fewer and fewer of the negative items would remain unfamiliar enough to qualify for the fast decision mode.

In consequence of these changes, one would expect times of positive responses to get progressively faster and also to be less and less affected by the size of the positive set. Because the negatives are getting more and more familiar during the session, they are more and more often having to be checked methodically against the entire memory set; therefore, the negative responses become progressively slower and also come more and more to depend on the size of the positive set.

The full rationale for this prediction cannot be presented here in a rigorous manner. However, the sketch in the left panel of Figure 11.2 should help. As the right panel in this figure shows, the results are just as the model specifies. Positive responses became faster and less dependent on set size as the session progressed, whereas negative responses became slower and more dependent on set size.

It is this aspect of the Atkinson and Juola (1973, 1974) model that makes contact with the process of perceptual learning. As symbols become more familiar through repetition our model of recognition for them changes. This comment anticipates the third implication of the Atkinson–Juola model. When an experiment is conducted with a set of items, all of which (positive and negative) are tremendously familiar and constantly recurring, we should expect very little use of the fast decision mechanism. In terms of the drawing on the left panel of Figure 11.2, it would be as if the shaded area were extended out to the left and right at the same time so as to include almost the whole area of the overlapping curves (except perhaps for the terminal serial position). This means the serial search must be enlisted on virtually every trial, which is what the results of Sternberg's original study show. The new model, therefore, which includes more complicated operations than Sternberg's, includes Sternberg's as a special case and furthermore stipulates what circumstances should lead to the application of that special case.

RECOGNITION MEMORY

As we have seen, one virtue of the Atkinson and Juola model is that it provides a framework from which to regard Sternberg's memory-scanning paradigm in the context of recognition memory in general. Treating recognition memory in its more general form is a mixed blessing. On the one hand, there is far greater generality in studying how humans discriminate which events have and have not occurred in their past experience than there is in timing the number of milliseconds elapsing between presentation of a test stimulus and a uniformly correct recognition response to it. On the other hand, however, there is a considerable loss in precision of formulation in the theories that surround the general problem of recognition as compared with the theoretical world of Sternberg's scanning experiments.

There are at least three separable sources of interest in recognition memory: (1) recognition as one of several measures of memory; (2) detailed theories of the recognition process; and (3) theories concerning the relation between recognition and other forms of retrieval, particularly recall. Of these the third is the most interesting because it generally subsumes answers to the first two issues; however, we shall treat the three approaches separately, if not equally.

The Measurement of Memory

Ebbinghaus (1964, originally published 1885) was alert to the problem that the apparent strength or durability of memories depends on how we go about measuring them. He invented the *relearning* method in the belief that it would be more sensitive than other measures. With this method of measuring memory, the amount of time, or number of trials, to learn material to some specified criterion is noted at the time of original acquisition. After the passage of some elapsed time, after which retention is to be measured, the same material is learned under exactly the same training routine and to the same criterion. If the material has been forgotten completely then relearning should be no easier than original learning, but if retention is perfect then the material should still be at criterion. Savings, as relearning scores are usually called, intermediate to these extremes can be represented as a proportional measure—for example, relearning has been 73% more rapid than original learning.

In addition to relearning there are three other measures of memory: In *recall,* there is some cue or instruction specifying the information to be remembered, and the subject must reproduce that material in written or oral form. Therefore, recall testing does not require training methods in which material must be mastered slowly, as does relearning. In *recognition,* of course, the information to be remembered is presented to the subject in some form and it is his job to decide whether or not it had indeed occurred during the presentation episode. In order to keep the subject honest, as it were, sometimes information from outside the presentation episode is presented for recognition, so that the task really becomes one of discriminating information which has or has not occurred in acquisition. There is a fourth measure, called *reconstruction,* in which the critical information is presented to the subject and his task is to organize it—usually with respect to order—in the same manner it has been organized during acquisition.

A little reflection will show that these four measures, sometimes called the four R's, are not really four different ways of testing memory. Reconstruction, for example, can be described as a form of recognition test in which memory for order is examined. Likewise, relearning and recall have a close relation, because most acquisition methods are themselves tests of recall repeated on successive trials. It is entirely proper, therefore, that our interest in the following pages be concentrated on recall and recognition. The other measures are just variants on them.

Several methods of testing memory for the same material were compared in a classic, although methodologically weak, study by Luh (1922); a methodologically sound replication by Postman and Rau (1957) led to similar conclusions. Luh showed recognition to be the most sensitive of the measures, that is, the measure of memory that gave highest scores and showed least deterioration with time. Recall was the most difficult measure and reconstruction and relearning were intermediate. Although Luh's experiment has been appearing in textbooks for over a generation, comparisons of the sort he made are basically a useless enterprise. For one thing, the numbers obtained as raw data are not commensurate: How do we compare a 50% savings in relearning trials to six items correctly recalled from a list of ten?

Even if the numerical measures can be brought into some kind of parity, however, the difficulty of each type of test can be radically altered by the specific circumstances of testing. A test of recall, for example, must include some specification of exactly which material it is that should be reproduced, but how much useful information is given in this recall instruction can vary enormously: A subject may be asked simply: "Write down all the words on the list that was just presented." Likewise, he may be asked: "Write down the word from the list that rhymes with BOARD and means a long weapon with a blade." This extreme contrast exemplifies the distinction between *free recall* and *cued recall,* but they are both recall measures and the distinction is not always as obvious as it seems here. The level of recall obtained would therefore depend on such factors as whether recall is cued or not and how informative the cues are. A second limitation on the generality of recall scores, as well as scores from the other measures, is that performance must always meet some latency criterion— giving the subject 1 sec versus 5 sec can make a large difference in how much he appears to remember.

Likewise, as every teacher knows, the difficulty of a multiple-choice recognition test varies as a function of what incorrect alternatives are used as distractors. The correct value of pi is easier to pick from among the set 48.0, 3.1416, 100.0, and 6.3842 than from among the set 3.4116, 4.3146, 3.1614, and 3.1416.

The point to remember is that memories cannot be observed directly but are manifest only through various measurement techniques, which themselves may greatly affect performance. Although this contribution frustrates the effort to make any general statement about how the methods differ in sensitivity, we shall see below that the comparison of recognition and recall has become the focus of a more sophisticated theoretical argument.

Process Models of Recognition

Here we offer an overview of the explicit proposals that have been advanced to cover recognition memory performance. How is it that a person can decide whether or not a certain piece of material has occurred before at a specified time and place? We know that S. Sternberg has constructed such a model, but only for the special case in which interest is in the speed of virtually perfect performance. There are four classes of ideas about recognition that we can now add to Sternberg's. It is interesting, parenthetically, to compare the current five-way partition of theories of recognition with an analysis of recognition theories written in 1915 (Woods, 1915); comparison shows that there is less novelty in the current "state of the art" of theory construction than we may have wished, although the early ideas were only poorly tied to experimental operations.

Tagging. Yntema and Trask (1963) proposed a retrieval model in which items occurring on a list are given labels, or tags, which encode the fact of that occurrence. This notion amounts to a theory of how episodic and semantic memory are related: There is a systematic network of locations, representing words, that remains stable (semantic memory), whereas episodic information consists of tags applied temporarily to this permanent structure. To verify that he has seen the word ULCER on a list, the subject consults the semantic-memory location of this word and determines that there is an occurrence tag attached. There is ordinarily no such tag on other words in nearby semantic memory that have not been presented on the list, so the subject can perform accurately on multiple-choice testing even when the test alternatives are somewhat similar. This theory accommodates a number of findings on recognition memory, such as the ability subjects have to make judgments of recency (Yntema & Trask, 1963) and the fact that nonlist words that are high associates of list words are sometimes incorrectly judged as having occurred (Anisfeld & Knapp, 1968). Recency discrimination would be based on the assumption that tags carry information not only about occurrence on a list but also about time of occurrence. False recognition on nonlist items is handled by the assumption that tagging sometimes misfires, such as when the subject thinks of PEN just after seeing the word PENCIL. The notion of tagging has proved useful to workers in conceptualizing memory, especially to those attached to metaphors drawn between humans and digital computers. However, these two examples of how a tagging theory works are sufficient to suggest that the theory assumes much of what needs to be explained. If recognition is governed by tagging, then we next need a theory of tagging.

Strength.   The strength (familiarity) view of recognition (Bernbach, 1967; Egan, 1958; Wickelgren & Norman, 1966) starts from the common intuition that very recent events seem strongly represented in the mind but that events from the distant past seem only weakly represented. It follows that one way of deciding whether a particular event has or has not occurred is to determine whether the memory for that event does or does not have a strong representation; if some items have occurred on a list, for example, then those specific items should appear stronger or more familiar than distractor items that have not appeared on the list.

Part of the Atkinson–Juola theory fits into this class, as is evident in Figure 11.2. It will be recalled also that we encountered this theory in connection with repetition effects in recency judgments (Chapter 9): The idea was that when it must be determined which of two words occurred more recently in a series, the decision could be based on which of the two traces is the stronger, as younger traces, on the average, would be stronger than older traces. The strength theory resembles the tagging theory in that episodic memory is portrayed as a transient modification of semantic memory, but the modification is not a labeling or tagging. Instead, there is an adjustment in some continuously variable quantity, strength, which is a property of each semantic memory location. There are two aspects of this theory that deserve special attention—the assumptions have to do with how a subject uses this memory representation in order to produce an overt recognition response.

One underlying idea that is central to the strength theory is that each entry in semantic memory has associated with it a sort of gauge or counter that indexes the momentary level of strength or familiarity for that entry. It is as if there were a bucket of liquid associated with each word, the level rising whenever the word occurred and the level falling with elapsed time since such occurrences. Continuing with the hydraulic metaphor, we may add that following occurrence of an item the liquid never quite returns to the initial state and therefore common words have inherently greater strength than uncommon words. Later in this chapter, we shall have occasion to examine an explicit model of this sort in more detail, the *logogen* model of Morton (1970). The main point concerning the memory representation envisaged by strength theory is its simple, unidimensional nature: When an item is recognized as having occurred, there is no reinstatement of the situation prevailing at the time of its occurrence because no information about that situation has been encoded, according to the strength theory. Instead, the decision that an item has occurred is based simply on the momentary quantity of familiarity, or strength, found at that item's semantic memory location. We turn now to the matter of a decision rule for translating the continuous reading, in terms of strength, into a recognition response, usually a dichotomous yes—no response.

The decision problem in recognition is usually handled by analogy with psychophysical detection situations—the subject in both cases must make a binary yes—no response based on the strength of a continuous input. In psychophysics the continuously variable input is the strength of some type of signal, whereas it is the amount of familiarity in recognition. Broadly speaking, there are two classes of theory covering either of these decision situations, the threshold model and the theory of signal detectability. In both, it is appreciated that the subject can be "correct"—that is, indicate that he has recognized a word that indeed has been presented for study—for two reasons. First, the subject can correctly indicate that he recognizes a target item because of the sensitivity of his memory, but second, he can get credit for correct recognition also on the basis of willingness to say "yes" even when the memory of an item is not particularly clear. The two theories differ on how memory combines with willingness to take risks in producing "yes" responses. (These can be only sketched here; the reader is referred to discussions of the subject by Kintsch, 1970, and Murdock, 1974.)

The high-threshold theory states that when an item is presented for a recognition decision, the subject has a recognition threshold in terms of strength: If an item exceeds this threshold it is recognized; otherwise, it is not recognized. If an item exceeds the threshold, of course, the subject says "yes." If its strength falls below the threshold, however, the subject does not necessarily make a negative response; he may guess that he saw the item. It all depends on how much he has to lose by being wrong in various ways. For example, if the subject gets a dollar for every item correctly recognized (that is, for every item from the study list to which he responds "yes") and if he loses nothing for incorrectly recognizing nonstudy items, then he should respond positively almost all the time whatever the strength of the item in memory. If he gets penalized for false alarms, incorrectly responding positively to nonstudy items, however, then he should never make a positive response unless the threshold is exceeded. Therefore, when a test item is presented, according to the high-threshold model, the strength observation falls either above or below the threshold. If it falls above then a positive response is given. If it falls below, the subject makes a guessing response. The probability of guessing "yes" is high or low depending on such factors as instructions, payoffs, and the subjects' inherent preferences for risks.

The theory of signal detectability holds, on the contrary, that there is no single threshold below which an item is unrecognized and above which it is recognized. Instead, it is claimed that when an observation is made of an item's momentary level of familiarity that observation is never conclusive. The reason a strength observation is never conclusive is that there is great variability in familiarity; items that have been studied on the input list have higher levels of strength than items that have not been studied, but many individual study items are weaker than some distractor (nonstudy) items and many distractors are stronger than some study items. This variability is shown in Figure 11.3 in the form of two overlapping distributions.

An analogy with jurisprudence may be helpful in rationalizing the approach of signal detection theory: The strength of evidence in a criminal trial can never be 100% conclusive, for no matter how strong the evidence pointing toward guilt there is always some possibility that perverse coincidences can doom an innocent man and, however trifling the evidence, it is always possible that a guilty man is the beneficiary of great luck. On the average, however, there will be stronger evidence for a guilty man than for an innocent man.

Inconclusive evidence can be resolved, in both memory and the courtroom, by application of a *decision criterion,* a rule stating that above a certain specified strength of evidence a positive response should be made and below that level a negative response should be made. By the nature of the distributions in Figure 11.3 there must be some occasions on which errors of commission occur (making a positive response to a nonstudy item, a *false alarm*) and some occasions on which errors of omission occur (making a negative response to a study item, a *miss*), just as there must be some cases in which the innocent are hung and some cases in which the guilty go free. However, the subject has some control over the balance between these two types of error. When a conservative criterion is adopted, only making a positive response when the evidence, or

signal distribution (handwritten margin note)

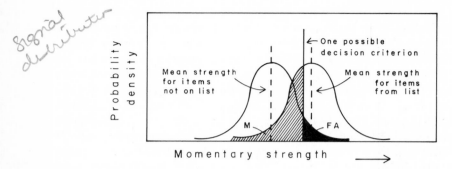

FIGURE 11.3 Probability density distributions showing how likely an observation of a given momentary strength is to have resulted from presentation of a test item that did not occur on the list of positive items (left distribution) or from a test item that had been on the list (right distribution). To the left of the decision criterion, subjects respond "no" to the test item and to the right they respond "yes." The abbreviations FA and M stand for false alarms (saying "yes" to a nonlist item) and misses (saying "no" to a list item), respectively.

strength, is very great, there may be few false alarms but many misses. When a lenient criterion is set, only making a negative response when the evidence is extremely weak, there may be many false alarms and few misses. Instructions and payoffs, among other considerations, affect setting of the criterion. The mathematical techniques of the theory of signal detectability permit measurement of sensitivity, which is proportional to the distance separating the two distributions of Figure 11.3, independent of the criterion applied by the subject.

  Context retrieval. In a systematic review of recall and recognition processes Tulving (1975) has identified Hollingworth (1913) as an early advocate of the position that the process of recognition is a matter of retrieving the context in which the target item has occurred. Hollingworth stated: "In recognition the focal element is present . . . and the question is whether or not this element will recall a more or less definite setting or background" (Hollingworth, 1913, pp. 532–533). Both he and, later, Norman (1968) contrasted the idea of recognition as retrieval of the experimental context with the idea of recall as just the reverse—given the context, what was the target item?

  Anderson and Bower (1972, 1974) have proposed a general theory of retrieval that includes a specific model of recognition that, in turn, includes this character. The essential distinction between their idea and those we have considered previously (and this is also a distinction that separates our next theory, the encoding specificity principle, from those we have examined until now) is that whereas the previous theories attribute recognition to some property of an item's independent trace per se, the theories to follow now attribute recognition to the item's relation to something that has occurred at the time of encoding.

According to Anderson and Bower the typical recognition situation is really a paired-associate task—the question is not whether the subject knows the item presented for recognition testing but whether there is an association between that item and a memorial representation of the relevant time and place. In short, asking whether a subject recognizes the word CUFFLINK from a prior list amounts to asking him whether he has an association between CUFFLINK and something like "MOST RECENT LIST." Anderson and Bower suppose that the relevant associations are not only between the item and a verbal representation, such as MOST RECENT LIST, but also with what they call context information ". . . physical characteristics of an item's presentation, implicit associations to the item, and some cognitive elements representing the list in question . . . the subject's general mood or attitude, his physical posture, and his physiological state, as well as any conspicuous external cues prevailing during the presentation of list *n*" (Anderson & Bower, 1972, p. 101). It is because of associations between items and cues of these types that a subject can determine that an item has occurred in one particular time and place rather than in another. We shall examine the detailed working of this theory in a later section.

Encoding specificity.   Another view that emphasizes what went on at the time of acquisition is the encoding specificity principle (Tulving, 1975; Tulving & Thomson, 1973): "Specific encoding operations performed on what is perceived determine what is stored, and what is stored determines what retrieval cues are effective in providing access to what is stored." (Tulving & Thomson, 1973, p. 369). What counts in recognition, according to this view, is the tendency for a particular retrieval cue to reinstate the particular cognitive state in which an item has been encoded originally. This state includes both a semantic or conceptual element as well as the more general class of context information, such as that proposed by Anderson and Bower. In recognition, the retrieval cue for the subject is the item itself plus the putative context in which it has appeared. However, it is not assured that the item must remind the subject of his original encoding: What if the item LIGHT, to use one of the examples from Tulving and Thomson (1973), is encoded originally as an illuminating source but then later, at the time of recognition testing, for some reason, the subject thinks of LIGHT in opposition to HEAVY. According to the encoding specificity principle the item is not recognized; even the item itself (that is, a spelling pattern) is not a guaranteed cue for reinstatement of the way in which that item of information has been encoded. We shall take up this theory in much greater detail below also. Strictly speaking, the encoding specificity principle is not a theory of recognition. Rather, it is a principle covering all of retrieval—that information in the memory trace must be combined with information provided by the retrieval cue, whether the retrieval cue is the item itself, as in recognition, or a representation of some aspect of its context, as in recall. As we shall see, however, encoding specificity is sufficiently different from the Anderson and Bower formulation to warrant separate treatment.

THE RELATION BETWEEN RECOGNITION
AND RECALL

There are two simple hypotheses about the way in which recognition and recall are related. According to one, recognition is basically the same as recall but somewhat easier. This assertion can be tied to the strength theory by the idea that recognition involves a lower threshold than recall. If memories vary in strength, therefore, as blades of grass vary in height, a low-threshold process will yield more successful retrieval than a high-threshold process, just as a low setting on the lawnmower cuts more grass than a high setting. The process is the same, but there is more retrieved in the case of recognition.

The second hypothesis is that recall and recognition are just the same except that recall entails an extra step. In recall, according to this idea, the subject must first implicitly generate, somehow, words that may have been on the list and then these generated words are subjected to a recognition test; but in recognition it is the experimenter who provides the items to be recognized, saving the subject the generation process. This hypothesis therefore identifies the greater difficulty of recall than of recognition with the fallibility of the generation process, or with its lengthiness. This last consideration, in turn, suggests that if we can devise a situation where the subject can be counted on to generate the same alternatives, by himself, that he is given by the experimenter in a recall test, there should be no difference in the difficulty of recall and recognition. This result was obtained by Davis, Sutherland, and Judd (1961); they showed that when the list of possibilities was narrowly restricted (say, to one of the ten digits from 0 to 9) then there was no advantage of recognition over recall but when the range of possibilities was large (say, all two-digit numbers) then the usual advantage of recognition was obtained (see also Slamecka, 1967).

As we shall observe below, the generate plus recognize hypothesis is in serious contention today. However, the first hypothesis we identified, the threshold-sensitivity hypothesis, is rather thoroughly discredited. The best reason for abandoning the simplicity of the threshold-sensitivity hypothesis is that it implies a uniform positive correlation between recognition and recall, but with recall always more difficult; any variable that improves recognition should also improve recall. However, there is a small list of experimental variables that appear to have opposite effects on recognition and recall performance.

In contrast, identification of experimental variables with effects on recognition opposite in direction to their effects on recall supports, to some extent, the second hypothesis, generation and recognition. This is because the generation–recognition hypothesis is a two-factor process. Take some variable that improves recall but damages recognition: This variable may be having a negative effect on the recognition subprocess but a positive effect on the generation subprocess. Provided the benefit for the ease of generation outweighs the harm for recognition, there is a positive net effect for the two-process measure, recall, and a negative net effect for the single-process measure, recognition. Therefore, the two-process hypothesis for the relation of recall and recognition not only allows experimental variables to have opposite effects on recall and recognition, but such a situation is indeed the best sort of evidence for it. We should therefore pause to consider the evidence on opposite recall and recognition effects.

Variables with Opposite Effects on Recognition and Recall

Although several variables have been reported as *interacting* with recognition versus recall, we shall be interested in this section only when there is evidence for a true crossover of effects, and not just absence of any effect with one retrieval measure. There are two well-documented cases, word frequency and intentional versus incidental learning.

Word frequency. Shepard (1967) showed his subjects a total of 540 single words, half high frequency and half low frequency in the language, as defined by the Thorndike–Lorge word count. In testing, there was a list of 60 pairs of words, each pair containing one of the 540 words studied and one comparable word that had not been on the study list. The frequency of the new and old words, respectively, defined four types of forced-choice test, high–high, high–low, low–high, and low–low, in which the subject had to discriminate items he had seen from those he had not. When the old word in the pair (the word actually seen on the study list) was high in frequency, correct recognition was either 82.1% or 86.7%, respectively, when the new word (the distractor) was of either high or low frequency; when the old word was low in frequency, correct choice was 93.0% or 92.0%, when the distractor was high or low in frequency, respectively. Whatever the frequency of the distractor, therefore, the subject was better off recognizing uncommon words than common words. However, we know (Deese, 1961; Hall, 1954) that recall is better for high-frequency words than for low-frequency words; Kinsbourne and George (1974) have shown the reversal of frequency effects between recall and recognition in a single experiment. Furthermore, the effect is robust and well replicated (McCormack & Swenson, 1972; A. I. Shulman, 1967).

A number of plausible artifacts have been ruled out. It could have been the case that rare words attract more attention within a list than commonplace words; if so, when words of the two types are mixed together then the rare words would enjoy the benefit of greater study at the expense of common words. However, the negative effect of frequency is obtained when the study list contains only a single band of frequency (Kinsbourne & George, 1974). Kinsbourne and George also showed that preexposure of a word served to increase its apparent frequency and reduce its recognition, over and above the effects of normative frequency. This last effect is important: If semantic and episodic memory are separate systems then one cannot expect a quick dose of repetitions at the beginning of an experiment to change the standing of a word with regard to frequency in a verbal repertoire that has been stable for many years. However, the result seems to show that the effects of normatively high frequency, poorer recognition, can be simulated with situational frequency. An alternative possibility is that preexposure reduced recognition by confusing subjects as to whether the word being tested was recognized on the basis of the preexposure list or the test list (R. J. Sternberg & Bower, 1974). If taken at face value, however, this result shows that possible structural differences between rare and common words (Landauer & Streeter, 1973) cannot be responsible for the frequency effect. We cannot dwell further on the effect of word frequency on recognition memory, except to reinforce the major point, which is that the influence is opposite to that found in recall.

Intentional versus incidental learning instructions. In recall there is a large mass of evidence comparing intentional learning instructions, where the subject is warned of an ultimate memory test, with incidental learning instructions, where the subject is led to believe there is not going to be such a test (recall the Hyde & Jenkins, 1969, study from Chapter 1). The size of the difference is quite variable (Postman, 1964) but it is generally intentional learning that has the edge in recall. However, it has been shown by Eagle and Leiter (1964; see also Estes & DaPolito, 1967) that, in recognition testing of the same material, incidental learning exceeds intentional learning.

Eagle and Leiter tested three groups of subjects on a 36-word list. One group, the intentional group, was told to try to remember the words. A second group, the intentional plus orienting task group, was told to classify each word with respect to its part of speech and also to try to remember the words. The third group, the incidental group, was told just that they should make the part of speech classification. All subjects were first tested for free recall and then they were tested on the same list with a four-alternative forced-choice test in which a word from the list was joined by a close associate of it and two distant associates of it. Setting aside the intention plus orienting task group, which was intermediate in all comparisons, our interest centers on the intentional and incidental groups. In recall, the intentional group got 15.2 correct and the incidental group got only 11.4; but in recognition the intentional group got 23.7 and the incidental group got 27.0, a sharp reversal.

The pattern of results we have just examined is not without interesting implications for education. Students cramming for an examination (a sort of superintentional self-instruction) can differ systematically from students learning out of interest in regard to their pattern of performance on essay and multiple-choice examinations.

One possibility is that the intentional learner focuses his attention more unevenly across the material than the incidental learner. As with the word-frequency effects in recognition and recall, we cannot pause to give a full discussion of the intentional–incidental difference (see Tversky, 1973)—the point of current importance is that the threshold-sensitivity hypothesis concerning recall and recognition cannot possibly accommodate variables that have opposite effects on recognition and recall measures. However, a two-process theory of the generation–recognition variety can handle this pattern of results. We now turn to a detailed consideration of the most powerful and elaborated of these theories.

The Anderson–Bower Retrieval Theory

Anderson and Bower (1972, 1974) start from the position we have taken here, that recognition cannot be a matter of applying a decision criterion to some single-dimensional strength or familiarity measure. They propose instead that recognition is a paired-associate retrieval process where the item itself is the instigating stimulus and the contextual information prevailing at the time of study is the response. Another closely related way of putting it (Slamecka, 1967) is that recognition tests are essentially tests of list differentiation—deciding when and where an item has occurred, not, as the strength theory has it, simply whether the item has occurred.

The Anderson and Bower theory includes specific statements about the organization of memory and the nature of associations, as well as about the details of retrieval (see also Anderson, 1972; Anderson & Bower, 1973). In their system the memory consists of nodes, or locations, as it were, which stand for concepts and corresponding words. These nodes are connected to one another through associative relations. Figure 11.4 shows one aspect of this system as it becomes modified during a list-learning experiment. Note that having decided that recognition is mainly a matter of associating items with their context, the list on which they have occurred, we can undertake to model recognition by constructing a theory of how a subject comes to a decision that a word has occurred on List N rather than on List $(N + 1)$.

The theory makes use of the idea of contextual information as a sort of stream of consciousness, denoted in the figure by the column of lower-case c's on the right; these contextual elements include just every imaginable salient source of stimulation that may occur during presentation of the list. Gastric pain, the sound of a bird's song, a siren in the distance, daydreaming about a romantic attachment, noticing a pattern of words on the list, estimating that there must be only a few words left to be presented, pondering the meaning of a word just presented—all these types of mental event, and more, qualify as contextual information. In common with most current psychological theories, which distinguish between stimulus information as given and stimulus information as encoded, Anderson and Bower assume that these contextual events are not floating

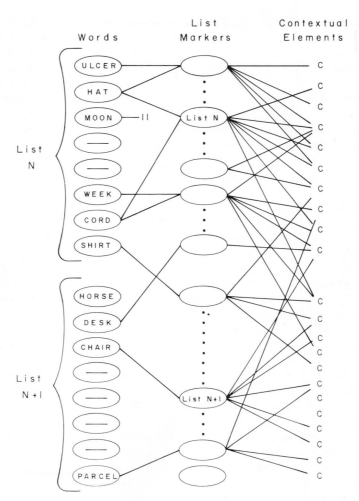

FIGURE 11.4 The memory structure associating list items to context according to the Anderson and Bower theory (only a fraction of the necessary connections are shown).

unprocessed in memory, but are encoded in bundles called "list markers." These list markers have the status of nodes, aggregations of encoded contextual information. As nodes, these list markers can become associated with the nodes representing words appearing on the list. The theory formally proposes a probabilistic tendency for each word presented to become associated with some list marker. Furthermore, there is a second probabilistic association formed between list markers and individual context elements.

It is useful to give a special status to one type of list marker, the *prototype list marker,* which is a concept standing for the identity of the list itself—in our example, the nodes in the central column with List N or List $(N + 1)$ identifications. These nodes and the relatively reliable associations they have with prevailing context elements, stand for the subject's tendency to "keep his mind on the job" by reminding himself constantly of what list he is studying (see Anderson & Bower, 1974, p. 408). In general the prototype list marker is associated with contextual elements from one particular list, but of course similarity of context from one list to another can lead to overlap, as shown in the figure, where two different lists share some context elements.

In a test of recognition, the subject is given some item and asked whether it has occurred in a specified context. The format of such a recognition test, therefore, is the question: "Did you see word X on List N?" In terms of the example memory structure shown in Figure 11.4, the subject might be asked whether he saw CORD on List N.

How does the subject go about answering this query according to the Anderson and Bower model? It depends on the exact form of the memory structure encoded. Sometimes, and as it happens for the word CORD, there is a *direct association* recording the proposition that a word has occurred on a particular list; it is as if the subject has said to himself, during the presentation interval for CORD, "I saw the word CORD on List N." In other cases, such as with the word WEEK, there is no direct proposition encoded about list membership and the subject must rely on a more indirect process, as follows.

Identification of the context for a word, such as WEEK, depends on the fact that the list marker associated with WEEK leads to some of the same contextual elements as does the prototype (List N) list marker. To retrieve the list identification of the word WEEK (that is, to recognize it) the subject starts with the list marker associated with WEEK and also with the List N list marker and counts the number of context elements that can be reached from both. The more of these there are, the more likely it is that WEEK has occurred on List N. Of course, however, because some contextual elements are associated both with the correct list marker and with the incorrect list marker, a by-product of the great similarity between the contexts when two similar lists are learned within the same laboratory, there can be some contextual elements reached from the item in question and the wrong list marker [that is, from both WEEK and List $(N + 1)$]. Still, on the average, there ought to be more convergence in the case of an appropriate prototype list marker than in the case of an inappropriate one. The amount of convergence on contextual elements expected from an item's list marker (the empty list markers in the center of Figure 11.4) and the appropriate prototype list marker as opposed to the inappropriate prototype list marker may be viewed as a quantity subject to a probabilistic error distribution. Once in a great while, therefore, there will be a misleading situation in which a word's list markers will be more fully associated with the incorrect prototype list marker than with the correct one. This situation is just the sort to which the theory of signal detectability is applied—when a binary decision must be reached on the basis of mixed evidence.

The application of signal-detectability theory to recognition within the Anderson and Bower model is shown in Figure 11.5. We have greatly simplified matters by assuming that there are only two possible lists on which an item can have occurred, corresponding to the two lists, N and $(N + 1)$, shown in the previous figure. The two distributions shown in Figure 11.5 operate in the same way as do distributions of familiarity, or strength, in the earlier explanation of signal-detectability theory. However, their psychological meaning is now quite different: Whereas the distributions of Figure 11.3 represent how familiar a recognition test item is if it either has or has not occurred on the specified list, the present distributions show how many converging associations there are, on the average, from items and prototype list markers—converging associations on contextual elements—if the item has or has not occurred on the specified list. Obviously in many cases the decision is difficult because it is quite possible for the item to have occurred on either list; this decision problem is resolved by application of a decision criterion.

Now, how does all of this relate to recall? The Anderson and Bower theory is a generation—recognition model and so far we have described only the recognition part of the system. In recall, there is a previous generation process that supplies candidates for the recognition system. The particular candidates for recognition, and their order of consideration, are given by a directed search process carried out along marked paths in an associative memory network. We need a few words about the network structure before considering the nature of the directed search. The associative memory network is the organized

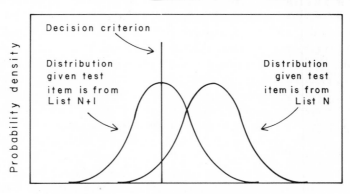

FIGURE 11.5 The decision aspect of recognition memory according to the Anderson and Bower theory. The illustration assumes that the item being tested did, in fact, occur on List N and that List $N + 1$ stands for all other possible contexts. The illustration therefore just underlines the expectation that there will be more common context elements between an item and the list on which it did occur than a list on which it did not occur.

Interitem associator

semantic memory store the subject has when he first walks into the laboratory—
the system of associations in which FAITH and CHARITY are closely related
but FAITH and RATTLESNAKE are only distantly related. During acquisition
of an episodic memory list, the idea is that both nodes and pathways between
nodes get marked with list markers. For simplicity let us assume that only the
prototype list markers—List *N*, for example—are involved in this marking procedure, not the entire machinery of Figure 11.4. The assumption that both
nodes and pathways are marked means that not only does FAITH get marked
with a List *N* designation, but also the association between FAITH and
CHARITY, if the subject happens to employ this association as a mediator
during acquisition of the list. If the subject thought of both words, but not
together, then each node would be marked, but not their association.

Anderson and Bower conceive that this marking of associations is a deliberate
strategy used by the subject to develop a way of recalling the list later. The
subject is most especially interested in following associations from one list word
that lead to another list word because then at recall, as the subject searches
through marked pathways, he encounters a high density of relevant items. The
flavor of this process is given in Figure 11.6. We see there several words from our
example list, marked in a way that is consistent with Figure 11.4

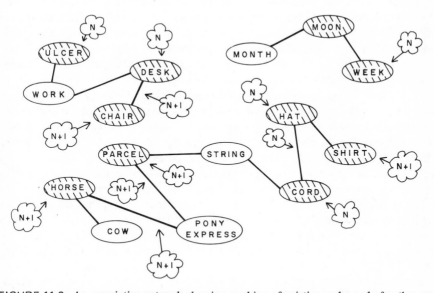

FIGURE 11.6 An associative network showing marking of existing nodes and of pathways
interconnecting these nodes. The items and some of their relations are taken from Figure
11.4; however, for simplicity, all list markers have been designated here as prototype list
markers, shown in small scalloped tags. Items that were presented on either of the two lists
are in shaded nodes. Some other items (PONYEXPRESS) have not been marked themselves
but interconnect two list items through marked pathways.

recognition

recall

recall vs.
recognition

We are now in a position to discuss the difference between recall and recognition. The level of recognition performance, as we have seen, is determined by associations from list items to relevant list markers, and their associated contextual elements. In ordinary terms, recognition is served by associating items with what has been going on at the time and place where the item has occurred, that is, paying attention to context. Recall, because it is so dependent on the tracing of pathways among list items through a marked semantic memory structure, is best served by ensuring a rich network of marked existing pathways. In contrast to recognition, then, recall is enhanced by attending to the stable semantic-memory relations among the words being presented on the list.

It is easy to see that these two objectives may be reciprocal, given that attention is limited: As the word CORD is being presented it may not be possible to attend both to (1) the knowledge that certain types of *hats* are decorated with cords—setting up a retrieval route for getting from HAT to CORD (and vice versa) in a generation–search process—and (2) the fact that as CORD is being presented the subject is expecting the list to be over soon and also reminds himself that he is studying List N. To the extent associations with contextual cues are formed at the expense of associations with other list items, through semantic memory, then it is quite possible to find variables that have opposite effects on recognition and recall performance. For example, instructions for intentional learning may focus the subject on intraverbal associations that may be useful in generating words at recall; such focusing may leave incidental learning at an advantage in recognition, as we saw earlier was the case.

An experiment by Tversky (1973) is quite consistent with the *reciprocity feature* of the Anderson and Bower model, that is, the idea that if a subject concentrates on marking pathways between list items it should aid free recall but, at the same time, such marking is at the expense of forming distinctive associations between items and the external context in which they occur. Tversky tested subjects with either recognition or recall for labeled-picture stimuli. The critical variable was whether the subjects expected to be tested by recognition or by recall. In comparing all four possible combinations of jointly expecting and getting either test, it turned out that whatever the test form subjects scored better if they had been expecting that form than if they had not. This is consistent with a strategy in which subjects expecting recall may have emphasized the formation of interitem associations whereas those expecting recognition may have emphasized item-to-context associations (see also Bernbach, 1973).

The Anderson and Bower (1972) model provides a framework for understanding an otherwise perplexing result that we encountered in Chapter 6. Recall that Woodward *et al.* (1973) obtained evidence against a simple notion of transfer from primary to secondary memory based on rehearsal. They presented words for free recall in a study of directed forgetting, in which each word on the list was followed by a cue telling the subject whether that particular word was to be remembered (for a monetary reward) or whether it could be forgotten. The main variable was the amount of time between exposure of the word and the cue assigning responsibility for the word. It was argued that during this time the word would surely be in a state of constant rehearsal, because it might be one of the important ones. Nonetheless Woodward *et al.* (1973) found that final free recall was unrelated to the amount of time in such a state of rehearsal, a result they took to support the distinction between low-level maintenance rehearsal and elaborative coding.

We mentioned in Chapter 6, however, that a final test of recognition showed a positive relation between the number of seconds a word was rehearsed awaiting the recall or forget signal and performance. Woodward *et al.* propose that maintenance rehearsal is not just useless behavior after all, but that it supports associations between the item being rehearsed and the context—the list discrimination mechanism of Anderson and Bower. This time spent increasing associations of items to their list context is not expected to assist in tests of free recall because free recall depends mainly on developing interitem associations. However, in recognition or in some other measure of list discrimination, increased encoding of the context in which items occur should permit them to be better remembered. Therefore, the term "maintenance rehearsal" may be somewhat condescending with regard to the process examined in Chapter 6 through the work of Woodward *et al.* (1973) Craik and Lockhart (1972), Craik and Watkins (1973), and Watkins and Watkins (1974). Items being rehearsed but not elaboratively encoded (or recoded) are in more than a holding pattern: They are being more and more securely fixed with regard to what was going on when they occurred.

Empirical separation of the two factors in recall.   Anderson and Bower performed a series of experiments the purpose of which was to tease apart the generation and recognition aspects of recall. The subjects received 15 successive lists with 16 words on each list. However, all the words used in the experiment came from a set of only 32; therefore, there had to be substantial overlap in the words used on adjacent lists. In fact, the lists were selected such that exactly eight words were shared between adjacent lists; otherwise, each list contained a random selection from the total pool of items. The instructions given subjects called for recalling, on each trial, only the words that had been presented on that particular trial, that is, from the most recent list. Anderson and Bower chose this novel method expecting it to bring the two components of retrieval to the surface in a particularly dramatic way: As trials go on, we should surely expect improving mastery of the total set of 32 words. This expectation follows from the likelihood that semantic associations among the 32 words would be discovered and marked as more potentially related words become discovered over the 15 trials. The more trials with members of the total set, the more existing pathways in semantic memory that can be exploited for this type

Factor I   *Factor II*

of organization. However, the retrieval of contextual information specific to each list may well become more and more difficult as trials continue. Precisely because each list contains many words common with the preceding list, those two lists ought to be difficult to differentiate, and increasingly so throughout the session of 15 lists. In terms of associations between a particular word and the contexts of successive lists, the tasks amount to the difficult A–B, A–D paradigm of transfer, where A stands for the similar context in which each list is learned.

Figure 11.7 shows the main result—the number of words recalled from each list. The scores in the figure have been corrected by subtracting intrusions from all but the immediately previous list; that is, each time the subject recalls a word from the set that has occurred earlier, but not on the most recent list, the subject loses credit for a word that he has correctly recalled from the most recent list. The main finding is that recall of items from the most recent list was a nonmonotonic function of the 15 trials; performance first improved as a function of trials, but later in the session performance declined with trials.

Anderson and Bower (1972) favored the interpretation that this curved relation between recall and trials reflected two opposed monotonic tendencies, the improvement in knowledge of the total set of words and a concomitant decline in ability to differentiate lists as separate events. Performance in this task requires both skills. (Notice that to ascribe a nonmonotonic relation such as that

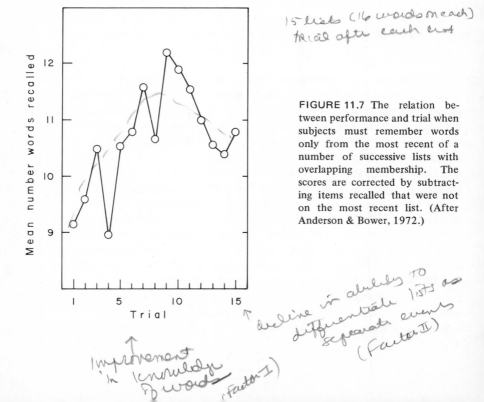

15 lists (16 words on each)
trial after each list

FIGURE 11.7 The relation between performance and trial when subjects must remember words only from the most recent of a number of successive lists with overlapping membership. The scores are corrected by subtracting items recalled that were not on the most recent list. (After Anderson & Bower, 1972.)

improvement in knowledge of words (Factor I)

decline in ability to differentiate lists as separate events (Factor II) in Figure 11.7 to two opposed monotonic functions requires an additional assumption: It must also be true that Factor I, the factor that improves performance as a function of trials, is changing faster than Factor II early in practice and that Factor II, the one that impairs performance as a function of trials, is changing faster late in practice than Factor I. Otherwise, for example, if the two monotonic tendencies were linear against time, there would not be a curved function from their combined influence).

In a second experiment they disposed of an uninteresting, but logically possible artifact—that the early improvement in Figure 11.7 simply represented warmup and the later decline, boredom. They repeated the experiment with 15 successive lists of a similar nature except that the words on each list were distinct to that list and never repeated elsewhere in the experiment. Under these conditions performance did not resemble that in Figure 11.7. In fact, there was a nonmonotonic function of exactly opposite inflection, an early deterioration over trials followed by a steady improvement in the later trials. At least we can be sure that the data of Figure 11.7 represent the operation of factors that occur on lists with overlapping word sets and not on discrete lists.

In a further effort to reinforce their interpretation of the inverted-U relationship between recall and trial, Anderson and Bower (1972) performed a study in which the same list construction rules as in the original study were used. In this new version however, the subject was asked to recall the 32 words from the total set on every trial. In addition the subject was asked to make a separate estimation, for each word, of his confidence that the word had occurred on the most recently presented list. The idea was to measure the growing structure for the total set and the declining list-differentiation separately.

Taking only those items both recalled and also assigned high confidence as being members of the most recent list, we can compare performance in this study with that of Figure 11.7. The assumption is that these items—those that are both recalled and given a confident placement in the most recent list—would have been recalled under the instructions of the first experiment. Anderson and Bower showed that indeed the course of performance for these specially defined items across the 15 trials was very similar to the data of Figure 11.7. Now, however, there is the opportunity to look at the two underlying components separately: There was a monotonic increasing function relating performance in recalling items from the total set of 32 across trials. That is, when the subject is given credit for each experimental word he recalls whatever his confidence that it has occurred on the last trial, he gets progressively better with no reversals. Recognition of list membership can be measured trial by trial also. On each trial the subject recalled some words that had occurred on the most recent list and others that had not. A measure of list discrimination, therefore, is the difference in confidence with which the subject rated truly recent items as being recent as opposed to nonrecent (not from the last list) items as being recent. This list-recognition score showed a steady decline over trials, just as the theory predicted.

Therefore, this experiment shows an operational separation of the two processes underlying retrieval—the search or generation process, which exploits the richness of semantic memory in order to identify pathways from one list item to another, and the process of list differentiation, which permits recognition of list items through associations with the context in which the list has been presented. Furthermore, the Anderson and Bower work makes manifest the possibility that these two factors can be affected in the opposite way by the same experimental variables.

Tulving's Encoding Specificity Principle

As we have seen the Anderson and Bower (1972) retrieval theory is a sophisticated version of the basic generation—recognition idea. It is sophisticated in two ways: First, it gives a plausible process explanation for the theoretical commodity that supports recognition. Rather than invoke such arbitrary mechanisms as strength or tags, the theory states that recognition is a decision based in a lawful manner on associations among list items and the stream of contextual events and markers representing them. The second point of sophistication in the Anderson—Bower theory is the situational control exerted over the generation process. Whereas simpler versions of the generation—recognition idea have portrayed the subject as covertly spewing out the entire contents of his semantic memory for the recognition monitor—say, everything remotely or closely associated with ULCER, then everything remotely or closely associated with the associates of ULCER, and so on—the Anderson and Bower subject simply follows the relevant semantic-memory paths, those paths marked during the active process of encoding the list.

With these important stipulations aside, it is useful to consider the points shared by the Anderson—Bower theory and others of the generation—recognition family, because this sets the stage for describing the position taken by Tulving and his associates in questioning the validity of all such theories.

The Anderson—Bower theory resembles other generation plus recognition theories in the assumption that recall involves two stages, whereas recognition involves only one. In recall the subject must get to some location in memory, through the generation subprocess, and then make a determination as to whether that location contains information sufficient to indicate occurrence on the list, through the recognition subprocess. In recognition it is the experimenter who gets the subject to the relevant memory location by presenting the word corresponding to that location, and thus one stage is bypassed. This assumption has the consequence that recognition ought always to be faster or easier than recall; it would be paradoxical, for all such theories, to demonstrate that recall, with a two-stage history, could be better than recognition, with only one of those same two stages.

Another assumption of most generation–recognition theories is inherent in what has been said already, but it deserves stating separately: When a written or spoken word is presented for study on a list and then presented again for a recognition test both of these two events involve the same memory location. Tulving has termed this assumption *transsituational identity*. The idea is that when the written word TALK occurs on two occasions there is automatically a potential matching between the test item and the memory because the word TALK is the same word both times. The alternative of special interest to Tulving has been that if TALK has been encoded in two different ways on two occasions, presentation and test, one cannot necessarily expect a matching between a test item and a memory. The major change between the 1972 and the 1974 version of the Anderson and Bower model is the abandonment of the transsituational identity assumption.

Recall versus recognition. In a paper called "When is recall higher than recognition?" Tulving (1968a) challenged the assumptions of generation–recognition retrieval theories. In the simple experiment reported in that article, subjects were required to learn 48 pairs of words by the traditional anticipation method of paired-associate learning. The anticipation trials continued until a subject had correctly anticipated the response term of each of the pairs on two trials; that is, until he could provide the response terms, given the stimuli as cues, twice without error. After they reached criterion, the subjects were tested for recognition of the response terms alone. Some of the pairs from the list were AIR–PORT, BACK–LOG, BASE–BALL, BATH–ROBE, and BIRTH–DAY. Note that these are not arbitrarily selected words but rather highly associated, or idiomatic, pairs. Tulving stated that these earlier materials were used because too much practice would have been required to learn 48 unrelated pairs of words. (We shall see below that it is not a matter of indifference whether the words within a pair are related to one another.) In the recognition test immediately following criterion, subjects received an alphabetical list of 96 words—48 of these were the response terms, PORT, LOG, BALL, ROBE, and DAY from the acquisition list and the other 48 were words that also formed high-frequency idioms with the stimulus terms, for the examples given these were PLANE, BONE, LESS, ROOM, and PLACE, respectively. For each word on the list the subject had simply to indicate whether the word had occurred on the previous list.

The results showed an average of 7.2 trials were required to reach a criterion of two perfect recitations of the original 48-pair list. All subjects achieved their second perfect trial immediately after their first, with no backsliding; therefore, Tulving concluded that an additional test of cued recall would have shown 100%

accuracy. However, in the recognition test performance was less than perfect; subjects failed to recognize 4.6 of the original response terms and incorrectly classified as "old" .9 items that had actually not been on the list. In terms of a decision-theory analysis of recognition the rate of *hits*, correct identification of items that had been on the list, was 90% (43.4/48) and the rate of *false alarms*, incorrect judgments that nonlist items had been on the list, was slightly less than 2% (.9/48). However one wants to evaluate recognition performance overall, recognition was worse than recall under the conditions of this experiment. The word from the list itself, PORT, was not as good a cue for the retrieval of the list-presentation episode of that word as was a related word, AIR. That is, access to the episode in which PORT occurred is better from the verbal context in which PORT was encoded, the cue AIR, than from the word PORT itself.

The generation–recognition theory of retrieval can rationalize a positive effect of retrieval cues—words given as hints, such as AIR in our example—in terms of a restriction in the amount of search or generation necessary prior to the recognition stage. Even though presenting AIR may restrict the search to all words associated with AIR, however, it can never reduce the search by as much as presenting PORT does, because restricting the search set to one item is the lowest limit possible. Tulving (1968a) sees this result as demonstrating not only the bankruptcy of generate plus edit models but also the value of considering retrieval of a word in the context of how it was encoded. When AIR and PORT are presented in close contiguity the word PORT is encoded in a manner that is quite different from that used when the word PORT is presented alone. Then, when PORT is exposed for a recognition test it is reasonable to expect on some occasions a failure to reinstate the encoding that has involved AIR. A closely related way of saying the same thing is that the memory trace is an aggregate of a word and the context in which it has been understood or encoded at the time of acquisition; this context may include other words that have been presented with the target. Now in any test of memory only a fragment of the aggregate is presented. One fragment of the whole can be the nominal target item PORT. Another fragment could be some aspect of the encoding context, such as the word AIR, or the cue *station where planes fly*. Finding better recall than recognition, according to this attitude, means that sometimes a cue presented with the target at learning can provide access to the stored aggregate idea better than the target item itself, separated from the context.

Tulving's demonstration used compound words. The phenomenon is quite generalizable, however, to other types of material, as we see in two further examples, one with lower-order materials by Watkins (1974b) and another with higher-order materials by Horowitz and Manelis (1972, 1973).

In the Watkins (1974b) experiment more or less unitary words were fractionated into parts for the paired-associate learning phase of the study, the design of which was quite similar to that of Tulving. Representative items, corresponding to AIR–PORT, BACK–LOG, and BASE–BALL in the Tulving study, were SPANI–EL, EXPLO–RE, and LIQU–EFY. Recognition distractor items, corresponding to PLANE, BONE, and LESS–which, it will be recalled, fit with the first three stimulus terms in Tulving's list–were SH, DE, and OR. So, the recognition test included both the correct word fragments EL, RE, and FY and also SH, DE, and OR. The test of cued recall, with the subject responding EL given SPANI as a stimulus, showed a mean of 72% correct responses. A forced-choice test of recognition, selecting EL versus SH, showed 52%. However, because chance guessing was measured at 14% for recall–the probability of coming up with EL in response to SPANI when the list had not even included that pair–and was equal to 50% for recognition, the true discrepancy between recognition and recall is more substantial. The standard correction for guessing yields 67% correct for recall and only 9% correct for recognition.

The Watkins (1974b) result exaggerates the Tulving (1968a) result by using materials that are a more extreme case of the whole's disguising the nature of the part. The point is exactly the same, however: Fragments of a larger whole can be unrecognizable unless they are adequate to reinstate the entire whole (PORT or EL is unrecognizable whereas AIR– or SPANI– serve to reinstate AIRPORT and SPANIEL). The important question for theory is to what extent this result generalizes to other learning. It may be that the stimulus materials used in these two studies exaggerate but do not distort the cohesiveness that always develops when verbal materials are entered into new combinations. This is the suggestion of the encoding specificity principle, that when a verbal component is encoded with another component each is fundamentally altered by becoming a part of a new whole.

Horowitz and Manelis (1973) have extended the generality of the Tulving–Watkins demonstration to two-word combinations that are controlled with regard to part–whole cohesiveness. Their experiment seems to show that the advantage of cued recall over recognition is not completely general across stimulus materials. In their experiment the learning materials were adjective–noun phrases. Some of the phrases were simple attributive phrases, such as HOT–MEAL: however, others were pairs that resemble those used by Tulving, such as HOT–DOG. Horowitz and Manelis term these latter phrases *idioms*.

The main theoretical distinction between idioms and ordinary phrases is the different degrees to which these materials have high *redintegrative probabilities*. "Redintegration" is a term that refers to a compound stimulus and the process whereby one part of the stimulus elicits the remaining parts (Horowitz & Manelis, 1972; Horowitz & Prytulak, 1969). With two-word phrases redintegrative power can be tested in free recall: When subjects almost never recall one part of the two-word phrase without also recalling the other part there is a high redintegrative probability (Horowitz & Prytulak, 1969). Such phrases as HOT–MEAL are low in redintegrative probability, that is, subjects may well often remember that either HOT or MEAL was on the list but fail to retrieve the other word. In contrast as we said above, such idioms as HOT—DOG are high in redintegrative probability. This variable therefore seems to capture what is peculiar about the Tulving (1968a) stimuli and permits us to enquire whether that peculiarity has been important for the results.

Subjects in the Horowitz and Manelis (1973) study received a list of 32 two-word items, 16 idioms, such as HOT—DOG, and 16 ordinary phrases, such as HOT—MEAL. One group was tested for recognition and another group for cued recall. In the recognition test 64 individual words were tested, half from the list and half new distractors, with adjectives and nouns used equally in each of these subsets. For each word the subject indicated with a yes or no whether he thought it had been on the list. Exactly the same list of 64 individual words was used in the cued-recall test. For each word that had not been on the list there was an instruction to copy the word. For each word that had, on the other hand, been on the list the subject was to supply the other word from the two-word unit.

The major result is shown in Table 11.1. Consider first performance on recognition. We see that words from ordinary phrases get recognized better than words from idioms and that nouns have an advantage over adjectives. Now, turning to cued recall we see this pattern reversed—idioms are better than phrases and adjectives are better than nouns. In comparing recognition with cued recall for phrases there is the normal advantage for recognition. However, when we examine recognition for adjectives from idioms (.42) in comparison with cued recall for the same words (.63) a clear advantage for recall is evident. That is, when the noun DOG is provided subjects can supply HOT with probability .63 whereas when HOT is presented for recognition they can perform only at a level of .42. (Notice that the effect is not symmetrical within the idiom, because

TABLE 11.1
Recognition and Recall
of Constituent Items
from Idioms and Phrases[a]

Test and target type	Type of pair	
	Idioms	Phrases
Recognition		
Nouns	.55	.58
Adjectives	.42	.46
Recall		
Nouns	.43	.29
Adjectives	.63	.39

[a]After Horowitz and Manelis (1973).

when HOT is presented as a cue for DOG recall is only .43 and when DOG is presented for recognition there is .55 probability of correct response. However, combining across nouns and adjectives there is a net superiority of recall over recognition—.53 versus .49.)

At the empirical level this result suggests that finding a cued-recall advantage over recognition depends on using materials with high cohesiveness and that Tulving may have gotten a different result with a different word list. In a recent study, Antognini (1975, Experiment 2) has shown just this. However, it does not make the results any the less interesting. Let us accept the theoretical position of Tulving (1968a) and of Horowitz and Manelis (1973) that either recognition or recall of information from the occurrence of HOT—DOG on the list requires retrieval of the aggregate higher-order unit HOT—DOG. What the results for idioms show is that subjects can somehow get back to the conglomerate when they are given DOG—resulting in either good recognition of DOG itself (.55) or in good recall of its made, HOT (.63). However, when subjects are given HOT, performance is relatively lower whether they have to recognize HOT itself (.42) or recall what went with it, DOG (.43). (We are to assume that in Tulving's study the left-hand member of each pair is satisfying the same semantic role as HOT in our example; these terms, that is, AIR from the pair AIR—PORT have not necessarily been adjectives but they may have been in a modifying relation anyway.)

Being able to get back to a higher-order unit from DOG but not as well from HOT implies there is an asymmetrical relationship between the elements of these two-word idioms. One possibility for this asymmetry is that, in general, modifiers are stored in semantic memory at the location of the nouns they modify. Another possibility is that both nouns and adjectives have, in some sense, their own location in semantic memory, but that diverging associations from adjectives are more numerous than from nouns. In this case to find a particular associative link, as between HOT and DOG, there is a lengthier search from HOT than from DOG. However, these speculations would have to be qualified immediately to account for the fact that with nonidiomatic adjective—noun phrases, the outcome was somewhat different. However, three points can and should be made before we move on to other matters:

1. There are indeed circumstances when recall of a particular unit, given an adequate cue, surpasses recognition of that unit alone. The circumstances that seem to be crucial are that the unit and the cue stand in a part—whole relation to some familiar larger unit. Theories of retrieval that imagine a search process through semantic memory and then a recognition or editing check are unable to account for the recall advantage. These theories need serious expansion to specify why part—whole associative relationships, such as HOT—DOG, do not fall under the same principles as ordinary associative relationships, such as HOT—MEAL.

2. Both the Tulving and Horowitz—Manelis results absolutely require some form of associative asymmetry between the abilities of the two parts of a unified whole, or conglomerate, to reinstate that unified whole. Otherwise, if HOT and DOG equally reinstated HOT—DOG and if AIR and PORT equally reinstated AIR—PORT then recognition and recall would not be different. Notice that the theory underlying this consideration includes an assumption that in order to decide whether he recognizes DOG as having occurred on the list, a subject determines whether he can recall an item that combines to produce a retained higher-order unit. This means recognition is dependent on an internal recall check, just the opposite model to that of the generate—edit position.

3. The differences between idioms and ordinary phrases suggest a new validity to the term *mental chemistry* used by John Stuart Mill and others of the British associationists (Boring, 1950; also see Chapter 12 of this book). Among the idioms there are parts combined into a whole such that they are later unrecognizable apart from that whole. Many questions seem testable when these fundamental ideas about the nature of associations are cast in this type of paradigm. For example, would all associations become, in this sense, chemical compounds given enough specific practice or strength? If one could distinguish, à la Paivio, between verbal and visual associations, would there be a difference in the degree of cohesiveness? These questions we must leave for future research.

The predicted effects of recall cues. Tulving (1975) has said that retrieval involves combining information stored in memory with cues of some sort designed to elicit that information. Sometimes the cues are very general—such as "Recall the list you just heard"—but sometimes the retrieval cues are very specific, such as: "Recall the item on the list you just heard that means the same thing as *automobile.*" A way in which to view the comparison between recognition and recall, which adheres to Tulving's general orientation, is as a comparison between the item itself as a retrieval cue versus some other information besides the item itself. In either case, the success of the retrieval effort ought to depend on the degree to which the cue reinstates the exact way in which the item has been encoded when it first occurs in the list—this notion is called the *encoding specificity principle.* One set of studies, reported by Thomson and Tulving (1970), was designed to examine this principle by comparing different cues for recall.

We may distinguish a strong and weak version of the encoding specificity principle. The weak version simply states that a retrieval cue, a piece of information presented as a hint or aid along with a recall instruction, should be more helpful if it is encoded with, or thought of, at the time the target item is learned than if not. The weak version of the encoding specificity principle is certainly reasonable, but it is almost truistic. Most theoretical positions on learning and memory, with the possible exception of strength theory, can assent to this prediction. For example Estes' stimulus fluctuation model makes the formal prediction that reinstatement of stimulus elements from the original learning situation are correlated with elicitation of the response that occurred in that situation. Indeed, it is hard to imagine how any theorist who believed in determinism as a philosophical doctrine could question the weak version of the encoding specificity principle, as we remarked in another context in Chapter 8.

The strong version is more interesting because it seems less truistic and therefore more capable of disproof. The strong version of the encoding specificity principle states that "...no cue, however strongly associated with the to-be-remembered unit, or otherwise related to it, can be effective unless the to-be-remembered item is specifically encoded with respect to that cue at the time of its storage" (Thomson & Tulving, 1970, p. 255). In other words, if an item is later to be an effective cue—which means it leads to better recall of some particular target word than can have occurred without any cue—it must be the case that the subject has somehow included the cue word in his encoding while studying the target word. If SCHIZOPHRENIA is one of a list of target words presented for learning, we can examine this proposition with respect to the potential cue, *paranoid*. If *paranoid* is an effective cue, that means recall of SCHIZOPHRENIA is better when *paranoid* is given as a cue than when subjects are left to their own devices. According to the Thomson–Tulving statement, PARANOID should only be effective, by this definition, if the subject has specifically encoded the word *paranoid* at the time he has learned SCHIZO-PHRENIA. The trick, of course, is to enter the subject's mind in order to determine what encoding operations have gone on as he has studied the target word. There are ways to approximate this knowledge, but first let us examine the type of theory that makes opposed predictions for this experimental situation.

According to theories of retrieval subscribing to the generation–recognition hypothesis, a cue word, such as *paranoid,* can facilitate recall of a target word SCHIZOPHRENIA by restricting the generation, or search, subprocess. That is, when asked for free recall of a list including SCHIZOPHRENIA the subject must depend on general search strategies for coming up with words to be tested against a recognition criterion—such search strategies as following associations from the recency buffer or retaining some categorical organization of the list items. However, when a cue word is given, such as *paranoid,* the subject has many fewer possible words to test against the recognition criterion, perhaps only three or four potential list items in semantic memory are suggested by this particular cue. Note that the advantage of associated retrieval cues in this instance is not dependent on the subjects' having thought of the cue word during study of the target word—the cue shortens the list of potential items to undergo the recognition check whether or not the cue has occurred to the subject previously.

A second theoretical attitude that yields contrasting predictions to those of the encoding specificity principle is found in the *logogen* model of Morton

(1970), a model originally formulated for the purpose of handling various aspects of perception, not memory. We shall digress in order to introduce the theory. The important idea behind the logogen model is the existence of dictionary units corresponding to words, letters, digits, or other unitary verbal items. These units, called "logogens," can be defined by their input and their output: When a logogen unit is excited, the consequence is a state of preparedness in a person for producing a response, a state of response availability. Morton illustrates this state of response availability with three situations: (1) a person sees the written word TABLE, (2) a person hears the spoken sound / teibəl /, and (3) a person is asked to free associate to the word CHAIR. The point is that in each case the word TABLE is on the tip of one's tongue, whatever has been its source, auditory, visual, or contextual–semantic. The logogen unit is built so as to receive input from auditory features, from visual features, or from semantic context. These sources of information combine their effects in the simplest possible manner—the logogen keeps track only of how much energy or input it is receiving, not from where that input has come, and when a critical threshold value is reached the unit is fired.

In perception one of the achievements of Morton's logogen model is predicting how stimulus information gets combined with context information. Consider the amount of stimulus energy, say visual duration, necessary for perceiving the word TABLE. In one case there is only the visual information from a brief exposure. In another condition the subject has been given a contextual cue prior to brief exposure of the word TABLE; the cue is a sentence, "I put the knife and fork on the _____." According to the model, that context sentence should result in some energy being fed into the logogen corresponding to TABLE, with the result that less stimulus energy is needed from the exposure in order to excite that logogen. In short, two independent sources of information about the same item combine.

This prediction has been confirmed by Tulving and Gold (1963). These authors measured the number of milliseconds a word had to be displayed before subjects could identify it, the duration threshold, as a function of the amount and relevance of a prior contextual cue. With a relevant context, the words presented before threshold measurement were helpful in identifying the critical target word: An eight-word context for the target PERFORMER was "The actress received praise for being an outstanding _____." Tulving and Gold found that with no context it took a 71-msec exposure to identify the word PERFORMER but with the sentence frame quoted above, this value was reduced to about 45 msec. There was therefore a tradeoff between the amount of context provided before a trial and the amount of visual stimulus energy needed on that trial.

To apply the logogen model to cuing effects in memory one needs only substitute the memory trace for the perceptual input. Again, the logogen unit would govern whether or not the subject could emit some target word in recall, but the excitation of the logogen would depend on (1) the amount of information carried by the memory trace and (2) the information contained in the context supplied by the retrieval cue. If the cue is strongly associated with the target, as in TABLE–CHAIR, then one ought to be able to recall the target word TABLE with less support from memory than when no cue is provided.

Of course, this application of the logogen reasoning to cued recall presupposes that the laws governing retrieval from semantic memory are applicable to episodic memory. Tulving clearly rejects this applicability; whereas the stimulus information and context operate as independent information sources in retrieval from semantic memory, he says, they must be nonindependent (specifically encoded together) in order for a retrieval cue to be effective in retrieving episodic memories.

Another useful remark about the logogen model is that Morton has made very clear the assumption that words are represented in logogen units by meaning and not by spelling. The words CHOP and CHOP, for example, referring respectively to a piece of meat and to a sudden action, are represented in the system by two different logogens, even though they happen to be spelled the same way in our language. In contrast, as we have seen, the handwritten, typed, printed, and spoken representations of a particular word are represented by the same logogen. Having examined three hypotheses about the effects of recall cues—the generation–recognition model, the logogen model, and the encoding specificity principle, we may now turn to the evidence.

Evidence of the effects of recall cues. There is no doubt that if a word is presented alone for study and then tested in company of a strongly associated retrieval cue there is a facilitation of recall in comparison with free, noncued recall (Thomson & Tulving, 1970, Experiment I). According to the logogen model, the strongly associated retrieval cue has fed enough excitation into the appropriate logogen unit that less memory trace is required than would be necessary for free recall. According to the generation–recognition model, the cue has restricted the set of possible targets through which the subject needs to search. According to the encoding specificity principle the strongly associated cue must have been encoded along with the target item at input, covertly.

To test these opposed interpretations we need a situation where the subject is encouraged to encode the target without any reference to the eventual, strongly associated retrieval cue and where the effects of that cue word can then be measured at retrieval. Thomson and Tulving (1970) report three experiments of this sort. In each the critical operation was presenting the target word in company with a weak associate under conditions where the subject was told to use the weak associate to aid retaining the target. If CHAIR were the target word, for example, the subject would have received the word *glue* as a retrieval cue for studying along with CHAIR. The question is then what happens when we test for the target CHAIR with a strongly associated retrieval cue, such as *table*.

(We are observing the convention of the Tulving group in writing target words all in upper-case letters and retrieval cue words in lower-case italics.)

In Experiment III of the Thomson and Tulving (1970) paper, 24 subjects received three successive lists of 24 words. On each of the first two lists, half the words were accompanied during the study phase by a strong associate and half accompanied by a weak associate. For these first two lists, which were designed to build up subjects' confidence that the cues presented along with target words would indeed help them recall the targets, the cues used in study were always presented at recall. Recall probability on these first two lists was .84 for words presented along with strongly associated cues and tested with these same cues and .75 for words presented along with weakly associated cues and tested with the same cues. Because noncued recall would have been somewhere between .30 and .40 we may be assured that subjects were using the cue words and that it was adaptive for them to do so.

The point of the experiment was a subtle change in cuing conditions in the third list. Just as before, half the items in this third list were presented in company with weakly associated retrieval cues and half were presented in company with strongly associated retrieval cues. However, at testing, some of the items were tested with new cues, which had not been seen at input. Of the 12 items studied with weak cues, half were tested with the same weak cues but the other half were tested with strong cues, which, although they were relevant to the target words, had never been seen by the subject. Likewise, of the words presented for study along with strongly associated cues, half were tested with the same cues and the other half were tested with new words that were weak associates of the target. All subjects were therefore challenged to show whether they could use unencoded cues on half the items they had studied. Because the first two lists more or less ensure that subjects have been encoding the targets only with respect to the cues presented overtly, we can examine the items switched between input and output to see whether new cues, not considered by the subject in study, can nonetheless assist recall.

The results are shown in Table 11.2. The main finding is for target items presented with weakly associated cues, such as CHAIR with *glue,* and switched at testing, to strongly associated novel cues, such as *table,* recall is not better than expected from free recall. Free recall from comparable lists in the first two experiments by Thomson and Tulving yielded average recall probabilities of around .30, whereas novel, strongly associated retrieval cues in the present study gave .33. When items had been studied in the presence of strongly associated retrieval cues, when CHAIR was studied in the presence of *table,* switching to a weak cue, such as *glue,* led to almost complete performance failure—.03. Therefore, the main result is that even though such a word as *table* leads to CHAIR with high normative probability, it is useless relative to the rate of free recall in retrieving the memory trace of the occurrence of CHAIR on a particular list when there is reason to expect the subject has not encoded the relation between CHAIR and *table* specifically at the time of study.

TABLE 11.2
Recall Probability as a
Function of Input and
Output Cues[a]

Input cue	Output cue	
	Strong	Weak
Strong	.833	.035
Weak	.326	.729

[a]After   Thomson   and
Tulving (1970).

(One puzzle in the data of Table 11.2 is the asymmetrical effect of a changed cue depending on whether its relation to the target is strong or weak, .326 versus .035, respectively. Clearly, this result shows that previous normative strength of association between retrieval cues and their corresponding target words plays some role in this experimental situation. However, it is not clear that this conclusion damages the encoding specificity principle.)

Testing the encoding specificity principle requires that we guard against the subjects' encoding items that we shall later be using as retrieval cues when the target words are being studied. The Thomson–Tulving procedure guards against this possibility by supplying the subject with something else to encode with the target. A second strategy is to find retrieval cues with associations with the target words so weak that we can be assured that few, if any, subjects encode the cue spontaneously while studying the target in isolation. Now the word *glue* is in such a relation to CHAIR: however, the weakness of the association back to CHAIR, given *glue* at recall, discourages us from predicting facilitation, and Thomson and Tulving have found indeed there is no facilitation under these conditions. How can we come up with a cue word that leads strongly to the target but that, at the time of study, is unlikely to have been encoded specifically with the target? Rightmer (1975) has developed the idea that *normatively asymmetrical* associations can be used for this purpose. Such a pair is *easy– HARD*. When given the word *easy*, subjects give HARD as an associate with probability .64; however, when given HARD, subjects come up with *easy* only with probability .05. For an entire list of words satisfying this asymmetrical criterion the average strength in one direction was .53 and in the other direction it was .01. The critical comparison is between free recall of the word HARD, and others like it, versus cued recall where *easy* is given as a stimulus for HARD. With the word HARD presented alone at input, we may be assured that subjects rarely, if ever, thought of the word easy, at least consciously. The strong version of the encoding specificity principle would be violated then by showing that *easy* is nonetheless an effective retrieval cue for HARD.

Rightmer's experiment did show a cuing effect when *easy* was used as a cue for HARD: Free recall of the targets was 13.5 words, out of a possible 24, whereas cued recall was 16.4 words, a gain in recall probability of from .56 to .68. How can we account for these discrepant results? When encoding of a cue word along with a target word is prevented by substituting another cue word—presenting CHAIR with *glue* in order to prevent the subject from thinking of *table*—the overlooked cue is ineffective in aiding recall. When encoding of a cue along with a target word is prevented by using cues that are extremely low-probability associates of the target, however, then the overlooked cue later turns out to be effective.

One possible reconciliation requires the assumption that words do not have a single unitary meaning but rather a pattern of meaning, or, alternatively, a population of meaning elements or vectors. If study of the word CHAIR in the presence of the word *glue* elicits some fraction of the total meaning of CHAIR, it becomes understandable that another word, such as *table*, which shares a different portion of CHAIR's total meaning, does not prove effective. It may be, however, that when a word is presented alone, as in Rightmer's experiment, the dominant meaning response on the average tends to include any strong cue, even though a particular cue word may not have been encoded. This line of reasoning requires a revision of the encoding specificity principle in which it is conceded that the specificity is in relation to a pattern of meaning rather than to a particular word, as originally claimed. However, there is another group of studies that we need to consider before making any concluding summary of these ideas.

Recognition failure of recallable words. A recent series of studies on the encoding specificity principle (Tulving & Thomson, 1973; Watkins & Tulving, 1975) returns to the comparison of recognition with recall. The main purpose of the 1973 experiments was to test the two-process, generation—recognition models of recognition. The method was to bring this generate—edit sequence to the surface by actually collecting free associates to strong retrieval cues for target words and then determining whether the subject could recognize those targets he generated. In the third experiment of the series, subjects received a list of 24 words, each paired with a weak associate, such as CHAIR presented in the company of *glue.* (On two previous lists subjects in this experiment had been given weak cues both in presentation and recall in order to make them trustful of the materials supplied as cues.) After studying the list the subjects were given a sheet with the corresponding 24 strong retrieval cues written in a column—such words as *table,* which had not been present on the study list but which were strongly related to words which had been presented. The instructions were to provide the first four words suggested by these strongly related cues, just as in a free-association experiment, without regard for what had happened on the study list.

The first question of interest was whether subjects did actually produce words from the list in the course of providing free associations—did they write down

CHAIR as one of the four free associates to *table?* (This phase of the study, of course, is an overt simulation of the "generate" process in generate plus edit models.) The answer is yes, in 66% of the cases the subject did produce a target word from the list in response to the strong cue. In the next phase of the experiment subjects were asked to look back over their free associates and determine whether there were any list targets among them. Here, subjects are being asked to perform the "edit" process from the generate plus edit notion. The question is whether having produced list items by free associating to new cues—that is, to cues not involved in the encoding during study—subjects are able to recognize these list items as such. Opposite each strong cue word, then, were four free associates, and the subject was told to circle whichever of the four words he considered most likely to have been on the previous list. Let us consider only those cases where there was a correct response in the sense that the target word had actually been produced as a free associate: Of these (66% of the original number of free-association tests) the rate of correct choice from the four alternatives given was 53.5%. That is, when the subject faced four alternatives he himself produced as free associates of the strongly related extralist cues, and when one of those four was an item that had been on the list, he was able to identify list items only 53.5% of the time.

If subjects had been guessing in this four-choice situation we would have expected 25% correct, so clearly there was some memory for the items generated by free association. However, perhaps 53.5% is too high a figure, for if the subjects are guessing occasionally they can get credit for lucky guesses one-quarter of the time. Assume that on trials where the subject guessed, he chose each of the four alternatives equally often. Assuming also that the subject was always guessing when in fact he chose the wrong item, then we could devise a way of correcting the obtained figure to include only trials where the correct response was based on an authentic memory for the list, and not on a lucky guess: With 53.5% correct there were 46.5% of the responses in error, where the subject chose one of the three nonlist alternatives from among his four free associates. Of these 46.5% choices to incorrect alternatives, one-third would have gone to each—about 15.5%. However, if, when the subject was guessing, he chose each of the three incorrect alternatives 15.5% of the time then he also chose the correct alternative 15.5% of the time—guessing is guessing. That means that mixed in with the 53.5% correct choices the subject is getting credit for all 15.5% guesses. His corrected recognition score ought therefore to be 53.5% minus 15.5%, or 38%. This method of correcting recognition scores for guessing is not the only possibility, and the assumptions underlying it offer a thorny set of problems for theory, but for present purposes we must be satisfied that it represents a reasonable estimate of what authentic recognition has occurred in this task setting (although see Antognini, 1975).

Now, so far this result has little importance; maybe subjects have simply forgotten most of the list items, leaving them with 38% retention whatever the circumstances of testing. However, for their last step in this experiment, Tulving and Thomson gave subjects the list of original cues that had been used at the time of study and found that recall based on these cues was 61%. In terms of our example, we can summarize the study as follows: Subjects studied CHAIR in the company of *glue*. They were then asked to free associate to the word *table*. With probability .66 one of the four items produced to the stimulus *table* was the word CHAIR, the target from the study list. When this was the case, however, subjects remembered that CHAIR had occurred on the list only 38% of the time. However, when they were given the word *glue* they showed that, after all, CHAIR was still well remembered by providing it 61% of the time in cued recall.

So again, recognition was shown to be clearly lower than cued recall. From the free-association part of the experiment we now know that studying CHAIR in the presence of *glue* does not weaken the association between *table* and CHAIR, because 66% of the time that link was expressed in the free-association phase of the experiment. The experimental task used by Tulving and Thomson has furthermore brought to the surface the two phases of the generate plus recognition theories of retrieval. However, the result fails to support simple models of this type, which suggest that subjects first use links in semantic memory to advance candidates for the recognition process, which, in turn, depends on some type of judgment of strength. These models are bound to predict an advantage of recognition over recall because the latter always involves one more step. Watkins and Tulving (1975) have shown that the failure to recognize recallable words is quite a general phenomenon and not restricted to the exact procedure of Tulving and Thomson (1973).

Interpretations of recognition failure of recallable words. The encoding specificity principle offers no explicit explanation for the Tulving and Thomson result, the fact that subjects cannot recognize list items they themselves have produced as free associates even though they can later recall these same items with their originally encoded cues. In answer to the numerous questions posed by their studies Tulving and Thomson conclude: "Specific encoding operations performed on what is perceived determine what is stored, and what is stored determines what retrieval cues are effective in providing access to what is stored" (Tulving & Thomson, 1973, p. 269). Therefore, a test of cued recall with a cue that had been included in the study list is expected to yield good performance because that original cue somehow makes contact with the encoding episode. Another cue, however, or even a letter by letter copy of the test word itself, can sometimes be ineffective in providing access to that same encoding episode. Why the item CHAIR fails to contact the *glue* + CHAIR episode, when the item *glue* does, is left by Tulving and Thomson to be a puzzle.

Tulving and Thomson do offer, although without enthusiasm, an explanation that is sufficient based on an extension of the common generate plus recognition models (see also Light, 1972; Reder, Anderson, & Bjork, 1974). The extension concerns how words are organized in semantic memory—by meaning or by spelling. If one wishes to make the assumptions that (1) words that mean different things but happen to have the same spelling, as BEAR and BEAR, are represented by two different locations in semantic memory; (2) when such a doubly stored word is presented in an experiment, different encoding contexts can lead to activation of the different meanings; and (3) activation of one word does not automatically lead to the activation of another word even if the second word is spelled the same as the first, then one can provide a clear understanding of the encoding specificity principle: What is specific about encoding is the activation of one meaning as determined by whatever semantic information the experimenter provides along with the target word. Anderson and Bower (1974) and Martin (1975) have made much the same point. Notice that Morton's (1970) logogen model was quite explicit in defining the word as a meaning and not as a spelling.

Consider a contrived example, where in the first phase of the Tulving–Thomson type of experiment the word IRON was presented with an associated retrieval cue *steel*. In the next phase of the study the subject was asked to free associate to the cue *laundry,* leading to to the four associates SOAP, KITCHEN, IRON, PRESS. Being asked to scan these words for any members of the previous list, the subject reports that he sees none, or perhaps he guesses. And he is right! The word IRON, meaning to press clothes, was really not on the list that was studied, even though another word with the same spelling was (IRON in the context *steel*). However, the subject quite well remembers that the IRON related to *steel* was a study item.

However, once one recognizes that a word is a meaning rather than a spelling, and that what is encoded during study is a fraction of some potential or alternative meanings, perhaps highly specific and context determined, then the general proposition becomes sensible and understandable that some retrieval cues bias against the specifically encoded meaning and impair retrieval of the learning episode. For example, *glue* may set up the encoding of certain aspects of the concept CHAIR that are particularly concerned with the structure of chairs and their construction. However, when *table* is presented and the subject thinks of the concept of CHAIR it is a specific evocation of the *table*–CHAIR unit that somehow masks the thoughts he has had earlier about how chairs are constructed. The result depends on how separated are the meanings activated by the spelling in the two episodes, encoding and recognition. It is possible that on at least seven items out of 24—enough to account for the average advantage of recall over recognition in the Tulving and Thomson experiment—the diversity has been sufficient to block recognition.

This scenario of the recognition-failure phenomenon (see Martin, 1975) depends for its persuasiveness on the use of homographic words, such as IRON. Light and Carter-Sobell (1970) showed that homographic nouns studied in the company of an adjective suggesting one of two possible meanings were very poorly recognized in the company of an adjective suggesting the other (*strawberry*–JAM versus *traffic*–JAM). However, is it fair to build our interpretation of the recognition-failure result on these homographic examples? After all, the Tulving and Thomson experiment has employed few, if any, items with such diverse meanings; the *glue*–CHAIR and *table*–CHAIR examples are not in the same category of ambiguity as IRON and JAM are.

Two recent experiments are relevant to this question of whether the recognition–failure phenomenon of Tulving and Thomson ought to be assigned to the "homograph explanation"–that extralist cues in the free-association phase of the experiment elicit different words than those learned initially in the presence of experimenter-supplied weak cues (even though the two words involved happen to have the same spelling). Reder *et al.* (1974) reasoned that if they could find stimulus words, targets, that have only a single very unambiguous meaning, then according to the homograph interpretation the rate of recognition failure ought to be low; one may expect, for example, the word RHINOCEROS to have little diversity in possible encodings to start with and that therefore a strong cue eliciting this word in the course of free association is likely to tap the same interpretation as an original intralist cue, in the Tulving and Thomson (1973) paradigm. Reder *et al.* (1974), in contrast, expected high-frequency words, such as WATER, would be likely to arouse more diverse encoding responses and, to that extent, there might be recognition failures. The results were entirely consistent with this expectation: The rate of recognition failure, both the absolute rate and the rate relative to cued recall, was much higher with the high-frequency words than with the low-frequency words. The authors suggest, in line with the homograph explanation, that what is learned is a particular sense of a word (WATER as a verb meaning to sprinkle a lawn or as a chemical compound) and encoding is specific to that particular sense.

Presumably different senses of a common word would possess different nodes in semantic memory, or different logogens; otherwise, if the different senses overlapped in their permanent memory representation, it should be possible for subjects to cross over from one to another at the time of testing. Watkins and Tulving (1975) warn that according to this theory the number of nodes necessary in the semantic memory becomes unreasonably large. The number of permanent memory representations for words would be unreasonably large if not only outright homographs and clearly separable meanings were accorded separate semantic-memory representations, but also different shades of meaning got their own independent locations. Deciding among these alternatives is of course a matter of degree but a recent study by Barclay, Bransford, Franks, McCarrell, and Nitsch (1974) illustrates the problem, as follows.

Barclay *et al.* (1974) presented target words, such as PIANO, in the company of either of two acquisition sentences: (1) "The man lifted the PIANO" or (2) "The man tuned the PIANO." In a subsequent test of cued recall (not recognition) subjects received both (1) *something heavy* and (2) *something with a nice sound* at separated points during a long series of tests. The point of the experiment was that Acquisition Sentence 1 and Recall Cue 1 go together, conceptually, and the (2) materials go together in the same way, but combinations of (1) and (2) provide mismatches. The finding was that subjects who had received Acquisition Sentence 1 did much better with Recall Cue 1 than with Recall Cue 2 but subjects who had received Acquisition Sentence 2 had this order of cue effectiveness reversed. If one wishes to make the leap from this cued-recall test to the free-association plus recognition test of Tulving and Thomson (1973) the suggestion is, for example, that the word PIANO may have been unrecognizable in the context of *something heavy* if it has been studied in the context of *piano tuning*. What this study then tells us is that the specificity of encoding pertains not just to grossly different meanings of homographic items but to very highly specific aspects of the same meaning pattern. Nobody is likely to claim that the PIANO implied by piano tuning is a different node in semantic memory from the PIANO implied by lifting a piano. However, this argument against the homograph interpretation depends on the unproved assumption that if the Barclay *et al.* (1974) study were recast into exactly the Tulving and Thomson paradigm it would indeed show the phenomenon of recognition failure for the items resembling PIANO.

The problems raised in this section, on the encoding specificity principle, are the focus of intense activity and controversy at the time this book is being written. A summary would therefore be risky. However, perhaps all workers can agree that the concept of an event, such as a word, is stored in memory by the specific meaning assigned to it at the time of study. In long-term episodic memory, at least, the spelling, voice quality, color of ink, and intonation in which these word concepts are presented make little difference (but see Kolers, 1975). To retrieve such a word, contact needs to be made with the stored meaning rather than with another meaning that was not stored at the time of acquisition. Although the language of this statement is closest to that used by Tulving and his collaborators, it is quite easily paraphrased in the context of a two-stage generation and recognition model with the properties of that of Anderson and Bower (1974); the main contention seems to be the level of discourse (Martin, 1975) at which we decide to define the unit of generation and recognition: The graphemic unit (where IRON is a single entry) is clearly ruled out by the encoding specificity experiments. The meaning unit (with homographic words having multiple entries) is a comfortable level of analysis for the Anderson and Bower (1974) version of generation–recognition theory. However, additional demonstrations, such as the Barclay *et al.* (1974) study, might make the meaning an uncomfortable level of analysis if it turned out that encoding was specific to extremely subtle shades of meaning.

Perhaps even a more important boundary consideration on the encoding specificity principle is the matter of the cohesiveness of the encoding compound into which the target enters. It will be recalled that Horowitz and Manelis (1973) showed that individual elements of idioms (HOT DOG) could not be recognized as well as they could be recalled when the other member of the pair was used as the recall cue. In contrast, they observed that with simple adjective–noun phrases lacking idiomatic cohesiveness (HOT MEAL) recognition of elements was always better than cued recall of them. This prompts us to ask whether Tulving and his associates have consistently used idiomatic pairs in their study lists; if so, the phenomenon of recognition failure is predictable from the Horowitz and Manelis findings.

The answer is that Tulving and his associates have not used phrases that one could call idiomatic (such as HOT DOG); however, the Tulving group has consistently given subjects study lists (putative cues plus target words) in which there has been a weak but nonzero prior normative relation between the cue word and the target word. Antognini (1975) has demonstrated that use of such weak normative associates is by no means an irrelevant procedural detail. In his study there was a comparison between weak normative pairs presented on the acquisition list (*butter*–SMOOTH) and ostensibly unrelated cue–target pairs (*glue*–SHEEP). For our purposes the result was very clear: With the weakly related cue–target pairs exactly the result of Tulving and Thomson was obtained, in that recognition of items elicited in free association (such as the word SMOOTH elicited as a free associate to *rough*) was poorer than recall of the original targets elicited by their own original cues. With unrelated pairs, however, recognition was better than recall, in conflict with the Tulving–Thomson (1973) pattern of results (but of course, exactly as one would predict from an extrapolation of the Horowitz–Manelis, 1973, finding).

To generalize broadly, we may say that the evidential base for the encoding specificity principle is secure with materials containing some potential normative relationship but not with arbitrarily paired materials, according to both the Horowitz and Manelis (1973) and the Antognini (1975) evidence. Why does this factor make a difference? There seem to be three related possibilities: First, it may be that normatively weak associates contain some inadvertent idioms by the definition of Horowitz and Manelis (perhaps *buttersmooth*). Second, it is possible that subjects can employ some device, such as visual imagery (see Baker, Santa, and Lamwers, 1975), to idiomatize materials where there is a sort of normative "head start." Finally, if one wishes to adhere to the homograph interpretation in the context of generation–recognition models, the use of a weak normative cue may systematically bias the interpretation of a word toward its most subordinate meaning entry, insuring that when the dominant meaning entry is elicited by the strong cue there is a recognition failure.

Whatever the reason, the applicability of the encoding specificity principle to related word pairs and its possible inapplicability to unrelated word pairs is of very broad theoretical significance for our understanding of the process of association. It suggests that there are emergent, gestalt properties of highly cohesive associations that are lacking from more arbitrary associations. When items enter into such a cohesive gestalt they lose their individual identity, whereas when they enter into a less cohesive bond they retain their individual identity. The distinction is exactly the distinction between the "mental compounding" of James Mill and the "mental chemistry" of John Stuart Mill (see Chapter 12). What is significant for the psychology of learning is that somehow through repetition and elaborative processing the same materials may pass from compounding relationship to the chemical relationship. An individual muscular gesture, the process of tying a shoelace, may well, at first for a child, be a highly distinctive and accessible response, whereas later, for an adult, the same gesture may be totally inaccessible as a separate act by virtue of having become an element of a coordinated, highly cohesive response. This example leads directly to the next chapter, the subject of which is sequential organization.

SUMMARY

Although the most compelling examples of the retrieval process, in intuitive terms, come from the retrieval of information stored in secondary memory or of facts stored in semantic memory, still, the analysis of retrieval is just as necessary logically in such apparently simple situations as pattern recognition of alphabetic characters during reading and Sternberg's task of deciding whether a test stimulus was a member of a just-exposed positive set. The evidence from this latter research setting is most consistent with a model based on serial exhaustive scanning by means of some nonverbal code. However, such observations as (1) the possibility of directed search among items in categorized lists, and (2) serial-position effects with regard to the slope of the latency versus positive-set size function, plus others (S. Sternberg, 1975), all suggest some boundary conditions on the simple exhaustive model must emerge. This is as it should be, for a model with no known boundary conditions is in some respects uninformative.

The model of Atkinson and Juola serves to integrate the Sternberg memory-scanning paradigm with the more general problem of recognition. The general mechanism in their model is a sort of tagging notion in which the semantic-memory location corresponding to an item receives strength marking its occurrence in an episodic context (on a list). Only if this evidence, or familiarity, is inconclusive, according to the Atkinson–Juola model, does the subject resort to the serial-scanning mechanism. We saw the tagging and strength notions recurring, in one form or another, throughout later sections of the chapter, although not necessarily associated with one another.

There are fundamentally only two measures of retention, recognition and recall. The important issues surrounding the comparison of these two retrieval procedures are not which is inherently "better" but in what respects, if any, they are distinct theoretically. In addition to Sternberg's model of serial scanning, there are four major process models for recognition: The notion of tagging is not a particularly rich concept by itself because it leaves unexplained the nature of the tags and also the process of using tags during recognition. The strength or familiarity theory takes a step toward filling in both; it specifies that the tags in question are variable quantities of a single commodity and that these strength values are translated into performance through the machinery of statistical decision theory. It is important to note that the application of statistical decision theory to recognition, in general, does not commit one to the strength theory. Anderson and Bower, for example, specifically reject the strength notion yet they make full use of the decision model.

The third process model for recognition is the context-retrieval theory of Anderson and Bower. Actually, it and Tulving's encoding specificity theory are both general theories of retrieval that subsume the process of recognition. Anderson and Bower stress the association of context elements jointly with the word in question and with a representation of the crucial aspect of the learning episode (such as the representation of a list). In Tulving's theory the stress is on the communality of recognition with recall: In both the subject must combine information from a retrieval cue with specific stored information dating from the learning episode; neither the target item nor the context has an inherent advantage in reinstating this encoding episode.

Having disposed of strength–familiarity theory because it fails to allow for variables with opposite effects on recognition and recall, our choice of how to rationalize the difference between these two retrieval measures amounts to an opposition of the generation–recognition model elaborated by Anderson and Bower and the encoding specificity principle of Tulving and his associates. The Tulving group bases its case mainly on poor performance (either recall or recognition) under conditions in which a strong retrieval cue is employed to probe for a word studied in the company of some different cue. This poor performance can easily be accommodated by a generation–recognition theory that assumes the nodes at which recognition information resides are specific to particular meanings of items and perhaps even to shades of meanings of items. The matter turns on how specific the representations held in these nodes ought to be. If there are different nodes for different shades of meaning the main character and attractiveness of generation–recognition models is sacrificed— specifically, the notion of tracing paths through an organized semantic memory and then retracing these paths for a recognition check, at retrieval, is lost if there are a couple of dozen nodes for a word, such as PIANO, each leading to multiple representations of other words, and so on.

The Tulving group, in contrast, has concentrated less on a process explanation of the retrieval-failure phenomenon than on its apparent inconsistency with early versions of generation–recognition theories. Perhaps workers from both points of view will do better to concentrate on why these cases of poor recognition or recall with strong extralist cues occur with stimuli studied in potential gestaltlike contexts and not those studied in arbitrary contexts. In any case, there can be no doubt that the processes of retrieval, long a neglected aspect of the acquisition–retention–retrieval trichotomy, has become in recent years the occasion for the posing of very basic issues in learning and memory.

12
Serial Organization in Learning and Memory

Learning is often not so much a matter of acquiring new behavior as it is a matter of organizing previously acquired behavior into new sequences. The point would be impossible to prove, but it is reasonable that truly new situations and truly new responses seldom occur once people are past childhood. Searching for exceptions to this generalization is instructive: A Westerner being served a new Oriental spice, an adult learning to feel, through proprioception, the unique wrist action associated with violin vibrato, a behavior-therapy client receiving a mild shock associated with photographs of some fetish object—these examples are so rare as to be exceptions that prove the rule. Furthermore, it is notable that these exceptions are all taken from situations far removed from the "higher mental processes;" we may be even more categorical in claiming that the rational, symbolic behavior which is relatively distinctive in humans is based almost entirely on novel rearrangements of familiar elements. Although it makes little difference to the analysis of human cognition, the same generalization on the rarity of truly new learning may apply to lower animals, at least when they are in their natural setting rather than in psychologists' laboratories.

HISTORICAL BACKGROUND

In the analysis of serial learning, more than in any other research area, experimental psychology is in contact with its ancient and recent historical roots. This is because theoretical accounts of serial learning have always taken as their point of departure the old philosophical problem of the *association of ideas*. The pivotal figure in joining the scientific method to the associationistic philosophical tradition was Hermann Ebbinghaus (1850–1909) but we shall have a glance at philosophical associationism before we cover Ebbinghaus.

Philosophical Associationism

One obvious phenomenological property of thought is its seriality and since ancient times philosophers, who owned the problem of thought until psychology became a viable discipline, have tried to rationalize the orderliness of thought through some principle of association of ideas. Good accounts of this aspect of associationism in the histories of philosophy and psychology may be found in Boring (1950), Robinson (1932), and Anderson and Bower (1973); here we pause only long enough to suggest the bare outline.

Aristotle identified three laws of association, in effect, three laws of learning—similarity, contrast, and contiguity, where contiguity included both spatial and temporal adjacency. (An additional law, *repetition,* can be seen as a special case of contiguity.) The next development of interest for us was not until 2000 years later, the emergence of the nineteenth-century British empiricist school. The empiricists, like Aristotle and most others, considered the idea to be the basic unit of thought; however, they rejected the nativist view, articulated by Plato and Descartes, that ideas were inborn in favor of the proposition that ideas were built up from experience (hence the term "empiricist").

James Mill (1773–1836) made one of the most systematic statements of the empiricist position. He divided mental content into two basic elements—sensations, which derived from external stimulation, and ideas, which were copies of sensations capable of being elicited internally. The association of ideas was mainly a result of contiguity, in time, of the sensations from which they were derived, as with the sight and sound of a trumpet or the succession of sounds of words in a prayer. There were three criteria for the strength of associations: permanence, which we would now term resistance to forgetting; certainty, which we would now call confidence and measure with rating scales; and spontaneity, which would correspond to our own measure of latency or reaction time. There were two antecedent conditions of association: frequency, which neither philosophers nor psychologists have been able to do without (although as we have seen in Chapter 6 the role of sheer frequency has been challenged); and vividness, which we would now be inclined to reject if the finding by Neisser and Kerr (1973) cited in Chapter 5 proves replicable. These laws of association were in effect the blueprints for a field of experimental investigation and, as we shall see presently, Ebbinghaus brought them into the laboratory.

While we are at it, however, it is useful to devote a few more remarks to British empiricism, because we find other interesting antecedents. The other major concern of James Mill, besides the laws for formation and strength of associations, was how simple ideas get combined into complex ideas. His notion was one of *mental compounding,* where the complex idea was unitary but made up of a conglomerate of simple ideas. The idea APPLE, for example, would be a conglomerate of associations among such ideas as RED, TREE, STEM, TART TASTE, PIE, CORE, and so on. Each of these subideas would be associated to the name APPLE and each would be called to mind by the complex idea and, possibly, by each other.

James Mill's son, John Stuart Mill (1806–1873) accepted much of his father's doctrine and his laws for association were only slightly different; however, he made a major departure on the nature of complex ideas. The younger Mill's idea on combination rules for simple ideas was *mental chemistry,* a term for a complex idea that originally derived from constituent simple ideas but which was qualitatively different from the sum of the simple constituents. By analogy, for example, water does not resemble either hydrogen or oxygen particularly, and a house can easily be imagined without specifically thinking of bricks or mortar. The opposition between mental compounding and mental chemistry has little to do with serial learning but it is prophetic of a whole class of theoretical controversy in the 1970s—the encoding specificity principle of Tulving (see Chapter 11 of this book). Tulving's position and that of Horowitz and Manelis are quite similar to John Stuart Mill's in that the association of two ideas results in a unique combination that may render the constituents unrecognizable by themselves.

The contributions of Ebbinghaus.   The encroachment of psychology into this branch of philosophy may be understood in reference to the old distinction between sensation and ideas: Weber, Fechner, and the other psychophysicists applied the methods of natural science to the study of sensations, whereas Ebbinghaus singlehandedly applied these same methods to the study of ideas.

Ebbinghaus received his doctoral degree at Bonn in philosophy at the age of 23, having had time off in the meantime to serve in the Franco-Prussian War. His next 7 years were spent in travel and a program of independent postdoctoral study which was absolutely crucial from the standpoint of his later activities: During this period he learned of Fechner's work, while in Paris, and he studied the British empiricist philosophers in England. Returning to Germany, he undertook the experiments on memory between 1879 and 1884, publishing the results in his magnificent 1885 book, *Memory: A Contribution to Experimental Psychology* (1964). He turned later in his career to research on vision and color perception; however, in the various editions of his textbook, *Grundzüge der Psychologie* (original publication in 1902), he had a good deal to say about memory, including reports of unpublished work of his own and also comments on the small experimental literature that had developed to that point. His students and theirs carried on the memory work in an unbroken arborization of intellectual genealogy that includes most of the scientists whose work is cited in this book.

It is quite clear that Ebbinghaus meant by the term *memory* the acquisition as well as the retention and retrieval stages of our modern trichotomy. His method included arranging artificial verbal materials, nonsense syllables, into serial lists and reading them to the beat of a metronome until they seemed just on the verge of being learned; then, he would look away from the sheet on which the entire list was printed, and try to recite the list. The measure of learning was the amount of time it took to reach this criterion. The measure of memory, following some lapse in time, was the percentage of this time saved in relearning the same material. As everyone knows, he himself was the only subject in this research. Rather than attempt a comprehensive review of the 1885 book here, we shall simply list some of the areas in which Ebbinghaus deserves priority:

1. As pointed out above, he was the first to undertake the systematic empirical study of learning and memory, in 1879. This same date places him among the pioneers of experimental psychology generally for it was in the same year that Wundt founded the first laboratory for experimental psychology.

2. He devised a system for constructing pronounceable syllables without meaning; these nonsense syllables, consonant–vowel–consonant combinations, were the major materials used in his experiments, although he also tried using words, numbers, and poetry. Many sources, especially introductory textbooks, harp on the invention of the nonsense syllable as if it were something approaching the invention of the wheel in importance, but in fact the nonsense syllable and using himself as the sole subject—the other widely noted fact about Ebbinghaus—are two of the least important contributions on this list in terms of their significance for the science of psychology.

3. With the possible exception of the psychophysicists, he was the first psychologist to understand error of measurement, distributions of observations about a mean value, and the idea that any difference between experimental conditions must be evaluated jointly against the size of the difference and the amount of error variability associated with the means. Boring (1950) reports that the second chapter of *Memory* was used for some years simply as a statistics source for psychology students.

4. After the Weber–Fechner psychophysical law, Ebbinghaus was responsible for the first mathematical model applied in psychology—his formulation of the logarithmic relation between savings and the passage of time since learning, the forgetting curve.

5. In the last chapter of *Memory* Ebbinghaus reported the first experiment in psychology, in the sense of deriving a testable implication from some theory and evaluating that implication as a hypothesis for differences among specially designed experimental and control groups. The German philosopher Herbart had expressed the notion that in a series of ideas there are not only associations between adjacent elements—the basic forward chain that leads through the series in an orderly manner—but also associations between elements that occupy nonadjacent, or remote, positions, say, between the third and seventh items. Ebbinghaus designed an experiment to test this hypothesis: He reasoned that

one could check on the existence of remote associations by learning two lists in succession, the second derived from the first.

If, in the course of learning the sequence $A-B-C-D-E-F-G-H-\cdots$, there are indeed associations being formed between such remote pairs as A and C, B and D, C and E, and so on, then a second list of the form $A-C-E-G-I-\cdots$ should be relatively easy to learn. Relative to what? There were two comparisons of importance. One was among conditions where the size of the gaps skipped in deriving the second list from the first was varied; the comparison would therefore be between a list with only one item skipped, $A-C-E-\cdots$, and a list with two skipped, $A-D-G-J-\cdots$, or three skipped, $A-E-I-M-\cdots$. This comparison tests for the possibility that the strength of remote associations is related to how remote they are. The other comparison of interest is between lists derived in the manner explained and a control condition in which the first and last syllables were retained as in the original list but the others drawn in random order. The results of the experiment were expressed in savings—how much more rapidly it was possible to learn a derived list than the corresponding original list. In the major part of the experiment Ebbinghaus learned 55 pairs of lists and in supplementary comparisons for the same experiment he learned an additional 44 pairs. The results confirmed the hypothesis. All conditions with regularly derived lists resulted in more savings than the random-order control and the closer the remote association being tested the greater the savings.

6. One aspect of this derived list experiment deserves separate mention in that it is the first appearance of the *logic of transfer* in learning research—the idea that we can find out what has been learned in a particular task, indirectly, by examining the effects of that first task on some specially designed second task. As Kausler (1974, p. 250) has noted perceptively, Ebbinghaus was sensitive to the need for special control conditions for the evaluation of specific transfer effects. In the derived-list experiment he anticipated the problem of separating response familiarization per se from specific sequential transfer effects by including the control condition with random linkages from the first list.

7. The same experiment shows his sensitivity to another problem in experimentation—what we now call *demand characteristics* of a task. He worried that while learning the transfer lists in the various conditions of his study, he would be consciously aware, also, of the particular condition under test and of its predicted difficulty according to the hypothesis. To measure the extent of this possible bias, he developed a parallel set of conditions in which, through a coding system, he eliminated this potential artifact. As it turned out there was not any difference, but the double-blind logic shows his highly refined sense for sources of experimental error.

8. Finally, some mention must be made of his remarkable writing style in *Memory*. In this respect he resembles not the overpoweringly turgid and rambling style of early German psychological literature, which followed him

closely in time, but rather he anticipates the crisp, pointed style of modern journal writing. For the book overall, and for individual research reports within it, Ebbinghaus follows the convention of first setting the problem and then dealing, in order, with the method for addressing that problem, the results generated by the method, and the probable meaning of the results in terms of the original hypotheses.

Ebbinghaus' theory.   So massive has been the authority of Ebbinghaus to subsequent workers that a review of his theory of serial verbal learning here will serve to set the stage for developments that did not occur until the 1960s. The basic principle of serial learning according to Ebbinghaus was that everything in the list became associated with everything else, subject to two qualifications: First, the strength of an association between two list items varied inversely with their degree of remoteness, that is, with how far apart they were in the series. Second, forward associations, for a particular degree of remoteness, were stronger than backward associations. From these qualifications it is clear that the basic mechanism that permits learning of a serial ordering is the formation of associations linking adjacent items in the forward direction. For a series, $A-B-C-D-E-F-G-\cdots N$, the links would be $A-B$, $B-C$, $C-D$, and so on. This *chaining hypothesis* was hardly considered hypothetical at all; it was (at least to most investigators) self-evidently true between the time of Ebbinghaus and recent times, when R. K. Young (1959) and others reopened the case.

Although the chaining hypothesis was accepted uncritically, still, the Ebbinghaus position on remote associations was not, and it is clear that he, too, thought remote associations were far more interesting that direct ones. The original derived list experiments were properly criticized on methodological grounds. For one thing, Ebbinghaus had used the method of whole presentation, in which all items appear on a sheet and the subject reads then in order. The serious danger was that he had inadvertantly swept his eyes between two items from remote list positions, making spatially noncontiguous items contiguous in terms of time so as to facilitate their acquisition on a subsequent derived list. Even more serious was the objection raised by Slamecka (1964) to Ebbinghaus' procedure of skipping a regular number of items when deriving a second list from an original one. Regular skipping means that the size of the gap separating remote associations to be tested in the derived list was always the same. With a regularity of this sort the possibility exists that the subject can discover the rule for derivation and use the first list to mediate acquisition of the second list. In an experiment of his own, Slamecka compared the Ebbinghaus procedure with one in which the *average* degree of remoteness on a derived list was set but the number of items skipped in deriving the second list from the first was variable, producing an irregular pattern; with this new procedure subjects did not show positive transfer.

There have been other techniques, besides the derived-list design, to establish the reality of remote associations. A thorough review of these is available (McGeoch, 1942, pp. 85–89). One method is just to take note of the errors subjects make in serial anticipation learning, a procedure in which each item is presented in order with the subject set to pronounce the next item; when items from the list are pronounced at the wrong time, they tend to be from a nearby position on the list and more often from a subsequent portion of the list (as would be expected from forward remote associations) than from a previous part of the list (as would be expected from backward remote associations). The same gradients of remote forward and backward associations occur when a single item is presented, after learning of a serial list, for spontaneous associations with other list items. However these methods have also been subject to a piercing critique by Slamecka (1964) and although some have undertaken to patch up the doctrine of remote associations (Bugelski, 1965; Dallett, 1965b), the current status of the issue is at best ambiguous. One problem is that the question has been out of fashion recently and little new evidence has accumulated since the Slamecka paper.

Our survey of the current state of theory concerning serial learning is organized around two issues. The first is the basic problem of what gets learned in serial learning and the second is the interpretation of the serial-position curve.

WHAT IS LEARNED IN SERIAL LEARNING?

Although it is true that theories are sometimes affected by new evidence, it is at least equally true that the nature of the evidence that can be collected is determined by the theoretical background of the research. The latter point is most particularly illustrated by the type of task that is chosen for experimentation. It is no accident that, over the years, there have been changes in theoretical fashions accompanied by changes in which tasks are most popular. In recent years, for example, the free-recall methodology has become popular in conjunction with interest in organizational processes in memory, which, it will be recalled from Chapter 10, are almost exclusively measured through recall order. During the long ascendancy of Ebbinghaus early in the twentieth century, it was the serial-learning task that was generally agreed to provide the quickest route to the truth. However, as theorists grappled with problems of interference and similarity in the 1940s, the serial methodology gave way to paired-associate learning. There was a perfectly logical reason: Although a stimulus–response analysis of serial learning was almost universally accepted, each item in the list serving both as a stimulus for the next item and as a response for the previous item, the stimuli and responses could not be manipulated independently of one another in an experiment. With paired-associate learning, however, stimulus and response similarity could easily be manipulated independently. For the research period that culminated in the Osgood transfer and retroaction surface (see Chapter 1 of this book) and in the interference theory of forgetting (see Chapter 8), therefore, serial learning took a back seat.

Theories of Serial Learning Based on Paired-Associate Learning

The conventional view of serial learning, still widely held, is that it can be analyzed into a paired-associate task where each list item is the response term of some pair. The major theoretical puzzle is finding out what the corresponding stimulus terms are. This presumption is shared by a group of formulations that has emerged from the first serious skepticism directed at Ebbinghaus's theory.

The chaining hypothesis. A set of experiments by R. K. Young (1959; see a detailed summary of this research in R. K. Young, 1968) disturbed the benign neglect in which serial-learning theory was held during what might be called the paired-associate age (1935–1960). Young's main experiment was actually a departure from conditions investigated by Primoff (1938); however, the earlier study had been ignored almost totally during the intervening years. The experimental compairson that Young offered was obvious and elegant, elegant by virtue of simplicity much in the same manner of the Slamecka (1968) paradigm for testing independence of storage in free-recall learning. If indeed when a subject learns a series $A-B-C-D-E-F- \cdots$ he is learning chained forward associations of the sort $A-B, B-C, C-D, D-E$, and so on, then once the list has been learned there ought to be perfect transfer to a *derived paired-associate* list with members $A-B, B-C, C-D$, and so on. The outcome of the experiment, repeated with extreme care on numerous occasions in Young's early papers, was that far from perfect positive transfer transfer was essentially zero! Although there had been facilitation on the first few trials of derived-list learning, the number of trials to reach a criterion of errorless performance was no lower for an experimental group given pairs of items from adjacent serial-list positions than for an appropriate control group.

The failure of transfer from serial to derived paired-associate lists was the topic of considerable research in the early and middle 1960s. As with any other research problem there were numerous refinements, methodological and conceptual, that attached to the growing literature. However, many of these refinements are quite specific to the experimental paradigms being used and they probably have little importance for the general problem of seriality in learning. One example illustrates how far experimenters have been willing to go in order to produce the Ebbinghaus result: Jensen (1962), himself greatly less committed to the chaining hypothesis than most workers at the time, pulled out all the stops in an effort to produce positive transfer. He (1) carried learning on the prior serial list to an overlearning criterion of three perfect trials; (2) took only four pairs of adjacent items over into the derived paired-associate list, a given item serving only once; (3) instructed subjects on the experimental design, the theoretical objectives of the research, and told them deliberately to transfer the serial-learning associations to paired-associate learning; and (4) gave them un-limited anticipation time during paired-associate learning. Still, there was only about 50% transfer—much less than one would have expected if the main component of serial learning were chaining.

We shall not review the vicissitudes of the chaining hypothesis through the 1960s here. The major problem was a confusion between the theoretical issue and the empirical issue. The theoretical issue was whether chained associations were formed during serial learning and the empirical issue was whether there would be positive transfer in trials to criterion in a paired-associate list derived appropriately from a prior serial list. As Postman (1968) has observed, the difficulty with trials to criterion as a performance measure is that it measures the time required to learn the most difficult pair on the list. With more sensitive measures of paired-associate performance the outcome is different. For one thing, as we have already seen, Young did obtain positive transfer in perfor-mance on early trials of serial paired-associate list learning. An experiment by Crowder (1968c) shows transfer, of the sort predicted by Ebbinghaus, in another paired-associate task—the continuous paired-associate method of Peterson et al. (1962).

In continuous paired-associate learning, as we saw in Chapter 9, there is an uninterrupted stream of presentation and test episodes, each lasting a few seconds, where a given pair is presented only once and then, after a variable lag, tested once through the presentation of its stimulus term alone. For example, a typical series would be $A–B, C–D, E–F, C–?, G–H, A–?, I–J, K–L, M–N, I–?, E–?, \ldots$, with several different lags imposed between the presentation and testing of the various pairs. Crowder (1968c) used the continuous paired-associate learning task as a transfer instrument for subjects who had just learned a serial list. If we denote the prior serial list by the usual sequence, $A–B–C–D–E–F–\cdots$, then the illustrative transfer pairs from above can serve as examples of what the adjacent group received in the second phase of the study. The nonadjacent group received the same items as the adjacent group but their pairs on the second task were from deliberately selected nonadjacent positions on the prior serial list, such as $A–I, B–L, C–K$, and so on. Within these two groups, adjacent and nonadjacent, there was a further subdivision according to the degree of learning required on the prior serial tasks; one pair of groups had only four trials, whereas the other had 12. So far, therefore, the experiment is a two by two design with adjacency and degree of prior learning the factors. An additional control group was tested, however, with a serial-learning task containing items *unrelated* to the subsequent paired-associate task. This group was to control for the possibility of nonspecific transfer effects and to determine whether negative transfer could be obtained in the nonadjacent groups.

The results of the Crowder (1968c) study are shown in Figure 12.1. The outcome was simple and clear: Both adjacent groups showed positive transfer and the nonadjacent groups showed negative transfer, with the amount of each related to the degree of prior serial learning. The control group was intermediate. Furthermore, there was, for the two adjacent groups, a positive correlation, across subjects, between the serial and paired-associate tasks, in terms of number of correct responses; however, for the nonadjacent groups there was not such a correlation. It would be tempting to speculate that if Young had used a more sensitive transfer measure than trials to criterion the entire controversy about "the stimulus" in serial verbal learning would have been avoided.

However, although we can now see that the evidence for chaining is abundant (see also Postman & Stark, 1967), it was not at all evident that this was the case following the initial transfer experiments, and therefore several alternative theories were devised. The main alternative to chaining was agreed to be the *serial-position hypothesis,* which states that each item in the serial list becomes associated with some representation of the position it occupies in the list. However there were variations on the basic opposition between chaining and position associations, including (1) the idea that two or more items in the list act as the stimulus for the following item, the *compound-stimulus hypothesis* (R. K. Young, 1962); (2) the compromise hypothesis that both chaining and serial-position associations are formed, with the chaining occurring for the outside portions of the list and the positional associations occurring for the internal portions (R. K. Young, Patterson, and Benson, 1963); and (3) the opposite

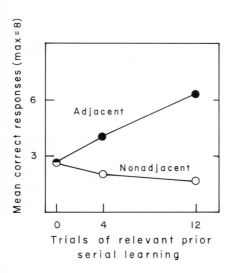

FIGURE 12.1 Mean correct responses in derived continuous paired-associate learning as a function of condition and degree of prior relevant serial learning. (After Crowder, 1968c.)

compromise hypothesis that both chaining and serial position links, with positional associations outside and chaining inside, are formed (Ebenholtz, 1963). Rather than weave through these variations on the chaining hypothesis, we shall turn to the major alternative, serial-position associations.

The serial-position hypothesis. The idea that a serial ordering can be learned by associating each item with some representation of its position rather than with the preceeding item is not actually new at all but extends back at least to a discussion in Ladd and Woodworth (1911, pp. 578–579). The ancestry usually cited for this idea is a mimeographed text by Woodworth and Poffenberger (1920, pp. 71–72) where the endorsed view is actually a combination hypothesis with chaining occurring at the interior positions of the list and serial-position associations on the outside positions. It is obvious, in any case, that obedience to the chaining doctrine was not absolute in the early years of our science.

There are several versions of what is meant by a position association, depending on whether the positional stimulus is an absolute number corresponding to locations in the list or, rather, some relative representation of position. Woodworth and Poffenberger thought that subjects would be unable to keep track of absolute positions in the middle of the list and that is why they adopted a chaining hypothesis for these items.

Several early studies gave evidence lending plausibility to the serial-position hypothesis. Melton and Irwin (1940) had parenthetically reported evidence supporting some such process in transfer between two unrelated serial lists: They observed that when an intrusion error from the first list was made on the second of two lists it was, more often than would be expected by chance, the item that had occupied the same position on the prior list; because the items on the lists were different, these serial-order intrusions were quite hard to rationalize on the basis of a simple chaining hypothesis (see also Fuchs & Melton, 1974).

In 1955 Schulz reported a study in which subjects were taught serial lists and then, after achieving some criterion, were given single items from the list and asked to identify the numerical position these items had occupied in the list. They were able to do this better than chance, although the degree of prior serial learning did not enhance performance as it should have if position associations were the basic underlying mechanism for serial learning. Schulz found also that performance at this backward position-identification task was better at the beginning and end of the list than in the middle, an important finding as it' allowed a ready explanation of the bowed serial-position curve.

Some of the best evidence for the serial-position hypothesis came from the research of Ebenholtz. In one of his studies (Ebenholtz, 1963; see also a review in Ebenholtz, 1972) there were three conditions in each of which a serial list was derived from a common prior serial list. The conditions are shown in Table 12.1. The letters *A*, *B*,. . . stand for items that have occurred on the common prior list

TABLE 12.1
Conditions in the Ebenholtz Experiment[a]

Prior serial list:	A	B	C	D	E	F	G	H	I	J	K · · ·
Derived serial lists:											
Coordinate	X	B	X	D	X	F	X	H	X	J	X · · ·
Disparate	X	H	X	J	X	L	X	B	X	D	X · · ·
Control	X	X	X	X	X	X	X	X	X	X	X · · ·

[a]After Ebenholtz (1963).

and the X's stand for filler items unrelated to the first list. The *control* condition has entirely new items on the transfer list and is therefore a baseline condition. The two conditions of interest, *coordinate* and *disparate,* should be almost equally favored according to the chaining hypothesis, because in each there are forward associations of just the same degree of remoteness, one item skipped (four for the coordinate and three for the disparate). However, if there is any merit to the serial-position hypothesis, then performance should be better in the coordinate than in the disparate condition because any particular transferred item occurs in its old serial position in the coordinate condition but in a far-removed serial position in the disparate condition. The result favored the serial-position hypothesis in that the coordinate condition produced clearly superior performance to the other two conditions, which did not themselves differ.

What we have been calling the serial-position hypothesis is probably best considered a class of propositions with something in common. One version, which some investigators have explicitly had in mind (Young, Hakes, & Hicks, 1967), states that serial learning is in fact a form of paired-associate learning where the stimulus terms for each item is the number representing its position in the list. A second version is that associations occur between items and some sort of relative positional cue, such as "next to the last" or "item before LEGEND" or "third item after start." These relative positional cues are left rather vague. They depend, however, on the concept of anchor points in serial learning (Glanzer & Peters, 1962): Ordinarily the first and last items are the most prominent anchor points. However, some unusually conspicuous item in the interior of the list can serve as an additional anchor, relative to which position new items can be added on successive trials. The superior performance on a built-in conspicuous item, itself, was discovered by von Restorff (1933) and is a natural consequence of the serial-position hypothesis. Murdock (1960a) proposed a theory holding that acquisition of items on a list was a function of the distinctiveness of their positions in the list; we shall have another look at Murdock's theory in the section of this chapter on the serial-position effect.

A third formulation of the serial-position hypothesis is based on a transformation between time and space. The time, or ordinality, dimension that defines the order of items in the list may be recoded, one-to-one, into an absolute or a relative spatial dimension. Although many of the workers in the field have apparently used these possibilities interchangeably, the temporal and spatial position dimensions, they have different implications in some cases. It is of course true that if the spatial representations we are starting to consider are simply numbered slots (fifth, sixth), or verbal descriptions of positions ("third from left" and so on) then absolutely nothing has been gained. If the spatial dimension more readily permits the use of *visual imagery,* however, then if we are to believe the message of Chapter 5 there can be important gains in performance. It must remain a matter for experimentation and analysis whether subjects normally make a transform into imaginal visual coding, but we know that if they are exhorted to do so by instructions their performance is enhanced, for, after all, the classic method of loci (see Chapter 5) is nothing more than a systematic application of the spatial-position mechanism where a well-learned list of very distinctive locations is, by previous learning, easily available to the subject. Bower (1971) has proposed that people develop a transsituational concept of "position within a linearly ordered series;" new serial arrays are then related to this abstract representation.

Objections to the paired-associate analysis of serial learning. The controversy that we have been examining, which has produced the chaining, serial-position, and compound-stimulus hypotheses, has been clearly circumscribed by a common underlying assumption that is seldom itself the subject of interest. That assumption is that there is really no such thing as serial learning and that the job of theory is to find exactly in what way serial learning is really nothing but a special case of paired-associate learning. Therefore, there was much talk of finding the so-called "functional stimulus" in serial learning, the nominal stimulus being the previous item, in the anticipation method, and the response being the item to be anticipated. Shared by the chaining and position hypotheses, and by variants on them, is the proposition that utterance of a single list item in anticipation learning or in some other method is the response and that the significant task for theory is reconstruction of what stimulus event elicits that response. The issue that we can now see to be of overriding importance in serial learning is whether to retain this stimulus—response view.

One reaction is to piece together a more adequate but more complicated stimulus—response theory, including such modulating factors as subjects' differential tendencies to select positional or sequential stimulus dimensions (Shuell & Keppel, 1967). Another reaction is to contemplate the more radical possibility that serial learning is not best described as an individual stimulus—response process at all, at least not a stimulus—response process where the response is isomorphic to the individual item to be learned. In the next sections we shall sketch three such alternatives, after a set of preliminary, nonevidential arguments.

Language, Skill, and Lashley

Unswerving loyalty to the anticipation method of serial verbal learning was an important factor in the long dominance of stimulus—response analysis although it would be hard to say whether the relationship was causal or consequential. Other varieties of sequential behavior might have suggested other models. A landmark paper by Lashley (1951) called "The problem of serial order in behavior" made exactly that point, with particular reliance on examples from language, speech, and skilled performance. This was, incidentally, the kind of landmark seen only in the rearview mirror—it was only years later, when cognitive, information-processing modes of theory were replacing stimulus—response analysis, that Lashley's paper received classic status; it was largely ignored by those in search of the functional stimulus in the early 1960s.

Lashley argued that the elementary units of language enter into so many different regroupings and reorderings, depending on the context, that language use could not depend on chained associations; there would just have to be too many associations and they would have to connect nearly all possible combinations. This is true whether the letter or the word is chosen as the elementary unit and Lashley concluded that there must be some higher level of organization which controls order in serial behavior. Another example is the ease of learning Piglatin, which is a system for fundamental reordering of sounds within words: If the new sound pattern for each word must be learned through individual chained associations, it should surely be harder than it is to learn Piglatin. However, it should be an easy task if one accepts that Piglatin represents the application of a perfectly simple abstract rule governing the order of sounds within a word. Lashley found evidence for rule-governed seriality in speech errors and typing mistakes; for example, the misplacement of a double letter—t-h-s-e-s rather than t-h-e-s-e—could be taken to suggest some kind of abstract letter-doubling instruction in the commands for spelling words, beyond the connections between each letter and its neighbor or the connection of each letter to its location within a word.

The same objections to stimulus—response theory as a model for language behavior, particularly the phenomena associated with syntax, were raised by linguists years later, after the Chomskian revolution (see Bever, Fodor, & Garret, 1968, for a particularly closely reasoned brief) but the issue is not even now settled to everyone's satisfaction (Halwes & Jenkins, 1971; Wickelgren, 1969b).

Lashley drew also on examples from human skill to discredit the chaining hypothesis for serial behavior; his points tell against a position-association theory as well. It is just preposterous to maintain that two individual notes in a sweeping arpeggio played on the piano are connected to some representation of a serial position in the sequence. Likewise, the coordinated twists and somersaults that go into a complicated performance in exhibition high diving seem incompatible with a model where elementary movements are related to the whole entirely through individual associations. Situations of this sort seem instead to require a theory that has two levels of organization. The simplest elementary responses are organized into intermediate units—in the piano arpeggio a "handful" of notes with a constant hand position, and in the exhibition dive, a particular trunk twist. These intermediate units are then organized into the proper sequence themselves, even though they are also divisible into still more elementary units. Lashley mentioned the various gaits of a horse, in which, again, there are quite similar elementary responses of leg muscles organized and ordered differently depending on whether one or another type of pacing is required. In the language of computers, the intermediate level of organization corresponds to *subroutines,* packages of commands, themselves divisible into elements, but which may also be rearranged and reorganized.

Lashley was apologetic about the inchoate flavor of his own ideas on serial order, having rejected the chaining doctrine. He suggested that a new approach to serial order could be found in a joint consideration of spatial and temporal organization. If memories are arrayed spatially then they must be scanned in some order to be activated in behavior. This scanning process could provide more flexibility in order than a more fixed chaining mechanism. It is more important to understand what Lashley is rejecting than to ponder how his temporal–spatial system may work. The objection is to any theory of serial order where the unit of theoretical analysis is restricted to the elementary response unit, on the piano the note or in speech the word. This restriction of analysis has been termed the "terminal meta-postulate" by Bever *et al.* (1968) and it is analyzed with great care by Anderson and Bower (1973, pp. 12–15). There is no room in such theories either for rule-governed ordering, as in Piglatin, or for subroutines, as in diving.

States of skill acquisition.   Our examples of skilled performance have been taken from the very highest levels of proficiency and this is by no means an accident. What about the eight year old painfully picking out an arpeggio note by note or the athlete first trying out a new routine? Or take tying a shoelace as exemplifying a complex skill—does the same theory do an equally adequate job in describing the first few awkward efforts as it does in describing the totally unconscious and expert process in the adult? Fitts (1964) has identified three stages in acquisition of skills, although different skills may place more or less emphasis on each of the three stages. First, it is necessary to establish an appropriate *cognitive set,* a conception of what constitutes the goal and how, in principle, it is accomplished. Another term for this first stage may be the "instructional stage," because it is best communicated verbally. Second, Fitts has suggested there is a stage of *stimulus–response associations,* a deliberate conscious phase in which the individual actions are carried out, usually slowly, and usually with concomitant verbal mediation. Here, the new golfer is slowly, carefully raising his club, saying to himself, ". . . eye on the ball, left arm straight, right elbow to the ribs, left knee flexed . . ." and so on. Depending on whether we define the unit of analysis in terms of molecular units or more global subroutines the Aristotelian–Ebbinghausian model may apply at this stage. The third stage of skill acquisition identified by Fitts is the *automatization* stage, when performance of the individual elements of the behavior becomes unconscious and does not require attention. Evidence for automatization comes from experiments in which two tasks are combined and it is shown that the interfering effect of one on another disappears when high degrees of practice are reached (Bahrick, Noble, & Fitts, 1954; Crowder, 1967b; LaBerge & Samuels, 1974).

The relevance of this three-stage analysis of skill learning should be clear. It may be that for serial ordering in general we need different theoretical models to apply to the early stages from those that apply to the later stages. Some data of Fleishman and Hempel (1956) show that this is a very likely possibility. Fleishman and Hempel were interested in how an extensive battery of very specialized skills, each measured with its own standardized test, would be predictive of overall performance on a highly complex skill—a complex timed discrimination task. Their findings were expressed in terms of the statistical weights assigned to each subskill in predicting the complex skill through multiple correlation. The major result of importance was that the relative weights changed drastically as a function of practice on the complex skill; early in practice, for example, verbal memory and spatial relations were good predictors of performance on the complex skill, whereas late in practice it was various measures of speed that accounted for most variance.

In the verbal-learning laboratory the subject almost never has a chance to progress to the final stage of skill learning—the level at which we can recite the Pledge of Allegiance, the months of the year, or the letters of the alphabet. Performance is instead abruptly terminated once some minimal criterion of accuracy and speed is achieved. This criterion usually represents a Stage-two proficiency, in terms of the Fitts analysis. However, even though measures of percent correct necessarily fail to show improvement after achievement of the typical accuracy criterion, we know (Peterson, 1965) that continued practice in verbal learning leads to steady gains in response speed even long after errors have ceased. It would probably not be difficult to demonstrate automatization in recitation of the alphabet, that is, to demonstrate that adults can recite the alphabet while they are performing some other cognitive task with no appreciable loss to performance on either task. Naturally, nothing like this state of proficiency is reached in laboratory serial-learning experiments. However, the transition between stages would not be abrupt and one might expect some regions of a list—particularly those areas favored by the serial-position effect—to show properties of advanced skills, whereas other regions of the list might still be governed by individual deliberate associations. By this view, which is eclectic almost to the point of promiscuity, not only is the quest for the functional stimulus futile, but even the effort to decide whether, in principle, a stimulus–response associative theory can or cannot explain serial learning is futile.

This ultimate futility need not have a paralytic effect on research, however; the range of theoretical machinery available to psychologists has been greatly extended by the evolution of models that go beyond stimulus–response associationism. What we have just been explaining, about how stages of serial skill learning may require different theoretical models, is that none of these newer conceptions is likely to be a panacea. In fact, models that violate the terminal meta-postulate by employing theoretical units different from the terminal response units (usually a word or syllable) have not proved simple to test. However predictions have been generated in certain cases and it should, in fairness, be held in mind that the chaining hypothesis has survived for generations on very little other than faith.

The theoretical positions we shall now review separate into two groups. The two groups share a major assumption about the structure of serial memory but they differ on the functional laws within these structures. The shared assumption about memory structure is that of a nested hierarchy, as shown in Figure 12.2. It is useful to risk repetition at this point in order to emphasize how the nested-hierarchy structure is a complete break with all stimulus–response associative theories from Aristotle through Ebbinghaus, right down to the subtlest compound-stimulus hypothesis devised by Young and his group. In the structure shown in Figure 12.2 there are intermediate levels of organization that participate, as units, in the theoretical sentences of the model; because these units are not the terminal items defining the string to be learned, their presence violates the terminal meta-postulate.

The two groups of nested-hierarchy theories separate on how the organization shown in Figure 12.2 comes about and in how it is used. The "nonassociative recoding" position, articulated by Jensen, Bower, and Johnson, relies on infor-

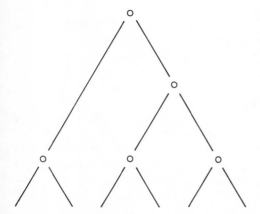

FIGURE 12.2 A nested hierarchical memory structure.

mation-processing machinery; great clarity at the gross level, such as can be simulated on a digital computer, is sacrificed for vagueness on the molecular level. To say, for example, that characters are grouped into a chunk and assigned a code is a clear formulation in that it can be realized without difficulty in a computer program; however, it leaves unspecified the processes responsible for the grouping and for code assignment. The *"multilevel-associative"* positions of Hebb, Sheffield, and Estes keep the Aristotelian faith in association through temporal contiguity but, by ignoring the terminal meta-postulate, they escape the limitations identified in Lashley's complaint.

Nonassociative Recoding into Higher-Order Responses

One perspective on serial order is that the response units are a nested hierarchy anyway: The list can be decomposed into words, the words can be decomposed into syllables, the syllables can be decomposed into letters, and the letters can be decomposed into phonemes or calligraphic strokes. As learning progresses, one can assume, the definition of the response simply climbs to more and more global units. The first time a child ties his shoelace the relevant response units are individual digital motions but years later the entire process has become a single response. This arm waving is of course unsatisfactory as an explanation, but the general notion has evolved into statements that have yielded testable consequences.

Jensen. Jensen (1962; Jensen & Rohwer, 1965) was among the few workers in serial learning during the 1960s who were sensitive to the objections raised by Lashley. Although the 1962 paper does not cite Lashley's manifesto, the 1965 paper does, and even in the earlier paper Jensen mentions the embarrassment caused for stimulus—response theories by the individual notes that go into rapid passages on the piano. Like Lashley, however, Jensen was more comfortable in grounds for rejecting conventional theories than in explicit alternatives. He was convinced by the serial to paired-associate transfer experiments that chaining and position associations played a small role, if any. Also, he noted that low correlations, across subjects, between serial and paired-associate learning skill were another source of negative evidence. Jensen's proposal for the mechanism of serial learning drew on theoretical machinery already accepted by his colleagues in verbal learning—the process of response integration. It will be recalled that the analysis of paired-associate learning into stages (see Chapter 1) includes not only the hookup of stimuli and responses but also the acquisition of response terms as unitary responses. For example, initially, the syllable BOJ would be a list of three letters but later in learning it would have become a single verbal response capable of entering into an association with some stimulus term.

The fact is, very little attention had ever been devoted to precisely how response integration occurs (although see Sheffield, 1946). Underwood (1963) mentioned that presumably response integration followed the chaining mechanism of serial learning; B–O, and O–J would then be the links permitting integration of BOJ. This is slightly dangerous to assume, however, because then there is the problem of avoiding an infinite regress of ever more elementary paired-associate and serial components alternating. Most workers were content to picture a vague process of response integration, whereby with continued repetition the response unit sort of jumped up one level from the individual letter to the syllable.

Jensen proposed that whatever the mechanism is that integrates B, O, and J into the unitary syllable BOJ also is the basic mechanism governing the transition of a serial list from a string of distinct elements to an integrated whole. In short, the whole list eventually becomes absorbed into a single response. Because the integration is gradual rather than sudden Jensen has suggested that distinctive items may serve as anchor points in determining where the integration process starts; ordinarily the items at either end of the list are the only distinctive ones and the integration process begins at these, working simultaneously in a forward and backward direction until they meet (see the discussion of Ribback & Underwood, 1950, below). Of course much is left out of this hypothesis and Jensen had no illusions that it was a complete theory. We are not told, for example, whether the entire list gets organized always into one gigantic response or whether there are sometimes intermediate-level response units, such as L–M–N–O–P or W–X–Y–Z in the alphabet. The Jensen hypothesis was therefore far from a real alternative to stimulus–response theories, but it was important for representing, in 1962, a deliberate effort to get around the terminal meta-postulate restriction that seemed to limit the generality of all currently available views on seriality.

Bower. What the Jensen position really needed was what always stands between good ideas and empirical support for them—some particularly relevant experimental operation or some particularly relevant performance measurement. Workers have provided both in the meantime. One important independent variable has been the insertion of *temporal pauses* or *rhythmic stress* within serial lists during presentation. The purpose of these devices is to induce the subject to define as an intermediate-level response the material that comes in between the demarcating features. The strategy is just exactly analogous to using categorized lists in the study of organization in free recall: It' is assumed the subject organizes or groups anyway, but in order to make the process transparent the experimenter builds the organizational principle into the list.

It would be hard to claim that explicit grouping is a modern innovation. After Ebbinghaus, one of the next major research efforts on human memory was reported by Müller and Schumann in 1894 (see Woodworth, 1938, pp. 28–30) and these authors used rhythmic grouping as one of their major independent variables. An article that brought temporal–rhythmic grouping to modern attention was a report by Wickelgren (1967). In Wickelgren's study pauses were used to punctuate lists of digits; the major findings were that such pauses facilitated performance, as compared to ungrouped control lists, and that the amount of facilitation was largest when the groups were of size three.

Bower and Winzenz (1969) used rhythmic stress to induce grouping of digit strings by their subjects. They were explicitly interested in the possibility that such strings are handled in the form of a nested hierarchy, such as we saw in Figure 12.2—each list decomposed into chunks, intermediate-level response units that, in turn, decompose into the terminal characters. In one of their studies Bower and Winzenz gave subjects the same memory-span strings on more than one trial, repeating experiments by Hebb (1961) and Melton (1963) that had shown performance was ordinarily improved on a string if it was repeated later in the session. Bower and Winzenz were able to show that this improvement from a repeated string occurred only if it was grouped in the same way on both occasions. For example, if the series *6475291* were presented once with rhythmic grouping *64'752'91* and then later again with the grouping changed to, say, *647'529'1* then there would be no improvement. However, if the same rhythmic breakdown were used on both occasions then there would be a gain from the first to the second trial with the same series. The same memory series, therefore, organized twice in the same way, shows the Hebb–Melton effect; however, a differently grouped version of the same series is no better than a completely new stimulus altogether. This result would have to be counted a minor catastrophe for any theories that include no higher units than the terminal characters. Even if such theories are modified to include the stress of the pause as a sort of special serial element in its own right, there is still the prediction of facilitation, because certain transitions, such as between the first two elements of the example used above, remain unchanged.

Bower and Springston (1970) used a converging operation for testing the same idea with prior experience from semantic as opposed to episodic memory. In their study subjects were responsible for immediate recall of 12-letter strings broken into groups by pauses within the string. The string included such familiar acronyms as IBM, TV, UCLA, FBI; in some cases the strings were broken by pauses so as to coincide with the acronyms, TV–IBM–TWA–USSR; but in other cases the pauses did not coincide, TVI–BMTW–AU–SSR. The finding was that the facilitation occasioned by familiar acronyms was heavily dependent on whether the grouping presented corresponded or not with the acronym boundaries. This and related demonstrations are rationalized in a systematic way by Anderson and Bower (1973, pp. 430–437); the Anderson–Bower model actually includes aspects of both the nonassociative and the associative versions of hierarchical theory being outlined here, but there is no way of boiling down their position to a few sentences.

Johnson.   N. F. Johnson (1970, 1972) has elaborated a step by step model of how the grouping process gets established and how it is used during the act of recall. Like Jensen and Bower, he assumes that the terminal elements become fused into chunks during learning. However, Johnson places much more emphasis on the higher-level unit that stands for chunked elements. This superordinate is called the *code,* a representation of the nested, subordinate information but not in any sense the sum of that information. For Johnson, the code in any serial recall task is much like the category name in clustering experiments, or the representation of the binary triplet *010* by the octal digit *2.* Having codes that stand for the information within a chunk without being simple conglomerates of that information means the codes themselves can be treated as constituent elements of still higher-level codes. As an example of a three-level nesting relation Johnson offers the familiar telephone number: At the highest level, there would be a single code representing the entire telephone number. This would break down into two codes, one for the area code and one for the individual number. The code for the individual number, in turn, would break down into the prefix plus the four-digit number. These two codes would, finally, break down into three and four terminal elements, respectively. There is the further assumption that the pieces of information organized under a code are distinguished by *order tags,* which allow their correct sequential retrieval.

Having many levels with codes at each level entails a responsibility for the theory to tell us how the entire sequence is *unpacked,* the order in which codes are decoded into their constituents. The rule Johnson provides is to start at a node, the highest code in the system first, and then retrieve all codes immediately subordinate to it. Of these, the one with the highest order tag is selected and the others are stored in short-term memory. The selected code is then decoded into its subordinates, which may themselves be still further codes or the actual terminal elements. Once the level of terminal elements is reached then the order tags on them determine which is recalled first, second, third, and so forth. When the terminal elements falling under a particular code have been exhausted, the process returns to the next highest level and retrieves the code with the next highest order tag, and on it continues until the whole string has been reproduced. In terms of our example with the telephone number, it would all start with decoding the superordinate *telephone number* into *area code* and *individual number.* With the latter stored in short-term memory, *area code* would be decoded into, say *three, one,* and *two;* these are terminal elements, and they would be recalled in the order of their tags. Next, the code *individual number* would be decoded into *prefix* and *number.* With the latter committed to storage, the prefix would be decoded to yield *nine-eight-five,* the terminal elements, and, following recall of the last of these, the four-digit number would be decoded.

One important part of Johnson's model is that each decoding operation is assumed to occur in all-or-none manner. That is, when a code is decomposed into its constituent elements, which constitute the chunk, the chunk is recalled as a unit or not at all. In other words, chunk boundaries are assumed to be decision points; if the subject is uncertain of one of the elements into which the current code should be decomposed, then he aborts the entire recall effort. Although the concept of an order tag certainly seems an arbitrary way around the problem of serial-order information, the all-or-none assumption has permitted experimental tests that are necessary conditions for the theory.

If subjects use chunk boundaries as decision points then there should be discontinuities in the correlation between recall at various adjacent positions. Consider the *transition error probability,* the probability of an error's occurring at a particular position given that the item in the previous position has been correct. Within a chunk the transition error probabilities should remain very low because, presumably, the subject would not have undertaken recall of that chunk unless he was in a position to retrieve all of its constituents. However, adjacent items belonging to different chunks should be the occasion for much higher transition error probabilities because uncertainty regarding any of the elements of the following chunk would have called for aborting the process at the end of the previous chunk. That is, in terms of our example, if the prefix were successfully retrieved but if any digit in the following four-digit number were uncertain, the subject would leave the entire four-digit sequence blank. Experiments (N. F. Johnson, 1970, 1972) have shown that when letter sequences are subdivided by pauses into groups the transition error probabilities are rather uniformly low for transitions within a chunk but jump dramatically for transitions between chunks.

It follows also that the larger the chunk, the more likely is recall to break down at the transition between it and its predecessor. To test this prediction Johnson had subjects learn letter sequences where there was always an initial group of three letters but various sizes of a second group. In one condition there was only the initial group and in others there were from one to four letters; the conditions could therefore be schematized as *ABC, ABC–D, ABC–DE, ABC–DEF,* and *ABC–DEFG.* As expected, the only differences among conditions were at the transition between the third and fourth items, where the probability of an omission following a correct response was an increasing function of the number of elements in the second chunk. (These sequences may seem too short for an immediate memory test, and they are, but Johnson used a procedure where they were the response terms in a short paired-associate list with digits as the stimuli.) Therefore, the subject omits the entire chunk when a code is decomposed into constituents about which there is some doubt.

Arguing analogously, we can make predictions for omission of the entire list. The first step is retrieval of the highest-level code, the superordinate *telephone number* in our example, and the next step is its decomposition into its constituents. The more constituents there are at any level the more likely an omission. Therefore, if the first superordinate leads to many intermediate-level codes there should be more omissions of the complete letter series than if there are fewer intermediate-level codes. In other words, we should expect more complete omissions for *ABC–DE–FG* than for *ABC–DEFG* because there are three chunks in the former and only two in the latter, even though both sequences have the same number of letters and even though, as we saw in the previous paragraph, there are other reasons why shorter chunks should be better. As the theory implied, however, Johnson found complete response omissions to depend on the number of chunks in the sequence and not in their sizes.

Finally, Johnson has advanced the *opaque container theory of codes*. This notion is that, although information is carried in the form of a code, that information cannot be consulted without a deliberate decoding process, just as one can carry a book in a foreign language in his hand but still depend on a laborious translation process in order to discover its meaning. This idea is very different from Jensen's notion of response elements congealing or absorbing into larger units and it is tempting to invoke the contrast between mental compounding of James Mill and the mental chemistry of John Stuart Mill. This aspect of the theory has been tested in the context of retroactive inhibition: The subject learns a sequence, in response to a paired-associate stimulus, and then must learn another sequence in response to the same stimulus term. The difference between the original and interpolated sequences is in the changing of a single letter from a chunk with three letters. The prediction of Johnson's theory is that an entirely new code must be devised for the changed chunk—a code as different from the original as would be necessary if all three letters were changed. In recall for the original sequence, this suggests that recall for all three letters within the chunk with one changed letter should be subject to high degrees of interference, whereas letters within unchanged chunks should not suffer any interference. By and large, a number of tests have supported this prediction (N. F. Johnson, 1972, p. 145).

The appraisal of Johnson's coding theory depends on what criteria one decides to apply. Estes (1972) has complained with complete justification that the theory leaves many of the most fundamental problems—order tags, coding mechanisms, decoding mechanisms—shrouded in mystery. However, the accomplishment seems more impressive if one looks at those aspects of the theory that have permitted experimental test—the nested-hierarchical structure, the all-or-none recall process, the opacity of codes. The experimental effects associated with these ideas are clearcut and nonintuitive. Indeed, these key results from Johnson's theory would hold true under a wide variety of assumptions about how the memory structure was established in the first place. That is, we can leave open the issues Johnson has chosen not to face but accept his views on how subjects deal with the nested-hierarchical structure once they have it.

A final comment: Johnson's theory was not initially developed to handle serial learning in the conventional sense but rather recall of sentences (N. F. Johnson, 1968), where chunks would be identified with constituent phrases as defined by syntax. This background suggests three more comments, in turn:

1. The theory is quite similar to one proposed by Yngve (1960) to cover the memory demands of producing and receiving sentences, which we shall inspect briefly later in this chapter.

2. It is noteworthy that the same assumptions can be carried intact from the domain of complex linguistic forms to that of simple, arbitrary strings of letters. From this one can conclude either that sentences are processed more simply than one may have supposed or that letter strings are processed with more complexity, or finally of course, that the theory is irrelevant.

3. The origin of the theory in memory for sentences can account partially for Johnson's relative neglect of the process of code assignment—the chunking structure of sentences is conventional and it is easy to regard it as self-evident.

Multilevel-Associative Theories

One distinguishing feature of the theories we have been examining is the absence of the ancient associative proposition that two mental events that occur in temporal contiguity tend to elicit each other on future occasions. [This needs to be qualified somewhat in light of the fact that in Anderson and Bower (1973, Chapter 7) Bower has moved toward a neoassociative position.] What distinguishes the theories to be considered now is that they simultaneously accept the associationistic assumption and reject the terminal meta-postulate, that only the ultimate response units can enter into associations.

Hebb. Apart from the dual-trace mechanism, an early form of distinction between short- and long-term storage, Hebb (1949) formulated no process theory for human learning; his main interest was in the organizational basis for perceptual learning. Because there is no scarcity of theories to review in this chapter, we shall not pause for long with Hebb, except to reinforce a single point: Hebb's psychological theory is a completely passive, connectionist, associative system in which elements are organized in the form of a nested, multilevel hierarchy.

The theory originates at the neural level, where it is assumed that by repeated temporal and spatial contiguity, two neurons become more likely to elicit each other by actually growing together (neurobiotaxis) somewhat at the synaptic juncture. A collection of these mutually facilitating units, caused by a single sensory event—say, a punctate visual fixation—is called a "cell assembly." With reorientation of the sensory apparatus, such as would occur in systematic scanning of a visual display, for example, there would be a tendency for different cell assemblies to be aroused repeatedly one after another. These temporally contiguous assemblies would then themselves become associated, forming a second level of organization. The principle can be extended still further upward. Units at one level become organized through associations until they form an organized whole and subsequently this higher-order, derivative unit can itself be an ingredient of another organized unit at still a higher level. Obviously, the theory is hierarchical enough to please, say, Mandler (see Chapter 10) but it is also a strict connectionist position. Subscription to the terminal meta-postulate is not compulsory for associative models, therefore, despite claims of those who would like to discredit all associative principles through pointing out the fatal consequences of the terminal meta-postulate (see Anderson & Bower, 1972, pp. 12–16, for more on this question).

Sheffield. In setting a theoretical context for research on the training of complex, sequential, mechanical-assembly skills, Sheffield (1961) outlined an unusually complete associative theory. (In fact, the theory to be described here was articulated as early as 1946 in Sheffield's doctoral dissertation; although never published, this dissertation had an appreciable influence on research in verbal learning.) The theory is complete in two major ways. It is designed to deal with serial behavior in general rather than simply with serial verbal learning or motor performance; therefore, it would in principle satisfy Lashley's admonition for those interested in seriality not to lose sight of such domains as language and skill. Sheffield's theory is complete in a second sense because it separates and deals with three distinct issues that have been of concern to associative theories from Aristotle on down—(1) the content of associations, (2) the process by which they are formed, and (3) the memory structure that results from the formation of associations. We may organize the theory in terms of these three headings.

The contents of the mind have always been a logical starting point for any associative theory; one needs to know what the elements are before discussing how they become connected. The most common treatment was the separation of sensations and ideas, following Aristotle, with ideas being internal copies of sensations derived from the physical world. Of course, this separation has for thousands of years defined the debate as to whether ideas are derived from sensations, as the empiricists hold, or are innate, as the nativists hold. Sheffield clearly falls on the empiricist side, with three, rather than two, basic kinds of mental event—the sensory response, the perceptual response, and the symbolic response. (It should be observed that the terms *response* and *event* should be read synonymously in the context of this theory; Sheffield makes it clear that these are completely central responses.)

A very straightforward distinction separates sensation and perception in Sheffield's system: Sensations are innate, whereas perceptions are learned. For example, a sensory event would be the central consequence of a particular flavor in a food; however, a representation of how that same food looked would be a perceptual event, provided that taste was the only stimulation. The third type of mental event, the symbolic response, is not only not an innate consequence of immediate stimulation, it is related to that stimulation through only an arbitrary code. The symbolic system of interest is, for humans, the verbal language. Therefore, whereas it is perfectly natural, although not innate, for the sight of an ice cube to lead to a perceptual event representing coldness, there is no nonarbitrary reason why the sight of an ice cube should lead to the letters *i-c-e* or to the auditory representation /aɪs/.

To these three types of mental content is applied the basic premise that events that occur in appropriate contiguity usually elicit one another mutually. This is how perceptual experience, and eventually symbolic experience, get built on sensation. To use Sheffield's example, the sight, smell, flavor, and texture of an orange all tend to occur together in the child's experience, along with the word representing an orange in the language and eventually the occurrence of any of these events will by itself tend to arouse the others. The term we encountered in Chapter 11, *redintegration,* is commonly used to cover this arousal by a stimulus of the full constellation of perceptual and symbolic events that have become associated with each other. Redintegration, in this system, is simply a necessary consequence of association by contiguity among diverse sensations, perceptions, and symbols that tend to be aroused together often. The principle of redintegration also subsumes some of the theoretical considerations we have dealt with in Chapter 5 about imagery. Most particularly Sheffield's theory is consistent with the dual-trace hypothesis of Paivio except that the latter does not go far enough, for not only a visual image is aroused by the word standing for an object, but also auditory, tactile, and olfactory imagery are aroused, as well as various interverbal associations.

In addition to the process assumptions of association by contiguity and redintegration of perceptual and symbolic responses, Sheffield's theory includes a limitation caused by incompatibility among responses or events. In the perception of an orange, for example, it is not claimed that at every instant every gustatory, olfactory, visual, tactile, or symbolic response is being simultaneously elicited. There may be an inherent incompatibility as, for example, between having perceptual imagery appropriate to both interpretations of an ambiguous figure, or between having tactile imagery for both the crust and filling of a pie. Even if the various components were not incompatible in some cases, any assumption of limited attention capacity would yield the same consequence. The total perceptual response, therefore, would be ". . .fairly labile, shifting from moment to moment in the particular constellation of conditioned sensory responses which constitute the momentary perception for the object" (Sheffield, 1961, p. 17).

Application of the basic contiguity assumption to response sequences is uncomplicated. If two responses, *a* and *b,* each depend on their own stimulus and if they are elicited by these independent stimului on a number of occasions, then there is a tendency for feedback cues from the first response to be sufficient to produce the second. This is the familiar chaining hypothesis of Ebbinghaus. Sheffield's theory of sequential organization takes on unique aspects when the above assumption is combined with the idea that the total response is a package of behavior only some of which is overt, say the pronunciation of a word. The response also includes various perceptual and symbolic responses—that is, events—that we cannot observe. Sheffield assumes that whichever of these fractional responses are not incompatible with earlier responses migrate forward in the sequence. In the sequence $a-b$, for example, there may be some components of b, call them b', that can actually occur compatibly with a and these should be elicited before the full overt b response. If c is supposed to follow b then the components c' would be elicited by b and anticipate actual occurrence of c. Furthermore, there may be aspects of c' that are compatible with both a and b—call these c''—and these should migrate still further forward and occur as responses to a. This derivation is based on the observation that conditioned responses tend to move forward in time when there is a sufficient delay before occurrence of the unconditioned stimulus.

The anticipatory tendencies implicit in a three-response sequence are shown in Figure 12.3. This process functions to integrate and coordinate the sequence beyond what would be possible with the simple chaining mechanism:

> Part of the subsequent response is present in the performance of the antecedent response, and cues from both a and b' are conditioned to performance of b. The response is also coordinated in that, instead of two discrete responses occurring one after the other, a blending of the two responses occurs in which all of b that is compatible with a occurs along with a and a graded transition from a to b characterizes the execution of the link. . . . Descriptively, then, the integration of a sequence is a process of moving forward in the sequence of all of those later parts which can occur simultaneously with earlier portions. This process results in a sequence more stable than a mere chain such as a-b-c. The reason it is more stable is that when a is initiated, b and c are immediately aroused in incipient form, which gives them prepotency over any incompatible responses. . . [Sheffield, 1961, p. 19].

Here, then, is a process assumption about the forward migration of response elements, which leads to a memory structure, as shown in Figure 12.3, that is quite different from that of most associative theories. It has the virtue of

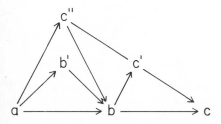

FIGURE 12.3 A memory structure for sequential tasks according to Sheffield's (1961) theory. In the basic sequence of responses, a, b, and c, there are components of later responses that are compatible with earlier responses (b', c', and c'') and can migrate forward to play an anticipatory, regulatory role early in the sequence. (After Sheffield, 1961.)

providing a means where the later portions of a sequence can be, as it were, in mind, from the very beginning. Even though a segment of an arpeggio on the piano may entail a sequence of very different muscular responses, many mutually incompatible ones, still, the sequence can be organized as a unit rather than as a chain. More importantly, the execution of a word within a sentence need not be isolated from its semantic and syntactic context; the entire idea of the sentence could, by a mechanism such as Sheffield's, be incipient on pronunciation of the first word. Of course, there would have to be limits; one would hardly expect the entire Gettysburg Address to be incipient, with the entire idea behind the totality aroused by the single word "Fourscore."

The second major structural assumption in Sheffield's theory is that a sequence breaks up into *natural units*—similar to the concept of the chunk—which themselves are subject to sequential organization of the type shown in Figure 12.3. Like Hebb's structural model, therefore, this system is a nested hierarchy, in clear violation of the terminal meta-postulate. A simple example is given in Figure 12.4, where arabic numerals stand for what Sheffield calls "superordinate sequences." Note that the superordinate symbol, 1, is attached only to one overt response, *a*. This distinguishes Sheffield's model from those of Rundus for free recall (Chapter 10) and of Johnson for serial recall. In these two models, and in that of Estes (to be covered next), the superordinates are connected simultaneously to each of the subordinate elements. A structure where the superordinate connects to all subordinates is fine for free recall but it poses difficulties for serial recall. Johnson was required, it will be remembered, to add the rather gratuitous assumption of *order tags* to permit the system to emit responses in order. Estes, however, as we shall see, has added a system of inhibitory associations. Serial order is quite natural in the system of Figure 12.4, however, because at any point there is only a single overt response coming up next in the associative network.

The difficulty in evaluating Sheffield's theory is in making contact with experimental data; his purpose was to provide an orientation for a research program in complex perceptual—motor training and not to attract partisans

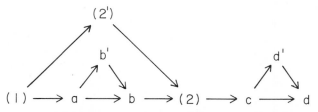

FIGURE 12.4 The superordinate sequence in Sheffield's theory. The numbers 1 and 2 stand for higher-order response units that are organized in the same manner as the simple constituents *a, b,* and *c.* (After Sheffield, 1961.)

among verbal-learning investigators. Sheffield therefore felt no responsibility for addressing directly such manifestations of serial learning as the serial-position effect, the problem of remote associations, or the relation between paired-associate and serial learning of the same items. The purpose was, rather, to guide a research program toward important questions in a systematic, rational way. We can, on an ad hoc basis, evaluate the theory against these and other considerations. (For example, the solution to Ebbinghaus' old concern with the existence of remote associations is a particularly interesting compromise—an item is connected with whichever aspects of remote items that, being compatible with earlier items, can move forward in the sequence.) However, there is always some way to accommodate new findings to a theory, so that such an ad hoc approach does not provide any general closure. Furthermore, in terms of its heuristic value to subsequent research on serial learning, the theory must be counted a total failure [although Sheffield's dissertation (1946) was widely read in the 1950s in connection with paired-associate familiarization effects].

Sheffield's theory and the one to follow, by Estes, may, as things develop, turn out to occupy critical positions conceptually: They remain in contact with the basic empiricist assumption about association through contiguity and yet at the same time they encompass certain information-processing concepts, such as nesting and coding. A pure chaining theory is unsatisfactory because of its inability to account for such data as the all-or-none recall of chunks in Johnson's research in addition to Lashley's more abstract objections, and yet a pure information-processing approach, such as Johnson's, leaves a great deal of the underlying process machinery assumed without explanation. It remains to be seen whether having the best of both worlds can confer lasting usefulness on these ideas. We conclude our survey with the theory of Estes (1972).

Estes. The present section completes our discussion of the model proposed by Estes in 1972. The short-term aspects of that model were covered in Chapter 6 and the reader may wish to review that material before proceeding here. The essence of the short-term coding model was (1) nested-hierarchical structure for memory traces, with higher-order control elements, or codes, governing subordinate constituents—words decomposed to letters, letters to features, and so on; (2) a system of reverberatory loops connecting each element to its immediate superordinate control element; and (3) the preservation of order information through cyclic reactivation of the reverberatory loops. This is a completely dynamic model of memory for order in that performance depends at any moment on the current state of the timing relations involved in these reverberatory loops. The reverberatory process is Estes' conceptualization of primary memory and accounts for our having the last few items in a state of ready accessibility, or consciousness. We are now interested in how this process extends to permit storage of information after primary memory is cleared by subsequent input.

Estes follows the assumptions of Waugh and Norman and of Atkinson and Shiffrin in assigning to *rehearsal* the promotion of information from primary to secondary memory; however, his view of rehearsal is quite explicit and different from theirs. First, let us consider what happens if rehearsal does not occur, a circumstance that would be approached, in the sense of an ideal experiment, by Brown–Peterson testing with a very demanding interpolated distractor activity. It will be recalled that when only the reverberatory loops are supporting performance there is a gradual deterioration caused entirely by accumulating error in the relative timing of the individual loops. Most especially, timing errors at the level of features combine to produce unacceptable characters that are dumped from the system altogether. The eventual consequence of the timing errors in reverberatory loops is that performance drops to zero, just as does the primary-memory component of performance in actual Brown–Peterson tasks.

Now, what does rehearsal accomplish to forestall this deterioration? Estes' assumption about rehearsal is that it produces specific inhibitory connections among each of the elements grouped under a particular control element. The structure is shown in Figure 12.5 for a three-level hierarchy, which may represent a two-word list, each word containing three letters. Excitatory associative connections are shown as solid lines and inhibitory connections as the dotted lines. It can be seen that the excitatory connections alone are not much help in

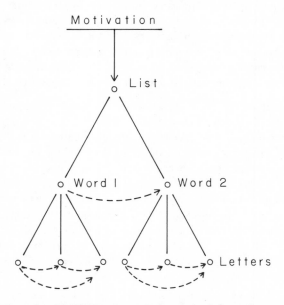

FIGURE 12.5 The role of inhibition in preserving order information according to Estes' theory: solid lines are excitatory and dashed lines are inhibitory. Retrieval starts with the highest node and works down, choosing the least inhibited lower node; following its selection, a node becomes temporarily refractory. (After Estes, 1972.)

preserving order information—one must rely on the fact that the looping process between each element and its control element has been set in motion at different times. However, adding inhibitory associations through rehearsal provides a clear structural basis (as opposed to the dynamic basis inherent in reverberatory looping) for order information. The stabilization of order through these inhibitory connections occurs because each element in a group has a different number of inhibitory links leading into it. Given the assumption that rehearsal establishes the inhibitory links shown in Figure 12.5, we can account for the stability of order information by following through the retrieval process. It is quite automatic: Given a motivational source, the highest-level control element is retrieved. From there we see that there are two excitatory connections down to the next level of control element. However, there is also an inhibitory link from the first of these to the second, and the first is therefore retrieved because the rule is that the more inhibitory links leading to an item the lower its probability of retrieval. The same logic applies at the next lower level, where each control element arouses three letters in an excitatory fashion; only the first of these letters is not the recipient of inhibitory associations and so it is retrieved first.

Thus far we have gotten the process to its first actual response, retrieval of the first letter of the first word. Now we need to know why the subject does not simply continue retrieving this letter for the rest of his life. The assumption is that a branch goes into a refractory period following retrieval of its terminal element. That is, following retrieval of the first letter in our example, that letter's association with its control element enters a refractory, dormant period. Being refractory, the inhibitory associations to other elements within the same group are not active and therefore the next item in the group can be retrieved. When the three letters of the first group have all been retrieved, their entire control element goes refractory and the process moves to the control element governing the second three-letter word. Once a long-term memory structure, such as that of Figure 12.5, is built up, therefore, there is no need for the dynamic reverberatory process at all. Furthermore, the structure is quite the same as that proposed by Johnson except that, whereas Johnson has had to assume order tags, Estes has assumed an associative process of inhibitory links. However, in both Johnson's system and in this one the course of retrieval is the same, moving systematically up and down branches and across the tree structure in the same sequence.

Estes (1972) has pointed out several empirical phenomena that are readily seen to be consequences of his model. The most interesting of these is the relation between performance on a series and the particular pattern of grouping imposed on it. Consider a list of six elements. There are two main ways to group this list into two segments—3–3 and 4–2. Shown in Figure 12.5 is the 3–3 arrangement and, by counting, one can see that there are eight excitatory associations and seven inhibitory connections. Now what would happen if the grouping were 4–2? By drawing out the associative connections this arrangement requires, it can readily be verified that there are again eight excitatory associations but this time eight rather than seven inhibitory connections. It is reasonable that the more associations of both types there are, the more difficult the series is to learn, under a particular grouping. With series of 12 items there are more possibilities, but again the one with the fewest associations in a subgroup size of three: 3–3–3–3. As Estes points out, this is exactly the finding obtained by Wickelgren (1967), that the best subgroup size for partitioning lists is three.

The model gives up an interesting prediction for the comparison between 4–4–4 and 3–3–3–3 groupings: There are 15 excitatory connections for 4–4–4 and 16 for 3–3–3–3; however, there are 21 inhibitory connections for 4–4–4 and 18 for 3–3–3–3. If it is the total number of connections that is correlated with difficulty, then which grouping pattern is more difficult should depend on whether or not rehearsal is possible. If rehearsal is prevented, then only the excitatory connections should determine performance and 4–4–4 becomes easier than 3–3–3–3; if rehearsal is allowed, however, then the easier pattern becomes 3–3–3–3. Absolute prevention of rehearsal is probably an unattainable goal, experimentally, but finding the predicted interaction would be a stunning victory for Estes' theory.

Estes' theory, like Sheffield's, has in some sense the best of both worlds. It is explicitly hierarchical, with an intermediate level of analysis that permits an acquisition process based on recoding and a retrieval process based on generation of lower nodes from higher nodes. Both properties are significant from the standpoint of language processing. However, the Sheffield and Estes theories are clearly associative at the molecular level; nothing is left to sophisticated homunculi or to some quasideistic Original Programmer, such as one needs sometimes to invoke with molar information-processing models. Unfortunately there is little in the way of evidence that specifically favors these theories as opposed to others. This seems to be the major area in which analysis of serial learning needs to move. There are, as we have seen, plenty of theories, new and old, but there are few empirical phenomena that are crucially relevant for these theories; one important exception follows.

Martin's analysis of subjective subsequences.   A significant common feature of the Bower, Johnson, Sheffield, and Estes theories is that the memory structure resulting from serial learning is not homogeneous; instead, it is organized as a nested hierarchy. However, because different lists would be broken up in different ways by a subject and because different subjects would organize the same materials differently, there was no obvious way of observing this grouped, hierarchical organization directly. One response to the difficulty of observing sequential, grouped memory structures has been for experimenters themselves to impose a prior grouping arrangement on sequential materials through the use of pauses, stress, or prior language groupings (see sections on Bower and Johnson).

This experimental strategy of contriving *a priori* organization in order to simulate what the subject is believed to do on his own is the same strategy we saw used in research on organization in free recall: The experiments on clustering with explicitly organized categorical lists may be viewed as efforts to bring to the surface that organizational behavior that the subject employs privately even if the learning materials are not categorically organized. In the field of free recall it was Tulving who managed to operationalize the private, improvised organization used with unrelated words through the measurement of subjective organization. E. Martin (1974) and E. Martin and Noreen (1974) have now performed a comparable operationalization for subjective sequences in serial learning.

The essential feature of Martin's strategy was to back off from the highly aggregated, highly counterbalanced data base modern experimental psychology has (quite properly) led us to value and to inspect instead the performance of individual subjects on a single list. Subjects in the Martin and Noreen study were given self-paced anticipation trials on the same fixed list of 32 words. After an initial study trial, subjects went through the list trying to guess the next word in the series until a trial occurred on which 21 of the 32 words were guessed correctly. After reaching this criterion, subjects were tested for free recall of all the list words by simply being asked to write as many as possible on a blank sheet of paper. Finally, there was a test of backward recall.

E. Martin and Noreen (1974) introduced the logic of their data analysis through the device of the *seriogram,* a semigraphical, semitabular display showing the history of a single subject with a particular list throughout the course of however many trials he required to reach criterion. An example taken from their paper is shown in Figure 12.6. In successive rows of the seriogram are the 32 list items. The columns of the latticelike display immediately to the right of the words represent the successive anticipation trials; this particular subject had seven. Within the matrix formed by the 32 words and the seven trials, a dot stands for a correct anticipation of a particular word on a particular trial. Dots are connected by lines when either (1) the same word has been correctly anticipated on two successive trials, or (2) two adjacent words have been correctly anticipated on a single trial. To the right of the lattice is the result of the free-recall trial that followed the criterion. Again, a dot indicates the word in question has been given in free recall and if words from adjacent positions on the list have been recalled as a cluster in free recall, these two items are connected by a line. Finally, the order in which such free-recall clusters have been emitted is given by the numerals of the far right.

The seriogram display makes apparent the formation of subjective subsequences for this subject. For example, Items 21, 22, and 23 seem to have been acquired as a unit, and more obviously, the first block of four items has also apparently been handled as an organized entity. The first four items constituted a block that was not expanded in the course of learning. The subsequence including Item 18, however, was an interesting case in which the size of the block was steadily increased.

Of course, the seriograms for other subjects might be less compelling than the one given in Figure 12.6. Martin and Noreen undertook to generalize their

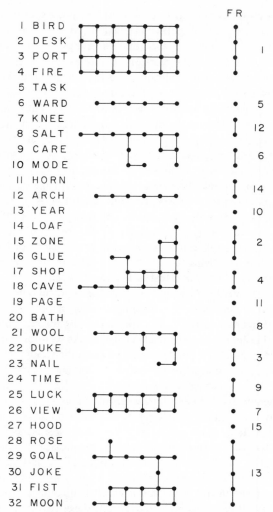

FIGURE 12.6   An example of a seriogram for a single subject learning a single 32-item list: FR is free recall. (After Martin & Noreen, 1974.)

analysis across subjects, but after they had extracted subjective subsequences from individual data. For this, clearly, they needed an explicit definition of a subjective subsequence. They adopted the following: A run of items is defined as a subjective subsequence if (1) the item just before the subsequence (that is, for example, Item 20 in the 21–22–23 subsequence of Figure 12.6) has itself never been a correct anticipation (in response, in the case of this example, to Item 19) and (2) if the sequence items have been correctly anticipated in a row either on the criterion trial or on at least two preceeding trials. This definition produced, for 48 subjects, each learning a single list, 146 subjective subsequences at least two items long.

We cannot detail here the list of properties adduced by Martin and Noreen for subjective subsequences. Several of the more interesting analyses focus on the status of the item just before a subsequence, such as Item 20 in the example. These items seem to have some of the properties of a retrieval cue for their subsequence. One may object that these items are simply unusually difficult ones, in view of their definition as never having been anticipated correctly. However, in free recall of subsequences with two or more items, these preceding items were recalled with probability .81, a figure only slightly lower than free recall of the first item within the subsequence (corresponding to Item 21 in the example), which was .92 for these subsequences. Neither is it just that these preceding items (items just before the first subsequence member) are inherently hard to anticipate, as if they took a long time to retrieve, because in backward anticipation they were given in response to the first subsequence member with probability .67. Furthermore, in free recall again, there was an overwhelmingly larger tendency for this preceding item to cluster with the item following it, that is, with the first member of the subsequence, than to cluster with the item preceding it.

These analyses are a start at understanding the dynamics and structural organization lying behind serial learning. In a further step, E. Martin (1974) has extended the subjective subsequence analysis to the serial-position effect (see below). His finding was that whereas access to groups, or getting into a subjective subsequence, was a function of where that subsequence occurred on the list, recalling the members of that group was independent of the group's location within the list. (This generalization should be understood as an implicit caveat on the theoretical analysis of the serial-position effect to follow but the theoretical problem is the same whether the unit is the individual word or the subsequence.)

Martin's work is a promising new avenue for the study of serial organization. It is to be hoped that further developments will see it combined with such explicit theoretical machinery as in Estes' model. It might be possible to infer exactly which words were connected in inhibitory relations, for example, and to derive consequences of these inhibitory relations for other tasks.

SERIAL-POSITION EFFECTS

In just about any learning task in which the ordering of items is required, and in many where it is not, there is better performance at the beginning and end of the series than elsewhere, with the hardest position occurring somewhere just beyond the middle. The advantage of the early items is called the primacy effect and the advantage of the last items is called the recency effect, as we have seen in previous chapters.

The traditional way of generating a serial-position function is to note errors occurring during repeated trials with the anticipation method of serial learning, with the subject trying to pronounce the name of each item as its predecessor is exposed, as in the Martin and Noreen study. Although the anticipation method was dominant during the period when theories of the serial position effect were being formulated with more enthusiasm than they are now, the effect occurs with other testing procedures. In fact, as we shall see below, the pervasiveness of the serial-position function is actually an embarrassment for certain explanations of it.

There are two dimensions of organization that distinguish ideas on why the serial-position effect occurs. The first is whether to have a single explanation that covers both the primacy and the recency effects or to have a separate explanation for each. The second dimension is whether or not to group together the serial-position functions that result from serial-list learning, serial recall in immediate memory (memory span), free recall, and still other situations; if it is assumed that serial-position effects occur in all these tasks for basically similar reasons then explanations that are too restrictively formulated to apply to just one or two of these may be inappropriate for others. These two dimensions are obviously related to one another and, together, they lie behind the organization of our discussion.

Single-Process Analyses

Among the ideas that include a consistent explanation for primacy and recency, we may distinguish analyses based on (1) intraserial interference, (2) distinctiveness of positional stimuli, and (3) processing order. It should be no surprise that these are not independent of the ideas advanced for the basic process of serial learning itself.

Interference. In an early contribution, Foucault (1928) suggested that the serial-position curve could be derived from gradients of retroactive and proactive inhibition within the list to be learned. The general idea is that items at the beginning are free from proactive inhibition and items at the end of the list are free from retroactive inhibition, whereas items in the middle are subject to both. With short lists there is not enough of either type of inhibition to do much damage but as length increases the two sources of inhibition cumulate in the interior. Foucault tried to find empirical verification for his theory by collecting memory-span data on school children. He first noted how performance on the first and last items decreased as a function of list length—these were to be measures of pure retroactive and proactive inhibition, respectively. From these estimates the goal was to predict performance in the interior positions.

However, it is not particularly difficult to understand that such a theory requires another strong package of assumptions. If retroactive and proactive inhibition are to be added, then in order to come up with a bow-shaped curve there must be a negatively accelerated function relating each source of interference to distance from the two ends of the list. That is, for the system to work, the buildup of proactive inhibition across the early serial positions must be occurring faster than the relieving of retroactive inhibition over those same positions; likewise, in the recency portion of the serial-position curve, the relief from retroactive inhibition must be occurring at a faster rate than the buildup of proactive inhibition over the same positions. Another way of accomplishing the same thing would be to have linear rather than negatively accelerated functions relating inhibition to list position but to combine the two sources of inhibition with a multiplicative function. Assumptions at this level were never worked out for the Foucault theory. Part of the difficulty was that retroactive and proactive inhibition were not themselves well understood and therefore the gains from using them to derive still further phenomena were not obvious.

Hull (1935) and his student Lepley (1934) undertook a comprehensive theory of serial learning and the serial position effect by a theoretical fusion of Ebbinghaus and Pavlov. Like Ebbinghaus they depended on adjacent forward associations as the basic mechanism of learning. Unlike Ebbinghaus, however, they attached a major theoretical role to remote associations. The Hull–Lepley view of remote associations called on the Pavlovian concept of *trace conditioned responses*—associations formed between the lingering stimulus trace of some event from the past and a current response event. Each item in the list was supposed to lay down a stimulus trace to which, one by one, all the subsequent responses would become attached. If there is the added assumption that all stimulus traces are chopped off when the last item occurs, before going back for another trial through the list, then these assumptions produce the memory structure shown in Figure 12.7.

The special feature of trace conditioned responses was thought by Pavlov to be *inhibition of delay*, which Hull and Lepley exploited to generate the serial-position function. Pavlov found that when animals were well into training on associations with a long delay between the conditioned stimulus and the unconditioned stimulus, they would withhold the conditioned response until just before the unconditioned stimulus. The question is what happens during the delay. Pavlov thought the response was held in check, during this period, by an inhibitory tendency. To support this idea of an inhibitory tendency during the delay period he showed that it was difficult to elicit some other, unrelated, stimulus–response association while the animal was waiting out the delay. In other words, an association is harder to elicit when bracketed within the delay period of some second association than when tested by itself. Applying this to

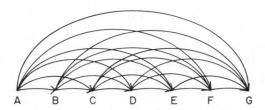

FIGURE 12.7 The memory structure assumed for explaining serial position effects by Hull and Lepley. Each item in the list is connected to all subsequent items. Any connection is inhibited to the extent there are other remote connections spanning it.

the serial-learning situation, Hull and Lepley reasoned that it should be harder to elicit an association from the middle of the list, say between C and D in the example of Figure 12.7, than one from either end of the list because the C–D association is bracketed with the A–E remote association and others.

How much inhibition should be working against each adjacent association can be determined simply by counting the number of remote connections spanning over a particular direct connection. Primacy and recency are thus explained because obviously there are more inhibitory links hindering the middle items than the outside items. One problem that arises immediately is the symmetry predicted by this model—whereas the obtained serial-position function usually shows more primacy than recency the Hull–Lepley theory produces a peak of errors in the exact middle of the list. Supplementary assumptions introduced by Hull, Hovland, Ross, Hall, Perkins, and Fitch (1940) were designed to meet this limitation.

A more serious difficulty with the Hull–Lepley theory is the assumption of discontinuity at the end of the list. Why does the last item on one trial not leave a stimulus trace that conditions to the first item on the next trial? This problem is brought into relief in a study by Glanzer and Peters (1962) in which the interval separating adjacent trials on the list was reduced to zero—that is, the last item on one trial was separated from the first item on the next trial by no more time than adjacent items, within the list, are separated from each other. Still, under these conditions, Glanzer and Peters obtained a reasonably normal serial-position function. Of course, there is always a way of patching up a theory to include, with more or less grace, an embarrassing datum; however, in this case such an epicycle would probably seriously undercut the greatest virtue of the Hull–Lepley position, its parsimony.

Before we dismiss the Hull–Lepley theory as a museum piece, however, we should pause to observe that the basic idea—a relation between difficulty and the number of remote inhibitory associations involved in a sequence—has re-emerged to play the central role in Estes' (1972) new theory. The difference is that Estes has not applied the idea to the differential difficulty of items within a sequence so as to yield a prediction for the serial-position function but such an extension is neither unreasonable nor complicated, as we shall see below.

Positional-stimulus distinctiveness. Another approach to a consistent account of primacy and recency is predicated on the assumptions that (1) some representation of serial position is an important stimulus component for the items on the list, and (2) the ends of the list are more distinctive, and therefore better stimuli, than the interior positions. Murdock (1960a), Ebenholtz (1972), and Bower (1971) have all articulated versions of this idea. There is obviously a natural affinity between what we called the *serial-position hypothesis* in our discussion of the acquisition process in serial learning and the present *positional-stimulus distinctiveness hypothesis* for the serial-position effect. However, it would be confusing to give them the same name and, because they are directed toward somewhat different aspects of serial learning, we shall try to distinguish these related ideas consistently with different terms.

Murdock's (1960a) treatment had the considerable virtue of relating two quite separate research areas within a single format. In experiments on *absolute judgment* subjects are shown stimuli representing values along some continuum, such as line lengths, and asked to apply consistent labels correlated with the values, such as 1, 2, . . . or *a, b, c,*. . . . The data show that the difficulty of this task increases with the number of values the subject must handle, with performance breaking down when more than about seven values are presented (G. A. Miller, 1956). The *anchor effects* observed in absolute judgments represent the fact that the performance breakdowns are not uniform across the range of values being tested; instead they come from the interior of that range. The extreme values tend to be better handled than the middle values. Murdock noted the similarity of this "endpoint anchor effect" to the superiority of terminal list positions over interior positions in serial recall. If one accepts the view that serial learning is a matter of associating serial positions with the corresponding items, then there is a methodological similarity between the absolute–judgments situation and the serial learning one: In serial learning, the stimulus items are the positional representations (such as "first," "second," and so on) and to each must be attached its response in a consistent manner. In both cases the subject is naming points along a single dimension.

Relating this dimensional aspect of serial learning to the concept of adaptation level and to the Weber–Fechner law from psychophysics, Murdock suggests that the apparent spacing of positions within the list should obey a logarithmic rule. The perceived differences between Positions 2 and 4, for example, should be the same as between Positions 4 and 8. Given this relation between actual and perceived position, Murdock defines the positional distinctiveness of a particular location as the relative perceived distance between that location and the locations of all other items in the series. In a list of three items, *A, B,* and *C,* where the locations are perceived as equally spaced, the middle item is an average of one position away from the other two, whereas either outside item is an average of 1.5 positions away from the other two; this three-item example generalizes to longer series and the logarithmic assumption produces the observed skewed nature of the function.

Bower (1971) has reviewed Murdock's theory in detail and has concluded that many of the predictions it makes cannot be distinguished from those of a somewhat different model, the assumptions of which are (1) that the effective stimulus in serial learning is the disparity in perceived locations of each position as opposed to the perceived midpoint (actually the adaptation level) of the series, and (2) that there are gradients of stimulus generalization surrounding each effective stimulus. The gist of the model is seen in the consideration that stimuli from the middle of the list "lose" responses through generalization to their neighbors in two directions, whereas stimuli from the ends of the dimension can generalize in only one direction. In some situations this model diverges in its predictions from Murdock's and Bower concludes that overall it fits the facts better.

Together with Ebenholtz (1972), Bower (1971) proposes, in addition to the generalization principle, implicit, abstract scales involved in serial-learning tasks, scales that can be represented by such neutral terms as "first," "second, . . ." without a necessary correlation with any particular dimension in the physical world. The evidence favoring such symbolic positional scales comes from experiments on transfer within and between different ordered dimensions. There is not space to recapitulate these studies here, except to note that they strongly imply a relative positional representation rather than an absolute one.

We shall return to the position-stimulus distinctiveness hypothesis later in this chapter. For the moment, the important points are that the various forms of this notion all share a dependence on sequential ordering beyond the level of the single pair and that the sequential representation is supplied internally by the subject.

Processing order.   To anyone who has ever served as a subject in a multiple-trial serial list-learning experiment, or to anyone who has closely inspected the protocol from such a study for a single subject (see Figure 12.6), there is one overwhelmingly obvious explanation for the serial-position function—it simply reflects the order in which subjects learn the items over successive trials: The first few recall efforts usually yield only the first handful of items and perhaps one or two from the end and gradually, as practice continues, the regions of mastery creep toward one another, meeting just past the middle point in the list. It was Ebbinghaus (1902, Volume I, pp. 624–626) who hit on measuring this differential difficulty by counting the number of promptings that were necessary, at each position in the list, before mastery.

(We may, incidentally, be almost completely assured that priority belongs once again to Ebbinghaus in discovery of the serial-position effect: For one thing, it is impossible to learn a serial list without noting the lawful order in which items are acquired. Second, Ebbinghaus was a compulsive enough scholar in his 1902 textbook to cite the research literature whenever possible, yet there is no outside reference in his discussion of the serial-position effect.)

There have been two systematic efforts to build a theoretical account of the serial-position function from the order of learning observation. Ribback and Underwood (1950) have suggested that serial learning is a chaining process that starts at the outside two positions on the list and works inward. This would produce a symmetrical function, of course, but they proposed a clever rationalization for the lopsidedness. Chain building from the beginning of the list, they said, is a forward paired-associate situation, whereas chain building from the end of the list is a backward paired-associate situation. Because backward associations are believed to be more difficult to establish than forward ones, it follows that the meeting point occurs closer to the end than to the beginning. The two-process theory was simulated in paired-associate learning as a means of verifying the theory independently of the serial-learning task to which it was meant to apply. Subjects first learned a given pair, say $X-Y$. Then one group was required to attach a third element, A, to the front end of the $X-Y$ association, giving the triple $A-X-Y$. A second group was required to attach the third element to the back end of the previous association, $X-Y-A$. The first task was harder than the second, confirming that the backward chain-building process would go on more slowly than the forward chain building, producing the crucial asymmetry.

The Ribback and Underwood hypothesis, for some reason, received little attention, even during the period of unquestioned dominance of pairwise associative learning during the 1950s and early 1960s. Even today, although the pairwise analysis of serial learning has been rather thoroughly discredited for reasons we have been discussing here, the hypothesis, and its experimental verification, provide an example of the best in the American functionalist tradition—an elegant application of a familiar simple principle (forward versus backward associations) to a new situation (serial acquisition) such as to explain a theoretical puzzle (the serial-position function) and the derivation of a new empirical consequence to test the whole package.

From a very different background orientation, Feigenbaum and Simon (1962) proposed a theory of the serial-position effect dependent, also, on the sequence of acquiring responses. Their approach is part of a much larger computer simulation model called EPAM, the elementary perceiver and memorizer (see Feigenbaum, 1970, for a review of this work). Perhaps the most interesting aspect of EPAM, and especially of an extension to it proposed by Hintzman (1968), is not actually the modeling of serial learning but rather the application of a device called a *discrimination net* to associative learning. Hintzman has shown that the discrimination-net mechanism is capable of generating a great number of the classic phenomena of verbal learning from relatively few assumptions.

The portion of the theory specifically developed by Feigenbaum and Simon for application to serial learning depends on two basic propositions that we have already encountered—the anchor point and the order of acquiring new segments of the list. Ordinarily, there are exactly two anchor points, the first and last items; the assumption is that the subject always initially learns the first two items on the list. From there, he selects new items to learn on a probabilistic basis from the two anchors defined (1) by the last item and (2) by whichever item is at the boundary of what has been learned at the beginning of the list. With these and other assumptions covering the independence and serial processing of items, Feigenbaum and Simon show data from computer simulations that are good matches against data derived from real subjects. As they point out, if some other items besides the first and last are made into potential anchor points, such as with the von Restorff phenomenon (the isolation of an item through a contrasting format or class) or with a list divided into sublists of different classes of item, the theory quite easily accommodates the regular perturbations observed in the resulting serial-position function.

Primacy and Recency in Two-Process Analyses

Give a subject a few trials of memory-span testing, with a new list of nine digits presented on each for immediate ordered recall, and he gives you back a serial-position curve roughly similar to the one Ebbinghaus reported; give your subject a few lists of 20 words for free recall and the same thing happens. The relative amounts of primacy and recency change as we move among testing situations but both remain prominent. This similarity in outcome between serial-list learning and these two immediate-recall situations, memory span and free recall, suggests that there may be a common underlying cause. However, if we take the theories covered in the previous section, those based on a single-process explanation for primacy and recency, with the intention of applying them to the memory-span and free-recall tasks, we stumble on two major difficulties.

First, several of the processes outlined in the previous section could never take place on a single trial. For example, the strategic explanations that have subjects departing from endpoints and learning towards the middle are very hard to apply to a single, fleeting experience with a list of nine digits. Similarly, Pavlov found that trace conditioned responses were painfully slow to learn in dogs and, although humans may be more talented in this sort of conditioning than dogs, one wonders whether it is indeed the same process going on.

The second reservation about applying the single-process explanations of the serial-position effect to free-recall and memory-span testing is still more serious.

In these latter situations there are well-documented arguments for ascribing primacy and recency to altogether different mechanisms. If these arguments are airtight then it becomes just as reasonable to apply the two-process models back to serial-list learning. We shall review the proposals for independent explanations of primacy and recency before we return to this problem.

Recency. In Chapter 6, on primary memory, we have dealt at length with the assignment of the free-recall recency effect to a highly accessible buffer store, limited to no more than three words, and fragile in the sense that the contents must be used right away or else they become displaced by new verbal activity. At various points we conjectured that this primary memory store was little more than persisting conscious awareness of what had just been happening, that is, of the extended present. The evidence allowing separation of this recency system from whatever type of storage supports performance in other list positions is the dependence of the recency effect on operations that have little effect on other items, such as interpolation of a distractor task between list presentation and recall. Independent, converging evidence on the properties of primary memory came from studies using the Brown–Peterson distractor method.

The other part of the argument is that there are numerous variables with major effects on all except the last few serial positions. Examples of these include presentation rate, meaningfulness, and subject-aptitude variables, among others. Together these considerations make a strong case for separate recency and prerecency factors in free recall.

In immediate serial recall, as occurs in memory span, the argument separating causes of recency and primacy must take a slightly different form, because the subject is not allowed to use information from his primary memory right after list presentation. As we saw in Chapter 3, however, there is actually not very much recency there to explain if the lists are presented visually and, if the lists are presented auditorily the recency effect may be shown to include a strong echoic-memory contribution. The main point is that whether echoic memory or primary memory, or some combination of them, is held responsible for the recency effect, these are mechanisms applying only to the end of the list and not possibly of any use in explaining the primacy effect.

Primacy. We turn now to the primacy effect. As both Tulving (1968b) and Crowder (1969) have observed in different contexts, there are fundamentally only two classes of hypothesis for primacy, active and passive. The passive approach holds that primacy is inherent within the mechanism for acquisition and retrieval of a list; for example, the spanning inhibitory tendencies that Hull has relied on are passive, as are the inhibitory processes described by Foucault. The active hypothesis holds that primacy results from some strategy applied to the list by the subject.

The usual strategy envisaged in the active approach is rehearsal, although in view of the new distinction between maintenance and elaborational rehearsal (see Chapter 6) we now want to be more specific about exactly what the crucial strategy is. That stipulated, the basic idea is that learning of any particular item occurs not only during the time it is being displayed but also after it has disappeared, if the subject has occasion to think back on earlier portions of the list while he is still receiving later portions. To the extent this occurs cumulatively, it stands to reason that the early items should be better recalled than the later items; they are better learned. In the simplest possible case, imagine the list $A-B-C-D-E$: After he receives A, the subject repeats it to himself, but after he receives B, he repeats the subsequence $A-B$, and so on. If number of repetitions were the major commodity determining later recall, then obviously there would be a monotonic primacy effect with better performance on an item the earlier in the list it occurred. One of the earliest references to this idea is in a paper by Welch and Burnett (1924).

There are at least three sources of evidence favoring the active theory and thus indirectly questioning the passive approach. First, recall the evidence on overt rehearsal procedures: Rundus (1971) has asked subjects to bring their covert verbalizations, during input of a free-recall list, to the surface through a sort of overt, stream of consciousness report. One of his major findings was that by the time the end of the list had been reached, there was a monotonic decreasing function relating the frequency with which an item had been rehearsed to the position it occupied in the list, that is, a monotonic primacy effect in rehearsal frequency.

The second type of evidence favoring an active over a passive approach to primacy comes from the study of individual differences. Again, the relevant evidence was covered in Chapter 6. Belmont and Butterfield (1971) found that, under constant task conditions, normal children showed a moderate primacy effect but retarded children showed none. Crowder (1969) found that among college students there was a relation between overall performance level and the primacy effect on a task (see below) that permitted relatively free application of behavioral strategies but that there was no relation between overall performance and primacy on a similar task with less opportunity for application of behavioral strategies.

The third line of evidence favoring some rehearsal-like process in primacy is found in the nature of those experimental operations that differentially affect the primacy effect as opposed to recall elsewhere in the list. The best example of this argument is an experiment by Sumby (1963; see Chapter 6 of this book) in which free recall has been compared for low- and high-frequency verbal items. We should expect rehearsal to be easier with the familiar items than with the unfamiliar items; and in fact there is a larger primacy effect with the high-frequency items and almost none with the low-frequency items, although the two stimulus classes are not different in recency. It must be mentioned that the theory predicts that presentation rate should affect primacy selectively, greater primacy being associated with slower rates, where the opportunity for all rehearsal is increased. However, the evidence here is not very good. The classic Glanzer and Cunitz (1966) finding on presentation rate and free recall is that the effect occurs everywhere except in the recency segment, but not differentially for the primacy effect. A consequence of preoccupation with primary memory, during the 1960s and afterwards, was that the distinction between a *prerecency* region of the curve, which includes the relatively long asymptote as well as primacy, and the primacy effect, as such, was blurred.

The final line of evidence favoring an active theory of primacy lies in experimental manipulations that have a presumptive effect on both primacy and on rehearsal. There are two such cases that we shall examine; first, an experiment reported by Bruce and Papay (1970): Consider a list of 50 words in which there is a signal to the subject, following the first 15 words, that he is responsible for retaining only words occurring from then on. This condition was compared with a condition in which only 35 words were presented, all to be recalled. If primacy is a matter of proactive inhibition building up inevitably over the early serial positions, or if primacy is caused by the formation of remote associations, then it should occur on the first words presented and not on the first words that the subjects need to recall. If primacy is caused by some voluntary, active process, such as differential rehearsal, however, then the subject should be able to "reset" the process when he receives the forget cue—the signal telling him to disregard the items presented so far—and he should enter the subsequent words as if it were the beginning of a fresh list. The results obtained by Bruce and Papay (1970, Experiment II) are in part shown in Figure 12.8. In the case of each curve on that figure, the subject was responsible for the same 35 words. In the control condition he received only 35 words in presentation, whereas in the experimental condition he received 15 words, followed by a signal to forget them, and then the additional 35 words. The serial-position curves are identical. In particular, primacy was the same with or without the block of 15 words occurring before the instruction to forget. This result, and those of a similar study by Waugh (1972), would be difficult to accommodate within a passive theory of the primacy effect.

In an experiment by Crowder (1969) immediate ordered recall was measured for lists of nine digits. In one condition each list was exactly nine digits long. In a second condition, however, there was a great deal of variability in list length, ranging from nine-digit lists to long streams of several dozen digits. In this second condition, called "variable context," almost all of the data were thrown away and only those trials with exactly nine digits presented were scored. In the constant- and variable-context conditions, therefore, performance was measured for recall of exactly the same stimuli, nine-digit lists, but the difference was in subjects' expectations for what they would hear during presentation. If the physical nature of the stimulus is what produces primacy, as the passive theory holds, then there should have been equal primacy in the two conditions because such factors as length and presentation rate were identical. However, the finding

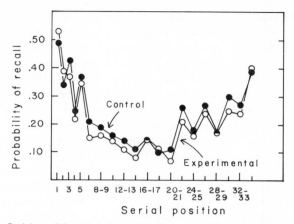

FIGURE 12.8 Serial position functions for 35-word lists (control condition) and for 50-word lists in which the subject was instructed to forget the first 15 words before he received the remaining 35 words (experimental condition). After the fifth position, each point on the horizontal axis represents two adjacent serial positions. (After Bruce & Papay, 1970.)

was that there was primacy only in the constant-context condition. Because the main difference between the conditions was in what the subject expected to hear during input of the stimulus lists, it is reasonable to infer that the primacy effect depends on some type of voluntary strategy applied during input rather than on structural properties.

Other Sources of Serial-Position Data

At this point the situation becomes confusing: We have basically two serial-position effects under study, the serial-position effect obtained under conditions of multitrial serial learning, usually by anticipation, and the one obtained under the one-shot memory-span or free-recall test. They are similar in that both show primacy and recency with the most difficult position skewed toward the end of the list. Because the serial-position effects obtained in these multitrial and one-trial situations are so similar, it would be a great pity to abandon the goal of explaining them in a consistent manner.

However, the models for multitrial serial learning apply only awkwardly to free recall and memory span. The interference hypothesis (Foucault, 1928; Hull, 1935; and variants of them) is almost ruled out by the evidence favoring active over passive theories of primacy. The hypotheses stressing acquisition-order strategies (Ribback and Underwood, 1950; Feigenbaum and Simon, 1962) are even more out of place in a task where the whole presentation episode was a fleeting, one time only glimpse at the list, as with memory span. The positional–dimensional hypothesis is perhaps less difficult to apply and we shall return to it presently.

The two-process model for position effects in single-trial situations are just about as unlikely in multitrial serial learning. At least, attribution of recency to an echoic store or to a fragile primary memory buffer is almost unthinkable in the context of a subject clamped into a rigid, paced anticipation schedule where each item must emerge in its fixed 2-sec slot. There is nothing wrong, however, with application of the primacy part of the two-process model to serial learning; that is, there could be active, selective processing working to the advantage of the early items provided the pacing of the rate of presentation were not too frantic.

Therefore, it should be noted, two hypotheses emerge relatively unscathed from this effort to apply theories of serial-position effects in multitrial situations to single-trial situations and vice versa: The idea that serial-position effects come from the greater distinctiveness, somehow, of the end items and the idea that primacy comes from an active processing schedule that favors early items. This point is important because we shall return to conclude that primacy probably comes from the differential processing at the beginning of the list and recency from the differential distinctiveness at the end of the list. However, if we take seriously our responsibility to formulate an account of serial-position effects that generalizes among all or most of the situations that yield a serial-position effect, there are several more groups of data to consider. These data further limit the hypotheses that we can apply consistently.

The conceptual position effect.   The ordinary assumption among students of verbal learning brought up in the tradition of Ebbinghaus has been that, at least in the laboratory, verbal items may be considered relatively independent of one another; furthermore, when this is not the case, workers in this tradition have probably wished it were. Since the earliest stirrings of the field of psycholinguistics, there has been another research tradition called *verbal behavior,* where the base assumption is that words in the natural language are interrelated and the task in the laboratory is to find out how. Measures of word associations (Deese, 1965) or the use of the semantic differential technique (Osgood *et al.,*1957) have been two ways of bringing verbal structure into the laboratory. Another approach is to assume the structure on the basis of intuition and observe its effects on behavior in a precise way. An ingenious experiment by DeSoto and Bosley (1962) fits this latter classification by examining, in a learning situation, the consequences of a conceptual dimension.

DeSoto and Bosley gave their subjects a list of 16 paired-associate items to be acquired in the conventional anticipation method. Although there were 16 stimulus terms, all boys' names, there were only four response terms, the words *freshman, sophomore, junior,* and *senior.* The measure of performance was the number of trials taken to reach a criterion of learning. The data were separated according to the response terms with the result that those pairs in which *freshman* was the response term required 13.3 trials, the *sophomore* pairs, 17.5 trials, with 16.4 and 14.6 trials, respectively, for the *junior* and *senior* associations. Nothing in the presentation procedure allowed a correlation between these four classes of associations and time or order, yet there were both primacy and recency in learning speed, a dependence on the natural order of the response terms that we might call the *conceptual position effect.*

Pollio and Draper (1966) replicated the phenomenon using neutral stimulus terms, the numerals 1, 2, 3, 4, and 5, rather than the school class designations. In both an experiment with nonsense syllables as stimulus terms and another with boys' names as stimulus terms, there was a conceptual position effect corresponding to the numerical progression.

Pollio (1968) has applied the technique of DeSoto and Bosley (1962) to somewhat more subtle stimulus dimensions than the class designations or the ordered numerals. In one study the stimulus terms were *beautiful, pretty, fair, homely,* and *ugly* and in another study they were *cold, cool, mild, warm,* and *hot.* The mean errors on the *beautiful–ugly* dimension were, respectively, 8.9, 15.0, 16.1, 15.8, and 13.1—a distribution of perfectly classic form although there was no seriality inherent in the task itself. With the *cold–warm* dimension the overall results were also consistent with a bowed, skewed curve. In closer analysis, Pollio showed that subgroups of subjects serving in the experiment at different times of the year produced characteristically distorted position curves; in winter, items paired with *cold* were fastest to learn, whereas in summer items paired with *hot* were fastest.

What does the conceptual position effect suggest for theory? If we wish, nothing—we can simply deny that it has anything to do with the traditional serial-position effect. If we accept that the form of the conceptual position effect is more than coincidental in its resemblance to the serial-position effect, however, then we encounter some of the familiar theoretical possibilities. Pollio and DeSoto themselves both favor a positional-stimulus distinctiveness view, where the endpoints of a conceptual dimension, as well as of a perceptual dimension, have inherently greater clarity or discriminability than interior positions along the dimension. Bower (1971) has chosen a similar explanation. It is also possible, however, that position along the conceptual dimension can affect a strategy having to do with order of acquisition, or that at least the primacy effect results from differential rehearsal. It is possible to render the acquisition-order and differential rehearsal interpretations very unlikely by showing that the conceptual position effect still occurs under short-term memory conditions, say, the continuous paired-associate task of Peterson, *et al.* (1962), where an association is presented only once for a second or two and then tested later, only once, after some specified lag. It is still possible that subjects differentially rehearse according to conceptual position, in such a single-shot method, but highly unlikely, and of course the order of acquisition is completely specified by the experimenter. Naturally, we may be opposing the acquisition-strategy and positional-distinctiveness hypotheses unnecessarily: Perhaps it is the factor of distinctiveness (anchor points) that determines rehearsal or order of acquisition strategies.

Serial-position effects in semantic memory. Returning again to Tulving's distinction between retrieval of memories that have been laid down in the laboratory (episodic memory) as opposed to knowledge in the semantic memory system, we find the pervasive bow-shaped curve wherever we look in semantic memory. In Figure 12.9 are shown data from subjects who have simply been asked to recall the names of all the presidents of the United States (Roediger & Crowder, 1976); data are given separately for those asked to indicate the order in which each president has served and for those asked simply to recall as many as possible without bothering to indicate their term. The impressive thing about these results, especially for ordered recall, is their regularity in view of the fact that "stimuli" are not counterbalanced against serial position. That is, the presidents are not anything like equally memorable on historical grounds, yet except for such overwhelming exceptions as Lincoln, a president can expect to be remembered according to a perfectly lawful function relating his time in office to the time of testing.

Koriat and Fischhoff (1974) stopped passersby on the campus of Hebrew University in Jerusalem and asked them two questions, timing the response to

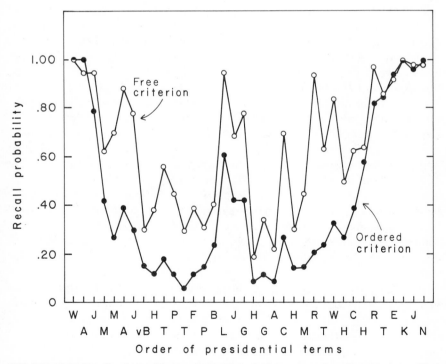

FIGURE 12.9 Recall of presidents of the United States as a function of the ordinal position of their term of office: open circles represent free recall and filled circles represent strict position scoring. (After Roediger & Crowder, 1976.)

each: What is the name of a country beginning with the letter g? What day of the week is it today? Times in seconds for correctly retrieving the day of the week, from Sunday through Friday, respectively, were 1.174, 1.451, 1.770, 1.850, 1.473, and .930, no data having been collected for Saturday. One might argue that the ravages of midweek fatigue slowed subjects down to produce the serial-position effect rather than some effect in retrieval from memory as such. However, the times to provide a country beginning with g were not a function of position within the week. The proportion of errors on day of week responses showed a regular serial-position effect also, ranging from 0.00 on Sunday to around .25 on Tuesday and Wednesday, and back to .08 on Friday. The authors propose two alternative models for this effect. First, there may be a serial-scanning procedure in which the days of the week are retrieved in order and matched against available evidence; to produce the bow-shaped function obtained this requires the assumption that sometimes the scan begins with the early part of the week and sometimes with the late part of the week. The alternative is somewhat closer to what we have been calling the positional-distinctiveness hypothesis, the transformation of the temporal stimulus dimension into a spatial or abstract dimension the endpoints of which are distinctive anchors.

The full range of situations in which a serial-position effect occurs therefore extends from an exposure of only a few seconds, to a new ordering of words or characters, to the retrieval of information that has been acquired decades ago and used more or less constantly in the meantime. After a college student who has learned the days of the week at around 5 years of age has experienced around 800 examples of each, why should he differentially rehearse the current day of the week more on Tuesdays than on Wednesdays? One would suppose, on the contrary, that with long practice, differentials in semantic memory owing to acquisition order or to unbalanced rehearsal would wash out. However, a basic retrieval process using some abstract or transformed dimension as the eliciting device—such as a commonplace version of the pegword or locus-method devices— might well retain differentials of discriminability built into the dimension. Therefore, these positional effects in semantic memory, if they are indeed to be grouped with other serial-position effects, tend to favor the positional (positional-stimulus distinctiveness) hypothesis, that is, the notion that there is some underlying linear ordering to which list items become related and that the endpoints of this underlying representation are more distinctive than the interior.

This argument is worth recapitulating: We have seen serial-position effects extending all the way from the most transient measures of episodic memory to some of the most well-learned knowledge people carry around with them. If all of these serial-position effects are based on the same causal mechanism, then we may be able to discard some hypotheses that are tied to the learning episode itself. Among such basically episodic mechanisms the association of the recency effect to primary memory is the most parochial: How can one maintain with a straight face that Hoover is better recalled than Taft because of a three-word buffer store that may represent the span of conscious awareness across time? Mechanisms associated with the primacy effect, such as (1) differential acquisition time and (2) differential rehearsal, are less inherently episodic than primary memory but somewhat the same argument applies. Is it likely that one rehearses what day it is more often on Tuesdays than on Wednesdays or that Van Buren is better remembered than Polk because of a differential learning time? These mechanisms can be generalized, but only with great awkwardness, back and forth between the episodic- and semantic-memory position effects. However, a mechanism that envisages some internalized abstract ordering scheme onto which both semantic and episodic arrays get mapped is sufficiently general to encompass the variety of serial-position effects observed.

Another Look at the Recency Effect

In many ways, then, the biggest problem is the recency effect in free recall, which has been tied to the concept of primary memory in Chapter 6. Clearly a primary-memory hypothesis makes no sense for the semantic-memory recency effects obtained above. This, in turn, is an inducement to scrutinize with great care how necessary it is to assign the free-recall recency effect to primary memory, an exercise that leads back to the "long-term memory recency effect" reported by Bjork and Whitten (1974).

It will be recalled from the end of Chapter 6 that Bjork and Whitten discovered that adding a distractor task between presentation and recall of a free-recall list did not eliminate the recency effect if periods of such a distractor activity were also inserted between the list items themselves. The inferential chain was that (1) the distractor activity following presentation ordinarily was adequate to remove the recency effect but (2) that same postpresentation task did not eliminate recency when the list items were spaced by interitem distractor activity and, therefore, (3) the recency effect ordinarily did not necessarily come from a primary-memory system subject to disruption from that particular distraction. It is now time to examine in detail the alternative recency mechanism proposed by Bjork and Whitten, for it converges on the same positional discriminability hypothesis that we have been working toward in this chapter.

As Bjork and Whitten pointed out, their results are consistent with a theory of recency that stresses the discriminability of items from each other in terms of time. There are several steps to the argument. First, they note (Experiment III) that there is no long-term (or short-term, for that matter) effect of recency when testing occurs by recognition rather than by recall for their experimental conditions. According to the conventional assumption that recognition and recall differ mainly in the complexity of the retrieval processes required, this finding permits the conclusion that the source of recency is located at the retrieval stage rather than at acquisition or during storage. The second part of the argument is a loose assumption that, somehow at retrieval, the subject looks back toward his memories for the recent past much as, when we are moving through space, we can look back over the most recent objects we have passed. The temporal–spatial parallel is too convenient to resist following further: The items in a memory list, being presented at a constant rate, pass by with the same regularity as do telephone poles when one is on a moving train. The crucial assumption is that just as each telephone pole in the receding distance becomes less and less distinctive from its neighbors, likewise each item in the memory list becomes less distinctive from the other list items as the presentation episode recedes into the past. Therefore, retrieval probability is being assumed to depend on discriminability of traces from each other.

The third assumption of this alternative theory of recency has to do with how discriminability of equally spaced events is related to the passage of time. Here again, the analogy with spatial perspective is all we have on which to fall back. Although two events that occur 2 sec apart do not ever change their objective separation, we seem to perceive time in such a way that later, say a full hour later, these two events are perceived subjectively to have occurred at the same time. One possibility for an index of temporal discriminability is an application of Weber's law stating that the necessary change in stimulus energy for a change in perceived intensity is a constant fraction of the baseline intensity. In terms of our temporal discriminability model, this would hold that the amount of time by which two adjacent memories would need to be separated in order to be discriminable would be a constant fraction of the distance back, in time, of the younger memory. For example, if the more recent of two traces that are just barely discriminable, in time, were 10-sec old and the other trace 15-sec old, we should expect that in another situation a trace 30-sec old would be barely discriminable from another trace 45-sec old. In terms of our telephone poles receding in space, the further away one is from two poles, the more widely spaced they must be in order to look separate.

These assumptions permit a theory of recency that holds up under every situation where recency is found, unlike the other possibilities we have considered. The recency effects in free recall, memory span, and serial learning are all subsumed under the assumption that coding late in the list is along a temporal dimension, from which retrieval is a function of temporal discriminability. Likewise, any other ordered series of memories would involve a process where the past is scanned from the present and where discriminability of recent items is a function of the distance from the end of the series. In episodic memory, distance from the end of the series may be defined in real time. In semantic memory, the point defining perspective on a series may be relative. Although in recalling presidents of the United States our *absolute* time perspective (including associations with particular dates) may work well, in recalling the seven deadly sins, in order, it may be necessary to assume a model where we place ourselves at the location of sin number seven and look back over the series.

It is recognized that this theory is closest to Murdock's (1960a) and Ebenholtz's (1972) proposals that distinctiveness of points along a dimension determines the ease with which they can be associated with new information. However, whereas Murdock has been anxious to fit both the primacy and recency effects this way, we are, for the moment, only concerned with recency.

This type of process has the virtue that it corresponds nicely with our conclusions concerning proactive inhibition in short-term memory (see Chapter 7). It will be recalled that we concluded, largely on the basis of a study by Gardiner, Craik, and Birtwistle (1972) and the arguments of Bennett (1975), that proactive inhibition was mainly a matter of discriminating the most recent memory traces from earlier ones. Therefore, the short-term memory proactive-inhibition phenomonon and the serial or free-recall recency effects may share a common mechanism. Note that this restores the intimate association between recency in free recall and the Brown–Peterson task in short-term memory; however, instead of depending on a primary-memory displacement rule, both are obeying the principle of temporal distinctiveness.

The model we have been examining works for recency but it is a disaster for primacy. If this single principle is applied to the whole list then the first item ought to be the very most difficult to retrieve because it, from the perspective of the retrieval point at the end of the list, has become most thoroughly merged with its neighbors.

There are three options for the accommodation of primacy: First, it may be assumed, more or less gratuitously, that by virtue of being in the first position or positions the primacy items enjoy a special form of distinctiveness, much in the way that any unusual item (different color, size, voice or what not) in the middle of the list shows its distinctiveness through the von Restorff isolation effect. Whereas Lincoln exerts such a von Restorff effect in the interior of the series by virtue of his accomplishments and the great events occurring during his tenure, therefore, we are suggesting that the distinctiveness of Washington may possibly derive partly from the simple fact of his having been the first president. A second accommodation of primacy within the implications of our temporal distinctiveness notions about recency is the assumption that a similar temporal distinctiveness holds for the primacy region when, for some reason, the perspective points shift toward the beginning of the list. That is, the series of temporally spaced events can be scanned either from the perspective of the last item (the model for a recency effect) or from the first item. It is not completely clear that this second alternative is different in its implications for performance than the first, although it may be somewhat more explicit about the expected form of the primacy effect.

The third alternative is to return to the proposition that primacy and recency are caused by different mechanisms. By this view, primacy is then attributed to something like differential degree (or quality) of processing at acquisition, despite our earlier skepticism that Polk is differentially rehearsed with comparison to Van Buren. This third resolution is consistent with the evidence reviewed above that primacy owes at least partly to active strategies at the time of input. Notice that accepting a differential processing hypothesis for primacy subscribes us not only to different explanations of primacy and recency but also to the attribution of these two effects to different stages. We have concluded that recency, mediated by temporal distinctiveness, occurs at the time of retrieval and now we are suggesting that the primacy effect is a consequence of events at acquisition.

LINGUISTIC ORGANIZATION

We complete this chapter with a brief survey of work that has been done on serial organization based on the natural language, rather than on materials contrived by an experimenter. Ebbinghaus was curious to compare the learning of meaningful material with the arbitrary lists of syllables with which he customarily dealt. He found (1964, originally published 1885, p. 51) that in learning stanzas from Byron's "Don Juan" he required only about a tenth the amount of work as in learning lists of nonsense syllables, an "extraordinary advantage" that he ascribed to rhyme, rhythm, meaning, and the natural language.

The organization of this section is an effort to tease out these various factors in their independent contributions to the staggering difference in difficulty between a list of items such as SWIFT–RABBITS–ARE–DIFFICULT–TO–CATCH as opposed to a list of items such as QZX–JPV–NZQ–RXY–TYG–ZQV–VJX. There are two objectives in this contrast: First, we shall try to show that these two types of list are separated by an orderly, gradual continuum rather than by a dichotomy. Second, we shall give a brief overview of research on memory for sentences.

Continuity Between Word Lists and Sentences

To provide further organization to our survey, we may distinguish between cases where the units, or items within a series, are originally independent of one another sequentially, and cases where the items are originally dependent on one another sequentially. With independent units the transition between nonsense and sense is defined by changes in the meaningfulness of the units. With units that have previous dependencies among them, it is primarily grammaticality which changes.

When there is no built-in structure to the sequencing of items in a list to be learned, ease of acquisition is a positive function of how closely the items resemble normal, meaningful words. Noble (1952) tested subjects with two-syllable items that ranged from nonwords (GOJEY) through rare words (ROSTRUM) to common words (KITCHEN) in carefully measured steps. The words were scaled for meaningfulness by determining the mean number of other words associatively elicited by the word in question within a 60-sec period. Noble found that in serial anticipation learning there was a reduction in trials to criterion of from about 32 with the least meaningful units to less than 16 with meaningful words, a 50% gain in learning trials owing entirely to the independent wordlikeness of the units on the list. The relation between meaningfulness and serial acquisition ease is so reliable and strong as to be almost uninteresting, although as we saw in Chapter 11 there are interesting relations among word frequency, recall, and recognition for tasks other than serial learning. By and large, the most important transitions between total nonsense and the sentences of the natural language are defined by the presence of sequential structure and its separation from meaning. Indeed, we shall see, eventually, that current theorists stress the importance of organization imposed from even beyond the level of the sentence.

The finite state grammar.   Among the first preoccupations of cognitive psychologists, when that field was reborn soon after the Second World War, was how to tie the methods of experimental psychology to problems of psycholinguistic relevance, most especially, to the production and reception of sentences. One early effort in this direction was inspired by *information theory,* a metric system for expressing communicative events in terms of the statistical distribution of the possible messages. The process model loosely implied by information theory, for sentence production, is a selection process in which a choice of each word is made on the basis of the previous word and the probabilitic connections between that previous word and all other words in the lexicon. As any of several texts in psycholinguistics explain (Deese, 1970; Slobin, 1971) this is a preposterous model of sentence production: It manifestly, and in a manner which renders generation of examples easy, fails to account for sentences where the subject and main verb are widely separated. However, the *finite state grammar* seems to have motivated much of the early research on grammaticality in memory.

G. A. Miller and Selfridge (1950) asked subjects for free recall of word strings that varied in their "order of approximation to English." At one end of this dimension was normal English text. At the other end, a zero order of approximation to English was based on randomly choosing words from the dictionary. The first order of approximation was constructed by taking the words in regular text and scrambling their order. The second-order approximation was constructed by giving a word to a person and asking for a second word that would form part of a normal sentence. This second word from this pair was then given to another subject with similar instructions. In a long string of words generated this way, each pair of words would be perfectly normal. To construct a third-order approximation to English, a pair of words from a sentence is given the first subject, with the instruction that he should add a third word such that all three can have been from a normal sentence. Then, to subject number two, the second and third words from number one's triple are passed, with instructions to add a third word, and so on. In this third-order approximation, therefore, triples of adjacent words would be perfectly sensible. Here is an example of a third-order approximation to English from the actual lists used by Miller and Selfridge: FAMILY WAS LARGE DARK ANIMAL CAME ROARING DOWN THE MIDDLE OF MY FRIENDS LOVE BOOKS PASSIONATELY EVERY KISS IS FINE. As the method for generation suggests, these words are, at any point, locally coherent but, of course, the whole thing tends to wander. Approximations were constructed to the seventh order, following the same generation rules. In the seventh order, for one more instance, each string of seven words would be quite coherent, but there would be a more restricted tendency for meandering over longer stretches: EASY IF YOU KNOW HOW TO CROCHET YOU CAN MAKE A SIMPLER SCARF IF THEY KNEW THE COLOR THAT IT.

The lists to be remembered were from ten to 50 words in length. The major finding was that performance improved as the order of approximation increased from zero to about the fifth order. However, there was little improvement after the fifth order, and particularly, no gain in going from the seventh order to text. This suggested that, in conformance with the finite-state grammar, it was the short-range dependencies that affected performance. However, a subsequent study by Marks and Jack (1952) has shown that when a scoring method is used that takes order information into account, there is a steadier gain, all across the range of order of approximation, including a sharp increment in going from seventh order to text.

The Miller and Selfridge experiment was a landmark in two major ways—it showed how the research methodology of experimental psychology could be applied to the study of language processing and it showed how the apparently vast gulf between arbitrary word lists and meaningful prose could be spanned with a carefully constructed stimulus continuum. The variable of order of approximation to English, however, can be seen to contain two distinguishable components, as we increase from second order to fifth order in the examples given above. First, the word lists gradually converge on a consistent semantic domain and, second, they increasingly obey the rules of grammar. These semantic and syntactic transitions can be separated experimentally.

A study of pure syntactic regularity was reported by G. A. Miller (1958). The learning materials were strings of letters from the vocabulary, G, S, N, and X. Each string was from four to seven letters in length and there were nine strings to a list; the learning task was multitrial free recall in which the nine strings could be reproduced in any order, after each presentation trial but, of course, the letters within any string had to be ordered correctly. The main variable had to do with the manner in which the individual strings were constructed. In one condition, they were random selections from the four-letter vocabulary. In the other condition they were constructed from the finite-state grammar shown in Figure 12.10. To read this grammar, picture a process that travels along the directed pathways from state to state. Each time the process goes from one numbered state to another, the indicated letter is placed into the string being generated. The operation of the grammar can be described by rules, which represent the consequences of the generation process. For example, all strings must begin with N or S and all strings must end in G. If there is an initial N then the next letter must be either N or G; however, if N occurs elsewhere than in the initial position, then the next letter can be either X or S; and so on, for many other rules.

Miller found that series, matched for length, were much easier to learn when produced by the grammar than when randomly selected. Because there is no possible difference in semantic reference, we may conclude that this effect is a result of the operation of pure syntax. One may object that the grammatical strings are more similar to one another than the random ones and that, because interitem similarity facilitates free recall (Watkins *et al.*, 1974), the results can be explained much more simply. However, Miller observed that the random lists were even harder to learn if they were preceded by grammatical lists than otherwise, which would indicate an effort by subjects to apply some abstract rule they had learned in the first task to the second task.

Separation of syntax and semantics. Marks and Miller (1964) sought to study the independent contributions of grammaticality and meaning to memorizing strings of words. For this purpose there were five sentences constructed of identical grammatical structure. (RAPID FLASHES AUGER VIOLENT STORMS. PINK BOUQUETS EMIT FRAGRANT ODORS. FATAL ACCIDENTS DETER CAREFUL DRIVERS. MELTING SNOWS CAUSE SUDDEN FLOODS. NOISY PARTIES AWAKE SLEEPING NEIGHBORS.) These were *base sentences,* obviously complete in both the syntactic and semantic attri-

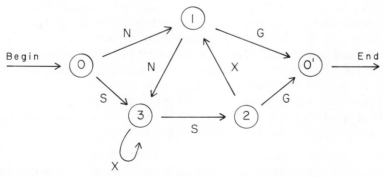

FIGURE 12.10 The finite-state grammar used by Miller (1958). As a generative process moves among the numbered states, the letters associated with each arrow are added to the string being produced. (After G. A. Miller, 1958.)

butes. By leaving the order of parts of speech unchanged but interchanging the particular words used among sentences, Marks and Miller produced a group of *anomalous sentences* (RAPID BOUQUETS DETER SUDDEN NEIGHBORS), which were acceptable syntactically but ridiculous in terms of meaning. By leaving the words within a sentence unchanged but scrambling their order, they produced *anagram strings* (RAPID AUGER VIOLENT FLASHES STORMS) which were ungrammatical but preserved at least something of the meaning from the original sentences. Finally there were *word lists,* anomalous both syntactically and semantically (RAPID DETER SUDDEN BOUQUETS NEIGHBORS).

Over five trials, subjects were presented five instances of one or another type of material and asked to recall them after each presentation. The result was that both syntax and semantics facilitated performance. That is, compared to the word-list control, syntax alone (anomalous sentences) or semantics alone (anagram strings) gave a clear advantage, and about the same degree of advantage. Furthermore, these results show the effects of syntax and semantics to be roughly additive; with the two factors combined performance is better than with either alone. Interestingly, although the anagram strings and anomalous sentences were recalled correctly to about the same extent the errors on each type of material were diagnostic—order errors predominated with the anagram strings and intrusions predominated in the anamolous sentences.

Although this research makes a strong case for the basic continuity of process separating arbitrary lists and items from natural sentences, it is not analytic about where the facilitation comes from with sentences or about the basic processes involved in remembering sentences. These issues are covered in the next section.

Memory for Sentences

Psychological research on memory for sentences can be understood in reference to changing fashions in linguistic and psycholinguistic theories of sentence production and comprehension. We have already seen that the early work of G. A. Miller and Selfridge (1950) has been motivated by the (inadequate) process model of information theory. (Indeed, taking information theory as a process model rather than as a metric system has been the cause of trouble and false starts in several areas.) Although we pretend to give nothing like an adequate survey of trends in conceptualizations of the sentence, our coverage is organized around several distinct psycholinguistic perspectives.

Transformational complexity. An immeasurable stimulus to the basically lethargic field of linguistics and to the embryonic field of psycholinguistics was publication of Chomsky's *Syntatic Structures* (1957). One idea that psychologists seized on was the transformational aspect of Chomsky's grammar. The type of idea involved is that two such sentences as *The philosopher pondered the issue gravely* and *Wasn't the issue pondered gravely by the philosopher?* are in fact very closely related sentences even though they differ greatly in word order, tense, and voice. Transformational grammar comprehends this basic similarity by assuming that people can select from among the various closely related versions of the same basic idea by application of simple transformational rules. Eight different versions of our example are shown in Figure 12.11 arranged so as to stress the three-dimensional structure underlying them— negative/affirmative, declarative/interrogative, active/passive. One way to associate this dimensional model with sentence processing (Mehler, 1963) is to adopt the schema with correction model: A sentence is retained as a kernel sentence (in simple, active, present, declarative form) plus a notation on the appropriate transformation. That is, such a sentence as *The tapes are not being released by the president* would be retained in two parts: (1) the kernel sentence *The president is releasing the tapes,* plus (2) a pair of transformational notations, active to passive and affirmative to negative.

From this hypothesis comes a direct prediction for behavior—the basic kernel sentence should be easier to remember than any transformation of it and, beyond that, the difficulty of transformations should depend on the number of steps through which the kernel sentence must be taken. The sentence *Aren't the tapes being released by the president?* therefore requires taking the kernel form through all three of the transformations shown in Figure 12.11, active to passive, affirmative to negative, and declarative to interrogative. Under the assumption that remembering these three transformational directives should require space in memory, we expect this to be the hardest form.

Savin and Perchonock (1965) performed an experiment testing this "space in memory" hypothesis. They read sentences from a wide range of trans-

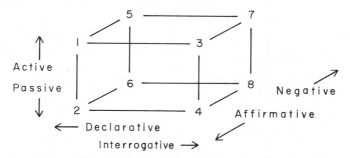

FIGURE 12.11 Eight sentences related by three binary dimensions. 1, The philosopher pondered the issue gravely. 2, The issue was pondered gravely by the philosopher. 3, Did the philosopher ponder the issue gravely? 4, Was the issue pondered gravely by the philosopher? 5, The philosopher did not ponder the issue gravely. 6, The issue was not pondered gravely by the philosopher. 7, Did not the philosopher ponder the issue gravely? 8, Was not the issue pondered gravely by the philosopher?

formational complexity to subjects and after each sentence a list of eight nouns was also presented. The subject was to listen to both the sentence and the nouns and then recall the sentence perfectly, followed by as many of the eight words as possible. The idea was that if transformationally complex sentences require more space in memory than simple sentences there should be less space left over to accommodate the nouns in the case of complex sentences than in the case of simple sentences. The results were beautifully consistent with this prediction, even to the extent that the space required for individual transformations was estimated, by converging comparisons, to be basically constant; that is, not only was recall of nouns worse the greater the complexity of the transformational derivation of the memory sentence, but also estimates of the amount of space consumed by a passive transformation agreed whether the space was measured by loss of memory for the unrelated nouns in moving from a simple interrogative to a passive interrogative or in moving from a kernel to a passive.

However, transformational complexity in the Savin and Perchonock experiment is confounded with sentence length and other studies (Wearing, 1970; Wright, 1968) have questioned the generality, if not replicability, of the finding that actives are remembered better than passives. As usually happens in such cases, it has been the appearance of more attractive models rather than embarrassing data that has turned attention from the transformational-complexity approach.

Phrase structure.   Another approach to a methodological handle on sentence memory has been to base a model on the immediate constituent phrase structure of sentences, to analyze a sentence by its more or less visible components, much in the manner many of us resisted in junior high school. The visible components of a sentence can be represented in an immediate constituent phrase marker, or tree diagram, that realizes certain rewrite rules. Such rewrite rules state that a sentence can be decomposed into a noun phrase and a verb phrase, that a noun phrase can be decomposed into a determiner (such as *the*) and a noun, that a verb phrase may be decomposed into a verb and a noun phrase, and so on. The flavor of this type of analysis can be seen in Figure 12.12, where a sentence is broken down into its corresponding tree diagram. It is a very grave problem that sometimes it is not obvious, even to experts, how a particular complex sentence ought to be analyzed; however, for simple sentences such as we deal with here there is ordinarily little uncertainty about how to construct the tree diagram.

The tree diagram in Figure 12.12 is similar to representations of hierarchical associative structures for arbitrary lists of items that we saw earlier in this chapter. The similarity is no coincidence. Johnson's coding theory, which we introduced earlier as a general-purpose conceptualization of serial learning, was in fact developed to cover the processing of sentences (N. F. Johnson, 1968). From the phrase structure for a sentence Johnson inferred the functional chunks into which the whole sequence would be partitioned. Given this partition, the theory specified aspects of the retrieval process with implications for such

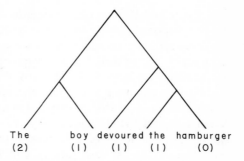

FIGURE 12.12 Phrase structure representation of the sentence "The boy devoured the hamburger." Below each word is the Yngve number, which indexes obligations on the speaker/hearer at that point in the sentence.

statistics as the transitional error probabilities. The interesting aspect of the evolution of Johnson's theory was that it turned out to apply just as well to haphazard lists of letters as to sentences. With letter lists, the occurrence of chunks is not tied to grammatical analysis, of course, but simply to experimenter-imposed pauses in presentation.

Johnson's analysis of sentence processing, and of list retrieval, by means of an ordered progression through a tree structure—retrieving elements nested below a particular node, then backing off to the next higher node, from left to right—was influenced by the work of Yngve (1960) on a processing model for sentences deriving from the phrase structure. Yngve was concerned with the number of *obligations* a speaker must have in mind at any particular point in producing a sentence; these obligations amount to demands made on memory and therefore they should determine the local difficulty of processing. Take a sentence in Figure 12.12, *The boy devoured a hamburger:* On pronunciation of the word *the,* the speaker is obligated to do two more things, provide a subject and a predicate. On saying *boy,* there is only one further obligation, to provide some predicate (which could be only a single word, such as *graduated*). However, when the following word, *devoured,* is transitive there has to be an object. Also, when *a* occurs, there is a clear responsibility to provide another noun. Now notice that these obligations we have detailed correspond perfectly with the number of left-branching segments above each word in the tree structure of Figure 12.12, 2–1–1–1–0. These are called *Yngve numbers* and they are taken to represent the momentary demands on memory—the number of things one must have in mind to complete—in order to make the utterance a good sentence.

The Yngve numbers work both ways. They can also be taken to represent a psychological process associated with the listener. The initial word *when,* for example, alerts the listener that at least four further structural components are coming along—a subject and predicate in the antecedent and a subject and predicate in the consequent. On the assumption that this alerting function of constituents concerning further constituents the speaker has obligated himself to provide is a function that occupies space in memory, the Yngve numbers represent the local difficulty of sentences at the receiving end as well as the production end.

E. Martin and Roberts (1966; see also Wearing & Crowder, 1971) have tested the proposition that a sentence as a whole may be characterized by the mean of all Yngve numbers associated with the individual words. This measure, called *mean depth,* should then give us a summary index of how heavy are the demands of a sentence on memory. As Martin and Roberts observed there is a systematic relation between mean depth and transformational complexity, so that, in an experiment such as that of Savin and Perchonok, it is impossible to know whether the relative difficulties were a function of one factor or of the other. Although mean depth of a sentence and its transformational complexity are correlated on the average, Martin and Roberts were able to devise sets of sentences in which they varied orthogonally, that is, in which different transformational histories were associated with sentences of identical mean depth and transformationally identical sentences had varying depth. In their experiment, the depth measure was a reliable predictor of performance; however, transformational complexity alone, had no influence (indeed, kernel sentences were recalled slightly worse than other types).

The psychological plausibility of the Yngve analysis is not constant across various sentences that can be used as examples. Rohrman (1968) has pointed out that sometimes early constituents are not predictive of later constituents, that is, that obligations for completing a sentence are not always accurately conveyed by previous words. In the simple sentence, *The glass broke,* the word *glass* has a depth of one; however, in the sentence *The glass pitcher broke,* the same word has a depth of two. Yet at the instant a listener hears the word *glass,* as he cannot be assumed to be psychic, we are in a quandry as to how his expectations for the rest of the sentence should be represented.

Deep-structure.   A basic part of Chomsky's transformational grammar was the distinction between deep and surface structure. Two sentences that are identical in their surface structure can be quite different in their deep structure, the underlying syntactic relations among the words. The classic example is the comparison between *John is easy to please* and *John is eager to please.* These two sentences have the same surface tree structure but quite different underlying deep structures; it is John who is getting pleased in one case and in the other case it is John doing the pleasing. Rohrman (1968) was interested in the possibility that in remembering sentences, we store the deep structure plus a transformational correction sufficient to generate the surface representation. This hypothesis is actually closer to Chomsky's position than the notion that we store the kernel's actual surface representation and work transformational corrections on it.

To test for the influence of deep structure Rohrman compared forms with identifcal surface-structure and differing deep-structure complexity. The materials were two-word *nominalizations,* a noun and a word modifying that noun. Two examples are *growling lions* and *raising flowers,* the former a subject nominalization and the latter an object nominalization. The important aspect of these two types of nominalization is that their underlying deep-structure representation are of different complexity: The representation of *growling lions* in deep structure is something like a simple statement, *lions growl,* whereas the representation of *raising flowers* involves a more complicated structure, *(somebody) raises flowers,* the subject left unspecified but still holding a position in the statement. Rohrman found that when presented with word pairs of these types, subjects performed better on the subject than on the object nominalizations, just as deep-structure considerations would predict.

Although Rohrman obtained the outcome predicted by considerations of deep structure in the face of stimulus materials with identical surface structures, however, there is still an alternate explanation of his results. The subject nominalizations—growling lions—consistently involve intransitive verbs whereas the object nominalizations—raising flowers—do not; there is therefore a con-founding of deep grammatical structure with stimulus materials. Paivio (1971b) maintains that associated with the different verbs participating in the two kinds of nominalizations were consistent differences in imagery potential; he showed that with imagery controlled there was no difference between subject and object nominalizations. By one view this demonstration destroys the significance of Rohrman's effect; however, by another view, the consistent difference in imagery between subject and object nominalizations is interpretable as part of the inherent deep-structure complexity between these two forms. There is no guarantee that deep structure is not itself coded in some abstract manner that is at least as close to visual imagery as to words; however, there seems to be no obvious way to untangle these possibilities with the research tools presently available.

Gist versus form.   The analyses that we have looked at so far are frank efforts to find experimental support for specific theories of grammar in sentences. A new direction was opened with an experiment by Sachs (1967) that questioned the functional significance of grammatical structure as opposed to meaning. Sachs argued that whether or not humans can retain the voice of a sentence, active or passive, makes little difference as compared with their retention for the gist of it. Whether "the dog bit the boy" or "the boy was bitten by the dog" is going to have little effect compared to the boy biting the dog. Sachs tested memory for aspects of form, such as voice, and compared it to memory for semantic content.

Her subjects were read a paragraph of prose comprising a coherent narrative. Somewhere in the narrative was a critical sentence about which the subject would receive a recognition test at the end of the passage. The item presented for recognition was either the exact sentence that had occurred earlier, a passive–active transformation of it, a word–order alteration, or a semantic alteration. The finding was that, immediately after the occurrence of the sentence to be tested, memory for all aspects of the sentence was quite good; however, when there was a separation of the critical sentence from its testing by another few sentences, then subjects were quite poor at detecting formal changes (word order or active–passive) but still easily able to detect changes in meaning.

The Sachs results should not be a surprise; what is, in retrospect, surprising is that investigators can have so steadfastly ignored the meaning of a sentence in favor of its form. Walter (1973) showed, furthermore, that the priority of semantic coding in memory depends on the occurrence of a sentence context. He has found that a synonym is a better cue for a word presented in a sentence than a homonym but when the same words are scrambled a homonym is better than a synonym. The Walter experiment therefore shows an influence of the sentence environment on semantic coding of a single word. Sachs' experiment shows evidence for semantic coding of whole sentence. We now turn to the possibility that, one level up, the semantic coding of a sentence is influenced by the environment of that sentence within a longer passage or paragraph.

Suprasentential context effects.   There are several approaches to human learning and memory from the perspective of the extended prose passage rather than the sentence or word. Kintsch (1974) has formulated a method of reducing prose passages down into their propositional structure in such a form as can be correlated with reading speed and later retention–comprehension tests. Rothkopf (1972) has investigated more pedagogically oriented questions concerning the acquisition of ideas within such passages as a function of orienting probe questions. However, our topic in these final pages of this chapter, is the process whereby wider levels of meaning influence the processing of narrower meaningful segments.

Dooling and Lachman (1971) presented the following passage to subjects in a recall experiment:

WITH HOCKED GEMS FINANCING HIM/ OUR HERO BRAVELY DEFIED ALL SCORNFUL LAUGHTER/ THAT TRIED TO PREVENT HIS SCHEME/ OUR EYES DECEIVE/ HE HAD SAID/ AN EGG/ NOT A TABLE/ CORRECTLY TYPIFIES THIS UNEXPLORED PLANET/ OUR THREE STURDY SISTERS SOUGHT PROOF/ FORGING ALONG SOMETIMES THROUGH CALM VASTNESS/ YET MORE OFTEN OVER TURBULENT PEAKS AND VALLEYS/ DAYS BECAME WEEKS/ AS MANY DOUBTERS SPREAD FEARFUL RUMORS ABOUT THE EDGE/ AT LAST/ FROM NOWHERE/ WELCOME WINGED CREATURES APPEARED/ SIGNIFYING MOMENTOUS SUCCESS.

For half the subjects the passage was preceded by a title suggesting the theme of Columbus discovering America and for the other half there was no title. The finding was that whether or not the passages were scrambled, there was an advantage to encoding the material with an appropriate title in mind. The point is that each of the sentences and phrases in the passage is *locally meaningful;* yet there is still a tangible effect of a unifying theme. Note how poorly this conclusion fits with the conclusion of Miller and Selfridge (1950) that in the progression from random words to coherent text it is only the short-range dependencies that affect performance. Data such as these should be the point of departure for every lecturer or writer: the responsibility is to be certain, before a paragraph of writing or speaking is undertaken, that the targets of communication have been provided with an orienting theme according to which information may be organized on the way in.

Bransford and Franks (1971) have carried the importance of the sentential context one step further in arguing that basically only the gist is remembered and nothing of the original medium in which it has been offered. This is, as it were, a "schema without correction" hypothesis. They gave subjects long lists of sentences that contributed to several complex ideas. One such complex idea was: *The rock which rolled down the mountain crushed the tiny hut at the edge of the woods,* Mixed in with other sentences pertaining to altogether different themes, subjects might have received sentences such as (1) The rock crushed the tiny hut at the edge of the woods; (2) The rock which rolled down the mountain crushed the tiny hut; (3) The rock which rolled down the mountain crushed the hut; but not such sentences as (4) The rock which rolled down the mountain crushed the hut at the edge of the woods; (5) The rock crushed the tiny hut; (6) The tiny hut was at the edge of the woods. After the entire presentation list, the task was to recognize whether such sentences as (1, 2, . . . 6) had or had not occurred verbatim. The test sentences were all consistent with the complex idea but only some of them had actually appeared on the list.

Bransford and Franks found that whether a sentence had been presented on the input list or not had almost no effect on recognition judgments. The apparent oldness of test sentences was, however, a function of how many of the elementary ideas were presented. That is, for two sentences that had not occurred on the list, the one incorporating more components of the complex idea was more likely to be judged old, as having been on the study list, than one incorporating fewer of the components. What little ability there was to discriminate old from new sentences was restricted to the simplest sentences. However, subjects were in no doubt at all concerning the description of the world inherent in the overall idea—test sentences that expressed relations violating the main theme were rejected as new with great confidence.

Anderson and Bower (1973, pp. 351–352) used the Bransford and Franks stimulus materials in a study with forced-choice testing, where subjects chose which, of a pair of test sentences, was the old one. They obtained considerably better discrimination of old and new sentences with the simplest one-idea level; subjects chose single-idea sentences that were old over new ones at about a three to one rate. However, in agreement with Bransford and Franks, Anderson and Bower obtained much poorer memory for the surface form of sentences containing more ideas. With four-idea sentences, for example, performance was not better than chance. For extended groups of related sentences, therefore, just as

Sachs has shown for sentences, subjects seem to retain little of the specific form in which semantic information arrives but they retain the message itself quite well.

To what extent is the comprehension that pervades memory in the Sachs (1967), Lachman and Dooling (1968), and Bransford and Franks (1971) experiments an active process of generating meaning as opposed to a more passive retention of meaning that is, in some sense, already there in the text? Although posed in that manner the question seems hopelessly philosophical, Bransford, Barclay, and Franks (1972) managed to formulate it in a testable manner. They were interested in whether subjects would jump beyond the facts given in a pair of sentences to draw inferences that, although logically correct, are not motivated by the task. Consider, for example, the following two pairs of sentences:

(1)   Three turtles are sitting beside a log. A fish swam under them; and
(2)   Three turtles are sitting on a log. A fish swam under them.

In the second, but not the first, pair, it is possible to infer that the fish has swum under the log as well as under the turtles. There is no particular reason for making this inference, but if the facilitation that owes to meaning is derived from a creative, generative process, then we may expect people to construct the entire scenario. Bransford *et al.* tested for this possibility by asking for recognition of test sentences stating that the fish swam *under the log.* The finding was that for subjects who had received Pair 1, there was little tendency to be fooled by the change in wording—little tendency to think (falsely state) that the "under the log" wording had occurred at the time of study. However, subjects who had received Pair 2, containing the unstated implication that the fish did swim under the log, were just as confident they had received the *under the log* wording as the—correct—*under them* wording. This false recognition could occur only if subjects had been going beyond the study sentences and generating a construction of the subject matter based on their own reasoning power or based on an actively constructed visual image.

In this section, then, we have followed the influence of linguistic organization from the individual unit in serial learning and its independent meaningfulness, through the context of a sentence on a word, the context of an extended paragraph on a sentence, and now, finally, to the influence of knowledge from outside the boundaries of the stimulus materials themselves.

SUMMARY

In the early sections of this chapter we have tried to demonstrate the historical continuity that flows through the analysis of serial organization in learning and memory. In the work of the British empiricists this continuity extends back beyond the beginnings of experimental psychology. In the work of Ebbinghaus, a focal interest in seriality marks exactly the beginnings of experimental psychology, a fusion of the enduring issues of association of ideas within philosophy with the methods of natural science.

The domination of Ebbinghaus' authority was challenged only in the early 1960s, by a reopening of the question of just what became learned in serial learning. A diversification of pairwise-associative hypotheses was one result of this return to the search for a basic mechanism, including, most importantly, hypotheses based on chaining and based on associations with absolute or relative positional cues. However, uncertainties about the evidence favoring such hypotheses made the field more receptive than it would otherwise have been to ideas rejecting altogether the underlying identity of serial and paired-associate learning.

The ideas of Jensen, Bower, and Johnson all make some appeal to a process of code formation, in which constituent items on the list become integrated into higher-order response units. These models sacrifice process specificity on the molecular level for an ability to predict grosser aspects of performance that are entirely foreign to earlier paired-associate models of serial learning (that is, chaining, and serial-position associations). The models of Sheffield and Estes provide a somewhat more balanced alternative; both accept a connectionist axiom but both include a hierarchical structure for memory that avoids the inherent difficulties of single-level associative systems.

Theoretical analysis of the serial-position effect is in such a state of untidiness that is almost embarrassing in view of the extreme reliability and pervasiveness of the phenomenon. One class of hypotheses for the serial-position effect includes the assumption that primacy and recency are caused by the same basic mechanism (interference, positional-stimulus discriminability, or processing order). These propositions seem, however, to be denied by the findings that primacy and recency are sensitive to different variables, especially the special relationship between the free-recall recency effect and primary memory.

At some point, the solution to the problem of serial-position effects must depend on our judgment as to whether all examples of the phenomonon, from short-term, long-term, or semantic memory experiments, are caused by the same principles. If we disregard such related phenomena as the conceptual position effect and serial-position data from semantic memory, then a combination of primary memory for recency (or possibly the Bjork and Whitten, 1974, temporal discriminability hypothesis) along with a differential-processing hypothesis for primacy seems to accommodate most of the data. If, in contrast, we regard all serial-position effects as likely manifestations of the same cause, then certain of these applications become unlikely and others impossible (for example, attribution of a semantic-memory recency effect to primary memory).

Perhaps the least damaged by these factors is the hypothesis that positional stimuli serve some cue function in serial learning and that the end positions are more distinctive cues than the interior positions. There are several versions of this notion: It is related to the Bjork and Whitten hypothesis that evenly spaced temporal events become less discriminable in a manner related to Weber's law with elapsed time following exposure of the series. The Murdock–Ebenholtz proposals rest on a pure assumption of positional associations and the relative distinctiveness of different positions per se. Bower's model proposes differential amounts of generalization working against accurate performance at different positions on the list. Not a great deal of work has yet been done to differentiate the predictions of these related hypotheses.

Of course, it would be preferable if the leading theoretical candidates for the serial-position effect meshed well with the leading candidates for the acquisition mechanism in serial learning. They do not, at the moment. Acceptable analysis of what gets learned in serial learning are tending to insist on a level of response organization in between the list and its terminal items (that is, an intermediate code). With no exceptions, however, the ideas we have seen on serial position treat the list as a homogeneous series. This is perhaps less of a problem than it seems to be, however. Martin (1974) showed that performance was influenced by serial position in gaining access to subjective subsequences but not in recalling items from within those units. Still, however, one needs a theory of serial-position effects with regard specifically to subsequence access. Moreover, if this theory of serial position is going to be needed only for subsequence access, the plausibility of the positional-discriminability hypothesis (that informational units are associated to positions and that the exterior positions are more discriminable than the interior ones) is greatly increased: If each item in the list is attached to some representation of relative or absolute position it stretches the imagination to conceive that Items 17 and 18 in a 30-item list can really be kept straight. However, if there are only six or eight subsequences in such a list that need to have their own distinctive positional referent, then the problem seems manageable.

In the final section of the chapter, experiments on linguistic organization of stimulus materials are seen to take a form that reflects prevailing attitudes within psycholinguistics. Beyond an exposition of these changing attitudes, the main point of the section has been to show that as we move along a dimension of complexity starting with isolated units and terminating with semantic constraints covering extended passages, there is a reasonably smooth transition without obvious emergent principles. As more and more "world knowledge" or semantic memory information is brought to bear on sequential materials there is a constantly shifting balance between prior learning and new episodic learning, but nowhere is there the suggestion that the principles for mixture change.

References

Abernathy, E. M. The effect of changed environmental conditions upon the results of college examinations. *Journal of Psychology,* 1940, **10,** 293–301.

Abra, J. C. List-1 unlearning and recovery as a function of the point of interpolated learning. *Journal of Verbal Learning & Verbal Behavior,* 1969, **8,** 494–500.

Adler, M. J. Individual differences in the organization of free recall. Ph.D. Dissertation, Yale University, 1969.

Anderson, J. R. FRAN: A simulation model of free recall. In G. Bower (Ed.), *The psychology of learning and motivation.* Vol. 5. New York: Academic Press, 1972. Pp. 315–378.

Anderson, J. R., & Bower, G. H. Recognition and retrieval processes in free recall. *Psychological Review,* 1972, **79**(2), 97–123.

Anderson, J. R., & Bower, G. H. *Human associative memory.* Washington, D.C.: Winston, 1973.

Anderson, J. R., & Bower, G. H. A propositional theory of recognition memory. *Memory & Cognition,* 1974, **2,** 406–412.

Anderson, J. R., & Lewis, C. Interference with real world knowledge. Paper presented at 15th annual meeting of the Psychonomics Society, Boston, November, 1974.

Anderson, R. C., & Watts, G. H. Response competition in the forgetting of paired associates. *Journal of Verbal Learning & Verbal Behavior,* 1971, **10,** 29–34.

Anisfeld, M., & Knapp, M. Association, synonymity, and directionality in false recognition. *Journal of Experimental Psychology,* 1968, **77,** 171–179.

Antognini, J. The role of extralist associate cues in retrieval from memory. Ph.D. Dissertation, Yale University, 1975.

Atkinson, R. C. Optimizing the learning of a second language. *Journal of Experimental Psychology,* 1972, **96,** 124–129.

Atkinson, R. C., Bower, G. H., & Crothers, E. J. *An introduction to mathematical learning theory.* New York: Wiley, 1965.

Atkinson, R. C., & Juola, J. F. Factors influencing speed and accuracy of word recognition. In S. Kornblum (Ed.), *Attention and Performance IV.* New York: Academic Press, 1973. Pp. 583–612.

Atkinson, R. C., & Juola, J. F. Search and decision processes in recognition memory. In D. H. Krantz, R. C. Atkinson, R. D. Luce, & P. Suppes (Eds.), *Contemporary developments in mathematical psychology.* Vol. 1. San Francisco: W. H. Freeman, 1974. Pp. 242–293.

Atkinson, R. C., & Shiffrin, R. M. Human memory: A proposed system and its control processes. In K. W. Spence & J. T. Spence (Eds.), *The psychology of learning and motivation.* Vol. 2. New York: Academic Press, 1968. Pp. 89–105.

Averbach, E., & Coriell, A. S. Short-term memory in vision. *Bell System Technical Journal,* 1961, **40,** 309–328.

Baddeley, A. D. Short-term memory for word sequences as a function of acoustic, semantic, and formal similarity. *Quarterly Journal of Experimental Psychology,* 1966, **18,** 362–365.

Baddeley, A. D. Closure and response bias in short-term memory for form. *British Journal of Psychology,* 1968, **59,** 139–145.

Baddeley, A. D. Retrieval rules and semantic coding in short-term memory. *Psychological Bulletin,* 1972, **78,** 379–385.

Baddeley, A. D., & Dale, H. C. A. The effect of semantic similarity on retroactive interference in long- and short-term memory. *Journal of Verbal Learning and Verbal Behavior,* 1966, **5,** 417–420.

Bahrick, H. P., Noble, M., & Fitts, P. M. Extratask performance as a measure of learning a primary task. *Journal of Experimental Psychology,* 1954, **48,** 298–302.

Baker, L., Santa, J. L., & Lamwers, L. L. The better the representation, the harder it is to retrieve. Paper presented at 46th Annual Meeting of Eastern Psychological Association. New York, April, 1975.

Barclay, J. R., Bransford, J. D., Franks, J. J., McCarrell, N. S., & Nitsch, K. Comprehension and semantic flexibility. *Journal of Verbal Learning and Verbal Behavior,* 1974, **13,** 471–481.

Barnes, J. M., & Underwood, B. J. "Fate" of first-list associations in transfer theory. *Journal of Experimental Psychology,* 1959, **58,** 97–105.

Bartlett, F. C. *Remembering: A study in experimental and social psychology.* Cambridge, England: Cambridge University Press, 1932.

Baxt, N. Über die Zeit welche nötig ist, damit ein Gesichtseindruck zum Bewusstsein kommt und über die Grösse (Extension) der Bewussten Wahrnehmung bei einem Gesichtseindruck von gegebener Dauer. *Pflüger's Archiv die gesammte Physiologie,* 1871, **4,** 325–336.

Belmont, J. M., & Butterfield, E. C. Learning strategies as determinants of memory deficiencies. *Cognitive Psychology,* 1971, **2,** 411–420.

Belmont, L., & Birch, H. G. Re-individualizing the repression hypothesis. *Journal of Abnormal & Social Psychology,* 1951, **46,** 226–235.

Bennett, R. W. Theoretical implications of proactive interference in short-term memory. *Human Performance Center Technical Report No. 33,* The University of Michigan, Ann Arbor, 1971.

Bennett, R. W. Proactive interference in short-term memory: Fundamental forgetting processes. *Journal of Verbal Learning & Verbal Behavior,* 1975, **14,** 123–144.

Bernbach, H. A. A forgetting model for paired-associate learning. *Journal of Mathematical Psychology,* 1965, **2,** 128–144.

Bernbach, H. A. Decision processes in memory. *Psychological Review,* 1967, **74,** 462–480.

Bernbach, H. A. Processing strategies for recognition and recall. *Journal of Experimental Psychology,* 1973, **99,** 409–412.

Bernbach, H. A. Rate of presentation in free recall: A problem for two-stage memory theories. *Journal of Experimental Psychology: Human Learning and Memory,* 1975, **104,** 18–22.

Bevan, W., & Steger, J. A. Free recall and abstractness of stimuli. *Science,* 1971, **172,** 597–599.

Bever, T. G., Fodor, J. A., & Garrett, M. A. A formal limit of associationism. In T. R. Dixon & D. L. Horton (Eds.), *Verbal behavior and general behavior theory.* Englewood Cliffs, New Jersey: Prentice-Hall, 1968. Pp. 582–585.

Bilodeau, I. McD., & Schlosberg, H. Similarity in stimulating conditions as a variable in retroactive inhibition. *Journal of Experimental Psychology,* 1951, **41,** 199–204.

Binford, J. R., & Gettys, C. Nonstationarity in paired-associate learning as indicated by a second-guess procedure. *Journal of Mathematical Psychology,* 1965, **2,** 190–195.

Birnbaum, I. M. Long-term retention of first-list associations in the *A–B, A–C* paradigm. *Journal of Verbal Learning and Verbal Behavior,* 1965, **4,** 515–520.

Birnbaum, I. M. Response selection and retroactive inhibition. *Journal of Experimental Psychology,* 1970, **85,** 406–410.

Bjork, E. L., & Healy, A. F. Short-term order and item retention. *Journal of Verbal Learning and Verbal Behavior,* 1974, **13,** 80–97.

Bjork, R. A., & Allen, T. W. The spacing effect: Consolidation or differential encoding? *Journal of Verbal Learning and Verbal Behavior,* 1970, **9,** 567–572.

Bjork, R. A., & Whitten, W. B. Recency-sensitive retrieval processes in long-term free recall. *Cognitive Psychology,* 1974, **6,** 173–189.

Boring, E. G. *A history of experimental psychology.* New York: Appleton-Century-Crofts, 1950.

Bousfield, A. K., & Bousfield, W. A. Measurement of clustering and of sequential constancies in repeated free recall. *Psychological Reports,* 1966, **19,** 935–942.

Bousfield, W. A. The occurrence of clustering in the recall of randomly arranged associates. *Journal of General Psychology,* 1953, **49,** 229–240.

Bousfield, W. A., & Cohen, B. H. The effects of reinforcement on the occurrence of clustering in the recall of randomly arranged associates. *Journal of Psychology,* 1953, **36,** 67–81.

Bousfield, W. A., & Sedgewick, C. H. An analysis of sequences of restricted associative responses. *Journal of General Psychology,* 1944, **30,** 149–165.

Bower, G. H. An association model for response and training variables in paired-associate learning. *Psychological Review,* 1962, **69,** 34–53.

Bower, G. H. Adaptation-level coding of stimuli and serial position effects. In M. H. Appley (Ed.), *Adaptation-level theory.* New York: Academic Press, 1971. Pp. 175–201.

Bower, G. H. Mental imagery and associative learning. In L. W. Gregg (Ed.), *Cognition in learning and memory.* New York: Wiley, 1972. Pp. 51–88. (a)

Bower, G. H. Stimulus sampling theory of encoding variability. In A. W. Melton & E. Martin (Eds.), *Coding processes in human memory.* Washington, D.C.: Winston, 1972. Pp. 85–123. (b)

Bower, G. H., & Reitman, J. S. Mnemonic elaboration in multilist learning. *Journal of Verbal Learning and Verbal Behavior,* 1972, **11,** 478–485.

Bower, G. H., & Springston, F. Pauses as recoding points in letter series. *Journal of Experimental Psychology,* 1970, **83,** 421–430.

Bower, G. H., & Winzenz, D. Group structure, coding, and memory for digit series. *Journal of Experimental Psychology Monograph Supplement,* 1969, **80**(2), 1–17.

Bracey, G. W. Two operations in character recognition: A partial replication. *Perception and Psychophysics,* 1969, **6,** 357–360.

Bransford, J. D., Barclay, J. R., & Franks, J. J. Sentence memory: A constructive versus interpretive approach. *Cognitive Psychology,* 1972, **3,** 193–209.

Bransford, J. D., & Franks, J. J. The abstraction of linguistic ideas. *Cognitive Psychology,* 1971, **2,** 331–350.

Bregman, A. S. Forgetting curves with semantic, graphic and contiguity cues. *Journal of Experimental Psychology,* 1968, **18,** 539–546.

Brelsford, J. W., Jr., & Atkinson, R. C. Recall of paired-associates as a function of overt and covert rehearsal procedures. *Journal of Verbal Learning and Verbal Behavior,* 1968, **7,** 730–736.

Briggs, G. E. Acquisition, extinction, and recovery functions in retroactive inhibition. *Journal of Experimental Psychology,* 1954, **47,** 285–293.

Broadbent, D. E. The role of auditory localization in attention and memory span. *Journal of Experimental Psychology,* 1954, **47,** 191–196.

Broadbent, D. E. *Perception and Communication.* New York: Pergamon, 1958.

Brooks, L. R. Spatial and verbal components of the act of recall. *Canadian Journal of Psychology,* 1968, **22,** 349–368.

Brown, J. Some tests of the decay theory of immediate memory. *Quarterly Journal of Experimental Psychology,* 1958, **10,** 12–21.

Bruce, D., & Papay, J. P. Primacy effects in single-trial free recall. *Journal of Verbal Learning and Verbal Behavior,* 1970, **9,** 473–486.

Bugelski, B. R. Presentation time, total time, and mediation in paired associate learning. *Journal of Experimental Psychology,* 1962, **63,** 409–412.

Bugelski, R. B. In defense of remote associations. *Psychological Review,* 1965, **72,** 169–174.

Bugelski, B. R., Kidd, E., & Segmen, J. Image as a mediator in one-trial paired-associate learning. *Journal of Experimental Psychology,* 1968, **76,** 69–73.

Buschke, H. Selective reminding for analysis of memory and learning. *Journal of Verbal Learning and Verbal Behavior,* 1973, **12,** 543–550.

Buschke, H. Spontaneous remembering after recall failure. *Science,* 1974, **184,** 579–581.

Carmichael, L. C., Hogan, H. P., & Walters, A. A. An experimental study of the effect of language on the reproduction of visually perceived form. *Journal of Experimental Psychology,* 1932, **15,** 73–86.

Carroll, J. B. The case for ideographic writing. In J. F. Kavanagh & I. G. Mattingly (Eds.), *Language by ear and by eye: The relationships between speech and reading.* Cambridge, Mass.: MIT Press, 1972. Pp. 103–109.

Chase, W. G., & Calfee, R. C. Modality and similarity effects in short-term recognition memory. *Journal of Experimental Psychology,* 1969, **81,** 510–514.

Cheng, C. Different roles of acoustic and articulatory information in short-term memory. *Journal of Experimental Psychology,* 1974, **103,** 614–618.

Cheng, N. Y. Retroactive effect and degree of similarity. *Journal of Experimental Psychology,* 1929, **12,** 444–458.

Chomsky, N. *Syntactic structures.* The Hague: Mouton, 1957.

Chorover, S. L., & Schiller, P. H. Short-term retrograde amnesia in rats. *Journal of Comparative and Physiological Psychology,* 1965, **59,** 73–78.

Cofer, C. N. On some factors in the organizational characteristics of free recall. *American Psychologist,* 1965, **20,** 261–272.

Cofer, C. N. Does conceptual organization influence the amount retained in immediate free recall? In B. Kleinmuntz (Ed.), *Concepts and the structure of memory.* New York: Wiley, 1967. Pp. 181–214.

Cofer, C. N., Bruce, D. R., & Reicher, G. M. Clustering in free recall as a function of certain methodological variations. *Journal of Experimental Psychology,* 1966, **71,** 858–866.

Cohen, B. H. Recall of categorized word lists. *Journal of Experimental Psychology,* 1963, **66,** 227–234.

Collyer, S. C., Jonides, J., & Bevan, W. Images as memory aids: is bizarreness helpful? *American Journal of Psychology,* 1972, **85,** 31–38.

Coltheart, M., & Glick, M. J. Visual imagery: A case study. *Quarterly Journal of Experimental Psychology,* 1974, **26,** 438–453.

Conrad, R. Acoustic confusions in immediate memory. *British Journal of Psychology,* 1964, **55,** 75–84.

Conrad, R. Order errors in immediate recall of sequences. *Journal of Verbal Learning and Verbal Behavior,* 1965, **4,** 161–169.

Conrad, R. Interference or decay over short retention intervals? *Journal of Verbal Learning and Verbal Behavior,* 1967, **6,** 49–54.

Conrad, R. Speech and reading. In J. F. Kavanagh & I. G. Mattingly (Eds.), *Language by ear and by eye: The relationships between speech and reading.* Cambridge, Massachusetts: MIT Press, 1972. Pp. 205–240. (a)

Conrad, R. Short-term memory in the deaf: A test for speech coding. *British Journal of Psychology,* 1972, **63,** 173–180. (b)

Conrad, R., & Hull, A. J. Information, acoustic confusion, and memory span. *British Journal of Psychology,* 1964, **55,** 429–432.

Conrad, R., & Hull, A. J. Imput modality and the serial position curve in short-term memory. *Psychonomic Science,* 1968, **10,** 135–136.

Conrad, R., & Rush, M. L. On the nature of short-term memory encoding by the deaf. *Journal of Speech & Hearing Disorders,* 1965, **30,** 336–343.

Cooley, R. K., & McNulty, J. A. Recall of individual CCC trigrams over short intervals of time as a function of mode of presentation. *Psychonomic Science,* 1967, **9,** 543–544.

Coons, E. E., & Miller, N. E. Conflict versus consolidation of memory traces to explain "retrograde amnesia" produced by ECS. *Journal of Comparative and Physiological Psychology,* 1960, **53,** 524–531.

Cooper, E. H., & Pantle, A. J. The total-time hypothesis in verbal learning. *Psychological Bulletin,* 1967, **68,** 221–234.

Cooper, F. S. How is language conveyed by speech? In J. F. Kavanagh & I. G. Mattingly (Eds.), *Language by ear and by eye: The relationships between speech and reading.* Cambridge, Massachusetts: MIT Press, 1972. Pp. 25–45.

Cooper, L. A., & Shepard, R. N. Chronometric studies of the rotation of mental images. In W. G. Chase (Ed.), *Visual information processing.* New York: Academic Press, 1973. Pp. 75–176.

Corballis, M. C. Rehearsal and decay in immediate recall of visually and aurally presented items. *Canadian Journal of Psychology,* 1966, **20**(1), 43–51.

Corcoran, D. W. J. An acoustic factor in letter cancellation. *Nature,* 1966, **210,** 658.

Corcoran, D. W. J. Acoustic factors in proof reading. *Nature,* 1967, **214,** 851.

Corcoran, D. W. J. *Pattern recognition.* Harmondsworth: Penguin, 1971.

Corman, C. N., & Wickens, D. D. Retroactive inhibition in short-term memory. *Journal of Verbal Learning and Verbal Behavior,* 1968, **7,** 16–19.

Craik, F. I. M. Short-term memory and the aging process. In G. A. Talland (Ed.), *Human aging and behavior.* New York: Academic Press, 1968. Pp. 131–168. (a)

Craik, F. I. M. Two components in free recall. *Journal of Verbal Learning and Verbal Behavior,* 1968, **7,** 996–1004. (b)

Craik, F. I. M. The fate of primary items in free recall. *Journal of Verbal Learning and Verbal Behavior,* 1970, **9,** 143–148.

Craik, F. I. M. Primary Memory. *British Medical Bulletin,* 1971, **27,** 232–236.

Craik, F. I. M., & Birtwistle, J. Proactive inhibition in free recall. *Journal of Experimental Psychology,* 1971, **91**(1), 120–123.

Craik, F. I. M., & Lockhart, R. S. Levels of processing: A framework for memory research. *Journal of Verbal Larning and Verbal Behavior,* 1972, **11,** 671–684.

Craik, F. I. M., & Watkins, M. J. The role of rehearsal in short-term memory. *Journal of Verbal Learning and Verbal Behavior,* 1973, **12,** 599–607.

Crowder, R. G. Prefix effects in immediate memory. *Canadian Journal of Psychology,* 1967, **21,** 450–461. (a)

Crowder, R. G. Short-term memory for words with a perceptual-motor interpolated activity. *Journal of Verbal Learning and Verbal Behavior,* 1967, **6,** 753–761. (b)

Crowder, R. G. The relation between interpolated-task performance and proactive inhibition in short-term retention. *Journal of Verbal Learning and Verbal Behavior,* 1968, 7, 577–583. (a)

Crowder, R. G. Intraserial repetition effects in immediate memory. *Journal of Verbal Learning and Verbal Behavior,* 1968, 7, 446–451. (b)

Crowder, R. G. Evidence for the chaining hypothesis of serial verbal learning. *Journal of Experimental Psychology,* 1968, 76, 497–500. (c)

Crowder, R. G. Behavioral strategies in immediate memory. *Journal of Verbal Learning and Verbal Behavior,* 1969, 8, 524–528.

Crowder, R. G. The sound of vowels and consonants in immediate memory. *Journal of Verbal Learning and Verbal Behavior,* 1971, 10, 587–596.

Crowder, R. G. Visual and auditory memory. In J. F. Kavanagh & I. G. Mattingly (Eds.), *Language by ear and by eye: The relationships between speech and reading.* Cambridge, Massachusetts: MIT Press, 1972. Pp. 251–275.

Crowder, R. G. Inferential problems in echoic memory. In P. Rabbitt & S. Dornic (Eds.), *Attention and performance.* V. London: Academic Press, 1975. Pp. 218–229.

Crowder, R. G., & Morton, J. Precategorical acoustic storage (PAS). *Perception & Psychophysics,* 1969, 5, 365–373.

D'Agostino, P. R., & DeRemer, P. Repetition effects as a function of rehearsal and encoding variability. *Journal of Verbal Learning and Verbal Behavior,* 1973, 12, 108–113.

Dallett, K. M. Practice effects in free and ordered recall. *Journal of Experimental Psychology,* 1963, 66, 65–71.

Dallett, K. M. "Primary memory": The effects of redundancy upon digit repetition. *Psychonomic Science,* 1965, 3, 237–238. (a)

Dallett, K. M. In defense of remote associations. *Psychological Review,* 1965, 72, 164–168. (b)

DaPolito, F. J. Proactive effects with independent retrieval of competing responses. Unpublished doctoral dissertation, Indiana University, Bloomington, 1966.

Darwin, C. J. Ear differences in the recall of fricatives and vowels. *Quarterly Journal of Experimental Psychology,* 1971, 23, 46–62.

Darwin, C. J., & Baddeley, A. D. Acoustic memory and the perception of speech. *Cognitive Psychology,* 1974, 6, 41–60.

Darwin, C. J., Turvey, M. T., & Crowder, R. G. An auditory analogue of the Sperling partial report procedure: Evidence for brief auditory storage. *Cognitive Psychology,* 1972, 3, 255–267.

Davis, R., Sutherland, N. S., & Judd, B. R. Information content in recognition and recall. *Journal of Experimental Psychology,* 1961, 61, 422–429.

Day, R. S., & Vigorito, J. M. A parallel between encodedness and the ear advantage: Evidence from a temporal order judgment task. *Journal of the Acoustical Society of America,* 1973, 53, 358.

Deese, J. Influence of inter-item associative strength upon immediate free recall. *Psychological Reports,* 1959, 5, 305–312.

Deese, J. From the isolated verbal unit to connected discourse. In C. N. Cofer (Ed.), *Verbal learning and verbal behavior,* New York: McGraw-Hill, 1961. Pp. 11–31.

Deese, J. *The structure of associations in language and thought.* Baltimore: The Johns Hopkins University Press, 1965.

Deese, J. *Psycholinguistics.* Boston: Allyn and Bacon, 1970.

Delprato, D. J. Specific-pair interference on recall and associative matching retention tests. *American Journal of Psychology,* 1971, 84, 185–193.

den Heyer, K., & Barrett, B. Selective loss of visual and verbal information in STM by means of visual and verbal interpolated tasks. *Psychonomic Science,* 1971, 25, 100–102.

DeSoto, C. B., & Bosley, D. D. The cognitive structure of a social structure. *Journal of Abnormal & Social Psychology*, 1962, **64**, 303–307.

Dick, A. O. Relations between the sensory register and short-term storage in tachistoscopic recognition. *Journal of Experimental Psychology*, 1969, **82**, 279–284.

Dick, A. O. On the problem of selection in short-term visual (iconic) memory. *Canadian Journal of Psychology*, 1971, **25**, 250–263.

Dillon, R. F., & Reid, L. S. Short-term memory as a function of information processing during the retention interval. *Journal of Experimental Psychology*, 1969, **81**, 261–269.

Doob, L. W. Eidetic imagery: A cross-cultural will-o'-the-wisp? *Journal of Psychology*, 1966, **63**, 13–34.

Dooling, D. J., & Lachman, R. Effects of comprehension on retention of prose. *Journal of Experimental Psychology*, 1971, 88(2), 216–222.

Duncan, C. P. The retroactive effect of electroshock on learning. *Journal of Comparative and Physiological Psychology*, 1949, **42**, 32–44.

Dyer, F. N. The Stroop phenomenon and its use in the study of perceptual, cognitive, and response processes. *Memory and Cognition*, 1973, **1**, 106–120.

Eagle, M., & Leiter, E. Recall and recognition in intentional and incidental learning. *Journal of Experimental Psychology*, 1964, **68**, 58–63.

Ebbinghaus, H. E. *Grundzüge der psychologie*. Leipzig: Von Veit, 1902.

Ebbinghaus, H. E. *Memory: A contribution to experimental psychology*. New York: Dover, 1964. (Originally published 1885; translated 1913.)

Ebenholtz, S. M. Position mediated transfer between serial learning and a spatial discrimination task. *Journal of Experimental Psychology*, 1963, **65**, 603–608.

Ebenholtz, S. M. Serial learning and dimensional organization. In G. H. Bower (Ed.), *The psychology of learning and motivation*. Vol. 5. New York: Academic Press, 1972. Pp. 267–314.

Egan, J. P. Recognition memory and the operating characteristic, Technical Note AFCRC-TN-58-51. Hearing and Communication Laboratory, Indiana University, Bloomington, 1958.

Ehrlich, M.-F. L'apprentissage verbal: Étude des processus d'activation et de structuration. *Monographies Françaises de Psychologie*, 1972, No. 22.

Ehrlich, S. Structuration and destructuration of responses in free-recall learning. *Journal of Verbal Learning & Verbal Behavior*, 1970, **9**, 282–286.

Ekstrand, B. R. Effect of sleep on memory. *Journal of Experimental Psychology*, 1967, **75**, 64–72.

Ekstrand, B. R. To sleep, perchance to dream (about why we forget). In C. P. Duncan, L. Sechrest, & A. W. Melton (Eds.), *Human memory: festschrift for Benton J. Underwood*, New York: Appleton-Century-Crofts, 1972. Pp. 59–82.

Elliott, L. L. Backward masking: Monotic and dichotic conditions. *Journal of the Acoustical Society of America*, 1962, **34**, 1108–1115.

Ellis, N. R. Memory processes in retardates and normals: Theoretical and empirical considerations. In N. Ellis (Ed.), *International review of research in mental retardation*. Vol. 4. New York: Academic Press, 1970. Pp. 1–32.

Elmes, D. G., Greener, W. I., & Wilkinson, W. C. Free recall of items presented after massed- and distributed-practice items. *American Journal of Psychology*, 1972, 85(2), 237–240.

Elmes, D. G., Sanders, L. W., & Dovel, J. C. Isolation of massed- and distributed-practice items. *Memory and Cognition*, 1973, **1**, 77–79.

Eriksen, C. W., & Johnson, H. J. Storage and decay characteristics of nonattended auditory stimuli. *Journal of Experimental Psychology*, 1970, **68**, 28–36.

Eriksen, C., Pollack, M., & Montague, W. Implicit speech: mechanism in perceptual coding? *Journal of Experimental Psychology*, 1970, **84**, 502–507.

Estes, W. K. Statistical theory of spontaneous recovery and regression. *Psychological Review,* 1955, **62,** 145–154.

Estes, W. K. The statical approach to learning theory. In S. Koch (Ed.), *Psychology: A study of a science.* Vol. II. New York: McGraw-Hill, 1959. Pp. 380–491.

Estes, W. K. Learning theory and the new "mental chemistry." *Psychological Review,* 1960, **67,** 207–223.

Estes, W. K. An associative basis for coding and organization in memory. In A. W. Melton & E. Martin (Eds.), *Coding processes in human memory.* Washington, D.C.: Winston, 1972. Pp. 161–190.

Estes, W. K., & DaPolito, F. Independent variation of information storage and retrieval processes in paired-associate learning, *Journal of Experimental Psychology,* 1967, **75,** 18–26.

Estes, W. K., Hopkins, B. L., & Crothers, E. J. All-or-none and conservation effects in the learning and retention of paired associates. *Journal of Experimental Psychology,* 1960, **60,** 329–339.

Feigenbaum, E. A. Information processing and memory. In D. A. Norman (Ed.), *Models of human memory.* New York: Academic Press, 1970. Pp. 451–468.

Feigenbaum, E. A., & Simon, H. A. A theory of the serial position effect. *British Journal of Psychology,* 1962, **53,** 307–320.

Fitts, P. M. Perceptual-motor skill learning. In A. W. Melton (Ed.), *Categories of human learning.* New York: Academic Press, 1964. Pp. 243–285.

Fleishman, E. A., & Hempel, W. E., Jr. Factorial analysis of complex psychomotor performance and related skills. *Journal of Applied Psychology,* 1956, **40,** 96–104.

Flexser, A. J., & Bower, G. H. How frequency affects recency judgments: A model for recency discrimination. *Journal of Experimental Psychology,* 1974, **103,** 706–716.

Foucault, M. Les inhibitions internes de fixation. *Année Psychologique,* 1928, **29,** 92–112.

Frost, N. Encoding and retrieval in visual memory tasks. *Journal of Experimental Psychology,* 1972, **95,** 317–326.

Frost, R. R., & Jahnke, J. C. Proactive effects in short-term memory. *Journal of Verbal Learning & Verbal Behavior,* 1968, **7,** 785–789.

Fuchs, A. F., & Melton, A. W. Effects of frequency of presentation and stimulus length on retention in the Brown–Peterson paradigm. *Journal of Experimental Psychology,* 1974, **103,** 629–637.

Fujisaki, H., & Kawashima, T. Some experiments on speech perception and a model for the perceptual mechanism. *Annual Report of the Engineering Research Institute, Volume 29,* Faculty of Engineering, University of Tokyo, Tokyo, 1970, 207–214.

Gardiner, J. M., Craik, F. I. M., & Birtwistle, J. Retrieval cues and release from proactive inhibition. *Journal of Verbal Learning & Verbal Behavior,* 1972, **11,** 778–783.

Gardiner, J. M., Thompson, C. P., & Maskarinec, A. S. Negative recency in initial free recall. *Journal of Experimental Psychology,* 1974, **103,** 71–78.

Garskof, B. E. Unlearning as a function of degree of interpolated learning and method of testing in the A–B, A–C and A–B, C–D paradigms. *Journal of Experimental Psychology,* 1968, **76,** 579–583.

Gartman, L. M., & Johnson, N. F. Massed versus distributed repetition of homographs: A test of the differential-encoding hypothesis. *Journal of Verbal Learning and Verbal behavior,* 1972, **11,** 801–808.

Gibson, E. J. Intralist generalization as a factor in verbal learning. *Journal of Experimental Psychology,* 1942, **30,** 185–200.

Glanzer, M. Distrance between related words in free recall: Trace of the STS. *Journal of Verbal Learning and Verbal Behavior,* 1969, **8,** 105–111.

Glanzer, M. Storage mechanisms in recall. In G. H. Bower & J. T. Spence (Eds.), *The psychology of learning and motivation.* Vol. 5. New York: Academic Press, 1972, Pp. 129–193.

Glanzer, M., & Ciark, W. H. The verbal loop hypothesis: Binary numbers. *Journal of Verbal Learning and Verbal Behavior,* 1963, **2,** 301–309.

Glanzer, M., & Cunitz, A. R. Two storage mechanisms in free recall. *Journal of Verbal Learning and Verbal Behavior,* 1966, **5,** 351–360.

Glanzer, M., & Peters, S. C. A re-examination of the serial position effect. *Journal of Experimental Psychology,* 1962, **64,** 258–266.

Glanzer, M., & Razel, M. The size of the unit in short-term storage. *Journal of Verbal Learning and Verbal Behavior,* 1974, **13,** 114–131.

Glassman, W. E. Subvocal activity and acoustic confusion in short-term memory. *Journal of Experimental Psychology,* 1972, **96,** 164–169.

Glaze, J. A. The association value of nonsense syllables. *Journal of Genetic Psychology,* 1928, **35,** 255–269.

Glenberg, A. M. Retrieval factors and the lag effect. Technical Report No. 49, Human Performance Center, The University of Michigan, Ann Arbor, 1974.

Glucksberg, S., & Cowan, G. N. Memory for nonattended auditory material. *Cognitive Psychology,* 1970, **1,** 149–156.

Goggin, J. First-list recall as a function of second-list learning method. *Journal of Verbal Learning and Verbal Behavior,* 1967, **6,** 423–427.

Goggin, J., & Martin, E. Forced stimulus encoding and retroactive interference. *Journal of Experimental Psychology,* 1970, **84,** 131–136.

Goodman, K. S. The psycholinguistic nature of the reading process. In K. S. Goodman (Ed.), *The psycholinguistic nature of the reading process.* Detroit: Wayne State University Press, 1968. Pp. 15–26.

Gorfein, D. S., & Jacobson, D. E. Memory search in a Brown–Peterson short-term memory paradigm. *Journal of Experimental Psychology,* 1973, **99,** 82–87.

Grant, K. W., & McCormack, P. D. Auditory and visual short-term memory with successive syllable presentation in both modalities. *Psychonomic Science,* 1969, **17,** 341–342.

Gray, C. R., & Gummerman, K. The enigmatic eidetic image: A critical examination of methods, data, and theory. *Psychological Bulletin,* 1975, **82,** 383–407.

Greenberg, R., & Underwood, B. J. Retention as a function of stage of practice. *Journal of Experimental Psychology,* 1950, **40,** 452–457.

Greeno, J. G. *Elementary theoretical psychology.* Reading, Mass.: Addison-Wesley, 1968.

Greeno, J. G. How associations are memorized. In D. A. Norman (Ed.), *Models of human memory.* New York: Academic Press, 1970. Pp. 257–284.

Greeno, J. G. Conservation of information-processing capacity in paired-associate memorizing. *Journal of Verbal Learning and Verbal Behavior,* 1970, **9,** 581–586.   (b)

Greeno, J. G., James, C. T., & DaPolito, F. J. A cognitive interpretation of negative transfer and forgetting of paired associates. *Journal of Verbal Learning and Verbal Behavior,* 1971, **10,** 331–345.

Greenspoon, J., & Ranyard, R. Stimulus conditions and retroactive inhibition. *Journal of Experimental Psychology,* 1957, **53,** 55–59.

Groninger, L. D. Mnemonic imagery and forgetting. *Psychonomic Science,* 1971, **23,** 161–163.

Guthrie, E. R. *The psychology of learning.* New York: Harper, 1935.

Guttman, N., & Julesz, B. Lower limits of auditory periodicity analysis. *Journal of the Acoustical Society of America,* 1963, **35,** 610.

Haber, R. N., & Haber, R. B. Eidetic Imagery: I. Frequency. *Perceptual & Motor Skills,* 1964, **19,** 131–138.

Hall, J. F. Learning as a function of word frequency. *American Journal of Psychology,* 1954, **67**, 138–140.

Hall, J. F. *Psychology of learning.* Philadelphia: Lippincott, 1966.

Halwes, T., & Jenkins, J. J. Problem of serial order in behavior is not resolved by context-sensitive associative memory models. *Psychological Review,* 1971, **78**, 122–129.

Hardyck, C. D., & Petrinovich, L. F. Subvocal speech and comprehension level as a function of the difficulty of the reading material. *Journal of Verbal Learning and Verbal Behavior,* 1970, **9**, 647–652.

Hardyck, C. D., Petrinovich, L. F., & Ellsworth, D. W. Feedback of speech muscle activity during silent reading: Two comments. *Science,* 1967, **157**, 581.

Harlow, H. F. The formation of learning sets. *Psychological Review,* 1949, **56**, 51–65.

Healy, A. F. Separating item from order information in short-term memory. *Journal of Verbal Learning and Verbal Behavior,* 1974, **13**, 644–655.

Hebb, D. O. *The organization of behavior: a neuropsychological theory.* New York: Wiley, 1949.

Hebb, D. O. Distinctive features of learning in the higher animal. In J. F. Delafresnaye (Ed.), *Brain mechanisms and learning.* New York: Oxford University Press, 1961.

Hebb, D. O. *A textbook of psychology.* Phildelphia: Saunders, 1966.

Hebb, D. O. Concerning imagery. *Psychological Review,* 1968, **75**, 466–477.

Hebb, D. O., & Foord, E. N. Errors of visual recognition and the nature of the trace. *Journal of Experimental Psychology,* 1945, **35**, 335–348.

Hellyer, S. Supplementary report: Frequency of stimulus presentation and short-term decrement in recall. *Journal of Experimental Psychology,* 1962, **64**, 650.

Hilgard, E. R., & Marquis, D. G. *Conditioning and learning.* New York: Appleton-Century-Crofts, 1940.

Hinrichs, J. V., Mewaldt, S. P., & Redding, J. The Ranschburg effect: Repetition and guessing factors in short-term memory. *Journal of Verbal Learning and Verbal Behavior,* 1973, **12**, 64–75.

Hintzman, D. L. Articulatory coding in short-term memory. *Journal of Verbal Learning and Verbal Behavior,* 1967, **6**, 312–316.

Hintzman, D. L. Explorations with a discrimination-net model for paired-associate learning. *Journal of Mathematical Psychology,* 1968, **5**, 123–162.

Hintzman, D. L. On testing the independence of associations. *Psychological Review,* 1972, **79**, 261–264.

Hintzman, D. L. Theoretical implications of the spacing effect. In R. L. Solso (Ed.), *Theories in cognitive psychology: The Loyola symposium.* Hillsdale, New Jersey: Lawrence Erlbaum Assoc., 1974. Pp. 77–99.

Hintzman, D. L., & Block, R. A. Repetition and memory: Evidence for a multiple-trace hypothesis. *Journal of Experimental Psychology,* 1971, **88**, 297–306.

Hintzman, D. L., Block, R. A., & Summers, J. J. Modality tags and memory for repetitions: Locus of the spacing effect. *Journal of Verbal Learning and Verbal Behavior,* 1973, **12**, 229–238.

Hirsch, I. J. Auditory perception of temporal order. *Journal of the Acoustical Society of America,* 1959, **31**, 759–767.

Hockey, G. R., Davies, S., & Gray, M. M. Forgetting as a function of sleep at different times of day. *Quarterly Journal of Experimental Psychology,* 1972, **24**, 386–393.

Hollingworth, H. C. Characteristic differences between recall and recognition. *American Journal of Psychology,* 1913, **24**, 532–544.

Horowitz, L. M. Free recall and ordering of trigrams. *Journal of Experimental Psychology,* 1961, **62**, 51–57.

Horowitz, L. M., & Manelis, L. Toward a theory of redintegrative memory: Adjective–noun phrases. In G. H. Bower (Ed.), *The psychology of learning and motivation.* Vol. 6. New York: Academic Press, 1972. Pp. 193–224.

Horowitz, L. M., & Manelis, L. Recognition and cued recall of idioms and phrases. *Journal of Experimental Psychology,* 1973, **100,** 291–296.

Horowitz, L. M., & Prytulak, L. S. Redintegrative memory. *Psychological Review,* 1969, **76,** 519–531.

Houston, J. P. Short-term retention of verbal units with equated degrees of learning. *Journal of Experimental Psychology,* 1965, **70,** 75–78.

Hovland, C. I. Experimental studies in rote learning theory: II. Reminiscence with varying speeds of syllable presentation. *Journal of Experimental Psychology,* 1938, **22,** 338–353.

Hovland, C. I. Experimental studies in rote learning theory. VI. Comparison of retention following learning to same criterion by massed and distributed practice. *Journal of Experimental Psychology,* 1940, **26,** 568–587.

Hudson, R. L. & Austin, J. B. Effect of context and category name on the recall of categorized word lists. *Journal of Experimental Psychology,* 1970, **86,** 43–47.

Hull, C. L. The conflicting psychologies of learning–a way out. *Psychological Review,* 1935, **42,** 491–516.

Hull, C. L., Hovland, C. I., Ross, R. T., Hall, M., Perkins, D. T., & Fitch, F. B. *Mathematico-deductive theory of rote learning.* New Haven, Connecticut: Yale University Press, 1940.

Hunt, E., & Love, T. How good can memory be? In A. W. Melton & E. Martin (Eds.), *Coding processes in human memory.* Washington, D.C.: Winston, 1972. Pp. 237–260.

Hunter, I. M. L. *Memory.* Baltimore: Penguin, 1964.

Hyde, T. S., & Jenkins, J. J. Differential effects of incidental tasks on the organization of recall of a list of highly associated words. *Journal of Experimental Psychology,* 1969, **82,** 472–481.

Jaensch, E. R. *Eidetic imagery.* (Translated by O. Oeser.) London: Kegan Paul, Trench, Trubner (New York: Harcourt Brace), 1930.

Jahnke, J. C. The Ranschburg effect. *Psychological Review,* 1969, **76,** 592–605.

Jahnke, J. C. The effects of intraserial and interserial repetition on recall. *Journal of Verbal Learning & Verbal Behavior,* 1972, **11,** 706–716.

James, W. *The principles of psychology.* New York: Dover, 1950. (Originally published in 1890.)

Jenkins, J. G., & Dallenbach, K. M. Oblivescence during sleep and waking. *American Journal of Psychology,* 1924, **35,** 605–612.

Jenkins, J. J., Mink, W. D., & Russell, W. A. Associative clustering as a function of verbal association strength. *Psychological Reports,* 1958,4,127–136.

Jenkins, J. J., & Russell, W. A. Associative clustering during recall *Journal of Abnormal & Social Psychology,* 1952, **47,** 818–821.

Jensen, A. R. Temporal and spatial effects of serial position. *American Journal of Psychology,* 1962, **75,** 390–400.

Jensen, A. R. & Rohwer, W. D., Jr. What is learned in serial learning? *Journal of Verbal Learning & Verbal Behavior,* 1965, **4,** 62–72.

Johnson, L. M. The relative effect of a time interval upon learning and retention. *Journal of Experimental Psychology,* 1939, **24,** 169–179.

Johnson, M. K. Organizational units in free recall as a source of transfer. *Journal of Experimental Psychology,* 1972, **94,** 300–307.

Johnson, N. F. Sequential verbal behavior. In T. R. Dixon & D. L. Horton (Eds.), *Verbal behavior and general behavior theory.* Englewood Cliffs, New Jersey: Prentice-Hall, 1968. Pp. 421–450.

Johnson, N. F. The role of chunking and organization in the process of recall. In G. H. Bower (Ed.), *The psychology of learning and motivation: Advances in research and theory.* Vol. 4. New York: Academic Press, 1970. Pp. 171–247.

Johnson, N. F. Organization and the concept of a memory code. In A. W. Melton & E. Martin (Eds.), *Coding processes in human memory*. Washington, D.C.: Winston, 1972. Pp. 125–159.

Johnston, W. A., Coots, J. H. & Flickinger, R. G. Controlled semantic encoding and the effect of repetition lag on free recall. *Journal of Verbal Learning & Verbal Behavior*, 1972, 11, 784–788.

Jonides, J., Kahn, R., & Rozin, P. Imagery instruction improves memory in blind subjects. *The Bulletin of the Psychonomic Society*, 1975, 5(5), 424–426.

Julesz, B. Binocular depth perception without familiarity cues. *Science*, 1964, 145, 256–362.

Kahneman, D. Method, findings, and theory in studies of visual masking. *Psychological Bulletin*, 1968, 70, 404–425.

Kahneman, D. *Attention and effort*. Englewood Cliffs, New Jersey: Prentice Hall, 1973.

Katona, G. *Organizing and memorizing*. New York: Columbia University Press, 1940.

Kausler, D. H. *Psychology of verbal learning and memory*. New York: Academic Press, 1974.

Keppel, G., & Rauch, D. S. Unlearning as a function of second-list error instructions. *Journal of Verbal Learning and Verbal Behavior*, 1966, 5, 50–58.

Keppel, G., & Underwood, B. J. Proactive inhibition in short-term retention of single items. *Journal of Verbal Learning and Verbal Behavior*, 1962, 1, 153–161.

Kincaid, J. P., & Wickens, D. D. Temporal gradient of release from proactive inhibition. *Journal of Experimental Psychology*, 1970, 86, 313–316.

Kinsbourne, M., & George, J. The mechanism of the word-frequency effect on recognition memory. *Journal of Verbal Learning and Verbal Behavior*, 1974, 13, 63–69.

Kintsch, W. All-or-none learning and the role of repetition in paired-associate learning. *Science*, 1963, 140, 310–312.

Kintsch, W. *Learning, Memory, and conceptual processes*. New York: Wiley, 1970.

Kintsch, W. *The representation of meaning in memory*. Hillsdale, N.J.: Erlbaum, 1974.

Kintsch, W., & Buschke, H. Homophones and synonyms in short-term memory. *Journal of Experimental Psychology*, 1969, 80, 403–407.

Kirsner, K., & Craik, F. I. M. Naming and decision processes in short-term recognition memory. *Journal of Experimental Psychology*, 1971, 88, 149–157.

Klapp, S. T. Implicit speech inferred from response latencies in same–different decisions. *Journal of Experimental Psychology*, 1971, 91, 262–267.

Kleinsmith, L. J., & Kaplan, S. Paired-associate learning as a function of arousal and interpolated interval. *Journal of Experimental Psychology*, 1963, 65, 190–193.

Kleinsmith, L. J., & Kaplan, S. Interaction of arousal and recall interval in nonsense syllable paired-associate learning. *Journal of Experimental Psychology*, 1964, 67, 124–126.

Köhler, W. *The mentality of apes*. New York: Harcourt, Brace, 1925.

Köhler, W. *Gestalt Psychology*. New York: Leveright (Meuter), 1947.

Kolers, P. A. Specificity of operations in sentence recognition. *Cognitive Psychology*, 1975, 7, 289–306.

Konorski, J. *Integrative activity of the brain: An interdisciplinary approach*. Chicago: University of Chicago Press, 1967.

Koppenaal, R. J. Time changes in the strengths of A–B, A–C lists: Spontaneous recovery? *Journal of Verbal Learning & Verbal Behavior*, 1963, 2, 310–319.

Koriat, A., & Fischhoff, B. What day is today? An inquiry into the process of time orientation, *Memory & Cognition*, 1974, 2, 201–205.

Kosslyn, S. M. Information representation in visual images. *Cognitive Psychology*, 1975, 7, 341–370.

Krechevsky, I. A study of the continuity of the problem solving process. *Psychological Review*, 1938, 45, 107–133.

Kreuger, W. C. The effect of overlearning on retention. *Journal of Experimental Psychology,* 1929, **12,** 71–78.

Kuhn, T. *The structure of scientific revolutions.* Chicago: University of Chicago Press, 1962.

LaBerge, D. Beyond auditory coding: A discussion of Conrad's paper. In J. F. Kavanagh & I. G. Mattingly (eds.), *Language by ear and by eye: relationships between speech and reading.* Cambridge, Massachusetts: MIT Press, 1972. Pp. 241–248.

LaBerge, D., & Samuels, S. J. Toward a theory of automatic information processing in reading. *Cognitive Psychology,* 1974, **6,** 293–323.

Lachman, R., & Dooling, D. J. Connected discourse and random strings: Effects of number of inputs on recognition and recall. *Journal of Experimental Psychology,* 1968, 77, 517–522.

Ladd, G. L. & Woodworth, R. S. *Elements of physiological psychology.* New York: Scribner's, 1911.

Lambert, W. E., & Paivio, A. The influence of noun–adjective ordering on learning. *Canadian Journal of Psychology,* 1956, **10,** 9–12.

Landauer, T. K. Rate of implicit speech. *Perceptual and Motor Skills,* 1962, **15,** 646.

Landauer, T. K. Interval between item repetitions and free recall memory. *Psychonomic Science,* 1967, **8,** 439–440.

Landauer, T. K. Reinforcement as consolidation. *Psychological Review,* 1969, 76, 82–96.

Landauer, T. K. Consolidation in human memory: Retrograde amnestic effects of confusable items in paired-associate learning. *Journal of Verbal Learning and Verbal Behavior,* 1974, **13,** 45–53.

Landauer, T. K., & Streeter, L. A. Structural differences between common and rare words: Failure of equivalence assumptions for theories of word recognition. *Journal of Verbal Learning and Verbal Behavior,* 1973, **12,** 119–131.

Lashley, K. S. The problem of serial order in behavior. In L. A. Jeffress (Ed.), *Cerebral mechanisms in behavior.* New York: Wiley, 1951. Pp. 112–136.

Leask, J., Haber, R. N., & Haber, R. B. Eidetic imagery among children: II. Longitudinal and experimental results. *Psychonomic Monograph Supplements,* 1969, 3(3, Whole No. 35), 25–48.

Lefton, L. A. Metacontrast: A review. *Perception & Psychophysics,* 1973, **13,** 161–171.

Lepley, W. M. Serial reactions considered as conditioned reactions. *Psychological Monographs,* 1934, **46,**(205).

Lester, O. P. Mental set in relation to retroactive inhibition. *Journal of Experimental Psychology,* 1932, **15,** 681–699.

Levonian, E. Short-term retention in relation to arousal. *Psychophysiology,* 1968, **4,** 284–293.

Liberman, A. M. The effect of interpolated activity in spontaneous recovery from experimental extinction. *Journal of Experimental Psychology,* 1944, **34,** 282–301.

Liberman, A. M., Cooper, F. S., Shankweiler, D. P., & Studdert-Kennedy, M. Perception of the speech code. *Psychological Review,* 1967, **74,** 431–461.

Light, L. L. Homonyms and synonyms as retrieval cues. *Journal of Experimental Psychology,* 1972, **96,** 255–262.

Light, L. L., & Carter-Sobell, L. Effects of changed semantic context on recognition memory. *Journal of Verbal Learning & Verbal Behavior,* 1970, **9,** 1–11.

Lindley, R. H. Effects of controlled coding cues in short-term memory. *Journal of Experimental Psychology,* 1963, **66,** 580–587.

Locke, J. L., & Fehr, F. S. Subvocal rehearsal as a form of speech. *Journal of Verbal Learning & Verbal Behavior,* 1970, **9,** 495–498.   (a)

Locke, J. L., & Fehr, F. S. Young children's use of the speech code in a recall task. *Journal of Experimental Child Psychology,* 1970, **10,** 367–373.   (b)

Locke, J. L., & Kutz, K. J. Memory for speech and speech for memory. *Journal of Speech & Hearing Research,* 1975, 18(1), 176–191.

Locke, J. L., & Locke, V. L. Deaf children's phonetic, visual, and dactylic coding in a grapheme recall task. *Journal of Experimental Psychology,* 1971, 89, 142–146.

Loess, H. Proactive inhibition in short-term memory. *Journal of Verbal Learning and Verbal Behavior,* 1964, 3, 362–368.

Loess, H., & Waugh, N. C. Short-term memory and intertrial interval. *Journal of Verbal Learning & Verbal Behavior,* 1967, 6, 455–460.

Loftus, G. R., & Patterson, K. K. Components of short-term proactive interference. *Journal of Verbal Learning and Verbal Behavior,* 1975, 14, 105–121.

Lorayne, H., & Lucas, J. *The memory book.* New York: Ballantine, 1974.

Lovelace, E. A., Powell, M., & Brooks, R. J. Alphabetic position effects in covert and overt alphabetic recitation times. *Journal of Experimental Psychology,* 1973, 99, 405–408.

Lowry, D. H. The effects of mnemonic learning strategies on transfer, interference, and 48-hour retention. *Journal of Experimental Psychology,* 1974, 103, 16–20.

Luh, C. W. The conditions of retention. *Psychological Monographs,* 1922, 31 (3, Whole No. 142).

Luria, A. R. *The mind of a mnemonist.* (Translated by L. Solotaroff.) New York: Basic Books, 1968.

Madigan, S. A. Intraserial repetition and coding processes in free recall. *Journal of Verbal Learning and Verbal Behavior,* 1969, 8, 828–835.

Madigan, S. A., & McCabe, L. Perfect recall and total forgetting: A problem for models of short-term memory. *Journal of Verbal Learning and Verbal Behavior,* 1971, 10, 101–106.

Mandler, G. Organization and memory. In K. W. Spence & J. T. Spence (Eds.), *The psychology of learning and motivation.* Vol. 1. New York: Academic Press, 1967. Pp. 327–372.

Mandler, G., & Pearlstone, Z. Free and constrained concept learning and subsequent recall. *Journal of Verbal Learning & Verbal Behavior,* 1966, 5, 126–131.

Marks, L. E., & Miller, G. A. The role of semantic and syntactic constraints in the memorization of English sentences. *Journal of Verbal Learning and Verbal Behavior,* 1964, 3, 1–5.

Marks, M. R., & Jack, O. Verbal context and memory span for meaningful material. *American Journal of Psychology,* 1952, 65, 298–300.

Marshall, G. R. Stimulus characteristics contributing to organization in free recall. *Journal of Verbal Learning and Verbal Behavior,* 1967, 6, 364–374.

Martin, E. Transfer of verbal paired associates. *Psychological Review,* 1965, 72, 327–343.

Martin, E. Verbal learning theory and independent retrieval phenomena. *Psychological Review,* 1971, 78, 314–332.

Martin, E. Stimulus encoding in learning and transfer. In A. W. Melton & E. Martin (Eds.), *Coding processes in human memory,* Washington, D.C.: Winston, 1972. Pp. 59–84.

Martin, E. Serial learning: A multilevel access analysis. *Memory & Cognition,* 1974, 2, 322–328.

Martin, E. Generation-recognition theory and the encoding specificity principle. *Psychological Review,* 1975, 82, 150–153.

Martin, E., & Greeno, J. G. Independence of associations tested: A reply to D. L. Hintzman. *Psychological Review,* 1972, 79, 265–267.

Martin, E., & Mackay, S. A. A test of the list-differentiation hypothesis. *American Journal of Psychology,* 1970, 83, 311–321.

Martin, E., & Noreen, D. L. Serial learning: Identification of subjective subsequences. *Cognitive Psychology,* 1974, 6, 421–435.

Martin, E., & Roberts, K. H. Grammatical factors in sentence retention. *Journal of Verbal Learning & Verbal Behavior,* 1966, 5, 211–218.

Martin, S. E. Nonalphabetic writing systems: Some observations. In J. F. Kavanagh & I. G. Mattingly (Eds.), *Language by ear and by eye: The relationships between speech and reading.* Cambridge, Mass.: MIT Press, 1972, Pp. 81–102.

Maskarinec, A. S., & Brown, S. C. Positive and negative recency effects in free recall learning. *Journal of Verbal Learning & Verbal Behavior,* 1974, **13**, 328–334.

Massaro, D. W. Preperceptual auditory images. *Journal of Experimental Psychology,* 1970, **85**, 411–417.

Massaro, D. W. Preperceptual images, processing time, and perceptual units in auditory perception. *Psychological Review,* 1972, 79(2), 124–145.

McCormack, P. D., & Swenson, A. L. Recognition memory for common and rare words. *Journal of Experimental Psychology,* 1972, **95**, 72–77.

McGaugh, J. L. Time-dependent processes in memory storage. *Science,* 1966, **153**, 1351–1358.

McGaugh, J. L., & Gold, P. E. Conceptual and neurobiological issues in studies of treatments affecting memory storage. In G. H. Bower (Ed.), *The psychology of learning and memory.* Vol. 8. New York: Academic Press, 1974. Pp. 233–264.

McGeoch, J. A. Forgetting and the law of disuse. *Psychological Review,* 1932, **39**, 352–370.

McGeoch, J. A. *The psychology of human learning.* New York: Longmans, Green, 1942.

McGeoch, J. A., & Irion, A. L. *The psychology of human learning.* New York: Longmans, Green, 1952.

McGovern, J. B. Extinction of associations in four transfer paradigms. *Psychological Monographs,* 1964, 78(16, Whole No. 593).

McGuigan, F. J. Covert oral behavior during the silent performance of language tasks. *Psychological Bulletin,* 1970, **74**, 309–326.

McGuire, W. J. A multiprocess model for paired-associate learning. *Journal of Experimental Psychology,* 1961, **62**, 335–347.

McLean, P. D. Induced arousal and time of recall as determinants of paired-associate recall. *British Journal of Psychology,* 1969, **60**, 57–62.

Mehler, J. Some effects of grammatical transformations on the recall of English sentences. *Journal of Verbal Learning and Verbal Behavior,* 1963, **2**, 346–351.

Melton, A. W. The end-spurt in memorization curves as an artifact of the averaging of individual curves. *Psychological Monographs,* 1936, 47(212), 119–134.

Melton, A. W. Comments on Professor Postman's paper. In C. N. Cofer (Ed.), *Verbal learning and verbal behavior,* New York: McGraw Hill, 1961. Pp. 179–193.

Melton, A. W. Implications of short-term memory for a general theory of memory. *Journal of Verbal Learning and Verbal Behavior,* 1963, **2**, 1–21.   (a)

Melton, A. W. Comments on Professor Peterson's paper. In C. N. Cofer & B. S. Musgrave (Eds.), *Verbal behavior and learning: Problems and processes.* New York: McGraw-Hill, 1963. Pp. 353–370.   (b)

Melton, A. W. Repetition and retrieval from memory. *Science,* 1967, **158**, 532.

Melton, A. W. The situation with respect to the spacing of repetitions and memory. *Journal of Verbal Learning and Verbal Behavior,* 1970, **9**, 596–606.

Melton, A. W., & Irwin, J. M. The influence of degree of interpolated learning on retroactive inhibition and the overt transfer of specific responses. *American Journal of Psychology,* 1940, **53**, 173–203.

Melton, A. W., & von Lackum, W. J. Retroactive and proactive inhibition in retention: Evidence for a two-factor theory of retroactive inhibition. *American Journal of Psychology,* 1941, **54**, 157–173.

Merryman, C. T. Retroactive inhibition in the A–B, A–D paradigm as measured by a multiple-choice test. *Journal of Experimental Psychology,* 1971, **91**, 212–214.

Miller, G. A. The magical number seven plus or minus two: Some limits on our capacity for processing information. *Psychological Review,* 1956, **63**, 81–97.

Miller, G. A. Free recall of redundant strings of letters. *Journal of Experimental Psychology,* 1958, **56,** 485–491.

Miller, G. A., Galanter, E., & Pribram, K. H. *Plans and the structure of behavior.* New York: Holt, Rinehart & Winston, 1960.

Miller, G. A., & Nicely, P. E. An analysis of perceptual confusions among some English consonants. *Journal of the Acoustical Society of America,* 1955, **27,** 338–352.

Miller, G. A., & Selfridge, J. A. Verbal context and the recall of meaningful material. *American Journal of Psychology,* 1950, **63,** 176–185.

Miller, N. E., & Stevenson, S. S. Agitated behavior of rats during experimental extinction and a curve of spontaneous recovery. *Journal of Comparative Psychology,* 1936, **21,** 205–231.

Miller, R. R., & Springer, A. D. Amnesia, consolidation and retrieval. *Psychological Review,* 1973, **80,** 69–79.

Minami, H., & Dallenbach, K. M. The effect of activity upon learning and retention in the cockroach. *American Journal of Psychology,* 1946, **59,** 1–58.

Moray, N., Bates, A., & Barnett, T. Experiments on the four-eared man. *Journal of the Acoustical Society of America,* 1965, **38,** 196–201.

Morton, J. Repeated items and decay in memory. *Psychonomic Science,* 1968, **10,** 219–220.

Morton, J. Interaction of information in word recognition. *Psychological Review,* 1969, **76,** 165–178.

Morton, J. A functional model for memory. In D. A. Norman (Ed.), *Models of human memory.* New York: Academic Press, 1970. Pp. 203–254.

Morton, J., Crowder, R. G., & Prussin, H. A. Experiments with the stimulus suffix effect. *Journal of Experimental Psychology,* 1971, **91,** 169–190.

Morton, J., & Halloway, C. M. Absence of a cross-modal "suffix effect" in short-term memory. *Quarterly Journal of Experimental Psychology,* 1970, **22,** 167–176.

Müller, G. E., & Pilzecker, A. Experimentalle Beiträge zur Lehre vom Gedächtnis. *Zeitschrift fur Pshchologie,* 1900, **1,** 1–300.

Murdock, B. B., Jr. The distinctiveness of stimuli. *Psychological Review,* 1960, **67,** 16–31. (a)

Murdock, B. B., Jr. The immediate retention of unrelated words. *Journal of Experimental Psychology,* 1960, **60,** 222–234. (b)

Murdock, B. B., Jr. The retention of individual items. *Journal of Experimental Psychology,* 1961, **62,** 618–625. (a)

Murdock, B. B., Jr. Short-term retention of single paired-associates. *Psychological Reports,* 1961, **8,** 280. (b)

Murdock, B. B., Jr. The serial position effect of free recall. *Journal of Experimental Psychology,* 1962, **64,** 482–488.

Murdock, B. B., Jr. Visual and auditory stores in short-term memory. *Quarterly Journal of Experimental Psychology,* 1966, **18,** 206–211. (a)

Murdock, B. B., Jr. Measurement of retention of interpolated activity in short-term memory. *Journal of Verbal Learning and Verbal Behavior,* 1966, **5,** 469–472. (b)

Murdock, B. B., Jr. Auditory and visual stores in short-term memory. *Acta Psychologica,* 1967, **27,** 316–324. (a)

Murdock, B. B., Jr. Recent developments in short-term memory. *British Journal of Psychology,* 1967, **58,** 421–433. (b)

Murdock, B. B., Jr. *Human memory: Theory and data.* Hillsdale, New Jersey: Lawrence Erlbaum Assoc., 1974.

Murdock, B. B., Jr., & vom Saal, W. Transpositions in short-term memory. *Journal of Experimental Psychology,* 1967, **74,** 137–143.

Murdock, B. B., Jr., & Walker, K. D. Modality effects in free recall. *Journal of Verbal Learning and Verbal Behavior,* 1969, **8,** 665–676.

Murray, D. J. Vocalization-at-presentation and immediate recall, with varying recall methods. *Quarterly Journal of Experimental Psychology,* 1966, **18,** 9–18.

Murray, D. J. The role of speech responses in short-term memory. *Canadian Journal of Psychology,* 1967, **21,** 263–276.

Naus, M. J. Memory search of categorized lists: a consideration of alternative self-terminating search strategies. *Journal of Experimental Psychology,* 1974, **102,** 992–1000.

Naus, M. J., Glucksberg, S., & Ornstein, P. A. Taxonomic word categories and memory search. *Cognitive Psychology,* 1972, **3,** 643–654.

Neisser, U. *Cognitive psychology.* New York: Appleton-Century-Crofts, 1967.

Neisser, U. Changing conceptions of imagery. In P. W. Sheehan (Ed.), *The function and nature of imagery.* New York: Academic Press, 1972. Pp. 233–251.

Neisser, U., & Kerr, N. Spatial and mnemonic properties of visual images. *Cognitive Psychology,* 1973, **5,** 138–150.

Newton, J. M., & Wickens, D. D. Retroactive inhibition as a function of the temporal position of interpolated learning. *Journal of Experimental Psychology,* 1956, **51,** 149–154.

Noble, C. E. The role of stimulus meaning (m) in serial verbal learning. *Journal of Experimental Psychology,* 1952, **43,** 437–446.

Norman, D. A. Toward a theory of memory and attention. *Psychological Review,* 1968, **75,** 522–536.

Norman, D. A. Memory while shadowing. *Quarterly Journal of Experimental Psychology,* 1969, **21,** 85–93.

Norman, D. A., & Rumelhart, D. E. A system for perception and memory. In D. A. Norman (Ed.), *Models of human memory.* New York: Academic Press, 1970, Pp. 19–64.

Noyd, D. E. Proactive and intra-stimulus interference in short-term memory for two-, three-, and five-word stimuli. Paper presented at meeting of the Western Psychological Association, Honolulu, June, 1965.

Olton, R. M. The effect of a mnemonic upon the retention of paired-associate verbal material. *Journal of Verbal Learning & Verbal Behavior,* 1969, **8,** 43–48.

Osgood, C. E. The similarity paradox in human learning: A resolution. *Psychological Review,* 1949, **56,** 132–143.

Osgood, C. E. *Method and theory in experimental psychology.* London and New York: Oxford University Press, 1953.

Osgood, C. E., Suci, G. J., & Tannenbaum, P. H. *The measurement of meaning.* Urbana, Illinois: University of Illinois Press, 1957.

Paivio, A. Abstractness, imagery, and meaningfulness in paired-associate learning. *Journal of Verbal Learning and Verbal Behavior,* 1965, **4,** 32–38.

Paivio, A. *Imagery and verbal processes.* New York: Holt, Rinehart & Winston, 1971. (a)

Paivio, A. Imagery and deep structure in the recall of English nominalizations. *Journal of Verbal Learning and Verbal Behavior,* 1971, **10,** 1–12. (b)

Paivio, A. Spacing of repetitions in the incidental and intentional free recall of pictures and words. *Journal of Verbal Learning and Verbal Behavior,* 1974, **13,** 497–511.

Paivio, A. Images, propositions, and knowledge. In J. M. Nicholas (Ed.), *Images, perception, and knowledge,* The Western Ontario Series in Philosophy of Science. Dordrecht: Reidel, in press.

Paivio, A., & Csapo, K. Concrete-image and verbal memory codes. *Journal of Experimental Psychology,* 1969, **80,** 279–285.

Paivio, A., & Csapo, K. Picture superiority in free recall: Imagery or dual coding? *Cognitive Psychology,* 1973, **5,** 176–206.

Paivio, A., Rogers, T. B., & Smythe, P. C., Why are pictures easier to recall than words? *Psychonomic Science*, 1968, **11**, 137–138.

Paivio, A., Smythe, P. C., & Yuille, J. C. Imagery versus meaningfulness of nouns in paired-associate learning. *Canadian Journal of Psychology*, 1968, **22**, 427–441.

Paivio, A., Yuille, J. C., & Madigan, S. Concreteness, imagery, and meaningfulness values for 925 nouns. *Journal of Experimental Psychology Monograph*, 1968, 76(1, Pt. 2).

Pellegrino, J. W. A general measure of organization in free recall for variable unit size and internal sequential consistency. *Behavior Research Methods and Instrumentation*, 1971, **3**, 241–246.

Peterson, L. R. Immediate memory: Data and theory. In C. N. Cofer & B. S. Musgrave (Eds.), *Verbal behavior and learning: Problems and processes*. New York: McGraw-Hill, 1963. Pp. 336–353.

Peterson, L. R. Paired-associate latencies after the last error. *Psychonomic Science*, 1965, **2**, 167–168.

Peterson, L. R. Concurrent verbal activity. *Psychological Review*, 1969, 76, 376–386.

Peterson, L. R. & Peterson, M. J. Short-term retention of individual verbal items. *Journal of Experimental Psychology*, 1959, **58**, 193–198.

Peterson, L. R., Saltzman, D., Hillner, K., & Land, V. Recency and frequency in paired-associate learning. *Journal of Experimental Psychology*, 1962, **63**, 396–403.

Peterson, L. R., Wampler, R., Kirkpatrick, M., & Saltzman, D. Effect of spacing presentations on retention of a paired-associate over short intervals. *Journal of Experimental Psychology*, 1963, **66**, 206–209.

Pisoni, D. B. Auditory and phonetic memory codes in the discrimination of consonants and vowels. *Perception and Psychophysics*, 1973, **13**, 253–260.

Pisoni, D. B., & Tash, J. Reaction times to comparisons within and across phonetic categories. *Perception and Psychophysics*, 1974, **15**, 285–290.

Pollio, H. R. Associative structure and verbal behavior. In T. R. Dixon & D. L. Horton (Eds.), *Verbal behavior and general behavior theory*. Englewood Cliffs, New Jersey: Prentice Hall, 1968. Pp. 37–66.

Pollio, H. R., & Draper, D. O. The effect of a serial structure on paired-associate learning. *Journal of Verbal Learning & Verbal Behavior*, 1966, **5**, 301–308.

Posner, M. I. Immediate memory in sequential tasks. *Psychological Bulletin*, 1963, **60**, 333–349.

Posner, M. I. *Cognition: An introduction.* Glenview, Illinois: Scott, Foresman, 1973.

Posner, M. I., Boies, S. J., Eichelman, W. H., & Taylor, R. L. Retention of visual and name codes of single letters. *Journal of Experimental Psychology Monograph*, 1969, 79(1, Pt. 2).

Posner, M. I., & Keele, S. W. Decay of visual information from a single letter. *Science*, 1967, **158**, 137–139.

Posner, M. I., & Konick, A. W. On the role of interference in short-term retention. *Journal of Experimental Psychology*, 1966, **72**, 221–231.

Posner, M. I., & Rossman, E. Effect of size and location of informational transforms upon short-term retention. *Journal of Experimental Psychology*, 1965, **70**, 496–505.

Postman, L. The present status of interference theory. In C. N. Cofer (Ed.), *Verbal learning and verbal behavior*. New York: McGraw-Hill, 1961. Pp. 152–179.

Postman, L. Transfer of training as a function of experimental paradigm and degree of first-list learning. *Journal of Verbal Learning and Verbal Behavior*, 1962, **1**, 109–118.

Postman, L. Differences between unmixed and mixed transfer designs as a function of paradigm. *Journal of Verbal Learning and Verbal Behavior*, 1966, **5**, 240–248.

Postman, L. Hermann Ebbinghaus. *American Psychologist*, 1968, **23**, 149–157.

Postman, L. Mechanisms of interference in forgetting. In G. A. Talland & N. C. Waugh (Eds.), *The pathology of memory*. New York: Academic Press, 1969. Pp. 195–210.

Postman, L. Organization and interference. *Psychological Review,* 1971, 78, 290–302.

Postman, L. A pragmatic view of organization theory. In E. Tulving & W. Donaldson (Eds.), *Organization of memory.* New York: Academic Press, 1972. Pp. 3–48.

Postman, L., Keppel, G., & Stark, K. Unlearning as a function of the relationship between successive response classes. *Journal of Experimental Psychology,* 1965, 69, 111–118.

Postman, L., & Phillips, L. W. Short-term temporal changes in free recall. *Quarterly Journal of Experimental Psychology,* 1965, 17, 132–138.

Postman, L., & Rau, L. Retention as a function of the method of measurement. *University of California Publications in Psychology,* Berkeley, 1957, 8, 217–270.

Postman, L., & Stark, K. Studies of learning to learn: IV. Transfer from serial to paired-associate learning. *Journal of Verbal Learning and Verbal Behavior,* 1967, 6, 339–353.

Postman, L., & Stark, K. Role of response availability in transfer and interference. *Journal of Experimental Psychology,* 1969, 79, 168–177.

Postman, L., Stark, K., & Fraser, J. Temporal changes in interference. *Journal of Verbal Learning and Verbal Behavior,* 1968, 7, 672–694.

Postman, L., & Underwood, B. J. Critical issues in interference theory. *Memory and Cognition,* 1973, 1, 19–40.

Potts, G. R. Distance from a massed double presentation or blank trial as a factor in paired-associate list learning. *Journal of Verbal Learning and Verbal Behavior,* 1972, 11, 375–386.

Pribram, K. H., Nuwer, M., & Baron, R. J. The holographic hypothesis of memory structure in brain function and perception. In D. H. Krantz, R. C. Atkinson, R. D. Luce, & P. Suppes (Eds.), *Contemporary developments in mathematical psychology.* Vol. II. New York: Freeman, 1974.

Primoff, E. Backward and forward association as an organizing act in serial and paired-associate learning. *Journal of Psychology,* 1938, 5, 375–395.

Puff, C. R. Role of clustering in free recall. *Journal of Experimental Psychology,* 1970, 86, 384–386.

Pylyshyn, Z. W. What the mind's eye tells the mind's brain: A critique of mental imagery. *Psychological Bulletin,* 1973, 80, 1–24.

Raeburn, V. P. Priorities in item recognition. *Memory and Cognition,* 1974, 2, 663–669.

Raymond, B. Short-term storage and long-term storage in free recall. *Journal of Verbal Learning and Verbal Behavior,* 1969, 8, 567–574.

Reder, L. M., Anderson, J. R., and Bjork, R. A. A semantic interpretation of encoding specificity. *Journal of Experimental Psychology,* 1974, 102, 648–656.

Reicher, G. M., Ligon, E. J., & Conrad, C. H. Interference in short-term memory. *Journal of Experimental Psychology,* 1969, 80, 95–100.

Reitman, J. S. Mechanisms of forgetting in short-term memory. *Cognitive Psychology,* 1971, 2, 185–195.

Reitman, J. S. Without surreptitious rehearsal, information in short-term memory decays. *Journal of Verbal Learning and Verbal Behavior,* 1974, 13, 365–377.

Restle, F. Significance of all-or-none learning. *Psychological Bulletin* 1965, 64, 313–325.

Ribback, A., & Underwood, B. J. An empirical explanation of the bowness of the serial position curve. *Journal of Experimental Psychology,* 1950, 40, 329–335.

Rightmer, D. R. Cuing effects in recognition and recall memory. Unpublished doctoral dissertation, Yale University, New Haven, Conn., 1975.

Riley, D. A. Memory for form. In L. Postman (Ed.), *Psychology in the making.* New York: Knopf, 1962. Pp. 402–465.

Robbins, D., & Wise, P. S. Encoding variability and imagery: Evidence for a spacing-type effect without spacing. *Journal of Experimental Psychology,* 1972, 95, 229–230.

Robinson, E. S. The "similarity" factor in retroaction. *American Journal of Psychology,* 1927, 39, 297–312.

Robinson, E. S. *Association theory today.* New York: The Century Co., 1932.

Rock, I. The role of repetition in associative learning. *American Journal of Psychology,* 1957, **70**, 186–193.

Rock, I. A neglected aspect of the problem of recall: The Höffding function. In J. M. Scher (Ed.), *Theories of the mind.* New York: Free Press, 1962. Pp. 645–659.

Roediger, H. L., III. Inhibition in recall from cueing with recall targets. *Journal of Verbal Learning and Verbal Behavior,* 1973, **12**, 644–657.

Roediger, H. L., III. Inhibiting effects of recall. *Memory and Cognition,* 1974, **2**, 261–269.

Roediger, H. L., III, & Crowder, R. G. The spacing of lists in free recall. *Journal of Verbal Learning and Verbal Behavior,* 1975, **14**.

Roediger, H. L., III, & Crowder, R. G. The serial position effect in recall of U.S. presidents. Unpublished manuscript, 1976.

Rohrman, N. L. The role of syntactic structure in the recall of English nominalizations. *Journal of Verbal Learning and Verbal Behavior,* 1968, **7**, 904–912.

Rothkopf, E. Z. Structural text features and the control of processes in learning from written materials. In J. B. Carroll & R. O. Freedle (Eds.), *Language comprehension and the acquisition of knowledge.* Washington, D.C.: Winston, 1972. Pp. 315–335.

Rundus, D. Analysis of rehearsal processes in free recall. *Journal of Experimental Psychology,* 1971, **89**, 63–77.

Rundus, D. Negative effects of using list items as recall cues. *Journal of Verbal Learning and Verbal Behavior,* 1973, **12**, 43–50.

Runquist, W. N. Retention of verbal associations as a function of strength. *Journal of Experimental Psychology,* 1957, **54**, 369–375.

Sachs, J. D. S. Recognition memory for syntactic and semantic aspects of connected discourse, *Perception and Psychophysics,* 1967, **2**, 437–442.

Savin, H. B. & Perchonock, E. Grammatical structure and the immediate recall of English sentences. *Journal of Verbal Learning and Verbal Behavior,* 1965, **4**, 348–353.

Schiller, P. H. Monoptic and dichoptic visual masking by patterns and flashes. *Journal of Experimental Psychology,* 1965, **69**, 193–199.

Schulz, R. W. Generalization of serial position in rote serial learning. *Journal of Experimental Psychology,* 1955, **49**, 267–272.

Shallice, T., & Warrington, E. K. Independent functioning of verbal memory stores: A neuropsychological study. *Quarterly Journal of Experimental Psychology,* 1970, **22**, 261–273.

Shaughnessy, J. J., Zimmerman, J., & Underwood, B. J. Further evidence on the MP–DP effect in free recall learning. *Journal of Verbal Learning and Verbal Behavior,* 1972, **11**, 1–12.

Sheffield, F. D. The role of meaningfulness of stimulus and response in verbal learning. Unpublished doctoral dissertation, Yale University, New Haven, Connecticut, 1946.

Sheffield, F. D. Theoretical considerations in the learning of complex sequential tasks from demonstration and practice. In A. A. Lumsdaine (Ed.), *Student response in programmed instruction.* Washington: National Academy of Sciences–National Research Council, Publication 943, 1961. Pp. 13–32.

Shepard, R. N. Recognition memory for words, sentences, and pictures, *Journal of Verbal Learning and Verbal Behavior,* 1967, **6**, 156–163.

Shepard, R. N. Form, formation, and transformation of internal representations. In R. Solso (Ed.), *Information processing and cognition: The Loyola Symposium.* Hillsdale, New Jersey: Lawrence Erlbaum, Assoc., 1975. Pp. 87–122.

Shepard, R. N., & Metzler, J. Mental rotation of three-dimensional objects. *Science,* 1971, **171**, 701–703.

Shiffrin, R. M. Memory search. In D. A. Norman (Ed.), *Models of human memory.* New York: Academic Press, 1970. Pp. 375–447.

Shiffrin, R. M. Information persistence in short-term memory. *Journal of Experimental Psychology,* 1973, **100,** 39–49.

Shuell, T. J., & Keppel, G. A further test of the chaining hypothesis of serial learning, *Journal of Verbal Learning and Verbal Behavior,* 1967, **6,** 439–445.

Shulman, A. I. Word length and rarity in recognition memory. *Psychonomic Science,* 1967, **9,** 211–212.

Shulman, H. G. Encoding and retention of semantic and phonemic information in short-term memory. *Journal of Verbal Learning and Verbal Behavior,* 1970, **9,** 499–508.

Shulman, H. G. Similarity effects in short-term memory. *Psychological Bulletin,* 1971, **75,** 399–415.

Siipola, E. M., & Hayden, S. D. Exploring eidetic imagery among the retarded. *Perceptual and Motor Skills,* 1965, **21,** 275–286.

Silverstein, A. Unlearning, spontaneous recovery, and the partial-reinforcement effect in paired-associate learning. *Journal of Experimental Psychology,* 1967, **73,** 15–21.

Skaggs, E. B. Further studies in retroactive inhibition. *Psychological Monographs,* 1925, No. 161.

Slamecka, N. J. An inquiry into the doctrine of remote associations. *Psychological Review,* 1964, **71,** 61–76.

Slamecka, N. J. Recall and recognition in list-discrimination tasks as a function of the number of alternatives. *Journal of Experimental Psychology,* 1967, **74,** 187–192.

Slamecka, N. J. An examination of trace storage in free recall. *Journal of Experimental Psychology,* 1968, **76,** 504–513.

Slamecka, N. J. Testing for associative storage in multitrial free recall. *Journal of Experimental Psychology,* 1969, **81,** 557–560.

Slamecka, N. J. The question of associative growth in the learning of categorized material. *Journal of Verbal Learning and Verbal Behavior,* 1972, **11,** 324–332.

Slamecka, N. J., Moore, T., & Carey, S. Part-to-whole transfer and its relation to organization theory. *Journal of Verbal Learning and Verbal Behavior,* 1972, **11,** 73–82.

Slobin, D. I. *Psycholinguistics.* Glenview, Illinois: Scott, Foresman, 1971.

Smith, A. D. Output interference and organized recall from long-term memory. *Journal of Verbal Learning and Verbal Behavior,* 1971, **10,** 400–408.

Smith, E. E. Choice reaction time: An analysis of the major theoretical positions. *Psychological Bulletin,* 1968, **69,** 77–110.

Smith, E. E., Barresi, J., & Gross, A. E. Imaginal versus verbal coding and the primary-secondary memory distinction. *Journal of Verbal Learning & Verbal Behavior,* 1971, **10,** 597–603.

Smith, W. G. The relation of attention to memory. *Mind,* 1895, **4,** 47–73.

Spence, K. W. An experimental test of the continuity and non-continuity theories of discrimination learning. *Journal of Experimental Psychology,* 1945, **35,** 253–266.

Sperber, R. D. Developmental changes in effects of spacing of trials in retardate discrimination learning and memory. *Journal of Experimental Psychology,* 1974, **103,** 204–210.

Sperling, G. The information available in brief visual presentations. *Psychological Monographs,* 1960, **74**(Whole No. 11).

Sperling, G. A model for visual memory tasks. *Human Factors,* 1963, **5,** 19–31.

Sperling, G. Successive approximations to a model for short-term memory. *Acta Psychologica,* 1967, **27,** 285–292.

Sperling, G. Short-term memory, long-term memory, and scanning in the processing of visual information. In F. A. Young & D. B. Lindsley (Eds.), *Early experience and visual information processing in perceptual and reading disorders.* Washington: National Academy of Sciences, 1970, Pp. 198–215.

Sperling, G., & Speelman, R. G. Acoustic similarity and auditory short-term memory: Experiments and a model. In D. A. Norman (Ed.), *Models of human memory*. New York: Academic Press, 1970. Pp. 151–202.

Standing, L., Conezio, J., & Haber, R. N. Perception and memory for pictures: Single-trial learning of 2560 visual stimuli. *Psychonomic Science,* 1970, **19,** 73–74.

Sternberg, R. J., & Bower, G. H. Transfer in part-whole and whole-part free recall: A comparative evaluation of theories. *Journal of Verbal Learning & Verbal Behavior,* 1974, **13,** 1–26.

Sternberg, R. J., & Tulving, E. The measurement of subjective organization in free recall. Unpublished manuscript, 1974.

Sternberg, S. High-speed scanning in human memory. *Science,* 1966, **153,** 652–654.

Sternberg, S. Memory-scanning: mental processes revealed by reaction-time experiments. *American Scientist,* 1969, **57,** 421–457. (a)

Sternberg, S. The discovery of processing stages: extensions of Donders' method. In W. G. Koster (Ed.), *Attention and performance II. Acta Psychologica,* 1969, **30,** 276–315. (b)

Sternberg, S. Memory scanning: New findings and current controversies. *Quarterly Journal of Experimental Psychology,* 1975, **27,** 1–32.

Strand, B. Z. Change of context and retroactive inhibition. *Journal of Verbal Learning and Verbal Behavior,* 1970, **9,** 202–206.

Stromeyer, C. F., III, & Psotka, J. The detailed texture of eidetic images. *Nature,* 1970, **225,** 346–349.

Stroop, J. R. Studies of interference in serial verbal reaction. *Journal of Experimental Psychology,* 1935, **18,** 643–662.

Studdert-Kennedy, M., Shankweiler, D., & Shulman, S. Opposed effects of a delayed channel on perception of dichotically and monotically presented CV syllables. *Journal of the Acoustical Society of America,* 1970, **48,** 599–602.

Sumby, W. H. Word frequency and serial position effects. *Journal of Verbal Learning and Verbal Behavior,* 1963, **1,** 443–450.

Symmes, J. S. Visual imagery in brain-injured children. *Perceptual & Motor Skills,* 1971, **33,** 507–514.

Talland, G. A. *Disorders of memory and learning.* New York: Penguin, 1968. (a)

Talland, G. A. Age and the span of immediate recall. In G. A. Talland (Ed.), *Human aging and behavior.* New York: Academic Press, 1968. Pp. 93–129. (b)

Talland, G. A., & Waugh, N. C. (Eds.), *The psychopathology of memory.* New York: Academic Press, 1969.

Tell, P. M. The role of certain acoustic and semantic factors at short and long retention intervals. *Journal of Verbal Learning and Verbal Behavior,* 1972, **11,** 455–464.

Theios, J., Smith, P. G., Haviland, S. E., Traupmann, J., & Moy, M. C. Memory scanning as a serial self-terminating process. *Journal of Experimental Psychology,* 1973, **97,** 323–336.

Thios, S. J. Memory for words in repeated sentences. *Journal of Verbal Learning and Verbal Behavior,* 1972, **11,** 789–793.

Thomasson, A. J. W. M. *On the representation of verbal items in short-term memory.* Nijmegen, Netherlands: Drukkerij Schippers, 1970.

Thompson, C. P., Hamlin, V. J., & Roenker, D. L. A comment on the role of clustering in free recall. *Journal of Experimental Psychology,* 1972, **94,** 108–109.

Thomson, D. M. Context effects in recognition memory. *Journal of Verbal Learning and Verbal Behavior,* 1972, **11,** 497–511.

Thomson, D. M., & Tulving, E. Associative encoding and retrieval: weak and strong cues. *Journal of Experimental Psychology,* 1970, **86,** 255–262.

Thorndike, E. L. *The psychology of learning.* New York: Teachers College, 1914.

Thurm, A. T., & Glanzer, M. Free recall in children: Long-term store versus short-term store.

Psychonomic Science, 1971, **23,** 175–176.

Townsend, J. T. A note on the identifiability of parallel and serial processes. *Perception and Psychophysics,* 1971, **10,** 161–163.

Trabasso, T., & Bower, G. H. *Attention in learning: Theory and research.* New York: Wiley, 1968.

Treisman, A. M. Monitoring and storage of irrelevant messages in selective attention. *Journal of Verbal Learning & Verbal Behavior,* 1964, **3,** 449–459.

Treisman, A. M. Strategies and models of selective attention. *Psychological Review,* 1969, **76,** 282–299.

Treisman, M., & Rostron, A. B. Brief auditory storage: A modification of Sperling's paradigm applied to audition. *Acta Psychologica,* 1972, **36,** 161–170.

Tulving, E. Subjective organization in free recall of "unrelated" words. *Psychological Review,* 1962, **69,** 344–354.

Tulving, E. Intratrial and intertrial retention: Notes towards a theory of free recall verbal learning. *Psychological Review,* 1964, **71,** 219–237.

Tulving, E. Subjective organization and the effects of repetition in multi-trial free recall verbal learning. *Journal of Verbal Learning and Verbal Behavior,* 1966, **5,** 193–197.

Tulving, E. When is recall higher than recognition: *Psychonomic Science,* 1968, **10,** 53–54. (a)

Tulving, E. Theoretical issues in free recall. In T. R. Dixon & D. L. Horton (Eds.), *Verbal behavior and general behavior theory.* Englewood Cliffs, New Jersey: Prentice-Hall, 1968, Pp. 2–36. (b)

Tulving, E. Episodic and semantic memory. In E. Tulving and W. Donaldson (Eds.), *Organization of memory.* New York: Academic Press, 1972. Pp. 381–403.

Tulving, E. Ecphoric processes in recall and recognition. In J. Brown (Ed.), *Recall and recognition.* London: Wiley, 1975 (in press).

Tulving, E., & Arbuckle, T. Y. Sources of intratrial interference in immediate recall of paired associates. *Journal of Verbal Learning and Verbal Behavior,* 1963, **1,** 321–334.

Tulving, E., & Colatla, V. Free recall of trilingual lists. *Cognitive Psychology,* 1970, **1,** 86–98.

Tulving, E., & Gold, C. Stimulus information and contextual information as determinants of tachistoscopic recognition of words. *Journal of Experimental Psychology,* 1963, **66,** 319–327.

Tulving, E., & Pearlstone, Z. Availability versus accessibility of information in memory for words. *Journal of Verbal Learning and Verbal Behavior,* 1966, **5,** 381–391.

Tulving, E., & Thomson, D. M. Encoding specificity and retrieval processes in episodic memory. *Psychological Review,* 1973, **80,** 352–373.

Turvey, M. T. The effects of rehearsing analysed information on the retrieval of unanalysed information. *Psychonomic Science,* 1966, **6,** 365–366.

Turvey, M. T. On peripheral and central processes in vision: Inferences from an information-processing analysis of masking with patterned stimuli. *Psychological Review,* 1973, **80,** 1–52.

Turvey, M. T., & Weeks, R. A. Effects of proactive interference and rehearsal on the primary and secondary components of short-term retention. *Quarterly Journal of Experimental Psychology,* 1975, **27,** 47–62.

Tversky, B. G. Pictorial and verbal encoding in a short-term memory task. *Perception and Psychophysics,* 1969, **6,** 225–233.

Tversky, B. G. Encoding processes in recognition and recall. *Cognitive Psychology,* 1973, **5,** 275–287.

Tzeng, O. J. L. Positive recency effect in a delayed free recall. *Journal of Verbal Learning and Verbal Behavior,* 1973, **12,** 436–439. (a)

Tzeng, O. J. L. Stimulus meaningfulness, encoding variability, and the spacing effect. *Journal of Experimental Psychology,* 1973, 99, 162–166. (b)

Underwood, B. J. The effect of successive interpolations on retroactive and proactive inhibition. *Psychological Monographs,* 1945, 59(3, Whole No. 273).

Underwood, B. J. Retroactive and proactive inhibition after five and forty-eight hours. *Journal of Experimental Psychology,* 1948, 38, 29–38. (a)

Underwood, B. J. "Spontaneous recovery" of verbal associations. *Journal of Experimental Psychology,* 1948, 38, 429–439. (b)

Underwood, B. J. Studies of distributed practice: VII. Learning and retention of serial nonsense lists as a function of intralist similarity. *Journal of Experimental Psychology,* 1952, 44, 80–87.

Underwood, B. J. Studies of distributed practice: VIII. Learning and retention of paired nonsense syllables as a function of intralist similarity. *Journal of Experimental Psychology,* 1953, 45, 133–142. (a)

Underwood, B. J. Studies of distributed practice: IX. Learning and retention of paired adjectives as a function of intralist similarity. *Journal of Experimental Psychology,* 1953, 45, 143–149. (b)

Underwood, B. J. Studies of distributed practice: X. The influence of intralist similarity on learning and retention of serial adjective lists. *Journal of Experimental Psychology,* 1953, 45, 253–259. (c)

Underwood, B. J. Interference and forgetting. *Psychological Review,* 1957, 64, 49–60.

Underwood, B. J. Stimulus selection in verbal learning. In C. N. Cofer & B. S. Musgrave (Eds.), *Verbal behavior and learning: problems and processes.* New York: McGraw-Hill, 1963. Pp. 33–48.

Underwood, B. J. Degree of learning and the measurement of forgetting. *Journal of Verbal Learning and Verbal Behavior,* 1964, 3, 112–129.

Underwood, B. J. A breakdown of the total-time law in free-recall learning. *Journal of Verbal Learning and Verbal Behavior,* 1970, 9, 573–580.

Underwood, B. J., & Ekstrand, B. R. An analysis of some shortcomings in the interference theory of forgetting. *Psychological Review,* 1966, 73, 540–549.

Underwood, B. J., & Ekstrand, B. R. Studies of distributed practice: XXIV. Differentiation and proactive inhibition. *Journal of Experimental Psychology,* 1967, 74, 574–580.

Underwood, B. J., & Freund, J. S. Effect of temporal separation of two tasks on proactive inhibition. *Journal of Experimental Psychology,* 1968, 78, 50–54.

Underwood, B. J., Ham, M., & Ekstrand, B. Cue selection in paired-associate learning. *Journal of Experimental Psychology,* 1962, 64, 405–409.

Underwood, B. J., & Keppel, G. One trial learning? *Journal of Verbal Learning and Verbal Behavior,* 1962, 1, 1–13.

Underwood, B. J., & Postman, L. Extra-experimental sources of interference in forgetting. *Psychological Review,* 1960, 67, 73–95.

Underwood, B. J., & Richardson, J. The influence of meaningfulness, intralist similarity, and serial position on retention. *Journal of Experimental Psychology,* 1956, 52, 119–126.

Underwood, B. J., & Schulz, R. W. *Meaningfulness and verbal learning.* Philadelphia: Lippincott, 1960.

von Restorff, H. Über die wirkung von bereichsbildungen im spurenfeld. *Psychologie Forschung,* 1933, 18, 299–342.

von Wright, J. M. Selection in visual immediate memory. *Quarterly Journal of Experimental Psychology,* 1968, 20, 62–68.

von Wright, J. M. On the problem of selection in iconic memory. *Scandanavian Journal of Psychology,* 1972, 13, 159–171.

Walker, E. L., & Tarte, R. D. Memory storage as a function of arousal and time with homogeneous and heterogeneous lists. *Journal of Verbal Learning and Verbal Behavior,*

1963, **2,** 113–119.

Walsh, D. A., & Jenkins, J. J. Effects of orienting tasks on free recall in incidental learning: "Difficulty," "effort," and "process" explanations. *Journal of Verbal Learning & Verbal Behavior,* 1973, **12,** 481–488.

Walter, D. A. The effect of sentence context on the stability of phonemic and semantic memory dimensions. *Journal of Verbal Learning and Verbal Behavior,* 1973, **12,** 185–192.

Ward, L. B. Reminiscence and rote learning. *Psychological Monographs,* 1937, **49.**

Washburn, M. F. *Movement and mental imagery.* Boston: Houghton Mifflin, 1916.

Watkins, M. J. Locus of the modality effect in free recall. *Journal of Verbal Learning and Verbal Behavior,* 1972, **11,** 644–648.

Watkins, M. J. The concept and measurement of primary memory. *Psychological Bulletin,* 1974, 81(10), 695–711.   (a)

Watkins, M. J. When is recall spectacularly higher than recognition? *Journal of Experimental Psychology,* 1974, **102,** 161–163.   (b)

Watkins, M. J., & Tulving, E. Episodic memory: When recognition fails. *Journal of Experimental Psychology: General,* 1975, **1,** 5–29.

Watkins, M. J., & Watkins, O. C. Processing of recency items for free recall. *Journal of Experimental Psychology,* 1974, **102,** 488–493.

Watkins, M. J., Watkins, O. C., Craik, F. I. M., & Mazuryk, G. Effect of verbal distraction on short-term storage. *Journal of Experimental Psychology,* 1973, **101,** 296–300.

Watkins, M. J., Watkins, O. C., & Crowder, R. G. The modality effect in free and serial recall as a function of phonological similarity. *Journal of Verbal Learning and Verbal Behavior,* 1974, **13,** 430–447.

Watkins, O. C., & Watkins, M. J. Build-up of proactive inhibition as a cue-overload effect. *Journal of Experimental Psychology: Human Learning and Memory,* 1975, **104,** 442–452.

Watson, J. B. *Psychology from the standpoint of a behaviorist.* Philadelphia: Lippincott, 1919.

Waugh, N. C. Immediate memory as a function of repetition. *Journal of Verbal Learning and Verbal Behavior,* 1963, **2,** 107–112.

Waugh, N. C. On the effective duration of a repeated word. *Journal of Verbal Learning and Verbal Behavior,* 1970, **9,** 587–595.

Waugh, N. C. Retention as an active process. *Journal of Verbal Learning and Verbal Behavior,* 1972, **11,** 129–140.

Waugh, N. C., & Norman, D. A. Primary memory. *Psychological Review,* 1965, **72,** 89–104.

Waugh, N. C., & Norman, D. A. The measure of interference in primary memory. *Journal of Verbal Learning and Verbal Behavior,* 1968, **7,** 617–626.

Wearing, A. J. The storage of complex sentences. *Journal of Verbal Learning and Verbal Behavior,* 1970, **9,** 21–29.

Wearing, A. J., & Crowder, R. G. Dividing attention to study sentence acquisition. *Journal of Verbal Learning and Verbal Behavior,* 1971, **10,** 254–261.

Weaver, G. E., McCann, R. L., & Wehr, R. J. Stimulus meaningfulness, transfer, and retroactive inhibition in the A–B, A–C paradigm. *Journal of Experimental Psychology,* 1970, **85,** 255–257.

Webb, L. W. Transfer of training and retroaction. *Psychological Monographs,* 1917, 24(104).

Weiss, W., & Margolius, G. The effect of context stimuli on learning and retention. *Journal of Experimental Psychology,* 1954, **48,** 318–322.

Welch, G. B., & Burnett, C. T. Is primacy a factor in association formation? *American Journal of Psychology,* 1924, **35,** 396–401.

Wendt, G. R. An interpretation of inhibtion of conditioned reflexes as competition between reaction systems. *Psychological Review,* 1936, **43,** 258–281.

Whitty, C. W. M., & Zangwill, O. L. (Eds.). *Amnesia.* London: Butterworths, 1966.

Wichawut, C., & Martin, E. Independence of A–B and A–C associations in retroaction. *Journal of Verbal Learning and Verbal Behavior,* 1971, **10,** 316–321.

Wickelgren, W. A. Acoustic similarity and retroactive interference in short-term memory. *Journal of Verbal Learning and Verbal Behavior,* 1965, **4,** 53–61.

Wickelgren, W. A. Phonemic similarity and interference in short-term memory for single letters. *Journal of Experimental Psychology,* 1966, **71,** 396–404.

Wickelgren, W. A. Rehearsal grouping and hierarchical organization of serial position cues in short-term memory. *Quarterly Journal of Experimental Psychology,* 1967, **19,** 97–102.

Wickelgren, W. A. Sparing of short-term memory in an amnesic patient: implications for a strength theory of memory. *Neuropsychologia,* 1968, **6,** 235–244.

Wickelgren, W. A. Auditory or articulatory coding in verbal short-term memory. *Psychological Review,* 1969, **76,** 232–235. (a)

Wickelgren, W. A. Context-sensitive coding, associative memory, and serial order in (speech) behavior. *Psychological Review,* 1969, **76,** 1–15. (b)

Wickelgren, W. A. The long and short of memory. *Psychological Bulletin,* 1973, **80,** 425–438.

Wickelgren, W. A., & Norman, D. A. Strength models and serial position in short-term recognition memory. *Journal of Mathematical Psychology,* 1966, **3,** 316–347.

Wickens, D. D. Characteristics of word encoding. In A. W. Melton & E. Martin (Eds.), *Coding processes in human memory.* Washington, D.C.: Winston, 1972. Pp. 191–215.

Wickens, D. D., Born, D. G., & Allen, C. K. Proactive inhibition and item similarity in short-term memory. *Journal of Verbal Learning and Verbal Behavior,* 1963, **2,** 440–445.

Wilkinson, W. C. Recency effects in long-term free recall. Unpublished doctoral dissertation. Yale University, 1975.

Williams, J. P. A. A selection artifact in Rock's study of the role of repetition. *Journal of Experimental Psychology,* 1961, **62,** 627–628.

Williams, M. The effects of experimental induced needs on retention. *Journal of Experimental Psychology,* 1950, **40,** 139–151.

Williams, M. Traumatic retrograde amnesia and normal forgetting. In G. A. Talland & N. C. Waugh (Eds.), *The pathology of memory.* New York: Academic Press, 1969. Pp. 75–80.

Williams, R. F., & Underwood, B. J. Encoding variability: Tests of the Martin hypothesis. *Journal of Experimental Psychology,* 1970, **86,** 317–324.

Wimer, C., & Lambert, W. E. The differential effects of word and object stimuli on the learning of paired-associates. *Journal of Experimental Psychology,* 1959, **57,** 31–36.

Wingfield, A., & Byrnes, D. L. Decay of information in short-term memory. *Science,* 1972, **176,** 690–692.

Wollen, K. A., Weber, A., & Lowry, D. Bizareness versus interaction of mental images as determinants of learning. *Cognitive Psychology,* 1972, **3,** 518–523.

Wood, G. Mnemonic systems in recall. *Journal of Educational Psychology Monographs,* 1967, 58(No. 6, Part 2).

Wood, G., & Clark, D. Instructions, ordering, and previous practice in free recall learning. *Psychonomic Science,* 1969, **14,** 187–188.

Woods, E. L. An experimental analysis of the process of recognizing. *American Journal of Psychology,* 1915, **26,** 313–317.

Woodward, A. E., Bjork, R. A., & Jongeward, R. H. Recall and recognition as a function of primary rehearsal. *Journal of Verbal Learning and Verbal Behavior,* 1973, **12,** 608–617.

Woodworth, R. S. *Experimental Psychology.* New York: Holt, 1938.

Woodworth, R. S., & Poffenberger, A. T. *Textbook of experimental psychology.* Mimeographed edition. New York: Columbia University, 1920.

Wright, P. Sentence retention and transformation theory. *Quarterly Journal of Experimental Psychology,* 1968, **20,** 265–272.

Yates, F. A. *The art of memory.* Middlesex, England: Penguin, 1966.

Yerkes, R. M. The mental life of monkeys and apes, a study of ideational behavior. *Behavioral Monographs*, No. 12, 1916.

Yngve, V. H. A model and a hypothesis for language structure. *Proceedings of the American Philosophical Society*, 1960, **104**, 444–466.

Yntema, D. B., & Trask, F. P. Recall as a search process. *Journal of Verbal Learning and Verbal Behavior*, 1963, **2**, 65–74.

Young, J. L. Effects of intervals between reinforcements and test trials in paired-associate learning. Technical Report No. 101, Institute for Mathematical Studies in the Social Sciences, Stanford University, 1966.

Young, R. K. A comparison of two methods of learning serial associations. *American Journal of Psychology*, 1959, **72**, 554–559.

Young, R. K. Tests of three hypotheses about the effective stimulus in serial learning. *Journal of Experimental Psychology*, 1962, **63**, 307–313.

Young, R. K. Serial learning. In T. R. Dixon & D. L. Horton (Eds.), *Verbal Behavior and General Behavior Theory*. Englewood Cliffs, New Jersey: Prentice-Hall, 1968. Pp. 122–148.

Young, R. K., Hakes, D. T., & Hicks, R. Y. Ordinal position number as a cue in serial learning. *Journal of Experimental Psychology*, 1967, **73**, 427–438.

Young, R. K., Patterson, J., & Benson, W. M. Backward serial learning. *Journal of Verbal Learning and Verbal Behavior*, 1963, **1**, 335–338.

Youtz, A. C. An experimental evaluation of Jost's laws. *Psychological Monographs*, 1941, **53**, No. 1 (Whole No. 238).

Yuille, J. C., & Paivio, A. Latency of imaginal and verbal mediators as a function of stimulus and response concreteness-imagery. *Journal of Experimental Psychology*, 1967, **75**, 540–544.

Author Index

A

Abernathy, E. M., 228, *479*
Abra, J. C., 238, 254, *479*
Adler, M. J., 341, *479*
Allen, C. K., 203, 204, *504*
Allen, T. W., 309, 310, 311, 312, 313, *481*
Anderson, J. R., 103, 127, 130, 165, 251, 289, 313, 315, 320, 338, 346, 351, 353, 376, 377, 381, 383, 386, 388, 389, 390, 404, 405, 406, 407, 412, 425, 430, 434, 435, 475, *479, 497*
Anderson, R. C., 242, *479*
Anisfeld, M., 373, *479*
Antognini, J., 395, 403, 408, *479*
Arbuckle, T. Y., 34, 347, *501*
Atkinson, R. C., 63, 156, 157, 158, 165, 166, 183, 228, 271, 272, 281, 292, 299, 303, 305, 307, 309, 367, 368, 369, *479, 480, 482*
Averbach, E., 32, 33, *480*
Austin, J. B., 345, *489*

B

Baddeley, A. D., 60, 62, 64, 96, 139, 167, *480, 484*
Bahrick, H. P., 426, *480*
Baker, L., 408, *480*
Barclay, J. R., 406, 407, 476, *480, 481*
Barnes, J. M., 232, *480*
Barnett, T., 48, 49, 50, 52, 65, *494*

Baron, R. J., 127, *497*
Barresi, J., 161, 162, 166, *499*
Barrett, B., 108, 109, 110, *484*
Bartlett, F. C., 95, *480*
Bates, A., 48, 49, 50, 52, 65, *494*
Baxt, N., 37, *480*
Belmont, J. M., 140, 141, 454, *480*
Belmont, L., 235, *480*
Bennett, R. W., 206, 213, 214, 251, 463, *480*
Benson, W. M., 420, *505*
Bernbach, H. A., 140, 178, 272, 335, 373, 386, *480*
Bevan, W., 112, 113, 116, *480, 482*
Bever, T. G., 424, 425, *480*
Bilodeau, I. McD., 228, *481*
Binford, J. R., 271, *481*
Birch, H. G., 235, *480*
Birnbaum, I. M., 238, 245, *481*
Birtwistle, J., 202, 212, 213, 251, 463, *483, 486*
Bjork, E. L., 189, *481*
Bjork, R. A., 143, 163, 164, 165, 169, 171, 211, 251, 309, 310, 311, 312, 313, 386, 387, 404, 406, 461, 477, *481, 497, 504*
Block, R. A., 282, 283, 284, 291, 314, 318, 319, 320, *488*
Boies, S. J., 99, 102, 103, 104, 105, 116, *496*
Boring, E. G., 396, 412, 414, *481*
Born, D. G., 203, 204, *504*
Bosley, D. D., 457, 458, *485*

Bousfield, A. K., 334, *481*
Bousfield, W. A., 324, 326, 334, *481*
Bower, G. H., 18, 27, 28, 103, 105, 106,
107, 114, 116, 118, 119, 122, 123, 127,
130, 165, 228, 251, 266, 270, 271, 272,
289, 297, 298, 300, 313, 315, 316, 317,
320, 321, 338, 351, 376, 377, 380, 381,
383, 386, 388, 389, 390, 405, 407, 412,
423, 425, 430, 434, 435, 449, 450, 458,
475, *479, 481, 486, 500, 501*
Bracey, G. W., 362, *481*
Bransford, J. D., 406, 407, 475, 476, *480,
481*
Bregman, A. S., 166, *481*
Brelsford, J. W., Jr., 63, *481*
Briggs, G. E., 231, *482*
Broadbent, D. E., 35, 133, 134, 178, 222,
482
Brooks, L. R., 107, 108, *482*
Brooks, R. J., 37, *492*
Brown, J., 18, 28, 105, 133, 176, *482*
Brown, S. C., 209, *493*
Bruce, D. R., 330, 455, 456, *482*
Bugelski, B. R., 114, 115, 125, 276, 417,
482
Burnett, C. T., 454, *503*
Buschke, H., 152, 153, 336, *482, 490*
Butterfield, E. C., 140, 141, 454, *480*
Byrnes, D. L., 178, 179, *504*

C

Calfee, R. C., 363, *482*
Carey, S., 338, *499*
Carmichael, L. C., 95, 96, *482*
Carroll, J. B., 83, *482*
Carter-Sobell, L., 405, *491*
Chase, W. G., 363, *482*
Cheng, C., 87, *482*
Cheng, N. Y., 235, *482*
Chomsky, N., 468, *482*
Chorover, S. L., 224, *482*
Clark, D., 338, *504*
Clark, W. H., 69, 89, *487*
Cofer, C. N., 328, 329, 330, 332, *482*
Cohen, B. H., 326, 330, 331, 332, 345, *481,
482*
Colatla, V., 148, *501*
Collyer, S. C., 116, *482*

Coltheart, M., 94, *482*
Conezio, J., 111, 113, *500*
Conrad, C. H., 186, *497*
Conrad, R., 13, 28, 61, 70, 71, 72, 73, 74,
75, 76, 184, 189, 198, 200, 216, *482, 483*
Cooley, R. K., 62, *483*
Coons, E. E., 223, *483*
Cooper, E. H., 276, *483*
Cooper, F. S., 40, 41, 64, 86, *483, 491*
Cooper, L. A., 102, *483*
Coots, J. H., 288, *490*
Corballis, M. C., 61, *483*
Corcoran, D. W. J., 82, 359, 364, *483*
Coriell, A. S., 32, 33, *480*
Corman, C. N., 196, 197, *483*
Cowan, G. N., 51, 65, *487*
Craik, F. I. M., 12, 15, 141, 143, 146, 147,
148, 149, 150, 156, 162, 163, 164, 168,
202, 212, 213, 251, 323, 366, 387, 463,
483, 486, 490, 503
Crothers, E. J., 269, 271, 272, *479, 486*
Crowder, R. G., 25, 26, 28, 48, 49, 50, 56,
57, 58, 59, 60, 62, 63, 64, 65, 141, 147,
150, 155, 156, 187, 188, 195, 209, 210,
216, 323, 419, 420, 426, 453, 454, 455,
459, 467, 472, *483, 484, 494, 498, 503*
Csapo, K., 113, 125, 126, *495*
Cunitz, A. R., 140, 141, 142, 147, 171,
455, *487*

D

D'Agostino, P. R., 286, 288, *484*
Dale, H. C. A., 139, *480*
Dallenbach, K. M., 220, 221, *489, 494*
Dallett, K. M., 56, 209, 417, *484*
DaPolito, F. J., 252, 380, *484, 486, 487*
Darwin, C. J., 48, 49, 50, 60, 62, 64, 65,
484
Davies, S., 222, *488*
Davis, R., 378, *484*
Day, R. S., 64, *484*
Deese, J., 326, 379, 457, 465, *484*
Delprato, D. J., 245, *484*
den Heyer, K., 108, 109, 110, *484*
DeRemer, P., 286, 288, *484*
DeSoto, C. B., 457, 458, *485*
Dick, A. O., 33, 34, 41, 42, *485*
Dillon, R. F., 196, 202, *485*

Doob, L. W., 92, *485*
Dooling, D. J., 474, 476, *485, 491*
Dovel, J. C., 286, *485*
Draper, D. O., 458, *496*
Duncan, C. P., 223, *485*
Dyer, F. N., 81, *485*

E

Eagle, M., 380, *485*
Ebbinghaus, H. E., 5, 6, 7, 90, 220, 236,
  264, 370, 413, 450, 464, *485*
Ebenholtz, S. M., 421, 422, 449, 450, 463,
  485
Egan, J. P., 373, *485*
Ehrlich, M.-F., 336, *485*
Ehrlich, S., 334, *485*
Eichelman, W. H., 99, 102, 103, 104, 105,
  116, *496*
Ekstrand, B. R., 16, 17, 220, 222, 248, 249,
  250, 251, *485, 502*
Elliott, L. L., 54, *485*
Ellis, N. R., 150, *485*
Ellsworth, D. W., 79, 82, *488*
Elmes, D. G., 285, 286, 291, *485*
Eriksen, C. W., 52, 65, 81, *485*
Estes, W. K., 188, 189, 191, 216, 228, 237,
  265, 266, 268, 269, 292, 294, 301, 348,
  352, 380, 433, 439, 440, 441, 448, *486*

F

Fehr, F. S., 77, 78, *491*
Feigenbaum, E. A., 451, 456, *486*
Fischhoff, B., 459, *490*
Fitch, F. B., 448, *489*
Fitts, P. M., 425, 427, *480, 486*
Fleishman, E. A., 426, *486*
Flexser, A. J., 316, 317, 321, *486*
Flickinger, R. G., 288, *490*
Fodor, J. A., 424, 425, *480*
Foord, E. N., 96, *488*
Foucault, M., 446, 456, *486*
Franks, J. J., 406, 407, 475, 476, *480, 481*
Fraser, J., 238, 239, 240, 241, 242, 243,
  246, 249, 262, *497*
Freund, J. S., 250, *502*
Frost, N., 126, *486*

Frost, R. R., 209, *486*
Fuchs, A. F., 201, 202, 203, 208, 215, 421,
  486
Fujisaki, H., 64, *486*

G

Galanter, E., 114, *494*
Gardiner, J. M., 141, 147, 212, 213, 251,
  463, *486*
Garrett, M. A., 424, 425, *480*
Garskof, B. E., 242, *486*
Gartman, L. M., 287, 288, *486*
George, J., 379, *490*
Gettys, C., 271, *481*
Gibson, E. J., 235, *486*
Glanzer, M., 17, 69, 89, 140, 141, 142, 146,
  147, 149, 150, 151, 152, 160, 171, 178,
  277, 279, 422, 448, 455, *486, 487, 500*
Glassman, W. E., 78, *487*
Glaze, J. A., 236, *487*
Glenberg, A. M., 275, 276, 289, 294, 299,
  300, 302, 308, *487*
Glick, M. J., 95, *482*
Glucksberg, S., 51, 65, 365, 366, *487, 495*
Goggin, J., 252, 259, *487*
Gold, C., 398, *501*
Gold, P. E., 224, *493*
Goodman, K. S., 82, *487*
Gorfein, D. S., 215, *487*
Grant, K. W., 62, *487*
Gray, C. R., 91, 94, *487*
Gray, M. M., 222, *488*
Greenberg, R., 234, *487*
Greener, W. I., 285, 291, *485*
Greeno, J. G., 252, 255, 256, 258, 270,
  278, 279, *487, 492*
Greenspoon, J., 228, *487*
Groninger, L. D., 120, *487*
Gross, A. E., 161, 162, 166, *499*
Gummerman, K., 91, 94, *487*
Guthrie, E. R., 228, 237, *487*
Guttman, N., 46, 65, *487*

H

Haber, R. B., 91, 92, 93, *487, 491*
Haber, R. N., 91, 92, 93, 111, 113, *487,
  491, 500*

Hakes, D. T., 422, *505*
Hall, J. F., 237, 379, *488*
Hall, M., 448, *489*
Halwes, T., 424, *488*
Ham, M., 16, 17, *502*
Hamlin, V. J., 330, *500*
Hardyck, C. D., 79, 82, *488*
Harlow, H. F., 265, *488*
Haviland, S. E., 367, *500*
Hayden, S. D., 92, *499*
Healy, A. F., 189, 192, *481, 488*
Hebb, D. O., 90, 94, 96, 134, 220, 222, 326, 430, 434, *488*
Hellyer, S., 134, 176, 177, *488*
Hempel, W. E., Jr., 426, *486*
Hicks, R. Y., 422, *505*
Hilgard, E. R., 237, *488*
Hillner, K., 291, 307, 419, 458, *496*
Hinrichs, J. V., 313, *488*
Hintzman, D. L., 83, 85, 254, 255, 273, 281, 282, 283, 284, 286, 289, 291, 314, 318, 319, 320, 451, *488*
Hirsh, I. J., 56, *488*
Hockey, G. R., 222, *488*
Hogan, H. P., 95, 96, *482*
Hollingworth, H. C., 376, *488*
Holloway, C. M., 60, *494*
Hopkins, B. L., 269, *486*
Horowitz, L. M., 25, 188, 392, 393, 394, 395, 407, 408, *488, 489*
Houston, J. P., 201, *489*
Hovland, C. I., 218, 235, 448, *489*
Hudson, R. L., 345, *489*
Hull, A. J., 61, 71, 74, 185, *483*
Hull, C. L., 447, 448, 456, *489*
Hunt, E., 95, *489*
Hunter, I. M. L., 114, *489*
Hyde, T. S., 15, 16, 26, 28, 168, 341, 380, *489*

I

Irion, A. L., 265, *493*
Irwin, J. M., 229, 230, 261, 421, *493*

J

Jack, O., 466, *492*
Jacobson, D. E., 215, *487*

Jaensch, E. R., 91, *489*
Jahnke, J. C., 209, 313, *486, 489*
James, C. T., 252, *487*
James, W., 132, *489*
Jenkins, J. G., 220, *489*
Jenkins, J. J., 15, 16, 26, 28, 168, 323, 326, 328, 341, 380, 424, *488, 489, 503*
Jensen, A. R., 418, 428,
Johnson, H. J., 52, 65, *485*
Johnson, L. M., 235, *489*
Johnson, M. K., 339, *489*
Johnson, N. F., 287, 288, 431, 432, 433, 434, 470, *486, 489, 490*
Johnston, W. A., 288, *490*
Jongeward, R. H., 143, 163, 164, 165, 169, 386, 387, *504*
Jonides, J., 116, 130, *482, 490*
Judd, B. R., 378, *484*
Julesz, B., 46, 65, 93, *487, 490*
Juola, J. F., 367, 368, 369, *479*

K

Kahn, R., 130, *490*
Kahneman, D., 43, 62, 63, *490*
Kaplan, S., 144, 161, 170, *490*
Katona, G., 14, *490*
Kausler, D. H., 415, *490*
Kawashima, T., 64, *486*
Keele, S. W., 97, 99, 131, *496*
Keppel, G., 200, 201, 202, 207, 240, 252, 269, 423, *490, 497, 499, 502*
Kerr, N., 127, 128, 129, 130, 412, *495*
Kidd, E., 114, 115, 125, *482*
Kincaid, J. P., 206, *490*
Kinsbourne, M., 379, *490*
Kintsch, W., 152, 153, 270, 271, 272, 374, 474, *490*
Kirkpatrick, M., 291, 292, 293, 294, 299, *496*
Kirsner, K., 366, *490*
Klapp, S. T., 81, *490*
Kleinsmith, L. J., 144, 161, 170, *490*
Knapp, M., 373, *479*
Köhler, W., 4, 265, *490*
Kolers, P. A., 407, *490*
Konick, A. W., 184, 185, 186, 193, 194, *496*
Konorski, J., 237, *490*

Koppenaal, R. J., 237, 238, 239, 262, *490*
Koriat, A., 459, *490*
Kosslyn, S. M., 130, *490*
Krechevsky, I., 265, *490*
Krueger, W. C., 235, *491*
Kuhn, T., 262, 364, *491*
Kutz, K. J., 77, *492*

L

LaBerge, D., 77, 83, 426, *491*
Lachman, R., 474, 476, *485, 491*
Ladd, G. L., 421, *491*
Lambert, W. E., 121, *491, 504*
Lamwers, L. L., 408, *480*
Land, V., 291, 307, 419, 458, *496*
Landauer, T. K., 37, 198, 224, 280, 380, *491*
Lashley, K. S., 14, 424, *491*
Leask, J., 92, 93, *491*
Lefton, L. A., 43, *491*
Leiter, E., 380, *485*
Lepley, W. M., 447, *491*
Lester, O. P., 235, *491*
Levonian, E., 144, *491*
Lewis, C., 353, *479*
Liberman, A. M., 41, 64, 86, 237, *491*
Light, L. L., 404, 405, *491*
Ligon, E. J., 186, *497*
Lindley, R. H., 18, 20, 27, 134, *491*
Locke, J. L., 75, 77, 78, *491, 492*
Locke, V. L., 75, *492*
Lockhart, R. S., 15, 168, 387, *483*
Loess, H., 201, 206, *492*
Loftus, G. R., 209, 215, *492*
Lorayne, H., 116, *492*
Love, T., 95, *489*
Lovelace, E. A., 37, *492*
Lowry, D. H., 116, 117, 120, 128, *492, 504*
Lucas, J., 116, *492*
Luh, C. W., 235, 371, *492*
Luria, A. R., 94, *492*

M

Mackay, S. A., 246, *492*

Madigan, S. A., 121, 142, 274, 281, 287, 288, 289, 291, 298, *492, 496*
Mandler, G., 323, 339, 340, 341, *492*
Manelis, L., 392, 393, 394, 395, 407, 408, *489*
Margolius, G., 235, *503*
Marks, L. E., 467, *492*
Marks, M. R., 466, *492*
Marquis, D. G., 237, *488*
Marshall, G. R., 328, 329, *492*
Martin, E., 23, 28, 225, 245, 246, 253, 255, 256, 258, 259, 260, 262, 348, 405, 407, 443, 444, 445, 472, 478, *487, 492, 504*
Martin, S. E., 83, *493*
Maskarinec, A. S., 141, 147, 209, *486, 493*
Massaro, D. W., 51, 54, 55, 56, 58, 65, *493*
Mazuryk, G., 156, *503*
McCabe, L., 142, *492*
McCann, R. L., 259, *503*
McCarrell, N. S., 406, 407, *480*
McCormack, P. D., 62, 379, *487, 493*
McGaugh, J. L., 223, 224, *493*
McGeoch, J. A., 198, 217, 218, 219, 220, 221, 224, 225, 226, 227, 228, 261, 265, 417, *493*
McGovern, J. B., 244, *493*
McGuigan, F. J., 82, *493*
McGuire, W. J., 21, 22, 28, 256, 271, *493*
McLean, P. D., 144, *493*
McNulty, J. A., 62, *483*
Mehler, J., 469, *493*
Melton, A. W., 4, 7, 134, 200, 201, 202, 203, 208, 215, 229, 230, 231, 236, 245, 251, 261, 274, 276, 281, 282, 291, 299, 421, 430, *486, 493*
Merryman, C. T., 243, 246, *493*
Metzler, J., 102, 116, 155, *498*
Mewaldt, S. P., 313, *488*
Miller, G. A., 69, 84, 86, 114, 323, 330, 449, 465, 466, 467, 468, 475, *492, 493, 494*
Miller, N. E., 223, 237, 238, 239, *483, 494*
Miller, R. R., 224, *494*
Minami, H., 221, *494*
Mink, W. D., 326, 328, *489*
Montague, W., 81, *485*
Moore, T., 338, *499*
Moray, N., 48, 49, 50, 52, 65, *494*
Morton, J., 38, 56, 57, 58, 59, 60, 65, 146,

278, 315, 316, 321, 374, 397, 405, *484, 494*
Moy, M. C., 367, *500*
Müller, G. E., 219, 220, *494*
Murdock, B. B., Jr., 20, 25, 62, 139, 140, 141, 144, 148, 180, 209, 374, 422, 449, 463, *494, 495*
Murray, D. J., 61, 63, 73, *495*

N

Naus, M. J., 365, 366, *495*
Neisser, U., 30, 43, 45, 127, 128, 129, 130, 412, *495*
Newton, J. M., 199, 240, *495*
Nicely, P. E., 84, 86, *494*
Nitsch, K., 406, 407, *480*
Noble, C. E., 464, *495*
Noble, M., 427, *480*
Noreen, D. L., 443, 444, *492*
Norman, D. A., 51, 52, 65, 135, 146, 177, 180, 183, 184, 194, 279, 323, 373, 376, *495, 503, 504*
Noyd, D. E., 201, 214, *495*
Nuwer, M., 127, *497*

O

Olton, R. M., 120, *495*
Ornstein, P. A., 365, 366, *495*
Osgood, C. E., 24, 28, 205, 225, 226, 237, 457, *495*

P

Paivio, A., 90, 92, 98, 112, 113, 114, 116, 118, 120, 121, 122, 123, 124, 125, 126, 127, 130, 277, 290, 291, 473, *491, 495, 496, 505*
Pantle, A. J., 276, *483*
Papay, J. P., 455, 456, *482*
Patterson, J., 420, *505*
Patterson, K. K., 209, 215, *492*
Pearlstone, Z., 8, 9, 26, 27, 28, 339, 340, 343, 345, *492, 501*
Pellegrino, J. W., 334, *496*
Perchonock, E., 469, *498*
Perkins, D. T., 448, *489*

Peters, S. C., 422, 448, *487*
Peterson, L. R., 18, 28, 105, 133, 136, 183, 196, 200, 291, 292, 293, 294, 299, 307, 419, 426, 458, *496*
Peterson, M. J., 18, 28, 105, 133, 136, 183, *496*
Petrinovich, L. F., 79, 82, *488*
Phillips, L. W., 140, 147, *497*
Pilzecker, A., 219, 220, *494*
Pisoni, D. B., 64, *496*
Poffenberger, A. T., 421, *504*
Pollack, M., 81, *485*
Pollio, H. R., 458, *496*
Posner, M. I., 97, 99, 102, 103, 104, 105, 116, 131, 156, 177, 184, 185, 186, 193, 194, 195, 196, *496*
Postman, L., 140, 147, 233, 237, 238, 239, 240, 241, 242, 243, 244, 245, 246, 247, 248, 249, 251, 252, 254, 256, 258, 260, 261, 262, 268, 324, 339, 343, 371, 419, 420, 496, 497, *502*
Potts, G. R., 285, *497*
Powell, M., 37, *492*
Pribram, K. H., 114, 127, *494, 497*
Primoff, E., 418, *497*
Prussin, H. A., 58, *494*
Prytulak, L. S., 393, *489*
Psotka, J., 93, *500*
Puff, C. R., 329, *497*
Pylyshyn, Z. W., 127, 130, *497*

R

Raeburn, V. P., 364, 366, *497*
Ranyard, R., 228, *487*
Rau, L., 371, *497*
Rauch, D. S., 252, *490*
Raymond, B., 147, 151, 152, *497*
Razel, M., 146, 147, 149, *487*
Redding, J., 313, *488*
Reder, L. M., 404, 406, *497*
Reicher, G. M., 186, 330, *482, 497*
Reid, L. S., 196, 202, *485*
Reitman, J. S., 118, 119, 180, 181, 182, *481, 497*
Restle, F., 272, *497*
Ribback, A., 429, 452, 456, *497*
Richardson, J., 235, *502*
Rightmer, D. R., 401, *497*

Riley, D. A., 95, *497*
Robbins, D., 312, *497*
Roberts, K. H., 472, *492*
Robinson, E. S., 226, 412, *497, 498*
Rock, I., 260, 265, 266, 268, 272, *498*
Roediger, H. L., III, 141, 147, 313, 346, 347, 459, *498*
Roenker, D. L., 330, *500*
Rogers, T. B., 112, *496*
Rohrman, N. L., 472, *498*
Rohwer, W. D., Jr., 428, *489*
Ross, R. T., 448, *489*
Rossman, E., 105, 195, 196, *496*
Rostron, A. B., 50, *501*
Rothkopf, E. Z., 474, *498*
Rozin, P., 130, *490*
Rumelhart, D. E., 180, *495*
Rundus, D., 143, 163, 281, 346, 348, 349, 350, 454, *498*
Runquist, W. N., 252, *498*
Rush, M. L., 73, *483*
Russell, W. A., 326, 328, *489*

S

Sachs, J. D. S., 473, 476, *498*
Saltzman, D., 291, 292, 293, 294, 299, 307 419, 458, *496*
Samuels, S. J., 426, *491*
Sanders, L. W., 286, *485*
Santa, J. L., 408, *480*
Savin, H. B., 469, *498*
Schiller, P. H., 43, 224, *482, 498*
Schiller, P. H., 43, 224, *482, 498*
Schlosberg, H., 228, *481*
Schulz, R. W., 240, 271, *498, 502*
Sedgewick, C. H., 324, *481*
Segmen, J., 114, 115, 125, *482*
Selfridge, J. A., 465, 468, 475, *494*
Shallice, T., 144, 161, *498*
Shankweiler, D., 40, 64, 86, *491, 500*
Shaughnessy, J. J., 284, 285, 291, *498*
Sheffield, F. D., 122, 428, 435, 436, 437, 438, 439, *498*
Shepard, R. N., 102, 111, 113, 116, 155, 379, *483, 498*
Shiffrin, R. M., 156, 157, 158, 165, 166, 182, 183, 228, 281, 292, 299, 303, 305, 307, 348, 350, *480, 498, 499*
Shuell, T. J., 423, *499*

Shulman, A. I., 379, *499*
Shulman, H. G., 166, 167, *499*
Shulman, S., 64, *500*
Siipola, E. M., 92, *499*
Silverstein, A., 238, *499*
Simon, H. A., 451, 456, *486*
Skaggs, E. B., 226, *499*
Slamecka, N. J., 338, 342, 343, 344, 345, 346, 378, 381, 416, 417, 418, *499*
Slobin, D. I., 465, *499*
Smith, A. D., 347, *499*
Smith, E. E., 161, 162, 166, 360, *499*
Smith, P. G., 367, *500*
Smith, W. G., 216, *499*
Smythe, P. C., 112, 124, *496*
Speelman, R. G., 71, *500*
Spence, K. W., 265, *499*
Sperber, R. D., 293, *499*
Sperling, G., 30, 31, 32, 33, 34, 35, 37, 38, 39, 47, 70, 71, 81, 104, 146, *499, 500*
Springer, A. D., 224, *494*
Springston, F., 430, *481*
Standing, L., 111, 113, *500*
Stark, K., 238, 239, 240, 241, 242, 243, 246, 249, 262, 420, *497*
Steger, J. A., 112, 113, *480*
Sternberg, R. J., 334, 338, 380, *500*
Sternberg, S., 354, 355, 356, 358, 359, 360, 361, 363, 364, 366, 409, *500*
Stevenson, S. S., 237, 238, 239, *494*
Strand, B. Z., 228, *500*
Streeter, L. A., 380, *491*
Stromeyer, C. F., III, 93, *500*
Stroop, J. R., 81, *500*
Studdert-Kennedy, M., 41, 64, 86, *491, 500*
Suci, G. J., 205, 457, *495*
Sumby, W. H., 140, 141, 454, *500*
Summers, J. J., 282, 283, 284, 291, 314, *488*
Sutherland, N. S., 378, *484*
Swenson, A. L., 379, *493*
Symmes, J. S., 92, *500*

T

Talland, G. A., 10, 11, 12, *500*
Tannenbaum, P. H., 205, 457, *495*
Tarte, R. D., 144, *502*
Tash, J., 64, *496*

Taylor, R. L., 99, 102, 103, 104, 105, 116, *496*

Tell, P. M., 153, 154, *500*

Theios, J., 367, *500*

Thios, S. J., 287, 288, *500*

Thomasson, A. J. W. M., 72, *500*

Thompson, C. P., 141, 146, 330, *486, 500*

Thomson, D. M., 281, 377, 396, 397, 399, 400, 401, 402, 404, 406, 407, 408, *500, 501*

Thorndike, E. L., 218, *500*

Thurm, A. T., 150, 151, *500*

Townsend, J. T., 359, *501*

Trabasso, T., 272, *501*

Trask, F. P., 315, 372, 373, *505*

Traupmann, J., 367, *500*

Treisman, A. M., 46, 50, 51, 65, *501*

Tulving, E., 8, 9, 26, 27, 28, 34, 148, 160, 251, 272, 322, 333, 334, 336, 337, 343, 345, 347, 376, 377, 391, 392, 393, 394, 395, 396, 397, 398, 399, 400, 401, 402, 404, 406, 407, 408, 453, *500, 501, 503*

Turvey, M. T., 43, 48, 49, 50, 104, 203, 216, *484, 501*

Tversky, B. G., 99, 100, 101, 126, 131, 381, 386, *501*

Tzeng, O. J. L., 172, 312, *501, 502*

U

Underwood, B. J., 5, 14, 16, 17, 27, 28, 200, 201, 202, 207, 231, 232, 233, 234, 235, 236, 237, 240, 243, 245, 246, 247, 248, 249, 250, 251, 254, 256, 258, 259, 260, 261, 262, 268, 269, 271, 278, 284, 285, 291, 302, 428, 429, 451, 456, *480, 487, 490, 497, 498, 502, 504*

V

Vigorito, J. M., 64, *484*

vom Saal, W., 25, *494*

von Lackum, W. J. 231, 236, *493*

von Restorff, 422, *497*

von Wright, J. M., 35, 41, 42, *502*

W

Walker, E. L., 144, *502*

Walker, K. D., 62, *495*

Walsh, D. A., 323, *503*

Walter, D. A., 474, *503*

Walters, A. A., 95, 96, *482*

Wampler, R., 291, 292, 293, 294, 299, *496*

Ward, L. B., 218, *503*

Warrington, E. K., 144, 161, *498*

Washburn, M. F., 61, *503*

Watkins, M. J., 25, 26, 28, 62, 63, 143, 146, 148, 149, 155, 156, 162, 163, 164, 170, 187, 188, 192, 209, 210, 215, 216, 323, 387, 392, 393, 402, 404, 406, 467, *483, 503*

Watkins, O. C., 25, 26, 28, 62, 63, 143, 155, 156, 170, 187, 188, 192, 209, 210, 215, 216, 387, 467, *503*

Watson, J. B., 78, 90, *503*

Watts, G. H., 242, *479*

Waugh, N. C., 10, 135, 146, 177, 180, 183, 184, 194, 206, 276, 278, 279, 323, 455, *492, 500, 503*

Wearing, A. J., 470, 472, *503*

Weaver, G. E., 259, *503*

Webb, L. W., 225, *503*

Weber, A., 116, 117, 128, *504*

Weeks, R. A., 203, 216, *501*

Wehr, R. J., 259, *503*

Weiss, W., 235, *503*

Welch, G. B., 454, *503*

Wendt, G. R., 237, *503*

Whitten, W. B., 171, 211, 251, 461, 476, *481*

Whitty, C. W. M., 10, *503*

Wichawut, C., 245, 260, *504*

Wickelgren, W. A., 85, 86, 145, 147, 189, 199, 216, 373, 424, 430, 442, *504*

Wickens, D. D., 196, 197, 199, 203, 204, 205, 206, 240, *483, 490, 495, 504*

Wilkinson, W. C., 172, 285, 291, *485, 504*

Williams, J. P. A., 268, *504*

Williams, M., 222, 235, *504*

Williams, R. F., 259, *504*

Wimer, C., 121, *504*

Wingfield, A., 178, 179, *505*

Winzenz, D., 430, *481*

Wise, P. S., 312, *497*

Wollen, K. A., 116, 117, 128, *504*

Wood, G., 116, 338, *504*

Woods, E. L., 372, *504*

Woodward, A. E., 143, 163, 164, 165, 169, 386, 387, *504*

Woodworth, R. S., 91, 95, 97, 116, 219, 421, 429, *491, 504*

Wright, P., 470, *504*

Y

Yates, F. A., 114, *504*
Yerkes, R. M., 265, *505*
Yngve, V. H., 434, 471, *505*
Yntema, D. B., 315, 372, 373, *505*
Young, J. L., 299, 307, *505*
Young, R. K., 416, 418, 420, 422, *505*

Youtz, A. C., 235, *505*
Yuille, J. C., 121, 123, 124, *496, 505*

Z

Zangwill, O. L., 10, *503*
Zimmerman, J., 284, 285, 291, *498*